C++

ALL-IN-ONE

by John Paul Mueller

for
dummies®
A Wiley Brand

C++ All-in-One For Dummies®, 4th Edition

Published by: **John Wiley & Sons, Inc.,** 111 River Street, Hoboken, NJ 07030-5774, www.wiley.com

Copyright © 2021 by John Wiley & Sons, Inc., Hoboken, New Jersey

Published simultaneously in Canada

For general information on our other products and services, please contact our Customer Care Department within the U.S. at 877-762-2974, outside the U.S. at 317-572-3993, or fax 317-572-4002. For technical support, please visit https://hub.wiley.com/community/support/dummies.

Wiley publishes in a variety of print and electronic formats and by print-on-demand. Some material included with standard print versions of this book may not be included in e-books or in print-on-demand. If this book refers to media such as a CD or DVD that is not included in the version you purchased, you may download this material at http://booksupport.wiley.com. For more information about Wiley products, visit www.wiley.com.

Library of Congress Control Number: 2020949804

ISBN: 978-1-119-60174-6

ISBN 978-1-119-60175-3 (ebk); ISBN 978-1-119-60173-9 (ebk)

Manufactured in the United States of America

SKY10022935_120120

Contents at a Glance

Table of Contents

Introduction

There are many general-purpose programming languages today, but few can claim to be the language of the millennium. C++ can make that claim, and for good reason:

>> It's powerful. You can write almost any program in it.

>> It's fast, and it's fully compiled. That's a good thing.

>> It's easy to use — if you have this book.

>> It's object oriented. If you're not sure what that is, don't worry. You can find out about it by reading this very book you're holding.

>> It supports functional programming techniques, which makes modeling math problems considerably easier and makes parallel processing easier. This book covers functional programming techniques, too.

>> It's portable. Versions are available for nearly every computer.

>> It's standardized. The American National Standards Institute (ANSI) and the International Standards Organization (ISO) both approve an official version.

>> It's continually updated to meet the changing challenges of the computer community.

>> It's popular. More people are using C++ because so many other people use it.

Sure, some people criticize C++. But most of these people don't truly understand C++ or are just having a bad day. Or both.

About This Book

This book is a hands-on, roll-up-your-sleeves experience that gives you the opportunity to truly learn C++. This edition starts out by helping you get a great C++ installation in place. A lot of readers wrote to tell me that they simply couldn't get C++ to work for them, and I listened by adding configuration instructions in Book 1, Chapter 1. You can find instructions for working with the Mac, Linux, and Windows throughout the book. The examples are also tested to work on all three platforms.

C++ All-in-One For Dummies, 4th Edition, is devoted to working with C++ wherever you want to use it. Book 1, Chapter 2 even includes techniques for writing C++ code on your mobile device, although writing a complex application on your smartphone would be understandably difficult because of the small device size.

At the very beginning, I start you out from square one. I don't assume any programming experience whatsoever. Everybody has to start somewhere. You can start here. Not to brag, but you are in the hands of a highly successful C++ developer who has shown thousands of people how to program, many of whom also started out from square one.

You already know C++? This book is great for you, too, because although I start discussing C++ from the beginning, I cover the important aspects of the language in depth. Even if you've used C++ in the past, this book gets you up to speed with the latest in C++ 14 and above innovations, including C++ 20 additions. Plus, this edition of the book focuses on all the latest programming strategies while removing some of the less used functionality of the past.

If you're interested in using the time-tested Object Oriented Programming (OOP) techniques that C++ developers have used for years, then Book 2 is where you want to look. You start with a view of classes, but eventually move into more advanced topics, including the use of programming patterns in Book 2 Chapter 4.

One of the most exciting additions to this edition is the use of functional programming techniques, which you can find in Book 3. Functional programming has become extremely popular because it makes modeling math problems significantly easier, and many people use functional programming techniques to solve modern data science problems. More important, functional programming can be a lot easier than earlier programming paradigms.

Every application out there has a bug or two. If you doubt this statement, just try to find one that is bug free—you won't. Book 4 includes all sorts of techniques you can use to make your application as bug free as possible before it leaves your machine and then help you find the bugs that others graciously point out later.

Book 5 is all about moving you from generalized programming strategies into the advanced strategies used by modern developers. It starts with a look at standardized structures for working with classes in a safe manner. The minibook takes you through

>> Simple structures, such as arrays

>> More advanced data management

>> The use of constructors, destructors, and exceptions

>> Templatized programming

>> Use of the Standard Library (originally called the Standard Template Library or STL).

Everyone needs to work with files at some point. You use local, network, and Internet files today on a regular basis. Book 6 is all about working with files in various ways. This book includes topics on working with data streams as well.

The Standard Library is immense and there are entire books written about its use. *C++ All-in-One For Dummies*, 4th Edition, focuses on providing you with a really good overview that you can use to drill down into more detailed topics later. Besides looking at the Standard Library in more detail, you discover how to work with User Defined Literals (UDLs) and how to create your own templates. This book also delves into the Boost library, which is the library that has added more to Standard Library than just about any other source. Check out Book 7, Chapters 4 and 5 to learn about Boost. If you use C++ and don't use Boost, you're really missing out!

C++ is standardized, and you can use the information in this book on many different platforms. I wrote the samples using Mac OS X, SUSE Linux (some of the beta readers used other flavors of Linux), and Windows systems (with some testing on my ASUS tablet as well). In order to make this happen, I used a compiler called *Code::Blocks* that runs on almost every computer (Windows, Linux, and Macintosh) and CppDroid for my tablet. It doesn't matter which device you're using!

To make absorbing the concepts easy, this book uses the following conventions:

>> Text that you're meant to type just as it appears in the book is in **bold**. The exception is when you're working through a step list: Because each step is bold, the text to type is not bold.

>> Web addresses and programming code appear in monofont. If you're reading a digital version of this book on a device connected to the Internet, you can click or tap the web address to visit that website, like this: https://www.dummies.com.

>> When you need to type command sequences, you see them separated by a special arrow, like this: File⇨New File. In this example, you go to the File menu first and then select the New File entry on that menu.

>> When you see words in *italics* as part of a typing sequence, you need to replace that value with something that works for you. For example, if you see "Type ***Your Name*** and press Enter," you need to replace *Your Name* with your actual name.

Foolish Assumptions

This book is designed for novice and professional alike. You can either read this book from cover to cover, or you can look up topics and treat the book as a reference guide — whichever works best for you. Keep it on your shelf, and have it ready to grab when you need to look something up. However, I've made some assumptions about your level of knowledge when I put the book together. The most important of these assumptions is that you already know how to use your device and work with the operating system that supports it. You also need to know how to perform tasks like downloading files and installing applications. A familiarity with the Internet is also required, and you need to know how to interact with it moderately well to locate the resources you need to work with the book. Finally, you must know how to work with archives, such as the ZIP file format.

Icons Used in This Book

As you read this book, you see icons in the margins that indicate material of interest (or not, as the case may be). This section briefly describes each icon in this book.

TIP

Tips are nice because they help you save time or perform some task without a lot of extra work. The tips in this book are time-saving techniques or pointers to resources that you should try so that you can get the maximum benefit from C++. Most important, many of these tips will help you make sense of the overwhelming quantity of libraries and tools that C++ developers have created over the years.

WARNING

I don't want to sound like an angry parent or some kind of maniac, but you should avoid doing anything that's marked with a Warning icon. Otherwise, you might find that your application fails to work as expected, you get incorrect answers from seemingly bulletproof code, or (in the worst-case scenario) you lose data. Given where C++ appears, you might also send the next rocket off to Mars prematurely, make someone's thermostat misbehave, or cause nationwide power outages. Really, warnings are for everyone!

TECHNICAL STUFF

Whenever you see this icon, think advanced tip or technique. You might find these tidbits of useful information just too boring for words, or they could contain the solution you need to get a program running. Skip these bits of information whenever you like.

REMEMBER

If you don't get anything else out of a particular chapter or section, remember the material marked by this icon. This text usually contains an essential process or a bit of information that you must know to work with C++, or to perform development tasks successfully.

Beyond the Book

If you want to email me, please do! Make sure you send your book-specific requests to:

John@JohnMuellerBooks.com

I get a lot of email from readers, so sometimes it takes me a while to answer. I try very hard to answer every book-specific question I receive, though, so I highly recommend contacting me with your questions. I want to ensure that your book experience is the best one possible. The blog category at http://blog. johnmuellerbooks.com/categories/263/c-all-in-one-for-dummies.aspx contains a wealth of additional information about this book. You can check out the website at http://www.johnmuellerbooks.com/.

This book isn't the end of your C++ programming experience — it's really just the beginning. I provide online content to make this book more flexible and better able to meet your needs. That way, as I receive email from you, I can address questions and tell you how updates to either Code::Blocks or the C++ language affect book content. You can also access other cool materials:

>> **Cheat Sheet:** You remember using crib notes in school to make a better mark on a test, don't you? You do? Well, a cheat sheet is sort of like that. It provides you with some special notes on things you can do with C++ that not every other developer knows. You can find the cheat sheet for this book at www. dummies.com and typing **C++ All-in-One For Dummies, 4th Edition** in the search field. It contains really neat information like the top ten mistakes developers make when working with C++, a list of header files that you use in most applications, and some of the C++ syntax that gives most developers problems.

>> **Updates:** Sometimes changes happen. For example, I might not have seen an upcoming change when I looked into my crystal ball during the writing of this book. In the past, such a situation simply meant that the book would become outdated and less useful, but you can now find updates to the book at www. dummies.com. In addition to these updates, check out the blog posts with

answers to reader questions and demonstrations of useful book-related techniques at http://blog.johnmuellerbooks.com/.

>> **Companion files:** Hey! Who really wants to type all the code in the book? Most readers would prefer to spend their time actually working through coding examples rather than typing. Fortunately for you, the source code is available for download, so all you need to do is read the book to learn C++ coding techniques. Each of the book examples even tells you precisely which example project to use. You can find these files by searching this book's title at www.dummies.com.

Just in case you're worried about Code::Blocks, you can find complete download and installation instructions for it in Book 1, Chapter 1. Don't worry about which platform you use. This chapter includes instructions for Mac OS X, Linux, and Windows.

Where to Go from Here

If you're just starting your C++ adventure, I highly recommend starting at either Book 1, Chapter 1 (for desktop developers) or Book 1, Chapter 2 (for mobile developers). You really do need to create a solid foundation before you can tackle the code in this book. If you're in a hurry and already have a C++ installation, you can always try starting with Book 1, Chapter 3.

Readers with a little more experience, who already know some C++ basics, can skip some of these introductory chapters, but you definitely don't want to skip Book 1, Chapter 8 because it contains a lot of pointer-related changes in current versions of C++. If you skip this chapter, you may find later that you have a hard time following the example code in the book because the newer examples use these pointer features.

An advanced reader with some idea of the current changes in C++ 20 could possibly skip Book 1, but scanning Book 2 is a good idea because there are some OOP changes you definitely want to know about. However, even for advanced readers, skipping Book 3 is a bad idea because modern development really is moving toward functional programming techniques.

1

Getting Started with C++

Contents at a Glance

and more . . .

Chapter **1**

Configuring Your Desktop System

This chapter is for those of you who have a desktop system and want to use it to create your application code. Chapter 2 discusses how to perform the same task using a mobile device (and provides you with some trade-offs between the two environments). Whether you use the desktop or the mobile solution, you need a copy of a compiler that supports C++ 20 features or some book examples won't work at all. This book relies on the GNU Compiler Collection (GCC) version 8.3 compiler because it provides great C++ 20 support (see https://en.cppreference.com/w/cpp/compiler_support). The best way to obtain the version 8.3 compiler for your desktop system is to follow the steps in this chapter.

Before you can do anything interesting at all with C++, you need a copy of it installed on your system. Of course, this means going online, finding the location of the software that's appropriate for your platform, and then downloading it as necessary. If you use an Integrated Development Environment (IDE) such as Code::Blocks (the IDE used throughout this book), you get a copy of C++ with your installation, so you don't need to worry about reading the first section of this chapter. This book relies on your having a compiler capable of compiling C++ 20 code, which is the latest version of the language available at the time of this writing.

REMEMBER

Even though this book focuses on working with C++ on the Mac, Windows, and Linux platforms, you can actually use the techniques it provides on a great many other desktop systems. With this in mind, you'll find an overview of using C++ with other IDEs. As your platform becomes more esoteric, you'll find that fewer of the book examples work because your platform may require special programming techniques. The best option for working with this book is using a copy of Code::Blocks 17.12 with C++ 20 support installed on the Linux, Mac, or Windows platform.

Obtaining a Copy of C++ 20

There is no product available named C++ 20. The C++ 20 standard simply says what the language contains and how someone should implement it. In other words, you can't just go online and get a copy of C++ 20; what you need to do instead is get a compiler vendor's implementation of the C++ 20 standard. For example, you can download the GNU Compiler Collection (GCC) version of C++ 20 from `https://gcc.gnu.org/releases.html`.

TIP

Every vendor will have a slightly different interpretation of this standard and could provide additions to the standard. In short, every compiler provides a unique version of C++. However, you also have the choice of not using the special features that the vendor provides, which means your source code is less susceptible to problems that occur when you use multiple compilers. The examples in this book are strictly written to the C++ 20 standard, so you shouldn't have a problem using them anywhere you want.

It's important that you also understand that a compiler is not the same as an Integrated Development Environment (IDE). The compiler is separate from the IDE in many cases and maintained by two separate parties. For example, the Code::Blocks IDE supports multiple compilers, and the GCC compiler works within multiple IDEs. The compiler is the important piece of software that turns your source code into an executable file that the operating system can run to produce the output you want.

The compiler you choose has to support the platforms you want to work with. For example, GCC supports Mac, Windows, and Linux development as well as some Acorn or (later) Advanced RISC Machine (ARM) processors (ARM doesn't officially stand for anything today). In fact, it may support other platforms by the time you read this chapter. Because it works in so many places, this book focuses on GCC, even though the examples will work with other compilers with some modification to overcome compiler differences.

Obtaining Code::Blocks

The Code::Blocks IDE provides an environment in which you can write source code, compile it, test it, and debug it as needed. The IDE doesn't actually compile the source code, but it does provide support for a compiler that does so. (It just so happens that it does its job in such a way that makes it appear that the compiler is part of the IDE.) You can choose from a number of compilers in Code::Blocks, but this book focuses on using GCC to ensure that the examples will run on as many platforms as possible. GCC comes with your copy of Code::Blocks when working with Windows, so you don't have to do anything special to work with it except select it during the installation process. (When working on a Mac or Linux system, you must install GCC separately — the compiler doesn't come with Code::Blocks.)

REMEMBER

This book is written using Code::Blocks version 17.12. That doesn't mean you can't use it with earlier or later versions of Code::Blocks. However, when working with other versions of Code::Blocks, you may find that you need to modify the code slightly. The modification is required in order to support the compiler that comes with that version of Code::Blocks. The IDE itself won't affect your ability to work with C++ 20.

REMEMBER

Code::Blocks comes in both binary form and source code form. You can download either form of version 17.12 from `http://www.codeblocks.org/downloads/5`. The link leads you to SourceForge, where you select the platform you want to use: Mac, Linux, or Windows. Click the folder link and you see a list of downloadable archive files for that platform. (Linux users will also have to choose their particular version of Linux.) Choosing the correct archive is important because different archives have different features.

TIP

When working with a Windows installation, make sure you use the `codeblocks-17.12mingw-setup.exe` installer to obtain a copy of GCC with Code::Blocks. Make absolutely certain that you don't install it to the `Program Files` folder on your system, because the application won't work there. Code::Blocks writes data to its host directory, and Windows won't allow applications to perform this task in the `Program Files` folder. Create a folder to which you have write privileges and install Code::Blocks there instead.

Now that you have an appropriate archive to use, it's time to install Code::Blocks on your machine. The "Installing Code::Blocks" section of this chapter tells you more about getting Code::Blocks installed on your particular system.

Installing Code::Blocks

Before you can use Code::Blocks as your IDE, you need to install it. The following sections describe how to install Code::Blocks on each of the main platforms supported by this book. The instructions in these sections assume that you've downloaded the binary version of Code::Blocks and that you aren't using a custom compiled version of the product.

WARNING

If you have an older version of Code::Blocks installed on your system, be sure to uninstall it before installing the new version. Also make sure that you tell the uninstaller to delete any old custom files in the folder so that you start with a fresh folder. Old files can cause errors to appear when you start Code::Blocks or perform common tasks.

Working with Windows

Code::Blocks comes with a Windows installer that will make the task of installing the IDE easier. The following steps help you work with the `codeblocks-17.12mingw-setup.exe` installer:

1. Double-click the file you downloaded from the Code::Blocks site.

You see the CodeBlocks Setup Wizard start. If you see a User Account Control dialog box, give the application permission to proceed by clicking Yes.

2. Click Next.

The licensing agreement appears. Read the licensing agreement so that you know the terms of usage for Code::Blocks.

3. Click I Agree.

The wizard displays a series of configuration options, as shown in Figure 1-1. This book assumes that you've performed the default, full installation.

4. Click Next.

The installation program asks where to install Code::Blocks on your system. Unlike many other applications, Code::Blocks will actually write data to this folder from time to time. The best idea is to use a folder to which you have write access. To ensure maximum compatibility, the book uses the `C:\CodeBlocks` folder for installation purposes. To keep from seeing any error messages, make sure that the path doesn't have any spaces in it (see the blog post at `http://blog.johnmuellerbooks.com/2016/04/20/spaces-in-paths/` for details).

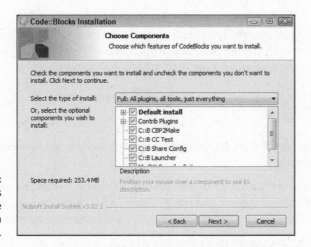

FIGURE 1-1:
The wizard asks
you to select the
configuration
options to use.

5. **Type** C:\CodeBlocks **in the Destination Folder field. Click Install.**

The installation program automatically creates the C:\CodeBlocks folder for you when it doesn't already exist. If the folder already exists because you previously installed an older version of Code::Blocks, you see a dialog box appear. Click Yes to allow installation to continue. You see all the files installed into the C:\CodeBlocks folder on your system.

The setup wizard may display a dialog box asking whether you want to start Code::Blocks. Click No if you see this dialog box.

6. **Click Next.**

You see a completion dialog box.

7. **Click Finish.**

The setup wizard ends.

TIP

If you find that the wizard has somehow managed not to select a compiler and/or debugger for you, you can perform this task manually. The "Selecting a compiler" section will help in this regard. In addition, the blog posts at http://blog.john muellerbooks.com/2011/04/06/checking-your-compiler-in-codeblocks/ and http://blog.johnmuellerbooks.com/2013/04/12/resetting-your-code blocks-configuration/ tell how to perform the additional setup. However, in most cases, the wizard will perform the required setup for you.

Working with Mac OS X

Installing Code::Blocks on a Mac requires a little extra work than it does in Windows. Code::Blocks requires Mac OS X 10.6 or later to install. You can get the version 17.12 file, codeblocks-17.12_OSX64.dmg, from https://sourceforge.net/

projects/codeblocks/files/Binaries/17.12/Mac/. If you experience a Mac Gatekeeper error during installation, please check out the blog post at http://blog.johnmuellerbooks.com/2016/03/21/mac-gatekeeper-error/.

The following steps tell you how to get a functional Code::Blocks installation on your Mac system.

1. **Download and install Xcode from the App Store to obtain a copy of GCC, if necessary.**

You can verify that you have the GNU GCC compiler installed by opening a terminal, typing **gcc -v**, and pressing Enter. If GCC is installed, you should see some version information along with some compiler instructions.

2. **Extract the Code::Blocks files into a folder.**

You see a number of files, including the Code::Blocks application, a readme file containing the latest update information, and a PDF file containing documentation.

3. **Open the** Applications **folder.**

You see the applications installed on your system.

4. **Drag the** CodeBlocks.app **file from the folder you used for extraction purposes to the** Applications **folder.**

The operating system adds Code::Blocks to the list of usable applications.

5. **Navigate to** https://developer.apple.com/downloads/.

This site requires that you sign up for a free developer ID. Simply follow the prompts onscreen to obtain your Apple ID. The sign-up process is free.

6. **Click the Command Line Tools for Xcode link.**

The operating system downloads the file and displays a package folder for you.

7. **Double-click the Command Line Tools package.**

The operating system installs the package for you, which enables access to GCC from Code::Blocks.

Using the standard Linux installation

There isn't a single set of steps for installing Code::Blocks on Linux, because each flavor of Linux has its own requirements. Code::Blocks directly supports:

>> Blag

>> Debian

>> Fedora

>> Gentoo

>> Platypux

>> Red Hat Package Manager (RPM)-based distributions (such as SUSE, Red Hat, Yellow Dog, Fedora Core, and CentOS)

>> Ubuntu

Each distribution type has its own set of instructions that you can find at http://wiki.codeblocks.org/index.php?title=Installing_Code::Blocks. Make sure you download and install the compiler, debugger, and IDE as needed by carefully following the instructions (typed at the terminal). The file that you download from http://www.codeblocks.org/downloads/26 contains the packages for a Code::Blocks installation, so you don't need to download each package separately as part of the installation process.

TECHNICAL STUFF

Some Linux installations have special requirements or experience limitations when working with Code::Blocks. The only apparent limitation that affects this book is the lack of Boost support for Red Hat and CentOS. Because of this limitation, you can't use the examples found in Book 7, Chapters 4 and 5. However, if you experience other limitations, please let me know about them at John@JohnMuellerBooks.com and I'll address them as part of a blog post for this book.

Using the graphical Linux installation

All versions of Linux support the standard installation discussed in the "Using the standard Linux installation" section of this chapter. However, a few versions of Debian–based Linux distributions, such as Ubuntu 12.x and above, provide a graphical installation technique as well. You'll need the administrator group (sudo) password to use this procedure, so having it handy will save you time. The following steps outline the graphical installation technique for Ubuntu, but the technique is similar for other Linux installations.

1. Open the Ubuntu Software Center **folder (the folder may be named Synaptics on other platforms).**

You see a listing of the most popular software available for download and installation, as shown in Figure 1-2. Your list will probably vary from the one shown in the screenshot.

2. Select Developer Tools (or Development) from the All Software drop-down list box.

You see a listing of developer tools, including Code::Blocks, as shown in Figure 1-3.

FIGURE 1-2:
The Ubuntu
Software Center
contains a list of
the most popular
software when
you open it.

FIGURE 1-3:
The Developer
Tools category
contains an entry
for Code::Blocks.

3. **Double click the Code::Blocks entry.**

   The `Ubuntu Software Center` provides details about the Code::Blocks entry and offers to install it for you, as shown in Figure 1-4.

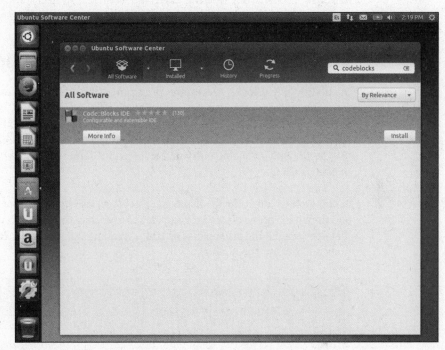

FIGURE 1-4:
It's possible to obtain additional information about Code::Blocks if necessary.

4. **Click Install.**

   Ubuntu begins the process of installing Code::Blocks. A progress bar shows the download and installation status. When the installation is complete, the Install button changes to a Remove button.

5. **Close the** `Ubuntu Software Center` **folder.**

   You see a Code::Blocks icon added to the Desktop. The IDE is ready for use.

Touring the Essential Code::Blocks Features

No matter how you install Code::Blocks for your platform, you eventually end up with an IDE with standardized characteristics. This is one of the best reasons to use an IDE such as Code::Blocks — you can use the same IDE no matter which platform you use.

REMEMBER

Your screenshots may look different from the ones shown in this book. Even though this book uses screenshots from the Windows version of Code::Blocks, the same features are provided for Code::Blocks installations on other platforms, though the IDE may not look precisely the same on those other platforms. The following sections describe the essential features you need to know about when working with Code::Blocks.

Starting Code::Blocks for the first time

Open the Code::Blocks executable program using the technique your platform usually requires. For example, when working with Windows or the Mac, you double-click the CodeBlocks icon. The first time you start Code::Blocks, you may see a Compilers Auto-detection dialog box. Select the GNU GCC Compiler entry (it may be the only available entry and selected by default), click Set as Default, and then click OK.

At this point, Code::Blocks displays a File Associations dialog box, similar to the one shown in Figure 1-5. It's a good idea to associate the IDE with your C++ files so that opening the file also opens the IDE — making it much easier to write applications and modify them later.

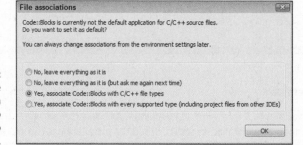

FIGURE 1-5:
Associate Code::Blocks with your C++ files to make it easier to manage them.

Select either of the Yes options in this list. You can associate Code::Blocks with other source code types, but for the purposes of this book, you only need to associate it with C++ files. Click OK to complete the action. At this point, you see the IDE.

After you set the file associations, Code::Blocks usually begins by opening the IDE and placing a tip dialog box in it, as shown in Figure 1-6. You can turn these tips off by clearing the Show Tips at Startup check box. The Tip of the Day link on the Start Here page (which you can display by choosing View⇨Start Page) also displays a tip when clicked. The tip is a random bit of information about using Code::Blocks more efficiently. You can see the next tip in the series by clicking Next Tip or disable the display of tips by clearing Show Tips at Startup. After you read the tip, click Close.

FIGURE 1-6:
Code::Blocks
provides a tips
dialog box that
contains helpful
information.

In some cases, the IDE will display a message similar to the one shown in Figure 1-7. What this message is saying is that you've made changes to the Code::Blocks configuration. Click Yes to save the changes.

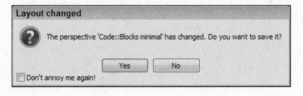

FIGURE 1-7:
Save your
changes to disk.

**TECHNICAL
STUFF**

Windows users may experience a problem at this point. If you install Code::Blocks in the C:\Program Files folder and don't have Administrator access (or if you simply opened the application as a regular user), you may find that you can't save any Code::Blocks settings, making using Code::Blocks an annoying experience. To use Code::Blocks without problems, make sure you have write access to the folder in which you installed it. The best policy is to install Code::Blocks to the C:\CodeBlocks folder on your system. As an alternative, you can right click the Code::Blocks icon and choose Run As Administrator from the context menu to run Code::Blocks with the required permissions.

Opening the sample projects

You obtain the source code for this book from the publisher site described in the Introduction. After you download the .zip file containing the source, you simply extract it to your hard drive. Don't attempt to run the source code inside the .zip file; doing so will display confusing messages in Code::Blocks and won't allow you to run the code.

The source code for this book is divided into books, chapters within books, and examples within chapters. To open the first example found in Chapter 3 of this book, for example, start by locating the \CPP_AIO\BookI\Chapter03\SayHello folder (or the equivalent on your platform). Within this folder is SayHello.cbp. The Code Blocks Project (.cbp) file extension contains everything that Code::Blocks needs to open the project and present it to you. When you get to this first project, you double-click SayHello.cbp and Code::Blocks automatically opens the project for you, as shown in Figure 1-8.

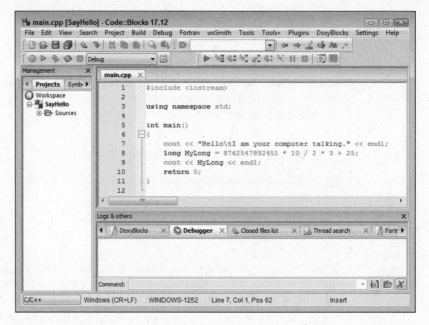

FIGURE 1-8:
Each example has a .cbp file associated with it that opens the example in Code::Blocks for you.

If you have chosen to allow tips, you'll actually see a Tip of the Day dialog box first, like the one shown earlier, in Figure 1-6. Click Close after you read the tip to see the project. Don't worry about the contents of this example for now. You'll discover how it works in Chapter 3. The only thing you need to know for now is how to open a project example so that you can follow along with the examples in the book.

TIP

When working with IDEs other than Code::Blocks, you can open the C++ (.cpp) file instead of the .cbp file. Opening the .cpp file will still display the code example for you. C++ stores source code in .cpp files, not as part of the .cbp files.

Viewing the essential windows

There are some windows that you use with every example in the book. As the book progresses, you'll be introduced to other windows, but the ones covered in the following sections are the windows that you need to know about in order to get started with Code::Blocks.

Using the Start Here window

The Start Here window, shown in Figure 1-9, does precisely as its name indicates — it gets you started with Code::Blocks. This window is automatically displayed when you open Code::Blocks directly, without opening a project first. It appears immediately after you clear the Tip of the Day dialog box.

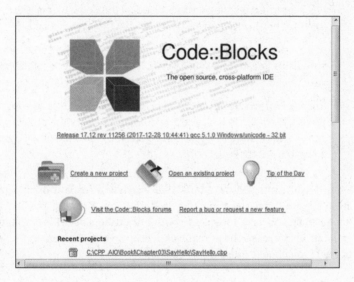

FIGURE 1-9:
Use the Start
Here window
to start a new
session.

This window is important because it also provides you with access to various Code::Blocks features and makes it possible for you to request changes. Here are the options you can access using this window:

>> **Create a New Project:** Before you can use Code::Blocks effectively, you need to create a project. A project acts as a container to hold the files used to create the application. It also stores settings used to configure the development environment and present that environment to you in a specific manner.

>> **Open an Existing Project:** Any time you want to re-create the environment you used during a previous coding session, you open an existing project. The project will automatically open any source code files that you had open and perform other tasks to make it easy for you to start right back up where you left off the previous day.

>> **Tip of the Day:** If you missed the Tip of the Day or you simply want to reactivate the feature, click this link. Code::Blocks displays the Tip of the Day dialog box, shown in Figure 1-6.

>> **Visit the Code::Blocks forums:** You can't communicate directly with the makers of Code::Blocks. However, you can communicate directly with other users and get peer support. The makers of Code::Blocks also monitor the forums, and you'll see them actively addressing issues that aren't handled with peer support.

>> **Report a Bug or Request a New Feature:** Every application on the planet has bugs (programming errors), including the Code::Blocks IDE. It's important to report bugs when you find them so that they can be fixed.

Anyone who uses an application long enough will likely come up with a spectacular idea for making it better. The makers of Code::Blocks want to hear your phenomenal idea, so contact them sooner than later.

>> **Recent Projects:** As you work with Code::Blocks, you'll create more than one project. Rather than look all over your hard drive for the project you need, you can use this feature to find it immediately. To open the project, just click on its link in the Recent Projects list.

REMEMBER

Even if you can't see the Start Here window after you open a project, you can always view it by selecting View⇨Start Page. Keeping the Start Here window handy makes it easy to access commonly used Code::Blocks features. However, you can also access these features using menus. For example, to create a new project, you choose File⇨New⇨Project.

Using the Management window

The purpose of an IDE is to help you manage your coding projects in various ways, so it's not surprising that Code::Blocks comes with a Management window, as shown in Figure 1-10. The Management window normally resides on the left side of the IDE's main window, but you can move it where you want by using the title bar to drag the window.

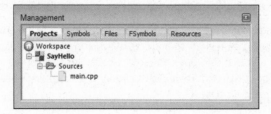

FIGURE 1-10:
The Management window helps you manage your Code::Blocks projects.

The Management window contains four tabs. (The Fortran Symbols, FSymbols, tab is never used in this book.) The following list describes the purpose of each tab:

>> **Projects:** Grouping in one place all of the files needed to create an application is a helpful method for managing it. A grouping of applications files is called a *project,* and helping you create and maintain projects is just one way in which Code::Blocks makes application development easier.

>> **Symbols:** Applications contain a number of symbols, such as the names of functions (named blocks of code). You use the Symbols tab to find specific symbols you need within an application. Don't worry too much about symbols now, but eventually you'll find that this tab helps save time and effort by making it easier to locate specific pieces of your application.

>> **Files:** Locating code and resources you need to add to the current project can be time consuming. The Files tab provides a method for navigating the file system. You can then right-click on files you need and use the context menu entries to perform tasks such as adding the file to your current project.

>> **Resources:** Graphical applications require the addition of dialog boxes and other visual elements that C++ treats as resources. The Resources tab contains a list of these resources so that you can find them easily and manage them in various ways.

**TECHNICAL
STUFF**

The Resources tab is a feature, used by advanced developers, which you generally don't need to worry about unless you decide to create graphical applications using a combination of C++ and the wxWidgets plug-in (installed automatically for Windows developers, but separately for both Mac and Linux developers). An explanation of how to create such applications is outside the scope of this book, but you can see a simple example of such a project at http://wiki.codeblocks.org/index.php?title=WxSmith_tutorial:_ Hello_world.

Using the Logs & Others window

Code::Blocks helps you track all sorts of activities. For example, when you create a new application from source code you write (a process called building), you see messages that tell you how the process went, as shown in Figure 1-11 (your messages may vary slightly). The examples in this book will help you understand when to use the various log tabs and other tabs (such as the Debugger tab) to better determine how your application works.

The tabs you see in this window depend on which options you have enabled in Code::Blocks and what task you're doing. Code::Blocks will usually select the tab you need automatically. If you want to close a particular tab, click the X next to its entry on the tab. To display a tab that you don't see, right-click any tab in the list and choose an entry from the Toggle option on the context menu.

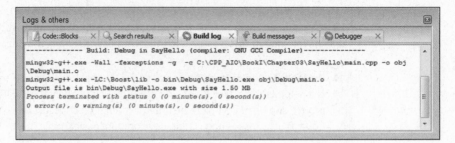

Selecting a compiler

Code::Blocks supports a host of compilers. This book uses GCC because it works on all of the target platforms and it provides great C++ 20 support. Most Code::Blocks installations also select this particular compiler automatically. So there are all kinds of great reasons to use GCC as a compiler. However, you might not have GCC selected on your system, and that could cause problems when running the examples. Not every compiler vendor provides great C++ 20 support, or your compiler vendor might implement a particular detail differently than GCC does. The following steps help you verify that GCC is the compiler selected for your system, and they help you change your configuration if it isn't:

1. **Open Code::Blocks.**

It doesn't matter if you select a project or not. Configuring the compiler will be the same whether you have a project loaded or not.

2. **Choose Settings⇨Compiler.**

You see the Compiler Settings dialog box, as shown in Figure 1-12.

3. **Click Global Compiler Settings in the left pane to display the global compiler settings.**

4. **Verify that the GNU GCC compiler (or an equivalent for your platform) is actually selected in the Selected Compiler list.**

The list could contain a number of GCC compiler entries. The best option is the GNU GCC Compiler setting because it offers maximum compatibility with the book examples. If the GNU GCC Compiler option (or an equivalent for your particular platform) is selected, proceed to Step 7.

5. **Select the GNU GCC Compiler option (or the equivalent for your platform) in the Select Compiler list.**

The Set As Default button becomes enabled after you make your selection.

6. **Click Set As Default.**

This step ensures that the GNU GCC compiler is used for all of your projects, even if you only want to open the downloaded source code.

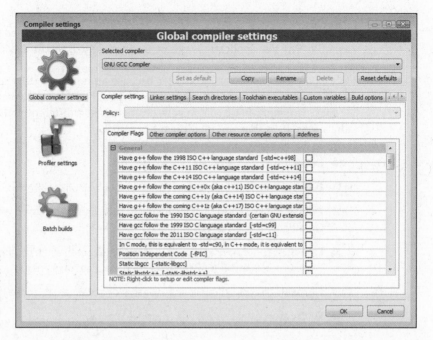

FIGURE 1-12:
Set Code::Blocks
to use the GCC
compiler to run
the examples in
this book.

7. **Click OK.**

8. **Close Code::Blocks.**

You see a Layout Changed dialog box.

9. **Click Yes.**

Your changes become permanent, and Code::Blocks closes.

Using Other IDEs

Even though this book will focus on the Code::Blocks IDE and the GCC compiler combination, the knowledge you gain can be used with any IDE and compiler combination. In fact, all you really need is the compiler. Most developers use an IDE, just because it makes things easy (and we all like things easy). You may find, though, that Code::Blocks simply doesn't provide the functionality you want or that it's too hard to use.

REMEMBER

The selection of an IDE is a personal thing, and most developers have specific reasons for choosing a particular IDE. In fact, I use several different IDEs and make my choice based on the needs of a particular project. So it's not even necessary to use the same IDE all the time. IDEs provide management features, while compilers control how the source code is interpreted and turned into an executable file. The two applications perform completely different tasks.

GCC is a great choice for a compiler because a number of IDEs support it. If you decide to use a different IDE from the one found in this book, that's fine with us. In fact, we congratulate you on your desire to take a different path! Here are some alternative IDEs that you might want to consider:

- **CodeLite:** https://codelite.org/
- **Dev-C++:** https://dev-c.soft32.com/free-download/?dm=2
- **Eclipse:** https://www.eclipse.org/downloads/ when used with C/C++ Development Tooling (CDT) (https://www.eclipse.org/cdt/)
- **Emacs:** https://www.gnu.org/software/emacs/) when used with the Emacs Code Browser (ECB) (http://ecb.sourceforge.net/)
- **Netbeans:** https://netbeans.apache.org/download/index.html
- **Qt Creator:** https://www.qt.io/developers/

» **Working with other mobile IDEs**

» **Using CppDroid to write code**

» **Getting CppDroid help**

Chapter 2

Configuring Your Mobile System

A t one time, developers relied exclusively on desktop systems to perform useful tasks because desktops provided the required computing power. Laptops came next, but essentially a laptop is a smaller form of a desktop. Today, however, developers rely on all sorts of mobile devices to write code. Even though someone could conceivably use a smartphone for the task, the majority of this activity occurs on high-powered tablet computers. The reason relates not so much to the power, but the form factor. A tablet offers more screen real estate to see your code and observe how it works. Keeping these two goals in mind and looking at the available Integrated Development Environments (IDEs), this chapter relies on Google CppDroid to make the leap from desktop systems to Android-powered tablet systems, such as the ASUS ZenPad 3S 10.

However, you shouldn't get the idea that CppDroid is the only game in town. You also find a description of a few other offerings in this chapter, and you can certainly try them if you like. The consistent issue with all of these offerings, though, is that they all currently lack C++ 20 support, so some book examples won't run on your tablet at all. If you want to ensure maximum compatibility with the book's code, procedures, and screenshots, you still need to rely on Code::Blocks running GCC.

After you get CppDroid installed, you need to know how to perform some basic tasks with it. This chapter doesn't provide a complete tutorial on using CppDroid, which is why it also discusses how to obtain help. However, you do discover how to interact with the book's code in this chapter, which is an essential part of the learning experience.

Obtaining CppDroid

Many IDEs are available for you to use to work with C/C++ code. However, most of them rely on the Windows, Linux, Mac OS X, and Solaris platforms (with Solaris appearing as an option far less often than the others). In addition, most of them are paid options, with Code::Blocks (http://www.codeblocks.org/) and Visual Studio Code (https://code.visualstudio.com/) being notable exceptions. However, to program on your Android device, you need an IDE that works with Android and provides some sort of cloud-based storage for the most part (PC-based IDEs use local storage). CppDroid offers a good Android-based solution that you can use in both online and offline mode without problem. Plus, the free option actually does work (but with limits; see the "Free versus paid software" sidebar for details). The following sections give you insights into working with CppDroid.

FREE VERSUS PAID SOFTWARE

You can often get by using free software on your mobile device. In some cases, you don't actually have a paid choice, but in other cases the paid option may offer features you won't use. Game software falls into this category, as do some kinds of productivity software. The paid version of an app often lacks ads, offers additional storage space, and frees up a few new features. You may also receive some level of support directly from the vendor, rather than rely on community support. Whether the paid version is worth your time depends on which features you use.

The free-versus-paid question skews toward paid when you start to work with an IDE. Many of the CppDroid features discussed in this chapter come with only the paid version, and the book assumes that you have the paid version when working with the code. However, you can probably work with a majority of the examples using the free version if you're willing to put up with the loss of some functionality, like real-time diagnostics and static analysis.

Understanding why CppDroid is such a great choice

You can find a number of C/C++ IDEs for Android in the Google Play Store. However, the choices come down to three products for most people (in order of preference):

» CppDroid

» C4Droid

» CxxDroid

REMEMBER

None of these products will completely replace a desktop IDE, but CppDroid comes very close. For example, CppDroid is the only one of the three products that has built-in support for graphics. You can obtain graphics support in CxxDroid using Qt (https://www.qt.io/) and a nonstandard header, graphics.h, but this means working in a manner that doesn't easily translate between desktop and mobile device. You can also use CxxDroid with Simple DirectMedia Layer (SDL) (https://www.libsdl.org/). C4Droid supports SDL using only a non-standard graphics.h file. You use Qt to develop business graphics software, while SDL works great for 2-D games.

If you want to develop 3-D games, you must use DirectX through Wine (https://www.androidpolice.com/2020/01/21/windows-compatibility-layer-wine-hits-v5-0-on-android/) or OpenGL (https://developer.android.com/guide/topics/graphics/opengl). There are add-ons, such as Unity (https://developer.android.com/games/develop/build-in-unity) and Unreal (https://docs.unrealengine.com/en-US/Platforms/Mobile/Android/index.html), but they actually layer on DirectX or OpenGL, so you're still using one of these two technologies, despite using them indirectly. Using any of these products on Android is difficult, and you should plan plenty of time to integrate these APIs into your IDE.

It's helpful to know precisely what CppDroid provides. Table 2-1 lists basic functionality, whether this functionality comes only with the paid version, and a brief overview of what you obtain with the basic functionality. As you work with CppDroid, you encounter some deficiencies, especially when running the standardized code in this book, but you also discover that you can run a lot of it without any sort of modification.

TABLE 2-1: **CppDroid Features**

Feature	Paid Only	Description
Add-ons manager		Even though CppDroid comes with all the basics you need, at some point you'll want to go beyond the basics, which is where add-ons come into play. An add-ons manager makes the task of knowing what you need to add a lot easier. Plus, you can easily get rid of items that you no longer need.
Auto indentation		Trying to keep your code readable means using indentation to see things like the start and finish of an if statement or other code block. Having configurable auto indentation means that you can choose how the code is indented, but you don't have to indent it manually.
Auto pairing		Locating a missing parenthesis or brace can drive you slowly nuts. Configurable auto pairing means that you determine how elements are paired, but the IDE helps you ensure that nothing needed to compile the code is missing.
Auto updates		Getting the latest software updates helps you write code that works with the newest trends in C/C++ development. You also get bug fixes, which is essential for the reliability and security of the code you create.
C/C++ code examples included	X	Because working with tablet-based IDEs can sometimes come with quirks, having a full set of C/C++ code examples is essential. These examples show how to work around the quirks so that you can execute your C/C++ code with just a few small modifications when necessary.
C++ tutorial and learn guide included	X	If you plan to work offline, it's essential to have a tutorial and learning guide for those times when you almost, but not quite, remember how to perform a particular task. Of course, you'll also want to keep this book handy.
Code complete	X	Automatically suggests how to complete statements that you type based on previous content. This feature reduces potential typos and makes you considerably more efficient, especially when working on the tiny keyboards found in tablets.
Compile C/C++ code		In some cases, such as when working with a web-based IDE, the C++ code you create is interpreted by ROOT (see https://en.wikitolearn.org/ROOT_for_beginners for more information about ROOT). Some tablet IDEs also require ROOT, but with CppDroid you get fully compiled C/C++ code output instead.
Dropbox support	X	Sharing your code with others is a lot easier when you have Dropbox support.
File and tutorial navigator		This feature provides an index into the documentation to tell you about C/C++ code constructs, including variables and methods.

Feature	Paid Only	Description
Google Drive support	X	Working from anywhere on a single piece of code means having access to that code from every environment you use. If your desktop system also supports Google Drive, you can switch between your desktop and tablet as the need arises.
Portrait/landscape UI		A tablet presents a constrained screen real estate environment. When an IDE forces you to use it in landscape mode only, you often see the IDE informational panes at the expense of seeing the code. Working in portrait mode lets you ignore most of the IDE panes while focusing on the code.
Problem fix suggestions	X	You get suggestions for a variety of coding issues, even if those issues may not necessarily result in a compilation error.
Real-time diagnostics (warnings and errors)	X	Real-time diagnostics enable you to find certain classes of errors in your code without having to compile it. The IDE monitors what you type and can point out issues like typos without compilation, which saves considerable time.
Smart syntax highlighting		Highlighting makes your code stand out so that you can see things like variables and keywords more easily.
Static analysis	X	Static analysis helps locate truly difficult-to-find bugs that include: memory leaks, mismatching allocation and deallocation, uninitialized variables usage, and array index out-of-bounds errors.
Theme-based code syntax highlighting	X	Themes let you highlight code syntax in a manner that makes sense to you. If you have visual problems, using themes can turn a difficult viewing experience into one that works well with your vision. The use of themes means that no one is stuck using a particular theme to highlight syntax; you see it the way that works best for you.
Works offline		The ability to work without an Internet connection means that you gain flexibility in where you can work. However, it also means that you must have access to everything you need as part of the local installation, which is something that CppDroid provides at the expense of additional local storage use.

Getting your copy of CppDroid

You obtain CppDroid from the Google App Store by searching for CppDroid. Unfortunately, it doesn't support every version of Android, so you may not actually see it if your device doesn't support it. Figure 2-1 shows how the page appears when you find it. To obtain a copy, all you need to do is tap Install.

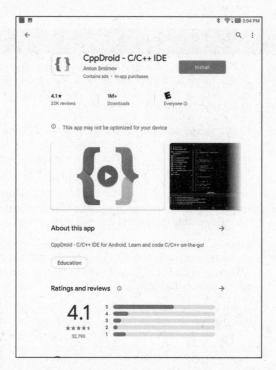

FIGURE 2-1:
Locating
CppDroid in
the Google Play
Store.

Ensuring you get a good install

After the CppDroid app installs on your tablet, you see the Open button as usual. However, instead of opening the app, you see something like the view in Figure 2-2. To work offline, CppDroid needs to install a number of libraries on your system. This process can take a while, so just wait for it to complete.

Extracting
"libclang" 3.4

37%   37/100

FIGURE 2-2:
Loading the
CppDroid
libraries for
offline use.

Considering Other Alternatives

You aren't limited to working with CppDroid, even though it's the tablet IDE used for the book. Most tablet IDEs will let you perform a basic set of tasks that will work well for the majority of the book examples. The only time you'll encounter difficulty is when working with examples that use new C++ features, rely on graphics in some way, or employ standard features not found in the tablet IDE. One of the advantages of these alternatives is that they might support your device when CppDroid doesn't. The following sections tell you about the best alternatives that provide maximum compatibility with the book examples.

Working with C4Droid

C4Droid has many of the same features as CppDroid. For example, it compiles your C/C++ code, so you don't need ROOT support. However, you can use it if desired. As with CppDroid, the app targets the educational market, but C4Droid doesn't enjoy the strong community support that CppDroid does (see the article at `https://www.androidrank.org/compare/c4droid_c_c_compiler_ide/cppdroid_c_c_ide/com.n0n3m4.droidc/name.antonsmirnov.android.cppdroid` for details). In contrast to CppDroid, no free version of C4Droid exists, but when compared to the price charged for most desktop IDEs, C4Droid is a bargain.

REMEMBER

Beside the graphics limitations noted earlier in the chapter, C4Droid has some other limits as well. The most important of these is that it currently supports only C++ 11, which means that any newer examples in the book won't run on it. You also need to download and separately install more products to get a fully functional IDE. The limited number of examples can also be a problem. Because the tablet environment can be different from working on the desktop, having a great list of examples can really help.

Getting multiple language support with AIDE

If you're looking for a single IDE that can do everything you need on your tablet, Android IDE (AIDE) (`https://www.android-ide.com/`) might be what you need. Unlike the other IDEs listed in this chapter, this one works with a slew of languages, including Java, C/C++, HTML5, CSS, and JavaScript. AIDE is also Android Studio and Eclipse compatible (limited to API level 27), so if you plan to create Android apps using a language such as Java, this might be the right choice for you. (Unfortunately, Google is focusing on the Kotlin language for Android development and has no plans to add Kotlin support to AIDE now.)

However, with such a flexible range of features comes complexity, which seems to be the major criticism of AIDE. The well-designed tutorials tend to help a little, but obviously not enough for a novice developer. Many users also complain that there is a plug-in for every need and all the plug-ins are paid, so this IDE can nickel-and-dime you to death.

REMEMBER

The C/C++ language support for AIDE comes from the Android Java C++ APK 3.2, which means that you can expect differences in support from the GNU Compiler Collection (GCC) used with Code::Blocks for the desktop application in this book. You may find that some examples won't work properly because of these differences, but all the simple (earlier) examples will work fine.

Using web-based IDEs

You can use a web-based IDE from any device, including your desktop, so in some cases, they represent the best in terms of device compatibility. A web-based IDE also provides an interpreted environment through ROOT in most cases. Consequently, when learning to develop apps in C/C++, you get instant feedback, which can save considerable time. As shown in Figure 2-3, the web-based offerings also tend to provide a simple interface that allows you to get right to work.

The example in Figure 2-3 is JDoodle (`https://www.jdoodle.com/online-compiler-c++17/`), which is one of the best C/C++ online offerings. This particular online IDE supports 72 programming languages. How well it supports all of them depends on the interpreter used. For the most part, you find that the JDoodle IDE provides an acceptable method of working with the code in the book. Because it also supports C++ 17, you can also run more of the examples than you can using a C/C++ app.

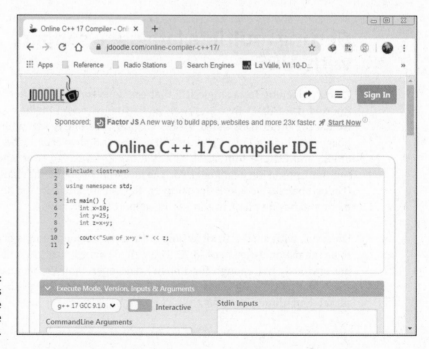

FIGURE 2-3:
Web-based IDEs tend to provide a very simple interface.

The problem with every one of the web-based IDEs is that you must use them online. In addition, there is a very good chance you won't be able to save your code, so they're mostly useful for experimentation and not long-term learning. However, even with these issues, here are some of the web-based IDEs you might consider as replacements for CppDroid in addition to JDoodle:

>> **C++ Shell (C++ 14):** http://cpp.sh/

>> **CodeChef (C++ 14):** https://www.codechef.com/ide

>> **Ideone (C++ 14):** https://ideone.com/SXNfC0

>> **OnlineGBD (C++ 17):** https://www.onlinegdb.com/online_c_compiler

>> **Rextester.com (Varies according to C compiler selected):** https://rextester.com/l/c_online_compiler_gcc

>> **RepLit (C++ 11):** https://repl.it/languages/cpp11

>> **TutorialsPoint (C++ 11):** https://www.tutorialspoint.com/compile_cpp11_online.php

Touring the Essential CppDroid Features

After you have CppDroid downloaded, you want to begin working with it. The following sections get you started with the basic features you need to work with the examples in this book. However, the IDE provides a lot more functionality than you find here, so spending time with the various examples and tutorials is a good idea as well.

Getting started with CppDroid

When the libraries are finally loaded, you see a screen similar to the one shown in Figure 2-4. The top left of this screen displays the name of the file (which you can change if you want). The top right contains buttons to Save, Compile, and Run your app.

Along the bottom of the screen, you see the current phase of working with your code:

>> **Diagnostics:** Shows errors that occur in your typing.

>> **Analysis:** Outputs the results of a compilation.

>> **Output:** Displays the output from your app.

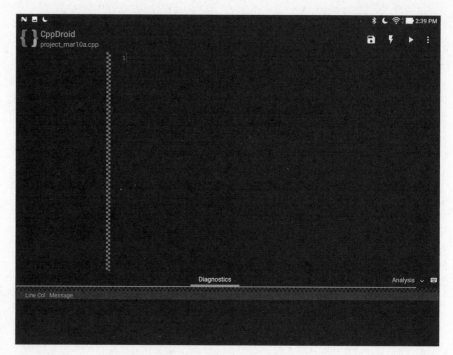

FIGURE 2-4:
Accessing the
basic CppDroid
user interface
features.

TIP

Tap the ellipsis button in the top-right corner and you see the menu shown in Figure 2-5. To obtain full functionality from CppDroid, you need to tap the Purchase entry and select the optional features you want to buy (see Table 2-1 for details). Choosing Premium will give you access to all the extra features at a reduced cost.

FIGURE 2-5:
Use the menu
to locate the
CppDroid
features and
options.

Accessing an example

CppDroid comes with both examples and tutorials you can use to learn more about the IDE and C/C++ in general. The tutorials work much like the examples—just with more content. To access the Hello World example, choose ...⇨Project⇨Examples⇨C++⇨For Beginners⇨HelloWorld. The display will now contain the code shown in Figure 2-6.

FIGURE 2-6:
Loading an example provides a quick way to see code in action.

```
1 #include <iostream>
2
3 int main()
4 {
5     std::cout << "Hello world!";
6 }
```

To compile this code, you touch the lightning icon. After it has compiled, you can run it by tapping the right-pointing arrow. The display will change to show the output. To clear the output, tap the left-pointing arrow in the upper left corner of the display.

Working with a simple online project

You can place the source code for this book on your Google Drive or Dropbox. Of course, you'll still need some method of accessing it. The following steps assume that you use Google Drive, but they also work with Dropbox. (When working with Dropbox, you place the code in the Dropbox\Apps\CppDroid folder.)

1. **Choose ...⇨Project⇨Open⇨From Google Drive.**

   You may have to log in at this point. After you log in, you may see a dialog box like the one shown in Figure 2-7 in which you give permission to access Google Drive from CppDroid. Tap Allow to allow the access. (This is a one-time step.)

2. **Locate the folder containing the code you want to access.**

   You see one or more .cpp files. For example, when working with the book's source code, you might choose the Book I\Chapter03\SayHello folder.

3. **Highlight the file you want to open and then tap Select.**

   CppDroid opens the file for you. Figure 2-8 shows an example of the HelloWorld.cpp file for Book 1, Chapter 3.

At this point, you can compile and run your application just as if you used Code::Blocks. The only difference is that you're doing it on your tablet.

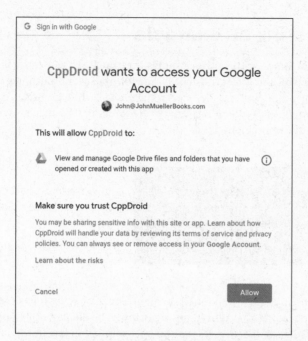

FIGURE 2-7:
Give permission
to access your
Google Drive.

FIGURE 2-8:
The file is
available for use
with your local
copy of CppDroid.

```cpp
1  #include <iostream>
2
3  using namespace std;
4
5  int main()
6  {
7      cout << "Hello\tI am your computer talking." << endl;
8      //long MyLong = 8762547892451; //* 10 / 2 * 3 + 25;
9      long MyLong = 2;
10     cout << MyLong << endl;
11     return 0;
12  }
13
```

Accessing your source code

To begin creating a new source code file, you choose ...⇨File⇨New. When you create a new file, CppDroid automatically gives it a default name. You can change the name by choosing ...⇨File⇨Rename. A single file can be part of a project, but you can also make a single file the entire project. For example, a Hello World app would consist of a single file.

You can store your source code locally, on Google Drive, or on Dropbox. When working online, the process is the same as when working with online source as described in the "Working with a simple online project" section of the chapter. The following list tells how you can store your source code locally to make it available at all times.

>> **To create a new project:** Choose ...⇨Project⇨New. When you see the New Project dialog box shown in Figure 2-9, type a project name and then tap either Create C Project or Create C++ Project.

>> **To open an existing project:** Choose ...⇨Project⇨Open, select one of the project sources: Recent, From Device, From Dropbox, or From Google Drive, and then select the project you want to open.

>> **To save an existing project:** Choose ...⇨Project⇨Save or ...⇨Project⇨Save As. When using Save As, you can choose a different location, such as Dropbox or Google Drive, and a new project name.

>> **To close an existing project:** Choose ...⇨Project⇨Close. CppDroid automatically saves your project to the default location with the current name if you haven't done so.

>> **To delete an existing project:** Choose ...⇨Project⇨Delete while the project is open for editing.

New Project

CREATE C PROJECT   CREATE C++ PROJECT

FIGURE 2-9:
Define a new local project.

Considering differences with the desktop environment

When you compare CppDroid with Code::Blocks, you find that CppDroid provides a much simpler interface with far fewer features. It works as a means to write code while on the road and for testing simple applications. You can't use CppDroid as a full-fledged development environment simply because it doesn't contain the features that such an environment provides, especially when it comes to things like debugging. In fact, the limits clearly present themselves on the Actions menu shown in Figure 2-10, where CppDroid limits you to completing code, performing analysis, compiling, and running the code with or without arguments.

FIGURE 2-10:
The list of actions
in CppDroid
is somewhat
limited.

TIP

Even with the limits, you can easily work with any example in the book that consists of a single file or doesn't rely on the latest C++ functionality. You need the desktop environment, however, to make most multifile examples work and to perform complex tasks. By working through the examples in this book on your tablet, you gain insights into what is and isn't possible for CppDroid, giving you another useful tool that you can use to code wherever and whenever you want.

Obtaining CppDroid Help

No matter how simple and straightforward the interface, no matter how many examples and tutorials supplied, every app will generate some number of questions. Consequently, you need access to help at some point to make things work. The following sections offer a quick overview of the help available for CppDroid.

Working with the Help documentation

The oddest part about working with CppDroid is that there isn't an actual Help file. When you open the ...⇨Help menu, you see the options shown in Figure 2-11.

FIGURE 2-11:
A list of Help
sources for
CppDroid.

The CppDroid blog contains the latest entries by the app author. What the blog provides is a running commentary of the problems that the developer is seeing and what is being done to fix them. You also see side posts on topics such as the number of people currently using CppDroid and other projects that the author is contemplating. Even so, this is where you go when you have a problem with the product and hope that the developer is addressing it. Figure 2-12 shows an example of the sort of blog posts you see.

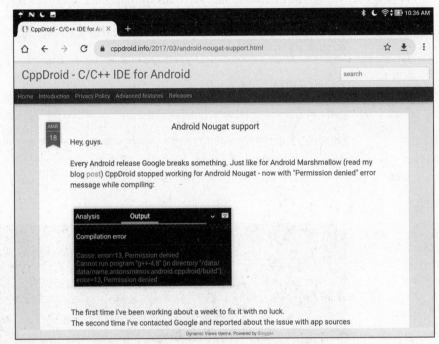

FIGURE 2-12:
The developer uses blog posts to help you find bug fixes.

When you find no apparent help for a particular problem, you choose the Post Feedback option on the Help menu to send the developer an email. Oddly enough, you may find that you have a hard time getting through with anything other than Gmail.

Getting community support

You can find a lot of articles about CppDroid online on various websites. The articles provide you with insights on how to use CppDroid and often answer questions that users have about it. In addition, you can find help using CppDroid at these sites:

>> **Reddit:** `https://www.reddit.com/r/cpp/search?q=cppdroid`

>> **SourceForge:** `https://sourceforge.net/` (search for CppDroid)

>> **StackOverflow:** `https://stackoverflow.com/search?q=CppDroid`

>> **AndroidForums:** `https://androidforums.com/apps/`
   `cppdroid-c-c-ide.5356/`

TIP

You might find additional locations for CppDroid information online. If you find one of these places and it seems to have good, consistent information, please let me know at John@JohnMuellerBooks.com so that I can share the information with other readers.

Using the free examples

The free examples often provide you with insights into how CppDroid works. For example, you may wonder how the static analysis feature works. To see a demonstration of static analysis, choose ...⇨Project⇨Examples⇨C++⇨For Developers⇨Static Analysis. After the file loads, choose ...⇨Actions⇨Analyze. Figure 2-13 shows the results.

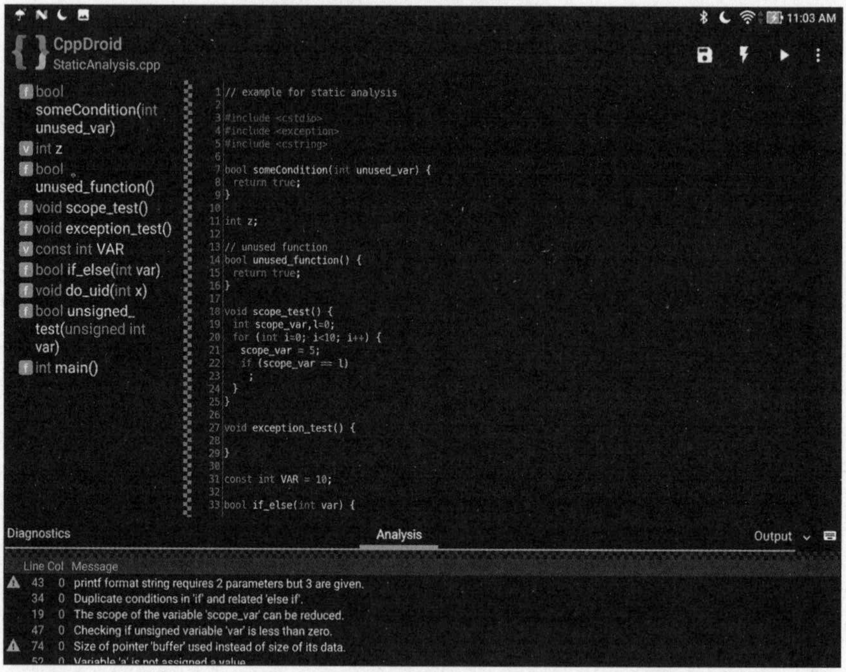

FIGURE 2-13:
Use an example to see how the static analysis feature works.

Notice that the output shows various problems with the code, such as the `printf` `format string requires 2 parameters, but 3 are given` at line 43, column

0 near the bottom of the screen. The output helps you locate problems with your code and fix them before you compile it.

Accessing the tutorials

The tutorials provide a multistep process for working with C++ within CppDroid. When you choose ...⇨Project⇨Tutorials⇨C++⇨For Beginners, you see two tutorial options:

>> CPlusPlus.com C++ Tutorial

>> LearnCpp.com C++ Tutorial

Both tutorials give you help with getting over the C++ learning curve from within the CppDroid environment. The IDE changes to show a tutorial outline in the left pane and the associated text in the right, as shown in Figure 2-14. You work directly from within the CppDroid environment, which means that you can better understand how CppDroid works when you finish.

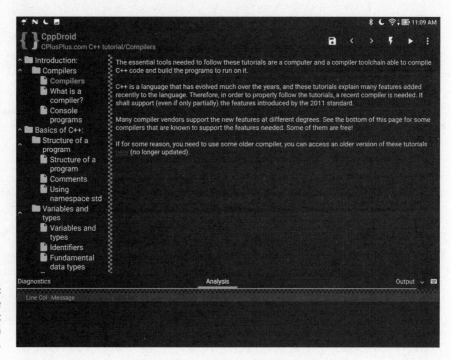

FIGURE 2-14:
The tutorials take you through basic processes within CppDroid.

IN THIS CHAPTER

» Organizing your applications into projects

» Typing code into the code editor

» Writing an application that writes to the screen

» Doing basic math

» Running your application

Chapter **3**

Creating Your First C++ Application

t's your lucky day. You have decided to learn one of the most popular programming languages on the planet. (C++ is the fourth most popular language according to the TIOBE Index at the time of this writing, at https://www.tiobe.com/tiobe-index/.) From the biggest skyscrapers housing huge Fortune 500 companies all the way down to the garages with the self-starting kids grinding out the next generation of software, people are using C++. Yes, there are other languages, but more programmers use C++ than any other language for desktop application, game, animation, media access, compiler, and operating system development. In this chapter, you start right out writing a C++ application.

As mentioned in Chapter 1, this book relies on your use of Code::Blocks as the IDE and on GCC as the C++ compiler. The procedures are written for the most current version of Code::Blocks (version 17.12) at the time of writing, so you may need to make allowances if you use a different Code::Blocks version, and the procedures won't work if you use another IDE. In addition, you may need to make minor changes to the code as the examples become more complex if you want to use other compilers.

You don't have to type the source code for this chapter manually. In fact, using the downloadable source is a lot easier. You can find the source for this chapter in the \CPP_AIO4\BookI\Chapter03 folder of the downloadable source. See the Introduction for details on how to find these source files.

Code::Blocks Creating a Project

Creating a computer application is usually a bigger job than you'd want to organize in your head. Application code is saved in files much like the documents in a word processor. But applications often have more than one source-code file. At big companies in big buildings in big cities, some applications are *really big* — hundreds of source-code files for just one application.

Understanding projects

Applications can contain a lot of source code. To keep all that source code together, programmers use a file that manages it all, called a *project*. A project has a few key elements:

>> A set of source-code files

>> (Optional) Resource information such as icons and sound files

>> A description of how to compile (build) the application

>> Integrated Development Environment (IDE) settings that tell how to set up the editor you use to write the application

>> Some general descriptions of the application being built, such as its name and the type of application it is

The *type of application* doesn't mean "word processor" or "really cool earth-shattering software," even if that's what your application is. This book uses *type* to mean your application's overall relationship with other applications:

>> Does this application run by itself?

>> Does this application add to or extend the functionalities of another application (such as Firefox)?

>> Does this application serve as a *library* (a bunch of code that you make available to another application)?

All this information, along with your source-code files, represents a project.

In the Code::Blocks IDE, you create a new project each time you start work on a new application. You provide a little information about the application you're working on, and then you begin writing your code. All the code for your application is stored in one place — in the project.

Defining your first project

To create a new project in Code::Blocks, start Code::Blocks and choose File➪New➪Project, or click Create a New Project on the Start Here page that appears when you start the application. A dialog box appears, as shown in Figure 3-1.

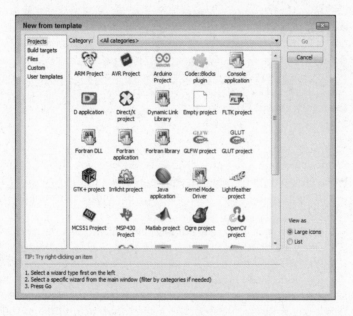

FIGURE 3-1:
The New from Template dialog box lets you select a new project type.

TIP

You see what appear to be way too many project types, including some that have nothing to do with C++, such as Fortran Application and Matlab Project. You can reduce the number of choices by selecting a category in the Category field. The best option for the projects in this book is Console.

When you create a C++ project in Code::Blocks, you choose from a list of several types of applications. They're shown as icons in the New from Template dialog box in alphabetical order. The following list shows some application types:

» **GTK+ Project:** This is a graphical application that includes, well, a window. You know the kind: It usually has a menu across the top and something inside it that you can either click or type into. It relies on the GNU Image Manipulation Program (GIMP) Toolkit (GTK), which provides an incredibly flexible interface that runs on a number of platforms including Linux, Mac, and Windows systems. Read more about GTK in the "What about all of those other projects?" sidebar.

» **Console Application:** This is an application that gets a paltry Console window instead of a graphical window. *Console* refers to a window with a command prompt. (Folks who recall the old days, before Windows, call it a *DOS box,* and you may know it as a *terminal window* when working with operating systems such as the Mac or Linux.)

» **Static library:** A *static library* is a set of C++ code that you use later in another project. It's like making a really great marinade that you won't use up today. You'll use some of it tomorrow and some of it after that.

» **Dynamic Link Library:** A Dynamic Link Library (DLL) is kind of like a static library except it is separated from the main application and gets its own file with a .DLL extension.

» **Empty project:** This blank project is as clean as a blank sheet of white typing paper, ready for you to fill 'er up.

TIP

Frankly, it's kind of a pain to use an empty project, because you have to tweak and set a bunch of things. So we never use this option.

For the samples in this chapter, create a Console Application. Follow these steps:

1. **In the New from Template dialog box, click the Console Application icon found on the Projects tab, and then click Go.**

The wizard asks which language you want to use.

2. **Highlight C++ and click Next.**

You see a list of project-related questions, as shown in Figure 3-2. These questions define project basics, such as the project name.

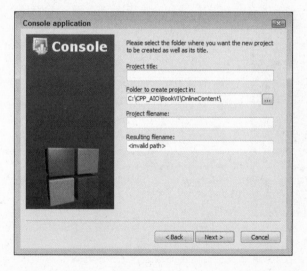

FIGURE 3-2:
Provide the name of your project for Code::Blocks.

3. **Type a name for your project in the Project Title field.**

The example uses SayHello as the project title. Notice that the wizard automatically starts creating an entry for you in the Project Filename field.

4. **Type a location for your project in the Folder to Create Project In field.**

The example uses C:\CPP_AIO4\BookI\Chapter03 as the folder name. You can also click the ellipsis button next to the Folder to Create Project In field to use the Browse for Folder dialog box to locate the folder you want to use. Notice that the wizard completes the entry in the Project Filename field.

5. **(Optional) Type a project filename in the Project Filename field.**

Code::Blocks fills in this field for you automatically based on the Project Title field entry, and there isn't a good reason to change it in most cases; however, in special circumstances, you may choose to do so. For example, if you have a project with multiple elements, you may want the project file to match the name of an overall project rather than the name of a particular entity within the project.

6. **Click Next.**

You see the compiler settings shown in Figure 3-3. Most of the projects in this book use the default compiler settings, which include the GNU GCC Compiler shown in the figure. However, if you look at the Compiler drop-down list, you see that Code::Blocks supports a number of compilers and you can add more to it. The other settings control the creation and location of a Debug version of the application (the version you use for finding problems in your code) and a Release version (the version that you send to a customer).

FIGURE 3-3:
Tell Code::Blocks where to place the Debug and Release versions of your application.

7. **(Optional) Change any required compiler settings.**

There generally isn't any good reason to change the compiler settings unless your project has a specific need, such as placing the output and object files in the same folder.

8. **Click Finish.**

The wizard creates the application for you. It then displays the Code::Blocks IDE with the project loaded. However, the source code file isn't loaded yet.

9. **Drill down into the SayHello workspace entries on the Projects tab of the Management window and double-click** `main.cpp`**.**

You see the source code file loaded so that you can edit it, as shown in Figure 3-4.

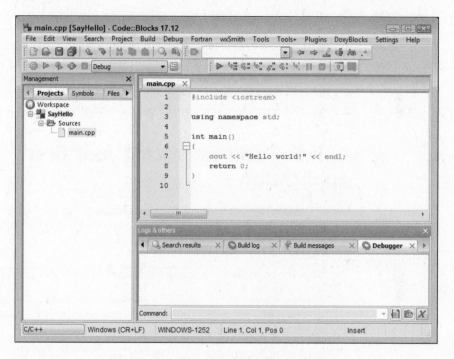

FIGURE 3-4: Use the Code::Blocks IDE to interact with your project.

The project window is organized side by side:

>> The left side is an Explorer view (called a *tree view*), which represents your project. At the top of the tree view is a workspace — the essential unit of a project. Below the workspace is the name of your project. Underneath that are the components of your project. In this case, only one component exists so far: the source-code file whose filename is `main.cpp`. Remember that, in order to program in C++, you enter code into a source-code file; this file, called `main.cpp`, is such a file for your SayHello project.

>> The right side (which actually takes up about three-quarters of the screen) is the source-code file itself.

This part works much like a word processor or an email editor, and you can type the code into the window. You notice that you already have some code there — a sort of starter code that came into being when you chose Console Application and created the project.

>> At the bottom of the display are a number of status windows. The Code::Blocks window tells you how the wizard created your application. Don't worry about these windows right now. You see them in action as the book progresses.

REMEMBER

Note that Figure 3-4 also shows some additional elements: a menu, several toolbars, and a status bar. You can right-click the toolbar area to show or hide toolbars as needed. Figure 3-4 shows the default toolbars when you first start a project. The status bar shows the language highlighting in use, some configuration settings, and your current position within the source file. You can change the highlighting used in the editor window by choosing a new language option in the drop-down menu on the left side of the status bar that currently shows C/C++.

Building and executing your first application

Okay, it's time to work with your first application. Use the following steps to save the file, build the application (make it into an executable that your operating system can use), and execute the application:

1. **Save the code file by choosing File⇨Save Everything or press Ctrl+Shift+S.**

Saving the files ensures that you have a good copy on disk should something go wrong. For example, you could completely crash the IDE if your application does the wrong thing.

2. **Choose Build⇨Build or press Ctrl+F9.**

This action creates the executable file. Building the code converts words you understand into code that your operating system understands. Notice that Code::Blocks automatically selects the Build Log window for you and you see the steps that Code::Blocks takes to create your application. At the end of the process, you should see something like `0 errors, 0 warnings` (`0 minutes, 1 seconds`) as the output (the precise amount of time may vary, but it should be short).

3. **Choose Build⇨Run or press Ctrl+F10.**

An output window like the one shown in Figure 3-5 opens, and you see your first application execute.

4. **Press Enter to stop application execution.**

The application window disappears and you see the Code::Blocks IDE again.

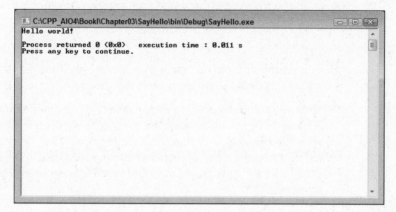

FIGURE 3-5:
Execute your first
application.

Well, that wasn't interesting, was it? But that's okay! The application starts out in a basic situation: You have a console window, and then when the application is finished doing whatever it must do, it shows the message Press any key to continue. — and when you do so, the application ends.

Typing the Code

The rightmost 75 percent or so of the Code::Blocks window is the *code editor*; it's where you type and change your code. Of all the tasks we just mentioned in the first part of this chapter, the nearest equivalent to using the Code::Blocks code editor is composing an email message.

WARNING

Word movement and selection actions look a bit strange on the screen. They ignore certain characters, such as *braces* — the curly characters { and }.

The code editor works like the editor in an email message. You can

>> Type code.

>> Move the *cursor* with the arrow keys (up, down, left, right) to the position where you want to type. The *cursor* is the little blinking vertical bar that shows where your text goes when you type. Some folks call it a *caret* or an *insertion point*.

>> **Click where you want to type.** Use the mouse to point where you want to type, and then click the mouse button. The cursor jumps to the spot where you click.

>> **Select text to delete or change.** You can select text in either of two ways:

 • Point with the mouse at the first or last character you want to select; then hold down the mouse button while you drag the mouse.

 • Move the cursor to the first or last character you want to select; then hold down the Shift key while you press the arrow keys.

>> **Scroll the text up and down (vertically) or left and right (horizontally)** with the scroll bars. The scroll bars work only when there is more text than you can see in the window, just like most other places in the Windows, Linux, and Mac worlds. You can scroll up and down (if there's enough text in the editor) by using Ctrl+↑ and Ctrl+↓ key combinations or the mouse wheel (assuming you have one).

>> **Scrolling changes only what you *see*.** You must use the mouse or the arrow keys to *select* what you see.

REMEMBER

After you play around a bit with the editor, you can use Table 3-1 to do a few of your favorite tasks. (Of course, if you're new to programming, you may not know yet whether these are your favorites — but they will be soon. Trust me.)

TABLE 3-1

Navigation and Edit Commands

Command	Keystroke or Action
Move the cursor	↑, ↓, ←, or →, Home, End
Move from word to word	Ctrl+← or Ctrl+→
Select with the mouse	Click the mouse in the text, and while the mouse button is down, drag the mouse
Select with the cursor	Shift+↑, Shift+↓, Shift+←, or Shift+→
Select the next word	Shift+Ctrl+→
Select the previous word	Shift+Ctrl+←
Select everything	Ctrl+A
Go to the top	Ctrl+Home
Go to the bottom	Ctrl+End

Starting with Main

When a computer runs code, it does so in a step-by-step, line-by-line manner. But your code is organized into pieces, and one of these pieces is the *main function,* or simply main( ), which is the part that runs first. main( ) tells the computer which *other* parts of the application you want to use. main( ) is the head honcho, the big boss.

How does the computer know what is main( )? You type lines of code between the *brace* characters, { and }. Here is the default application that Code::Blocks produces when you create a Console Application project:

```
#include <iostream>

using namespace std;

int main()
{
    cout << "Hello world!" << endl;
    return 0;
}
```

The word main is required, and it tells the computer where main( ) is. You might also see main( ) shown as

```
int main(int argc, char *argv[])
```

Don't worry about the words around main( ) for now. You discover what these words mean later in the chapter. For now, all you need to know is that every C++ application has a main( ) function.

REMEMBER

The computer performs the code line by line. If a line is blank, the computer just goes to the next line. When you write lines of code, you are instructing the computer to do something (which is why some people refer to lines of code as *instructions*).

Showing Information

Ready to type some code and try it out? Go for it! This code will open the famous console window and write some words to it.

First, make sure that you still have the Code::Blocks IDE open and the SayHello project open, as in this chapter's preceding examples. If not, follow these steps:

1. **Start Code::Blocks if it's not already running.**

   You see the Start page for the Code::Blocks IDE.

2. **Click the** SayHello.cbp **project found in the Recent Projects list.**

   Code::Blocks opens the project for you.

If the main.cpp code isn't showing in the rightmost 75 percent of the window, double-click main.cpp in the tree view on the left. It immediately opens. (If you don't see the tree view, click the little tab at the top that says Projects; it's next to a tab that says Symbols.)

Follow these steps carefully. Make sure that you type everything exactly as given here:

1. **Position the cursor on the line with the opening brace.**

   In this case, that's Line 6. You can see the line number on the left side of the code editor.

2. **Press the Enter key.**

   The cursor should be in the fifth column. If it isn't — if it stays in the first column — press the spacebar four times.

3. **Type the following line of code exactly as it appears here.**

   Put no spaces between the two less-than (<) symbols. Make sure that you remember the final semicolon at the end. Here's the line:

   ```
   cout << "Hello, I am your computer talking." << endl;
   ```

4. **Delete the line of code that looks like this:**

   ```
   cout << "Hello world!" << endl;
   ```

In the end, your code will look like the following example (the new line that you typed is shown here in bold):

```
#include <iostream>

using namespace std;

int main()
```

```
{
    cout << "Hello, I am your computer talking." << endl;
    return 0;
}
```

If you don't type your code correctly, the computer can tell you. This step *compiles* the application: The computer makes sure that what you wrote is okay and then translates it into a *runnable* application. (Don't worry too much about what that means. For now, just think of it as making sure that your application is okay.)

To find out whether your application is good to go, choose Build⇨Build.

If all is well, you see a window in the lower-left of the main Code::Blocks window with the really happy message, 0 errors, 0 warnings (0 minutes, 1 seconds) (the precise time you see may vary). A message like Yourock! might be nicer, but 0 errors, 0 warnings (0 minutes, 1 seconds) ain't all that bad.

If you didn't type the line correctly, all is not lost, because the computer will tell you what you did wrong. For example, you might type couts instead of cout. In this case, you will see something like what is shown in Figure 3-6. A list with columns appears at the bottom of your screen.

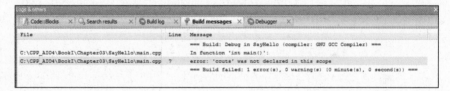

» The leftmost column shows the name of the file where the error was. In this case, the error was in main.cpp, the only file you were working on.

» The middle column shows the *line number* of the problem (in this case, 7).

» The rightmost column of the list makes a basic attempt to tell you what you did wrong, like this:

```
error: 'couts' was not declared in this scope
```

When the compiler doesn't recognize a word, it says that the word is not declared. In other words, the compiler doesn't know what couts is. (The word should be cout.)

If you want to see the problem, you can point at the error report line and double-click. The bad line appears in the code editor, with a little red box next to the line. The line is also highlighted normally. As soon as you press an arrow key, the highlight vanishes.

Thus, if you press the → key a few times and get to the word `couts` and then delete the letter `s`, you can try again. If you choose Build⇨Build, this time you see the happy message `0 errors, 0 warnings (0 minutes, 1 seconds)`. Excellent!

No errors means that the application is good enough to run. So run it!

Choose Build⇨Run. A console appears with text that looks like this:

```
Hello I am your computer talking.

Process returned 0 (0x0)   execution time : 0.030 s
Press any key to continue.
```

See what happened? There is now a message that says, `Hello, I am your computer talking.` Apparently, the thing you typed caused that message to appear. (Go ahead and press Enter to close the console.)

And in fact, that's exactly what happened. That's how you make a message appear on the console screen. The steps look like this:

1. **Type** cout.

   Although cout looks like it's pronounced "cowt," most programmers say "see-out." Think of it as shorthand for *console output*. (But don't type *console output* in its place, because the compiler won't accept that.)

2. **After the word** cout, **type a space and then type two less-than signs (make sure to leave that single space before them).**

   These less-than signs just mean that the data that follows will be sent to cout for display on the console. The data that follows, some text, is in double quotes. That's the way the computer knows where it starts and ends. The words and stuff inside these double quotes is called a *string* because it's a bunch of letters strung together. The computer knows where the string starts because there's a double quote, and it knows where the string ends because there's a double quote. The computer doesn't display these two sets of double quotes when the application runs.

   Then some weirdness follows. There's another set of less-than signs, which means you want to write more to the console. But what follows? It's endl. Notice this is not in quotes. Therefore, you aren't saying that you want the strange barely pronounceable word "endl" to appear on the screen. Instead, you're using a special notation that tells the computer that you want to end the current line and start fresh on the next line. And if you look at the output, you notice that the words that follow (the message about pressing the any key) are, indeed, on the next line. Note that endl is pronounced "end-el."

So that's not so bad after all. Here's a recap:

>> The word cout means you want to write to the console.

>> The << symbols together (with no space between them!) mean the thing that follows is what you want to write.

>> After the << symbol, you tell the computer what you want to write. It can either be a string of letters, symbols, and other characters (all inside quotes), or it can be the word endl.

>> You can put multiple items in a row and have them appear on the console that way, provided you start the line with cout and precede each item with the << symbols.

Oh, and if you have a sharp eye, you may notice one more thing not mentioned yet; a semicolon appears at the end of the line. In C++, every line must end with a semicolon. That's just the way it's done.

REMEMBER

Statements in C++ end with a semicolon.

TECHNICAL STUFF

Saying that *every* line must end with a semicolon is not quite accurate. You can break any line of code into multiple lines. The computer doesn't mind. You could just as easily have written your code as the following two lines:

```
cout << "Hello, I am your computer talking."
    << endl;
```

This is fine, provided that you don't split any individual word (such as cout and endl) or the << symbols or the string. In effect, any place you have a space occurring "naturally" in the code, you can start a new line, if you want.

REMEMBER

Strings, the text in this example, must stay together on a single line between double quotes as shown, unless you break it into two strings, each with its own set of double quotes like this:

```
cout << "Hello, I am your" <<
    " computer talking."
    << endl;
```

Notice that you must also add << between each string segment. Then, when the whole statement is finished, you end with a semicolon. Think of the semicolon as a signal to the computer that the old statement is finished.

Doing some math

You can get the computer to do some math for you; you can use the same cout approach described in the preceding section; and you can throw in some numbers and arithmetic symbols.

REMEMBER

Although addition uses the familiar plus sign (+) and subtraction uses the familiar minus sign (−), multiplication and division use symbols you might not be familiar with. To multiply, you use the asterisk (*); to divide, you use the forward slash (/).

Table 3-2 shows the four common math symbols.

TABLE 3-2

Math Symbols

Symbol	Function
+	Addition (plus)
−	Subtraction (minus)
*	Multiplication (times)
/	Division (divided by)

Yep, it's now math-with-weird-symbols time. Continue with the source code you already have. Click somewhere on the line you typed — you know, the one that looks like this:

```
cout << "Hello, I am your computer talking." << endl;
```

Press End so that the cursor moves to the end of the line. Then press Enter so that you can start a new line between the cout line and the line that starts with the word return.

TIP

Whenever you want to insert a line between two other lines, the easiest way to get it right is to go to the first of those two lines, press End, and then press Enter. Doing so inserts a new, blank line in the right place.

After you press Enter, you notice that something happened: The cursor is not at the start of the newly inserted line; instead, it has four spaces and it's indented flush with the other lines. That's not a mistake. Believe it or not, it's a serious lifesaver. Well, okay, maybe not a lifesaver, but it's almost as good as those little candies that everybody loves. The reason is that often you indent your code (this particular code is indented four spaces); if you're typing lots of code, it's a bummer to have to type four spaces (or press the Tab key) every time you start a new line. So Code::Blocks considerately (and automatically) does the indentation for you.

TIP

If, for some reason, your code didn't automatically indent and the cursor is loitering at the beginning of the line, the auto-indent feature is not turned on. It *should* be on by default, but if it isn't, here's how to turn it on:

1. Choose Settings⇨Editor.

The Configure Editor dialog box, shown in Figure 3-7, appears. It should automatically show the General Settings/Editor Settings tab, but you can select this tab if needed.

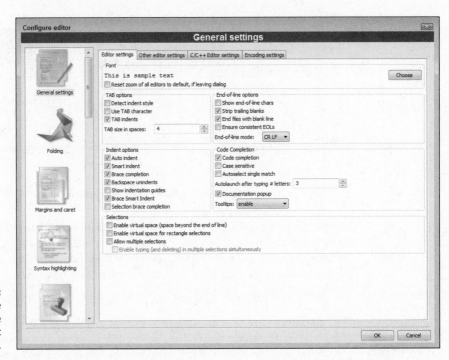

FIGURE 3-7: Configure the editor to use automatic indents.

2. **Make sure that the Tab Indents check box is selected and then click OK.**

3. **When you're back in the code, press Backspace to delete your new line and then try pressing Enter again.**

Behold! The code automatically indents.

4. **After your new, blank line appears and indents itself, type the following:**

```
cout << 5 + 10 << endl;
```

The beginning and the end of this line are just like those of the line you typed earlier. The difference is the middle — instead of typing a string, you type a math problem: 5 plus 10. Note that you put spaces around the 5, around the +, and around the 10 — but not between the 1 and 0. If you put a space there, the computer gets confused (it doesn't know that you meant to write a single two-digit number). When you're finished, your code should look like the following code snippet (here, the new line you typed is shown in bold and the first cout is broken to fit in the book):

```
#include <iostream>

using namespace std;

int main()
{
    cout << "Hello, I am your computer talking." <<
        endl;
    cout << 5 + 10 << endl;
    return 0;
}
```

5. **Save your work by choosing File➪Save Everything.**

TIP

Instead of choosing File➪Save Everything, you can recognize that the only thing that changed is the source-code file you're currently working on. If you see the blinking cursor in the code editor, you know that the code editor is active. If not, click somewhere in your code to activate the editor. When you see the blinking cursor, press Ctrl+S. This saves your file.

TIP

The computer world uses an adage that goes something like this: "Save early, save often." Get in the habit of pressing Ctrl+S every so often. You won't wear out your hard drive, and the keyboard is pretty durable. Every time you type a few lines of code, press Ctrl+S. Before you compile, press Ctrl+S. When you feel paranoid that the last Ctrl+S didn't stick, you can press Ctrl+S. When you're stuck at a traffic light, you press Ctrl+S.

Now you can tell the computer to compile your code. If you haven't saved it, do so now by pressing Ctrl+S. Then choose Build⇨Build. If you typed everything correctly, you should see the magical message `0 errors, 0 warnings (0 minutes, 1 seconds)` appear in the Build Log window. But if not, don't worry; you can easily fix it. Look at your code and find the difference between the line we wrote earlier and your code. Here it is again, just for safe measure:

```
cout << 5 + 10 << endl;
```

There is a space after `cout`, a space after `<<`, a space after `5`, a space after `+`, a space after `10`, and a space after `<<`. And there is a semicolon at the end. Make sure that these are all correct.

Then when you successfully compile and see the happy message `0 errors, 0 warnings`, you are ready to run your application. Choose Build⇨Run.

A console window opens, and you should see the following:

```
Hello I am your computer talking.
15

Process returned 0 (0x0)    execution time : 0.015 s
Press any key to continue.
```

Notice that the second line is the answer to the math problem 10 + 5. That means the computer knows how to do math, more or less correctly.

Ordering the operations

If you want, you can play around with some more complicated problems. For example, you can try something like this:

```
cout << 5 + 10 / 2 * 3 + 25 << endl;
```

What do you think the answer will be? The answer depends on computer rules for the order in which it performs math problems. These are called *orders of operation*. Multiplication and division take precedence over addition and subtraction. Therefore, the computer does all the multiplication and division first from left to right; then it does the addition and subtraction from left to right. Figure 3-8 shows the order in which the computer does this particular math problem.

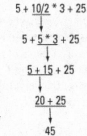

$$5 + \underline{10/2} * 3 + 25$$
$$\downarrow$$
$$5 + \underline{5 * 3} + 25$$
$$\downarrow$$
$$\underline{5 + 15} + 25$$
$$\downarrow$$
$$\underline{20 + 25}$$
$$\downarrow$$
$$45$$

FIGURE 3-8:
The computer
likes to use
orders of
operation.

Going overboard

The computer actually has various limits, including when it comes to math. If you try something like this:

```
cout << 12345678 * 100 / 2 * 3 * 3 << endl;
```

a warning message shows up in the error window when you try to compile:

```
warning: integer overflow in expression [-Woverflow]
```

This message is bad. It means that you can't rely on the answer, which is 1,260,587,804 in this case, when it should be 5,555,555,100. You can use a programming calculator to see why this problem occurs. When you input 12345678, the resulting value takes up to bit 23 of the 32-bit integer, as shown in Figure 3-9.

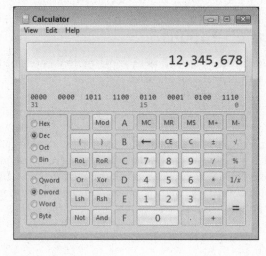

FIGURE 3-9:
A programmer
calculator comes
in handy when
working with
numbers.

When you multiply the initial value by 100, the bits now extend up to bit 30 of the 32-bit integer, as shown in Figure 3-10. At this point, the value is in jeopardy of running out of bits to use. Only the topmost bit is left.

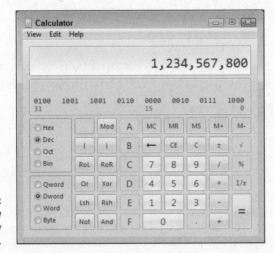

FIGURE 3-10:
You can see how overruns occur by doing the math.

Dividing by 2 buys you some room — the value is back down to bit 29. Multiplying by 3 produces a correct output value of 1,851,851,700. However, multiplying by 3 the second time causes an overflow. The value actually decreases, which is not what you'd expect from a multiplication. The value from the programmer calculator matches the value output by the application. In both cases, you see the result as an overflow of the number of available bits. Using the programmer calculator helps you see what is happening in a visual way.

TECHNICAL STUFF

The greatest positive number you can use is 2,147,483,647. The greatest negative number is −2,147,483,647. However, if you're willing to stick to only positive numbers and 0, the computer can make some adjustments inside and handle a higher positive number. In that case, your numbers can range from 0 to 4,294,967,295.

Pairing the parentheses

If you want to get around the order in which the computer does its math, you can add parentheses. For example, if you use the following line, the computer does the final operation (+) before it does the others:

```
cout << 5 + 10 / 2 * (3 + 25) << endl;
```

Whereas previously, without the parentheses, this thing came out to be 45, now it comes out to be 145. First the computer does the 3 + 25 to get 28. Then it begins

Creating Your First C++ Application

with the multiplication and division, from left to right. So it takes 10 / 2 to get 5, and then multiplies that by (3 + 25), or 28, to get 140. Then it starts with the addition and subtraction from left to right. So it adds 5 to this to get the final number, 145.

Tabbing your output

Just as you can write a string of letters and numbers to the console, you can also write a tab. For example, change the following line from your application

```
cout << "Hello, I am your computer talking." << endl;
```

to:

```
cout << "Hello\tI am your computer talking." << endl;
```

In the preceding code, you replaced the comma and space with a backslash and then a lowercase t. But when you compile and run this application (remember to *compile it first!*), it won't print exactly what's in the double quotes. Here's what you see:

```
Hello    I am your computer talking.
```

The extra space in the displayed line is a *tab space*, just as if you had pressed the Tab key while typing this. (Is that slick, or what?)

There's a complication to using the backslash: You can't just type a backslash (or a double quote, for that matter) and expect to see it on the screen. A couple of workarounds will show the actual characters:

» Really want to display a backslash, not a special character? Use a backslash followed by another backslash. (Yes, it's bizarre.) The compiler treats only the *first* backslash as special. When a string has two backslashes in a row, the compiler treats the second backslash as, well, a backslash.

For example, the following line of code has *two* backslashes:

```
cout << "\\tabc" << endl;
```

The following text shows up at the console:

```
\tabc
```

>> If a string starts with a double quote and ends with a double quote, how in the world would you actually *print* a double quote? Type a backslash and then a double quote, as in the following code:

```
cout << "Backslash and double quote are \"." << endl;
```

When that code runs in an application, you see this on the screen:

```
Backslash and double quote are ".
```

TIP

C++ programmers use the term *escape-sequence* to refer to any special character in a string that starts with a backslash. This is an outdated bit of vocabulary — maybe not as old as "methinks," but it does date back to the original C language of the 1970s. Back then, you made special characters appear on console screens by first pressing the Esc key.

Let Your Application Run Away

The word *execute* refers to running your application, but you need to compile (or *build*, using the Code::Blocks terminology) the application before you run it. The compilation process transforms your application into an executable file. An *executable file* is a special type of file that contains an application you can run on your computer. When you run your word processor application, you run an executable file containing the word processor application.

TECHNICAL
STUFF

After the computer compiles (builds) your application, it performs a step called *linking*. People often refer to these two steps together as simply *compiling.* Indeed, this book often uses the term to mean both steps together. If you're curious about what goes on here, take a look at Appendix A. It has a section devoted to the compiling and linking processes.

Whenever you want to run your application, you first compile it and then run it. If you make more changes to your application, you must compile it again before running it. Otherwise, the executable file won't have your changes.

Because you almost always use Build and Run in sequence, the kind people who built Code::Blocks included a special menu item called Build and Run on the Build menu. The computer first compiles your code, and then it immediately runs the application if there are no errors. If there are errors, the compiler doesn't run the application, and the errors are reported as usual. (You can also perform a build and run by pressing F9.)

Table 3-3 lists keyboard shortcuts for compiling.

TABLE 3-3

Keyboard Shortcuts for Compiling and Running

Action	Keyboard Shortcut
Build	Ctrl+F9
Run	Ctrl+F10
Build and run	F9

Chapter **4**

Storing Data in C++

Everyone loves to store things away. The closet is a perfect example of a place to store things. You may have boxes in your closets that you haven't opened in years. Perhaps you inadvertently created a time capsule. Or just a fire hazard. When you program a computer, you can also store things away. Most people know that a computer has two kinds of memory: memory inside a chip and memory on a hard drive. But most people use the term *memory* in reference to chip memory; the other is referred to as simply the hard drive. When you type a business letter in a word processor, the letter is stored in memory. After you choose File⇔Save, the letter gets stored on the hard drive, but as long as you still have the letter open in the word processor, it's generally still in memory.

The best way to think of memory is as a set of storage bins, much like the ones in the closets that you're afraid of. When you write a computer application, you reserve some storage bins, and you give each storage bin a name. You also say what type of thing can be stored in the storage bin. The technical term for such a storage bin is a *variable.*

In this chapter, you discover how you can use these storage bins in your applications.

REMEMBER

You don't have to type the source code for this chapter manually. In fact, using the downloadable source is a lot easier. You can find the source for this chapter in the \CPP_AIO4\BookI\Chapter04 folder of the downloadable source. See the Introduction for details on how to find these source files.

Putting Your Data Places: Variables

When you write an application, you specify that you want to make use of one or more storage bins called *variables.* You can put different kinds of things in these storage bins. The difference between these computer storage bins and those in your closet, however, is that each computer storage bin can hold only *one thing at a time.*

You can put many different types of things into your variables, too. For example, you can put numbers in a storage bin, or you can put a string in a storage bin. (However, each storage bin contains a unique kind of data — you can't put a number into a storage bin designed for a string.) Book 1, Chapter 3 advises that a *string* is simply a bunch of letters, digits, punctuation marks, or other characters all strung together. As for numbers, they can be either *integers* (which are positive whole numbers, negative whole numbers, and 0) or numbers with a decimal point, such as 3.11 or 10.0, which (for various reasons) are called floating-point numbers.

REMEMBER

The term *floating-point number* refers to a number that has a decimal point and something to the right of the decimal point (even if it's just a 0). When you see the term *floating point,* you can remember what it means by focusing on the word *point* in its name. Think of decimal point.

TECHNICAL STUFF

If you are already familiar with the term *variable* from other fields (such as astronomy, in which variable refers to a kind of star), be careful not to apply their definitions here. Even if they're from fields similar to computer science, such as data science or math, some significant differences are involved. For example, in algebra, a variable represents an unknown quantity, and you can solve for a variable. But in C/C++ programming, it's simpler than that: A *variable* is simply a storage bin with an associated name.

Creating an integer variable

In your C++ application, you can easily write a line of code that creates a variable. Although what you're doing at that point is simply writing code (and the variable doesn't actually get created until you run the application), people often refer to this process as *creating a variable*. A variable has three aspects, as shown in Table 4-1.

TABLE 4-1

A Variable Has Three Aspects

Aspect	What It Means
Name	The name you use in your application to refer to the variable
Type	The type of information that the variable can hold
Value	The actual thing that the storage bin holds

The following list describes the items in Table 4-1 in more detail.

>> **Name:** Every variable must have a name. In your application, you refer to the variable by this name. For example, you may have a variable called count, and you may have a variable called LastName. Or you could have a variable called MisterGates.

>> **Type:** When you create a variable, you must specify the type of information the variable can hold. For example, one variable may hold an integer, and another variable may hold a single character. After you pick a type for the variable in your application, you can put only things of that type into the variable.

>> **Value:** At any given moment, a variable holds a single value. For example, an integer variable might hold the number 10, and a character variable might hold the character a. In your application, you can store something in a variable, and later you can store something else in the variable. When you store something else, the variable forgets what was previously inside it. So, in this sense, you can think of a computer as having a one-track mind.

The code for the SimpleVariable example, shown in Listing 4-1, demonstrates how to create a variable. This is a full application that you can run.

LISTING 4-1: Creating a Variable

```cpp
#include <iostream>

using namespace std;

int main()
{
    int mynumber;
    mynumber = 10;
    cout << mynumber << endl;
    return 0;
}
```

Take a careful look at Listing 4-1. Remember that the computer starts with the code inside the braces that follow the word `main`, and it performs the code line by line.

The first line inside `main` looks like this:

```
int mynumber;
```

When you declare a variable, the first thing you specify is the type of thing the variable can hold. Here, you use the word `int`. This word is the C++ word for *integer*. Thus, the variable that you're declaring can hold an integer. Next is the name of the variable. This variable is named `mynumber`. Then a semicolon ends the variable declaration.

Notice that, in this line, you've covered two of the three aspects of variables: You have given the variable a name, and you have told the computer what type of thing you want the variable to hold. The order seems a little odd — in C++, you first say the type and then the name. That's just the way it's done in C++, and a good reason stands behind it, which you can read about in "Declaring multiple variables," later in this chapter.

The next line looks like this:

```
mynumber = 10;
```

This line puts something in the variable. It puts the number 10 in it. Because you already know that the variable can hold an integer, you're allowed to put in a 10 because it is an integer. If you had tried to put something other than an integer in the variable, the compiler would have given you an error. The compiler makes sure that you put into a variable only the type of thing that you said you would. The compiler is good at keeping you in line. And of course you noticed that the statement ends with a semicolon. In C++, every statement ends with a semicolon.

REMEMBER

To put something in a variable, you type the variable's name, an equals sign (surrounded by optional spaces), and the value. You then end the line with a semicolon. This line of code is an *assignment.* Or you can say that you are *setting* the variable to the value. The next line is this:

```
cout << mynumber << endl;
```

Book 1, Chapter 3 describes what this line does. It's a `cout` statement, which means that it writes something on the console. As you can probably guess, this code tells the computer to write the value of `mynumber` on the console. It does not write the string `mynumber`. Rather, it writes whatever happens to be stored in the storage bin. The previous line of code puts a 10 in the storage bin, and so this line prints a 10 on the console. When you run the application, you see this:

```
10
```

TIP

Think of it like this: When you type the variable's name, you are accessing the variable. The exception to this is when the variable's name appears to the left of an equals sign. In that case, you are setting the variable. You can do two things with a variable:

>> **Set the variable:** You can set a variable, which means that you can put something inside the storage bin.

>> **Retrieve the value:** You can get back the value that is inside the variable. When you do so, the value stays inside it; you are not, so to speak, *taking it out.*

REMEMBER

When you retrieve the value that is in a variable, you are not removing it from the variable. The value is still inside the variable.

Declaring multiple variables

Many years ago, when the original C programming language first appeared (which was the language that served as the predecessor to C++), many developers thought it odd that they had to first say the type of the variable and then the name. But this actually works out well because it makes declaring multiple variables of the same type easy. If you want to declare three integer variables in a row, you can do it all in one shot, like this:

```
int tom, dick, harry;
```

This statement declares three separate variables. The first is called tom; the second is called dick; and the third is called harry. Each of these three variables holds an integer. You have not put anything in any of them, so you may follow that with some code to stuff each of them full with a number. For example, this code puts the number 10 in tom, the number 20 in dick, and the number 3254 in harry.

```
tom = 10;
dick = 20;
harry = 3254;
```

REMEMBER

When you run your applications, the computer executes the statements in the order that they appear in your code. Therefore, in the preceding code, the computer first creates the three storage bins. Then it puts a 10 inside tom. (Now doesn't that sound yummy?) Next, dick gets a 20. And finally, harry consumes a 3254.

Changing values

Although a variable can hold only one thing at a time, you can still change what the variable holds. After you put something else in a variable, it forgets what it originally had. So when people accuse you of being forgetful, you can just say, "Yes, but you should see that computer I work with all day long!"

You put something new in the variable in the same way you originally put something in it. Look closely at the code for the ChangeVariable example in Listing 4-2. Notice that the first part of the application is just like Listing 4-1. But then you add two more lines (shown in bold) that look pretty much like the previous two: The first one sticks 20 in the same variable as before, and the next one writes this new value out to the console.

LISTING 4-2: **Changing a Variable**

```
#include <iostream>

using namespace std;

int main()
{
    int mynumber;
    mynumber = 10;
    cout << mynumber << endl;

    mynumber = 20;
    cout << mynumber << endl;
    return 0;
}
```

As before, the line where you put something new in the variable follows the same format: There's an equals sign, with the variable on the left and the new value on the right. As described earlier in this chapter, this statement is an assignment statement.

REMEMBER

When you see a single equals sign by itself, the item on the left side is the variable or item that receives the information that is on the right side.

Setting one variable equal to another

Because you can do only two direct things with variables — put something in and retrieve the value — setting one variable equal to another is a simple process of retrieving the value of one variable and putting it in the other. This process is often referred to as *copying* the variable from one to another. For example, if you have two integer variables — say, start and finish — and you want to copy the value of start into finish, you would use a line of code like the following:

```
finish = start;
```

REMEMBER

Don't let the language confuse you. Although you want to copy the value of start into finish, notice that the first thing you type is **finish**, and then the equals sign, and then **start**. The left side of the equals sign is what *receives* the value; it is an assignment statement.

REMEMBER

When you copy the value of one variable to another, the two variables must be the same type. You cannot, for instance, copy the value from a string variable into an integer variable. If you try, the compiler issues an error message and stops.

After the computer runs this copy statement, the two variables hold the same thing. The code for CopyVariable, shown in Listing 4-3, is an example of copying one variable to another.

LISTING 4-3: **Copying a Value from One Variable to Another**

```cpp
#include <iostream>

using namespace std;

int main()
{
    int start = 50;
    int finish;
    finish = start;
    cout << finish << endl;
    return 0;
}
```

Initializing a variable

When you create a variable, it starts as an empty storage bin. Before it can be of much use, you need to put something in it.

WARNING

If you try to retrieve the contents of a variable before you actually put anything in it, you end up with what computer people fondly call "unpredictable results." What they really mean to say is, "Don't do this because who knows what's in it." It's kind of like if you go in the attic and you discover that the former owners left behind a big, ominous box. Do you *really* want to look inside it? With variables, the problem you run into is that the computer memory has something stored in that particular place where the variable now sits, and that stored item is probably just some number left over from something else. But you can't know in advance what it is. So always make sure that you place a value inside a variable before you try to retrieve its contents, a process called *initializing the variable.*

You can initialize a variable in two ways. The first way is by declaring the variable and then assigning something into it, which takes two lines of code:

```
int mynumber;
mynumber = 153;
```

But the other way is a bit quicker. It looks like this:

```
int mynumber = 153;
```

This method combines both strategies into one neat little package that is available for you to use whenever you want. You see variables initialized both ways in this book, depending what is clearer or more convenient at the time.

Creating a great name for yourself

Every variable needs to have a name. But what names can you use? Although you are free to use names such as Fred, Zanzibar, or Supercount1000M, there are limits to what C++ will allow you to use.

MYTHIS AND MYTHAT

As you progress through your computer programming life (in addition to your anticipated life as a millionaire), you're likely to notice that, for some reason, some computer programmers seem to favor variable names that start with the word *My.* Other computer programmers despise this practice and completely distance themselves from it. You may have seen such computer identifiers as MyClass, MyNumber, MyHeight, MyName, MyCar, MyWhatASurprise, MyLar, MyStro, and MyOpic. There really isn't any problem using names that start with *My,* especially in training exercises.

WARNING

Although most C++ code is in lowercase, you are free to use uppercase letters in your variable names. However, C++ distinguishes between the two. Therefore, if you have a variable called count, you cannot access it later in your application by calling it Count with a capital C. The compiler treats the two names as two different variables, which makes C++ case sensitive. But on the other hand, please don't use two separate variables in the same application — one called count and one called Count. Although the compiler doesn't mind, the mere humans that may have to read your code or work on it later might get confused.

Here are the rules you need to follow when creating a variable name:

>> **Characters:** You can use any uppercase letter, lowercase letter, number, or underscore in your variable names. Other symbols (such as spaces or the ones above the number keys on your keyboard) are not allowed in variable names. The only catches are that

- The first character cannot be a number.

- The variable name cannot consist of only numbers.

>> **Length:** Most compilers these days allow you to have as many characters in the variable name as you want. Just to be sure, and to prove I'm easily amused, I successfully created a variable in Code::Blocks with a name that's more than 1,000 characters in length. However, I wouldn't want to have to type that name over and over. Instead, I recommend keeping variable names long enough to make sense but short enough that you can type them easily. Most people prefer anywhere from five to ten characters or so.

Examples of acceptable variable names are Count, current_name, address_1000, and LookupAmount. Some variable names are legal, but not easily understood, such as _, __, and _12 — none of which tell you what the variable contains. Table 4-2 lists some variable names that are not allowed.

TABLE 4-2

Examples of Bad Variable Names

Bad Variable Name	Why It's Not Allowed
12345	It has only numbers (and it starts with a number, which is wrong as well).
A&B	The only special character allowed is the underscore, _. The ampersand (&) is not allowed.
1abc	A variable name cannot start with a number.

Manipulating Integer Variables

A potter who is creating an elegant vase is said to manipulate the clay. Likewise, you can manipulate variables to create a thing of abstract beauty. But in this case, manipulation means simply that you can do arithmetic. You can easily do the usual addition, subtraction, multiplication, and division. Book 1, Chapter 3, introduces the characters that you use for the arithmetic operations. They are:

» + for addition

» - for subtraction

» * for multiplication

» / for division

You can, however, perform another operation with integers, and it has to do with remainders and division. The idea is that if you divide, for example, 16 by 3, the answer in whole numbers is *5 remainder 1*. Another way of saying this is that 16 doesn't divide by 3 evenly, but 3 "goes into" 16 five times, leaving a remainder of 1. This remainder is sometimes called a *modulus*. Computer people actually have an important reason for calling it *modulus* rather than *remainder*, and that's because people in the computer field like to use confusing terms.

REMEMBER

When working with integer variables, remember the two basic things you can do with variables: You can put something in a variable, and you can retrieve it from a variable. Therefore, when working with an integer variable, the idea is that you can retrieve the contents, do some arithmetic on it, and then print the answer or store it back into the same variable or another variable.

Adding integer variables

If you want to add two integer variables, use the + symbol. You can either print the result or put it back into a variable.

The AddInteger example adds two variables (start and time) and then prints the answer to the console. The addition operation is shown in bold.

```
#include <iostream>

using namespace std;

int main()
{
```

```
    int start;
    int time;

    start = 37;
    time = 22;

    cout << start + time  << endl;
    return 0;
}
```

REMEMBER

This code starts with two integer variables called start and time. It then sets start to 37 and sets time to 22. Finally, it adds the two variables (to get 59) and prints the results. When you see start + time, + is the *operator* that tells what action to perform, and start and time are the *operands* upon which the operator acts.

In this example, however, the computer doesn't actually do anything with the final sum, 59, except print it. If you want to use this value later, you can save it in its own variable. The AddInteger2 example demonstrates how to save the result in a variable; the storage operation is shown in bold:

```
#include <iostream>

using namespace std;

int main()
{
    int start;
    int time;
    int total;
    start = 37;
    time = 22;
    total =  start + time;
    cout << total << endl;
    return 0;
}
```

In this code, you declare the integer variable total along with the others. Then after you store 37 in start and 22 in time, you add the two and save the total in the variable called total. Then you finally print the value stored in total.

You can also add numbers themselves to variables. The following line adds 5 to start and prints the result:

```
cout << start + 5 << endl;
```

Or you can save the value back in another variable, as in the following fragment:

```
total = start + 5;
cout << total << endl;
```

This example adds 5 to start and saves the new value in total.

When you use code such as total = start + 5;, although you are adding 5 to start, you are not actually changing the value stored in start. The start variable itself remains the same as it was before this statement runs. Rather, the computer figures out the result of start + 5 and saves that value inside total. Thus, total is the only variable that changes here.

Here's where things get a little tricky in the logical arena. This might seem strange at first, but you can actually do something like this:

```
total = total + 5;
```

If you have taken some math courses, you might find this statement a little bizarre, just like the math courses themselves. But remember that total is a variable *in computer programming*, and that definition is a bit different from the math world.

This statement really just means you're going to add 5 to the value stored in total, and you'll take the value you get back and store it *back in total*. In other words, total will now be 5 greater than it was to begin with. The AddInteger3 example shows this technique in action:

```
#include <iostream>

using namespace std;

int main()
{
    int total;
    total = 12;
    cout << total << endl;

    total = total + 5;
    cout << total << endl;

    return 0;
}
```

When you run this application, you see the following output on the console:

```
12
17
```

Notice what took place. First, you put the value 12 inside total and print the value to the console. Then you add 5 to total, store the result back in total, and print the new value of total to the console.

Now, it's no big secret that we computer people are lazy. After all, why would we own computers if we weren't? And so the great makers of the C++ language gave us a bit of a shortcut for adding a value to a variable and storing it back in the variable. The line

```
total = total + 5;
```

is the same as

```
total += 5;
```

We computer folks also have a special way of pronouncing +=. We say "plus equal." So for this line, we would say, "Total plus equal five."

TIP

Think of the total += 5 notation as simply a shortcut for total = total + 5;.

You can also use the += notation with other variables. For example, if you want to add the value in time to the value in total and store the result back in total, you can do this

```
total = total + time;
```

or you can use this shortcut:

```
total += time;
```

If you are adding just 1 to a variable, which is called *incrementing the variable*, you can use an even shorter shortcut. It looks like this:

```
total++;
```

This is the same as total = total + 1; or total += 1;.

Table 4-3 summarizes the different things you can do that involve the addition of variables. Note that when you see ++, which is the *increment operator*, it's pronounced *plus plus*, not *double plus*.

TABLE 4-3 **Doing Things with Addition**

What You Can Do	Sample Statement
Add two variables	`cout << start + time << endl;`
Add a variable and a number	`cout << start + 5 << endl;`
Add two variables and save the result in a variable	`total = start + time;`
Add a variable and a number and save the result in a variable	`total = start + 5;`
Add a number to what's already in a variable	`total = total + 5;`
Add a number to what's already in a variable by using a shortcut	`total += 5;`
Add a variable to what's already in a variable	`total = total + time;`
Add a variable to what's already in a variable by using a shortcut	`total += time;`
Add 1 to a variable	`total++;`

Subtracting integer variables

Everything you can do involving the addition of integer variables you can also do with subtraction. For example, you can subtract two variables, as shown in the `SubtractVariable` example in Listing 4-4.

AND NOW THE ANSWER TO THE GREAT QUESTION

In C++, as well as in the original C language (upon which C++ is based), the ++ operator adds 1 to a variable, which finally allows an answer to The Great Question: Where did the name C++ come from? When the guy who originally designed C++, Bjarne Stroustrup, needed a name for his language, he decided to look into its roots for the answer. He had based the language on C; and in C, to add 1 to something, you use the ++ operator. And because he felt that he added only 1 thing to the language, he decided to call the new language C++.

Okay, that's not quite true; Bjarne actually added a great deal to the language. But that entire great deal can be thought of as just one thing made of lots of smaller things. What did he add? The main thing of those smaller things is the capability to do object-oriented programming. Object-orientation is something you find in the next chapter. And by the way, the originator of C++, Mr. Stroustrup, is still alive and still doing work for the language at AT&T. You can see his web page at http://www.stroustrup.com/.

LISTING 4-4: **Subtracting Two Variables**

```cpp
#include <iostream>

using namespace std;

int main()
{
  int final;
  int time;

  final = 28;
  time = 18;

  cout << final - time << endl;
  return 0;
}
```

When this application runs, the console shows the number 10, which is 28 - 18. Remember that, as with addition, the value of neither final nor time actually change. The computer just figures out the difference and prints the answer on the console without modifying either variable.

You can also subtract a number from a variable, and (as before) you still aren't changing the value of the variable, as in the following example:

```cpp
cout << final - 5 << endl;
```

You can subtract one variable from another and save the result in a third variable:

```cpp
start = final - time;
```

And you can change the value in a variable by using subtraction, as in the following four sample lines of code. This first subtracts time from final and saves the result back in final:

```cpp
final = final - time;
```

Or you can do the same thing by using the shortcut notation:

```cpp
final -= time;
```

Storing Data in C++

Or you can do the same thing with a number:

```
final = final - 12;
```

And (as before) you can alternatively do the same thing with a shortcut:

```
final -= 12;
```

Finally, as with addition, you have a shortcut to a shortcut. If you want only to subtract 1, you can simply use two minus signs, as in

```
Final--;
```

This line is pronounced *minus minus*. The -- is the *decrement operator* and when applied to a variable is called *decrementing the variable*.

Multiplying integer variables

To do multiplication in C++, you use the asterisk (*) symbol. As with addition and subtraction, you can multiply two variables, or you can multiply a variable by a number. You can either print the result or save it in a variable. For example, you can multiply two variables and print the results to the console with the following line:

```
cout << length * width << endl;
```

Or you can multiply a variable by a number, as in this line:

```
cout << length * 5 << endl;
```

And as with addition and subtraction, you can multiply two variables and save the result in a third variable:

```
area = length * width;
```

Also, you can use multiplication to modify a variable's value, as in

```
total = total * multiplier;
```

Or, to use the shortcut:

```
total *= multiplier;
```

PREFIX VERSUS POSTFIX

The ++ and −− operators can appear as a *prefix* (before the variable name) or a *post-fix* (after the variable name) operator. However, they behave differently depending on where they appear. A prefix operator is applied before anything else happens, while a postfix operator is applied afterward. Consider this code:

```
int final = 10;
cout << final++ << endl;
cout << final << endl;
```

The output from this code is

```
10
11
```

because the postfix ++ operator is added after the cout. However, with this code:

```
int final = 10;
cout << ++final << endl;
cout << final << endl;
```

the output in this case is

```
11
11
```

because the prefix ++ operator is added before the cout. The same holds true for the −− operator. Code with a prefix operator like this:

```
int final = 10;
cout << --final << endl;
cout << final << endl;
```

produces an output of

```
9
9
```

because the operator is applied before the cout. Using prefix or postfix operators, when applied correctly, can reduce the amount of code you write and possibly make your code easier to read.

And (as before) you can do the same with just a number:

```
total = total * 25;
```

or this:

```
total *= 25;
```

WARNING

Note that there is no ** operator used to multiply a value by 1 or by itself. Consequently, the compiler will raise an error if you type total**;.

Dividing integer variables

Although addition, subtraction, and multiplication are straightforward with integer variables, division is a bit trickier. The chief reason is that, with whole numbers, sometimes you just can't divide evenly. It's like trying to divide 21 tortilla chips *evenly* among five people. You just can't do it. Either somebody will feel cheated, or everyone will get four chips, and one will be left over for everyone to fight over. Of course, you could break every chip into five pieces, and then each person gets ⅕ of each chip, but then you're no longer working with whole numbers — just a bunch of crumbs.

If you use a calculator and type 21 divided by 5, you get 4.2, which is not a whole number. If you want to stick to whole numbers, you have to use the notion of a remainder. In the case of 21 divided by 5, the remainder is 1, as you figured out with the tortilla chips. The reason is that the highest multiple of 5 in 21 is 20 (because 5 times 4 is 20), and 1 is left over. That lonely 1 is the remainder.

So in terms of strictly whole numbers, the answer to 21 divided by 5 is 4 *remainder 1*. And that's how the computer does arithmetic with integers: It gets two different answers: The *quotient* and the *remainder.* In math terms, the main answer (in the example, 4) is the *quotient.* What's left over is the *remainder.*

Because two different answers to a division problem may occur, C++ uses two different operators for figuring these two different answers.

To find the quotient, use the slash (/). Think of this character as the usual division operator, because when you deal with numbers that divide evenly, this operator gives you the correct answer. Thus, 10 / 2 gives you 5, as you would expect. Further, most people just call this the division operator, anyway.

To find the remainder, use the percent sign (%). This is often called the *modulus operator.*

The DivideInteger example, shown in Listing 4-5, takes two numbers and prints their quotient and remainder. Then it does it again for another pair of numbers. The first pair has no remainder, but the second pair does.

LISTING 4-5: **Finding Quotients and Remainders**

```cpp
#include <iostream>

using namespace std;

int main()
{
    int first, second;
    cout << "Dividing 28 by 14." << endl;
    first = 28;
    second = 14;
    cout << "Quotient  " << first / second << endl;
    cout << "Remainder " << first % second << endl;

    cout << "Dividing 32 by 6." << endl;
    first = 32;
    second = 6;
    cout << "Quotient  " << first / second << endl;
    cout << "Remainder " << first % second << endl;
    return 0;
}
```

When you run this application, you see the following output:

```
Dividing 28 by 14.
2
0
Dividing 32 by 6.
5
2
```

TIP

The code in Listing 4-5 uses a couple new tricks in addition to (or divided by?) the division tricks. For one, it combines the variable declarations of first and second variables into one statement. A comma separates the variable names and the type (int) only once. Next, you combine the output of strings and numbers into a single cout statement. You did this for four of the cout statements. That's acceptable, as long as you string them together with the << signs between each of them.

You have access to all the usual goodies with both the division (/) and modulus (%) operators. For example, you can store the quotient in another variable, as you can with the remainder:

```
myQuotient = first / second;
myRemainder = first % second;
```

And you have shortcuts available:

```
int first = 30;
first /= 5;
cout << first << endl;
```

In this case, the value of first becomes 6 because 30 / 5 is 6. And in the following case, the value of first becomes 3 because the remainder of 33 divided by 6 is 3:

```
int first = 33;
first %= 5;
cout << first << endl;
```

Characters

Another type of variable you can have is a character variable. A *character variable* can hold a single — *just one* — character that C++ stores as a number. It holds a value between –127 and 128 (char or signed char) or between 0 and 255 (unsigned char). Normally, a *character* is anything that can be typed, such as a letter of the alphabet, a digit, or another symbol you see on the computer keyboard, but a character can also hold nonprintable values found in an ASCII table (see https://en.cppreference.com/w/cpp/language/ascii). Some of these unprintable characters are *control characters* (so called because they control the appearance of text on the screen), such as the tab, carriage return, and newline character.

To use a character variable, you use the type name char. To initialize a character variable, you put the character inside *single* quotes. (If you use double quotes, the compiler issues an error message because double quotes create a string, which can contain multiple characters rather than a single character.) The following is an example of a character:

```
char ch;
ch = 'a';
```

```
cout << ch << endl;
```

The character variable here is called ch, which is initialized to the character a. It's surrounded by single quotes. The code then prints it by using cout.

Null character

One important character in the programming world is the *null* character. Deep down inside the computer's memory, the computer stores each character by using a number, and the null character's number is 0. There's nothing to actually see with the null character; this book can't contain a picture of it for you to hang on your wall. (Bummer.) The book can only describe it. Yes, every once in a while, computer people have to become philosophers. But the null character is important because it is often used to signify the end of something — not the end of the world or anything big like that, but the end of some data.

To notate the null character in C++, use \0, as in

```
char mychar = '\0';
```

Nonprintable and other cool characters

In addition to the null character, several other cool characters are available — some that have a look to them and can be printed and some that do not and cannot. The null character is an example of a *nonprintable* character. You can try to print one, but you get either a blank space or nothing at all, depending on the compiler.

But some characters are special in that they do something when you print, though you can't type them directly. One example is the newline character. The *newline* character (\n) symbolizes the start of a new line of text. In all cases, the computer places the *insertion point*, the place where it adds new characters, on the next line. If you are printing some text to the console and then you print a newline character, any text that follows will be on the next line. Most compilers these days start the text at the far left end of the next line (Column 1), but some compilers start the text in the next column on the next line, as in the following output. In this case, the text appears on the next line, but it starts at Column 4 rather than at the far left end (Column 1):

```
abc
   def
```

Here, you print abc, and then a newline, and then def. Notice that the def continues in the same position it would have been had it been on the first line. For the compilers used in this book, however, printing abc, and then a newline, and finally def results in this output:

```
abc
def
```

But to accommodate the fact that some other compilers sometimes treat a newline as just that (start a new line but don't go anywhere else), the creators of the computers gave you another special character: the carriage return. (Can you hear the crowd say, "Ooooh!"?)

The *carriage return* character (\r) places the insertion point at the start of the line, but not on a new line (which means that if you use just a carriage return on a computer expecting both a carriage return and a newline, you overwrite what's already on the line). That's true with pretty much every C++ compiler.

The "Tabbing your output" section of Book 1, Chapter 3, describes the tab character (\t) and other characters that start with a backslash. These are individual characters, and you can have them inside a character variable, as in the following example, which prints the letter *a*, and then a tab, and then the letter *b*. Notice that, to get the tab character to go into the character variable, you have to use the \ and then a t:

```
char ch = '\t';
cout << "a" << ch << "b" << endl;
```

Book 1, Chapter 3 mentions that to put a double quote inside a string, you need to precede the double quote with a backslash so that the computer won't think that the double quote is the end of the string. But because a character is surrounded by single quotes, you don't need to do this. You can just put a double quote inside the character, as in

```
char ch = '"';
```

Of course, that raises an important question now: What about single quotes? This time, you *do* have to use the backslash:

```
char ch = '\'';
```

And finally, to put a backslash inside a character, you use two backslashes:

```
char ch = '\\';
```

REMEMBER

When the compiler sees a backslash inside a string or a character, it treats the backslash as special and looks at whatever follows it. If you have something like '\' with no other character inside the single quotes following it, the compiler thinks the final quote is to be combined with the backslash. And then it moves forward, expecting a single quote to follow, representing the end. Because a single quote doesn't appear, the compiler gets confused and issues an error. Compilers are easily confused — kind of gives you more respect for the human brain.

CARRIAGE RETURN, NEWLINE, OR BOTH?

Depending on what platform you use (such as Windows, Linux, or Mac) and on which applications you use, the effect of the carriage return, newline, or a combination of both varies. In some cases, it's really enough to drive you quite nuts. The form that seems to work best in all situations is the combination of the carriage return and linefeed (\r\n). Sometimes, you can also use the linefeed and carriage return combination (\n\r), but oddly enough, it doesn't always produce the same result as \r\n. Here is a quick sampling based on platform:

- **Windows:** \r\n
- **Linux:** \n
- **Older Mac:** \r
- **Acorn BBC and RISC:** \n\r

This list doesn't even get into the domain of mainframes and other computers, which can use very odd combinations like \025. Sometimes a single character doesn't produce any result at all. For example, when working with Windows Notepad, you must provide the \r\n combination because using \n alone won't do anything. However, when importing a file using some C++ libraries, all you want is the \n because the library will see the \r as a second line. This is the reason that many developers use just \n, which, as previously mentioned, doesn't show up in some editors.

So, there isn't a pat answer to the question of which character to use, and you need to experiment to ensure that using \r, \n, \r\n, or \n\r will actually work the way you want it to in the situation you're dealing with. When in doubt, rely on \r\n until you know that the combination won't work.

WHAT IS THAT SYMBOL?

Never known to turn down the chance to invent a new word, computer people have come up with names for characters that may not always match the names you know. You've already heard the use of the word *dot* for a period when surfing the Internet. And for some characters that already have multiple names, computer folks may use one name and not the other. And sometimes, just to throw you off, they use the usual name for something. The following are some of the names of symbols that computer people like to use:

.	Dot *(but not* period *or* decimal point*)*
@	At
&	Ampersand *(but not* and*)*
#	Pound *(but not* number sign*)*
!	Bang *(though most people still say* exclamation point*)*
~	Tilde
%	Percent
*	Star *(not* asterisk*)*
(	Left paren *or* left parenthesis
)	Right paren *or* right parenthesis
[	Left square bracket *or* left bracket
]	Right square bracket *or* right bracket
==	Equal-equal *(not* double equal*)*
++	Plus-plus *(not* double plus*)*
--	Minus-minus *(not* double minus*)*
/	Forward slash
\	Backslash
{	Left brace *or* left curly brace *or* open brace

Strings

If any single computer word has become so common in programming that most computer people forget that it's a computer word, it's *string*. Book 1, Chapter 3 introduces strings and describes what they are, and it gives examples of them. In short, a *string* is simply a set of characters strung together. The compiler knows the start and end of a string in your code based on the location of the double quotes.

You can create a variable that can hold a string. The type you use is string. The CreateString example, shown in Listing 4-6, demonstrates how to use a string variable.

LISTING 4-6: **Using Brackets to Access Individual Characters in a String**

```cpp
#include <iostream>

using namespace std;

int main()
{
    string mystring;
    mystring = "Hello there";
    cout << mystring << endl;
    return 0;
}
```

When you run this application, the string Hello there appears on the console. The first line inside main() creates a string variable called mystring. The second line initializes it to "Hello there". The third line prints the string to the console.

Getting a part of a string

Accessing the individual characters within a string is easy. Take a look at the IndividualCharacter example shown in Listing 4-7.

LISTING 4-7: **Using the string Type to Create a String Variable**

```
#include <iostream>

using namespace std;

int main()
{
    string mystring;
    mystring = "abcdef";
    cout << mystring[2] << endl;
    return 0;
}
```

Notice that the ninth line, the cout line, has the word mystring followed by a 2 inside brackets ([]). When you run this application, here's what you see:

```
c
```

That's it, just a letter c, hanging out all by itself. The 2 inside brackets means that you want to take the *second* character of the string and only that character. But wait! Is c the second character? Your eyes may deceive you, but it looks like that's the third character. What gives?

REMEMBER

Turns out that C++ starts numbering the positions inside the string at 0. So for this string, mystring[0] is the first character, which happens to be a. And so, really, mystring[2] gets the *third* character. Yes, life gets confusing when you try to hold conversations with programmers, because sometimes they use the phrase *the third character* to mean the third position; but sometimes they use it to mean what's really the *fourth* position. But to those people, the fourth position is actually the fifth position, which is actually the sixth position. Life among computer programmers can be confusing. In general, this book uses *fourth position* to mean the fourth position, which you access through mystring[3]. (The number inside brackets is called an *index*.)

A string is made of characters. Thus, a single character within a string has the type char. This means that you can do something like this (as shown in the IndividualCharacter2 example):

```cpp
#include <iostream>

using namespace std;

int main()
{
    string mystring;
    mystring = "abcdef";
    char mychar = mystring[2];
    cout << mychar << endl;
}
```

In this example, mychar is a variable of type char. The mystring[2] expression *returns* an item of type char. Thus, the assignment is valid. When you run this, you once again see the single character in the third position:

```
c
```

Changing part of a string

Using the bracket notation, you can also change a character inside a string. The following code, for example, changes the second character in the string (that is, the one with index 1) from a b to a q:

```cpp
string x = "abcdef";
x[1] = 'q';
cout << x << endl;
```

This code writes the string aqcdef to the console.

Storing Data in C++

Adding onto a string

Any good writer can keep adding more and more letters to a page. And the same is true with the string type: You can easily add to it. The following lines of code use the += operator, which was also used in adding numbers. What do you think this code will do?

```
string mystring;
mystring = "Hi ";
mystring += "there";
cout << mystring << endl;
```

The first line declares the string mystring. The second line initializes it to "Hi ". But what does the third line do? The third line uses the += operator, which appends something to the string — in this case, "there". Thus, after this line runs, the string called mystring contains the string "Hi there", and that's what appears on the console when the cout line runs. The fancy programmer term for adding something to a string is *concatenation*.

You can also do something similar with characters. The following code snippet adds a single character to a string:

```
string mystring;
mystring = "abcdef";
mystring += 'g';
cout << mystring << endl;
```

This code creates a string with "abcdef" and then adds a 'g' character to the end to get "abcdefg". Then it writes the full "abcdefg" to the console.

Adding two strings

You can take two strings and add them together by using a + sign, just as you can do with integers. The final result is a string that is simply the two strings pushed together, side by side. For example, the following code adds first to second to get a string called third:

```
string first = "hello ";
string second = "there";
string third = first + second;
cout << third << endl;
```

This code prints the value of third, which is simply the two strings pushed together — in other words, "hello there". (Notice that the string called first has a space at its end, which is inside quotes and, therefore, part of the string.) You can also add a *string constant* (that is, an actual string in your application surrounded by quotes) to an existing string variable, as shown here:

```
string first = "hello ";
string third = first + "there";
cout << third << endl;
```

WARNING

You may be tempted to try to add two string constants together, like so:

```
string bigstring = "hello " + "there";
cout << bigstring << endl;
```

Unfortunately, this won't work. The reason is that (deep down inside its heart) the compiler just wants to believe that a string constant and a string are fundamentally

Storing Data in C++

different. But really, you don't have a good reason to do this, because you can accomplish the same thing with this code:

```
string bigstring = "hello there";
cout << bigstring << endl;
```

TECHNICAL STUFF

You can do a lot more with strings. But first, you need to understand something called a function. If you're curious about functions, read Book 1, Chapter 6, which covers all the nitty-gritty details.

Making Decisions Using Conditional Operators

One of the most important features of computers, besides allowing you to surf the web and allowing telemarketers to dial your telephone automatically while you're eating, is the capability to make comparisons. Although this topic may not seem like a big deal, computer technology did not start to take off until the engineers realized that computers could become much more powerful if they could test a situation and do one task or another task, depending on the situation.

You can use many ways to write a C++ application that can make decisions; see Book 1, Chapter 5, for a discussion about this topic. But one way that is quite handy is the use of the *conditional operator.*

Think about this process: If two integer variables are equal, set a string variable to the string "equal". Otherwise, set it to the string "not equal". In other words, suppose that you have two integer variables, called first and second. first has the value 10 in it, and second has the value 20 in it. You also have a string variable called result. Now, to follow the little process just described: Are the two variables equal? No, they are not, so you set result to the string "not equal".

Now do this in C++. Look carefully at the following code. First, you declare the variables first, second, and result:

```
int first = 10;
int second = 20;
string result;
```

So far, so good. Notice that you didn't yet initialize the string variable result. But now you're going to write a single line of code that performs the process just described. First, look over the following example, and see whether you can figure out what it's doing. Look carefully at the variables and what they may do, based on the process described earlier. Then the text explains what the code does.

```
result = (first == second) ? "equal" : "not equal";
```

The preceding line is probably one of the more bizarre-looking lines of C++ code that you'll see in this book. First, you discover what it means. Then you break it into parts to understand why it means what it does.

In English, this means `result` gets `"equal"` if `first` is equal to `second`; otherwise, it gets `"not equal"`.

Now break it into two parts. A single equals sign indicates that the left side, `result`, receives what is on the right side. So you need to figure out that crazy business on the right side:

```
(first == second) ? "equal" : "not equal"
```

When you see this strange setup, consider the question mark to be the divider. The stuff on the left of the question mark is usually put in parentheses, as shown in the following:

```
(first == second)
```

This line actually compares `first` to `second` and determines whether they are equal. Yes, the code shows *two* equals signs. In C++, that's how you test whether two things are equal. Now move to the part on the right of the question mark:

```
"equal" : "not equal"
```

This is, itself, two pieces divided by a colon, so if `first` is indeed equal to `second`, `result` gets the string `"equal"`. Otherwise, it gets the string `"not equal"`. Take a look at the whole thing one more time:

```
result = (first == second) ? "equal" : "not equal";
```

Once again, consider what it means: If `first` is equal to `second`, `result` gets `"equal"`; otherwise, it gets `"not equal"`.

Remember that the storage bin on the left side of the single equals sign receives what is on the right side. The right side is an *expression,* which comes out to be a string of either `"equal"` or `"not equal"`. The whole EqualityCheck example is shown in Listing 4-8.

LISTING 4-8: **Using the Conditional Operator to Do Comparisons**

```cpp
#include <iostream>

using namespace std;

int main()
{
    int first = 10;
    int second = 20;
    string result;

    result = first == second ? "equal" : "not equal";

    cout << result << endl;
    return 0;
}
```

Telling the Truth with Boolean Variables

In addition to integers and strings, another type in C++ can be pretty useful. This type is called a Boolean variable. Whereas an integer variable is a storage bin that can hold any integer value, a Boolean variable can hold only one of two different values: a true or a false. Boolean values take their name from George Boole, the father of Boolean logic. You can read about him at: http://mathshistory.st-andrews.ac.uk/Biographies/Boole.html.

The type name for a Boolean variable is bool. Therefore, to declare a Boolean variable, you use a statement like this:

```cpp
bool finished;
```

This line declares a Boolean variable called finished. Then you can put either a true or a false in this variable, as in the following:

```cpp
finished = true;
```

or

```cpp
finished = false;
```

BOOLEAN VARIABLES AND CONDITIONAL OPERATORS

You can use Boolean variables with conditional operators. In a conditional operator such as

```
result = (first == second) ? "equal" : "not equal";
```

the item (`first == second`) actually works out to be a Boolean value — either `true` or `false`. Therefore, you can break up this code into several lines. Even though breaking something into several lines seems a little backward, developers do it all the time. The reason for breaking code into lines is that sometimes, when you are programming, you may have an expression that is extremely complex — much more complex than `first == second`. As you grow in your C++ programming ability, you start to build more complex expressions and then start to realize just how complex they can become. Often, breaking expressions into multiple smaller pieces is more manageable. To break this example into multiple lines, you can do this (as shown in the `EqualityCheck2` example):

```
string result;
bool isequal;
isequal = (first == second);
result = isequal ? "equal" : "not equal";
```

The second line declares a Boolean variable called `isequal`. The third line sets it to the value `first == second`. In other words, if `first` *is* equal to second, then `isequal` gets the value `true`. Otherwise, `isequal` gets the value `false`. In the fourth line, `result` gets the value "equal" if `isequal` is `true`; or `result` gets the value "not equal" if `isequal` is `false`.

The reason that this code works is that the item on the left side of the question mark is a *Boolean expression,* which is just a fancy way of saying that the code requires a Boolean value. Therefore, you can throw in a Boolean variable if you prefer, because a Boolean *variable* holds a Boolean *value.*

When you print the value of a Boolean variable by using code like this:

```
cout << finished << endl;
```

you see either a 1 for `true` or a 0 for `false`. The reason is that, deep down inside, the computer stores a 1 to represent `true` and a 0 to represent `false`.

Reading from the Console

Throughout this chapter and the preceding chapter, you see many examples of how to write information to the console. But just writing information is sort of like holding a conversation where one person does all the talking and no listening. Getting some feedback from the users of your applications would be nice. Fortunately, getting feedback is easy in C++. Writing to the console involves the use of cout in a form like this:

```
cout << "hi there" << endl;
```

Reading from the console (that is, getting a response from the user of your application) uses the cin object. (It's pronounced "see-in".) Next, instead of using the goofy-looking << operator, you use the equally but backwardly goofy >> operator.

TECHNICAL STUFF

The << operator is often called an *insertion operator* because you are writing to (or *inserting into*) a stream. A *stream* is nothing more than a bunch of characters going out somewhere. In the case of cout, those characters are going out to the console. The >> operator, on the other hand, is often called the *extraction operator*. The idea here is that you are extracting stuff from the stream. In the case of cin, you are pulling letters from the stream that the user is, in a sense, sending into your application through the console.

The ReadString example, shown in Listing 4-9, demonstrates how you can read a string from the console.

LISTING 4-9: **Using the Conditional Operator to Make Comparisons**

```cpp
#include <iostream>

using namespace std;

int main()
{
    string name;
    cout << "Type your name: ";
    cin >> name;
    cout << "Your name is " << name << endl;
    return 0;
}
```

When you run this code, you see the console ask you to type your name, and then it stops. That's because it's waiting for your input. Notice that the insertion point appears immediately after the text "Type your name:". That's because the first cout statement lacks the usual endl. It's normal to leave the insertion point, or cursor, on the same line as the question to avoid confusing the user. Type a name, such as Fred, without spaces and press Enter. The console then looks like this:

```
Type your name: Fred
Your name is Fred
```

The first line includes the name you typed, and the second line is whatever appears after you press Enter. Notice what happens: When you type a word and press Enter, the computer places that word in the name variable, which is a string. Then you can print name to the console by using cout.

You can also read integers, as in the following code (in the ReadInt example):

```cpp
#include <iostream>

using namespace std;

int main()
{
    int x;
    cout << "Type your favorite number: ";
    cin >> x;
    cout << "Your favorite number is " << x << endl;
    return 0;
}
```

This sample code reads a single integer into the variable x and then prints it to the console.

REMEMBER

By default, cin reads in characters from the console based on spaces. If you put spaces in your entry, only the first word gets read. cin reads the second word the next time the application encounters a cin >>.

Storing Data in C++

Chapter **5**

Directing the Application Flow

As you program in C++, many times you need to present the computer with a choice, allowing it to do one thing in one situation and something else in another situation. For example, you may have an application that asks for a user's password. If the password is correct, the application continues; but if the password is incorrect, the application asks the user to reenter the password. After some number of times — usually three — the application performs yet another task when the user enters the incorrect password. Such situations are called *conditions*. In the case of the password, the condition is whether the password is correct.

You may also encounter situations in which you want several lines of code to run over and over. These are *loops*, and you can specify conditions under which the loop runs. For example, you may want to check the password only three times; and if the user fails to enter it correctly the third time, you may bar access to the system. This is a loop, and the loop runs under the condition that a counter has not exceeded the value of 3.

In this chapter, you consider different ways to evaluate conditions within your applications and cause different sections of code to run based on those conditions. The chapter helps you understand how you can use C++ commands called *if statements,* which are similar to what-if situations in real life. You also see how to use other C++ statements (such as do-while) to perform *loops* (repeating the same application sections a number of times).

To make the explanations clear, this chapter gives you real-world examples that you can feel free to incorporate into your life. The examples usually refer to groups of friends and how you can get money from them. So, you see, the benefits of this chapter are twofold: You find out how to program by using conditions and loops, and you find out how to make money off your unsuspecting friends.

REMEMBER

You don't have to type the source code for this chapter manually. In fact, using the downloadable source is a lot easier. You can find the source for this chapter in the \CPP_AIO4\BookI\Chapter05 folder of the downloadable source. See the Introduction for details on how to find these source files.

Doing This or Doing That

As you go through life, you're always faced with decisions. For example, when you bought this book, you faced the following decision: Should I buy this great *For Dummies* book that's sure to tell me just what I need to know, or should I buy some other book?

When you're faced with a decision, you usually have options that offer different results — say, Plan A and Plan B. Making a decision requires making a choice that results in the execution of either Plan A or Plan B. For example, if you approach a stoplight that has just turned yellow, you must either slam on the brakes or floor the accelerator. If you slam on the brakes, the car will stop just in time (you hope). If you floor the accelerator, the car will speed up and you'll go sailing through the intersection just before the stoplight turns red. The choice is this: Press the brake, or press the accelerator. The plan looks like this:

> If I press the brake, I will stop just in time.
>
> If I press the accelerator, I will speed through the intersection.

Computers are faced with making decisions too, although their decisions are usually a little less exciting and don't usually yield the possibility of police interaction. Computer decisions are also usually simpler in nature. That is, a computer's decisions mostly focus around such issues as comparing numbers and strings of characters. For example, you may be writing a computer application for a bank. The user of your application (that is, the bank customer) has a choice of Plan A, Make a Deposit, or Plan B, Receive a Cash Withdrawal when interacting with an account. If the user chooses to make a deposit, your application adds to the account balance the amount of the deposit. If the user chooses to make a withdrawal, your application instead subtracts the withdrawal amount from the account balance.

In C++, decisions usually take the form of an `if` statement, which is code that starts with the `if` keyword followed by a condition, which is often a numerical condition wherein two numbers are compared and then two blocks of code appear: one that runs if the condition is satisfied and one that runs if it is not.

Evaluating Conditions in C++

Most decisions that the computer makes are based on conditions evaluated by comparing either two numbers or two characters. For numerical comparisons, you may compare a variable to a number, as in the following statement:

```
x > 10
```

This comparison evaluates whether the variable x holds a value greater than the number 10. If x is indeed greater than 10, the computer sees this condition as `true`. If x is not greater than 10, the computer sees the condition as not true (`false`).

Developers often use the word *satisfied* with conditions. For the condition x > 10, if x is greater than 10, developers say the condition is satisfied. It's kind of like, "We're satisfied if our IRS tax refund is five figures." For this, if the condition is x > 9999, and you receive a $10,000 refund, the condition is satisfied.

For character comparisons, you may compare whether two characters are equal, as in the following statement:

```
mychar == 'A'
```

This comparison evaluates whether `mychar` contains the letter A. Notice that you use two equals signs, not just one. Using a single equals sign would assign the value A to `mychar`.

To test whether the character is not equal to something, you use the somewhat cryptic-looking `!=` operator. Think of the `!` as meaning *not*, as in

```
mychar != 'X'
```

Finding the right C++ operators

Each statement in the previous section uses an *operator* to specify the comparison to make between the numbers or the strings. Table 5-1 shows you the types of operators available in C++ and the comparisons that they help you make in your applications.

TABLE 5-1   **Evaluating Numerical Conditions**

Operator	What It Means
<	Less than
<=	Less than or equal to
>	Greater than
>=	Greater than or equal to
==	Equal to
!=	Not equal to

Some operators in this table — and how you use them — can be a bit annoying or downright frightening. The following list gives examples:

>> The operator that tests for equality is *two* equals signs. It looks like this:

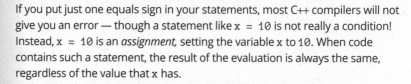

```
x == 10
```

When the computer finds this statement, it checks to see whether x equals 10.

WARNING

If you put just one equals sign in your statements, most C++ compilers will not give you an error — though a statement like x = 10 is not really a condition! Instead, x = 10 is an *assignment,* setting the variable x to 10. When code contains such a statement, the result of the evaluation is always the same, regardless of the value that x has.

>> The operator that tests for inequality is an exclamation mark followed by an equals sign. For the condition x != 10, the condition evaluates as true only if x is not equal to 10 (x is equal to something other than 10).

>> When you're testing for greater-than or less-than conditions, the condition x > 10 is not true if the value of x is equal to 10. The condition x > 10 is true only if x is actually greater than, but not equal to, 10. To also test for x being equal to 10, you have two choices:

- If you're working with integers, you can test whether x > 9. In that case, the condition is `true` if x equals 10, or 11, or 12, and so on.

- You can use the greater-than-or-equal-to operator to determine equality x >= 10. This condition also is true if x equals 10, 11, and so on.

REMEMBER

To test for all whole numbers greater than or equal to 10, the condition x > 9 works only if you're working with integers. If you're working with floating-point numbers (refer to Book 1, Chapter 4, for information on the types of numbers you can work with in C++), the statement x > 9 won't work the way you want. The number 9.1 is greater than 9, and it's not greater than or equal to 10. So if you want greater than or equal to and you're not working with integers, use the >= operator.

CONSIDERING THE NEW SPACESHIP OPERATOR

C++ 20 comes with a new operator that will eventually make your life easier. It's called the spaceship operator and looks like this: <=>. The spaceship operator performs a *three-way comparison,* which means that it can tell you whether a < b, a == b, or a > b, all in one operation. This is one of those cases when you might want to skip this sidebar and come back to it after you've read through later in the book (such as Book 5, Chapter 2), but this chapter is the most appropriate place to include information about the spaceship operator.

The spaceship operator appears as part of the std::strong_ordering class, so that's how you see it referred to in many cases. Instead of an output of true or false, this operator outputs –1 (std::strong_ordering::less) when a < b, 0 (std::strong_ordering::equal) when a == b, and 1 (std::strong_ordering::greater) when a > b. Using this different form of output means that you need to write your conditional statements differently than normal.

If you try to use the spaceship operator in a copy of C++ that doesn't support it, you receive an error message because the compiler won't be able to understand what <=> means. As of this writing, Code::Blocks doesn't implement the spaceship operator, so you need to test the spaceship operator somewhere else. One of the few online

(continued)

(continued)

compilers that fully implements this operator is Wandbox (https://wandbox.org/). You can see how this operator works using this code:

```cpp
#include <iostream>
#include <cstdlib>

int main()
{
    std::strong_ordering result = 1 <=> 1;
    bool out1 = result < 0;
    bool out2 = result == 0;
    bool out3 = result > 0;

    std::cout << out1 << std::endl;
    std::cout << out2 << std::endl;
    std::cout << out3 << std::endl;
}
```

In this case, the outputs are 0 (which is false), 1 (which is true), and 0 because 1 really does equal 1. The std::strong_ordering type doesn't provide cout functionality, so you have to create a bool comparison for it. Instead of comparing the value of result to 0, you can also use std::strong_ordering constants like this: result == std::strong_ordering::equal. Obviously, this is an extremely simple example and you normally use the spaceship operator to perform complex comparisons. In Book 5, Chapter 2, you begin to see how it's possible to reduce the amount of code needed for comparing two structures using the spaceship operator. For now, just know that the operator exists and it can perform complex comparisons.

Combining multiple evaluations

When you make evaluations for application decisions, you may have more than one condition to evaluate. For example, you might say, "If I get a million dollars, or if I decide to go into debt up to my eyeballs, I will buy that Lamborghini." In this case, you would buy the car under two conditions, and either can be true. Combining conditions like this is called an *or* situation: If this is true or if that is true, something happens.

To evaluate two conditions together in C++, you write them in the same statement and separate them with the *or* symbol (||), which looks like two vertical bars. Other programming languages get to use the actual word *or*, but C++ uses the strange, unpronounceable symbol that you might call *The Operator Previously Known As Or*. The following statement shows it performing live:

```
(i < 10 || i > 100)
```

WARNING

This condition is useful for some kinds of range checking for which you want to exclude the middle of a range and check only for the extremes. In this case, an i value of 50 (the middle of the range) would evaluate to false. If you use the *or* operator (||), accidentally ending up with a condition that is *always* true is easy. For example, the condition (x < 100 || x > 0) is always going to be true. When x is –50, it's less than 100, so the condition is true. When x is 500, it's greater than 0, so it's true.

In addition to an *or* condition, you can have something like this: "If I get a million dollars and I feel really bold, I will buy a Lamborghini." Notice that this uses the word *and.* In this case, you do it only if both situations are true. (Remember that with *or*, you do it if either situation is true.) In C++, the *and* operator is *two* ampersands: &&. This makes more sense than the *or* operator because the & symbol is often associated with the word *and.* The *and* comparison in C++ looks like this:

```
(i > 10 && i < 100)
```

This example checks to see whether a number is more than 10 *and* less than 100. That would mean the number is in the range 11 through 99.

Combining conditions by using the && and || operators is a use of *logical operators.*

TIP

To determine whether a number is within a certain range, you can use the *and* operator (&&), as you see earlier in this chapter.

WARNING

With the *and* operator, accidentally creating a condition that is never true is easy. For example, the condition (x < 10 && x > 100) will never be true. No single number can be both less than 10 and simultaneously greater than 100.

Including Evaluations in C++ Conditional Statements

Computers, like humans, evaluate conditions and use the results of the evaluations as input for making a decision. For humans, the decision usually involves alternative plans of action, and the same is true for computers. The computer needs to know what to do if a condition is true and what to do if a condition is not true. To decide on a plan of action based on a condition that your application evaluates, you use an if statement, which looks like this:

```
if (x > 10)
{
    cout << "Yuppers, it's greater than 10!" << endl;
}
```

This example translates into English as: If x is greater than 10, write the message

```
"Yuppers, it's greater than 10!"
```

In an if statement, the part inside the parentheses is called either the *test* or the *condition.* You usually apply *condition* to this part of the if statement and use the word *test* as a verb, as in "I will test whether x is greater than 10."

REMEMBER

In C++, the condition for an if statement always goes inside parentheses. If you forget the parentheses, you get a compile error.

You can also have multiple plans of action. The idea is simply that if a condition is true, you will do Plan A. Otherwise, you will do Plan B. This is an *if-else block,* which appears in the next section.

Deciding what if and also what else

When you write code for a comparison, usually you want to tell the computer to do something if the condition is true and to do something else if the condition is not true. For example, you may say, "If I'm really hungry, I will buy the Biggiesuper-sizemondohungryperson french fries with my meal for an extra nickel; otherwise, I'll go with the small." In the English language, you often see this kind of logic with the word *otherwise:* If such-and-such is true, I will do this; otherwise, I will do that.

In C++, you use the else keyword for the *otherwise* situation. The IfElse example demonstrates how to use the else keyword, as shown in the following code:

```
#include <iostream>

using namespace std;

int main()
{
    int i;
    cout << "Type any number: ";
    cin >> i;
```

```
    if (i > 10)
    {
        cout << "It's greater than 10." << endl;
    }
    else
    {
        cout << "It's not greater than 10." << endl;
    }

    return 0;
}
```

In this code, you test whether a number is greater than 10. If it is, you print one message. If it is not, you print a different message. Notice how the two blocks of code are distinct. The first block immediately follows the if statement; it's the code that runs if the condition is true. The next block is preceded by the else keyword, and this block runs if the condition is false.

WARNING

Think carefully about your else code block when dealing with numbers. If you are testing whether a number is greater than 10, for instance, and it turns out that the number is not greater than 10, the tendency of most people is to assume that it must, therefore, be *less than 10*. But that's not true. The number 10 itself is not greater than 10, but it's not less than 10, either. So the opposite of *greater than 10* is simply *not greater than 10*. If you need to test the full range of numbers using a simple if statement, create an if statement that uses either >= or <= (refer to Table 5-1 for a listing of operators).

Going further with the else and if

When you are working with comparisons, you often have multiple comparisons going on. For example, you may say, "If I go to Mars, I will look for a cool red rock; otherwise, if I go to the moon, I will jump up really high; otherwise, I will just look around wherever I end up, but I hope there will be air."

The IfElse2 example, shown in the following code, demonstrates how to combine the if and else keywords to check for multiple alternatives:

```
#include <iostream>

using namespace std;

int main()
{
```

```
    int i;
    cout << "Type any number: ";
    cin >> i;

    if (i > 10)
    {
        cout << "It's greater than 10." << endl;
    }
    else if (i == 10)
    {
        cout << "It's equal to 10" << endl;
    }
    else
    {
        cout << "It's less than 10." << endl;
    }

    return 0;
}
```

Here you can see having several different conditions, and only one can be true. The computer first checks to see whether i is greater than 10. If i is greater, the computer prints a message saying that i is greater than 10; but if it isn't greater, the computer checks to see whether i equals 10. If so, the computer prints a message saying that i is equal to 10. Finally, the computer assumes that i must be less than 10, and it prints a message accordingly. Notice there is no condition for the final else statement (you can't have a condition with else statements). But because the other conditions failed, you know, by your careful logic, that i must be less than 10.

Be careful when you are thinking through such if statements. You could have a situation where more than one condition can occur. For example, you may have something like the example shown in IfElse3:

```
#include <iostream>

using namespace std;

int main()
{
    int i;
    cout << "Type any number: ";
    cin >> i;
```

```
if (i > 100)
{
  cout << "It's greater than 100." << endl;
}
else if (i > 10)
{
  cout << "It's greater than 10" << endl;
}
else
{
  cout <<
    "It's neither greater than 100 nor greater than 10."
    << endl;
}

return 0;
}
```

Think about what would happen if i is the number 150. The first condition, i > 100, is true. But so is the second condition, i > 10. The number 150 is greater than 100, and 150 is also greater than 10. So which block will the computer execute? Or will it execute both blocks?

The computer executes only the first condition that is satisfied. Thus, when i is 150, the computer prints the message "It's greater than 100." It doesn't print the other messages. In fact, the computer doesn't even bother checking the other conditions at that point. It just continues with the application.

Repeating Actions with Statements That Loop

You see loops all the time. A child runs around in circles until getting quite dizzy and falling over (laughing, in all likelihood). While driving, you see a roundabout and navigate it successfully or go around for another try. During exercise, you perform a given number of repetitions to obtain a desired fitness result. All these examples reflect real-life loops. Computers also deal with loops, as defined in the following sections.

Understanding how computers use loops

Suppose that you're writing an application to add all the numbers from 1 to 100. For example, you may want to know how much money you will get if you tell 100 people, "Give me one dollar more than the person to your left." With a mastery of copy-and-paste, you could do something like this (with the first person giving you a dollar, the second giving you two dollars, the third giving you three dollars, and so on):

```
int x = 1;      // First person.
x = x + 2;      // Person two gives you 2, for a total of 3
x = x + 3;      // Person three gives you 3, for a total of 6
x = x + 4;      // Person four gives you 4, for a total of 10
```

and so on until you get to x = x + 100. As you can see, this code could take a long time to type, and you would probably find it a tad frustrating, too, no matter how quickly you can choose the Edit⇨Paste command (or press Ctrl+V). Fortunately, the great founders of the computer world recognized that not every programmer is a virtuoso at the piano with flying fingers and that applications often need to do the same thing over and over. Thus, they created a helpful tool: the for loop. A for loop executes the same piece of code repeatedly a certain number of times. And that's just what you want to do in this example.

Looping situations

Several types of loops are available, and in this section you see how they work. Which type of loop you use depends on the situation. The preceding section methods one loop type: the for loop. The idea behind a for loop is to have a counter variable that either increases or decreases, and the loop runs as long as the counter variable satisfies a particular condition. For example, the counter variable might start at 0, and the loop runs as long as the counter is less than 10. The counter variable *increments* (has one added to it) each time the loop runs, and after the counter variable is not less than 10, the loop stops.

Another way to loop is to simplify the logic a bit and say, "I want this loop to run as long as a certain condition is true." This is a while loop, and you simply specify a condition under which the loop continues to run. When the condition is true, the loop keeps running. After the condition is no longer true, the loop stops.

Finally, there's a slight modification to the while loop: the do-while loop. The do-while loop is used to handle one particular situation that can arise. When you have a while loop, if the condition is not true when everything starts, the computer skips over the code in the while loop and does not even bother executing it. But sometimes you may have a situation in which you would want the code to always execute at least once. In that case, you can use a do-while loop.

Table 5-2 shows the types of loops. As the chapter progresses, you see examples of using all three loop types.

TABLE 5-2

Choosing Your Loops

Type of Loop	Appearance
for	for (x=0; x<10; x++) { }
while	while (x < 10) { }
do-while	do { } while (x < 10)

You may want to use these loops in these situations:

>> for **loop:** Use a for loop when you have a counter variable and you want it to loop while the counter variable increases or decreases over a range. It's a good choice if you know how many times you want the loop to execute.

>> while **loop:** Use the while loop when you have a condition under which you want your code to run. It's a good choice when you want to perform the test at the beginning of the loop. The test may fail immediately, so the loop may not execute even once.

>> do-while **loop:** Use the do-while loop when you have a condition under which you want your code to run and you want to ensure that the loop always runs at least once, even if the condition is not satisfied. It's a good choice when the code inside the loop prepares the variables that the test uses, so the loop must execute at least once.

Looping for

Using the for loop provides precise control over how many times the code performs a task. In addition, it's extremely flexible because you also have control over how the counter variable updates. While you can use a for loop for situations when you don't know how many times you need to perform a task, such as streaming content from the Internet, it still provides the basis for code that is less susceptible to errors because you always know precisely how long the loop will continue. With this in mind, the following sections tell you more about the for loop.

Performing a simple for loop

To use a for loop, you use the for keyword and follow it with a set of parentheses that contains information regarding the number of times the for loop executes.

For example, when adding the numbers from 1 to 100, you want a variable that starts with the number 1; then you add 1 to x, increase the variable to 2, and add the next number to x again over and over. The common action here that doesn't change each time is the "add it to x" part, and the part that changes is the variable, called *a counter variable*.

The counter variable, therefore, starts at 1 and goes through 100. Does it include 100? Yes. And with each iteration, you add 1 to the counter variable. The for statement looks like this:

```
for (i = 1; i <= 100; i++)
```

This statement means that the counter variable, i, starts at 1, and the loop runs over and over while i is less than or equal to 100. After each iteration, the counter variable increments by 1 because of the i++ statement.

The following list describes the three portions inside the parentheses of the for loop:

>> **Initializer:** You use this first portion to set up the counter variable.

>> **Condition:** It's the condition under which the loop continues to run.

>> **Finalizer:** In this third portion, you specify what happens after each cycle of the loop.

REMEMBER

Three items are inside the for loop, and you separate them with semicolons. If you try to use commas, your code will not compile.

Now the line of code from a few paragraphs back doesn't do anything for each iteration other than add 1 to i. To tell the computer the work to do with each iteration, follow the for statement with a set of braces containing the statements you want to execute with each iteration. Thus, to add the counter variable to x, you would do this:

```
for (i = 1; i <=100; i++)
{
    x += i;
}
```

Note that if the for loop only executes one statement, you don't have to include the braces. This example would add i to x with each loop. Of course, you must create x and assign an initial value to it to make the loop work. The ForLoop example demonstrates the for loop in its final form, complete with the way to write the final value of x to the console after the loop is finished:

```cpp
#include <iostream>

using namespace std;

int main()
{
    int x = 0;
    int i;

    for (i = 1; i <= 100; i++)
    {
        x += i;
    }

    cout << x << endl;
    return 0;
}
```

When you run this example, you see an output of 5050. Notice a few things about this block of code.

1. You declare both variables that you're working with: x and i.

2. The for statement initializes the counter variable, specifies the condition under which it continues running, and tells what to do after each iteration. In this example, the for loop starts with i = 1, and it runs as long as i is less than or equal to 100. For each iteration, the computer adds the value of i to x; the process that adds the value to x is the code inside the braces.

3. The computer adds 1 to i, which you specify as the third item inside the parentheses. The computer does this part, adding 1 to i, only after it finishes executing the stuff inside the braces.

Meddling with the middle condition

The middle portion of the for statement specifies a condition under which to continue doing the stuff inside the for loop. It must eventually evaluate to false or the loop will continue forever. In the case of the preceding example, the condition is i <= 100, which means that the stuff inside the braces continues to run as long as i is less than or equal to 100.

GETTING A SMALL PERFORMANCE BOOST

It's possible to get a small, but sometimes noticeable, performance boost by declaring your counter variable within the `for` statement. The following code runs precisely the same as the code used in the "Performing a simple for loop" section, but it uses one less line of code by initializing `i` within the `for` statement using `int i = 1;`. The trade-off is that it may be less clear in some situations where the function you write is longer and `i` becomes inaccessible when the `for` loop terminates.

```cpp
#include <iostream>

using namespace std;

int main()
{
    int x = 0;

    for (int i = 1; i <= 100; i++)
    {
        x += i;
    }

    cout << x << endl;
    return 0;
}
```

In this example, you want the loop to iterate for the special case in which `i` is 100, which still satisfies the condition `i <= 100`. If you instead say `i < 100`, the loop won't execute for the case in which `i` equals 100. The loop will stop short of the final iteration. In other words, the computer would add only the numbers 1 through 99. And if your friends are gathering money for you, you'd be cheated out of that final $100. And, by golly, that could make the difference as to whether you pay rent this month.

WARNING

The question of when the loop stops can get kind of confusing. If you go crazy and tell the compiler that you want to add the numbers 1 up to but not including 100, you need a condition such as `i < 100`. If you say up to 100, it's not clear exactly which you want to do — include the 100 or not. If that's the case and you're writing the application for someone else, you would want to ask for clarification. (Unless you're the 100th friend, in which case you may get out of paying your dues.)

In the example you've been using, the condition i <= 100 and the condition i < 101 have essentially the same meaning. If the condition is i < 101, the application operates the same. But that's true only because the example uses integers to count up to and including 100. If you instead add floating-point numbers, and increment the counter by 0.1 after each iteration, these two conditions (i <= 100 and i < 101) aren't the same. With i <=100, i gets up to 99.5, 99.6, 99.7, 99.8, 99.9, and finally 100, after which the loop stops. But i < 101 would also include 100.1, 100.2, up to and including 100.9.

You can see that the two conditions are not the same by playing with the ForLoop2 example. When you run this example with a condition of i <= 100, the output is 50050. However, when you run this example with a condition of i < 101, the output is 51055.5. (Remember to rebuild the application after you make any changes to it.)

```cpp
#include <iostream>

using namespace std;

int main()
{
    double x = 0.0;

    for (double i = 0.1; i <= 100; i += 0.1)
    {
        x += i;
    }

    cout << x << endl;
    return 0;
}
```

Now notice the third item in the for statement: i+=0.1. Remember that this item is the same as i = i + 0.1. Therefore, this third item is a complete statement. A common mistake is to instead include just a partial statement, as in i + 0.1. Unfortunately, some compilers allow a partial statement to get through with only a warning. C++ is notorious for letting you do things that don't make a whole lot of sense, though newer compilers tend to fix these errors.

Yes, it's true: The entire statement i = i + 1 is considered to have a side effect. In medicine, a *side effect* is an extra little goodie you get when you take a pill that the doctor prescribes. For example, to cure your headache with medicine, one side effect may be that you experience severe abdominal pains — not something you want. But in computers, a side effect can be something that you may want. In this case, you want the counter to be incremented. The partial statement i + 0.1 returns only a value and doesn't put it anywhere; that is, the partial statement doesn't change the value of i — it has no side effects.

If you try this at home by replacing one of the for loops in the earlier examples with just i + 0.1, your loop runs forever until you manually stop the application. The reason for this action is that the counter always stays put, right where it started, and it never increments. Thus, the condition i <= 100 is always satisfied.

REMEMBER

The final portion of the for statement must be a complete statement in itself. If the statement simply evaluates to something, it will not be used in your for loop. In that case, your for loop can run forever unless you stop it.

Going backward

If you need to count backward, you can do that with a for loop as well. For example, you may be counting down the number of days remaining before you get to quit your job because you learned C++ programming and you are moving on to an awesome new job. Or you may be writing an application that can manipulate that cool countdown timer that they show when the space shuttle launches. Counting up just isn't always the right action. It would be a bummer if every day were one day more before you get to quit your job and move to an island. Sometimes, counting backward is best.

To count backward, you set up the three portions of the for loop. The first is the initial setup, the second is the condition under which it continues to run, and the third is the action after each iteration. For the first portion, you set the counter to the starting value, the top number. For the condition, you check whether the number continues to be greater than or equal to the final number. And for the third portion, you *decrement* the counter (reduce its value by 1) rather than increment it. Thus, you would have this:

```
for (i=10; i>=5; i--)
```

This line starts the counter variable i at 10. (Note the lack of spaces between i, =, and 10—the compiler doesn't care whether you use spaces or not, the spaces are there, or not, for you.) The for loop decrements i by 1 after each iteration, and thus i moves to 9, then 8, then 7, and so on. This process continues as long as i is at least 5. Thus, i counts 10, 9, 8, 7, 6, 5. The whole application might look like the ForCountdown example, shown here:

```
#include <iostream>

using namespace std;
```

```
int main()
{
    for (int i=10; i>=5; i--)
    {
        cout << i << endl;
    }

    return 0;
}
```

When you run this code, you see the following output:

```
10
9
8
7
6
5
```

Using multiple initialization variables

If you need multiple counter variables, the for loop can handle it. Each portion of the for statement can have multiple items in it, separated by commas. For example, the following code uses two counter variables, as demonstrated in the ForLoopMultiVariable example:

```
#include <iostream>

using namespace std;

int main()
{
  string A = "Hello";
  string B = "1122334455";

  for (int i = 0, j = 0; i < 5; i++, j += 2)
  {
    cout << A[i] << B[j] << endl;
  }

  return 0;
}
```

In this case, you work with two strings: A and B. String B is twice as long as string A, but you want to combine the two. So, you need to access the string index of B using j by incrementing it twice the amount of i. This type of processing can happen in C++, so it's good to keep in mind the fact that using multiple variables in a for loop isn't always bad. The output you see from this example looks like this:

```
H1
e2
13
14
o5
```

The problem with using multiple variables comes when you start to create really complex and convoluted code. Here is an example of when what is happening with the for loop becomes harder to understand:

```
for (int i = 0, j=10; i <= 5, j <=20; i++, j+=2)
{
    cout << i << " " << j << endl;
    x += i + j;
}
```

Look carefully at it because it's a bit confusing (in fact, you learn a little something about the complexity shortly). To understand this example, look at each portion separately. The first portion starts the loop. Here, the code creates two counters — i and j; i starts at 0, and j starts at 10.

So far, easy enough. The second portion says that the loop will run as long as the following two conditions are true: i must be less than or equal to 5, and j must be less than or equal to 20.

Again, not too bad. The final portion says what must happen at the end of each iteration: i is incremented by 1, and j is incremented by 2.

Thus, you have two counter variables. And it's not too bad, except that you might imagine doing something like this instead:

```
for (int i = 0, j=20; i <= 5, j >= 10 ; i++, j-=2)
{
    cout << i << " " << j << endl;
    x += i + j;
}
```

If you look carefully, you'll notice that aside from i, j starts out at 20 and the loop runs as long as j is at least 10, and that with each iteration, 2 is subtracted from j. In other words, j is counting down by 2 from 20 to 10.

But i is counting up from 0 to 5. Thus, you have two loops: one counting up and one counting down.

Code can become extremely confusing—look at the following gem from the For-LoopComplex example:

```
#include <iostream>

using namespace std;

int main()
{
  int x = 0;
  for (int i=0, j=10; i<=5, j<=20;
    i++, j+=2, cout << i+j << endl, x+=i+j)
  {
  }

  return 0;
}
```

It's hard to tell what it does just by looking at it. Running the code will give you an output of

```
13
16
19
22
25
28
```

The truth is, this kind of code is just too complicated — best to stick with simpler code. Although you may know what this code means, your coworkers will only get frustrated trying to decode it. And if you write code just for fun at home, six months from now — when you go back and look at this code — you might have trouble figuring it out yourself!

One thing to notice about this particular example is that the `for` conditions reside on two lines. At least the line isn't so long that you need to scroll it within the editor. Using shorter code lines is usually helpful.

TIP
Putting too much inside the `for` statement itself is easy to do. In fact, if you're really clever, you can put almost everything inside the `for` loop and leave nothing but an empty pair of braces, as shown in the preceding example. But remember, just because your code is clever doesn't mean that what you did was the best way to do it. Instead, sticking to the common practice of using only one variable in the `for` statement is a good idea (as is not using multiple statements within each portion).

TIP

Keeping your applications clear so that other people can figure out what you were trying to do when you wrote the code is always a good idea. Some people seem to think that if they keep their applications complicated, they're guaranteeing themselves job security. Oddly, all the people I know like that tend to leave their jobs and have trouble getting good references. (Imagine that!)

TECHNICAL STUFF

You may recall that with the `++`, you can have both `i++` and `++i`. The first is a *post-increment,* and the second is a *pre-increment.* You may be tempted to try something like this: `for (int i = 0; i <= 5; ++i)`. Although it looks cool and some people prefer it, the truth is that it doesn't change anything. The `++i` still takes place at the end of the loop, not at the beginning, as you might hope. Using pre-increment just makes code confusing; use `i++` in your `for` loops and avoid `++i`.

Working with ranges

A *range* is a series of values that go from one value to another value and include the values in between. For example, the range a through d is a, b, c, and d. An integer range of 1 through 5 is 1, 2, 3, 4, and 5. You see ranges in action multiple times in this book, but the main discussion appears in Book 5, Chapter 6. For now, this chapter works with an incredibly simple range.

To make this example work, you must configure GCC to use a minimum of C++ 17. Choose Settings⇨Compiler to display the Compiler Settings dialog box shown in Figure 5-1. Select the Have G++ Follow the Coming C++ 1z (aka C++ 17) setting option; then click OK. If you don't select this option, the example will fail to build properly. Remember that if you build a project using the wrong options, you must rebuild it by choosing Build⇨Rebuild after setting the correct options.

FIGURE 5-1:
Configure GCC to
use the C++ 17
standard.

Now that the compiler is configured, you can use the code that follows, which also appears in the ForLoopRange example, to test a for loop using a range. In this case, the range is from 1 through 5:

```cpp
#include <iostream>

using namespace std;

int main()
{
  int range[] = {1, 2, 3, 4, 5};

  for (int i : range)
  {
    cout << i << endl;
  }

  return 0;
}
```

Don't worry too much about what may appear to be confusing code; it all makes sense as you progress. The int range[] = {1, 2, 3, 4, 5}; line of code creates an *array* — a series of values within a single variable. Think of it as a box with partitions in which you can place a single value in each partition. Book 5, Chapter 1 tells you more about working with arrays.

REMEMBER

The for loop condition looks really strange. The condition looks like this: int i : range. The code creates an int value i that receives one value from the range for each iteration of the loop. The range (:) operator appears between the range declaration (i) and the range expression (range). This is a somewhat new feature of C++, and you'll find it extremely useful for processing storage containers like arrays.

After i receives a value, the code outputs it to the screen using cout. What you see as output is the values 1 through 5 — each on a separate line. Of course, you might think this is all smoke and mirrors. So, try changing one of the values in the array and you see that the output changes to match the array content.

Placing a condition within the declaration

Sometimes you need to perform data manipulation within a for loop in a way that's more convenient than trying to manipulate it in a code block. You can actually create a special kind of condition within a for loop declaration in which the condition does something like access a part of a string or array. The ForLoopCondition example demonstrates how to perform this task, as shown here:

```cpp
#include <iostream>

using namespace std;

int main()
{
  string hello = "Hello";
  for (int i = 0; char c = hello[i]; i++)
  {
    cout << c << endl;
  }
  return 0;
}
```

Notice that the middle condition, which normally checks for a particular value or performs some other logical function, actually creates a new char variable, c, and places a letter from the hello string into it based on the value of i. After scratching your head for a while looking for the means of ending the loop, you determine that when the loop gets to the end of the string, it automatically ends.

TIP

This is a handy way of working with all sorts of data when you don't know how large the data is at the outset. The for loop continues processing the string until it runs out of letters, so you don't have to worry about the string size.

Letting C++ determine the type

The previous section tells you about placing a condition within a for loop to manipulate data of uncertain size. The example assumes that the data is of a specific type, but you may not know the type. Starting with C++ 11 (which means that you must configure GCC with the Have G++ Follow the Combine C++ 1z (aka C++ 17) setting, as described in the "Working with ranges" section, earlier in this chapter), you can tell C++ to determine what type to use automatically. You do this using the auto keyword, as shown in the ForLoopCondition2 code here:

```cpp
#include <iostream>

using namespace std;

int main()
{
  string hello = "Hello";
  int values[] = {1, 2, 3, 4, 5, 0};

  for (int i = 0; auto c = hello[i]; i++)
  {
    cout << c << endl;
  }

  return 0;
}
```

As shown, the for loop will process the values in hello just as it did for the example in the previous section. However, this time you don't specify that c is a char; you use auto instead. Now, try replacing hello with values in the for loop so that it looks like this:

```cpp
for (int i = 0; auto c = values[i]; i++)
{
  cout << c << endl;
}
```

Instead of outputting Hello one letter at a time, you now see the numbers 1 through 5, one on each line. So, the same for loop now works for data of two different types: string and int. Using this approach gives you additional flexibility at the cost of a little code readability.

Notice that the for loop doesn't output the 0 in the values array; rather, it uses the 0 to determine the ending point of the array. If you didn't include this 0, the for loop would continue until it found a 0, which means you could see quite a bit of garbage onscreen.

Looping while

Often, you find that for loops work only so well. Sometimes, you don't want a counter variable; you just want to run a loop over and over as long as a certain situation is true. Then, after that situation is no longer the case, you want to stop the loop.

For example, instead of saying that you'll have 100 people line up and each one will give you one more dollar than the previous person, you may say that you will continue accepting money like this as long as people are willing to give it.

In this case, you can see that the condition under which the giving continues to operate is the statement "as long as they're willing to give it."

To do this in C++, you use a while statement. The while keyword is followed by a set of parentheses containing the condition under which the application is to continue running the loop. Whereas the general for statement's parentheses include three portions that show how to change the counter variable, the while statement's parentheses contain only a condition. The WhileLoop example demonstrates a simple while loop, as shown here:

```
#include <iostream>

using namespace std;

int main()
{
    int i = 0;
    while (i <= 5)
    {
        cout << i << endl;
        i++;
    }
```

```
    cout << "All Finished!" << endl;
    return 0;
}
```

This code runs while i is less than or equal to 5. Thus, the output of this application is

```
0
1
2
3
4
5
All Finished!
```

Notice that you must declare i outside the while loop using int i = 0;. If you were to try to declare the while loop using while (int i <= 5), the compiler would complain.

The while loop is handy if you don't have a particular number of times you need the loop to run. For example, consider a situation in which your application is reading data from the Internet. Unless you control the Internet data source, you don't know how much data it can provide. (Many other situations can arise in which you don't know how much data to read, but Internet applications commonly experience this problem.) Using a while loop, the code can continue reading data until your application has read it all. The Internet data source can simply *stream* the data to your application until the data transfer is complete.

Often, for this kind of situation, you create a Boolean variable called done and start it out as false. The while statement is simply

```
while (!done)
```

This line translates easily to English as "while not done, do the following." Then, inside the while loop, when the situation happens that you know the loop must finish (such as the Internet data source has no more data to read), you set

```
done = true;
```

The WhileLoop2 example demonstrates how to do this sort of process, as shown here:

```cpp
#include <iostream>

using namespace std;

int main()
{
    int i = 0;
    bool done = false;
    while (!done)
    {
        cout << i << endl;
        i++;
        if (i > 5)
            done = true;
    }
    cout << "All Finished!" << endl;
    return 0;
}
```

In the case of the Internet data example, after you encounter no more data, you would set done to true. The variable used to control the loop condition must change or the loop will continue to run forever. In the case of your friends giving you money, after one of them refuses, you would set done to true.

Doing while

The while statement has a cousin in the family: the do-while statement. A loop of this form is similar to the while loop, but with an interesting little catch: The while statement goes at the end, which means the loop always executes at least one time. The DoWhileLoop example demonstrates how to use this kind of loop, as shown here:

```cpp
#include <iostream>

using namespace std;

int main()
{
    int i = 15;
```

```
      do
      {
          cout << i << endl;
          i++;
      }
      while (i <= 5);
      cout << "All Finished!" << endl;
      return 0;
}
```

Notice here that the loop starts with the do keyword, and then the material for the loop follows inside braces, and finally the while statement appears at the end. The idea is that you're telling the computer "Do this while such-and-such is true," where *this* is the stuff inside braces and the *such-and-such* is the condition inside parentheses. Because the condition is evaluated at the end, after everything else is done, the output from this example is a little different from the other while loop examples:

```
15
All Finished!
```

WARNING

If you had used a while loop here, the loop wouldn't have executed at all because i is set to 15. However, because this is a do-while loop, you see the output of 15. Having the loop run at least once can be a problem sometimes, and if you don't want that behavior, consider using a while loop instead of a do-while loop.

Breaking and continuing

Sometimes, you may write an application that includes a loop that does more than simply add numbers. You may find that you want the loop to end under a condition that's separate from the condition in the loop declaration. Or you may want the loop to suddenly skip out of the current loop and continue with the next item in the loop when the item being processed is incorrect in some way. When you stop a loop and continue with the code after the loop, you use a break statement. When you quit the current cycle of the loop and continue with the next cycle, you use a continue statement. The next two sections show you how to do this.

REMEMBER

Even though the examples in the following sections rely on a for loop, the break and continue statements also work for while and do-while loops.

Breaking

Suppose that you are writing an application that reads data over the Internet, and the loop runs for the amount of data that's supposed to come. But midway through the process, you may encounter some data that has an error in it, and you may want to get out of the `for` loop immediately.

C++ includes a handy little statement that can rescue you in such a situation. The statement is called `break`. Now, nothing actually breaks, and it seems a bit frightening to write an application that instructs the computer to break. But this use of the term *break* is more like in "break out of prison" than "break the computer." But instead of breaking out of prison, it breaks you out of the loop.

The ForLoop3 example that follows demonstrates this technique. This sample checks for the special case of `i` equaling 5. You could accomplish the same result by changing the end condition of the `for` loop, but at least it shows you how the `break` statement works.

```cpp
#include <iostream>

using namespace std;

int main()
{
    for (int i=0; i<10; i++)
    {
        cout << i << " ";
        if (i == 5)
        {
            break;
        }
        cout << i * 2 << endl;
    }
    cout << "All Finished!" << endl;
    return 0;
}
```

In the preceding code, the first line inside the `for` loop, `cout << i << " ";`, runs when `i` is 5. But the final line in the `for` loop, `cout << i * 2 << endl;`, does not run when `i` is 5 because you tell it to break out of the loop between the two `cout` statements.

Also notice that when you break out of the loop, the application does not quit. It continues with the statements that follow the loop. In this case, it still prints the message "All Finished!"

WARNING

You can leave empty the second portion of the for statement (the condition) by simply putting a blank between the spaces. Then, to get out of the loop, you can use a break statement. However, doing this makes for messy code. You should treat messy code like you treat a messy house: Although sometimes not everyone minds it, the truth is that most people don't care to see a messy house. And you really don't want other people to see your messy house — or your messy code. Yes, as a programmer, being a little self-conscious is sometimes a good thing.

Continuing

In addition to the times when you may need to break out of a loop for a special situation, you can also cause the loop to end its current iteration; but instead of breaking out of it, the loop resumes with the next iteration.

For example, you may be, again, reading data from over the Internet, and doing this by looping a specified number of times. In the middle of the loop, you may encounter some bad data. But rather than quit out of the loop, you may want to simply ignore the current piece of bad data and then continue reading more data.

To do this trick, you use a C++ statement called continue. The continue statement says, "End the current iteration, but continue running the loop with the next iteration."

The ForLoop4 example that follows shows a slightly modified version of the previous example, in the "Breaking" section. When the loop gets to 5, it doesn't execute the second cout line. But rather than break out of the loop, it continues with 6, and then 7, and so on until the loop finishes on its own:

```cpp
#include <iostream>

using namespace std;

int main()
{
    int i;
    for (i=0; i<10; i++)
    {
        cout << i << " ";
        if (i == 5)
```

```
        {
            cout << endl;
            continue;
        }
        cout << i * 2 << endl;
    }
    cout << "All Finished!" << endl;
    return 0;
}
```

Nesting loops

Many times, you need to work with more than one loop. For example, you may have several groups of friends, and you want to bilk the individual friends of each group for all you can get. You may host a party for the first group of friends and make them each give you as much money as they have. Then, the next week, you may hold another party with a different group of friends. You would do this for each group of friends. You can draw out the logic like this:

```
For each group of friends,
    for each person in that group
        bilk the friend for all he or she is worth
```

This is a nested loop. But if you do this, don't be surprised if this is the last time your friends visit your nest.

A *nested loop* is simply a loop inside a loop. Suppose that you want to multiply each of the numbers 1 through 10 by 1 and print the answer for each multiplication, and then you want to multiply each of the numbers 1 through 10 by 2 and print the answer for each multiplication, and so on, up to a multiplier of 10. Your C++ code would look like the ForLoop5 example:

```
#include <iostream>

using namespace std;

int main()
{
    for (int x = 1; x <= 10; x++)
    {
        cout << "Products of " << x <<endl;
        for (int y = 1; y <= 10; y++)
```

```
        {
            cout << x * y << endl;
        }
        cout << endl;
    }
    return 0;
}
```

In this example, you have a loop inside a loop. The inner loop can make use of x from the outer loop. Beyond that, nothing is magical or bizarre about this code. It's just a loop inside a loop. And yes, you can have a loop inside a loop inside a loop inside a loop. You can also place any loop inside any other loop, like a `while` loop inside a `for` loop.

Notice you have a `cout` call before and after the inner loop. You can do this; your inner loop need not be the only thing inside the outer loop.

WARNING

Although you can certainly have a loop inside a loop inside a loop inside a loop, the deeper you get, the more potentially confusing your code can become. It's like the dozens of big cities in America that are promising to build an outer loop (a road that surrounds the outside of the city to help move traffic faster). Eventually, that outer loop won't be big enough, so the cities have to build another and another. That's kind of a frightening prospect, so try not to get carried away with nesting.

**TECHNICAL
STUFF**

If you put a `break` statement or a `continue` statement inside a nested loop, the statement applies to the innermost loop it sits in. For example, the `ForLoop6` example that follows contains three loops: an outer loop, a middle loop, and an inner loop. The `break` statement applies to the middle loop, as shown here:

```
#include <iostream>

using namespace std;

int main()
{
    for (int x = 1; x <= 3; x++)
    {
        for (int y = 1; y < 3; y++)
        {
            if (y == 2)
                break;
            for (int z = 1; z < 3; z++)
            {
                cout << x << " " << y;
```

```
                cout << " " << z << endl;
            }
        }
    }
    return 0;
}
```

You can see that when y is 2, the for loop with the y in it breaks. But the outer loop continues to run with the next iteration.

» Writing your own great functions

» Fun with strings

» Manipulating `main()`

Chapter **6**

Dividing Your Work with Functions

People generally agree that most projects throughout life are easier when you divide them into smaller, more manageable tasks. That's also the case with computer programming — if you break your code into smaller pieces, it becomes more manageable.

C++ provides many ways to divide code into smaller portions. One way is through the use of what are called functions. A *function* is a set of lines of code that performs a particular job. In this chapter, you discover what functions are and how you can use them to make your programming job easier.

REMEMBER

You don't have to type the source code for this chapter manually. In fact, using the downloadable source is a lot easier. You can find the source for this chapter in the \CPP_AIO4\BookI\Chapter06 folder of the downloadable source. See the Introduction for details on how to find these source files.

Dividing Your Work

If you have a big job to do that doesn't involve a computer, you can divide your work in many ways. Over the years of studying process management, people have pretty much narrowed the division of a job to two ways: using nouns and using verbs.

Yes, that's right. Back to good old English class, where everyone learned about nouns and verbs. The idea is this: Suppose that you're going to go out back and build a flying saucer. You can approach the designing of the flying saucer in two ways.

First, you could just draw up a plan of attack, listing all the steps to build the flying saucer from start to finish. That would, of course, be a lot of steps. But to simplify it, you could instead list all the major tasks without getting into the details. It might go something like this:

1. Build the outer shell.

2. Build and attach the engine.

That's it. Only two steps. But when you hire a couple dozen people to do the grunt work for you while you focus on your day trading, would that be enough for them to go on? No, probably not. Instead, you could divide these two tasks into smaller tasks. For example, Step 2 might look like this:

2a. Build the antigravity lifter.

2b. Build the thruster.

2c. Connect the lifter to the thruster to form the final engine.

2d. Attach the engine to the outer shell.

That's a little better; it has more detail. But it still needs more. How do you do the "Build the antigravity lifter" part? That's easy, but it requires more detail, as in the following steps:

2aa. Unearth the antigravity particles from the ground.

2ab. Compress them tightly into a superatomizing conductor.

2ac. Surround with coils.

2ad. Connect a 9-volt battery clip to the coils.

And, of course, each of these instructions requires even more detail. Eventually, after you have planned the whole thing, you will have many, many steps, but they will be organized into a hierarchy of sorts, as shown in Figure 6-1. In this drawing, the three dots represent places where other steps go — they were left off so that the diagram could fit on the page.

This type of design is a *top-down* design. The idea is that you start at the uppermost step of your design (in this case, "Build flying saucer") and continue to break the steps into more and more detailed steps until you have something manageable. For many years, this was how computer programming was taught.

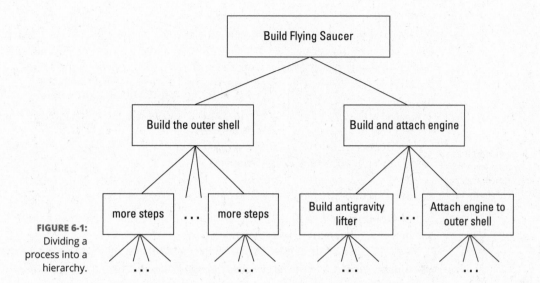

FIGURE 6-1:
Dividing a
process into a
hierarchy.

Although this process works, people have found a slightly better way. First, before breaking the steps (which are the verbs), you divide the thing you're building into parts (the nouns). In this case, you kind of do that already, in the first two steps. But instead of calling them steps, you can call them *objects*. One object is the outer shell, and one object is the engine. This way, two different factories can work on these in sort of a division of labor. Of course, the factories would have to coordinate their activities; otherwise, the two parts may not fit together when they're ready to go. And before you figure out exactly how to build each of these objects, it would be a good idea to describe each object: what it does, its features, its dimensions, and so on. Then, when you finally have all that done, you can list the exact features and their details. And finally, you can divide the work with each person designing or building a different part.

As you can see, this second approach makes more sense. And that's the way programmers divide their computer applications. But at the bottom of each method is something in common: The methods are made of several little processes. These processes are called *functions*. When you write a computer application, after you divide your job into smaller pieces called objects, you eventually start giving these objects behaviors. And to code these behaviors, you do just as you did in the first approach: You break them into manageable parts, again, called functions. In computer programming terms, a *function* is simply a small set of code that performs a specific task. But it's more than that: Think of a function as a machine. You can put one or more things into the machine; it processes them, and then it spits out a single answer, if anything at all. One of the most valuable diagrams you can have draws a function in this manner, like a machine, as shown in Figure 6-2.

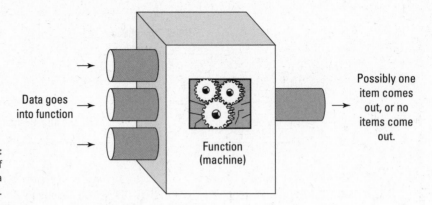

FIGURE 6-2:
You can think of a function as a machine.

Data goes into function

Function (machine)

Possibly one item comes out, or no items come out.

This machine (or function) has three main parts:

» **Inputs:** The function can receive data through its inputs. These data elements can be numbers, strings, or any other type. When you create such a machine, you can have as many inputs as you want (or even zero, if necessary).

» **Processor:** The processor is the function itself. In terms of C++, this is actually a set of code lines.

» **Output:** A function can *return* something when it has finished doing its thing. In C++, this output is in the form of numbers, strings, or any other type.

To make all this clear, try out the FirstFunction code in Listing 6-1. (Don't forget the second line, #include<math.h>, which gives you some math capabilities.)

LISTING 6-1: **Seeing a Function in Action**

```
#include <iostream>
#include <math.h>

using namespace std;

int main()
{
    cout << fabs(-10.5) << endl;
    cout << fabs(10.5) << endl;
    return 0;
}
```

When you run this application, you see the following output:

```
10.5
10.5
```

In this code, you use a function or machine called `fabs()` (usually pronounced "ef-abs," for floating-point absolute). This function takes a number as input and returns as output the absolute value of the number.

REMEMBER

The absolute value of a number is simply the positive version of the number. The absolute value, for example, of −5 is simply 5. The absolute value of 12 is still 12. An absolute value is almost always positive because the absolute value of 0 is 0, but 0 is the origin, which is neither positive nor negative (see `http://www.math.com/school/subject1/lessons/S1U1L10DP.html` for details). The reason for the `f` before the name `abs` is that it uses floating-point numbers, which are simply numbers with decimal points.

So the first line inside `main()` *calls* `fabs()` for the value −10.5. The `cout` then takes the output of this function (that is, the *result*) and prints it to the console.

Then the second line does the same thing again, except that it takes the absolute value of the number 10.5.

And where is the processor for this function? It's not in your code; it's in another file, and the following line ensures that your application can use this function:

```
#include <math.h>
```

You have seen functions in many places. If you use a calculator and enter a number and press the square root button, the calculator runs a function that calculates the square root.

But functions can be more sophisticated than just working with numbers. Consider this statement carefully: When you are using a word processor and you highlight a word and check the spelling of the word, the application calls a function that handles the spelling check. This function does something like the following:

```
This is a function to check the spelling of a single word.
Inputs: A single word.
Look up the word
If the word is not found
    Find some suggestions.
    Open a dialog box through which you (the user)
        can change the word by either typing a new word
```

```
        or picking one of the selections, or just leaving
        it the same.
    If you made a change,
        Return the new spelling.
    Otherwise
        Return nothing.
  Otherwise
    Return nothing
```

Notice how the if statements are grouped with indentations. The final otherwise goes with the first if statement because its indentation matches that of the if statement.

So that's a function that performs a spelling check. But consider this: When you do not highlight a word but run the spelling checker, the spelling checker runs for the whole document. That's another function. Here it is.

```
This function checks the spelling of the entire document
For each word in the document
    Check the spelling of the single word
```

How does the computer do the step inside the for loop, "Check the spelling of the single word?" It calls the function described earlier. This process is called *code reuse*. You have no reason to rewrite the entire function again if you already have it somewhere else. And that's the beauty of functions.

Calling a Function

When you run the code in a function, computer people say that you are *calling* the function. And just like every good person, a good function has a name. When you call a function, you do so by name.

TIP

Often, when writing an application and developing code to call a function, developers say that they are calling a function. This is partly computerspeak and partly a strange disorder in which developers start to relate just a little *too* much to the computer.

To call a function, you type its name and then a set of parentheses. Inside the parentheses, you list the items you want to send to the inputs of the function. The term used here is *pass*, as in "You pass the values to the function."

For example, if you want to call the fabs() function, you type the name, fabs, an open parenthesis, the number you want to pass to it, and then a closed parenthesis, as in the following example:

```
fabs(-10.5)
```

But by itself, this line does not do anything with regard to the application as a whole. The fabs() function returns a value — the absolute value of -10.5, which comes out to be 10.5 — and you probably want to do something with that value. You could, for example, print it to the console:

```
cout << fabs(-10.5) << endl;
```

Or you could store it away in another variable. But there's a catch. Before you can do that, you need to know the *type* that the function returns. Just as with a variable, a function return value has a type. In this case, the type is a special type called double (which stands for double precision floating point). The double type is a floating-point type that can hold many digits in a single number. To save the result of fabs(), you need to have a variable of type double. The Fabs2 example, shown in Listing 6-2, does this.

LISTING 6-2: **Seeing Another Way to Use fabs()**

```
#include <iostream>
#include <math.h>

using namespace std;

int main()
{
  double mynumber = fabs(-23.87);
  cout << mynumber << endl;
  return 0;
}
```

This code declares a double variable called mynumber. Then it calls fabs(), passing it -23.87 and returning the value into mynumber. Next, it prints the value in mynumber to the console.

When you run this application, you see the following, which is the absolute value of -23.87:

```
23.87
```

USING AUTO FOR FUNCTIONS

In general, specifically defining the type of the variable you use to receive output from a function makes your code more readable. However, there are situations for which you may not know the precise output type or different versions of the function output different types (which is very confusing). In this case, you begin by setting GCC to use C++ 17, as described in the "Working with ranges" section of Book 1, Chapter 5. Then, you can write the Fabs2 example shown in Listing 6-2, as shown in the following UsingAuto example:

```
#include <iostream>
#include <math.h>

using namespace std;

int main()
{
  auto mynumber = fabs(-23.87);
  cout << mynumber << endl;
  return 0;
}
```

The result is the same as the Fabs2 example. The difference is that mynumber is now of type auto, where C++ automatically detects the data type for you, instead of double, where you explicitly define the data type.

Passing a variable

You can also pass the value of a variable into a function. The Fabs3 example in Listing 6-3 creates two variables: One is passed into the function, and the other receives the result of the function.

LISTING 6-3: **Seeing Yet Another Way to Use fabs()**

```
#include <iostream>
#include <math.h>

using namespace std;

int main()
```

```
{
    double start = -253.895;
    double finish = fabs(start);
    cout << finish << endl;
    return 0;
}
```

This code creates two variables; the first is called start, and the second is called finish. It initializes start with a value of -253.895. Next, it calls fabs(), passing it the value of start. It saves the return value in finish, and prints the value in finish. When Fabs3 runs, you see the following appear on the console:

```
253.895
```

TIP

Saving a function result to a variable is useful if you need to use the result several times over. For example, if you need the absolute value of -253.895 for whatever reason and then a few lines later you need it again, you have a choice: You can either call fabs(-253.895) each time or call it once, save the result in a variable, and then use the variable each time you need it. The advantage to saving it in a variable is that you might later say, for example, "Oh, wait! I didn't just want the absolute value! I wanted the negative of the absolute value!" Then you only have to change one line of code — the line where it calls fabs(). If, instead, you had called fabs() several times, you would have had to change it every time you called it. And by the way, in case you're curious about how to take the negative of the absolute value and store it in a variable, you just throw a minus sign in front of it, like so:

```
finish = -fabs(start);
```

Passing multiple variables

Some functions like to have all sorts of goodies thrown their way, such as multiple parameters. As with functions that take a single value, you put the values inside a single set of parentheses. Because you have multiple values, you separate them with commas. The Pow1 example, shown in Listing 6-4, uses a function called pow() to calculate the third power of 10. (That is, it calculates 10 times 10 times 10. Yes, *POW!*). Make sure that you include the math.h line in the include section so that you can use the pow() function.

Seeing Yet One More Function in Action

```cpp
#include <iostream>
#include <math.h>

using namespace std;

int main()
{
    double number = 10.0;
    double exponent = 3.0;
    cout << pow(number, exponent) << endl;
    return 0;
}
```

When you run the application, you see 10 to the third power, which is 1,000:

```
1000
```

You can also pass a mixture of variables and numbers, or just numbers. The following code snippet also calculates the third power of 10 but passes an actual number, 3.0, for the power:

```
double number = 10.0;
cout << pow(number, 3.0) << endl;
```

Or you can pass only numbers:

```
cout << pow(10.0, 3.0) << endl;
```

Writing Your Own Functions

And now the fun begins! Calling functions is great, but you get real power (ooh!) when you write your own, specialized functions. Before writing a function, remember the parts: the inputs, the main code or processor, and the single output (or no output). The inputs, however, are called *parameters*, and the output is called a *return value*. The following sections fill you in on the details.

Defining the AddOne() function

The AddOne example, shown in Listing 6-5, provides both a custom function and code in main() that calls the custom function. (The function is placed outside main() — before it, in fact.)

LISTING 6-5: **Writing Your Very Own Function**

```cpp
#include <iostream>

using namespace std;

int AddOne(int start)
{
  int newnumber = start + 1;
  return newnumber;
}

int main()
{
  int testnumber = 20;
  int result = AddOne(testnumber);
  cout << result << endl;
  return 0;
}
```

REMEMBER

Notice that this example lacks the #include <math.h> entry found in earlier examples. You need to add an entry to the include section of your code only when you use a feature of that include file. In this case, the example relies on standard math features that are part of the basic C++ language, so you don't need any additional code.

Using the downloadable source will save you time and ensure that the example runs the first time you try it. However, you might choose to type it manually. Because there's a good bit of code, you may get some compiler errors at first; look carefully at the lines with the errors and find the difference between your code and what's here in the book. After you run the example, you see:

21

Seeing how AddOne() is called

You can start reviewing this code by seeing how to call `AddOne()`. Look at these lines of `main()`:

```
int testnumber = 20;
int result = AddOne(testnumber);
cout << result << endl;
```

You can probably put together some facts and determine what the function does. First, the example is called `AddOne()`, which is a good indication in itself. Second, when you run the application, the number 21 appears on the console, which is one more than the value in `testnumber`; it adds one. And that, in fact, is what the function does. It's amazing what computers can do these days.

TIP

When you write your own functions, try to choose a name that makes sense and describes what the function does. Writing a function and calling it something like `process()` or `TheFunction()` is easy, but those names don't accurately describe the function.

Taking the AddOne() Function apart

Now, look at the `AddOne` function. Here are a few high-level observations about it:

>> **Position:** The function appears *before* `main()`. Because of the way the compiler works, it must know about a function before you call it. And thus, you put it before `main()`. (You can do this in another way that is discussed in the "Forward references and function prototypes" section, later in this chapter.)

>> **Format:** The function starts with a line that seems to describe the function (explained later in this section), and then it has an open brace and, later, a closing brace.

>> **Code:** The function has code in it that is just like the type of code you could put inside a `main()`. The code consists of these elements:

- **Performing a task:** The code begins by performing a task, like this:

```
int newnumber = start + 1;
```

- The code declares an integer variable called `newnumber`. Then it initializes it to `start` plus 1. But what is `start`? That's one of the inputs.

- **Returning a result:** This line appears at the end of the function:

```
return newnumber;
```

- This is the output of the function, or the *return value*. When you want to return something from a function, you just type the word `return` and then indicate what you want to return. From the first line in the `AddOne()` function, you can see that `newnumber` is one more than the number passed into the function. So this line returns the `newnumber`.

Considering the AddOne() parameter

`AddOne()` takes just one parameter called `start`, which comes from the first line of the function:

```
int AddOne(int start)
```

The entry in parentheses is the parameter. Notice it looks like a variable declaration; it's the word `int` (the type, or integer) followed by a variable name, `start`. That's the parameter — the input — to the function, and you can access this parameter throughout the function using a variable called `start`. You can use the input to the function as a variable.

If you had written `result = AddOne(25);` in `main()`, then, throughout the function, the value of `start` would be 25. Likewise, if you had written

```
result = AddOne(152);
```

then, throughout the function, the value of `start` would be 152.

But here's the outstanding thing about functions (or, at least, one of the loads of outstanding things about functions): You can call the function several times over. In the same `main()`, you can have the following lines

```
cout << AddOne(100) << endl;
cout << AddOne(200) << endl;
cout << AddOne(300) << endl;
```

which would result in this output:

```
101
201
301
```

In the first call to `AddOne`, the value of `start` would be 100. During the second call, the value would be 200, and during the third call, it would be 300.

Understanding the AddOne() name and type

Look at the `AddOne()` header again:

```
int AddOne(int start)
```

The word `AddOne` is the name of the function, as you've probably figured out already. And that leaves the thing at the beginning — the `int`. That's the *type* of the return value. The final line in the function before the closing brace is

```
return newnumber;
```

The variable `newnumber` inside the function is an integer. And the return type is `int`. That's no accident: As programmers have all heard before, friends don't let friends return something other than the type specified in the function header. The two must match in type. And further, examine this line from inside `main()`:

```
int result = AddOne(testnumber);
```

The type of `result` is also an integer. All three match. Again, no accident. You can copy one thing to another (in this case, the function's return value to the variable called `result`) only if they match in type. And here, they do — they're both integers.

Notice one more thing about the function header: It has no semicolon after it. This is one of the places you do *not* put a semicolon. If you do, the compiler gets horribly confused. The Code::Blocks compiler shows an error that says, `"error: expected unqualified-id before '{' token."`

Finally, ponder this line of code for a moment:

```
testnumber = AddOne(testnumber);
```

This line takes the value stored inside `testnumber`, passes it into `AddOne()`, and gets back a new number. It then takes that new number and stores it back into `testnumber`. Thus, `testnumber`'s value changes based on the results of the function `AddOne()`.

Improving On the Basic Function

Not all functions work precisely the same way. You can create functions that have multiple parameters or no parameters. There is no law that says that a function must absolutely provide a return value. The following sections discuss variations on the basic function theme discussed in the previous section.

Using multiple parameters or no parameters

You don't need to write your functions with only one parameter each. You can have several parameters, or you can have none. It may seem a little strange that you would want a function — a machine — that accepts no inputs. But you may run into lots of cases where this may be a good idea. Here are some ideas for functions:

>> **Day:** Determines the day and returns it as a string, as in "Monday" or "Tuesday"

>> **Number-of-users:** Figures out the current number of users logged in to a web-server computer

>> **Current font:** In a text editor application (such as Notepad), returns a string containing the current font name, such as "Arial"

>> **Editing time:** Returns the amount of time you have been using the word processor application

>> **Username:** If you are logged on to a computer, gives back your username as a string, such as "Elisha"

All functions in this list have something in common: They look up information. Because no parameters are in the code, for the functions to process some information, they have to go out and get it themselves. It's like sending people out into the woods to find food but not giving them any tools: It's totally up to them to perform the required tasks, and all you can do is sit back and watch and wait for your yummy surprise.

If a function takes no parameters, you write the function header as you would for one that takes parameters, and you include the parentheses; you just don't put anything *in* the parentheses, as the UserName example in Listing 6-6 shows. So if nothing good is going in, there really can be something good coming back out, at least in the case of a function with no parameters.

LISTING 6-6: **Taking No Parameters**

```
#include <iostream>

using namespace std;

string Username()
{
  return "Elisha";
}

int main()
{
  cout << Username() << endl;
  return 0;
}
```

When you run Listing 6-6, you see the following output:

```
Elisha
```

Your function can also take multiple parameters. The ConnectNames example, shown in Listing 6-7, demonstrates the use of multiple parameters. Notice that the function, ConnectNames(), takes the two strings as parameters and combines them, along with a space in the middle. Notice also that the function uses the two strings as variables.

LISTING 6-7: **Taking Multiple Parameters**

```
#include <iostream>

using namespace std;

string ConnectNames(string first, string last)
{
  return first + " " + last;
}

int main()
{
  cout << ConnectNames("Richard", "Nixon") << endl;
  return 0;
}
```

In the function header in Listing 6-7, you see the type name string for each parameter. Each parameter requires its own type entry or the compiler displays an error. Here are some points about this code:

>> **You didn't create variables for the two names in** main( ). Instead, you just typed them as string constants (that is, as actual strings surrounded by quotes).

>> **You can do calculations and figuring right inside the** return **statement.** That saves the extra work of creating a variable. In the function, you could create a return variable of type string, set it to first + " " + last, and then return that variable, as in the following code:

```
string result = first + " " + last;
return result;
```

But instead, the example shows how to do it all on one line, as in this line:

```
return first + " " + last;
```

Although you can save yourself the work of creating an extra variable and just put the whole expression in the return statement, sometimes that's a bad thing. If the expression is really long, like the following:

```
return (mynumber * 100 + somethingelse / 200) *
   (yetanother + 400 / mynumber) / (mynumber + evenmore);
```

it can get just a tad complicated. Breaking it into variables, such as in this example, is best:

```
double a = mynumber * 100 + somethingelse / 200;
double b = yetanother + 400 / mynumber;
double c = mynumber + evenmore;
return a * b / c;
```

Returning nothing

In the earlier section "Using multiple parameters or no parameters," you see a list of functions that take no parameters; these functions go and bring back something, whether it's a number, a string, or some other type of food.

One such example gets the username of the computer you're logged in to. But what if you are the great computer guru, and *you* are writing the application that actually logs somebody in? In that case, your application doesn't ask the computer what the username is — your application *tells* the computer what the username is, by golly!

In that case, your application would call a function, like SetUsername(), and pass the new username. The resulting function could do any of the following for a return value:

» It could return the name

» It could return a message saying that the username is not valid or something like that

» It may not return anything at all

Look at the case in which a function doesn't return anything. In C++, the way you state that the function doesn't return anything is by using the keyword void as the return type in the function header. The SetUserName example, shown in Listing 6-8, demonstrates this approach.

LISTING 6-8: **Returning Nothing at All**

```
#include <iostream>

using namespace std;

void SetUsername(string newname)
{
```

```
    cout << "New user is " << newname << endl;
}

int main()
{
    SetUsername("Harold");
    return 0;
}
```

When you run the application, you see

```
New user is Harold
```

Notice the `SetUsername()` function header: It starts with the word `void`, which means that it returns nothing at all. It's like outer space: There's just a big void with nothing there, and nothing is returned, except for static from the alien air-waves, but we won't go there. Also notice that, because this function does not return anything, there is no `return` statement.

Now, of course, this function really doesn't do a whole lot other than print the new username to the console, but that's okay; it shows you how you can write a function that does not return anything.

A function of return type `void` returns nothing at all.

REMEMBER

Do not try to return something in a function that has a return type of `void`. *Void* means that the function returns nothing at all. If you try to put a `return` statement in your function, you get a compile error.

Keeping your variables local

Everybody likes to have their own stuff, and functions are no exception. When you create a variable inside the code for a function, that variable will be known only to that particular function. When you create such variables, they are called *local variables,* and people say that they are local to that particular function. (Well, *computer people* say that, anyway.)

To see a local variable at work, consider the code in the `PrintName` example:

```
#include <iostream>

using namespace std;
```

```
void PrintName(string first, string last)
{
  string fullname = first + " " + last;
  cout << fullname << endl;
}

int main()
{
  PrintName("Thomas", "Jefferson");
  return 0;
}
```

Notice in the PrintName() function that you declare a variable called fullname. You then use that variable in the second line in that function, the one starting with cout. But you cannot use the variable inside main(). If you try to, as in the following code, you get a compile error:

```
int main()
{
  PrintName("Thomas", "Jefferson");
  cout << fullname << endl;
  return 0;
}
```

However, you can *declare* a variable called fullname inside main(), as in the PrintName2 example. But, if you do that, this fullname is local only to main(), whereas the other variable, also called fullname, is local only to the PrintName() function. In other words, each function has its own variable; they just happen to share the same name. But they are *two separate variables*:

```
#include <iostream>

using namespace std;

void PrintName(string first, string last)
{
  string fullname = first + " " + last;
  cout << fullname << endl;
}

int main()
{
  string fullname = "Abraham Lincoln";
  PrintName("Thomas", "Jefferson");
```

```
    cout << fullname << endl;
    return 0;
}
```

REMEMBER

When two functions declare variables by the same name, they are two separate variables. If you store a value inside one of them, the other function does not know about it. The other function only knows about its own variable by that name. Think of it this way: Two people could each have a storage bin labeled Tools in their closet. If Sally puts a hammer in her bin labeled Tools at her house and Hal opens another bin also labeled Tools at *his* house, he won't see Sally's hammer. As a result, the output from this example is:

```
Thomas Jefferson
Abraham Lincoln
```

WARNING

If you use the same variable name in two different functions, forgetting that you are working with two different variables is very easy. Do this only if you are sure that no confusion can occur.

TIP

If you use the same variable name in two different functions (such as a counter variable called index, which you use in a for loop), matching the case is usually a good idea. Don't use count in one function and use Count in another. Although you can certainly do that, you may find yourself typing the name wrong when you need it. But that won't cause you to access the other one. (You can't, because it is in a different function.) Instead, you get a compile error, and you have to go back and fix it. Being consistent is a time-saver.

Forward references and function prototypes

All examples in this chapter place the function code above the code for main(). The reason is that the compiler scans the code from start to finish. If it has not yet encountered a function but sees a call to it, it doesn't know what it's seeing, and it issues a good old compile error.

Such an error can be especially frustrating and can cause you to spend hours yelling at your computer. Nothing is more frustrating than looking at your application and being told by the compiler that it's wrong, yet knowing that it's correct because you know that you wrote the function.

You can, however, place your functions after main(); or you can even use function prototypes to put your functions in other source code files (a topic you find in Book 1, Chapter 7).

What you can do is include a function prototype. A *function prototype* is nothing more than a copy of the function header. But rather than follow it with an open brace and then the code for the function, you follow the function header with a semicolon and you are finished. A function prototype, for example, looks like this:

```
void PrintName(string first, string last);
```

Then you actually write the full function (header, code, and all) later. The full function can even be later than main() or later than any place that makes calls to it.

Notice that this example looks just like the first line of a function. In fact, it's possible to cheat! To write it, you simply copy the first line of the original function you write and add a semicolon. The PrintName3 example, shown in Listing 6-9, shows how to use this technique.

LISTING 6-9: Using a Function Prototype

```
#include <iostream>

using namespace std;

void PrintName(string first, string last);

int main()
{
  PrintName("Thomas", "Jefferson");
  return 0;
}

void PrintName(string first, string last)
{
  string fullname = first + " " + last;
  cout << fullname << endl;
}
```

Notice that the function header appears above main() and ends with a semicolon. Next comes main(). Finally, you see the PrintName() function itself (again, with the header but no semicolon this time). Thus, the function comes after main().

"Whoop-de-do," you say. "The function comes after." But why bother when now you have to type the function header twice?

This step truly is useful. If you have a source code file with, say, 20 functions, and these functions all make various calls to each other, it could be difficult to carefully order them so that each function calls *only* functions that are above it in the source code file. Instead, most programmers put the functions in some logical order (or maybe not), and they don't worry much about the calling order. Then they have all the function prototypes toward the top of the source code file, as shown previously in Listing 6-9.

TIP

When you type a function prototype, many people say that you are specifying a *forward reference*. This phrase simply means that you are providing a reference to something that happens later. It's not a big deal, and it mainly comes from some of the older programming languages.

Writing two versions of the same function

Sometimes you may want to write two versions of the same function, with the only difference being that they take different parameter types. For example, you may want a function called `Combine()`. One version takes two strings and puts the two strings together, but with a space in the middle. It then prints the resulting string to the console. Another version adds two numbers and writes all three numbers — the first two and the sum — to the console. The first version would look like this:

```
void Combine(string first, string second)
{
  cout << first << " " << second << endl;
}
```

There's nothing magical or particularly special about this function. It's called `Combine()`; it takes two strings as parameters; it doesn't return anything. The code for the function prints the two strings with a space between them. Now the second version looks like this:

```
void Combine(int first, int second)
{
  int sum = first + second;
  cout << first << " " << second << " " << sum << endl;
}
```

Again, nothing spectacular here. The function name is `Combine()`, and it doesn't return anything. But this version takes two integers, not two strings, as parameters. The code is also different from the previous code in that it first computes the sum of the inputs and then prints the different numbers.

REMEMBER

Overloading, or using one name for multiple functions, is somewhat common in C++. The `Combine` example, shown in Listing 6-10, contains the entire code. Both functions are present in the listing.

LISTING 6-10: **Writing Two Versions of a Function**

```cpp
#include <iostream>

using namespace std;

void Combine(string first, string second)
{
  cout << first << " " << second << endl;
}

void Combine(int first, int second)
{
  int sum = first + second;
  cout << first << " " << second << " " << sum << endl;
}

int main()
{
  Combine("David","Letterman");
  Combine(15,20);
  return 0;
}
```

You see each function called in `main()`. The compiler chooses which function to call based on the arguments you provide. For example, when viewing this call:

```cpp
Combine("David","Letterman");
```

you see two strings. So, the compiler knows to use the first version, which takes two strings. Now look at the second function call:

```cpp
Combine(15,20);
```

This call takes two integers, so the compiler knows to use the second version of the function.

REMEMBER

When you overload a function, the parameters must differ (or must appear in a different order). For example, the functions can take the same type of information but use a different number of parameters. Of course, the previous example shows that the parameters can also vary by type. You can also have different return types, though they must differ by more than just the return type, and varying the parameter names doesn't count. The compiler will see `Combine(string A, string B)` and `Combine(string First, string Second)` as the same function.

Calling All String Functions

To get the most out of strings, you need to make use of some special functions that cater to the strings. However, using these functions is a little different from the other functions used so far in this chapter. Rather than just call the function, you first type the variable name that holds the string, and then a period (or *dot*), and then the function name along with any arguments.

TECHNICAL STUFF

The reason you code string functions differently is because you're making use of some object-oriented programming features. Book 2, Chapter 1 describes in detail how these types of functions (called *methods*) work. The following sections describe some common functions and tell you how to use them.

Inserting a string into a string

One function that you can use is `insert()`. You can use this function if you want to insert more characters into another string. For example, if you have the string `"Something interesting and bizarre"` and you insert the string `"seriously "` (with a space at the end) into the middle of it starting at index 10, you get the string `"Something seriously interesting and bizarre"`.

REMEMBER

When you work with strings, the first character is the 0th index, and the second character is the 1st index, and so on. The following lines of code perform an insert by using the `insert()` function at index 10, even though you perform the insertion at letter 11:

```
string words = "Something interesting and bizarre";
words.insert(10, "seriously ");
```

The first of these lines simply creates a string called `words` and stuffs it full with the phrase `"Something interesting and bizarre"`. The second line does the insert. Notice the strange way of calling the function: You first specify the variable name, `words`, and then a dot, and then the function name, `insert`. Next, you follow it with the parameters in parentheses, as usual. For this function, the first parameter is the index where you want to insert the string. The second parameter is the actual string you are going to insert. After these two lines run, the string variable called `words` contains the string `"Something seriously interesting and bizarre"`.

Removing parts of a string

You can also erase parts of a string by using a similar function called `erase()`. The following line of code erases 16 characters from the `words` string starting at index 19:

```
words.erase(19,16);
```

Consequently, if the variable called `words` contains the string `"Something seriously interesting and bizarre"`, after this line runs, it will contain `"Something seriously bizarre"`.

Replacing parts of a string

Another useful function is `replace()`. This function replaces a certain part of the string with another string. To use `replace`, you specify where in the string you want to start the replacement and how many characters you want to replace. Then you specify the string with which you want to replace the old, worn-out parts.

For example, if your string is `"Something seriously bizarre"` and you want to replace the word `"thing"` with the string `"body"`, you tell `replace()` to start at index 4 and replace 5 characters with the word `"body"`. To do this, you enter:

```
words.replace(4, 5, "body");
```

TIP

Notice that the number of characters you replace does not have to be the same as the length of the new string. If the string starts out with `"Something seriously bizarre"`, after this `replace()` call the string contains `"Somebody seriously bizarre"`.

Using the string functions together

The `OperatingOnStrings` example, shown in Listing 6-11, demonstrates all these functions working together.

LISTING 6-11: **Operating on Strings**

```
#include <iostream>

using namespace std;

int main()
{
```

```
string words = "Something interesting and bizarre";
cout << words << endl;
words.insert(10, "seriously ");
cout << words << endl;
words.erase(19,16);
cout << words << endl;
words.replace(4, 5, "body");
cout << words << endl;
return 0;
}
```

When you run this application, you see the following output:

```
Something interesting and bizarre
Something seriously interesting and bizarre
Something seriously bizarre
Somebody seriously bizarre
```

The first line is the original string. The second line is the result of the insert() function. The third line is the result of the erase() function. And the final line is the result of the replace() function.

Understanding main()

All applications so far in this chapter have had a main(), which is a function. Notice its header, which is followed by code inside braces:

```
int main()
```

You can see that this is definitely a function header: It starts out with a return type and then the function name, main(). This is just one form of the main() function — the form that Code::Blocks uses by default. However, you may decide that you want to give users the ability to provide input when they type the name of your application at the console. In this case, you use this alternative form of the main() function that includes two parameters:

```
int main(int argc, char *argv[])
```

WHO, WHAT, WHERE, AND WHY RETURN?

The main() function header starts with the type int. This means that the function main() returns something to the caller. The result of main() is sometimes used by the computer to return error messages if the application, for some reason, didn't work or didn't do what it was supposed to do. But here's the inside scoop: Outputting a return value doesn't work in the graphical environment that most people use.

For Windows computers, the return value isn't normally used when you run the application outside Code::Blocks. The return type is specifically designed to work with batch files (files with a BAT extension that originally appeared as part of DOS, or Disk Operating System). You also see them used in scripts and as part of PowerShell. Consequently, unless you plan to work with command line utilities (and many people still do), just return 0. (The other time you want to return a non-zero value is when working in Code::Blocks. A non-zero return value appears highlighted in red in the Build Log, alerting you to the error condition.)

Some Unix and Linux systems also use the return value of main() for the same reason that Windows does — to indicate success or failure and to provide an error code when there is a failure. These computers may run hundreds of command-line applications. If one of these applications returns something other than 0, another application detects the error and notifies somebody.

Notice that the second form of main() has two parameters:

- » int argc: Tells you how many arguments appear on the command line.
- » char *argv[]: Provides a list of the command-line arguments in an array.

A *command-line argument* is something you type in the Windows Command Prompt or at the Linux Terminal window after the name of the application (the *command* you want to execute). When you run an application, especially from the command prompt, you type the name of the application and press Enter. But before pressing Enter, you can follow the application name with other words that are generally separated by spaces.

Many of the commands you use in Terminal window and the Command Prompt have an application name and then various arguments. The command usually tells you about these arguments when you enter a special argument such as /? or --h. An argument preceded by a slash (/) or two dashes (--) is a *switch* because it affects how the command works. Figure 6-3 shows an example of the dir (directory) command using the /? switch to tell you about the other arguments (including other switches) available with dir.

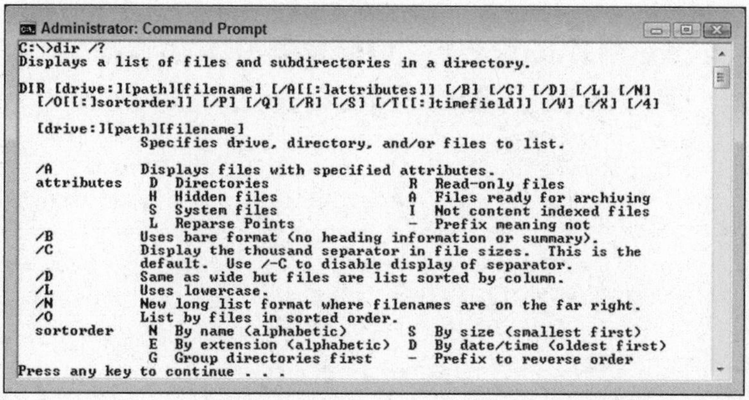

FIGURE 6-3:
Command-line apps often have switches and arguments.

To make these switches and their associated arguments work, the `main()` function must process the input. You determine how many command-line arguments the user supplied using `argc`, and then access them using `argv`. Book 2, Chapter 2 deals with the topic arrays. An *array* is a sequence of variables stored under one name. The `argv` variable is one such animal. To access the individual variables stored under the single umbrella known as `argv`, you do something like this:

```
cout << argv[0] << endl;
```

In this example, you use brackets as you did when accessing the individual characters in a string. When working with the `/?` switch, you see `/?` as the output. You can access the command-line parameters using a `for` loop. The `CommandLineParameters` example, shown in Listing 6-12, demonstrates this technique.

LISTING 6-12: **Accessing the Command-Line Parameters**

```cpp
#include <iostream>
#include <stdlib.h>

using namespace std;

int main(int argc, char *argv[])
{
  for (int index=1; index < argc; index++)
  {
    cout << argv[index] << endl;
  }

  return 0;
}
```

SETTING THE COMMAND-LINE PARAMETERS IN CODE::BLOCKS

If you attempt to run the example in Code::Blocks by choosing Build ⇨ Run with the default settings, the example doesn't output anything. To add command-line arguments, choose Project ⇨ Set Program's Arguments. You see the Select Target dialog box, where you can type the command-line arguments in the Program Arguments field. Type **Hello World I Love You!** in this field, one argument to a line, as shown in the figure, and click OK. You're ready to run the example, which outputs:

```
Hello
World
I
Love
You!
```

REMEMBER

Notice that the for loop begins at index = 1 rather than index = 0. The first item in the argv list is always the execution path and the name of the application. This information can come in handy at times, but normally you want the remaining arguments to change the way your application works.

Chapter **7**

Splitting Up Source Code Files

Just as you can divide your work into functions, so you can divide your work into multiple source code files. The main reason to do so is to help keep your project manageable. Also, with multiple source code files, you can have several people working on a single project, each working on a different source code file at the same time.

The key to multiple source files is knowing where to break the source code into pieces. As with anything else, if you break the source code in the wrong place, it will, well, break.

In this chapter, you discover how to divide your source code into multiple files (and in all the right places). The examples use Code::Blocks, but most modern IDEs work in about the same manner. You create multiple files and import them into a *project* (a description of what you want to do), which then manages the files for you and ensures that the right files are compiled at the right time.

REMEMBER

You don't have to type the source code for this chapter manually. In fact, using the downloadable source is a lot easier. You can find the source for this chapter in the \CPP_AIO4\BookI\Chapter07 folder of the downloadable source. See the Introduction for details on how to find these source files.

Creating Multiple Source Files

In the sections that follow, you see how to create multiple source code files using one of two techniques: You can rely on the IDE to perform all the required setups for you, or you can manually add the file and perform the required setups by editing a build file.

When you create a second source code file, this code becomes part of your project. And when you compile, the compiler compiles all the source code files in your project, assuming that you have changed them since the last time you compiled. You can put your functions in separate source code files, and they can call each other. In this way, they all work together in the single application. The section "Sharing with Header Files," later in this chapter shows how you can have a function call another function in a different source file.

REMEMBER

You can't break up a single function and put it into two source files. The compiler requires that your functions stay in one piece in a single source file.

Adding a new source code file

If you're using Code::Blocks, cutting your application into multiple source code files is as easy as cutting a cake. The AddFiles example assumes that you have started with an existing project using the process found in Book 1, Chapter 2. The following steps show how to add another file to this existing project.

1. **Choose File ⇨ New ⇨ File.**

    You see the New from Template dialog box, shown in Figure 7-1. Notice that you can choose from a header, a source code, or an empty file (among other non-C++ possibilities). Normally, you choose either the C/C++ Header or C/C++ Source option. The Empty File option is for non-source files, such as a text file used as a ReadMe.

2. **Highlight the template you want to use and click Go.**

    You see a wizard associated with the particular file you've chosen. The example uses a new C++ Header File named my_stuff.h.

3. **Click Next to get past the initial Welcome page.**

    If you chose the Empty File template, skip to Step 7. When using the C/C++ Header or C/C++ Source templates, you see a language selection page.

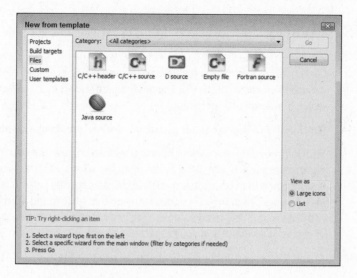

FIGURE 7-1:
The New from Template dialog box lets you select a new file type.

4. **Highlight the language you want to use — either C or C++ — and click Next.**

The wizard asks what you want to call the file, where you want to store it, and which builds should use the file, as shown in Figure 7-2. (More on these choices in Steps 5–8.)

FIGURE 7-2:
Provide the file information required by the wizard.

5. **Type a path and filename for the file in the Filename with Full Path field.**

You must provide the full path, even if you want the file in the current folder. Click the ellipsis to display the Select Filename dialog box, where you can choose the location of the file. The default path shown in the Select Filename dialog box is the current folder.

6. **(Optional) Provide a header guard word when creating a header file.**

You don't need to worry about how to use headers now, but you use them to perform tasks such as making declarations like #include statements. Adding a header more than once into an application can cause all sorts of problems, and the application might not compile, even though it would normally do so without the multiple header copies. The header guard word keeps the number of copies of the header in your application to one.

7. **Check the individual builds that should use the file.**

As an alternative, you can click All to add the file to all builds.

REMEMBER

A *debug* version of your application will contain special information that you can use to find program errors. A *release* version of your application is smaller and executes faster. Each version has a purpose, so developers usually need to create both at some point.

8. **Click Finish.**

The wizard adds the new file to your project. Code::Blocks automatically opens the file so that you can begin editing it. You also see the file you added in the Management window, as shown in Figure 7-3. In this case, you see both the source files and a header file. Notice that the source files appear in dark type and the header file appears in gray type. This shows that the source files are compiled to create the project and the header file isn't. The "Sharing with Header Files" section, later in this chapter, discusses in more detail how the compiler works with header files.

TIP

If Code::Blocks doesn't automatically open the file you added, you can open it by double-clicking its name in the Management Window tree (see Figure 7-3). When you do, an additional tab appears at the top of your source code files. These tabs represent the different files that are open. You can click a tab to have that file's code appear in the source code window. When you click another tab, the window shows the source for that file instead. And, thankfully, Code::Blocks remembers any changes you make if you switch to another tab. So you can bounce all around the screen and switch all you want, and the computer shouldn't get confused.

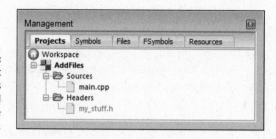

FIGURE 7-3:
The Management
window displays
the files used
to compile the
project.

After you have multiple files in your project, you can put some of your source in one file and some in another. But before you do, you may want to read some of the other sections in this chapter because they explain how to properly divide your source code without having it end up like cake that got smooshed while you were trying to cut it.

Removing an existing source code file

If you add a file to Code::Blocks that you really don't need, right-click the file in the Management window and choose Remove File from Project from the context menu. The file will disappear from the project but still appear in the directory in which you created it.

If you later decide that you really do want that file, right-click the project entry in the Management window, choose Add Files from the context menu, and select the file you want to add back into the project using the options in the Add Files to Project dialog box.

Creating a project with multiple existing files

Sometimes you have a number of existing files, but no project to hold them. For example, you might be moving from another IDE to Code::Blocks. That would mean that you'd have the source files from the other IDE, but no project file that Code::Blocks would recognize. Don't worry: You can put existing files into a Code::Blocks project. The following steps tell you how to perform this process (you can see the result by opening the CopiedFiles project):

1. **Choose Create a New Project on the Code::Blocks Start page.**

You see the New from Template dialog box used to create all the examples so far in this book.

2. **Choose the Empty Project template and click Go.**

You see an Empty Project welcome dialog. You can skip this dialog box the next time by selecting Skip this Page Next Time. The Empty Project template lets you create a project shell without any files in it.

3. **Click Next.**

You see the Empty Project configuration dialog box, shown in Figure 7-4. This is where you supply the name of the project, not the files used in the project.

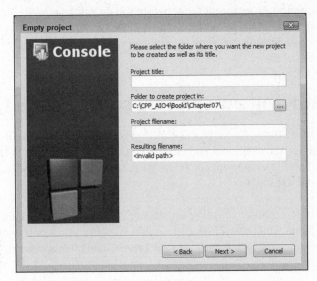

4. **Type a name for the project in the Project Title field.**

The example uses CopiedFiles. Notice that the wizard automatically fills in the Project Filename field for you.

5. **Click Next.**

The wizard asks you to supply the usual information for the compiler, debug configuration, and release configuration. The default settings will work fine in most cases.

6. **Click Finish.**

Code::Blocks creates an empty project for you where you can add files as needed.

7. **Right-click the CopiedFiles project entry in the Management window and choose Add Files from the context menu.**

You see the Add Files to Project window, shown in Figure 7-5. Only the project (.cbp) file appears because this is an empty project.

Of course, you need to add files to your project to make it useful. For the purposes of this example, you can use the files found in the AddFiles example created in the previous section of the chapter. For real-world use, you need to know the locations of the files you want to use to create your new project.

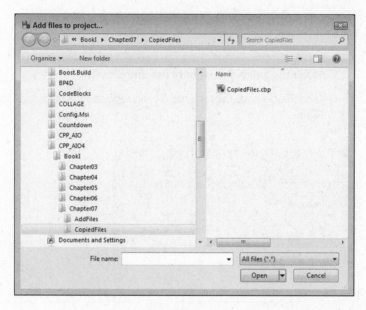

FIGURE 7-5:
The current directory doesn't contain any code files.

8. **Navigate to the** AddFiles **folder, shown in Figure 7-5.**

   Notice that you see a main.cpp and my_stuff.h file in the folder. (You may also see other files that you can safely ignore for now.)

9. **Locate and highlight the files you want to copy to the new project, which are** main.cpp **and** my_stuff.h **in this case.**

TIP

   Use the Ctrl+click method to select multiple files from the list. Code::Blocks makes it easy to select multiple files in a single pass so that you don't have to open the Add Files to Project dialog box multiple times.

10. **Click Open.**

   Code::Blocks displays a dialog box asking which builds to add the files to, as shown in Figure 7-6. The exact appearance of the dialog box will vary by the number of files you select.

Splitting Up Source Code Files

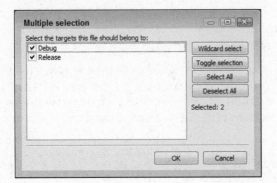

FIGURE 7-6:
Select the builds where the files are used.

11. **Select the builds you want to use and click OK.**

Code::Blocks adds the required file references to the project, as shown in Figure 7-7.

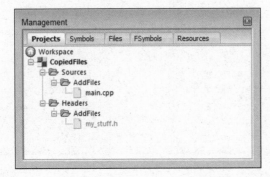

FIGURE 7-7:
The new project now contains references to the selected files.

WARNING

Notice that the references in Figure 7-7 still show the original location of the files. In this case, these files come from the AddFiles project. If you change the file in the original project, it also changes in the new project.

You also notice that the File➪Save command is disabled. That's because you can't save changes to file references in the project that references them; you must make changes in the original project. However, now that you have a reference to the file, you can make changes to it, and then use the File➪Save As command to create local copies of the files with your changes in them. Don't use the File➪Save command; create a local copy using File➪Save As instead.

Unfortunately, just creating the local copies doesn't change your project. To remove the references from the original project, right-click the project entry in the Management window (which is CopiedFiles for the example) and choose Remove Files from the context menu. You see the Multiple Selection dialog box, shown in Figure 7-8, where you can choose which references to remove and which to keep.

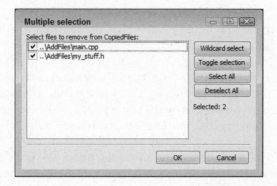

After you remove the references you no longer need, you can use Steps 7 through 11 in the preceding list to add the local copies of the files to the current project. The Management window will change to show that you're using local copies of the files, rather than copies found in another project.

Getting multiple files to interact

Before two source files can work together, they must somehow find out about each other. Just because they're both sitting on the computer doesn't mean that they know about each other. Computers are kind of goofy about that sort of thing. To get two source files to finally open up and get to know each other, you need to tell each of them about what's in the other file.

When you write a function, normally the function must appear before any calls to it appear within the same source file. That's because of the way the compiler parses the code: If the compiler encounters a call to a function but has not yet heard of that function, it issues an error. But the way around this is to use a function prototype. A *function prototype* is simply the header line from a function, ending with a semicolon, as in the following:

```
void BigDog(int KibblesCount);
```

Later in the source file is the actual function, with this header line duplicated. But instead of a semicolon, the function would have an open brace, the function code, and a closing brace, as in the following:

```
void BigDog(int KibblesCount)
{
  cout << "I'm a lucky dog" << endl;
  cout << "I have " << KibblesCount << " pieces of food"
    << endl;
}
```

Splitting Up Source
Code Files

So, after the function prototype, you can call the function whether the function code itself is before or after the call.

REMEMBER

For the compiler to understand a function call, all it needs at the point that the code makes the call is a function *prototype.* It's up to the *linker* (the special application that takes the object file created by the compiler and creates an executable from it by linking everything together) to determine whether that function really exists.

Because the function call needs only a function prototype, you can put the function *itself* in another source code file. You could, therefore, have two separate source code files, as in the MultipleSourceFiles example, shown in Listings 7-1 and 7-2. (The first source code file — main.cpp — is shown in Listing 7-1, and the second source code file — mystuff.cpp — is shown in Listing 7-2.)

LISTING 7-1: **Calling a Function with Only a Prototype**

```
void BigDog(int KibblesCount);

int main() {
  BigDog(3);
  return 0;
}
```

LISTING 7-2: **Using a Function from a Separate File**

```
#include <iostream>

using namespace std;

void BigDog(int KibblesCount) {
  cout << "I'm a lucky dog" << endl;
  cout << "I have " << KibblesCount << " pieces of food"
    << endl;
}
```

Listings 7-1 and 7-2 break the function away from the prototype. When you compile these two files together as a single application (either by pressing F9 in Code::Blocks or by choosing Build⇨Build and Run), they all fit together nicely. You can then run the application, and you see this somewhat interesting output:

```
I'm a lucky dog
I have 3 pieces of food
```

REMEMBER

Notice that main.cpp doesn't contain either #include <iostream> or using namespace std; because it doesn't have any calls to cout, just the call to BigDog(). You do have to put the #include <iostream> and using namespace std; lines at the start of the mystuff.cpp file because mystuff.cpp does use cout.

Sharing with Header Files

Breaking apart source code into multiple files is easy, but soon you may run into a problem. If you have a function — say, SafeCracker() — and this function is extremely useful and is likely to be called many times from within several other source code files, you would need a prototype for SafeCracker() in every file that calls it. The prototype may look like this:

```
string SafeCracker(int SafeID);
```

But there is an easier way of adding the prototype instead of adding it to every file that uses the function. Simply put this line inside its own file, called a *header file*, and give the filename an .h or .hpp extension. (It's your choice which extension you use, because it really doesn't matter; most developers use .h.) For this example, you place the line string SafeCracker (int SafeID); in a file called safestuff.h.

Then, instead of typing the header line at the start of each file that needs the function, you type

```
#include "safestuff.h"
```

You would then have the three source code files used for the `MultipleSource Files2` example, shown in Listings 7-3, 7-4, and 7-5:

>> `main.cpp`: Calls the function

>> `safestuff.h`: Contains the function prototype

>> `safestuff.cpp`: Contains the actual code for the function whose prototype appears in the header file

Lots of files, but now the code is broken into manageable pieces. Also, make sure that you save all three of these files in the same directory.

LISTING 7-3: **Including the Header File in the main File**

```
#include <iostream>
#include "safestuff.h"

using namespace std;

int main()
{
  cout << "Surprise, surprise!" << endl;
  cout << "The combination for Safe 12 is: " << endl;
  cout << SafeCracker(12) << endl;
  cout << "Let's check on Safe 11 too: " << endl;
  cout << SafeCracker(11) << endl;
  return 0;
}
```

LISTING 7-4: **Containing the Function Prototype in the Header File**

```
#ifndef SAFESTUFF_H_INCLUDED
#define SAFESTUFF_H_INCLUDED

using namespace std;

string SafeCracker(int SafeID);

#endif // SAFESTUFF_H_INCLUDED
```

LISTING 7-5: **Containing the Actual Function Code**

```cpp
#include <iostream>
using namespace std;

string SafeCracker(int SafeID)
{
  if (SafeID == 12)
    return "13-26-16";
  else
    return "Safe Combination Unknown";
}
```

Before you compile this application, you need to know a few things about how the compilation process works:

>> When you compile a .cpp file, the compiler outputs a .o (for object) file that is then linked by the linker with all the other .o files to create an .exe (executable) file. In addition to the .o files from your project, the linker also links in any library files or external code that your application accesses.

>> The compiler doesn't compile the header file into a separate .o file. With the application in Listings 7-3 through 7-5, the compiler creates only two output files: main.o and safestuff.o (you can see them in the CPP_AIO4\BookI\Chapter07\MultipleSourceFiles2\obj\Debug folder).

>> When the compiler reads the main.cpp file and reaches the #include "safestuff.h" line for the header file, it verifies that it hasn't read the safestuff.h file before and included it within the .o file.

>> If the safestuff.h file hasn't been read before, the compiler temporarily switches over and reads the header file, pretending that it's still reading the same main.cpp file. As it continues, it compiles everything as if it's all part of the main.cpp file.

REMEMBER

If you include the safestuff.h header file in other source code files, the compiler adds the content to those source files as well. Compile and run the code in Listings 7-3 through 7-5. When you run the application, you see the following output:

```
Surprise, surprise!
The combination for Safe 12 is:
13-26-16
Let's check on Safe 11 too:
Safe Combination Unknown
```

TIP

If you have a source file containing some functions, creating a header file that contains the associated function prototypes is generally a good practice. Then you can name the header file the same as the source file, except with a different extension. In this example, you use the safestuff.h file to hold the prototype for the safestuff.cpp file.

Adding the header only once

Code::Blocks includes several lines in the header file by default. These lines create a symbol that tells the compiler whether a header file is already included in the source file so that the compiler doesn't add it twice. Adding a header twice is an error because then you'd define the forward reference for a function twice. Here is what you see when you initially create a header file with Code::Blocks:

```
#ifndef SAFESTUFF_H_INCLUDED
#define SAFESTUFF_H_INCLUDED
#endif // SAFESTUFF_H_INCLUDED
```

When you type the header code into Code::Blocks, type it between the #define SAFESTUFF_H_INCLUDED and #endif // SAFESTUFF_H_INCLUDED lines. The section "Using the Mysterious Header Wrappers," later in this chapter, describes these automatic entries in detail.

Using angle brackets or quotes

You may have noticed something about the code in Listing 7-3. When including the safestuff.h file, you don't put it inside angle brackets, as with the #include <iostream> line. Instead, you put it inside quotes:

```
#include "safestuff.h"
```

That's because programmers for years have been fighting over the rules of *where* exactly on the hard drive to put the header files. The question is whether to put them in the same directory or folder as your project or to place them in a directory all by themselves.

REMEMBER

Regardless of where you put your header files, here is the rule for when to use quotes and when to use brackets: The compiler looks in several directories to find header files. And it can, possibly, look in the same directory as the source file. If you use angle brackets (that is, less-than and greater-than signs), as in #include <string>, the compiler doesn't look in the same directory as the source file. But if you use double quotes, as in #include "safestuff.h", the compiler *first* looks in the same directory as the source file. And if the compiler doesn't find the header file there, it looks in the remaining directories, as it would with angle brackets.

Some people always use double quotes. That way, whether the header file is in the same file as the source file or not, the compiler should find it. Most professional programmers today always use angle brackets. This forces programmers to put their header files in a common area. With really big projects, programmers like to have a directory dedicated to source files and another directory dedicated to header files. No header file is ever in the same directory as the source file.

TIP

For small projects, some people like to lump all the source and header files into a single directory. These people typically use angle brackets around system header files (such as #include <string>) and use double quotes around their own header files. The projects in this book generally follow this rule. The example header files are in the same directory as the source files and use double quotes for #include lines. System headers use angle brackets for the #include lines.

TIP

If you follow the same approach used here, you immediately know whether the #include line refers to one of your own header files or another header file. If it refers to your own, it has double quotes.

If you start working on a large C++ project, you will probably find that project managers use the rule of always using angle brackets. For large projects, this is typically the best policy.

TIP

If you try to compile and you get a No such file or directory error on the #include line, it's probably because you put the header file in a source file directory but used angle brackets instead of double quotes. Try switching that line to double quotes.

Sharing Variables among Source Files

When you declare a variable inside a function, it remains local to the function. But you may want functions to share a single *global* variable: One function may store something, and another may read its contents and write it to the console. To do this, declare the global variable outside a function. Declaring the global variable inside a source file works until you try to share it among multiple source files. If you're not careful, the source files end up with a separate copy of the global variable. Within a single source file, the global variable can be shared among functions but not among source files. That could be confusing.

There's a trick to making this work. Declare the variable inside one and only one of the source files. Then you declare it *again* inside one (and only one) header file, but you precede it with the word *extern,* as in extern int DoubleCheeseburgers;.

The GlobalVariable example, shown in Listings 7-6, 7-7, and 7-8, demonstrates the use of a single global variable that is shared among multiple source files.

LISTING 7-6: **Making Use of a Global Variable**

```
#include <iostream>
#include "sharealike.h"

using namespace std;

int main()
{
  DoubleCheeseburgers = 20;
  EatAtJoes();
  return 0;
}
```

LISTING 7-7: **Using the sharealike.h Header File to Declare a Global Variable**

```
#ifndef SHAREALIKE_H_INCLUDED
#define SHAREALIKE_H_INCLUDED

extern int DoubleCheeseburgers;
void EatAtJoes();

#endif // SHAREALIKE_H_INCLUDED
```

LISTING 7-8: **Declaring Global Variable Storage in the sharealike.cpp File**

```
#include <iostream>
#include "sharealike.h"

using namespace std;

int DoubleCheeseburgers = 0;

void EatAtJoes() {
  cout << "How many cheeseburgers today?" << endl;
  cout << DoubleCheeseburgers << endl;
}
```

Be careful when you do this; getting it exactly right is very tricky. You declare the variable once inside the header file, but you must remember the word extern. That tells the various files, "This variable is declared elsewhere, but here's its name and type so that you can use it." (It's okay that the file that defines the variable also includes the header file, which contains the extern declaration. In this case, extern says that the variable is declared somewhere, not that it's declared externally outside this file.) Then you declare the variable in one of the source files, *without* the word extern; this creates the actual storage bin for the variable. Finally, you include the header file in each of your source files that uses the global variable.

WARNING

It's a bad idea to declare any variable without initializing it. If you don't initialize the variable, you have no idea of what it contains. Not initializing the variable could lead to difficult-to-find errors. Global variables are even worse in this regard because now you don't even have a good idea of precisely where to search. Fortunately, Code::Blocks does help you in this regard. You can right-click any occurrence of a global variable and choose Find Occurrences Of: *<Variable Name>* from the context menu.

Using the Mysterious Header Wrappers

When you include a header file, you usually want to include it only *once* per source file. But that can create a problem: Suppose that you have a huge software project, and several header files include another of your header files, called superheader.h. If you include all these other header files, how can you be sure to pick up the superheader.h file only once?

The answer looks strange but does the trick. You start each header file with these lines:

```
#ifndef SHAREALIKE_H_INCLUDED
#define SHAREALIKE_H_INCLUDED
#endif
```

REMEMBER

Depending on which C++ IDE you use, your editor may add these lines automatically, just as Code::Blocks does. In this case, you type the header file content between the #define SHAREALIKE_H_INCLUDED and #endif lines. However, if your IDE doesn't add the lines automatically, be sure to add them so that your code looks like the code in Listing 7-7. Otherwise, the compiler may spout errors that you may not recognize immediately.

These *header wrappers,* as they are often called, ensure that the code in the header gets processed only once per source code file each time you compile. The wrappers use special lines called *preprocessor directives.* Basically, the *second* line defines something that is sort of like a variable but is used only during compilation; this something is called a *symbol.* In this case, the symbol is called SHAREALIKE_H_INCLUDED.

The first line checks to see whether this symbol has been defined. If *not,* the compiler proceeds with the lines of code that follow. The next line defines the symbol, so now it's actually defined for later. Then the compiler does all the rest of the lines in the file. Finally, the last line, #endif, simply finishes the very first line.

Now consider what could happen if you include this same file twice, as in

```
#include "sharealike.h"
#include "sharealike.h"
```

(That can happen indirectly if you include two different files that each include sharealike.h.) The *second* time the compiler goes through sharealike.h, it sees the first line, which checks to see whether the SHAREALIKE_H symbol is defined. But this time it is! So instead of going through all the lines again, the compiler skips to the #endif line that normally appears at the end of the file. Thus, your header file is processed only once per source code file. Use the following rule to make using headers easier:

REMEMBER

When you create a header file, be sure to put the header wrappers around it. You can use any symbol name you like, as long as it uses only letters, numbers, and underscores and doesn't start with a number and isn't already a variable name in your source or a C++ word. But most people base their choice on some variation of the filename itself, such as MYFILE_H or MYFILE_H_ or even _MYFILE_H_. Code::Blocks, by convention, adds _INCLUDED to each symbol name, but it's not necessary that you follow suit unless you want to.

Chapter **8**

Referring to Your Data Through Pointers

Where do you live? Don't say it out loud, because thousands of people are reading this book and you don't want them all to know. So just think about your address. Most places have some sort of address so that the mail service knows where to deliver your packages and the cable guy can show up sometime between now and 5:00 next Thursday. (So make sure that you're there.)

Other things have addresses, too. For example, a big corporation in an office building likely has all its cubes numbered. Offices in buildings usually have numbers, and apartments normally have numbers, too.

Now suppose that someone named Sam works in office number 180. Last week, however, Sam got booted out the door for spending too much time surfing the web. Now Sally gets first dibs on office number 180, even though she's not taking over Sam's position. Sam moved out; Sally moved in. Same office — different person staying there.

The computer's memory works similarly. Every little part of the computer's memory is associated with a number that represents its location, or *address.* In this chapter, you discover that after you determine the address of a variable stored in memory, you can do powerful things with it, which gives you the tools to create powerful applications.

TIP

If any single topic in C++ programming is most important, it is the notion of pointers. Therefore, if you want to become a millionaire, read this chapter. Okay, so it may not make you a millionaire, but suggesting it *could* give you the incentive to master this chapter. Then you can become an ace programmer and make lots of money.

REMEMBER

You don't have to type the source code for this chapter manually. In fact, using the downloadable source is a lot easier. You can find the source for this chapter in the \CPP_AIO4\BookI\Chapter08 folder of the downloadable source. See the Introduction for details on how to find these source files.

Understanding the Changes in Pointers for C++ 20

If you don't understand pointers at all, you might want to first read the rest of the chapter, starting with "Heaping and Stacking the Variables," and return to this first section later. Readers who already know something about pointers need to be aware of the changes in pointers for C++ 20, which is why it appears first. The essential thing to remember as you move to C++ 20 (where new is deprecated) and then to C++ 23 (where new is removed) is that pointers are going to change.

C++ will always need pointers, of course, but long-time C++ users have always seen pointers as a burden, while new C++ users see pointers as some sort of heroic nightmare rite of passage. The goal, then, is to make pointers easier and more consistent to use as C++ continues to grow and mature. The following sections discuss how C++ pointers are changing in C++ 20.

Avoiding broken code

A *raw* pointer, one that you allocate using the new operator, serves important purposes in your code. You often see it used for these purposes:

>> **Dynamic allocation:** Allows an application to allocate more memory as needed

>> **Runtime polymorphism:** Allows an application to pass pointers that may point to different kinds of data at different times

>> **Nullable references:** Handles instances in which a pointer doesn't point to anything

>> **Avoiding copies:** Uses a single copy of an object instead of creating multiple copies, which reduces the risk of errors

As your knowledge of C++ increases, you soon discover that these are critical application needs, so replacing the raw pointer will be quite difficult. Fortunately, you don't have to use the new C++ 20 features immediately, even if you're using a C++ compiler. You control whether your application uses the new approach through compilation directives:

```
#feature <no_pointers> //opt-in to no pointers
#feature <cpp20>        //opt-in to all C++20 features
```

Consequently, you don't have to worry about your existing code suddenly breaking. The idea is to make the transition from raw pointers to something better as smooth and transparent as possible. Given the realities of C++ development, you likely will see some sort of legacy support for a long time. However, to move forward, you must adapt to the new realities of pointers in C++.

Considering the issues

At this point, you might wonder why raw pointers are such a problem. After all, a pointer is simply an address in memory that looks something like 0x9caef0. The value it contains is the address, and by *dereferencing* the pointer, looking at the address to which it points, you see the value that the pointer references. It's just like the address for your house. You send mail to the address, but the address isn't your house — it's simply a pointer to your house.

At this point, it doesn't sound as if using pointers would be a problem, despite being a bit convoluted. The reason for using pointers in the first place is to avoid carrying large objects around in your code. You can leave the object, like a house, sitting in one place and simply point to it as needed. Imagine having to carry your house around with you. Besides having a horrible backache, doing so would be inconvenient and make your house harder to find. Instead, you give someone who wishes to mail you a letter or visit you in your home the address. Early applications had to use every tiny bit of memory and CPU processing cycles efficiently or face performance issues. Pointers allowed early applications to perform well by simply pointing at big objects in memory, rather than passing them around.

PLACING A HEX ON C++

Sooner or later in your computer programming, you encounter a strange way of notating numbers on the computer. This strange way is called *hexadecimal,* or sometimes just *hex*. In C++, you can recognize a hex number because it starts with the characters 0x. These characters aren't actually part of the number; they just notate it in the same way as double quotes denote a string. Whereas the usual decimal numbers consist of the digits 0, 1, 2, 3, 4, 5, 6, 7, 8, and 9, a hex number consists of these digits plus six more: A, B, C, D, E, and F. That makes a total of 16 digits. A good way to picture counting with regular decimal numbers is to use the odometer in a car, which (if you're honest) goes only forward, not backward. It starts out with 00000000 (assuming eight digits, which is a lot). The rightmost digit runs from 0 through 9, over and over. When any digit reaches 9 and all digits to the right of that are 9, the next digit to the left goes up by 1. For example, when you reach 00000999, the next digit to the left goes up by 1 as each 9 goes back to 0, to get 00001000.

With hex numbers, you count this same way, except that instead of stopping at 9 to loop back, you then go to A, and then B, and then up to F. And then you loop back. So the first 17 hex numbers are, using eight digits, 00000000, 00000001, 00000002, 00000003, 00000004, 00000005, 00000006, 00000007, 00000008, 00000009, 0000000A, 0000000B, 0000000C, 0000000D, 0000000E, 0000000F, 00000010. Notice that when you hit F at the end, the number wraps around again, adding 1 to the next digit to the left. When working with hex numbers, you may see such numbers as 0xAAAA0000 and 0x0000A3FF. And incidentally, 1 more than each of these is 0xAAAA0001 and 0x0000A400.

The biggest problem with pointers is the same problem incurred by house addresses. You need to think about the number of times you've received your neighbor's mail (and vice versa). Likewise, applications can have invalid pointers, and when the code tries to process this invalid address, it often crashes the application. Of course, the worst problem is the null pointer, 0x000000, which you expect to point to something. A null pointer points to nothing.

Another problem with pointers is that you spend a lot of time managing them, and who can remember all that code! Every time you work with pointers, you risk:

>> **Creating a memory leak:** By not deallocating the pointer so you can reuse the memory, the memory becomes inaccessible to the application. You could actually run out of memory despite having memory available. The memory becomes available again after the operating system frees it once the application terminates.

>> **Using memory that hasn't been initialized:** The memory location could contain anything and if you act on the data in that memory location, your application will act oddly or simply crash.

>> **Obtaining the wrong data:** The application could point to the wrong location and you might not know it. This means that the application is using the wrong data, which could result in unanticipated output or data damage.

Writing cleaner and less bug-prone code

To write cleaner code with fewer bugs, you need to find a way to get the effects of a pointer without any of the disadvantages of pointers. The C++ committee has been working on this issue. For example, `std::auto_ptr` is *deprecated* (set for deletion, but still allowed) in C++ 11 and removed in C++ 17. Here are some modern ways of getting past pointers:

>> **Using smart pointers:** Boost (explained in Book 7, Chapter 4) has provided access to smart pointers for a long time, and many developers use them because they make both dynamic allocation and runtime polymorphism easier to deal with. Using a smart pointer, such as `std::unique_ptr` or `std::shared_ptr`, eliminates the need for you to manage memory manually. Instead, the smart pointer addresses memory management needs for you so that you can concentrate on writing business logic rather than performing low-level programming tasks.

>> **Relying on optional pointers:** C++ 17 introduced `std::optional` as the means for working with nullable references. When an optional pointer is null, it has a value of `std::nullopt`, which is actually an important thing to know when dealing with them. The only problem is that the implementation is flawed because it lacked support for references (pointers to pointers) and had no *monadic* (entity operator) interface (see `http://www.open-std.org/jtc1/sc22/wg21/docs/papers/2017/p0798r0.html` for a discussion of this extremely advanced concept not covered in this book). The short version is that it didn't do what raw pointers could do, but these problems are fixed in C++ 20.

>> **Passing objects around:** A modern computer isn't nearly as resource limited as those in the past were, so modern languages commonly pass objects around rather than create pointers to them. This solution addresses the need to eliminate unwanted copies. C++ 20 provides two solutions for this task, both of which rely on the idea of using the object `obj`, which is outside the function, to directly construct the object being initialized inside the function and that is

returned from it. You can view this optimization as: `T obj = f();`, where `f()` is a function that initializes `obj` of type `T`. Here is how the optimizations differ:

- **Return Value Optimization (RVO):** In this case, you could have a function that looks like this:

```
T f() {
    ... // Do something here.
    return T(constructor arguments);
}
```

In this case, you could create three objects of type `T`: the unnamed temporary object created by the `return` statement; the temporary object returned by `f()` to the caller; and the named object, `obj`, copied from the return from `f()`. Using RVO eliminates the two temporary objects by initializing `obj` directly with the arguments passed inside the body of `f()`. This is actually a complex topic that's well outside the purview of this book, but you can read a discussion of the details of this topic at `https://shaharmike.com/cpp/rvo/`.

- **Named Return Value Optimization (NRVO):** This form of optimization goes a step further than RVO when the `return` statement uses a named value, as shown here:

```
T f() {
    ... // Do something here.
    T result(constructor arguments);
    return result;
}
```

This technique effectively replaces the hidden object and the named object inside the function with the object used for holding the result. The only caveat is that `result` must be unique so that the compiler knows which object inside `f()` to use to construct the memory in `obj`. NRVO is a particular kind of copy elision (the process of joining together or merging of objects) discussed in detail at `https://en.cppreference.com/w/cpp/language/copy_elision`.

Heaping and Stacking the Variables

C++ applications use two kinds of memory:

>> **Heap:** A common area in memory where you can store global variables. This is where you also store objects and variables that you allocate from memory.

>> **Stack:** The area where the computer stores both function information and local value type variables for those functions. The stack also stores pointers to local object type variables for functions.

REMEMBER

Function storage is a little more complicated because each function gets its own little private area at the top of the stack. It is called a stack because it's treated like a stack of papers: You can put something on the top of the stack, and you can take something off the top of the stack, but you can't put anything in the middle or bottom. In addition, you can't take anything from the middle or bottom. (You can, however, peek at the values from any place in the stack and change those values — it's the memory block that isn't removed.) The computer uses this stack to keep track of all your function calls.

Suppose that you have a function called GoFishing(). The function GoFishing() calls StopAndBuyBait(). Depending on the complexity of the bait business, StopAndBuyBait() may call PayForBait(), which calls GetOutCash(). How can the computer keep track of all this mess? It uses the stack. Begin with the following code:

```
int GoFishing() {
    int baitMoney = 2;
    int numberWorms = StopAndBuyBait(baitMoney);
    if (numberWorms > 0) {
        return true;
    }
    return false;
}

int StopAndBuyBait(int customerMoney) {
    if (customerMoney > 0) {
        int wormsBought = customerMoney * 20;
        return wormsBought;
    }
    return 0;
}
```

The customer starts out with $2.00. When stopping in the store, the clerk asks for the money. If the customer does have money, the clerk provides 20 worms for each $1.00. The customer determines whether there was enough money to buy any worms. If so, it's time to go fishing. The stack for each of these calls appears in a *stack frame,* which the application treats as a single entity for that function. This code uses two stack frames, one for each function call, as shown in Figure 8-1.

Application Stack

Top of Stack

StopAndBuyBait Stack Frame

int wormsBought

Return Address

int customerMoney

GoFishing Stack Frame

int numberWorms

int baitMoney

Return Address

FIGURE 8-1:
The two
stack frames
used for the
example code.

REMEMBER

From a stack perspective, the code begins by creating a stack frame for
GoFishing(). On this stack frame, it creates a variable holding a pointer with
the return address of the caller (which is unknown in this case). Adding a value
to the stack is called *pushing*. GoFishing() creates two variables, baitMoney and
numberWorms. From a stack perspective, because GoFishing() creates baitMoney
first, it also appears first on the stack.

When GoFishing() calls StopAndBuyBait(), it passes a single argument that
GoFishing() sees as baitMoney. However, StopAndBuyBait() sees the parameter
as customerMoney. The arguments that GoFishing() passes to StopAndBuyBait()
appear first as parameters within the stack frame that the application creates
for StopAndBuyBait(), followed by the return address for GoFishing(). Consequently, before StopAndBuyBait() executes even a single line of code, its stack
frame already has two variables on it.

At this point, StopAndBuyBait() optionally creates a local variable, wormsBought.
Notice that in the stack frame, parameters appear first, followed by the return
address of the caller and then the local variables. When StopAndBuyBait() determines what to return to GoFishing(), it places this value in numberWorms because
numberWorms is set to receive this return value.

CONVERTING BETWEEN HEXADECIMAL AND DECIMAL

Every hex number has a decimal equivalent. When you make a list showing decimal numbers side by side with hex numbers, you see, for example, that 0x0000001F is next to the decimal number 31. Thus, these two numbers represent the same quantity of items, such as apples.

You can represent hex numbers by using either uppercase or lowercase letters. However, do not mix cases within a single number because it makes the number incredibly hard to read and other developers will make mistakes. Don't use 0xABab0000. Instead, use either 0xabab0000 or 0xABAB0000.

If you want to convert between hex and decimal, you can use the Hex to Decimal Converter application at https://www.binaryhexconverter.com/hex-to-decimal-converter or the Decimal to Hex Converter application at https://www.binaryhexconverter.com/decimal-to-hex-converter. These two applications make it easy to convert between the two numbering systems, and you can use them on any device that supports a browser.

To convert a hex number to decimal, select the Hex to Decimal Converter application and type the hex number into the Hex Value field by using the number keys and the letters *A* through *F*, such as FB1263. (You don't need to type the zeroes at the beginning, such as 00FB1263 — they don't show up — nor do you type the 0x used in C++.) After you finish typing it all, click Convert. The application instantly transforms the hex number into a decimal number! In this case, you see 16454243. You can go the other way, too: If you have a decimal number, such as 16454243, you can select the Decimal to Hex Converter application, type its value into the Decimal Value field, and click Convert to convert it to hex. If you convert 16454243 to hex, you get back FB1263, which is what you started with.

The Windows calculator also makes it easy to convert between hex and decimal when placed in Programmer view, as shown in the following figure. The calculator also supports binary (base 2) and octal (base 8) numbers. Just select the base you want to use and the calculator performs the conversion automatically. (The precise Calculator features you have for performing this task depend on your version of Windows. The blog post at http://blog.johnmuellerbooks.com/2012/01/30/examining-the-calculator-in-windows-7/ complains about the changes that Windows 7 brought. Windows 10 offers more of the same.)

(continued)

(continued)

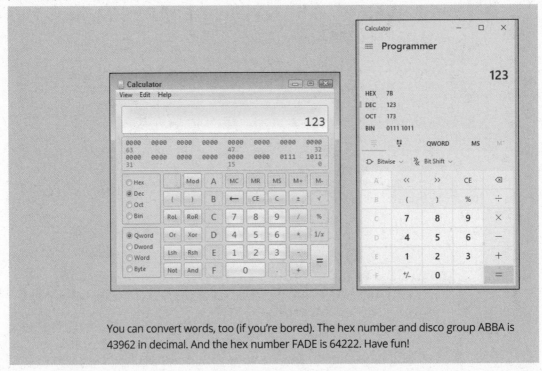

You can convert words, too (if you're bored). The hex number and disco group ABBA is 43962 in decimal. And the hex number FADE is 64222. Have fun!

REMEMBER

The application then starts to dismantle the StopAndBuyBait() stack frame by *popping* (removing) the values off the stack. It throws wormsBought away (if StopAndBuyBait() created it) because the application has already placed this value in numberWorms. The application saves the GoFishing() return address for later use. It then throws customerMoney away and removes the stack frame.

The return address is a pointer to a specific place in memory that marks the continuation point in the code for GoFishing(). So, the next step is to read the next processing instruction for GoFishing() that comes after the return from StopAndBuyBait().

Getting a variable's address

Because every variable lives somewhere in memory, every variable has an address. If you have a function that declares an integer variable called NumberOfPotholes, then when your application calls this function, the computer will allocate space for NumberOfPotholes somewhere in memory.

REMEMBER

If you want to find the address of the variable NumberOfPotholes, you simply throw an ampersand (&) in front of it. Listing 8-1 shows the VariableAddress example, which obtains the address of a variable and prints it.

LISTING 8-1: **Using the & Character to Obtain the Address of a Variable**

```
#include <iostream>

using namespace std;

int main() {
  int NumberOfPotholes = 532587;
  cout << &NumberOfPotholes << endl;
  return 0;
}
```

When you run this application, a hexadecimal number appears on the console. This number may or may not match ours, and it may or may not be the same each time you run the application. The result depends on exactly how the computer allocated your variable for you and the order in which it did things. This could be very different between versions of compilers. When you run Listing 8-1, you see something like the following (it varies with each run):

```
0x22ff74
```

REMEMBER

The output you see from this application is the address of the variable called NumberOfPotholes. In other words, that number is the hex version of the place where the NumberOfPotholes variable is stored in memory. The output is not the *content* of the variable or the content of the variable converted to hex; rather, it's the address of the variable in hex.

Knowing the address of a variable doesn't tell you about the variable content, but C++ programmers use addresses in other ways:

>> Modifying the variable content directly using what are called pointer variables. A *pointer variable* is just like any other variable except that it stores the *address of* another variable.

>> Performing any of the tasks mentioned in the "Avoiding broken code" section of the chapter.

>> Modifying values pointed at by the address indirectly using any of a number of math techniques.

>> Comparing entities such as objects based on their pointers.

Referring to Your Data Through Pointers

To declare a pointer variable, you need to specify the type of variable it will point to. Then you precede the variable's name with an asterisk, as in the following:

```
int *ptr;
```

This line declares a variable that *points to* an integer. In other words, it can contain *the address* of an integer variable. And how do you grab the address of an integer variable? Easy! By using the & notation! Thus, you can do something like this:

```
ptr = &NumberOfPotholes;
```

This line puts the address of the variable NumberOfPotholes in the ptr variable. Remember that ptr doesn't hold the number of potholes; rather, it holds the address of the variable called NumberOfPotholes.

TIP

You specify the type of pointer by the type of item it points to. If a pointer variable points to an integer, its type is *pointer to integer.* In C++ notation, its type is int * (with a space between them) or int* (no space); you are allowed to enter it with or without a space. If a pointer variable points to a string, its type is *pointer to string,* and notation for this type is string *.

REMEMBER

The ptr variable holds an address, but what's at that address? That address is the location in memory of the storage bin known as NumberOfPotholes. Right at that spot in memory is the data stored in NumberOfPotholes.

TIP

Think this pointer concept through carefully. If you have to, reread this section a few times until it's locked in your head. Then meditate on it. Wake up in the night thinking about it. Call strangers on the telephone and chitchat about it. The more you understand pointers, the better off your programming career will be — and the more likely you are to make a million dollars.

Changing a variable by using a pointer

After you have a pointer variable holding another variable's address, you can use the pointer to access the information in the other variable. That means you have two ways to get to the information in a variable: Use the variable name itself (such as NumberOfPotholes), or use the pointer variable that points to it.

If you want to store the number 6087 in NumberOfPotholes, you can do this:

```
NumberOfPotholes = 6087;
```

Or you can use the pointer. To use the pointer, you first declare it as follows:

```
ptr = &NumberOfPotholes;
```

Then, to change NumberOfPotholes, you don't just assign a value to it. Instead, you throw an asterisk in front of it, like so:

```
*ptr = 6087;
```

If ptr points to NumberOfPotholes, these two lines of code will have the same effect: Both will change the value to 6087. This process of sticking the asterisk before a pointer variable is called *dereferencing* the pointer. Look at the DereferencePointer example, shown in Listing 8-2, which demonstrates all this.

LISTING 8-2: **Modifying the Original Variable with a Pointer Variable**

```
#include <iostream>

using namespace std;

int main() {
  int NumberOfPotholes;
  int *ptr;

  ptr = &NumberOfPotholes;
  *ptr = 6087;

  cout << NumberOfPotholes << endl;
  return 0;
}
```

In Listing 8-2, the first line of main() declares an integer variable, and the second line declares a pointer to an integer. The next line takes the address of the integer variable and stores it in the pointer. Then the fourth line modifies the original integer by dereferencing the pointer. And just to make sure that the process worked, the next line prints the value of NumberOfPotholes. When you run the application, you see the following output:

```
6087
```

You can also read the value of the original variable through the pointer. Look at the ReadPointer example, shown in Listing 8-3. This code accesses the value of `NumberOfPotholes` through the pointer variable, `ptr`. When the code gets the value, it saves it in another variable called `SaveForLater`.

LISTING 8-3: **Accessing a Value through a Pointer**

```cpp
#include <iostream>

using namespace std;

int main() {
    int NumberOfPotholes;
    int *ptr = &NumberOfPotholes;
    int SaveForLater;

    *ptr = 6087;
    SaveForLater = *ptr;
    cout << SaveForLater << endl;

    *ptr = 7000;
    cout << *ptr << endl;
    cout << SaveForLater << endl;
    return 0;
}
```

When you run this application, you see the following output:

```
6087
7000
6087
```

Notice that the code changes the value through `ptr` again — this time to 7000. When you run the application, you can see that the value did indeed change, but the value in `SaveForLater` remained the same. That's because `SaveForLater` is a separate variable, not connected to the other two. The other two, however, are connected to each other.

Pointing at a string

Pointer variables can point to any type, including strings. However, after you say that a variable points to a certain type, it can point to only that type. That is, as with any variable, you cannot change its type. The compiler won't let you do it.

To create a pointer to a string, you simply make the type of the variable `string *`. You can then set it equal to the address of a string variable. The `StringPointer` example, shown in Listing 8-4, demonstrates this idea.

LISTING 8-4: **Pointing to a String with Pointers**

```cpp
#include <iostream>

using namespace std;

int main() {
  string GoodMovie;
  string *ptrToString;

  GoodMovie = "Best in Show";
  ptrToString = &GoodMovie;

  cout << *ptrToString << endl;
  return 0;
}
```

In Listing 8-4, you see that the pointer named `ptrToString` points to the variable named `GoodMovie`. But when you want to use the pointer to access the string, you need to dereference the pointer by putting an asterisk (*) in front of it. When you run this code, you see the results of the dereferenced pointer, which is the value of the `GoodMovie` variable:

```
Best in Show
```

You can change the value of the string through the pointer, again by dereferencing it, as in the following code:

```cpp
*ptrToString = "Galaxy Quest";
cout << GoodMovie << endl;
```

The code dereferences the pointer to set it equal to the string "GalaxyQuest". Then, to show that it truly changed, the code prints the `GoodMovie` variable. The result of this code, when added at the end of Listing 8-4 (but prior to the `return 0`), is

```
Galaxy Quest
```

You can also use the pointer to access the individual parts of the string, as shown in the `StringPointer2` example in Listing 8-5.

LISTING 8-5: **Using Pointers to Point to a String**

```cpp
#include <iostream>

using namespace std;

int main() {
  string AMovie;
  string *ptrToString;

  AMovie = "L.A. Confidential";
  ptrToString = &AMovie;

  for (unsigned i = 0; i < AMovie.length(); i++) {
    cout << (*ptrToString)[i] << " ";
  }
  cout << endl;

  return 0;
}
```

When you run this application, you see the letters of the movie appear with spaces between them, as in

```
L . A .   C o n f i d e n t i a l
```

WARNING

When you access the characters of the string through a pointer, you need to put parentheses around the asterisk and the pointer variable. Otherwise, the compiler gets confused and first tries to access the index in brackets with the variable name and afterward applies the asterisk. That's backward, and it doesn't make sense to the computer, so the compiler gives you an error message. But you can make it all better by using parentheses, as shown in Listing 8-5.

This application loops through the entire string, character by character. The string's `length()` function tells how many characters are in the string. The code inside the loop grabs the individual characters and prints them with a space after each.

Notice that i is of type unsigned rather than int. The length() function returns an unsigned value rather than an int value, which makes sense because a string can't have a negative length. If you try to use an int for i, the compiler displays the following warning:

```
warning: comparison between signed and unsigned integer
```

The application still runs, but you need to use the correct data types for loop variables. Otherwise, when the loop value increases over the amount that the loop variable can support, the application will fail. Trying to find such an error can prove frustrating even for the best developers. It's important to not ignore warnings even if they appear harmless.

TIP

You can also change the individual characters in a string through a pointer. You can do this by using a line like (*ptrToString)[5] = 'X';. Notice you still need to put parentheses around the variable name along with the dereferencing character.

TIP

The length of a string is also available through the pointer. You can call the length() function by dereferencing the pointer, again with the carefully placed parentheses, such as in the following:

```
for (unsigned i = 0; i < (*ptrToString).length(); i++) {
  cout << (*ptrToString)[i] << " ";
}
```

Pointing to something else

When you create a pointer variable, you must specify the type of data it points to. After that, you cannot change the type of data it points to, but you can change *what* it points to. For example, if you have a pointer to an integer, you can make it point to the integer variable called ExpensiveComputer. Then, later, in the same application, you can make it point to the integer variable called CheapComputer. Listing 8-6 demonstrates this technique in the ChangePointer example.

LISTING 8-6: **Using Pointers to Point to Something Else and Back Again**

```
#include <iostream>

using namespace std;

int main() {
  int ExpensiveComputer;
```

(continued)

LISTING 8-6: *(continued)*

```cpp
int CheapComputer;
int *ptrToComp;

ptrToComp = &ExpensiveComputer;
*ptrToComp = 2000;
cout << *ptrToComp << endl;

ptrToComp = &CheapComputer;
*ptrToComp = 500;
cout << *ptrToComp << endl;

ptrToComp = &ExpensiveComputer;
cout << *ptrToComp << endl;
return 0;
}
```

This code starts out by initializing all the goodies involved — two integers and a pointer to an integer.

Next, the code points the pointer to ExpensiveComputer and uses the pointer to put 2000 inside ExpensiveComputer. It then writes the contents of Expensive-Computer, again by using the pointer.

Then the code changes what the pointer points to. To do this, you set the pointer to the address of a different variable, &CheapComputers. The next line stores 500 in CheapComputers. And, again, you print it.

Now, just to drive home the point, in case the computer isn't listening, you then point the pointer back to the original variable, ExpensiveComputer. But you don't store anything in it. This time, you simply print the cost of this high-powered supermachine. You do this again by dereferencing the pointer. And when you run the application, you see that ExpensiveComputer still has 2000 in it, which is what was originally put in it. This means that after you point the pointer to something else and do some finagling, the original variable remains unchanged.

TIP

Be careful if you use one pointer to bounce around several different variables. It's easy to lose track of which variable the pointer is pointing to.

Tips on pointer variables

This section contains tips on using pointer variables. You can declare two pointer variables of the same type by putting them together in a single statement, as you can with regular variables. However, you must precede *each one* with an asterisk, as in the following line:

```
int *ptrOne, *ptrTwo;
```

WARNING

If you try to declare multiple pointers on a single line but put an asterisk only before the first pointer, only that one will be a pointer. The rest will not be. This can cause serious headaches later because this line compiles fine:

```
int *ptrOne, Confused;
```

Here, Confused is not a pointer to an integer; rather, it's just an integer. Beware!

TIP

Some people like to put the asterisk immediately after the type, as in the following example, to emphasize the fact that the type is *pointer to integer*:

```
int* ptrOne;
```

However, this approach makes it easy to leave out the asterisks for any pointer variables that follow.

Creating New Raw Pointers

It isn't possible to predict some kinds of memory use in your application, but the requirements aren't known when you write the code. For example, streaming data from the Internet or creating new records in a database are both examples of unpredictable memory use. When working with unpredictable memory requirements, you *allocate* (request memory) and *deallocate* (release the memory you requested) as needed in a process called *dynamic memory management.* You use the *heap*, an area of unallocated memory, to perform dynamic memory management.

Most modern programming languages provide a means for managing memory for you. The reason for using this strategy is that older memory management techniques are error prone. You often see these common memory errors using older methods:

>> Code tries to use the memory without allocating it first.

>> Memory remains allocated after use, creating a memory leak.

>> Uninitialized memory contains random data.

Consequently, most modern languages simply allow you to create and delete variables using one simple approach, and a process called *garbage collection* (the freeing of unused memory) occurs in the background. C++ is moving in this direction. However, the transition is taking some time.

Up to this point, you allocated memory using various approaches including the new keyword. Using new simply meant that you needed memory for a specific purpose. The new keyword is deprecated in C++ 20 and will disappear altogether in C++ 23. The following sections begin with two examples of using new because you see new used in all current existing code of any complexity at this point. The remaining three sections tell you about the updated C++ 20 method of managing memory.

Using new

To declare a storage bin on the heap using existing methods, first you need to set up a variable that will help you keep track of the storage bin. This variable must be a pointer variable.

Suppose that you already have an integer declared out on the heap somewhere. (You see how to do that in the next paragraph.) Oddly enough, such variables don't have names. Just think of it as an integer on the heap. Then, with the integer variable, you could have a *second* variable. This second variable is not on the heap, and it's a pointer holding the address of the integer variable. So if you want to access the integer variable, you do so by *dereferencing* (looking at the address of) the pointer variable.

To allocate memory on the heap, you need to do two things: First, declare a pointer variable. Second, call a function named new. The new function is a little different from other functions in that you don't put parentheses around its parameter. For this reason, it's actually an *operator*. Other operators are + and – and are for adding and subtracting integers. These other operators behave similarly to functions, but you don't use parentheses.

To use the new operator, you specify the type of variable you want to create. For example, the following line creates a new integer variable:

```
int *somewhere = new int;
```

After the computer creates the new integer variable on the heap, it stores the address of the integer variable in somewhere. And that makes sense: somewhere is a pointer to an integer, so it's prefaced by the * (pointer) operator. Thus, somewhere holds the address of an integer variable. The UseNew example, shown in Listing 8-7, demonstrates how pointers work when using new.

LISTING 8-7: **Allocating Memory by Using new**

```
#include <iostream>

using namespace std;

int main() {
  int *ptr = new int;
  *ptr = 10;
  cout << *ptr << endl;
  cout << ptr << endl;
  return 0;
}
```

When you run this application, you see this sweet and simple output (the second value will change each time you run the example):

```
10
0x73af10
```

In this application, you first allocate a pointer variable, which you call ptr. Then you call new with an int type, which returns a pointer to an integer. You save that return value in the ptr variable.

Then you start doing your magic on it. Okay, so it's not all that magical, but you save a 10 in the memory that ptr points to. And then you print the value stored in the memory that ptr points to.

To see for yourself that ptr is pointing to a memory location and not the actual value of 10, the code also prints ptr without dereferencing it (using the * operator). The output is a hexadecimal value such as 0x9caef0, but this output will change each time because the memory allocation occurs in a different location on the heap each time.

As you can see, ptr contains the address of the memory allocated by the new operator. But unlike regular variables, the variable pointed at by ptr doesn't have a name. And because it doesn't have a name, the only way you can access it is through the pointer. It's kind of like an anonymous author with a publicist. If you want to send fan mail to the author, you have to go through the publicist. Here, the only way to reach this unnamed but famous variable is through the pointer.

But this doesn't mean that the variable has a secret name such as BlueCheese and that, if you dig deep enough, you might discover it; it just means that the variable has no name. Sorry.

REMEMBER

When you call new, you get back a pointer. This pointer is of the type that you specify in your call to new. You can then store the pointer only in a pointer variable of the same type.

TIP

When you use the new operator, the usual terminology is that you are *allocating memory on the heap.*

By using pointers to access memory on the heap, you can take advantage of many interesting C++ features. For example, you can use pointers along with something called an array. An *array* (as described in Book 5, Chapter 1) is simply a large storage bin that has multiple slots, each of which holds one item. If you set up an array that holds pointers, you can store all these pointers without having to name them individually. And these pointers can point to complex things, called objects. (Book 2, Chapter 1 covers objects and Book 2, Chapter 2 discusses arrays.) You could then pass all these variables (which could be quite large, if they're strings) to a function by passing only the array, not the strings themselves. That step saves memory on the stack.

In addition to objects and arrays, you can have a function allocate memory and return a variable pointing to that memory. Then, when you get the variable back from the function, you can use it, and when you finish with the variable, delete it (freeing the memory). Finally, you can pass a pointer into a function. When you do so, the function can actually modify the data the pointer references for you. (See "Passing Pointer Variables to Functions" and "Returning Pointer Variables from Functions," later in this chapter, for details.)

Using an initializer

When you call new, you can provide an initial value for the memory you are allocating. For example, when allocating a new integer, you can, in one swoop, also store the number 10 in the integer. The Initializer, example shown in Listing 8-8, demonstrates how to do this.

LISTING 8-8: **Putting a Value in Parentheses to Initialize Memory That You Allocate**

```cpp
#include <iostream>

using namespace std;

int main() {
  int *ptr = new int(10);
  cout << *ptr << endl;
  return 0;
}
```

This code calls new, but also provides a number in parentheses. That number is put in the memory initially, instead of being assigned to it later. This line of code is equivalent to the following two lines of code:

```
int *ptr = new int;
*ptr = 10;
```

TECHNICAL STUFF

When you initialize a value in the new operator, the technical phrase for what you are doing is *invoking a constructor.* The reason is that the compiler adds a bunch of code to your application — code that operates behind the scenes. This code is the *runtime library.* The library includes a function that initializes an integer variable if you pass an initial value. The function that does this is known as a *constructor.* When you run it, you are *invoking* it. Thus, you are invoking the constructor. For more information on constructors, see Book 2, Chapter 1.

Freeing Raw Pointers

When you allocate memory on the heap by calling the new operator and you're finished using the memory, you need to let the computer know, regardless of whether it's just a little bit of memory or a lot. The computer doesn't look ahead into your code to find out whether you're still going to use the memory. So in your code, when you are finished with the memory, you *free* the memory.

The way you free the memory is by calling the delete operator and passing the name of the pointer:

```
delete MyPointer;
```

This line would appear after you're finished using a pointer that you allocated by using new. (Like the new operator, delete is also an operator and does not require parentheses around the parameter.)

The FreePointer example, shown in Listing 8-9, provides a complete demonstration of allocating a pointer, using it, and then freeing it. Note the use of the replace() method, which first appears in the "Replacing parts of a string" section of Book 1 Chapter 6. You use the arrow operator (->) to access this string method of phrase. The "Using classes and raw pointers" section of Book 2 Chapter 1 describes the arrow operator in more detail.

LISTING 8-9: **Using delete to Clean Up Your Pointers**

```cpp
#include <iostream>

using namespace std;

int main() {
  string *phrase =
    new string("All presidents are cool!!!");
  cout << *phrase << endl;

  (*phrase)[20] = 'r';
  phrase->replace(22, 4, "oked");
  cout << *phrase << endl;

  delete phrase;
  return 0;
}
```

When you run this application, you see the following output:

```
All presidents are cool!!!
All presidents are crooked
```

This code allocates a new string and initializes it, saving its address in the pointer variable called `phrase`. The code outputs the phrase, manipulates it, and then writes it again. Finally, the code frees the memory used by the phrase.

TIP

Although people usually say that you're *deleting the pointer* or *freeing the pointer*, you're actually freeing the *memory* that the pointer points to. The pointer can still be used for subsequent new operations.

WARNING

When you free memory, the memory becomes available for other tasks. However, immediately after the call to `delete`, the pointer still points to that particular memory location, even though the memory is free. Using the pointer without pointing it to something else causes errors. Therefore, don't try to use the pointer after freeing the memory it points to until you set the pointer to point to something else through a call to `new` or by setting it to another variable.

Whenever you free a pointer, a good habit is to set the pointer to the value 0 or `nullptr` (when using C++ 11 or above). Then, whenever you use a pointer, first check whether it's equal to 0 (or `nullptr`) and use it only if it's not 0. This strategy always works because the computer will never allocate memory for you at address 0. So the number 0 can be reserved to mean *I point to nothing at all.*

The following code sample shows how to use this strategy. First, this code frees the pointer and then clears it by setting it to 0:

```
delete ptrToSomething;
ptrToSomething = 0;
```

The reason to use nullptr in place of 0 when you can is that nullptr is clearer — it says precisely what you're doing to the pointer. This code checks whether the pointer is not 0 before using it:

```
ptrToComp = new int;
*ptrToComp = 10;
if (ptrToComp != 0) {
  cout << *ptrToComp << endl;
}
```

WARNING

Call delete only on memory that you allocated by using new. Although the Code::Blocks compiler doesn't seem to complain when you delete a pointer that points to a regular variable, it serves no purpose to do so. You can free only memory on the heap, not local variables on the stack. In addition, you should avoid freeing the same pointer multiple times because doing so can create hard-to-find bugs; the application may have already reallocated that memory for some other purpose.

WARNING

An older method of freeing a pointer involves setting the pointer to NULL. Code::Blocks raises an error when you attempt to use NULL normally because NULL isn't part of the standard and it's considered outdated. However, you may have a lot of older code that uses NULL. In this case, you must add #include <cstddef> to your code to allow it to compile. However, it would be better to update the code to use either 0 or nullptr.

Working with Smart Pointers

As mentioned previously in the chapter, smart pointers are the direction that C++ is taking, so you need to use them in all new application development. The reason is simple: Using smart pointers reduces the amount of code you must create, reduces errors, makes applications more efficient, and virtually eliminates many common application issues, such as memory leaks. The following sections offer an overview of smart pointers. Most of the code will run with C++ 17, but some of the items are C++ 20 specific.

Creating smart pointers using std::unique_ptr and std::shared_ptr

Smart pointers do a lot of work for you when it comes to memory management, so you should use them in new projects and when converting old projects. The biggest advantage of smart pointers is that they automatically deallocate resources for you, so you don't encounter problems like memory leaks in your applications. However, they can do a lot more for you by enforcing good programming practices through the compiler. No longer can you create code that's easy to crash because you're attempting to use a pointer that doesn't point anywhere. You also gain access to unique functions and operators that help you better understand how memory is used.

REMEMBER

This section discusses two smart pointer classes from an overview perspective: `unique_ptr` and `shared_ptr`. The main difference between them is that a `unique_ptr` is the only pointer that can point to a resource. If you attempt to copy a `unique_ptr` to another pointer, the compiler will complain. Using a `unique_ptr` keeps you from making copies that could cause problems in deallocating a resource. However, there are times when you actually do need to copy pointers, such as dealing with a multithreaded environment. In this case, you use a `shared_ptr` because you can copy a `shared_ptr` to another pointer. In fact, it even includes a function that tells you how many references currently exist to the resource. Whether you use `unique_ptr` or `shared_ptr`, both object types wrap a raw pointer in an object that performs all the management tasks for you.

Normally you use `unique_ptr` when working in an environment where you don't need to copy pointers. Using `unique_ptr` makes your code significantly safer and more bulletproof. The `UniquePtr` example, shown in Listing 8-10, gets you started on using `unique_ptr`.

RESOLVING SMART POINTER EXPERIMENTATION PROBLEMS

Working with the new pointer types can prove frustrating when you continually see errors instead of results. When you encounter problems using Code::Blocks to work with new pointer types, make sure you have the correct version installed and the right settings configured. If you still have problems, consider trying the techniques on https://wandbox.org/, which can sometimes provide better results because the pointer methodologies are new. In some cases, you may find that old habits are getting in the way of new processes, so it's also essential to verify that your code is written to use the new pointer types.

LISTING 8-10: Using a unique_ptr to Perform Common Tasks

```
#include <iostream>
#include <memory>

using namespace std;

int main() {
  unique_ptr<int> ptr1(new int());
  *ptr1 = 100;
  cout << "ptr1 value: " << *ptr1 << endl;

  int myValue = 42;
  unique_ptr<int> ptr2(&myValue);
  cout << "ptr2 value: " << *ptr2 << endl;

  unique_ptr<int> ptr3 = make_unique<int>(99);
  cout << "ptr3 value: " << *ptr3 << endl;
  cout << "ptr3 address: " << ptr3.get() << endl;

  unique_ptr<int> ptr4;
  ptr4 = move(ptr3);
  if (ptr3 == nullptr) {
    cout << "ptr3 is nullptr." << endl;
  }
  cout << "ptr4 value: " << *ptr4 << endl;
  cout << "ptr4 address: " << ptr4.get() << endl;

  return 0;
}
```

The example shows three ways to create a `unique_ptr`:

» Use the `new` operator.

» Create a variable and point to it.

» Employ the `make_unique()` function.

In all three cases, you get a `unique_ptr` with the value you specify. Notice that you must specify the pointer type using `<int>` (for an `int` value). As with other pointers, you can't really create a generic pointer that can point to anything.

REMEMBER

A `unique_ptr` provides you with a number of functions. Unlike most pointers, you can't simply specify the pointer name and obtain its address because `unique_ptr` exercises stricter control over accessing the address information. You must use the `get()` function instead, as shown in the code.

As previously mentioned, you can't make one `unique_ptr` equal to another `unique_ptr`. However, you can use the `move()` function to move the address of one `unique_ptr` to another `unique_ptr`. The `swap()` function simply swaps addresses between two pointers.

This example also shows the use of `nullptr`. As you can see, using `nullptr` is clearer than using `0` in your code. Here is the output from this example:

```
ptr1 value: 100
ptr2 value: 42
ptr3 value: 99
ptr3 address: 0x5daf28
ptr3 is nullptr.
ptr4 value: 99
ptr4 address: 0x5daf28
```

To really understand `unique_ptr` versus `shared_ptr`, you need to compare usage side by side. The `SharedPtr` example, shown in Listing 8-11, demonstrates some differences that you need to consider when choosing between the two pointer objects.

LISTING 8-11: **Using a shared_ptr for Copying**

```cpp
#include <iostream>
#include <memory>

using namespace std;
```

```cpp
int main() {
    int myValue = 42;
    shared_ptr<int> ptr1(new int(myValue));
    cout << "ptr1 value: " << *ptr1 << endl;
    cout << "ptr1 use count: " << ptr1.use_count()
        << endl;

    shared_ptr<int> ptr2 = ptr1;
    cout << "ptr2 value: " << *ptr2 << endl;
    cout << "ptr1 address: " << ptr1 << endl;
    cout << " ptr2 address: " << ptr2 << endl;
    cout << "ptr1 use count: " << ptr1.use_count()
        << endl;

    ptr2.reset();
    cout << "ptr1 use count: " << ptr1.use_count()
        << endl;

    ptr1.reset();
    cout << "ptr1 use count: " << ptr1.use_count()
        << endl;

    return 0;
}
```

When working with a shared_ptr, you can make one pointer equal to another pointer, as this example shows. The code demonstrates that both ptr1 and ptr2 point to the same memory location and have the same value. Consequently, the resource (not the pointers) is shared between the two pointers.

To make it easier to determine how many references a resource has, you use the use_count() function. Each additional reference increments the count so that you're never in the dark as to how many references the resource has.

Of course, now you need some way to remove references when they're no longer needed. To perform this task, you use reset(). The code uses ptr2.reset() to remove the second reference to myValue. As shown in the following output, the use count decreases each time you reset() a pointer.

```
ptr1 value: 42
ptr1 use count: 1
ptr2 value: 42
ptr1 address: 0x6caf08
```

```
ptr2 address: 0x6caf08
ptr1 use count: 2
ptr1 use count: 1
ptr1 use count: 0
```

WARNING

The important thing to remember about copying pointers is that copying a pointer only copies the pointer address, not the underlying reference. Consequently, if you copy a pointer to an array, there is still just one array, but now you have two references to that array. To create a copy of an array, you would need to create a second array of the same size and copy the data, index by index, from the first array to the second array.

TECHNICAL STUFF

Some significant differences exist between the C++ 17 and the C++ 20 versions of the smart pointer classes. One of the most important changes from a coding perspective is that C++ 20 relies on the spaceship operator (see the "Considering the new spaceship operator" sidebar of Book 1, Chapter 5 for details) in place of the !=, <, <=, >, and >= operators. If you try to use these operators in a C++ 20 application, you see an error message. See https://en.cppreference.com/w/cpp/memory/ unique_ptr and https://en.cppreference.com/w/cpp/memory/shared_ptr for other version differences that could cause errors when updating your code.

Defining nullable values using std::optional and std::nullopt

An optional value is one that may or may not be there. For example, a caller may supply an int value when calling your function, or may send nothing at all. In some cases, when an error occurs, the value may simply not exist. C++ developers have tried to come up with all sorts of solutions to the problem of values not being provided, but none of them is as good as using optional. If a value doesn't appear in the optional object, it's easy to check using nullopt.

You may wonder why optional appears in this chapter. After all, it should possibly appear in Book 1, Chapter 6 when working with functions. In many respects, optional appears as a pointer because it supports many of the same features as unique_ptr and shared_ptr do. For example, you have access to the reset() and swap() functions, as described at https://en.cppreference.com/w/cpp/ utility/optional. It's actually easier to understand optional after you get to this point in the book, which is why it appears here.

The Optional example, shown in Listing 8-12, demonstrates how to create a function that could receive a string, but then again, perhaps not. (Note that this example may not run in Code::Blocks because of problems in GCC. Currently, you must change the `#include <optional>` to read `#include <experimental/optional>` because the support is experimental. There are other necessary changes as well, which you can see in the `OptionalExperimental` project in the downloadable source code.)

LISTING 8-12: ## Using optional to Avoid Instances of Nothing

```cpp
#include <iostream>
#include <optional>

using namespace std;

void myFunction(optional<string> name = nullopt) {
  if (name == nullopt) {
    cout << "I wish I knew your name!" << endl;
  } else {
    cout << "Hello " << name.value() << "!" << endl;
  }
}

int main() {
  myFunction();
  myFunction("Sarah");
  return 0;
}
```

In this case, you see `myFunction()`, which accepts nothing or a `string`. If the caller sends nothing, then `name` equals `nullopt`. On the other hand, if the caller sends a `string`, the code uses `name.value()` to obtain the `string` and print it onscreen. Note that you can't access the `string` directly but must call `value()` instead. Here is the output from this example:

```
I wish I knew your name!
Hello Sarah!
```

WARNING

You might be tempted to think that `nullopt` somehow equals `nullptr`. However, this isn't the case. If you try to replace the `nullopt` check in Listing 8-12 with (`ptr1 == nullptr`), the compiler will complain loudly that you're using the wrong data type.

Passing Pointer Variables to Functions

One of the most important uses for pointers is this: If a pointer points to a variable, you can pass the pointer to a function, and the function can modify the original variable. This functionality lets you write functions that can actually modify the variables passed to them. Even though this section discusses raw pointers, the same techniques work with smart pointers.

Normally, when you call a function and you pass a few variables to the function, the computer just grabs the values out of the variables and passes those values. Take a close look at the VariablePointer example, shown in Listing 8-13.

LISTING 8-13: A Function Cannot Change the Original Variables Passed into It

```
#include <iostream>

using namespace std;

void ChangesAreGood(int myparam) {
  myparam += 10;
  cout << "Inside the function:" << endl;
  cout << myparam << endl;
}

int main() {
  int mynumber = 30;
  cout << "Before the function:" << endl;
  cout << mynumber << endl;

  ChangesAreGood(mynumber);
  cout << "After the function:" << endl;
  cout << mynumber << endl;

  return 0;
}
```

Listing 8-13 includes a function called ChangesAreGood() that modifies the parameter it receives. (It adds 10 to its parameter called myparam.) It then prints the new value of the parameter.

The main() function initializes an integer variable, mynumber, to 30 and prints its value. It then calls the ChangesAreGood() function, which changes its parameter.

After coming back from the ChangesAreGood() function, main() prints the value again. When you run this application, you see the following output:

```
Before the function:
30
Inside the function:
40
After the function:
30
```

Before the function call, mynumber is 30. And after the function call, it's still 30. But the function added 10 to its parameter. This means that when the function modified its parameter, the original variable remains untouched. The two are separate entities. Only the value 30 went into the function. The actual variable did not. It stayed in main(). But what if you write a function that you *want* to modify the original variable?

A pointer contains a number, which represents the address of a variable. If you pass this address into a function and the function stores that address into one of its own variables, its own variable also points to the same variable that the original pointer did. The pointer variable in main() and the pointer variable in the function both point to the same variable because both pointers hold the same address.

That's how you let a function modify data in a variable: You pass a pointer. But when you call a function, the process is easy because you don't need to make a pointer variable. Instead, you can just call the function, putting an & in front of the variable. Then you're not passing the variable or its value — instead, you're passing the address of the variable.

The VariablePointer2 example, shown in Listing 8-14, is a modified form of Listing 8-13; this time, the function actually manages to modify the original variable.

LISTING 8-14: **Using Pointers to Modify a Variable Passed into a Function**

```cpp
#include <iostream>

using namespace std;

void ChangesAreGood(int *myparam) {
  *myparam += 10;
  cout << "Inside the function:" << endl;
```

(continued)

LISTING 8-14:   *(continued)*

```
  cout << *myparam << endl;
}

int main() {
  int mynumber = 30;
  cout << "Before the function:" << endl;
  cout << mynumber << endl;

  ChangesAreGood(&mynumber);
  cout << "After the function:" << endl;
  cout << mynumber << endl;

  return 0;
}
```

When you run this application, you see the following output:

```
Before the function:
30
Inside the function:
40
After the function:
40
```

Notice the important difference between this and the output from Listing 8-13: The final line of output is 40, not 30. The variable was modified by the function!

To understand how this happened, first look at main(). The only difference in main() is that it has an ampersand (&) in front of the mynumber argument in the call to ChangesAreGood(). ChangesAreGood() receives the address of mynumber.

Now the function has some major changes. The function header takes a pointer rather than a number. You perform this task by adding an asterisk (*) so that the parameter is a pointer variable. This pointer receives the address being passed into it. Thus, it points to the variable mynumber. Therefore, any modifications made by dereferencing the pointer will change the original variable. The following line changes the original variable.

```
  (*myparam) += 10;
```

TECHNICAL STUFF

The `ChangesAreGood()` function in Listing 8-14 no longer modifies its own parameter. The parameter holds the address of the original `mynumber` variable, and that never changes. Throughout the function, the pointer variable `myparam` holds the `mynumber` address. And any changes the function performs are on the dereferenced variable, which is `mynumber`.

Returning Pointer Variables from Functions

Functions can return values, including pointers. To set up a function to return a pointer, specify the type followed by an asterisk at the beginning of the function header. The `ReturnPointer` example, shown in Listing 8-15, demonstrates this technique. The function returns a pointer that is the result of a `new` operation.

LISTING 8-15:	**Returning a Pointer from a String Involves Using an Asterisk in the Return Type**

```
#include <iostream>
#include <sstream>
#include <stdlib.h>

using namespace std;

string *GetSecretCode() {
  string *code = new string;
```

(continued)

LISTING 8-15: *(continued)*

```cpp
    code->append("CR");

    int randomnumber = rand();
    ostringstream converter;
    converter << randomnumber;
    code->append(converter.str());

    code->append("NQ");
    return code;
}

int main() {
    string *newcode;

    for (int index = 0; index < 5; index++) {
        newcode = GetSecretCode();
        cout << *newcode << endl;
    }

    return 0;
}
```

The `main()` function creates a pointer to a `string` named `newcode`. `GetSecret-Code()` returns a pointer to a `string`, so `newcode` and the function return value match. When you use `newcode`, you must dereference it.

When you run this application, you see something like the following output:

```
CR41NQ
CR18467NQ
CR6334NQ
CR26500NQ
CR19169NQ
```

WARNING

Never return from a function the address of a local variable in the function. The local variables live in the stack space allocated for the function, not in the heap. When the function is finished, the computer frees the stack space used for the function, making room for the *next* function call. If you try this, the variables will be okay for a while, but after enough function calls follow, the variable's data will get overwritten.

RANDOM NUMBERS AND STRINGS

Some special code appears in GetSecretCode( ) that requires explanation. The call to int randomnumber = rand( ); generates a random number. To obtain a random number and convert it to a string, you add two more include lines:

```
#include <stdlib.h>
#include <sstream>
```

The first line provides access to the rand( ) function. The second line provides access to the ostringstream type. Here are the three lines that perform the magic:

```
int randomnumber = rand();
ostringstream converter;
converter << randomnumber;
```

The first of these creates a random number by calling rand( ), which returns an int. The next line creates a variable of type ostringstream, which is a type that's handy for converting numbers to strings. A variable of this type has features similar to that of a console. You can use the insertion operator (<<), except that instead of going to the console, anything you write goes into a string of type ostringstream (which comes from the words *output, string,* and *stream;* usually, things that allow the insertion operator << or the extraction operator >> to perform input and output are called *streams*). You can add the resulting string onto the code string variable using:

```
code->append(converter.str());
```

The part inside parentheses — converter.str( ) — returns an actual string version of the converter variable. You use the append( ) function to add the string to code.

TECHNICAL STUFF

Just as the parameters to a function are normally values, a function normally *returns* a value. In the case of returning a pointer, the function is still returning just a value — it is returning the value of the pointer, which is a number representing an address.

2
Understanding Objects and Classes

Contents at a Glance

Chapter **1**

Working with Classes

B ack in the early 1990s, the big buzzword in the computer world was *object-oriented*. For anything to sell, it had to be *object-oriented*. Programming languages were object-oriented. Software applications were object-oriented. Computers were object-oriented. Unfortunately, object-oriented was simply a cool catchphrase at the time that meant little in real terms. Often, ideas begin poorly formed and gain resolution as people work to implement the idea in the real world.

Now it's possible to explore what object-oriented *really* means and how you can use it to organize your C++ applications. In this chapter, you discover object-oriented programming and see how you can do it in C++. Although people disagree on the strict definition of object-oriented, in this book it means programming with objects and classes.

Understanding Objects and Classes

Consider a pen, a regular, old pen. Here's what you can say about it:

» **Ink Color:** Black

» **Shell Color:** Light gray

- » **Cap Color:** Black
- » **Style:** Ballpoint
- » **Length:** Six inches
- » **Brand:** Paper Mate
- » **Ink Level:** 50 percent full
- » **Capability #1:** Write on paper
- » **Capability #2:** Break in half
- » **Capability #3:** Run out of ink

Now, look around for other things, such as a printer. Here's a description of a printer:

- » **Kind:** Laser
- » **Brand:** HP
- » **Model:** MFP M479fdw
- » **Ink Color:** Color
- » **Case Color:** Cream
- » **Input trays:** One
- » **Output trays:** One
- » **Connection:** Ethernet/Wi-Fi/ Wi-Fi Direct
- » **Capability #1:** Reads print job requests from the device
- » **Capability #2:** Prints on sheets of paper
- » **Capability #3:** Prints a test page
- » **Capability #4:** Needs the toner cartridges replaced when empty

These lists describe the objects you might see. They provide dimensions, color, model, brand, and other details. The lists also describe what the objects can do. The pen can break in half and run out of ink. The printer can take print jobs, print pages, and have its cartridges replaced.

When describing what objects can do, you carefully write it from the perspective of the object itself, not from the perspective of the person using the object. A good way to name the capability is to test it by preceding it with the words "I can" and see if it makes sense. Thus, because "I can *write on paper*" works from the perspective of a pen, the list contains *write on paper* for one of the pen's capabilities. But is seeing all the objects in the universe possible, or are some objects hidden? Certainly, some objects are physical, like atoms or the dark side of the moon, and you can't see them. But other objects are abstract. For example, you may have a credit card account. What is a credit card account, exactly? A credit card account is abstract because you can't touch it — it has no physical presence. The following sections of the chapter examine various kinds of objects: those with physical representations and those that are abstract.

USING ENUMERATIONS

Someone may think that the number 12 is a good representation of the color blue, and the number 86 is a good representation of the color red. Purple? That's 182. Beige? That's getting up there — it's 1047. Yes, this sounds kind of silly. But suppose that you want to create a variable that holds the color blue. Using the standard types of integers, floating-point numbers, characters, and letters, you don't have a lot of choices. In the old days, people would just pick a number to represent each color and store that number in a variable. Or, you could have saved a string, as in blue. But C++ presents a better alternative. It's called an *enumeration*, which mates a human-understandable term like blue to a computer-friendly value like 12. Remember that for each type, there's a whole list of possible values. An integer, for example, can be a whole number within a particular range. (This range varies between computers, but it's usually pretty big.) Strings can be any characters, all strung together. But what if you want a value called blue? Or red? Or even beige? Then you need enumerations. This line creates an enumeration type:

```
enum MyColor {blue, red, green, yellow, black, beige};
```

You now have a new *type* called MyColor, which you can use the same way you can use other types, such as int, double, or string. For example, you can create a variable of type MyColor and set its value to one of the values in the curly braces:

```
MyColor inkcolor = blue;
MyColor shellcolor = black;
```

The variable inkcolor is of type MyColor, and its value is blue. The variable shellcolor is also of type MyColor, and its value is black.

Classifying classes and objects

When you pick up a pen, you can ask somebody, "What type of object is this an instance of?" Most people would probably say, "a pen." In computer programming, instead of using *type of object,* you say *class.* This thing in your hand belongs to the pen class. Now if you point to the object parked out in the driveway and ask, "What class does that belong to?" the answer is, "class Car." Of course, you could be more specific. You may say that the object belongs to class 2020 Ford Taurus.

When you see a pen, you might ask what class this object belongs to. If you then pick up another pen, you see another example of the same class. One class; several examples. If you stand next to a busy street, you see many examples of the class called car. Or you may see many examples of the class Ford Explorer, a few instances of the class Toyota Corolla, and so on. It depends on how you *classify* those objects roaring down the road. Regardless, you likely see several examples of any given class.

So when you organize things, you specify a *class,* which is the type of object. And when you're ready, you can start picking out examples (or *instances*) of the class. Each class may have several instances. Some classes have only one instance. That's a *singleton class.* For example, at any given time, the class United States President would have one instance.

CLASS NAMES AND CLASS FILES

In Listings 1-3 and 1-5, nearby in this chapter, you see the filenames match the name of the class. Common practice when creating a class is to put the class definition in a header file of the same name as the class but with an .h extension. And you put the class method code in a source code file of the same name as the class but this time with a .cpp extension. You also capitalize the filenames the same as the class name; thus, the files are called Pen.h and Pen.cpp. Naming the files the same as classes has lots of advantages:

- You automatically know the name of the header file you need to include if you want to use a certain class.

- It provides a general consistency, which is always good in reducing the complexities of programming.

- When you see a header file, you know what class is probably inside it.

Describing methods and data

If you choose a class, you can describe its characteristics. However, because you're describing only the class characteristics, you don't actually specify them. You may say the pen has an ink color, but you don't actually say *what* color. That's because you don't yet have an example of the class Pen. You have only the class itself. When you finally find an example, it may be one color, or it may be another. So, if you're describing a class called Pen, you may list the characteristics presented in the introduction to this section.

You don't specify ink color, shell color, length, or any of these *properties* (terms that describe the class) as actual values. You're listing only general characteristics for all instances of the class Pen. That is, every pen has these properties. But the actual values for these properties might vary from instance to instance. One pen may have a different ink color from another, but both might have the same brand. Nevertheless, they are both separate instances of the class Pen.

After creating an instance of class Pen, you can provide values for the properties. For example, Table 1-1 lists the property values of three actual pens.

TABLE 1-1 **Specifying Property Values for Instances of Class Pen**

Property Name	First Pen	Second Pen	Third Pen
Ink Color	Blue	Red	Black
Shell Color	Grey	Red	Grey
Cap Color	Blue	Black	Black
Style	Ballpoint	Fountain	Felt-tip
Length	5.5 inches	5 inches	6 inches
Brand	Office Depot	Parker	Paper Mate
Ink Level	30%	60%	90%

In Table 1-1, the first column holds the property names. The second column holds property values for the first pen. The third column holds the property values for the second pen, and the final column holds the property values for the third pen. All the pens in the class share properties. But the values for these properties may differ from pen to pen. When you *instantiate* (build or create) a new Pen, you follow the list of properties, giving the new pen instance its own values. You may make the shell purple with yellow speckles, or you may make it transparent. But you would give it a shell that has some color, even if that color is *transparent*.

In Table 1-1, you didn't see a list of *methods* (ways of interacting with the Pen class to exercise its capabilities). But all these pens have the same methods:

>> **Method #1:** Write on paper

>> **Method #2:** Break in half

>> **Method #3:** Run out of ink

Unlike properties, methods don't change from instance to instance. They are the same for each class.

When you describe classes to build a computer application using a class, you are modeling. In the preceding examples, you modeled a class called Pen. In the following section, you implement this model by writing an application that mimics a pen using the Pen class.

If you work with enums (the code form of enumerations), you need to decide what to name your new type. For example, you can choose MyColor or MyColors. Many people, when they write a line such as enum MyColor {blue, red, green, yellow, black, beige};, make the name plural (MyColors) because this is a list of colors. It's best to make the term singular, as in MyColor, because you use only one color at a time. When you declare a variable, it makes more sense: MyColor inkcolor; would mean that inkcolor is a *color* — not a group of *colors*.

Implementing a class

To implement a class in C++, you use the keyword class. And then you add the name of the class, such as Pen. You then add an open brace, list your properties and methods, and end with a closing brace.

Most people capitalize the first letter of a class name in C++, and if their class name is a word, they don't capitalize the remaining letters. Although you don't have to follow this rule, many people do. You can choose any name for a C++ class provided it is not a C++ keyword; it consists only of letters, digits, and underscores; and it does not start with a number.

The PenClass example, shown in Listing 1-1, contains a C++ class description that appears inside the Pen.h header file. (See Book 1, Chapter 7, for information on how to put code in a header file.) Review the header file, and you see how it implements the different characteristics. The properties of a header file are just like variables: They have a type and a name. The methods are implemented using functions. All this code goes inside curly brackets and is preceded by a class header. The header gives the name of the class. And, oh yes, the word *public* is stuck in there, and it has a colon after it. The "Accessing members," section later in this chapter explains the word `public`. By itself, this code isn't very useful, but you put it to use in Listing 1-2, an application that you can actually compile and run.

LISTING 1-1: **Pen.h Contains the Class Description for Pen**

```
#ifndef PEN_H_INCLUDED
#define PEN_H_INCLUDED
using namespace std;
enum Color {
  blue,
  red,
  black,
  clear,
  grey
};

enum PenStyle {
  ballpoint,
  felt_tip,
  fountain_pen
};

class Pen {
public:
  Color InkColor;
  Color ShellColor;
  Color CapColor;
  PenStyle Style;
  float Length;
  string Brand;
  int InkLevelPercent;

  void write_on_paper(string words) {
    if (InkLevelPercent <= 0) {
      cout << "Oops! Out of ink!" << endl;
    }
    else {
      cout << words << endl;
```

(continued)

LISTING 1-1: *(continued)*

```
      InkLevelPercent = InkLevelPercent - words.length();
    }
  }

  void break_in_half() {
    InkLevelPercent = InkLevelPercent / 2;
    Length = Length / 2.0;
  }

  void run_out_of_ink() {
    InkLevelPercent = 0;
  }
};
#endif // PEN_H_INCLUDED
```

REMEMBER When you write a class, you always end it with a semicolon. Write that down on a sticky note and hang it on the refrigerator. The effort spent in doing this will be well worth avoiding the frustration of wondering why your code won't compile.

REMEMBER In a class definition, you describe the characteristics and capabilities (that is, supply the properties and methods, respectively).

Note in Listing 1-1, earlier in this chapter, that the methods access the properties. However, we said that these variables don't have values yet, because this is just a class, not an *instance* of a class. How can that be? When you create an instance of this class, you can give values to these properties. Then you can call the methods. And here's the really great part: You can make a *second instance* of this class and give it its own values for the properties. Yes, the two instances will each have their own sets of properties. And when you run the methods for the second instance, these functions operate on the properties for the second instance. Isn't C++ smart? Now look at Listing 1-2. This is a source file that uses the header file in Listing 1-1. In this code, you see the Pen class in action.

LISTING 1-2: **main.cpp Contains Code That Uses the Class Pen**

```
#include <iostream>
#include "Pen.h"

using namespace std;

int main() {
  Pen FavoritePen;
```

```
FavoritePen.InkColor = blue;
FavoritePen.ShellColor = grey;
FavoritePen.CapColor = blue;
FavoritePen.Style = ballpoint;
FavoritePen.Length = 5.5;
FavoritePen.Brand = "Office Depot";
FavoritePen.InkLevelPercent = 30;

Pen WorstPen;
WorstPen.InkColor = red;
WorstPen.ShellColor = red;
WorstPen.CapColor = black;
WorstPen.Style = fountain_pen;
WorstPen.Length = 5.0;
WorstPen.Brand = "Parker";
WorstPen.InkLevelPercent = 60;

cout << "This is my favorite pen" << endl;
cout << "Color: " << FavoritePen.InkColor << endl;
cout << "Brand: " << FavoritePen.Brand << endl;
cout << "Ink Level: " << FavoritePen.InkLevelPercent
    << "%" << endl;
FavoritePen.write_on_paper("Hello I am a pen");
cout << "Ink Level: " << FavoritePen.InkLevelPercent
    << "%" << endl;

return 0;
}
```

There are two variables of class Pen: FavoritePen and WorstPen. To access the properties of these objects, you type the name of the variable holding the object, a dot (or period), and then the property name. For example, to access the InkLevelPercent member of WorstPen, you type:

```
WorstPen.InkLevelPercent = 60;
```

Remember, WorstPen is the variable name, and this variable is an object. It is an object or an instance of class Pen. This object has various properties, including InkLevelPercent.

You can also run some of the methods that are in these objects. This code calls:

```
FavoritePen.write_on_paper("Hello I am a pen");
```

This called the function write_on_paper() for the object FavoritePen. Look at the code for this function, which is in the header file, Listing 1-1:

```
void write_on_paper(string words) {
  if (InkLevelPercent <= 0) {
    cout << "Oops! Out of ink!" << endl;
  }
  else {
    cout << words << endl;
    InkLevelPercent = InkLevelPercent - words.length();
  }
}
```

This function uses the variable called InkLevelPercent. But InkLevelPercent isn't declared in this function. The reason is that InkLevelPercent is part of the object and is declared in the class. Suppose you call this method for two different objects, as in the following:

```
FavoritePen.write_on_paper("Hello I am a pen");
WorstPen.write_on_paper("Hello I am another pen");
```

The first of these lines calls write_on_paper() for the FavoritePen object; thus, inside the code for write_on_paper(), the InkLevelPercent refers to Ink-LevelPercent for the FavoritePen object. It looks at and possibly decreases the variable for that object only. But WorstPen has its *own* InkLevelPercent property, separate from that of FavoritePen. So in the second of these two lines, write_on_paper() accesses and possibly decreases the InkLevelPercent that lives inside WorstPen. In other words, each object has its own InkLevelPercent. When you call write_on_paper(), the function modifies the property based on which object you are calling it with. The first line calls it with FavoritePen. The second calls it with WorstPen. When you run this application, you see the following output:

```
This is my favorite pen
Color: 0
Brand: Office Depot
Ink Level: 30%
Hello I am a pen
Ink Level: 14%
```

You should notice something about the color line. Here's the line of code that writes it:

```
cout << "Color: " << FavoritePen.InkColor << endl;
```

THE STRING CLASS

If you've been reading the previous chapters of Book 1 (and now this first chapter of Book 2), and trying the applications, you have seen the string type. Now for the big secret: string is actually a class. When you create a variable of type string, you are creating an object of class string. That's why, to use the string functions, you first type the variable name, a dot, and then the function name: You are really calling a method for the string object that you created. Similarly, when you work with pointers to strings, instead of a dot you can use the –> notation to access the methods. (See "Using classes and raw pointers," later in this chapter, for more information.) When working with newer versions of C++, the string class is part of the std namespace, which is why you add using namespace std; to the beginning of your code. If you use an older version of C++, the string class appears as part of the string file. In this case, you include <string> to provide the necessary header files to declare the string class.

This line outputs the InkColor member for FavoritePen. But what type is InkColor? It's the new Color enumerated type. But something is wrong. It printed 0 despite being set as follows:

```
FavoritePen.InkColor = blue;
```

The code sets it to blue, not 0. Unfortunately, that's the breaks with using enum. You can use it in your code, but *under the hood*, it just stores numbers. When printed, you get a number. The compiler chooses the numbers for you, and it starts the first entry in the enum list as 0, the second as 1, then 2, then 3, and so on. Thus, blue is stored as 0, red as 1, black as 2, clear as 3, and grey as 4. Fortunately, people have found a way to create a new class that handles the enum for you (that is, it *wraps* around the enum), and then you can print what you really want: blue, red, black, clear, and grey. Book 2, Chapter 2 has tips on how to do this astounding feat.

REMEMBER

Remember that you can create several *objects* (also called *instances*) of a single class. Each object gets its own properties, which you declare in the class. To access the members of an object, you use a period, or dot.

Separating method code

When you work with functions, you can either make sure that the code to your function is positioned before any calls to the function, or you can use a *forward reference,* also called a *function prototype.* Book 1, Chapter 6 discusses this feature.

When you work with classes and methods, you have a similar option. Most C++ programmers prefer to keep the code for their methods outside the class definition. The reason for placing them outside is to make the code easier to read; you don't end up with a single, huge block of code that is incredibly difficult to follow. In addition, someone using the class may not care about how the methods work, so keeping things simple is the best option. The class definition contains only method prototypes, or, at least, mostly method prototypes. If the method is one or two lines of code, people may leave it in the class definition.

When you use a method prototype in a class definition, you write the prototype by ending the method header with a semicolon where you would normally have the open brace and code. If your method looks like this:

```
void break_in_half() {
    InkLevelPercent = InkLevelPercent / 2;
    Length = Length / 2.0;
}
```

a method prototype would look like this:

```
void break_in_half();
```

After you write the method prototype in the class, you write the method code again outside the class definition. However, you need to doctor it up just a bit. In particular, you need to throw in the name of the class, so that the compiler knows which class this method goes with. The following is the same method described earlier, but with the class information included. You separate the class name and method name with a *scope resolution operator* (::) that links the method to the class:

```
void Pen::break_in_half() {
    InkLevelPercent = InkLevelPercent / 2;
    Length = Length / 2.0;
}
```

You put the method after your class definition. And you would want to put the method code inside one of your source code files if your class definition is in a header file.

TIP

You can use the same method name in different classes. As are variables in different functions, method names are associated with a particular class using the scope resolution operator. Although you don't want to go overboard on duplicating method names, if you feel a need to, you can certainly do it without a problem.

For example, toString() is a common method name and you often see it provided with a wide range of classes in your application.

The PenClass2 example, shown in Listings 1-3 and 1-4, contains the modified version of the Pen class that appeared earlier in this chapter in Listing 1-1. You can use these two files together with Listing 1-2, which hasn't changed.

LISTING 1-3: **Using Method Prototypes with the Modified Pen.h file**

```
#ifndef PEN_H_INCLUDED
#define PEN_H_INCLUDED

using namespace std;
enum Color {
  blue,
  red,
  black,
  clear,
  grey
};

enum PenStyle {
  ballpoint,
  felt_tip,
  fountain_pen
};

class Pen {
public:
  Color InkColor;
  Color ShellColor;
  Color CapColor;
  PenStyle Style;
  float Length;
  string Brand;
  int InkLevelPercent;
  void write_on_paper(string words);
  void break_in_half();
  void run_out_of_ink();
};

#endif // PEN_H_INCLUDED
```

LISTING 1-4: **Containing the Methods for Class Pen in the New Pen.cpp File**

```cpp
#include <iostream>
#include "Pen.h"

using namespace std;

void Pen::write_on_paper(string words) {
  if (InkLevelPercent <= 0) {
    cout << "Oops! Out of ink!" << endl;
  }
  else {
    cout << words << endl;
    InkLevelPercent = InkLevelPercent - words.length();
  }
}

void Pen::break_in_half() {
  InkLevelPercent = InkLevelPercent / 2;
  Length = Length / 2.0;
}

void Pen::run_out_of_ink() {
  InkLevelPercent = 0;
}
```

All the functions from the class are now in a separate source (.cpp) file. The header file now just lists prototypes and is a little easier to read. The source file includes the header file at the top. That's required; otherwise, the compiler won't know that Pen is a class name, and it will get confused (as it so easily can).

The parts of a class

Here is a summary of the parts of a class and the different ways classes can work together:

>> **Class:** A class is a type. It includes properties and methods. *Properties* describe the class, and *methods* describe its behaviors.

>> **Object:** An *object* is an instance of a class. Think of the class as a blueprint and the object as the building created from the blueprint. You need only one blueprint to build multiple buildings of precisely the same type. Each building is an instance of that blueprint.

>> **Class definition:** The class definition describes the class. It starts with the word *class,* and then has the name of the class, followed by an open brace and closing brace. Inside the braces are the members of the class.

>> **Property:** A *property* is a characteristic in a class, such as a color, style, or other descriptive element. You list the properties inside the class (normally before any methods, but there is no rule that says you must do so). Each instance of the class gets its own copy of each property.

>> **Method:** A *method* is a capability of a class — some task that the class can perform. As with properties, you list methods inside the class. When you call a method for a particular instance, the method accesses the properties for the instance.

When you divide the class, you put part in the header file and part in the source code file. The following list describes what goes where:

>> **Header file:** Put the class definition in the header file. Properties appear as part of the class definition within the header. You can include the method code inside the class definition if it's a short method. Most people prefer not to put any method code longer than a line or two in the header — in fact, many don't put any method code at all in the header. You may want to name the header file the same as the class but with an .h or .hpp extension. Thus, the class Pen, for instance, might be in the file Pen.h.

>> **Source file:** If your class has methods, and you didn't put the code in the class definition, you need to put the code in a source file. When you do, precede the function name with the class name and the scope resolution operator (::). If you named the header file the same as the class, you probably want to name the source file the same as the class as well but with a .cpp extension.

Working with a Class

Many handy tricks are available for working with classes. In this section, you explore several clever ways of working with classes, starting with the way you can hide certain parts of your class from other functions that are accessing them.

Accessing members

When you work with an object in real life, there are often parts of the object that you interact with and other parts that you don't. For example, when you use the computer, you type on the keyboard but don't open the box and poke around with a wire attached to a battery. For the most part, the stuff inside is off-limits except when you're upgrading it.

In object terminology, the words *public* and *private* refer to properties and methods. When you design a class, you might want to make some properties and methods freely accessible by class users. You may want to keep other members tucked away. A *class user* is the part of an application that creates an instance of a class and calls one of its methods. In Listing 1-2, earlier in the chapter, main() is a class user. If you have a function called FlippityFlop() that creates an instance of your class and does a few things to the instance, such as change some its properties, FlippityFlop() is a class user. In short, a user is any function that accesses your class.

When designing a class, you may want only specific users calling certain methods. You may want to keep other methods hidden away, to be called only by other methods within the class. Suppose you're writing a class called Oven. This class includes a method called Bake(), which takes a number as a parameter representing the desired oven temperature. Now you may also have a method called TurnOnHeatingElement() and one called TurnOffHeatingElement().

Here's how it would work. The Bake() method starts out calling TurnOnHeating Element(). Then it keeps track of the temperature, and when the temperature is correct, it calls TurnOffHeatingElement(). You wouldn't want somebody walking in the kitchen and calling the TurnOnHeatingElement() method without touching any of the dials, only to leave the room as the oven gets hotter and hotter with nobody watching it. You allow the users of the class to call only Bake(). The other two methods, TurnOnHeatingElement() and TurnOffHeatingElement(), are reserved for use only by the Bake() function.

REMEMBER

You bar users from calling functions by making specific functions *private*. Functions that you want to allow access to you make *public*. After you design a class, if you write a function that instantiates an object based on that class that tries to call one of an object's private methods, you get a compiler error when you try to compile it. The compiler won't allow you to call it.

The OvenClass example, shown in Listing 1-5, defines a sample Oven class and a main() that uses it. Look at the class definition. It has two sections: one private and the other public. The code for the functions appears after the class definition. The two private functions don't do much other than print a message. (Although they're also free to call other private functions in the class.) The public function, Bake(), calls each of the private functions, because it's allowed to.

LISTING 1-5: **Using the Public and Private Words to Hide Parts of Your Class**

```cpp
#include <iostream>

using namespace std;

class Oven {
private:
  void TurnOnHeatingElement();
  void TurnOffHeatingElement();
public:
  void Bake(int Temperature);
};

void Oven::TurnOnHeatingElement() {
  cout << "Heating element is now ON! Be careful!" << endl;
}

void Oven::TurnOffHeatingElement() {
  cout << "Heating element is now off. Relax!" << endl;
}

void Oven::Bake(int Temperature) {
  TurnOnHeatingElement();
  cout << "Baking!" << endl;
  TurnOffHeatingElement();
}

int main() {
  Oven fred;
  fred.Bake(875);
  return 0;
}
```

When you run this application, you see some messages:

```
Heating element is now ON! Be careful!
Baking!
Heating element is now off. Relax!
```

Nothing too fancy here. Now if you tried to include a line in your `main()` such as the one in the following code, where you call a private function

```
fred.TurnOnHeatingElement();
```

you see an error message telling you that you can't do it because the function is private. In Code::Blocks, you see this message:

```
error: 'void Oven::TurnOnHeatingElement()' is private
```

When you design your classes, consider making all the functions private by default, and then only make those public that you want users to access. Some people, however, prefer to go the other way around: Make them all public, and only make those private that you are sure you don't want users to access. There are good arguments for either approach; however, the preference in this book is to make public only what must be public. This approach minimizes the risk of some other application that's using that class creating errors by calling things the programmer doesn't really understand.

You don't necessarily need to list the private members first followed by the public members. You can put the public members first if you prefer. Some people put the public members at the top so they see them first. That makes sense. Also, you can have more than one private section and more than one public section. For example, you can have a public section, a private section, and then another public section, as in the following code:

```
class Oven {
public:
    void Bake(int Temperature);
private:
    void TurnOnHeatingElement();
    void TurnOffHeatingElement();
public:
    void Broil();
};
```

Using classes and raw pointers

This and other sections of the chapter discuss the use of raw pointers with objects. In the "Understanding the Changes in Pointers for C++ 20" section of Book 1, Chapter 8, you discover that there are other pointer types, including smart and optional pointers. Because most code still relies on raw pointers to work with objects, the majority of this chapter focuses on their use.

As with any variable, you can have a pointer variable that points to an object. As usual, the pointer variable's type must match the type of the class. This creates a pointer variable that points to a Pen instance:

```
Pen *MyPen;
```

The variable MyPen is a pointer, and it can point to an object of type Pen. The variable's own type is pointer to Pen, or in C++ notation, Pen *. Because you're always working with pointers when interacting with objects, you leave *ptr* off the variable name to save typing time and focus attention on the variable's purpose, which is to serve as your personal pen.

REMEMBER

A line of code like Pen *MyPen; creates a variable that serves as a pointer to an object. But this line, by itself, does not actually create an instance. By itself, it points to nothing. To create an instance, you have to call new. This is a common mistake among C++ programmers; sometimes people forget to call new and wonder why their applications crash.

After you create the variable MyPen, you can create an instance of class Pen and point MyPen to it using the new keyword, like so:

```
MyPen = new Pen;
```

Or you can combine both Pen *MyPen; and the preceding line:

```
Pen *MyPen = new Pen;
```

Now you have two variables: You have the actual object, which is unnamed and sitting on the heap. (See the "Heaping and Stacking the Variables" section of Book 1, Chapter 8, for more information on pointers and heaps.) You also have the pointer variable, which points to the object: two variables working together. Because the object is out on the heap, the only way to access it is through the pointer. To access the members through the pointer, you use a special notation — a minus sign followed by a greater-than sign. It bears a passing resemblance to an arrow (and is therefore called the *arrow operator*), as the following line makes clear:

```
MyPen->InkColor = red;
```

This goes through the MyPen pointer to set the InkColor property of the object to red.

As with other variables you created with new, after you are finished using an object, you should call delete to free the memory used by the object pointed to by MyPen. To do so, start with the word delete and then the name of the object pointer, MyPen, as in the following:

```
delete MyPen;
```

CREATING A PEN.CPP AND PEN.H REFERENCE

To use this example and others in the chapter that reference Pen.cpp and Pen.h, you must include Pen.cpp and Pen.h from the PenClass2 example using the technique described in the "Creating a project with multiple existing files" section of Book 1, Chapter 7. Notice that because Pen.h doesn't appear in the current directory, you must make a relative reference (the ../PenClass2/ part) to it in Listing 1-6. As shown in the following figure, if you add Pen.cpp and Pen.h to the project first, and then type the #include " statement, Code::Blocks will actually provide the relative reference for you.

REMEMBER

Store a 0 in the pointer after you delete the object it points to. When you call delete on a pointer to an object, you are deleting the object itself, not the pointer. If you don't store a 0 in the pointer, it still points to where the object *used to be*.

The PenClass3 example, shown in Listing 1-6, demonstrates the process of declaring a pointer, creating an object and pointing to it, accessing the object's members through the pointer, deleting the object, and clearing the pointer back to 0.

LISTING 1-6:	**Managing an Object's Life**

```cpp
#include <iostream>
#include "../PenClass2/Pen.h"

using namespace std;

int main() {
  Pen *MyPen;
  MyPen = new Pen;
  MyPen->InkColor = red;
```

```
    cout << MyPen->InkColor << endl;
    delete MyPen;
    MyPen = 0;
    return 0;
}
```

TIP

Table 1-2 reiterates the process (steps) shown in Listing 1-6 in a more formal way. The table is called "Steps to Using Objects" rather than something more specific such as "Using Objects with Pointers" because the majority of your work with objects will be through pointers. Therefore, this is the most common way of using pointers.

TABLE 1-2

Steps to Using Objects

Step	Sample Code	Action
1	`Pen *MyPen;`	Declares the pointer
2	`MyPen = new Pen;`	Calls new to create the object
3	`MyPen->InkColor = red;`	Accesses the members of the object through the pointer
4	`delete MyPen;`	Deletes the object
5	`MyPen = 0;`	Clears the pointer

Now that you have an overview of the process through Listing 1-6 and understand the basics through Table 1-2, you can see how to formalize the procedure. The following steps describe precisely how to work with raw pointers and objects:

1. **Declare the pointer.**

   The pointer must match the type of object you intend to work with, except that the pointer's type name in C++ is followed by an asterisk, *.

2. **Call** new, **passing the class name, and store the results of** new **in the pointer.**

   You can combine Steps 1 and 2 into a single step.

3. **Access the object's members through the pointer with the arrow operator, ->.**

   You could dereference the pointer and put parentheses around it, but everyone uses the shorthand notation.

4. **When you are finished with the pointer, call** delete.

This step frees the object from the heap. Remember that this does not delete the pointer itself, but frees the object memory.

5. **Clear the pointer by setting it to** 0.

TIP

If your delete statement is at the end of the application, you don't need to clear the pointer to 0 because the pointer is going out of scope. The pointer won't exist any longer, so setting it to 0 isn't essential, but it's good practice because you get into the habit of doing it in places where clearing the pointer to 0 would be important.

Using classes and smart pointers

If you're working with C++ 17 or above, you probably want to use smart pointers with your objects, rather than the labor-intensive and error-prone raw pointers. The SmartPtr example, shown in Listing 1-7, shows the same process as Listing 1-6 but uses smart pointers instead. You still need to add Pen.cpp and Pen.h from PenClass2.

LISTING 1-7: **Managing an Object's Life Using Smart Pointers**

```cpp
#include <iostream>
#include <memory>
#include "../PenClass2/Pen.h"

using namespace std;

int main() {
  unique_ptr<Pen> MyPen;
  MyPen.reset(new Pen());
  MyPen->InkColor = red;
  cout << MyPen->InkColor << endl;
  MyPen.reset();
  return 0;
}
```

REMEMBER

You wouldn't ordinarily assign an object to a unique_ptr as a separate step, but this example shows you how by using reset(). In this case, you actually reset MyPen to point to a new object, new Pen(), which must include the opening and closing parentheses. If you were to do this in an application, reset() would take care of freeing any old object before pointing MyPen to any new object. The "Creating smart pointers using std::unique_ptr and std::shared_ptr" section of Book 1, Chapter 8 shows the standard approach to creating smart pointers.

Notice that you still use the arrow operator to assign the color red to MyPen->InkColor and to retrieve the value later. This part of the code appears the same as when using a raw pointer. The final step is to free the object memory using reset(). The pointer will automatically delete itself, saving you a line of code in this example.

Passing objects to functions

When you write a function, normally you base your decision about using pointers on whether or not you want to change the original variables passed into the function. Suppose you have a function called AddOne(), and it takes an integer as a parameter. If you want to modify the original variable, you can use a pointer (or you can use a reference). If you don't want to modify the variable, just pass the variable *by value*.

The following prototype represents a function that can modify the variable passed into it:

```
void AddOne(int *number);
```

And this prototype represents a function that cannot modify the variable passed into it:

```
void AddOne(int number);
```

With objects, you can do something similar. For example, this function takes a pointer to an object and can, therefore, modify the object:

```
void FixFlatTire(Car *mycar);
```

This version doesn't allow modification of the original object:

```
void FixFlatTire(Car mycar);
```

However, unlike a primitive type, the function gets its own instance. In other words, every time you call this function, it creates an entirely new instance of class Car. This instance would be a duplicate copy of the myCar object that is an instance of class Car — it wouldn't be the same instance.

When you work with objects, a complete copy is not always a sure thing. The original object may have properties that are pointers to other objects, but the object copy may not get copies of those pointers. The properties that contain pointers may end up blank (due to a lack of proper copying technique), point to the same values as the original (a shallow copy), or point to new variables (a deep copy). The difference is the kind of copy that the object provides:

>> **Shallow:** C++ copies the object and its property values precisely as provided in the original object. If the original object doesn't rely on any sort of dynamic memory allocation, as is the case when working the primitives, the copy will work precisely as planned.

>> **Deep:** C++ not only copies the original object, but also allocates memory for any objects pointed to by the original object. So, the copy not only copies the original object, but any objects pointed to by that object. The two copies are completely separate.

TECHNICAL STUFF

A problem occurs when any of the subsidiary objects also have pointers to other objects. Now you have an entirely new level of objects to worry about. The topic of shallow and deep copying can become incredibly complex. If you want to know more, check out the article at https://www.learncpp.com/cpp-tutorial/915-shallow-vs-deep-copying/.

TIP

The smart move with objects is to always pass objects as pointers. Don't pass objects directly into functions. Yes, it risks bad code changing the object, but careful C++ programmers want the actual object, not a copy. Having access to the original outweighs the risk of an accidental change. This chapter explains how to prevent accidental changes by using the const parameters in the next section.

Because your function receives its objects as pointers, you continue accessing them by using the arrow operator. For example, the function FixFlatTire() may do this:

```
void FixFlatTire(Car *mycar) {
  mycar->RemoveTire();
  mycar->AddNewTire();
}
```

Or, if you prefer references, you would do this:

```
void FixFlatTire2(Car &mycar) {
  mycar.RemoveTire();
  mycar.AddNewTire();
}
```

Remember that pointers contain the address of an object, while a reference is simply another name (alias) for an object. Even though the reference is still an address, it's the actual address of the object, rather than a pointer to the object. (Book 1, Chapter 8 discusses pointers in more detail.) In this code, because you're dealing with a reference, you access the object's members using the dot operator (.) rather than the arrow operator (->).

TIP

Another reason to use only pointers and references as parameters for objects is that a function that takes an object as a parameter usually wants to change the object. Such changes require pointers or references.

Using const parameters in functions

A *constant* is a variable or object that another function can't change even when you pass a reference to it to another function. To define a variable or an object as constant, unchangeable, you use the const keyword. For example, to define a variable as constant, you use:

```
const int MyInt = 3;
```

If someone were to come along and try to use this code:

```
MyInt = 4;
```

The compiler would display an error message saying, error: assignment of read-only variable 'MyInt'. The same holds true for a function using a const primitive like this one:

```
void DisplayInt(const int Value) {
  cout << Value << endl;
}
```

It's possible to display Value or interact with it in other ways, but trying to change Value will raise an error. This version will raise an error because Value is being changed:

```
void DisplayInt(const int Value) {
  Value += 1;
  cout << Value << endl;
}
```

The const keyword is useful when working with objects because you generally don't want to pass an object directly. That involves copying the object, which is messy. Instead, you normally pass by using a pointer or reference, which would allow you to change the object. If you put the word const before the parameter, the compiler won't allow you to change the parameter. The PenClass4 example that appears in Listing 1-8 has const inserted before the parameter. The function can look at the object but can't change it.

```
#include <iostream>
#include "../PenClass2/Pen.h"

using namespace std;

void Inspect(const Pen *Checkitout) {
  cout << Checkitout->Brand << endl;
}

int main() {
  Pen *MyPen = new Pen();
  MyPen->Brand = "Spy Plus Camera";
  Inspect(MyPen);
  return 0;
}
```

Now suppose that you tried to change the object in the Inspect function. You may have put a line in that function like this:

```
Checkitout->Length = 10.0;
```

If you try this, the compiler issues an error. In Code::Blocks, you get: error: assignment of member 'Pen::Length' in read-only object.

REMEMBER

If you have multiple parameters, you can mix const and non-const. If you go overboard, this can be confusing. The following line shows two parameters that are const and another that is not. The function can modify only the members of the object called one.

```
void Inspect(const Pen *Checkitout, Spy *one,
             const Spy *two);
```

Using the this pointer

Consider a function called OneMoreCheeseGone(). It's not a method, but it takes an object of instance Cheese as a parameter. Its prototype looks like this:

```
void OneMoreCheeseGone(Cheese *Block);
```

This is just a simple function with no return type. It takes an object pointer as a parameter. For example, after you eat a block of cheese, you can call:

```
OneMoreCheeseGone(MyBlock);
```

Now consider this: If you have an object on the heap, it has no name. You access it through a pointer variable that points to it. But what if the code is currently executing inside a method of an object? How do you refer to the object itself?

C++ has a secret variable that exists inside every method: this. It's a pointer variable. The this variable always points to the current object. So if code execution is occurring inside a method and you want to call OneMoreCheeseGone(), passing in the current object (or block of cheese), you would pass this.

The following sections discuss what you might call the standard use of this, the version of this that exists in most code now. Once you understand the standard use of this, you move on to modifications to this that occur in C++ 20. Like most pointer usage in C++ 20, this has undergone changes to make it safer, smarter, and easier.

Defining standard this pointer usage

This section tells you how this is used for application development in most applications today. The CheeseClass example, shown in Listing 1-9, demonstrates this.

LISTING 1-9: **Passing an Object from Inside Its Methods by Using the this Variable**

```
#include <iostream>

using namespace std;

class Cheese {
public:
  string status;
  void eat();
  void rot();
};

int CheeseCount;

void OneMoreCheeseGone(Cheese *Block) {
  CheeseCount--;
```

(continued)

LISTING 1-9: *(continued)*

```
  Block->status = "Gone";
};

void Cheese::eat() {
  cout << "Eaten up! Yummy" << endl;
  OneMoreCheeseGone(this);
}

void Cheese::rot() {
  cout << "Rotted away! Yuck" << endl;
  OneMoreCheeseGone(this);
}

int main() {
    Cheese *asiago = new Cheese();
    Cheese *limburger = new Cheese();

    CheeseCount = 2;
    asiago->eat();
    limburger->rot();

    cout << endl;
    cout << "Cheese count: " << CheeseCount << endl;
    cout << "asiago: " << asiago->status << endl;
    cout << "limburger: " << limburger->status << endl;
    return 0;
}
```

The this listing has four main parts. First is the definition for the class called Cheese. The class contains a couple of methods.

Next is the function OneMoreCheeseGone() along with a global variable that it modifies. This function subtracts one from the global variable and stores a string in a property, status, of the object passed to it.

Next come the actual methods for class Cheese. (You must put these functions after OneMoreCheeseGone() because they call it. If you use a function prototype as a forward reference for OneMoreCheeseGone(), the order doesn't matter.)

Finally, main() creates two new instances of Cheese. Then it sets the global variable to 2, which keeps track of the number of blocks left. Next, it calls the eat()

function for the asiago cheese and rot() for the limburger cheese. And then it prints the results of everything that happened: It displays the Cheese count, and it displays the status of each object.

When you run the application in Listing 1-9, you see this output:

```
Eaten up! Yummy
Rotted away! Yuck

Cheese count: 0
asiago: Gone
limburger: Gone
```

The first line is the result of calling asiago->eat(), which prints one message. The second line is the result of calling limburger->rot(), which prints another message. The third line is simply the value in the variable CheeseCount. This variable was *decremented* once each time the computer called OneMoreCheeseGone(). Because the function was called twice, CheeseCount went from 2 to 1 to 0. The final two lines show the contents of the status variable in the two objects. (One-MoreCheeseGone() stores "Gone" in these variables.)

Take a careful look at the OneMoreCheeseGone() function. It operates on the current object provided as a parameter by setting its status variable to the string Gone. The eat() method calls it, passing the current object using this. The rot() method also calls it, again passing the current object via this.

Changes to the this pointer in C++ 20

Unless you're actually working with C++ 20 at a somewhat detailed level, you can probably skip this section and not really lose much. Of course, you may just be curious and learning something new is always a good thing.

C++ 20 brings a few changes to the this pointer with it. Even though you don't see anything about functional programming until Book 3, it's important to know that like the examples in this chapter, you can use the this pointer in a lambda expression. A *lambda expression* is a mathematically based approach to dealing with certain kinds of programming problems that is concise and easier to understand than some standard C++ approaches. You can also pass a lambda expression, essentially a kind of function, to other functions as you would any other argument. The change of the use of the this pointer for lambda expressions is simply a clarification — you must now actually declare use of the this pointer before you're allowed to use it. You can get an overview of lambda expressions in the "Using Lambda Expressions for Implementation" section of Book 3 Chapter 1 and read about using lambda expressions in your code in Book 3 Chapter 2. The discussion at `http://www.open-std.org/jtc1/sc22/wg21/docs/papers/2018/p0806r2.html` will fill in some very technical details if you're interested.

It's important to note that the C++ definition of an object as described in this chapter differs from the definition used by some other languages. There is lengthy and involved discussion of the topic at `https://blog.panicsoftware.com/objects-their-lifetimes-and-pointers/`, but the point is that if you understand objects as described in this chapter, then you know how C++ developers view them. You may have noticed that there is a great deal of emphasis in this chapter on destroying objects by releasing their storage. The "Starting and Ending with Constructors and Destructors" section of this chapter discusses another technique, which is to call a destructor. However, until C++ 20, standard objects, such as `string`, don't have a destructor as such, the calling of it is a *no-op* (a no operation, nothing happens). Because the manner in which objects are destroyed is changing, so is the use of the `this` pointer, which relies on the existence of an object to work.

TECHNICAL STUFF

The `this` pointer can also come into play in situations that most people are unlikely to see unless they're performing advanced tasks. For example, you can use the `this` pointer to access initialized members of a partially constructed object—one that hasn't had every member fully initialized.

Overloading methods

You may want a method in a class to handle different types of parameters. For example, you might have a class called `Door` and a method called `GoThrough()`. You might want the `GoThrough()` method to take as parameters objects of class `Dog`, class `Human`, or class `Cat`. Depending on which class is entering, you might want to change the `GoThrough()` function's behavior.

A way to handle this is by *overloading* the `GoThrough()` function. C++ lets you design a class that has multiple methods that are all named the same. However, the parameters must differ between these methods. With the `GoThrough()` method, one version will take a `Human`, another a `Dog`, and another a `Cat`.

View the code for the `DoorClass` example in Listing 1-10 and notice the `GoThrough()` methods. There are three of them. To use these methods, `main()` creates four different objects — a cat, a dog, a human, and a door. It then sends each creature through the door.

LISTING 1-10:

Overloading Functions in a Class

```cpp
#include <iostream>

using namespace std;

class Cat {
public:
  string name;
};

class Dog {
public:
  string name;
};

class Human {
public:
  string name;
};

class Door {
private:
  int HowManyInside;
public:
  void Start();
  void GoThrough(Cat *acat);
  void GoThrough(Dog *adog);
  void GoThrough(Human *ahuman);
};

void Door::Start() {
  HowManyInside = 0;
}

void Door::GoThrough(Cat *somebody) {
  cout << "Welcome, " << somebody->name << endl;
  cout << "A cat just entered!" << endl;
  HowManyInside++;
}

void Door::GoThrough(Dog *somebody) {
  cout << "Welcome, " << somebody->name << endl;
  cout << "A dog just entered!" << endl;
```

(continued)

LISTING 1-10:   *(continued)*

```cpp
      HowManyInside++;
}

void Door::GoThrough(Human *somebody) {
   cout << "Welcome, " << somebody->name << endl;
   cout << "A human just entered!" << endl;
   HowManyInside++;
}

int main() {
   Door entrance;
   entrance.Start();

   Cat *SneekyGirl = new Cat;
   SneekyGirl->name = "Sneeky Girl";
   Dog *LittleGeorge = new Dog;
   LittleGeorge->name = "Little George";
   Human *me = new Human;
   me->name = "John";

   entrance.GoThrough(SneekyGirl);
   entrance.GoThrough(LittleGeorge);
   entrance.GoThrough(me);

   delete SneekyGirl;
   delete LittleGeorge;
   delete me;
   return 0;
}
```

The application allows dogs and cats to enter like humans. The beginning of this application declares three classes, Cat, Dog, and Human, each with a name member. Next is the Door class. A private member, HowManyInside, tracks how many beings have entered. The Start() function activates the door. Finally, the class contains the overloaded functions. They all have the same name and the same return type. You can have different return types, but for the compiler to recognize the functions as unique, they must differ by parameters. These do; one takes a Cat pointer; one takes a Dog pointer; and one takes a Human pointer.

Next is the code for the methods. The first function, Start() sets HowManyInside to 0. The next three functions are overloaded. They do similar things, but they write slightly different messages. Each takes a different type.

The first step in main() is to create a Door instance. The code doesn't use a pointer to show that you can mix pointers with stack variables in an application. After creating the Door instance, the code calls Start(). Next, the code creates three creature instances: Cat, Dog, and Human, and sets the name property for each.

The calls to the entrance.GoThrough() method passes a Cat, a Dog, and a Human (all in order). Because you can see the Door class, you know the code calls three different methods that are all named the same. But when *using* the class, you consider them one method that accepts a Cat, a Dog, or a Human. That's the goal of overloading: to create what feels like *versions* of the one function. Here's what you see when you run this application:

```
Welcome, Sneeky Girl
A cat just entered!
Welcome, Little George
A dog just entered!
Welcome, John
A human just entered!
```

Starting and Ending with Constructors and Destructors

You can add two special methods to your class that let you provide special startup and shutdown functionality: a *constructor* and a *destructor.* The following sections provide details about these methods.

Starting with constructors

When you create a new instance of a class, you may want to do some basic object setup. Suppose you have a class called Apartment, with a private property called NumberOfOccupants and a method called ComeOnIn(). The code for ComeOnIn() adds 1 to NumberOfOccupants.

When you create a new instance of Apartment, you probably want to start NumberOfOccupants at 0. The best way to do this is by adding a special method, a *constructor,* to your class. This method has a line of code such as

```
NumberOfOccupants = 0;
```

Whenever you create a new instance of the class Apartment, the computer first calls this constructor for your new object, thereby setting NumberOfOccupants to 0. Think of the constructor as an *initialization function:* The computer calls it when you create a new object.

To write a constructor, you add it as another method to your class, and make it public. You name the constructor the same as your class. For the class Apartment, you name the constructor Apartment(). The constructor has no return type, not even void. You can have parameters in a constructor; see "Adding parameters to constructors," later in this chapter. Listing 1-11, later in this section, shows a sample constructor along with a *destructor,* which is covered in the next section.

Ending with destructors

When you delete an instance of a class, you might want some *cleanup* code to straighten things out before the object memory is released. For example, your object may have properties that are pointers to other objects. It's essential to delete those other objects. You put cleanup code in a special function called a destructor. A *destructor* is a finalization function that the computer calls before it deletes your object.

The destructor function gets the same name as the class, except it has a tilde, ~, at the beginning of it. (The tilde is usually in the upper-left corner of the keyboard.) For a class called Squirrel, the destructor would be ~Squirrel(). The destructor doesn't have a return type, not even void, because you can't return anything from a destructor (the object is gone, after all). You just start with the function name and no parameters. The next section, "Sampling constructors and destructors," shows an example that uses both constructors and destructors.

TIP

Constructors and destructors are a way of life for C++ programmers. Nearly every class has a constructor, and many also have a destructor.

Sampling constructors and destructors

The WalnutClass example, shown in Listing 1-11, uses a constructor and destructor. This application involves two classes, the main one called Squirrel that demonstrates the constructor and destructor, and one called Walnut, which is used by the Squirrel class.

LISTING 1-11: **Initializing and Finalizing with Constructors and Destructors**

```cpp
#include <iostream>

using namespace std;

class Walnut {
public:
  int Size;
};

class Squirrel {
private:
  Walnut *MyDinner;
public:
  Squirrel();
  ~Squirrel();
};

Squirrel::Squirrel() {
  cout << "Starting!" << endl;
  MyDinner = new Walnut;
  MyDinner->Size = 30;
}

Squirrel::~Squirrel() {
  cout << "Cleaning up my mess!" << endl;
  delete MyDinner;
}

int main() {
  Squirrel *Sam = new Squirrel;
  Squirrel *Sally = new Squirrel;

  delete Sam;
  delete Sally;
  return 0;
}
```

The Squirrel class has a property called MyDinner that is a pointer to a Walnut instance. The Squirrel constructor creates an instance of Walnut and stores it in MyDinner. The destructor deletes the instance of Walnut. In main(), the code creates two instances of Squirrel. Each instance gets its own Walnut to eat.

Each Squirrel creates its Walnut when it starts and deletes the Walnut when the Squirrel is deleted.

Notice in this code that the constructor has the same name as the class, Squirrel(). The destructor also has the same name, but with a tilde, ~, tacked on to the beginning of it. Thus, the constructor is Squirrel() and the destructor is ~Squirrel(). Destructors never take parameters and you can't call them directly, but the runtime calls them automatically when it's time to destroy an object.

When you run this application, you can see the following lines, which were spit up by the Squirrel in its constructor and destructor. (You see two lines of each because main() creates two squirrels.)

```
Starting!
Starting!
Cleaning up my mess!
Cleaning up my mess!
```

If the Walnut class also had a constructor and destructor, and you made the MyDinner property a variable in the Squirrel class, rather than a pointer, the computer would create the Walnut instance after it creates the Squirrel instance, but before it calls the Squirrel() constructor. It then deletes the Walnut instance when it deletes the Squirrel instance, after calling the ~Squirrel() destructor. The code performs these steps for each instance of Squirrel.

CONSTRUCTORS AND DESTRUCTORS WITH STACK VARIABLES

Listing 1-11 creates two Squirrels on the heap by using pointers and calling

```
Squirrel *Sam = new Squirrel;
Squirrel *Sally = new Squirrel;
```

But you could also create them on the stack by declaring them without pointers:

```
Squirrel Sam;
Squirrel Sally;
```

If you do this, the application will run fine, provided that you remove the delete lines. You do not delete stack variables. The computer calls the destructor when the main() function *ends*. That's the general rule with objects on the stack: They are created when you declare them, and they stay until the function ends.

Adding parameters to constructors

Like other methods, constructors allow you to include parameters. When you do, you can use these parameters in the initialization process. To use them, you list the arguments inside parentheses when you create the object. Because constructors have parameters, you can create multiple overloaded constructors for a class by varying the number and type of parameters.

TECHNICAL STUFF

Although int has a constructor, it isn't a class. However, the *runtime library* (that big mass of code that gets put in with your application by the linker) includes a constructor and destructor that you can use when calling new for an integer.

Suppose that you want the Squirrel class to have a name property. Although you could create an instance of Squirrel and then set its name property, you can specify the name directly by using a constructor. The constructor's prototype looks like this:

```
Squirrel(string StartName);
```

Then, you create a new instance like so:

```
Squirrel *Sam = new Squirrel("Sam");
```

The constructor is expecting a string, so you pass a string when you create the object.

The SquirrelClass example, shown in Listing 1-12, presents an application that includes all the basic elements of a class with a constructor that accepts parameters.

LISTING 1-12: **Placing Parameters in Constructors**

```
#include <iostream>

using namespace std;

class Squirrel {
private:
    string Name;
public:
    Squirrel(string StartName);
```

(continued)

LISTING 1-12: *(continued)*

```
      void WhatIsMyName();
};

Squirrel::Squirrel(string StartName) {
    cout << "Starting!" << endl;
    Name = StartName;
}

void Squirrel::WhatIsMyName() {
    cout << "My name is " << Name << endl;
}

int main()
{
    Squirrel *Sam = new Squirrel("Sam");
    Squirrel *Sally = new Squirrel("Sally");

    Sam->WhatIsMyName();
    Sally->WhatIsMyName();

    delete Sam;
    delete Sally;
    return 0;
}
```

In main(), you pass a string into the constructors. The constructor code takes the StartName parameter and copies it to the Name property. The WhatIsMyName() method writes Name to the console.

Building Hierarchies of Classes

When you start going crazy describing classes, you usually discover *hierarchies* of classes. For example, you have a class Vehicle that you want to divide into classes: Car, PickupTruck, TractorTrailer, and SUV. The Car class is further divided into the StationWagon, FourDoorSedan, and TwoDoorHatchback classes.

Or you could divide Vehicle into car brands, such as Ford, Honda, and Toyota. Then you could divide the class Toyota into models, such as Prius, Avalon, Camry, and Corolla. You can create similar groupings of objects for the other class hierarchies; your decision depends on how you categorize things and how the hierarchy is used. In the hierarchy, class Vehicle is at the top. This class has properties you find in every brand or model of vehicle. For example, all vehicles have wheels. How many they have varies, but it doesn't matter at this point, because classes don't have specific values for the properties.

Each brand has certain characteristics that might be unique to it, but each has all the characteristics of class Vehicle. That's called *inheritance.* The class Toyota, for example, has all the properties found in Vehicle. And the class Prius has all the properties found in Toyota, which includes those inherited from Vehicle.

Creating a hierarchy in C++

In C++, you can create a hierarchy of classes. When you take one class and create a new one under it, such as creating Toyota from Vehicle, you are *deriving* a new class, which means Toyota is a *child* of Vehicle in the hierarchy.

To derive a class from an existing class, you write the new class as you would any other class, but you extend the header after the class name with a colon, :, the word public, and then the class you're deriving from, as in the following class header line:

```
class Toyota : public Vehicle {
```

When you do so, the class you create (Toyota) *inherits* the properties and methods from the *parent* class (Vehicle). For example, if Vehicle has a public property called NumberOfWheels and a public method called Drive(), the class Toyota has these members, although you didn't write the members in Toyota.

The VehicleClass example, shown in Listing 1-13, demonstrates class inheritance. It starts with a class called Vehicle, and a derived class called Toyota. You create an instance of Toyota in main() and call two methods for the instance, MeAndMyToyota() and Drive(). The definition of the Toyota class doesn't show a Drive() function. The Drive() function is inherited from the Vehicle class. You can call this function like a member of the Toyota class because in many ways it *is.*

LISTING 1-13: **Deriving One Class from Another**

```cpp
#include <iostream>

using namespace std;

class Vehicle {
public:
  int NumberOfWheels;

  void Drive() {
    cout << "Driving, driving, driving..." << endl;
  }
};

class Toyota : public Vehicle {
public:
  void MeAndMyToyota() {
    cout << "Just me and my Toyota!" << endl;
  }
};

int main() {
  Toyota MyCar;
  MyCar.MeAndMyToyota();
  MyCar.Drive();
  return 0;
}
```

When you run this application, you see the output from two functions:

```
Just me and my Toyota!
Driving, driving, driving...
```

Understanding types of inheritance

When you create a class, its methods can access both public and private properties and methods. Users of the class can access only the public properties and methods. When you derive a new class, it *cannot* access the private members in the parent class. Private members are reserved for a class itself and not for any derived class. When members need to be accessible by derived classes, there's a specification you can use beyond public and private: *protected.*

REMEMBER

Protected members and private members work the same way from a user perspective, but derived classes can access both protected and public members. Private members are hidden from both users and derived classes. Always use protected members when possible when you plan to derive classes from a parent class.

Creating and Using Object Aliases

An *alias* is another name for something. If your name is Robert, someone could use an alias of Bob when calling your name. Both Robert and Bob point to the same person — you. However, the names are actually different. One is your real name, Robert, and the other is your alias, Bob. In real life, using aliases can make things easier: saying Bob is definitely easier than saying Robert (although not by much). Using aliases in C++ applications can make things easier, too.

REMEMBER

One of the most common reasons to use an alias in C++ is to change the manner in which an object is accessed. Moving a pointer to an object is always going to be easier than moving the object itself because a pointer is simply a number that specifies the address of the object. The object could contain complex data and pointers to yet other objects. Moving objects is complicated and messy, so developers try to avoid it at all cost.

However, sending a pointer to someone gives the recipient access to the original data. The recipient could modify the data in ways that you don't want. So, you could create an alias of the original object that is a constant. No one can modify a constant. The ObjectAlias example, shown in Listing 1-14, demonstrates how to create a constant alias of a string object. The same technique works with any other sort of object you might want to work with.

LISTING 1-14: **Creating an Object Alias**

```
#include <iostream>

using namespace std;

int main() {
  string OriginalString = "Hello";
  const string &StringCopy(OriginalString);
  OriginalString = "Goodbye";
  cout << OriginalString << endl;
  cout << StringCopy << endl;
  return 0;
}
```

The code begins by creating a string named OriginalString that contains a value of Hello. It then creates a const string alias of OriginalString named StringCopy. When the code changes the value of OriginalString, the value of StringCopy is also changed because StringCopy points to the same location in memory. So when you run this example, you see output of

```
Goodbye
Goodbye
```

It may not seem like you've accomplished anything, but if you try to modify the value of StringCopy, Code::Blocks outputs an error message like this:

```
error: passing 'const string {aka const
std::basic_string<char>}' as 'this' argument of
'std::basic_string<_CharT, _Traits, _Alloc>&
std::basic_string<_CharT, _Traits,
_Alloc>::operator=(const _CharT*) [with _CharT = char;
_Traits = std::char_traits<char>; _Alloc =
std::allocator<char>; std::basic_string<_CharT, _Traits,
_Alloc> = std::basic_string<char>]' discards qualifiers
[-fpermissive]|
```

The point is that you can't modify the value of StringCopy, but you can modify the value of OriginalString. Sending StringCopy to someone who needs access to the value is safe. Just to ensure that you understand what is happening, try making StringCopy a standard string rather than a const string. You'll be able to modify the value, and the modification will now affect OriginalString as well. StringCopy truly is an alias of OriginalString, but as a const string, it's an alias that prevents modification of the underlying string value.

Chapter **2**

Using Advanced C++ Features

his chapter will amaze you because C++ has amazing advanced features. It begins by helping you understand how to leave notes for yourself so that you don't embarrass yourself in front of your boss when you forget how your code works. Comments can do a lot more, but for the most part, they're there to help you remember.

The next sections are all about helping your code jump through new hoops. You discover that you can turn an `int` into a `string`, connect with the user at the command line, and tell the compiler to do something new with your code as part of a preprocessor directive. In case that isn't enough, you also find out new ways to create variables using constants, enums, and random numbers.

The final sections are about working with code using switches so that you don't have to keep creating huge `if...else if` statement chains. You also gain knowledge of the humble array, which will make your life considerably easier in so many ways that space doesn't allow total disclosure. Suffice it to say that storing lists of data elements in a convenient form is just the start.

Filling Your Code with Comments

Your boss is irritable because that rush job you did was a little too rushed and now the application keeps crashing. So, you have your boss standing there, right behind you, wanting you to explain your code, except that you can't. Your nervousness makes all the code look like a jumble of alien words that you swear you didn't write, even though you know you did. Why can't you remember? At this point, you'd just love to go somewhere and hide for a while, but the boss is smoking mad and you'll never make your escape. You can avoid this situation and many others in which your memory about your code is apt to fail. To remember what your code does, you put comments into it. A *comment* is simply some words in the code that the compiler ignores and include for the benefit of the humans reading the code. Comments are also quite useful for colleagues who come by to help you out of jams, or to allow someone to fix your code over the weekend when you'd much rather spend time at the beach. Comments are essential to good coding. For example, you may have some code like this:

```
total = 10;
for (i = 0; i < 10; i++)
{
    total = (total + i) * 3;
}
```

But this code may not be clear to you if you put it away for six months and come back later to look at it. So instead, you can add some comments. You denote a comment in C++ by starting a line with two slashes, like this:

```
// Initialize total to the number
// of items involved.
total = 10;

// Calculate total for the
// first ten sets.
for (i = 0; i < 10; i++)
{
    total = (total + i) * 3;
}
```

Now anyone working on the project can understand what the code does. Note the white space between the groups of code. Using white space helps someone looking at the code see where one thought ends and another begins. You should always include white space in your code so that everyone can read the code more easily. Of course, you could put in comments like this:

```
// My salary is too low
// I want a raise
total = 10;

// Someday they'll recognize
// my superior talents!
for (i = 0; i < 10; i++)
{
    total = (total + i) * 3;
}
```

However, comments like this don't have much use in the code; besides, they may have the reverse effect from the one you're hoping for! The compiler ignores comments; they're meant for other humans. You can write whatever you want as comments, and the compiler pretends that it's not even there.

TIP

A comment begins with //, and it can begin anywhere on the line. In fact, contrary to what you might think, you can even put comments at the end of a line containing C++ code, instead of on a separate line. Using comments on a code line lets you focus a comment on just that line, as follows:

```
int subtotal = 10;  // Initialize subtotal to 10.
```

This comment gives a little more explanation of what the line does. You usually use line comments like this when you want to tell others what kind of information a variable holds or explain a complex task. Normally, you explain blocks of code as shown earlier in this section.

TIP

You can use two kinds of comments in C++. One is the double slash (as already described). The other kind of comment begins with a slash-asterisk, /*, and ends with an asterisk-slash, */. The comments go between these *delimiters* (special character sequences) and can span several lines, as in the following example:

```
/* This application separates the parts of the
   sandwich into its separate parts. This
   process is often called "separation of
   parts".
   (c) 2020 Sandwich Parts Separators, Inc.
*/
```

This is all one comment, and it spans multiple lines. You normally use this kind of comment to provide an overview of a task or describe the purpose of a function. This kind of comment also works well for the informational headings that some large company applications require. As with other comments, you can put these anywhere in your code, as long as you don't break a string or word in two by putting a comment in the middle. Much of the code in the remainder of this chapter has comments in it so that you can see how to use comments and so that you can get a few more ideas about how the code works.

Some beginning programmers get the mistaken idea that comments appear in the application window when the application runs. That is not the case. A comment does not write anything to the console. To write things to the console, use cout.

Converting Types

Sometimes, you just don't have the type of things you want. You might want to trade in your 2014 Ford Taurus for that brand-new Porsche. But, needless to say, unless you have plenty of money, that might be difficult.

But converting between different types in C++ — now, *that's* a lot easier. For example, you may have a string variable called digits, and it holds the string "123". Further, you want to somehow get the numbers inside that string into an integer variable called amount. Thus, you want amount to hold the value 123; that is, you want to convert the string to a number.

Understanding how int and string conversions work

In Listing 2-1, later in this chapter, you see how you can convert between numbers and strings. Book 1, Chapter 8 shows some sample code for converting a number to a string. This example employs that same technique along with a similar technique for converting a string back to a number.

Converting strings is an interesting concept in C++ because an outstanding feature lets you *write to* and *read from* a string just as you would to and from a console. For example, although you can write a number 12 out to a console by using code like this:

```
cout << 12;
```

you can actually do the same thing with strings: You can write a number 12 to a string, as in

```
mystring << 12;
```

After this line runs, `mystring` contains the value `"12"`. However, to do this, you need to use a special form of string called a `stringstream`. In the never-ending world of computer terminology, a *stream* is something that you can write to and read from in a flowing fashion (think about bits flowing through a wire — much as a stream flows along a waterbed). For example, you might write the word `"hello"` to a `stringstream`, and then the number `87`, and then the word `"goodbye"`. After those three operations, the string contains the value `"hello87goodbye"`.

Similarly, you can read from a stream. In the section "Reading from the Console," later in this chapter, you discover how you can read from a console by using the › notation. When you read from the console, although your application stops and waits for the user to enter something, the real stream technology takes place *after* the user types something and presses Enter: After the console has a series of characters, your application reads in the characters as a stream, one character after another. You can read a string, and then a series of numbers, and another string, and so on.

With `stringstream`, you can do something similar. You would fill the string with something rather than have the user fill it, as in the case of a console. From there, you can begin to read from the string, placing the values into variables of different types. One of these types is `int`. But because the `stringstream` is, at heart, just a string, that's how you convert a string of digits to an integer: You put the digit characters in the string and read the string as a stream into your integer.

The only catch to using these techniques is that you need to know in advance which kind of streaming you want to do. If you want to write to the `stringstream`, you create an instance of a class called `ostringstream`. (The *o* is for *output*.) If you want to read from a `stringstream`, you create an instance of a class called `istringstream`. (The *i* is for *input*.)

Seeing int and string conversions in action

The `TypeConvert` example, shown in Listing 2-1, demonstrates several kinds of `int` and string conversions that include *truncating* (lopping the decimal portion off) and *rounding* (bringing the number value up or down to the nearest whole number). The listing also includes two handy functions that you may want to save for your own programming experience later. One is called `StringToNumber()` (converts a string to a number) and the other is called `NumberToString()` (converts a number to a string). This example includes plenty of comments as well as demonstrates some extremely simple onscreen formatting using the tab (`\t`) escape character (see the "Tabbing your output" section of Book 1, Chapter 3 for details).

LISTING 2-1: **Converting Between Types Is Easy**

```cpp
#include <iostream>
#include <sstream>   // for istringstream, ostringstream

using namespace std;

int StringToNumber(string MyString) {
  // Converts from string to number.
  istringstream converter(MyString);
  // Contains the operation results.
  int result;

  // Perform the conversion and return the results.
  converter >> result;
  return result;
}

string NumberToString(int Number) {
   // Converts from number to string.
  ostringstream converter;

  // Perform the conversion and return the results.
  converter << Number;
  return converter.str();
}

int main() {
  // Contains the theoretical number of kids.
  float NumberOfKids;
  // Contains an actual number of kids.
  int ActualKids;

  /* You can theoretically have 2.5 kids, but in the
     real world, you can't. Convert the theoretical number
     of kids to a real number by truncating NumberOfKids
     and display the results. */
  NumberOfKids = 2.5;
  ActualKids = (int)NumberOfKids;
  cout << "Float to Integer" << "\tTruncated" << endl;
  cout << NumberOfKids << "\t\t\t" << ActualKids << endl;

  // Perform the same task as before, but use a
  // theoretical 2.1 kids this time.
```

```
NumberOfKids = 2.1;
ActualKids = (int)NumberOfKids;
cout << NumberOfKids << "\t\t\t" << ActualKids << endl;

// This time we'll use 2.9 kids.
NumberOfKids = 2.9;
ActualKids = (int)NumberOfKids;
cout<<NumberOfKids<<"\t\t\t"<<ActualKids<<endl<<endl;

// This process rounds the number, instead of
// truncating it. We do it using the same three
// numbers as before.
NumberOfKids = 2.5;
ActualKids = (int)(NumberOfKids + .5);
cout << "Float to Integer" << "\tRounded" << endl;
cout << NumberOfKids << "\t\t\t" << ActualKids << endl;

// Do it again using 2.1 kids.
NumberOfKids = 2.1;
ActualKids = (int)(NumberOfKids + .5);
cout << NumberOfKids << "\t\t\t" << ActualKids << endl;

// Do it yet again using 2.9 kids.
NumberOfKids = 2.9;
ActualKids = (int)(NumberOfKids + .5);
cout<<NumberOfKids<<"\t\t\t"<<ActualKids<<endl<<endl;

// In this case, use the StringToNumber() function to
// perform the conversion.
cout << "String to number" << endl;
int x = StringToNumber("12345") * 50;
cout << x << endl << endl;

// In this case, use the NumberToString() function to
// perform the conversion.
cout << "Number to string" << endl;
string mystring = NumberToString(80525323);
cout << mystring << endl;
return 0;
}
```

REMEMBER

The comments in Listing 2-1 give you a complete dialogue of how the code works, so no discussion of it here is needed. Of course, you do want to see the output, which appears in Figure 2-1. The important thing to remember is that rounding is different from truncating in the results that it produces, and each method is appropriate at specific times depending on the rules you want to use. For example, when calculating, in whole dollars, how much someone owes you, you don't want to rely on truncating or you'll end up with less money.

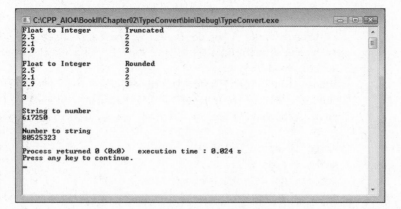

FIGURE 2-1:
The formatted output shows the difference between truncating and rounding.

Considering other conversion issues

Another kind of conversion that's useful is converting floating-point numbers (that is, numbers with a decimal point) and integers and vice versa. In C++, this conversion is easy: You just copy one to the other, and C++ takes care of the rest.

The only catch is that when C++ converts from a float to an integer, it always *truncates.* That is, it doesn't round up: When it converts 5.99 to an integer, it doesn't go up to 6; it goes *down* to 5. But there's an easy trick around that: Add 0.5 to the number before you convert it. If the number is in the upper half (that is, from 0.5 to 0.9999 and so on), then adding 0.5 first takes the number above or equal to the upper whole number. Then, when the function rounds the number, the number rounds *down* to the *upper* whole number. For example, if you start with 4.6, just converting it outputs 4. But if you add 0.5, the 4.6 becomes 5.1, and then when you convert that, you get 5. It works!

Going in the other direction is even easier: To convert an integer to a float, you just copy it. If i is an integer and f is a float, you just set it as follows to convert it:

```
f = i;
```

REMEMBER

Whenever you convert from a float to an int or from an int to float, you must tell the compiler that you know what you're doing by adding (int) or (float) in front of the variable. Adding these keywords is called *coercion* or *type conversion*. The act of coercing one type to another is called *casting.* For example, the following line tells the compiler that you know you're converting from a float to an int:

```
ActualKids = (int)NumberOfKids;
```

If you leave out the (int) part, the compiler normally displays a warning like this one:

```
warning: converting to 'int' from 'float'
```

Using the proper coercion code is important because it also tells other developers that you really do intend to perform the type conversion. Otherwise, other developers will point to that area of your code and deem it the source of an error, when it might not be the true source. Using proper coding techniques saves everyone time.

Reading from the Console

Throughout this book, you have used the console to see example output. You can also use the console to get information from the user — a topic briefly mentioned in the "Reading from the Console" section of Book 1, Chapter 4. To use the console to get information from the user, instead of using the usual << with cout to write to the console, you use the >> operator along with cin (pronounced "see-in").

In the old days of the C programming language, reading data from the console and placing it in variables was somewhat nightmarish because it required you to use pointers. In C++, that's no longer the case. If you want to read a set of characters into a string called MyName, you just type

```
cin >> MyName;
```

That's it! The application pauses, and the user can type something at the console. When the user presses Enter, the string the user typed goes into the MyName string.

WARNING

Reading from the console has some catches. First, the console uses spaces as delimiters. That means that if you put spaces in what you type, only the letters up to the space are put into the string. Anything after the space, the console saves for the next time your application calls cin. That situation can be confusing. Second, if you want to read into a number, the user can type any characters, not just numbers. The computer then goes through a bizarre process that converts any letters into a meaningless number. Not good.

The ReadConsoleData example, shown in Listing 2-2, shows you how to read a string and then a number from the console. Next, it shows you how you can force the user to type only numbers. And finally, it shows how you can ask for a password with only asterisks appearing when the user types.

To make these last two tasks work correctly you use the conio library. This library gives you better access to the console, bypassing cin. This example also uses the StringToNumber() function, described in the "Seeing int and string conversions in action" section, earlier in this chapter.

LISTING 2-2: **Having the User Type Something**

```cpp
#include <iostream>
#include <sstream>
#include <conio.h>

using namespace std;

int StringToNumber(string MyString) {
  // Holds the string.
  istringstream converter(MyString);
  // Holds the integer result.
  int result;

  // Perform the conversion.
  converter >> result;
  return result;
}

string EnterOnlyNumbers() {
  string numAsString = ""; // Holds the numeric string.
  char ch = getch();       // Obtains a single character.

  // Keep requesting characters until the user presses
  // Enter.
  while (ch != '\r') {  // \r is the enter key
    // Add characters only if they are numbers.
    if (ch >= '0' && ch <= '9') {
      cout << ch;
```

```
      numAsString += ch;
    }

    // Get the next character from the user.
    ch = getch();
  }

  return numAsString;
}

string EnterPassword() {
  // Holds the password string.
  string numAsString = "";
  // Obtains a single character from the user.
  char ch = getch();

  // Keep requesting characters until the user presses
  // Enter.
  while (ch != '\r') { // \r is the enter key
    // Display an asterisk instead of the input character.
    cout << '*';
    // Add the character to the password string.
    numAsString += ch;
    // Get the next character from the user.
    ch = getch();
  }

  return numAsString;
}

int main() {
  // Just a basic name-entering
  string name;
  cout << "What is your name? ";
  cin >> name;
  cout << "Hello " << name << endl;

  // Now you are asked to enter a number,
  // but the computer allows you to enter anything!
  int x;
  cout << endl;
  cout << "Enter a number, any number! ";
```

(continued)

LISTING 2-2:   *(continued)*

```
cin >> x;
cout << "You chose " << x << endl;

// This time you can only enter a number.
cout << endl;
cout << "This time enter a number!" << endl;
cout << "Enter a number, any number! ";
string entered = EnterOnlyNumbers();
int num = StringToNumber(entered);
cout << endl << "You entered " << num << endl;

// Now enter a password!
cout << endl;
cout << "Enter your password! ";
string password = EnterPassword();
cout << endl << "Shhhh, it's " << password << endl;
return 0;
}
```

The first parts of main() are straightforward. It calls cin >> name; to read a string, name, from the console; then main() prints Hello plus name to the console. Next, main() calls cin >> x; to read and print an integer from the console.

Calling EnterOnlyNumbers() ensures that the user can enter only digits. The first thing EnterOnlyNumbers() does is declare a string called numAsString. When the user types a letter or number, it comes in as a character, so the code saves them one by one in a string variable (because a string is really a *character string*). To find out what the user types, EnterOnlyNumbers() calls getch(), which returns a single character. (For example, if the user presses Shift+A to produce a capital *A*, getch() returns the character A.)

TECHNICAL STUFF

AVOIDING GETCH() FUNCTION PROBLEMS

Some compilers complain if you use the getch() function. If you want to use it, try the _getch() function instead. Both functions perform the same task. Some vendors claim that _getch() is compliant with the International Standards Organization (ISO), but it isn't. The getch() and _getch() functions are useful, low-level library functions that you can use without hesitation, but they don't appear as part of any standard. The GNU GCC compiler, provided with Code::Blocks, can use either form of the function.

After retrieving a single character, EnterOnlyNumbers() starts a loop, watching for the '\r' character, which represents a carriage return. The loop continues processing characters until the user presses the Enter key. At that point, the character received by getch() is '\r', so the loop exits and returns the number as a string.

Inside the loop, EnterOnlyNumbers() tests the *value* of the character, seeing whether it's in the range '0' through '9'. Yes, characters are associated with a sequence, and fortunately, the digits are all grouped together. So it's possible to determine whether the character is a digit character by checking to see whether it's in the range '0' through '9':

```
if (ch >= '0' && ch <= '9')
```

If the user presses a number key, the code enters the if statement. Because the user pressed a number key, the code writes the value to the console and adds the digit character to the end of the string. The code has to write it to the console because, when it calls getch(), the computer doesn't automatically print anything. But that's a good thing here, because after leaving the if statement, the code calls getch() again for another round. Thus, if the user pressed something other than the Enter key or a number, the character the user pressed doesn't even appear on the console, and it doesn't get added to the string, either.

TIP

The EnterPassword() routine is similar to the EnterOnlyNumbers() routine, except that it allows the user to enter any character (including spaces). So no if statement is filtering out certain letters. And further, instead of printing only the character that the user types, it prints an asterisk: *. That gives the feeling of a password entry, which is a good feeling.

When you run this application, you get output similar to the following:

```
What is your name? Hank
Hello Hank

Enter a number, any number! abc123
You chose 0

This time you'll only be able to enter a number!
Enter a number, any number! 5001
You entered 5001

Enter your password! *****
Shhhh, it's hello
```

The first line went well; there aren't any spaces so the name Hank made it into the output. But then when asked to enter a number, the user types abc123. The output of 0 indicates that cin can't convert the input to an int. If you type 123abc instead, you see 123 as the output. The next section doesn't allow the user to type anything but numbers because it calls EnterOnlyNumbers(). In the final two lines, the user enters a password, and you can see that the computer displays asterisks after each key press. This is because EnterPassword() contains the line cout << '*';. You see the actual password output as the last on the screen.

Understanding Preprocessor Directives

When you compile an application, the first thing the compiler does is run your code through something called a preprocessor. The preprocessor simply looks for certain statements in your code that start with the # symbol. You have already seen one such statement in every one of your applications: #include. These preprocessor statements are known as directives because they tell the preprocessor to do something; they direct it. The following sections tell you more about the preprocessor and describe how it works.

Understanding the basics of preprocessing

Think of the preprocessor as just a machine that transforms your code into a temporary, fixed-up version that's all ready to be compiled. For example, look at this preprocessor directive:

```
#include <iostream>
```

If the preprocessor sees this line, it inserts the entire text from the file called iostream (yes, that's a filename; it has no extension) into the fixed-up version of the source code. Suppose that the iostream file looks like this:

```
int hello = 10;
int goodbye = 20;
```

Just two lines are all that's in it. (Of course, the real iostream file is much more sophisticated.) And suppose that your own source file, MyProgram.cpp, has this in it (as found in the Preprocessor example):

```
#include <iostream>

int main()
```

```
{
  std::cout << "Hello world!" << std::endl;
  return 0;
}
```

Then, after the preprocessor finishes its preprocessing, it creates a temporary fixed-up file (which has the lines from the iostream file inserted into the MyProgram.cpp file where the #include line had been) to look like this:

```
int hello = 10;
int goodbye = 20;

int main()
{
  std::cout << "Hello world!" << std::endl;
  return 0;
}
```

In other words, the preprocessor replaced the #include line with the contents of that file. Now, the iostream file could have #include lines, and those lines would be replaced by the contents of the files *they* refer to. As you may imagine, what started out as a simple application with just a few lines could actually have hundreds of lines after the preprocessor gets through with it.

Creating constants and macros with #define

The preprocessor also provides you with a lot of other directives besides #include. One of the more useful ones is the #define directive. Here's a sample #define line:

```
#define MYSPECIALNUMBER 42
```

After the preprocessor sees this line, every time it encounters the word MYSPECIALNUMBER, it replaces it with the word 42 (that is, whatever sequence of letters, numbers, and other characters follow the definition). In this case, #define creates a kind of constant where the word is easier to understand than the value associated with it. But #define also lets you create what are called *macros*, which are a sort of script. This line defines the oldmax() macro:

```
#define oldmax(x, y) ((x)>(y)?(x):(y))
```

SEEING THE PREPROCESSOR IN ACTION

You may want to see how the preprocessor actually works. To see it in action, you must open a Windows command prompt or a terminal window to the location of your source code, such as C:\CPP_AIO4\BookII\Chapter02\Preprocessor. The next thing you need to know is where Code::Blocks is located on your system, such as C:\CodeBlocks\MinGW\bin. At this point, you can type a special GCC compiler command with the name of the .CPP file you want to check out, such as Main.cpp, and a special command-line switch, –E. For a Windows system, you can probably type **\CodeBlocks\MinGW\bin\GCC -E main.cpp >> Preprocessed.cpp** and press Enter.

The –E command-line switch tells the GCC compiler you normally use with Code::Blocks to output only preprocessed code. The >> operator tells Windows to place the output in Preprocessed.cpp rather than display it onscreen. When you run the default Code::Blocks code through the preprocessor it contains somewhere around 16,497 lines! You can see the output in Preprocessed.cpp, which is included in the Preprocessor folder of the downloadable source code. Many of those are blank lines, for various reasons, but nevertheless, it's a very big file!

You actually have access to a second preprocessor. To access the second preprocessor, type **\CodeBlocks\MinGW\bin\CPP main.cpp >> Preprocessed2.cpp** and press Enter in the same folder as your source code (as in the previous example using GCC). CPP stands for C preprocessor and it's interesting to look at its output, which is precisely the same as using GCC with the –E command-line switch.

In looking at the preprocessor output, you see a combination of actual code and what are called line markers. A *line marker* is a kind of preprocessor comment that tells you where something comes from. Here is a small sample of what you see when you pre-process the main.cpp file of the Preprocessor example. Some lines have been pur-posely shortened, with the missing content replaced by an ellipsis (...):

```
# 1 "main.cpp"
# 1 "<built-in>"
# 1 "<command-line>"
# 1 "main.cpp"
# 1 "C:/CodeBlocks/MinGW/lib/.../include/c++/iostream" 1 3
# 36 "C:/CodeBlocks/MinGW/lib/.../include/c++/iostream" 3
```

The comments all take the same form: the line number within the target file; the name of the target file; and processing flags used with the target file. So, the example starts in main.cpp line 1, looks for the built-in and command-line entries but doesn't find them, and then starts again with `main.cpp` line 1. None of these entries has flags. The next line does. It appears on `main.cpp` line 1 with the `#include <iostream>` directive. The preprocessor opens `iostream` and starts processing it on line 36. Both these lines have flags with these meanings:

1. Start a new file (`iostream` in the example code).

2. Return to the previous file.

3. The following text comes from a system header file, so the compiler should ignore certain warnings.

4. The following text should be treated as if it is wrapped in an `extern "C"` block.

This is enough information to get you started in understanding how preprocessed output works. You can learn more at `https://gcc.gnu.org/onlinedocs/gcc-3.4.6/cpp/Preprocessor-Output.html`.

After the preprocessor sees this line, it replaces every occurrence of `oldmax()` followed by two arguments with `((x)>(y)?(x):(y))`, using the appropriate substitutes for `x` and `y`. For example, if you then have this line

```
q = oldmax(abc, 123);
```

the preprocessor replaces the line with

```
q = ((abc)>(123)?(abc):(123));
```

and does nothing more with the line. Book 1, Chapter 4, refers to the output code as a conditional operator. The variable `q` is set to the value in `abc` if the `abc` value is greater than `123`; otherwise, the `q` gets set to `123`.

WARNING

However, the preprocessor doesn't have an understanding of the conditional operator, and `q` doesn't get set to anything during preprocessing. All the preprocessor knows is how to replace text in your source code file. The preprocessor replaced the earlier line of code that contained `oldmax()` with the next line containing the conditional operator. That's it. The preprocessor doesn't run any code, it doesn't make the comparison, and it doesn't put anything in `q`. The preprocessor just changes the code.

Notice that `#define oldmax(x, y)` places `x` and `y` in parentheses. This is because `oldmax()` takes two arguments, `x` and `y`, and the parentheses serve to tell the compiler that they are arguments. Consequently, q = oldmax(abc, 123); is oldmax() with the required arguments, abc and 123.

WARNING

Although you can still use #define statements in C++, in general you should simply create a function instead of a macro or use a constant instead of a symbol. Symbols and macros are used in older and outdated styles of programming. However, you still see them used for some purposes, such as conditional compilation, which appears in the next section of the chapter.

Performing conditional compilation

At times, you may want to compile one version of your application for one situation and compile another for a different situation. For example, you may want to have a *debug* version of your application that has in it some extra goodies that spit out special information for you that you can use during the development of your application. Then, after your application is ready to ship to the masses so that millions of people can use it, you no longer want that extra debug information. To accomplish this transition between debug and production versions, you can use a conditional compilation like this:

```
#ifdef DEBUG
    cout << "The value of j is " << j << endl;
#else
    cout << j << endl;
#endif
```

The lines that begin with # are preprocessor directives. The preprocessor has its own version of if statements. In your code, you can have a line like the following, with nothing after it:

```
#define DEBUG
```

This line *defines* a symbol (rather than a constant with a value). It works just like the symbols described earlier, except that it's not set to be replaced by anything. You can also define such symbols in the command-line options to GCC or whichever compiler you use.

In Code::Blocks, you choose Project ⇨ Build Options. In the Project Build Options dialog box that opens, click the Compiler Settings tab, followed by the #defines subtab, as shown in Figure 2-2. You type your define symbols as shown in the figure. Be sure to place each symbol on a separate line.

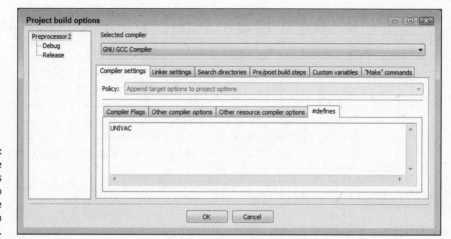

FIGURE 2-2:
Provide the compiler options you want to use to change the application output.

REMEMBER

Code::Blocks provides a special method for setting Debug or Release builds. You choose Build ⇨ Select Target and then choose the build you want from the menu. Notice that there are three entries in the left pane of Figure 2-2. Selecting Preprocessor2 lets you add defines, such as HAL2000, that affect both Debug and Release builds. Selecting Debug lets you add defines that affect only the Debug build, such as DEBUG. Note that selecting a particular build target doesn't automatically create a symbol, such as DEBUG, for you.

Now, when the preprocessor starts going through your application and gets to the #ifdef DEBUG line, it checks to see whether the DEBUG symbol is defined. If the symbol is defined, it spits out to its fixed-up file the lines that follow, up until the #else line. Then it skips any lines that follow that, up until the #endif line. For the earlier example in this section, if DEBUG is defined, the block of code starting with #ifdef DEBUG through the line #endif is replaced by the code in the first half of the block:

```
cout << "The value of j is " << j << endl;
```

But if the DEBUG symbol is *not* defined, the preprocessor skips over the lines up until the #else, and spits out the lines that follow, up until the #endif. In this case, it's replaced by the code following the #else line:

```
cout << j << endl;
```

REMEMBER

When the preprocessor goes through your file, it's only creating a new source code file the compiler uses to create an executable. That means that these #ifdef lines affect your application only when the compiler runs the preprocessor. When you compile the application and run it, these #ifdef lines are gone. So remember that #ifdef lines don't affect how your application runs — only how it compiles.

Exercising the basic preprocessor directives

It's time to see the various preprocessor directives in action. The Preprocessor2 example, shown in Listing 2-3, demonstrates all the preprocessor directives discussed in this chapter so far. In addition, you see predefined macros demonstrated, such as __FILE__. The C++ standard and your compiler provide *predefined macros* to allow you to output information such as the current filename without having to develop these macros yourself. You can see a list of predefined macros at https://riptutorial.com/cplusplus/example/4867/predefined-macros.

LISTING 2-3: **Using Many Different Preprocessor Directives**

```cpp
#include <iostream>

using namespace std;

#ifdef UNIVAC
const int total = 200;
const string compname = "UNIVAC";
#elif defined(HAL2000)
const int total = 300;
const string compname = "HAL2000";
#else
const int total = 400;
const string compname = "My Computer";
#endif

// This is outdated, but you might see it on
// occasion. Don't write code that does this!
#define oldmax(x, y) ((x)>(y)?(x):(y))
#define MYSPECIALNUMBER 42

int main() {
  cout << "Welcome to " << compname << endl;
  cout << "Total is:" << endl;
  cout << total << endl << endl;

  // Try out the outdated things.
  cout << "*** max ***" << endl;
  cout << oldmax(5,10) << endl;
  cout << oldmax(20,15) << endl;
  cout << MYSPECIALNUMBER << endl << endl;
```

```
    // Here are some standard redefined macros.
    cout << "*** Predefined Macros ***" << endl;
    cout << "This is file " << __FILE__ << endl;
    cout << "This is line " << __LINE__ << endl;
    cout << "Compiled on " << __DATE__ << endl;
    cout << "Compiled at " << __TIME__ << endl << endl;

    // Here's how some people use #define, to
    // specify a "debug" version or "release" version.
    cout << "*** total ***" << endl;
    int i;
    int j = 0;
    for (i = 0; i<total; i++)
    {
        j = j + i;
    }

#ifdef DEBUG
    cout << "The value of j is " << j << endl;
#else
    cout << j << endl;
#endif

    return 0;
}
```

When you run Listing 2-3 without any symbols using the Release target (choose Build ⇨ Select Target ⇨ Release), you see this output:

```
Welcome to My Computer
Total is:
400


*** max ***
10
20
42


*** Predefined Macros ***
This is file C:\CPP_AIO\BookI\Chapter09
    \Preprocessor2\main.cpp
This is line 35
Compiled on Apr 23 2020
```

```
Compiled at 15:19:38

*** total ***
79800
```

Note, at the beginning, that the code tests for the symbol UNIVAC. But that if block is a bit more complex because it also has an #elif (else if) construct. The language of the preprocessor has no elseifdef or anything like it. Instead, you have to write it like so:

```
#elif defined(HAL2000)
```

With this block, the preprocessor checks for the symbol UNIVAC; if the preprocessor finds UNIVAC, it spits out these lines:

```
const int total = 200;
const string compname = "UNIVAC";
```

Otherwise, the preprocessor looks for HAL2000; if the preprocessor finds it, it adds these lines to the fixed-up code:

```
const int total = 300;
const string compname = "HAL2000";
```

And finally, if neither UNIVAC nor HAL2000 is set, the preprocessor adds these lines:

```
const int total = 400;
const string compname = "My Computer";
```

Remember that in each case, these two lines are sent out to the fixed-up version in place of the entire block starting with #ifdef UNIVAC and ending with #endif. If you add UNIVAC to the #defines tab of the Project Build Options dialog box shown previously in Figure 2-2, you change how the preprocessor configures its output. To see the following output, you must choose Build ⇨ Rebuild, and then Build ⇨ Run, rather than use the Build ⇨ Build and Run command as normal.

```
Welcome to UNIVAC
Total is:
200

*** max ***
10
```

```
20
42

*** Predefined Macros ***
This is file C:\CPP_AIO\BookI\Chapter09
    \Preprocessor2\main.cpp
This is line 35
Compiled on Apr 23 2020
Compiled at 15:26:56

*** total ***
19900
```

To see a different output version, replace UNIVAC with HAL2000 in the #defines tab of the Project Build Options dialog box shown previously in Figure 2-2. Choose Build⇨Select Target⇨Debug to change the executable type. Finally, rebuild your application by choosing Build⇨Rebuild. Here is what you see when you choose Build⇨Run.

```
Welcome to HAL2000
Total is:
300

*** max ***
10
20
42

*** Predefined Macros ***
This is file C:\CPP_AIO\BookI\Chapter09\
    Preprocessor2\main.cpp
This is line 37
Compiled on Dec 18 2013
Compiled at 10:30:23

*** total ***
The value of j is 44850
```

TIP

The downloadable source includes a project file that has all the required defines included with it. If you type this source yourself, you must create the appropriate defines as well or the output won't match what you see in the book. Simply selecting a debug build, for example, won't provide the DEBUG define for you.

Using Constants

When you're programming, you may sometimes want a certain fixed value that you plan to use throughout the application. For example, you might want a string containing the name of your company, such as "Bob's Fixit Anywhere Anyhoo". And you don't want someone else working on your application to pass this string into a function as a reference and modify it by mistake, turning it into the name of your global competitor, "Jims Fixum Anyhoo Anytime". That could be bad. Or, if you're writing a scientific application, you might want a fixed number, such as pi = 3.1415926 or root2 = 1.4142135.

You can create such constants in C++ by using the const keyword. When you create a constant, it works just like a variable, except that you can't change it later in the application. For example, to declare your company name, you might use

```
const string CompanyName = "Bobs Fixit Anywhere Anyhoo";
```

Of course, you can always modify this particular string in your code, but later in your code, you can't do something like this:

```
CompanyName = CompanyName + ", Inc.";
```

The compiler issues an error for that line, complaining that it's a constant and you can't change it.

After you declare the CompanyName constant, you can use it to refer to your company throughout your code. The Constants example in Listing 2-4 shows you how to do this. Note the three constants toward the top called ParkingSpaces, StoreName, and pi. In the rest of the application, you use these just like any other variables — except that you don't try to change them.

LISTING 2-4: **Using Constants for Permanent Values That Do Not Change**

```
#include <iostream>

using namespace std;

const int ParkingSpaces = 80;
const string StoreName = "Joe's Food Haven";
const float pi = 3.1415926;

int main() {
  cout << "Important Message" << endl;
```

```
cout << "Here at " << StoreName << endl;
cout << "we believe you should know" << endl;
cout << "that we have " << ParkingSpaces;
cout << " full-sized" << endl;
cout << "parking spaces for your parking" << endl;
cout << "pleasure." << endl;
cout << endl;
cout << "We do realize that parking" << endl;
cout << "is tight at " << StoreName << endl;
cout << "and so we are going to double our" << endl;
cout << "spaces from " << ParkingSpaces << " to ";
cout << ParkingSpaces * 2;
cout << ". Thank you again!" << endl << endl;
float radius = 5;
float area = radius * radius * pi;
cout << "And remember, we sell " << radius;
cout << " inch radius apple pies" << endl;
cout << "for a full " << area << " square" << endl;
cout << "inches of eating pleasure!" << endl;
return 0;
}
```

When you run this application, you see the following:

```
Important Message
Here at Joe's Food Haven
we believe you should know
that we have 80 full-sized
parking spaces for your parking
pleasure.

We do realize that parking
is tight at Joe's Food Haven
and so we are going to double our
spaces from 80 to 160. Thank you again!

And remember, we sell 5 radius inch apple pies
for a full 78.5398 square
inches of eating pleasure!
```

TIP

The biggest advantage to using constants is this: If you need to make a change to a string or number throughout your application, you make the change only once. For example, if you have the string "Bob's Fixit Anywhere Anyhoo" pasted a gazillion times throughout your application, and suddenly you incorporate and need to change your application so that the string says "Bob's Fixit Anywhere Anyhoo, LLC", you would need to do some serious search-and-replace work. But if you have a single constant in the header file for use by all your source code files, you need to change it only *once*. You modify the header file with the new constant definition and recompile your application, and you're ready to go.

TIP

There's a common saying in the programming world: "Don't use any magic numbers." The idea is that if, somewhere in your code, you need to calculate the number of cows that have crossed over the bridge to see whether the bridge will hold up and you know that the average weight of a cow is 632 pounds, don't just put the number 632 in your code. Somebody else reading it may wonder where that number came from. Instead, make an AverageCowWeight constant and set it equal to 632. Then use AverageCowWeight anytime you need that number. Plus, if cows evolve into a more advanced species and their weight changes, all you need to do is make one change in your code — you change the header file containing the const declaration. Here's a sample line that declares AverageCowWeight:

```
const int AverageCowWeight = 632;
```

You don't have to create most common mathematical constants in your code. Instead, you add #include <math.h> to the top of your code and then use the constants as defined at @@@https://www.gnu.org/software/libc/manual/html_node/Mathematical-Constants.html. For example, if you want to use the value of pi in your code, you use the M_PI constant.

Unfortunately, the math header isn't part of the ANSI standard, so sometimes you have to jump through hoops to use it. Older compilers may require that you add #define _USE_MATH_DEFINES at the top of the source code file before any #include statements.

WARNING

If you have the Code::Blocks compiler set to use the C++ 11 or above standard, the __STRICT_ANSI__ define (added by default) will keep you from using a constant, such as M_PI, in your code. To overcome this issue, add the line #undef __STRICT_ANSI__ to the beginning of your code. Here is a short example of what you need to do:

```
#undef __STRICT_ANSI__

#include <iostream>
#include <math.h>

using namespace std;

int main()
{
    cout << M_PI << endl;
    return 0;
}
```

TIP

C++ 20 and above developers have some relief from this problem in the form of `std::numbers::pi` that you access with `#include <numbers>` (see https://en.cppreference.com/w/cpp/numeric).

Using Switch Statements

Many times in programming, you may want to compare a variable to one thing, and if it doesn't match, compare it to another and another and another. To do this with an `if` statement, you need to use a whole bunch of `else if` lines. Using `if` statements works out pretty well, but you can do it in another way: Use the `switch` statement.

WARNING

The approach shown in this section doesn't work for all types of variables. In fact, it works with only the various types of integers and characters. It won't even work with character strings. However, when you need to make multiple comparisons for integers and characters, using this approach is quite useful.

Here's a complete `switch` statement that you can refer to as you read about the individual parts in the paragraphs that follow. This `switch` compares x to 1, and then 2, and, finally, includes a catchall section called `default` if x is neither 1 nor 2:

```
int x;
cin >> x;
switch (x)
{
```

```
    case 1:
        cout << "It's 1!" << endl;
        break;
    case 2:
        cout << "It's 2!" << endl;
        break;
    default:
        cout << "It's something else!" << endl;
        break;
}
```

To use the `switch` statement, you type the word **switch** and then the variable or expression that you want to test in parentheses. Suppose that x is type `int` and you want to compare it to several different values. You would first type

```
switch (x) {
```

The preceding item in parentheses isn't a comparison; it's a variable. You can also put complex expressions inside the parentheses, but they must evaluate to either an integer or a character. For example, if x is an integer, you can test

```
switch (x + 5) {
```

REMEMBER

because x + 5 is still an integer. A `switch` statement compares only a single variable or expression against several different items. If you have complex comparisons, you instead use a compound `if` statement.

After the header line for the `switch` statement, you list the values you want to compare the expression to. Each entry starts with the word `case` followed by the value to compare the expression against, and then a colon, as in

```
case 1:
```

Next is the code to run in the event that the expression matches this case (here, 1).

```
cout << "It's 1" << endl;
```

To complete a specific `case`, you add the word `break`. Every `case` in the `switch` statement usually has a `break` line, which ends the `case`. If you leave out the `break` statement (either purposely or accidentally), when the computer runs this case, execution continues with the next `case` statement code.

TIP

Note the end of the example `switch` block has a final `default` case. It applies to the situation when none of the preceding cases applies. The `default` case isn't required; you can leave it off if you don't need it. However, if you do include it, you put it at the end of the `switch` block because it's the catchall `case`.

The `SwitchStatement` example in Listing 2-5 is a complete application that demonstrates a `switch` statement. It also shows you how you can make a simple, antiquated-looking *menu* application on the console. You don't need to press Enter after you choose the menu item; you just press the key for your menu selection. That's thanks to the use of `getch()` rather than `cin`.

LISTING 2-5: **Making Multiple Comparisons in One Big Block**

```cpp
#include <iostream>
#include <conio.h>

using namespace std;

int main() {
  // Display a list of options.
  cout << "Choose your favorite:" << endl;
  cout << "1. Apples " << endl;
  cout << "2. Bananas " << endl;
  cout << "3. Lobster " << endl;

  // Obtain the user's selection.
  char ch = getch();

  // Continue getting user selections until the user
  // enters a valid number.
  while (ch < '1' || ch > '3') {
    ch = getch();
  }

  // Use a switch to display the user's selection.
  cout << "You chose " << ch << endl;
  switch (ch) {
  case '1':
    cout << "Apples are good for you!" << endl;
    break;
  case '2':
    cout << "Bananas have plenty of potassium!" << endl;
    break;
```

(continued)

LISTING 2-5: **_(continued)_**

```
case '3':
  cout << "Expensive, but you have good taste!" << endl;
  break;
}

return 0;
}
```

Supercharging enums with Classes

When you work with classes, you can use a technique called _wrapping_, which helps you manage a resource. Book 2, Chapter 1 discusses the enum keyword and shows how you can use it to create your own types. However, when you print the enumeration, you don't see the word, such as red or blue; you see a number. The DisplayEnum example, shown in Listing 2-6, is a simple class that _wraps_ an enum type by converting the number into a human readable form, which is a kind of resource management. You can use this class with enum ColorEnum, as main() demonstrates. When you run this application, you see the single word red in the console.

LISTING 2-6: **Creating a Class for enums**

```
#include <iostream>

using namespace std;

class Colors {
public:
  enum ColorEnum {blue, red, green};
  Colors(Colors::ColorEnum value);
  string AsString();
protected:
 ColorEnum value;
};

Colors::Colors(Colors::ColorEnum init) {
  value = init;
}

string Colors::AsString() {
```

```cpp
  switch (value) {
    case blue:
      return "blue";
    case red:
      return "red";
    case green:
      return "green";
    default:
      return "Not Found";
  }
}

int main() {
  Colors InkColor = Colors::red;
  cout << InkColor.AsString() << endl;
  return 0;
}
```

In this example, the `switch` statement doesn't include any `break` statements. Instead, it uses `return` statements. The `return` causes the computer to exit the function entirely, so you have no reason to worry about getting out of the `switch` statement. You may wonder why the `switch` statement includes a `default` clause. After all, it will never get called. In this case, if you don't supply a `default` clause, the compiler displays the following message:

```
warning: control reaches end of non-void function
```

Whenever possible, add the code required for your application to compile without warnings. Adding the `default` clause simply ensures that the `AsString()` function always returns a value, no matter what happens. In addition, having the `default` clause will make it apparent that a color has been added to the `enum`, but isn't handled by the `switch` statement.

The expression `Colors::red` may be unfamiliar to you. That means you're using the `red` value of the `ColorEnum` type. However, because `ColorEnum` is declared inside the class `Color`, you can't just say `red`. You have to first say the class name, and then two colons, and then the value. Thus, you type **Colors::red**.

The code in `main()` creates the `InkColor` instance and sets it not to a `Color` object but to an `enum`. This works because C++ has a neat little trick: You can create a constructor that takes a certain type. In this case, `Color` has a constructor that takes a `ColorEnum`. Then when you create a `stack` variable (not a pointer), you can just set it equal to a value of that type. The computer will *implicitly* call the constructor, passing it that value.

ADDING COUT CAPABILITIES

It would be nice if the Colors class allowed you to just call cout, as in cout << Ink Color << endl; without having to call Ink Color.AsString() to get a string version. C++ has a capability called *operator overloading*, which is a technique for extending the functionality of an operator. When you type **something cout <<** followed by a variable, you are calling a function: <<. Several versions of the << functions (they are overloaded) are available; each has a different type. For example, int handles the cases when you write out an integer, as in int x = 5;, and then cout << x;. Because the << function doesn't use parentheses, it is an *operator*.

To add cout capabilities to your class, just write another << function for your class. Here's the code. This is not a class method; it goes *outside* your class. Add it to Listing 2-6 anywhere after the class declaration but before main(). Here goes:

```
ostream& operator << (ostream& out, Colors& inst)
{
    out << inst.AsString();
    return out;
}
```

Because this function is an operator, you have to throw in the word operator. The type of cout is ostream, incidentally; thus, you take an ostream as a parameter and you return the same ostream. The other parameter is the type you are printing: in this case, it's a Colors instance, and once again, it's passed by reference. After you add this code, you can change the line cout << InkColor.As String() << endl; to simply

```
cout << InkColor << endl;
```

Working with Random Numbers

Sometimes, you need the computer to generate random numbers for you. But computers aren't good at doing tasks at random. Humans can toss dice or flip a coin, but the computer must do things in a predetermined fashion. The computer geniuses of the past century have come up with algorithms that generate *pseudorandom numbers*. These numbers are almost random or seemingly random. They're sufficiently random for many purposes.

The only catch with these random-number generators is that you need to *seed* them, that is, provide them with an input value as a starting point for the calculation. If you provide the same seed each time, the starting output number is the same, as is the sequence of additional output numbers. Consequently, pseudorandom-number generators need some sort of seed that changes in an apparently random fashion. Fortunately, the seconds component of the current time is a changeable input that appears random when used correctly. When you run an application, most likely you won't start running it at precisely the same second in time. The RandomNumber example shown in Listing 2-7 shows how to generate a random number.

LISTING 2-7: **Seeding the Random-Number Generator**

```cpp
#include <iostream>
#include <time.h>
#include <stdlib.h>

using namespace std;

int main()
{
  // Seed the random-number generator
  time_t now;
  time(&now);
  srand(now);

  // Print out a list of random numbers
  for (int i=0; i<5; i++)
  {
      cout << rand() % 100 << endl;
  }

  return 0;
}
```

The example follows a process that you often see when working with random numbers. To obtain the time, you must include time.h. Initializing and using the random-number generator requires that you include stdlib.h.

1. Obtain the current time to start the random-number generator by creating a variable called now of a special type called time_t (which is just a number).

2. Call the time() function, passing the address of now, which obtains the number of seconds since January 1, 1970.

3. Initialize the random number using the time seed by calling srand().

4. Create a random number based on the seed by calling rand().

Each time you call rand(), you receive a new random int. However, the number may not be in the range you want. To limit the numbers in the range from 0 through 99, the code uses the *modulus 100* of the number. (That's the remainder when you divide the number by 100.) The first time you run Listing 2-7, you may see the following output:

```
19
69
85
83
47
```

The *second* time, you may see this output. It's different than before:

```
79
67
38
72
73
```

Storing Data in Arrays

Most programming languages support a data structure called an array. An *array* is a list of variables, all stored side by side in a row. You access them through a single name. Each variable in the array must be of the same type. This section tells you how to work with arrays for data storage purposes in a simple manner. A more detailed discussion of creating and using arrays in an advanced way appears in the "Building Up Arrays" section of Book 5, Chapter 1.

When you create an array, you specify how many items the array holds. For example, you can have an array of 100 integers. Or you can have an array of 35 strings or an array of 10 pointers to the class BrokenBottle. If the code you're working with represents a type, you can create an array out of it.

When you create an array, you give it a name. You can access the array's *elements* (items) by using that name followed by an *index* number in brackets. The first element is always 0. Thus, if you have an array of five integers called AppendixAttacks, the first element is AppendixAttacks[0]. The second is AppendixAttacks[1], and then AppendixAttacks[2], AppendixAttacks[3], and finally AppendixAttacks[4].

REMEMBER

Because an array starts with element number 0, the final element in the array has an index that is 1 less than the size of the array. Thus, an array of 89 elements has indexes ranging from 0 to 88.

Declaring and accessing an array

Here's how you declare an array:

```
int GrilledShrimp[10];
```

This line declares an array of 10 integers called GrilledShrimp. You first put the type (which is really the type of each element in the array), and then the name for the array, and then the number of elements in brackets. And because this declares 10 integers, their indexes range from 0 to 9.

To access the first element of the array, you put the number 0 in brackets after the type name, as in

```
GrilledShrimp[0] = 10;
```

Often, people use a loop to fill in an array or access each member. People usually call this *looping through the array*. The ArrayLoop example, in Listing 2-8, shows how to create and use a basic array.

LISTING 2-8: **Using a Loop to Loop Through the Array**

```cpp
#include <iostream>

using namespace std;

int main() {
    int Values[5];
    int VSize = sizeof(Values)/sizeof(*Values);
    cout << "Array count: " << VSize << endl;

    for (int i=0; i < VSize; i++) {
        Values[i] = i * 2;
        cout << Values[i] << endl;
    }

    return 0;
}
```

It's never a good idea to hard-code the length of your array anywhere in your code because the array length could change. Rather, calculate the size of the array using the sizeof() function. The example shows you how to perform this task by obtaining the actual length of Values in bytes and dividing it by the size of the individual array elements, which requires *Values. The result, VSize, is the number of array elements. When you use a for loop to loop through the array, you set the counter variable, i, to end the loop when it equals or exceeds the value of VSize.

When you use arrays, don't go beyond the array bounds. Due to some old rules of the early C language, the compiler doesn't warn you if you write a loop that goes beyond the upper boundary of an array. You may not get an error when you run your application, either.

Arrays of pointers

Arrays are particularly useful for storing *pointers* — a variable that contains the address of an item in memory — to objects. If you have lots of objects of the same type, you can store them in an array.

Although you can store the actual objects in the array, most people don't because they take up too much space. Most people fill the array with pointers to the objects. To declare an array of pointers to objects, remember the asterisk in the type declaration, like this:

```
CrackedMusicCD *missing[10];
```

The ArrayPointer example, shown in Listing 2-9, declares an array of pointers. In this example, after declaring the array, you fill the elements of the array with zeroes. Remember that each element is a *pointer*; that way, you can immediately know whether the element points to something by just comparing it to 0. If it's 0, it's not being used. If it has something other than 0, it has a pointer in it.

LISTING 2-9: **Using an Array to Store a List of Pointers to Your Objects**

```
#include <iostream>

using namespace std;

class CrackedMusicCD {
public:
  string FormerName;
  int FormerLength;
```

```
  int FormerProductionYear;
};

int main() {
  CrackedMusicCD *Missing[10];
  int SMissing = sizeof(Missing)/sizeof(*Missing);

  for (int i=0; i < SMissing; i++) {
    Missing[i] = 0;
  }
  return 0;
}
```

If you want to create a whole group of objects and fill the array with pointers to these objects, you can do this kind of thing:

```
for (int i=0; i < SMissing; i++) {
    Missing[i] = new CrackedMusicCD;
}
```

Because each element in the array is a pointer, if you want to access the properties or methods of one of the objects pointed to by the array, you need to *dereference* the pointer — obtain the value pointed to by the pointer — by using the shortcut -> notation:

```
Missing[0]->FormerName = "Shadow Dancing by Andy Gibb";
```

This sample line accesses the FormerName property of the object whose address is in the first position of the array. When you're finished with the object pointers in the array, you can delete the objects by calling delete for each member of the array, as in this example:

```
for (int i=0; i < SMissing; i++) {
    delete Missing[i];
    Missing[i] = 0;
}
```

TIP

The preceding code, clears each array element to 0. That way, the pointer is *reset* to 0 and no longer points to anything after its object is gone.

Passing arrays to functions

Sometimes you need to pass an entire array to a function. Though passing entire objects to arrays can be unwieldy, passing an entire array can be dangerous. Arrays can be enormous, with thousands of elements. If each element is a pointer, each element could contain several bytes, which works with smaller arrays, but could cause problems with arrays containing thousands of elements. When you pass a huge array on the stack, you may *overflow* the application's stack — meaning the application crashes. Fortunately, the compiler automatically treats arrays as pointers for you, but you still need to understand what is happening underneath the cover.

As with passing objects, your best bet is to pass an array's address. You pass the function a pointer to the array. But passing an array's address to a function is confusing to code. The ArrayPassing example, shown in Listing 2-10, is a sample that passes an array, without directly coding any pointers and addresses.

LISTING 2-10: Passing an Array to a Function by Declaring the Array in the Function Header

```cpp
#include <iostream>

using namespace std;

const int MyArraySize = 10;

void Crunch(int myarray[], int size) {
  for (int i=0; i<size; i++) {
    cout << myarray[i] << endl;
  }
}

int main() {
  int BigArray[MyArraySize];

  for (int i=0; i<MyArraySize; i++)
  {
    BigArray[i] = i * 2;
  }

  Crunch(BigArray, MyArraySize);
  return 0;
}
```

When you run this application, it prints the nine members of the array. The array appears in the function header without specifying a size. This means that you can pass an array of any size to the function. The size parameter defines the array size for the function. This example uses a constant rather than calculating the array size; then if you decide later to modify the application by changing the size of the array, you need to change only the one constant at the top of the application. Otherwise, you risk missing one of the 10s.

The example doesn't actually pass BigArray to Crunch. Instead, it passes the array's address. When you pass an array this way, the compiler writes code to pass a pointer to the array. You don't worry about it. The name of an array is actually a pointer to the first element in the array.

@@@Thus, BigArray (as an argument) is the same as &(BigArray[0]). (You put parentheses around the BigArray[0] part so that the computer knows that the & refers to the combination of BigArray[0], not just BigArray.) So you could have used this in the call:

```
Crunch(&(BigArray[0]), MyArraySize);
```

Adding and subtracting pointers

You can do interesting things when you add numbers to and subtract numbers from a pointer to an array element that is stored in a pointer variable as an address. If you take the address of an element in an array and store it in a variable, such as one called cur (for current), as in

```
cur = &(Numbers[5]);
```

where Numbers is an array of integers, you can access the element at Numbers[5] by dereferencing the pointer, as in

```
cout << *cur << endl;
```

Then you can add and subtract numbers from the pointer, like these lines:

```
cur++;
cout << *cur << endl;
```

The compiler knows how much memory space each array element takes. When you add 1 to cur, it advances to the next element in the array. And so the cout that follows prints the next element — in this case, Numbers[6].

The `PointerArithmetic` example, shown in Listing 2-11, shows how to move about an array. The code declares a variable called `cur`, which is a pointer to an integer. The array holds integers, so this pointer can point to elements in the array.

LISTING 2-11: **Moving by Using Pointer Arithmetic**

```cpp
#include <iostream>

using namespace std;

int main() {
  int Numbers[10];
  int SNumbers = sizeof(Numbers) / sizeof(*Numbers);

  for (int i=0; i<SNumbers; i++)
  {
      Numbers[i] = i * 10;
  }

  int *cur = Numbers;
  cout << *cur << endl;
  cur++;
  cout << *cur << endl;
  cur += 3;
  cout << *cur << endl;
  cur--;
  cout << *cur << endl;
  return 0;
}
```

The code begins with `cur` pointing to the first element. The array name is the address of the first element. The code then adds and subtracts from the value of `cur` to point to other array elements. When you run the application, here is the output you see:

```
0
10
40
30
```

You can't do multiplication and division with pointers.

REMEMBER

Chapter **3**

Planning and Building Objects

S tep outside for a moment and look down. What is the thing you are standing on? (Hint: It's giant, it's made of rock and sand and stone and molten lava, and it's covered with oceans and land.) The answer? A thing! (Even a planet is a thing.) Now go back inside. What's the thing that you opened — the thing with a doorknob? It's a thing, too! It's a slightly different kind of thing, but a thing nevertheless. What are you standing in inside? Okay, you get the idea. Everything you can imagine is a thing — or, to use another term, an *object*.

Over the years, researchers in the world of computer programming have figured out that one of the better ways to program computers is to divide whatever it is you're trying to model into a bunch of objects. These objects have *methods* (capabilities) and *properties* (characteristics). (Eventually they have relationships, but that comes later.)

In this chapter, you see how to make use of objects to create a software application. In the process, you get to twist some of the nuts and bolts of C++ that relate to objects and get tips on how to get the most out of them.

REMEMBER

You don't have to type the source code for this chapter manually. In fact, using the downloadable source is a lot easier. You can find the source for this chapter in the \CPP_AIO4\BookII\Chapter03 folder of the downloadable source. See the Introduction for details on how to find these source files.

Recognizing Objects

Think of an *object* as anything that a computer can describe. Just as physical things have characteristics, such as size, weight, and color, objects in an application can have *properties* — say, a particular number of accounts, an engine, or even other objects that it contains., A car, for example, contains engines, doors, and other objects.

Further, just as you can use real-world objects in certain ways because they have particular capabilities, an object in an application can use *methods.* For example, it might be able to withdraw money or send a message or connect to the Internet.

Here's an example of modeling an object by thinking about how it's put together and how you use it. Outside, in front of your house, you might see a mailbox. That mailbox is an object. A mailbox is a useful device. You can receive mail, and depending on the style (kind) of mail, you can send mail. (The style of mail is important — you can send a letter because you know how much postage to attach, but you can't send a package because the amount of postage is unknown.) Those are the mailbox's *methods.* And what about its characteristics? Different mailboxes come in different shapes, sizes, colors, and styles. So those are four *properties.* Now, some mailboxes, such as the kind often found at apartment buildings, are great big metal boxes with several little boxes inside, one for each apartment. The front has doors for each individual box, and the back has a large door for the mail carrier to fill the boxes with all those wonderful ads addressed to your alternative name: Resident.

In this case, you could think of the apartment mailbox as one big mailbox with lots of little boxes, or you could think of it as a big container for smaller mailboxes. In a sense, each of the little boxes has a front door that a resident uses, and the back of each one has an entry that the mail carrier uses. The back opens when the big container door opens.

So think about this: The mail carrier interacts with the container, which holds mailboxes. The container has a big door, and when that door opens, it exposes the insides of the small mailboxes inside, which open, too. Meanwhile, when a resident interacts with the system, he or she interacts with only his or her own particular box.

Take a look at Figures 3-1 and 3-2. Figure 3-1 shows the general look of the back of the mailbox container, where the mail carrier can open the container and put mail in all the different boxes. Figure 3-2 shows the front of the container, with the boxes open so that residents can take out the mail.

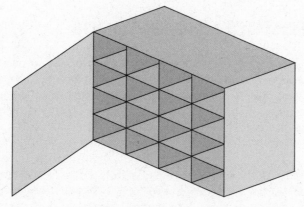

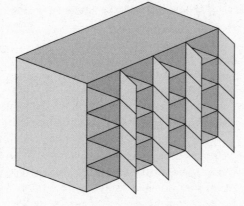

So far, there are two kinds of objects here: the container box and the mailboxes. But wait! There are multiple mailboxes. So, really, you have one container box and multiple mailboxes. But each mailbox is pretty much the same, except for a different lock and a different apartment number, right? In Figure 3-2, each box that's open is an example of a single mailbox. The others are also examples of the type of object called mailbox. In Figure 3-2, you can see 16 examples of the objects classified as mailbox. In other words, Figure 3-2 shows 16 instances of the class called `Mailbox`. All those mailboxes are inside an instance of the class that you would probably call `Mailboxes`.

TIP

There is no hard-and-fast rule about naming your classes. However, most developers use a singular name for objects and a plural name for collections. A single `Mailbox` object would appear as part of a `Mailboxes` collection. Using this naming convention makes it easier for other developers to understand how your code works. Of course, the most important issue is consistency. After you decide on a naming convention, use the same convention all the time.

OTHER MODELING METHODS

Computer scientists use a variety of modeling methods to create programs that reflect what the code is supposed to do. Object-oriented programming (OOP) techniques work best when modeling real-world objects. The object need not be something you would necessarily touch, such as a bank account, but it does exist in the real world, and using objects makes modeling the item easier. That's why this chapter focuses so much on real-world objects.

However, other sorts of modeling exist, and you experience one of these other models in Book 3 in the form of functional programming. Unlike OOP, functional programming excels at modeling abstractions. Trying to model an abstraction, such as statistical analysis, using OOP can prove difficult. Functional programming also has other advantages when performing certain kinds of tasks that require a lot of memory and high-speed processors.

You have also experienced procedural programming in the early examples of this book in which the code follows a set of steps to accomplish a task. In fact, most of the examples in Book 1 fall into this category.

Even though this book doesn't cover them, C++ can also adapt to several other models. Event-driven programming allows you to react to user interactions with the application, and you can perform whatever task the user needs no matter how the user makes the request (see the article at http://www.husseinsspace.com/teaching/udw/1996/cnotes/chapsix.htm). Reactive programming is especially adept at processing data streams (see the library at http://reactivex.io/RxCpp/). Automata programming is used for various kinds of automation, including robots and factory automation (see the article at https://www.tutorialspoint.com/cplusplus-program-to-perform-finite-state-automaton-based-search). The point is that you may find developers who use just one modeling method, but it's often better to know multiple techniques so that you can use an approach that works best for your particular need.

Observing the Mailboxes class

What can you say about the Mailboxes collection object?

>> The Mailboxes collection contains 16 mailbox instances.

>> The Mailboxes collection object is 24 inches by 24 inches in front and back, and it is 18 inches deep.

>> When the carrier unlocks the mailboxes and pulls, its big door opens.

» When the mailboxes' big door opens, it exposes the insides of each contained mailbox.

» When the mail carrier pushes on the door, the door shuts and relocks.

By using this list, you can discover some of the properties and methods of the Mailboxes collection. The following list shows its properties:

» Width: 24 inches

» Height: 24 inches

» Depth: 18 inches

» Mailboxes: 16 Mailbox objects inside

And here's a list of some of the Mailboxes collection methods:

» Open its door.

» Give the mail carrier access to the mailboxes.

» Close its door.

Think about the process of the carrier opening or closing the door. Here we seem to have a bizarre thing: The mail carrier asks the Mailboxes collection to close its door, and the door closes. That's the way you need to look at modeling objects: Nobody does anything to an object. Rather, someone asks the object to do something, and the object does it itself.

For example, when you reach up to shove a slice of pizza into your mouth, your brain sends signals to the muscles in your arm. Your brain sends out the signals, and your arms move up, and so does the pizza. The point is that you make the command; then the arms carry it out, even though you feel like you're causing your arms to do it.

Objects are the same way: They have their methods, and you tell them to do their job. You don't do it for them. At least, that's the way computer scientists view it. The more you think in this manner, the better you understand object-oriented programming.

REMEMBER

The Mailboxes collection contains 16 Mailbox objects. In C++, that means the Mailboxes collection has as properties 16 different Mailbox instances. These Mailbox instances could contain an array or some other collection, and most likely the array holds pointers to Mail instances within the Mailbox object.

Observing the Mailbox class

Consider the characteristics and capabilities of the Mailbox class. Each Mailbox has these properties:

>> Width: 6 inches

>> Height: 6 inches

>> Depth: 18 inches

>> Address: A unique integer

And each Mailbox has these methods:

>> Open its door.

>> Close its door.

Notice that the methods are from the perspective of the Mailbox, not the person opening the Mailbox.

Now think about the question regarding the address printed on the Mailbox. There are 16 different Mailbox objects, and each one gets a different number. So it's possible to say this: The Mailbox class includes an address, which is an integer. Each instance of the Mailbox class gets its own number. The first may get 1, the second may get 2, and so on. So you have two concepts here for representing the mailboxes in code:

>> **Mailbox class:** This is the general description of a mailbox. It includes no specifics, such as the actual address. It simply states that each mailbox has an address.

>> **Mailbox instance:** This is the actual object. The Mailbox instance belongs to the class Mailbox. There can be any number of instances of the Mailbox class.

Think of the Mailbox class as a cookie cutter — or, in C++ terminology, the *type*. The Mailbox instance is an actual example of the class. In C++, you can create a variable of class Mailbox and set its Address integer to 1. Then you can create another variable of class Mailbox and set its Address integer to 2. Thus, you've created two distinct Mailbox objects, each of class Mailbox.

But all these Mailbox instances have a width of 6, a height of 6, and a depth of 18 inches. These properties are the same throughout the Mailboxes collection. Thus, you would probably not set those manually; instead, you would probably set them in the constructor for the class Mailbox. Nevertheless, the values of width, height, and depth go with each instance, not with the class; and the instances could, conceivably, each have their own width, height, and depth. However, when you design the class, you would put a stipulation in the class that these properties can't be changed.

Finding other objects

If you are dealing with a Mailboxes instance and an instance of Mailbox, you can probably come up with some other classes. When you start considering the *parts* involved, you can think of the following objects:

>> Lock: Each Mailbox instance would have a Lock, and so would the Mailboxes instance.

>> Key: Each Lock instance would require one or more Key instances.

>> Mail: Each Mailbox instance can hold several Mail instances. The carrier puts these in the Mailbox instances, and the residents take them out.

>> LetterOpener: Some residents would use these to open the Mail.

So you now have four more types of objects (Lock, Key, Mail, and LetterOpener). But are these classes necessary? Their need depends on the application you're building. In this case, you're modeling the mailbox system simply as an exercise. Therefore, it's possible to choose the desired classes. But if this were an actual application for a post office, for example, you would have to determine whether the classes are necessary for the people using the software. If the application is a training exercise for people learning to be mail carriers, the application may need more detail, such as the Key objects. If the application were a video game, it may need all the classes mentioned and even more.

TIP

In deciding whether you need certain classes, you can follow some general rules. First, some classes are so trivial or simple that it doesn't make sense to include them. For example, a letter opener serves little purpose beyond opening mail. If you're designing a Mail class, you would probably have the method OpenEnvelope. Because some people would use a letter opener and others wouldn't, you have little reason to pass into that method a LetterOpener instance. Therefore, you would probably not include a class as trivial as LetterOpener. But then again, when writing a game that involves a Mail instance, you may allow use of a LetterOpener instance, but not a Scissors instance, to open the letter.

Planning and Building Objects

Encapsulating Objects

People have come up with various definitions for what exactly object-oriented means. The phrase *various definitions* in the preceding sentence means that there aren't simple discussions around a table at a coffeehouse about what the term means. Rather, there are outright arguments! One of the central points of contention is whether C++ is object-oriented. In such discussions, one of the words that usually pops up is *encapsulation*, which hides data values within the class and prevents unauthorized access to them. People who defend C++ as being object-oriented point out that it supports encapsulation.

Considering the Application Programming Interface

Encapsulation is an important concept because it helps you create easier-to-use, safer, and more reliable applications. In the world of computer programming, encapsulation refers to the process of creating a stand-alone object that can take care of itself and do what it must do while holding on to information. For example, to model a cash register, an application would encapsulate the cash register by putting everything about the register (its methods and properties) into a single class.

REMEMBER

To keep data within the class safe, you would make some methods and properties public (accessible through an Application Programming Interface, API) and others private (accessible only through the class). Some methods and properties can be *protected*, so derived classes could access them, but they still wouldn't be public. The combination of public methods and properties used by other developers to access the class is the class's API.

Understanding properties

In Chapter 1 of this minibook, you see how to build classes and instantiate objects from them. The examples in that chapter are straightforward, and all you really deal with are properties and methods. A property in Chapter 1 is essentially a variable, such as `Color InkColor;`. However, real-world classes work a little differently. You create a class member, which is actually the property from Chapter 1, and access it through methods that consist of the following:

>> **Setter:** A special method used to set (modify) the value of a property.

>> **Getter:** A special method used to get (read) the value of a property.

When viewed in this way, a property can consist of a setter (write-only), getter (read-only), or both (read/write). The property is never actually touched as part of the API. Here are the reasons you want to use this approach:

- Using a getter, it's possible to ensure that the value supplied by the caller is the right type, the correct length, and is in a specific range. You can also verify that the data doesn't contain viruses and other nasty stuff.

- Using a getter or a setter (depending on access), you can change the format of data from its internal representation to its external representation. For example, you could represent money as strings externally and floating-point values internally.

- Employing properties can allow you to perform security checks and other measures to keep data safe.

- Using getters and setters also makes it easier to set a breakpoint for debugging (discussed in Book 4 Chapter 2).

- Increasing property functionality can make it possible to manage resources in various ways, such as allowing access only at given times (configurable by an administrator).

Methods also access properties, but in a different manner than properties do. When designing a cash register class, you'd probably have a property representing the total dollar amount that the register contains—the methods that use the class wouldn't directly modify that value. Instead, they'd call various methods to perform transactions. One transaction might be Sale(). Another transaction might be Refund(); another might be Void(). These would be the capabilities of the register in the form of public methods, and they would modify the cash value inside the register, making sure that it balances with the sales and returns. If a method could just modify the cash value directly, the balance would get out of whack. Encapsulation, then, is this:

- You combine the use of methods and properties to access class members, hiding some of them and making some accessible.

- Some methods perform specific tasks that may access more than one property.

- The accessible methods and properties together make up the API of the object.

- When you create an object, you create one that can perform on its own. In other words, the users of the class tell it what to do (such as perform a sales transaction) by calling its methods or properties and supplying parameters, and the object does the work.

Choosing between private and protected

The cash amount would be a private or protected property. It would be hidden from the caller. As for which it would be, private or protected, that depends on whether you expect to derive new classes from the cash register class and whether you want these new classes to have access to the members.

In the situation of a cash register, you probably wouldn't want other parts of the application to access the cash register total if you're worried about security, so you might choose private. On the other hand, if you think that you'll create derived classes that have added features involving the cash (such as automatically sending the money to a bank via an electronic transaction), you'd want the members to be protected. In general, developers often choose protected, rather than private, because they've been bitten too many times by using classes that have too many private members. In those cases, you're unable to derive useful classes because everything is private!

Defining a process

The encapsulation process matters more than simply enclosing code in an easily accessed form. When you design objects and classes, you encapsulate your information into individual objects. If you keep the process in mind, you'll be better off. Here are the things you need to do every time you design a class:

>> **Encapsulate the information.** Combine the information into a single entity that becomes the class. This single entity has properties representing its characteristics and methods representing its capabilities.

>> **Clearly define the public interface of the class.** Provide a set of properties and methods that are public, and make the class members either protected or private.

>> **Write the class so that it knows how to do its own work.** The class's users should need only to call the methods in the public interface, and these public methods should be simple to use.

>> **Think of your class as a black box.** The object has an interface that provides a means so that others can use it. The class includes details of how it does its thing; users only care that it does it. In other words, the users don't see into the class.

» **Never change the class interface after you publish the class.** Many application errors occur when a developer changes how methods, properties, events, or access methods in the class work after publishing the class. If application developers rely on one behavior and the class developer introduces a new behavior, all applications that rely on the original behavior will break. You can always add to a class interface but never subtract from it or modify it. If you find that you must introduce a new behavior to `Sale()`, add the new behavior to a new method, `Sale2()`.

Implementing properties

A common saying in object-oriented programming is that you should never make your properties public. The idea is that if users of the object can easily make changes to the object's properties, a big mess could result. Previous sections mention properties and then talk about special methods as well. There are two methods of accessing property values in C++, and most developers today implement both when possible:

» **Getter/setter as a method:** You can use separate getter and setter methods, such as `setValue()` and `getValue()`. This is the approach that you can easily use with all versions of C++ and is the only officially supported technique.

» **Property approach:** Developers who have a background in other languages, such as C#, prefer the property approach, in which you have the object name, a dot, and then the property you want to change, such as `MyObject.Value`. The selection of getter or setter is automatic, based on context. To implement this approach, you must either use the correct C++ language product, such as Microsoft C++, or create a specialized class.

TIP

The article at `https://www.codeproject.com/Articles/118921/C-Properties` tells you about the Microsoft approach to creating properties, which involves creating a standard getter, setter, or both and then relying on `__declspec()` to define the property. The discussion at `https://stackoverflow.com/questions/8368512/does-c11-have-c-style-properties` describes a number of methods you can use with standards-based C++, including the creation of a template. The point is that you can use the property approach with C++, but it requires some additional work.

The `ImplementProperties` **example**, shown in Listing 3-1, demonstrates the process for working with read-only, read/write, and write-only properties for a class.

LISTING 3-1: **Working with Properties**

```cpp
#include <iostream>

using namespace std;

class MyDog {
protected:
  string _Name;
  int _Weight = 300;
  bool _IsHealthy = false;

public:
  // Properties
  string getName() {
    return _Name;
  }

  int getWeight() {
    return _Weight;
  }
  void setWeight(int Weight) {
    if (Weight > 0)
      _Weight = Weight;
  }

  void setIsHealthy(bool IsHealthy) {
    if (_Weight > 200)
      _IsHealthy = false;
    else
      _IsHealthy = IsHealthy;
  }

  // Methods
  MyDog(string Name);
  void DoDogRun();
};

MyDog::MyDog(string Name) {
  if (Name.length() == 0)
    throw "Error: Couldn't create MyDog!";

  MyDog::_Name = Name;
}
```

```cpp
void MyDog::DoDogRun() {
  if (MyDog::_IsHealthy)
    cout << MyDog::_Name << " is running!" << endl;
  else if (MyDog::_Weight > 200)
    cout << MyDog::_Name << " is too fat to run!" << endl;
  else
    cout << MyDog::_Name
      << " is unhealthy; see vet first!" << endl;
}

int main() {
  MyDog *ThisDog;

  try {
    // Uncomment to generate an error.
    //ThisDog = new MyDog("");

    ThisDog = new MyDog("Fred");
  } catch (const char *msg) {
    cerr << msg << endl;
    return -1;
  }

  cout << ThisDog->getName() << " needs exercise."
    << endl;
  ThisDog->DoDogRun();

  ThisDog->setWeight(100);
  ThisDog->DoDogRun();

  ThisDog->setIsHealthy(true);
  ThisDog->DoDogRun();

  delete ThisDog;
  ThisDog = 0;

  return 0;
}
```

The code begins by creating protected properties. The default dog doesn't have a name, but it does weigh 300 pounds and is definitely unhealthy. The properties provide setter and getter code as needed. For example, you don't want to change the dog's name after you create it, but you do want to change its weight as needed. Keeping the dog's health state a secret provides personal protections for the dog, so you can set it, but you can't get it. Notice how you use the getters and setters to interact with the data. For example, you can't set the dog's weight to a negative amount.

REMEMBER

Because you can't change the dog's name after you create the dog, the constructor has to accept a name. Notice how this constructor code includes exception handling. If someone tries to create the object without supplying a name, the constructor will throw an exception and not create a new MyDog object. Consequently, when you create ThisDog, you must enclose it within a try...catch block, as shown in Listing 3-1. The error message shows the problem onscreen:

```
Error: Couldn't create MyDog!
```

At this point, you can interact with ThisDog in the same way that you interact with any other object. The example discovers that the poor dog needs exercise, but you can't exercise the dog at first because he's too fat. Even after losing weight, Fred needs to become healthy before going out for a good run. However, look at the setIsHealthy() code. If Fred weighs more than 200 pounds, the code ignores that the input value indicates that Fred still isn't healthy. Here is the output from this example:

```
Fred needs exercise.
Fred is too fat to run!
Fred is unhealthy; see vet first!
Fred is running!
```

Building Hierarchies

One of the great powers in C++ is the capability to take a class and build new classes from it. When you use any of the available C++ libraries, such as the Standard C++ Library, you will probably encounter many classes — sometimes dozens of classes — that are all related to each other. Some classes are derived from other classes, although some classes are stand-alone. This gives programmers great flexibility. It's good for a class library to be flexible because when you're using a flexible library, you have many choices in the different classes you want to use.

Establishing a hierarchy

When you design a class, you have the option of deriving the class you're creating from an original base class — creating a child/parent relationship. The new class inherits the capabilities and characteristics of the base class. Normally, the members that are public in the base class will remain public in the derived class. The members that are protected in the base class will remain protected in the derived class; thus, if you derive even further, those final classes will also inherit the protected members. Private members, however, live only in the base class.

Suppose you have a base class called FrozenFood, and from there you derive a class called FrozenPizza. From FrozenPizza, you then derive a class called DeepDishPizza. FrozenFood is at the top of the hierarchy. It includes various members common to all classes. Now suppose that the FrozenFood class has the following properties:

» int Price (private): This is a private variable that represents the price of the product.

» int Weight (protected): This is a protected variable that represents the weight of the product.

The FrozenFood class also has these methods:

» constructor: The constructor is public and takes a price and a weight as parameters. It saves them in the Price and Weight properties, respectively.

» GetPrice(): This is a public access method that returns the value in the private Price property.

» GetWeight(): This is a public access method that returns the value in the protected Weight property.

To make this concept clearer, it helps to list these items in a box, putting the name of the class (FrozenFood) at the top of the box. Then the box has a horizontal line through it, and under that you list the properties. Under the properties, you have another line, and then a list of methods, as shown in Figure 3-3.

FIGURE 3-3: You can draw a class by using a box divided into three horizontal sections.

FrozenFood
−int Price #int Weight
+FrozenFood(int APrice, int AWeight); +int GetPrice(); +int GetWeight();

Note that in this figure, you can describe the visibility of each property and method:

>> **+:** Public

>> **-:** Private

>> **#:** Protected

TECHNICAL STUFF

Even though Figure 3-3 is helpful in assisting anyone in visualizing a class and ultimately class relationships, it's part of a technique called the Unified Modeling Language (UML) — a topic associated with software engineering and not discussed further in this book. If you're interesting in learning more about UML, you can find tutorials at `https://www.tutorialspoint.com/uml/index.htm` and `https://www.visual-paradigm.com/guide/uml-unified-modeling-language/uml-class-diagram-tutorial/`. You can write great code without using UML and, today, most developers rely on it only when working on large projects that would be hard to manage otherwise.

Protecting members when inheriting

In C++, you have options for how you derive a class. To understand this, remember that when you derive a class, the derived class inherits the members from the base class. With the different ways to derive a class, you can specify whether those inherited members will be public, protected, or private in the derived class. Here are the options:

>> **Public:** When you derive a new class as public, all members that were public in the base class will remain public in this derived class.

>> **Protected:** When you derive a new class as protected, all members that were public in the base class will now be protected in this new class. This means the members that were public in the base class will not be accessible by users of this new class.

>> **Private:** When you derive a new class as private, all members in the base class that this new class can access will be private. This means that these members will not be accessible by any classes that you later derive from this new class or by users of the class.

Think of it as an order of diminishing accessibility: The highest access is public. When a member is public, users can access the member. The middle access is protected. Users cannot access protected members, but derived classes will have access to the protected members. The lowest access is private. Users cannot access private members, and derived classes can't, either.

REMEMBER

To put protection during inheritance in perspective, consider the FrozenFood class and its children. When working with the FrozenPizza derived class, you see a combination of the members in FrozenFood and additional FrozenPizza members. However, only the methods in the FrozenFood portion of FrozenPizza can access the private members of the FrozenFood portion. Nevertheless, the methods in the FrozenFood portion of FrozenPizza and the private members of FrozenFood are part of the derived class.

When you derive a class as public, the base class portion of the derived class remains unchanged: Those items that were private remain in the base class portion; therefore, the derived class does not have access to them. Those that were protected are still protected, and those that were public are still public.

But when you derive a class as protected, the base class portion is different from the original base class: Its public members are now protected members of this derived class. The actual base class itself did not change; only the base class portion of the derived class becomes protected. Thus, the members that were public in the base class but are now protected in the derived class are not accessible to other methods and classes.

And finally, if you derive a class as private, the base class portion is again different from the original base class: All its members are now private. Because its members are private, any classes you derive from this newly derived class can't access these members: They're private. However, as before, the original base class itself didn't change.

In C++, you specify the type of inheritance you want in the header line for the derived class. Look at the InheritedMembers example, shown in Listing 3-2. Notice the three classes at the top of the listing: FrozenFood, FrozenPizza, and DeepDishPizza. FrozenFood is the base class of FrozenPizza, and FrozenPizza is the base class of DeepDishPizza. Figure 3-4 shows this relationship using arrows to point toward the base class.

Planning and Building Objects

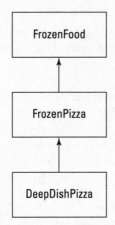

FIGURE 3-4:
The arrows in
this UML diagram
point toward the
base class.

LISTING 3-2: **Specifying the Access Levels of the Inherited Members**

```cpp
#include <iostream>

using namespace std;

class FrozenFood {
private:
  int Price;
protected:
  int Weight;
public:
  FrozenFood(int APrice, int AWeight);
  int GetPrice();
  int GetWeight();
};

class FrozenPizza : public FrozenFood {
protected:
  int Diameter;
public:
  FrozenPizza(int APrice, int AWeight, int ADiameter);
  void DumpInfo();
};

class DeepDishPizza : public FrozenPizza {
private:
  int Height;
public:
  DeepDishPizza(int APrice, int AWeight, int ADiameter,
                int AHeight);
```

```cpp
    void DumpDensity();
};

FrozenFood::FrozenFood(int APrice, int AWeight) {
  Price = APrice;
  Weight = AWeight;
}

int FrozenFood::GetPrice() {
  return Price;
}

int FrozenFood::GetWeight() {
  return Weight;
}

FrozenPizza::FrozenPizza(int APrice, int AWeight,
                         int ADiameter) :
                         FrozenFood(APrice, AWeight) {
  Diameter = ADiameter;
}

void FrozenPizza::DumpInfo() {
  cout << "\tFrozen pizza info:" << endl;
  cout << "\t\tWeight: " << Weight << " ounces" << endl;
  cout << "\t\tDiameter: " << Diameter << " inches"
    << endl;
}

DeepDishPizza::DeepDishPizza(int APrice, int AWeight,
                            int ADiameter, int AHeight) :
                            FrozenPizza(APrice, AWeight,
                                        ADiameter) {
  Height = AHeight;
}

void DeepDishPizza::DumpDensity() {
    // Calculate pounds per cubic foot of deep-dish pizza
  cout << "\tDensity: ";
  cout << Weight * 12 * 12 * 12 * 14 /
          (Height * Diameter * 22 * 16);
  cout << " pounds per cubic foot" << endl;
}
```

(continued)

LISTING 3-2: *(continued)*

```cpp
int main() {
  cout << "Thin crust pepperoni" << endl;
  FrozenPizza pepperoni(450, 12, 14);
  pepperoni.DumpInfo();
  cout << "\tPrice: " << pepperoni.GetPrice()
    << " cents" << endl;

  cout << "Deep dish extra-cheese" << endl;
  DeepDishPizza extracheese(650, 21592, 14, 3);
  extracheese.DumpInfo();
  extracheese.DumpDensity();
  cout << "\tPrice: " << extracheese.GetPrice()
    << " cents" << endl;
  return 0;
}
```

When you run Listing 3-2, you see the following output:

```
Thin crust pepperoni
        Frozen pizza info:
                Weight: 12 ounces
                Diameter: 14 inches
        Price: 450 cents
Deep dish extra-cheese
        Frozen pizza info:
                Weight: 21592 ounces
                Diameter: 14 inches
        Density: 35332 pounds per cubic foot
        Price: 650 cents
```

The first five lines show information about the object of class FrozenPizza. The remaining lines show information about the object of class DeepDish Pizza, including the fact that it weighs 21,592 ounces (which happens to be 1349.5 pounds), It has a density of 35,332 pounds per cubic foot.

The derivations are all public. Thus, the items that were public in FrozenFood are still public in FrozenPizza and DeepDishPizza. Note where the different information in the output comes from. The line Frozen pizza info: and the two lines that follow (Weight: and Diameter:) come from the public method DumpInfo(), which is a member of FrozenPizza. DumpInfo() is public in the FrozenPizza class. Since DeepDishPizza derives from FrozenPizza as public, DumpInfo() is also a public member of DeepDishPizza.

Try changing the header for DeepDishPizza from

```
class DeepDishPizza : public FrozenPizza
```

to

```
class DeepDishPizza : protected FrozenPizza
```

You're changing the word public to protected. Make sure that you change the correct line. Compile and run the application. You see an error that looks similar to this one:

```
In function 'int main()':
error: 'void FrozenPizza::DumpInfo()' is inaccessible
error: within this context
error: 'FrozenPizza' is not an accessible base of
  'DeepDishPizza'
error: 'int FrozenFood::GetPrice()' is inaccessible
error: within this context
error: 'FrozenFood' is not an accessible base of 'DeepDishPizza'
```

This message refers to the extracheese.DumpInfo(); line in main(). DumpInfo() is now a protected member of DeepDishPizza, thanks to the word protected in the class header. By putting the word protected in the class definition, you're saying the inherited members that are currently public will instead be protected. Because the DumpInfo() member is protected, you can't call it from main(). However, DumpInfo() is still public in the FrozenPizza class, so this call is fine:

```
pepperoni.DumpInfo();
```

TIP

Note that you can double-click the error: within this context line to jump directly to the code that is trying to access the hidden member, rather than look at the initial error. Using this technique saves you time looking for the errant code.

Change the line back to a public inheritance, as it was in Listing 3-2: class DeepDishPizza : public FrozenPizza.

And now change the header of FrozenPizza so that it looks like this:

```
class FrozenPizza : private FrozenFood
```

Again, make sure to change the correct lines. Compile and run the application to see the following error:

```
In function 'int main()':|
error: 'void FrozenPizza::DumpInfo()' is inaccessible|
error: within this context|
error: 'FrozenPizza' is not an accessible base of
   'DeepDishPizza'|
error: 'int FrozenFood::GetPrice()' is inaccessible|
error: within this context|
error: 'FrozenFood' is not an accessible base of 'DeepDishPizza'|
```

This error refers to the line inside DeepDishPizza::DumpDensity() where the code is trying to access the Weight member. The compiler doesn't allow access now because the member, which was public in the original FrozenFood class, became private when it became a part of FrozenPizza. And because it's private in FrozenPizza, the derived class DeepDishPizza can't access it from within its own methods. Make sure to change back the header of FrozenPizza so that it looks like this: class FrozenPizza : public FrozenFood.

Overriding methods

One of the cool things about classes is that you can declare a method in one class, and then when you derive a new class, you can give that class a different version of the same method. This is called *overriding* the method. For example, if you have a class FrozenFood and a derived class FrozenPizza, you may want to include a method in FrozenFood called BakeChemistry(), which modifies the food when it's baked. Because all foods are different, the BakeChemistry() method would be different for each class derived from FrozenFood.

In C++, you can provide a different version of the method for the different derived classes by adding the word virtual before the method name in the base class declaration, as in this line of code:

```
virtual void BakeChemistry();
```

This line is the prototype inside the class definition. Later, you would provide the code for this method. In the class for your derived class, you would then just put the method prototype, without the word virtual:

```
void BakeChemistry();
```

And as before, you would include the code for the method later on. For example, you might have something like the following example. First, here are the classes:

```cpp
class FrozenFood {
private:
  int Price;
protected:
  int Weight;
public:
  FrozenFood(int APrice, int AWeight);
  int GetPrice();
  int GetWeight();
  virtual void BakeChemistry();
};

class FrozenPizza : public FrozenFood {
protected:
  int Diameter;
public:
  FrozenPizza(int APrice, int AWeight, int ADiameter);
  void DumpInfo();
  void BakeChemistry();
};
```

You can see the word virtual in the FrozenFood class, and then you see the method declaration again in the FrozenPizza class. Now, here are the BakeChemistry() methods:

```cpp
void FrozenFood::BakeChemistry() {
  cout << "Baking, baking, baking!" << endl;
}

void FrozenPizza::BakeChemistry() {
  cout << "I'm getting crispy!" << endl;
}
```

Note that the word virtual doesn't appear in front of the methods; it appears only in the class declaration. Now, whenever you make an instance of each class and call BakeChemistry() for each instance, you call the one for the given class. Consider the following two lines of code:

```cpp
FrozenPizza pepperoni(450, 12, 14);
pepperoni.BakeChemistry();
```

Because pepperoni is an instance of FrozenPizza, this code calls the BakeChemistry() for the FrozenPizza class, not for the FrozenFood class. You may not want any code in your base class for the BakeChemistry() method. If so, you can do this:

```
virtual void BakeChemistry() {}
```

The reason to take this approach is that you don't need code in the base class, but you do want code in the derived classes, and you want them to be different versions of the same code. The idea, then, is to provide a basic, default set of code that the classes inherit if they don't override the method. And sometimes, that basic, default set of code is simply nothing. So you would put only an open brace and a closing brace, and you can do that inside the class itself:

```
class FrozenFood
{
private:
  int Price;
protected:
  int Weight;
public:
  FrozenFood(int APrice, int AWeight);
  int GetPrice();
  int GetWeight();
  virtual void BakeChemistry() {}
};
```

Specializing with polymorphism

Suppose you have a method called Bake() and you want it to take as a parameter a FrozenFood instance. If you derive FrozenPizza from FrozenFood and then derive DeepDishPizza from FrozenPizza, by the "is a" rule, objects of the class FrozenPizza and DeepDishPizza are both examples of FrozenFood objects. This is true in general: If you have a class called Base and you derive from that a class called Derived, instances of class Derived are also instances of class Base. Therefore, if you have a method called Bake() and you declare it as follows, you are free to pass to this method a FrozenFood instance or to pass an instance of any class derived from FrozenFood, such as FrozenPizza or DeepDishPizza:

```
void Bake(FrozenFood *)
{
  cout << "Baking" << endl;
}
```

Suppose that in this Bake() method, you set the oven temperature to a fixed amount, turn on the oven, and then cook the food. Every food behaves differently in the oven. For example, a deep-dish frozen pizza might rise and become thicker, but a regular frozen pizza will become crispier but not get any thicker.

You don't really want to put all the different food types inside the Bake() method, with if statements for each food type. Instead, you can put the actual baking chemistry in the class for the food itself. The FrozenPizza would have its own BakeChemistry() method, and the DeepDishPizza would also have its own Bake-Chemistry() method. Then the Bake() method would call BakeChemistry() for whatever object it receives as a parameter. C++ knows how to do this because of the virtual methods. The Bake() method doesn't even know or care what type of FrozenFood it receives. It just calls BakeChemistry() for whatever object it receives. And when you modify the application by writing a new class derived from FrozenFood and give it its own BakeChemistry() method, you can pass an instance of this class to Bake(), without even having to modify Bake(). This whole process is called *polymorphism.*

REMEMBER

Polymorphism is one of the most powerful aspects of object-oriented programming. The idea is that you can expand and enhance your application by adding new classes derived from a common base class. Then you have to make very few (if any) modifications to the rest of your application. Because you used virtual methods and polymorphism, the rest of your application automatically understands the new class you created. In essence, you are able to snap in the new class, and the application will run just fine.

Getting abstract about things

When you create a base class with a virtual method and then derive other classes, you may want to override the virtual method in all the derived classes. Furthermore, you may want to make sure that nobody ever creates an instance of the base class. You do this because the base class might contain basic things that are common to all the other classes, but the class itself doesn't make much sense as an instance. For example, no one would want you to go to the store and pick up a frozen food without specifying the sort of frozen food to get. Consequently, it doesn't make much sense to have an instance of a class called FrozenFood.

REMEMBER

Philosophers have a word to describe such things: *abstract.* The class FrozenFood is abstract; it doesn't make sense to create an instance of it. In C++, you can make a class abstract, but when you do, the compiler won't allow you to make any instances of the class.

In C++, you don't actually specify that the class is abstract. The word *abstract* doesn't appear in the language. To specify that the class is abstract, you add at least one virtual method that has no code. But instead of just putting an empty code block, as in {}, you follow the method prototype in the class definition with = 0 (called the *pure specifier,* which makes the method a *pure virtual method* or an *abstract virtual method,* depending on which you prefer), as in

```
class FrozenFood
{
private:
  int Price;
protected:
  int Weight;
public:
  FrozenFood(int APrice, int AWeight);
  int GetPrice();
  int GetWeight();
  virtual void BakeChemistry() = 0;
};
```

In this class definition, the method BakeChemistry() has = 0 after it (but before the semicolon). The = 0 transforms the virtual method into an abstract virtual method, which transforms the class into an abstract class.

After you create an abstract class, you must also modify the derived classes by overriding the abstract virtual method. Otherwise, the derived classes will also be abstract. When your class is abstract, you can't create instances of it. To override the abstract virtual method, you override as you would with any virtual method. This class includes a method that overrides the BakeChemistry() method:

```
class FrozenPizza : public FrozenFood
{
protected:
  int Diameter;
public:
  FrozenPizza(int APrice, int AWeight, int ADiameter);
  void DumpInfo();
  void BakeChemistry();
};
```

Then you provide the code for the BakeChemistry() method, as in

```
void FrozenPizza::BakeChemistry()
{
  cout << "I'm getting crispy under this heat!" << endl;
}
```

There's nothing magical about defining the override method, but you are required to override it if you want to create an instance of this class.

Chapter **4**

Building with Design Patterns

When you work as a developer, eventually you start to notice that you do certain things repeatedly. For example, when you need to keep track of how many instances of a certain class you create, you define a static property called something like `int InstanceCount;`, include a line that increments `InstanceCount` in the constructor, and include a line that decrements `InstanceCount` in the destructor. You make `InstanceCount` private and include a static method that retrieves the value, such as `getInstanceCount()`.

Because you use it so often, it becomes a pattern. The first time you used it, you had to think about it — how to design and implement it. Now, you barely have to think about it; you just do it. Thus, it's a *design pattern* that you use.

This chapter takes a practical look at design patterns that you use when creating applications. It helps you understand why using design patterns reduces development time, makes code less error prone, and improves application efficiency. The chapter delves just a bit into history and usage, with the usage considerations relying on the singleton pattern as a starting point.

You also see how to create and use two common design patterns: observer and mediator. You may or may not actually use these patterns in your applications, but by seeing how they're put together, you can find or create other patterns that will make your development process easier.

Delving Into Pattern History

Way back in 1995, a book became an instant bestseller in the computer programming world: *Design Patterns: Elements of Reusable Object-Oriented Software,* by Erich Gamma, Richard Helm, Ralph Johnson, and John Vlissides. The four authors of this groundbreaking book would become known in the field of programming as The Gang of Four.

The Gang of Four drew on a body of knowledge in the field of architecture — not software architecture, but rather the field of those people who build tall buildings, brick-and-mortar style. That kind of architecture has been around for at least two-and-a-half centuries, so the field is more mature than the field of software development. And, in the field of building design, people have come up with common ways to design and build buildings and towns, without having to start over from scratch every time with a new set of designs. Christopher Alexander wrote a book in 1977 called *A Pattern Language* (see http://www.patternlanguage.com/ca/ca.html for details), which teaches the major concepts of building architecture by using patterns. The Gang of Four drew on this knowledge and applied it to software development principles.

In their book, The Gang of Four point out something that seems obvious in hindsight (but then again, great discoveries are often deceptively simple): The best software developers reuse techniques in the sense of patterns. The description of the class that keeps an instance count is an example of a technique that can be used over and over.

Now, if you heavily explore the field of object-oriented programming (and computer science in general, really), you often see the term *reusable.* One of the goals of object-oriented programming is to make code reusable by putting it in classes. You then derive your own classes from these classes, thereby reusing the code in the base classes.

You could probably put an instance-counting class in a base class and always derive from it. But for some other designs, using a base class doesn't always work. Instead, software developers apply the same design to a new set of classes. The design is reused, but not the code. That's the idea behind design patterns. You don't just write up your design patterns and stuff them into a bunch of base classes. Instead, you know the patterns. Or you keep a list or catalog of them. You can find a list of the seven most important design patterns at https://medium.com/educative/the-7-most-important-software-design-patterns-d60e546afb0e.

Introducing a Simple Pattern: the Singleton

In this section, you discover how to create a design pattern so that you can see what it is and, more important, how you can use it. You look at a situation in which you need a class that allows only one instance to exist at any given time. You've come across this need many times. For example, you may have a class that represents the computer itself. You want only one instance of it. You also may have a class that represents the planet Earth. Again, you need only one instance. If people try to create a second instance of the class in their code, they will receive a compiler error. The following sections discuss how to perform this task in C++ using the *singleton pattern* (which ensures that only one instance exists at a time).

Using an existing pattern

You could spend a couple hours coming up with an approach to the problem of creating only a single instance. Or you could look at a pattern that already exists somewhere, such as what this section shows you.

To understand how to create the singleton pattern, you need to first understand an unusual concept that many C++ programmers don't usually consider: You can make a constructor of a class private or protected, which prevents someone from directly creating an instance of a class. To make this process work, you include a static method that creates the instance for you. Static methods don't have an instance associated with them. You call them directly by giving the class name, two colons, and the method name. Fortunately, the static method is a member of the class, so it can call the constructor and create an instance for you.

Here's how you make a singleton class: First, make the constructor private. Next, add a public static method that does the following:

1. Checks to see whether a single instance of the class already exists. If so, it returns the instance's pointer.

2. Creates a new instance and returns its pointer if an instance doesn't already exist.

Finally, where do you store this single instance? You store its pointer in a static property of the class. Because it's static, only one property is shared throughout the class, rather than a separate variable for each class instance. Also, make the variable private so that users can't just modify it at will.

And, voilà — you have a singleton class! Here's how it works: Whenever you need the single instance of the class, you don't try to create it. (You'll get a compile error! Yes, the compiler itself won't let you do it.) Instead, you call the static method.

WARNING

The singleton pattern won't prevent different programs on the same machine from creating multiple instances of the class (one for each application). This pattern works only within a single application. Consequently, if you need to ensure that a class isn't instantiated more than once on a machine as a whole, you need to use some form of globally unique identifier at the operating system level, a topic that's outside the scope of this book.

Creating a singleton pattern class

It's time to see the singleton pattern at work. Listing 4-1 from the Singleton example shows how to create such a class:

LISTING 4-1: **Creating a Singleton Class**

```
class Planet {
private:
  static Planet *inst;
  Planet() {}
  ~Planet() {}
public:
  static Planet *GetInstance();
};

Planet *Planet::inst = 0;

Planet *Planet::GetInstance() {
  if (inst == 0)      {
    inst = new Planet();
  }
  return inst;
}

int main() {
  Planet *MyPlanet = Planet::GetInstance();
  cout << "MyPlanet address: " << MyPlanet << endl;

  Planet *MyPlanet2 = Planet::GetInstance();
  cout << "MyPlanet2 address: " << MyPlanet2 << endl;
  return 0;
}
```

To use this class, you can't create an instance directly. Instead, you call the Get-Instance() method:

```
Planet *MyPlanet = Planet::GetInstance();
```

REMEMBER

You call this any time you want to get a copy of the single instance, which may include creating an instance when one doesn't exist. Every time you call GetInstance(), you always get a pointer to the same instance. When you run this code, you see output like this, which confirms that MyPlanet and MyPlanet2 both point to the same instance:

```
MyPlanet address: 0x3faf08
MyPlanet2 address: 0x3faf08
```

Look at the constructor: It's private. Therefore, if you attempt something like this somewhere outside the class (such as in main()):

```
Planet MyPlanet;
```

you get a compiler error. In Code::Blocks, you get this error:

```
error: 'Planet::Planet()' is private
error: within this context
```

Or if you try to create a pointer, you get the same error when you call new:

```
Planet *MyPlanet = new Planet();
```

The singleton pattern is about creating and destroying a single instance as needed, so you don't want anything deleting the instance that the application creates. Just as you would make the constructor private, you would also make the destructor private, as shown in Listing 4-1. If you try to delete an instance after you obtain it, as in

```
Planet *MyPlanet = Planet::GetInstance();
delete MyPlanet;
```

then once again you receive an error message — this time, for the destructor:

```
error: 'Planet::~Planet()' is private
error: within this context
```

You may be tempted to make a constructor that takes a parameter. You could pass parameters into the GetInstance() method, which would in turn pass them to the constructor. This would work the first time, but there's a catch: Remember that after the GetInstance() method creates the instance, it never does so again. That means it won't call the constructor again. Therefore, if you have a class that looks like this:

```
class Planet
{
private:
  static Planet *inst;
  Planet(string name)
  {
    cout << "Welcome to " << name << endl;
  }
  ~Planet() {}
public:
  static Planet *GetInstance(string name);
};
```

and your GetInstance() method has this code in it:

```
Planet *Planet::GetInstance(string name)
{
  if (inst == 0)
  {
    inst = new Planet(name);
  }
  return inst;
}
```

and you make two calls like this:

```
Planet *MyPlanet = Planet::GetInstance("Earth");
Planet *MyPlanet2 = Planet::GetInstance("Venus");
```

the results may not be as you expect. You end up with only one instance, which gets created with the first line — the one with "Earth" passed in. In your second call to the GetInstance() method, GetInstance() sees that an instance already exists and does not even use the "Venus" parameter. So be careful if you're using parameters in constructors.

Watching an Instance with an Observer

A common task in computer programming is when one or more instances of a class (or different classes) need to keep an eye on a certain object and perform various actions when that object changes. In other words, the class that keeps an eye on the others is an observer, hence the name of the pattern. The following sections tell you about the observer pattern and describe its use.

Understanding the observer pattern

You may write an application that monitors various activities around your house when you're away. Your application could be configurable; you could set it up so that the user can choose various actions to take if something goes awry. You might have the following options:

>> The application saves a note in a file so that you can later review it.

>> The application sends an email (or text for that matter) to you.

>> If the computer is linked to a telephone security system, it can notify the police.

>> The robotic dog can receive a signal to go on high alert.

Each of these actions can exist in a different class, each with its own code for handling the situation. The one about saving a note to a file is easy: You would open a file, write to it, and close the file. The email example might involve obtaining a Simple Mail Transfer Protocol (SMTP) library, using it to create a message object, and then sending the message. To notify the police, your computer would have to be hooked up to an online security system that's accessible via the phone lines or perhaps via the Internet, and the police would need a similar system at their end. The class for this would send a signal over the lines to the police, much like the way a secret button that notifies the police of a robbery at a gas station works. Finally, you might have a similar contraption hooked up to the brain of your little robotic watchdog, Fido; after receiving a high-voltage jolt, Fido can go on high alert and ward off the intruders. These situations use Observer classes (each class derives from a base class called Observer).

Now, you would also have a class whose object detects the problem in the house. This object might be hooked up to an elaborate security system, and when the change takes place, the computer calls a method inside this object. We call this class the Subject class. So think about what is happening here:

1. When a security issue happens, the computer calls a method inside the single Subject instance.

2. The Observer classes have objects that watch the Subject instance. The method in the Subject class then calls methods in each of the Observer objects. These methods take the appropriate action, whether it's write to a file, notify the police, zap the robotic dog, or whatever.

Here's the catch: The people using your computer application can determine which Observer classes they want to respond to the event (possibly, via an Options dialog box). The ability of the user to determine which Observer classes to use means that the design must be flexible. In order to obtain this flexibility, you need to add the following requirement: You might add new Observer classes as they come up, so the Subject class must accommodate them all. One Observer might signal a helicopter to fly in and chase a robber who's making a getaway. But you can't be sure what you'll come up with next. All you know is that you may add Observer subclasses and instances of these subclasses. Here are the issues that come up when designing such a set of classes:

>> You could keep a long list of instances inside the Subject class, and whenever an event takes place, the event handler calls a routine in all the Observer instances. The Observer instances then decide whether they want to use the information. The problem with this situation is that you have to call a method within the Observer classes (call into the class), even if the individual instances don't want the information.

>> You could have each Observer instance constantly check the Subject instance, looking for an event. (This process is called *polling*.) The problem here is that this process can push the computer to its limits, believe it or not: If every single Observer instance is constantly calling into the Subject class, you'll have a lot of activity going on for possibly hours on end, keeping the CPU nice and toasty. That's not a good idea, either.

>> You can perform polling using the observer pattern, which won't overextend the CPU. In this pattern, the Observer class contains a method called Respond(). Meanwhile, the Subject class includes a list of Observer instances. Further, the Subject class includes a method called Event, which the computer calls whenever something happens, such as a break-in. The application adds and removes Observer instances to and from the Subject's list of Observer instances, based on the options the people choose when using your application.

As you can imagine, this is a recurring pattern that a lot of applications use. Although zapping a robotic dog might not be commonplace, other applications use this general model. For example, in some C++ editors, you can open the same document in multiple windows, all under one instance of the editor application. When you change the code in one window, you immediately see the change in the other windows. Each class probably has a window, and these windows are the `Observer` classes. The `Subject` represents the underlying document.

Defining an observer pattern class

This section discusses how to create an `Observer` class. The `Observer` class contains a method called `Respond()`, which is a purely abstract function in the class declaration — meaning that the derived classes must create their own version of the `Respond()` function. It's up to the derived classes to respond to the event in their own ways. The following lines from the `AddRemoveItems` example (see Listing 4-2, later in the chapter) show how to create the `Observer` class:

```
class Observer {
public:
   virtual void Respond() = 0;
};
```

As you can see, there's not much here, so the example adds some derived classes. Here are a couple:

```
class Dog : public Observer {
public:
   void Respond();
};

class Police : public Observer {
protected:
   string name;
public:
   Police(string myname) { name = myname; }
   void Respond();
};
```

And here are the `Respond()` methods for these two classes. For now, to keep it simple, they just write something to the console:

```
void Dog::Respond() {
   cout << "Bark bark" << endl;
}
```

```
void Police::Respond() {
   cout << name << ": 'Drop the weapon! Now!'" << endl;
}
```

Again, so far, there's nothing particularly interesting about this. These lines of code represent just a couple methods that do their thing, really. When the next step rolls around, though, things get exciting. Here's the Subject class:

```
class Subject {
protected:
   int Count;
   Observer *List[100];
public:
   Subject() { Count = 0; }
   void AddObserver(Observer *Item);
   void RemoveObserver(Observer *Item);
   void Event();
};
```

This class has a list of Observer instances in its List member. The Count member is the number of items in the list. Two methods for adding and removing Observer instances are available: AddObserver() and RemoveObserver(). A constructor initializes the list by just setting its count to 0, and there's the Event() method. Here's the code for the AddObserver() and RemoveObserver() methods. These functions simply manipulate the arrays:

```
void Subject::AddObserver(Observer *Item) {
   List[Count] = Item;
   Count++;
}

void Subject::RemoveObserver(Observer *Item) {
   int i;
   bool found = false;
   for (i=0; i < Count; i++) {
      if (!found && List[i] == Item) {
         found = true;
         List[i] = List[i+1];
      }
   }
   if (found) {
      Count--;
   }
}
```

The RemoveObserver() function uses some little tricks (again, a pattern!) to remove the item. It searches through the list until it finds the item; after that, it continues through the list, pulling items back one slot in the array. And finally, if it finds the item, it decreases Count by 1. The Event() method looks like this:

```
void Subject::Event() {
  int i;
  for (i=0; i < Count; i++) {
    List[i]->Respond();
  }
}
```

This code climbs through the list, calling Respond() for each item in the list. When you put this all together, you can have a main() that sets up these items. Here's one possibility:

```
Dog Fido;
Police TJHooker("TJ");
Police JoeFriday("Joe");
Subject Alarm;
Alarm.AddObserver(&Fido);
Alarm.AddObserver(&TJHooker);
Alarm.AddObserver(&JoeFriday);
Alarm.RemoveObserver(&TJHooker);
Alarm.Event();
```

The code creates three Observer instances (one dog and two cops) and a Subject instance called Alarm. It then adds all three instances to the list; but then TJ Hooker backs out, so the code removes him from the list.

To test the additions, the code calls Event(). (Normally you call Event() when an actual break-in event occurs.) And when you run this code, you get the responses of each of the registered observers:

```
Bark bark
Joe: 'Drop the weapon! Now!'
```

Notice that the TJHooker Observer didn't respond, because it isn't in the list and didn't receive a notification. It's still an instance.

REMEMBER

In this example, the three observers (Fido, TJ Hooker, and Joe Friday) are *watching* the alarm, ready to respond to it. They are observers, ready for action. The alarm is their subject of observation. That's why the code uses the Observer and Subject pattern.

Observers and the Standard C++ Library

TECHNICAL STUFF

If you're interested in using templates and the Standard C++ Library, you can make the Subject class a bit more sophisticated by using a list rather than an array. (A list allows you to easily add and remove items without constantly rebuilding the list, as you would need to do with an array.) You can do this by using the standard list class. The only catch is that the list class doesn't seem to do well with abstract classes. So you need to "de-abstractify" your Observer class, which you do by setting it up like this:

```
class Observer {
public:
  virtual void Respond() {}
};
```

Then you can modify the Subject class and its methods, like so:

```
class Subject {
protected:
  list<Observer *> OList;
public:
  void AddObserver(Observer *Item);
  void RemoveObserver(Observer *Item);
  void Event();
};

void Subject::AddObserver(Observer *Item) {
  OList.push_back(Item);
}

void Subject::RemoveObserver(Observer *Item) {
  OList.remove(Item);
}

void Subject::Event() {
  list<Observer *>::iterator iter;
  for (iter=OList.begin(); iter!=OList.end(); iter++) {
      Observer *item = (*iter);
      item->Respond();
  }
}
```

Note that the list saves pointers to Observer; not the Observer instances themselves. That's because, by default, the list class makes a copy of whatever you put in the array. If you put in an actual instance, the list class will make a copy (which creates problems with derived classes because the list copies only the object being stored as an `Observer` instance, not a class derived from `Observer`). With pointers, a copy of a pointer still points to the original object, and therefore the items in the list are the originals (at least their addresses are in the list). The list can also add and remove items without needing the program to loop through all the items, as occurs when using an array.

Automatically adding an observer

When you have an application that lets its users configure various observers, you may want to create and delete observers based on the configurations. In that case, it's possible to add an `Observer` to a `Subject`'s list automatically when you create the `Observer`, and to remove the `Observer` from the list when you delete the `Observer`. To do this, you can call the `AddObserver()` method from within the constructor and call the `RemoveObserver()` method from within the destructor.

To make this technique work, you need to tell the object who the `Subject` is by passing the name as a parameter to the constructor. The following code does this. Note that you have to move the `Subject` class above the `Observer` class because the `Observer`'s constructor and destructor call into `Subject`. Also, note the `AddObserver()` and `RemoveObserver()` functions are protected. However, to allow the `Observer` class to use these functions, you need to add the word `friend` followed by the word `Observer` in the `Subject` class. The code for the complete `AddRemoveItems` application is in Listing 4-2.

LISTING 4-2: Adding and Removing Items in the Constructor and Destructor

```cpp
#include <iostream>

using namespace std;

class Observer;

class Subject {
  friend class Observer;
protected:
  int Count;
  Observer *List[100];
  void AddObserver(Observer *Item);
  void RemoveObserver(Observer *Item);
public:
  Subject() { Count = 0; }
  void Event();
};
```

(continued)

LISTING 4-2: *(continued)*

```cpp
class Observer {
protected:
  Subject *subj;
public:
  virtual void Respond() = 0;
  Observer(Subject *asubj) {
    subj = asubj;
    subj->AddObserver(this);
  }
  virtual ~Observer() { subj->RemoveObserver(this); }
};

class Dog : public Observer {
public:
  void Respond();
  Dog(Subject *asubj) : Observer(asubj) {}
};

class Police : public Observer {
protected:
  string name;
public:
  Police(Subject *asubj, string myname) :
    Observer(asubj) {
      name = myname; }
  void Respond();
};

void Dog::Respond() {
  cout << "Bark bark" << endl;
}

void Police::Respond() {
  cout << name << ": 'Drop the weapon! Now!'" << endl;
}
void Subject::AddObserver(Observer *Item) {
  List[Count] = Item;
  Count++;
}
void Subject::RemoveObserver(Observer *Item) {
  int i;
  bool found = false;
```

```
    for (i=0; i < Count; i++) {
      if (!found && List[i] == Item) {
        found = true;
        List[i] = List[i+1];
      }
    }
    if (found)    {
      Count--;
    }
  }

void Subject::Event() {
    int i;
    for (i=0; i < Count; i++) {
      List[i]->Respond();
    }
}

int main() {
  Subject Alarm;
  Police *TJHooker = new Police(&Alarm, "TJ");
  cout << "TJ on the beat" << endl;
  Alarm.Event();
  cout << endl;
  cout << "TJ off for the day" << endl;
  delete TJHooker;
  Alarm.Event();
  return 0;
}
```

Notice the Dog(Subject *asubj) : Observer(asubj) {} line of code in the list-ing. This line tells the application to call the base class constructor first with the subject. This action ensures that the base object, Observer, is correctly instantiated before Dog is instantiated. If you don't do this, then the instantiation of Dog will fail because Dog won't have access to the resources in the base class that it needs.

Mediating with a Pattern

The idea behind the *mediator* pattern is that it performs the work of organizing class communication when you have classes that interact in a complex way. That way, only the underlying mediator class needs to know about all the instances.

The instances themselves communicate only with the mediator. The following sections describe the basis for this pattern and demonstrate how it works.

Defining the mediator pattern scenario

Suppose that you're designing a sophisticated, complex model of a car. You're going to include the following parts, each of which will have its own class:

>> The engine

>> The electrical supply (for technically minded folks, the battery and alternator combined)

>> The radio

>> The wheels

>> The brakes

>> The headlights

>> The air conditioner

>> The road

Part of your task is to model the behaviors that these classes provide:

>> When the amount of electricity produced changes, the headlights get brighter or dimmer.

>> When the amount of electricity produced increases or decreases, the radio volume increases or decreases.

>> When the engine speed increases or decreases, the amount of electricity produced increases or decreases.

>> When the engine speeds up, the wheels accelerate.

>> When the air conditioner turns on, the amount of electricity available decreases.

>> When the air conditioner turns off, the amount of electricity available increases.

>> When the road angle increases due to going uphill, the speed of the wheels decreases.

>> When the road angle decreases because the car is going downhill, the speed of the wheels increases.

>> When the brakes come on, the speed of the wheels decreases.

This list represents nine objects interacting with each other in different ways. You could try to make all the objects communicate directly with each other. In the code, making them communicate would mean that most of the classes would have to contain references to objects of the other classes. That technique could get pretty confusing.

Figure 4-1 shows a hierarchy of the interactions between classes that demonstrates that you don't have to have every class communication directly with every other class.

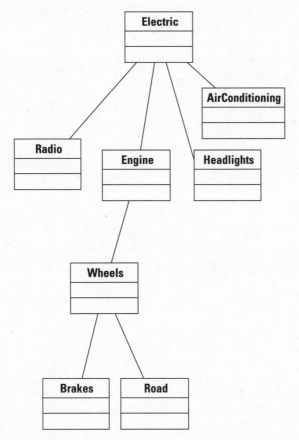

Building with Design Patterns

FIGURE 4-1:
A model of the hierarchy between classes.

Outlining the car example

In the example, when there's a hill, the road angle either increases or decreases, depending on the side of the hill you're on (uphill or downhill). The road does not need to know about all the other car parts. Instead, it just informs the mediator of the change. The mediator then informs the necessary car parts.

This may seem like overkill because the car parts should be able to talk with each other directly. The idea is that if you enhance this application later, you may want to add more car parts. Rather than connecting the new car part to all the necessary existing car parts, you just make a connection with the mediator object. Suppose that you add a new part called an automatic transmission. When the car begins to climb a hill, the automatic transmission might detect the change in grade and automatically shift to a lower gear, resulting in an increase to the engine speed. To add this class, you only need to define its behavior and specify how it responds to various events, and then hook it up to the mediator. You also modify the mediator so it knows something about the automatic transmission's behavior. Thus, you don't need to hook it up to all the other instances. Figure 4-2 shows how the application classes look with the mediator in place.

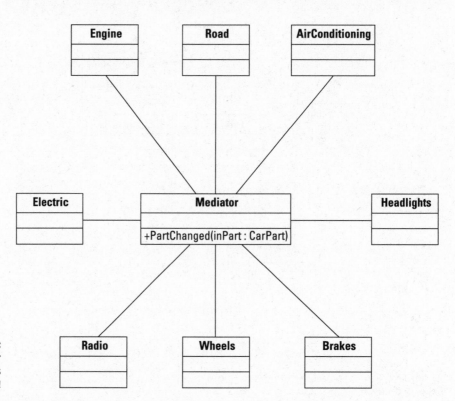

FIGURE 4-2: A mediator certainly cleans things up!

One thing not shown in Figure 4-2 (for the purpose of avoiding clutter) is that all the various car parts (including the road!) derive from a base class called CarPart. This class will have a single member: a pointer to a Mediator instance. Each of the car parts, then, will inherit a pointer to the Mediator instance.

PUTTING UP A FAÇADE (PATTERN)

In the CarParts example, it would be cumbersome to have to manipulate the car system by paying separate attention to all the different parts, such as the engine and the wheels, simultaneously. Imagine what life would be like if you had to drive a car while constantly worrying about every little thing. Instead, the example uses a CarControls class through which you can interact with the system. The CarControls class is a pattern itself, called a Façade pattern. (A *façade* is the front of something — it's a French word.) This pattern is also a front: It's the interface into the system through which you interact. That way, you don't have to keep track of the individual classes. When you add a class through which users can interact with the system, you are using a Façade pattern.

The Mediator class has a PartChanged() method. This is the key function: Anytime any of the car parts experiences a change, it calls PartChanged(). Remember that a car part can experience a change in only one of two ways: through an outside force unrelated to the existing classes (such as the driver pushing the gas pedal or turning the steering wheel) or through the Mediator instance. If the change comes from the Mediator instance, it was triggered through one of the other objects. Consider the following steps:

1. The driver pushes the gas pedal by calling a method in the Engine instance.

2. The Engine instance changes its speed and then tells the Mediator of the change.

3. The Mediator instance knows which objects to notify of the change. For this change, it notifies the wheels to spin faster and the amount of electricity produced to increase.

Here's another possible sequence:

1. The road has a hill. To tell the car about the hill, the main routine calls a method in the Road instance. The hill has a 10 degree incline.

2. The Road instance notifies Mediator of the change.

3. The Mediator instance handles this by figuring out how much to decelerate; it then notifies the wheels to slow down.

So you can see that most of the application smarts are in the Mediator class.

TIP

Using the mediator pattern may seem to break the rules for using OOP techniques. The example puts the smarts in the Mediator class. Elsewhere, you may hear that objects must be able to do their own work. But that's not really a contradiction. In fact, the Mediator class is handling all the smarts dealing with collaborations between objects. After the Mediator instance figures out, for example, that the wheels must spin faster, it notifies the wheels and tells them to spin faster. That's when the wheels take over and do their thing. At that point, they know how to spin faster without outside help from other classes and objects. So it's not a contradiction, after all.

Creating the car example

It's time to put everything you've discovered into coded form. The following sections break the car example into manageable pieces, but you need all the pieces before running the example.

Working with the car parts header

The CarParts example begins in Listing 4-3. This is a header file that contains the class declarations for the car parts. Each class provides behaviors appropriate for that part, such as starting and stopping the engine.

LISTING 4-3:   **Using the carparts.h File**

```
#ifndef CARPARTS_H_INCLUDED
#define CARPARTS_H_INCLUDED

#include "mediator.h"

class CarControls; // forward reference

class CarPart {
protected:
  Mediator *mediator;
  CarPart(Mediator *med) : mediator(med) {}
  void Changed();
};

class Engine : public CarPart {
protected:
  friend class Mediator; friend class CarControls;
  int RPM;
  int Revamount;
```

```cpp
public:
  Engine(Mediator *med) : CarPart(med),
      RPM(0), Revamount(0) {}
  void Start();
  void PushGasPedal(int amount);
  void ReleaseGasPedal(int amount);
  void Stop();
};

class Electric : public CarPart {
protected:
  friend class Mediator; friend class CarControls;
  int Output;
  int ChangedBy;
public:
  Electric(Mediator *med) : CarPart(med),
      Output(0), ChangedBy(0) {}
  void ChangeOutputBy(int amount);
};

class Radio : public CarPart {
protected:
  friend class Mediator; friend class CarControls;
  int Volume;
public:
  Radio(Mediator *med) : CarPart(med), Volume(0) {}
  void AdjustVolume(int amount) { Volume += amount; }
  void SetVolume(int amount) { Volume = amount; }
  int GetVolume() { return Volume; }
};

class Wheels : public CarPart {
protected:
  friend class Mediator; friend class CarControls;
  int Speed;
public:
  Wheels(Mediator *med) : CarPart(med), Speed(0) {}
  int GetSpeed() { return Speed; }
  void Accelerate(int amount);
  void Decelerate(int amount);
};
```

(continued)

LISTING 4-3: *(continued)*

```cpp
class Brakes : public CarPart {
protected:
  friend class Mediator; friend class CarControls;
  int Pressure;
public:
  Brakes(Mediator *med) : CarPart(med), Pressure(0) {}
  void Apply(int amount);
};

class Headlights : public CarPart {
protected:
  friend class Mediator; friend class CarControls;
  int Brightness;
public:
  Headlights(Mediator *med):CarPart(med), Brightness(0) {}
  void TurnOn() { Brightness = 100; }
  void TurnOff() { Brightness = 0; }
  void Adjust(int Amount);
  int GetBrightness() { return Brightness; }
};

class AirConditioner : public CarPart {
protected:
  friend class Mediator; friend class CarControls;
  int Level;
  int ChangedBy;
public:
  AirConditioner(Mediator *med) : CarPart(med),
      Level(0), ChangedBy(0) {}
  void TurnOn();
  void TurnOff();
  bool GetLevel() { return Level; }
  void SetLevel(int level);
};

class Road : public CarPart {
protected:
  friend class Mediator; friend class CarControls;
  int ClimbAngle;
  int BumpHeight;
  int BumpWhichTire;
```

```
public:
  Road(Mediator *med) : CarPart(med) {}
  void ClimbDescend(int angle);
  void Bump(int height, int which);
};
```

```
#endif // CARPARTS_H_INCLUDED
```

These classes know little of each other. That's a good thing. However, they do know all about the mediator, which is fine. This example uses an important small feature of the American National Standards Institute (ANSI) version of C++. Notice the constructor line in the Engine class definition:

```
Engine(Mediator *med) : CarPart(med),
    RPM(0), Revamount(0) {}
```

After the constructor definition, you see a colon and the name of the base class, CarPart. This calls the base class constructor. Then there's a comma and the name of a property (RPM) and a value in parentheses, which together form an initializer. When you create an instance of Engine, the RPM variable will get set to 0. Further, the Revamount variable will also get set to 0. Using the constructor with an initializer causes the constructor to behave just like this code:

```
Engine(Mediator *med) {
    RPM = 0;
    Revamount = 0;
}
```

Working with the mediator and car controls header

In Listing 4-4 you see the header file for the mediator along with a special class called CarControls, which provides a central place through which you can control the car. You may have noticed the CarControls friend class accesses the car parts in carparts.h. This file includes several forward declarations and it knows about the various CarParts classes. This file also includes a Mediator derived class that provides a general interface to the whole system.

LISTING 4-4: **Using the mediator.h File**

```
#ifndef MEDIATOR_H_INCLUDED
#define MEDIATOR_H_INCLUDED

// Define all of the required forward references.
class CarPart;
class Engine;
class Electric;
class Radio;
class SteeringWheel;
class Wheels;
class Brakes;
class Headlights;
class AirConditioner;
class Road;

class Mediator {
public:
  Engine *MyEngine;
  Electric *MyElectric;
  Radio *MyRadio;
  SteeringWheel *MySteeringWheel;
  Wheels *MyWheels;
  Brakes *MyBrakes;
  Headlights *MyHeadlights;
  AirConditioner *MyAirConditioner;
  Road *MyRoad;
  Mediator();
  void PartChanged(CarPart *part);
};

class CarControls : public Mediator {
public:
  void StartCar();
  void StopCar();
  void PushGasPedal(int amount);
  void ReleaseGasPedal(int amount);
  void PressBrake(int amount);
  void Turn(int amount);
  void TurnOnRadio();
  void TurnOffRadio();
  void AdjustRadioVolume(int amount);
  void TurnOnHeadlights();
  void TurnOffHeadlights();
```

```
    void ClimbHill(int angle);
    void DescendHill(int angle);
    void TurnOnAC();
    void TurnOffAC();
    void AdjustAC(int amount);
    int GetSpeed();
    CarControls() : Mediator() {}
};

#endif // MEDIATOR_H_INCLUDED
```

Creating the car parts methods

The methods for all the car parts appear in Listing 4-5. Note that these functions never call the functions in other car parts.

LISTING 4-5: **Presenting the carparts.cpp File**

```
#include <iostream>
#include "carparts.h"

using namespace std;

void CarPart::Changed() {
  mediator->PartChanged(this);
}

void Engine::Start() {
  RPM = 1000;
  Changed();
}

void Engine::PushGasPedal(int amount) {
  Revamount = amount;
  RPM += Revamount;
  Changed();
}

void Engine::ReleaseGasPedal(int amount) {
  Revamount = amount;
  RPM -= Revamount;
  Changed();
}
```

(continued)

LISTING 4-5:   *(continued)*

```
void Engine::Stop() {
  RPM = 0;
  Revamount = 0;
  Changed();
}

void Electric::ChangeOutputBy(int amount) {
  Output += amount;
  ChangedBy = amount;
  Changed();
}

void Wheels::Accelerate(int amount) {
  Speed += amount;
  Changed();
}

void Wheels::Decelerate(int amount) {
  Speed -= amount;
  Changed();
}

void Brakes::Apply(int amount) {
  Pressure = amount;
  Changed();
}

void Headlights::Adjust(int Amount) {
  Brightness += Amount;
}

void AirConditioner::TurnOn() {
  ChangedBy = 100 - Level;
  Level = 100;
  Changed();
}

void AirConditioner::TurnOff() {
  ChangedBy = 0 - Level;
  Level = 0;
  Changed();
}
```

```
void AirConditioner::SetLevel(int newlevel) {
  Level = newlevel;
  ChangedBy = newlevel - Level;
  Changed();
}

void Road::ClimbDescend(int angle) {
  ClimbAngle = angle;
  Changed();
}

void Road::Bump(int height, int which) {
  BumpHeight = height;
  BumpWhichTire = which;
  Changed();
}
```

REMEMBER

You can see that each method calls Changed() after each change. This function is in the base class, and it calls into the Mediator's PartChanged() method, which does all the hard work. Also note that in some of the car parts classes, the Mediator doesn't respond to their changes (such as the Wheel class), but the methods still call Change(). The reason is that you may add features whereby the Mediator would respond to these changes. Then you won't have to check to see whether you included a Change() call; it's already there. This approach helps avoid the problem of wondering why Mediator isn't doing what it's supposed to do when the code forgets to call Change().

Creating the mediator and car control methods

Listing 4-6 contains the mediator source code and the source code for the Car-Controls class. This code appears in mediator.cpp.

LISTING 4-6: **Presenting the mediator.cpp File**

```
#include <iostream>
#include "carparts.h"
#include "mediator.h"

using namespace std;
```

(continued)

LISTING 4-6:   *(continued)*

```
Mediator::Mediator() {
  MyEngine = new Engine(this);
  MyElectric = new Electric(this);
  MyRadio = new Radio(this);
  MyWheels = new Wheels(this);
  MyBrakes = new Brakes(this);
  MyHeadlights = new Headlights(this);
  MyAirConditioner = new AirConditioner(this);
  MyRoad = new Road(this);
}

void Mediator::PartChanged(CarPart *part) {
  if (part == MyEngine) {
    if (MyEngine->RPM == 0) {
      MyWheels->Speed = 0;
      return;
    }
    if (MyEngine->Revamount == 0) {
      return;
    }
    // If engine increases, increase the electric output
    MyElectric->ChangeOutputBy(MyEngine->Revamount / 10);
    if (MyEngine->Revamount > 0)
      MyWheels->Accelerate(MyEngine->Revamount / 50);
  }
  else if (part == MyElectric) {
    // Dim or brighten the headlights
    if (MyHeadlights->Brightness > 0)
      MyHeadlights->Adjust(MyElectric->ChangedBy / 20);
    if (MyRadio->Volume > 0)
      MyRadio->AdjustVolume(MyElectric->ChangedBy / 30);
  }
  else if (part == MyBrakes)
    MyWheels->Decelerate(MyBrakes->Pressure / 5);
  else if (part == MyAirConditioner)
    MyElectric->ChangeOutputBy(
      0 - MyAirConditioner->ChangedBy * 2);
  else if (part == MyRoad) {
    if (MyRoad->ClimbAngle > 0) {
      MyWheels->Decelerate(MyRoad->ClimbAngle * 2);
      MyRoad->ClimbAngle = 0;
    }
```

```
      else if (MyRoad->ClimbAngle < 0) {
        MyWheels->Accelerate(MyRoad->ClimbAngle * -4);
        MyRoad->ClimbAngle = 0;
      }
    }
}

void CarControls::StartCar() {
  MyEngine->Start();
}

void CarControls::StopCar() {
  MyEngine->Stop();
}

void CarControls::PushGasPedal(int amount) {
  MyEngine->PushGasPedal(amount);
}

void CarControls::ReleaseGasPedal(int amount) {
  MyEngine->ReleaseGasPedal(amount);
}

void CarControls::PressBrake(int amount) {
  MyBrakes->Apply(amount);
}

void CarControls::TurnOnRadio() {
  MyRadio->SetVolume(100);
}

void CarControls::TurnOffRadio() {
  MyRadio->SetVolume(0);
}

void CarControls::AdjustRadioVolume(int amount) {
  MyRadio->AdjustVolume(amount);
}

void CarControls::TurnOnHeadlights() {
  MyHeadlights->TurnOn();
}
```

(continued)

LISTING 4-6:   *(continued)*

```
void CarControls::TurnOffHeadlights() {
  MyHeadlights->TurnOff();
}

void CarControls::ClimbHill(int angle) {
  MyRoad->ClimbDescend(angle);
}

void CarControls::DescendHill(int angle) {
  MyRoad->ClimbDescend( 0 - angle );
}

int CarControls::GetSpeed() {
  return MyWheels->Speed;
}

void CarControls::TurnOnAC() {
  MyAirConditioner->TurnOn();
}

void CarControls::TurnOffAC() {
  MyAirConditioner->TurnOff();
}

void CarControls::AdjustAC(int amount) {
  MyAirConditioner->SetLevel(amount);
}
```

The CarControls part runs a bit long, but it's handy because it provides a central interface through which you can operate the car.

REMEMBER

The workhorse of the pattern, however, is in the Mediator class. This code consists of a bunch of if statements that look at the change that took place and then call into other classes to modify the objects of the other classes. That's the whole goal with the mediator pattern: It has a Mediator class containing a general function that looks for changes and then changes other classes.

Driving the car

Now it's finally time to try the mediator pattern by running the car through its paces. Listing 4-7 shows the various classes in action.

LISTING 4-7: **Running the Car through Its Paces**

```cpp
#include <iostream>
#include "mediator.h"
#include "carparts.h"

using namespace std;

int main() {
  // Create a new car.
  Mediator *MyCar = new Mediator();

  // Start the engine.
  MyCar->MyEngine->Start();
  cout << "Engine Started!" << endl;

  // Accelerate.
  MyCar->MyWheels->Accelerate(20);
  cout << "The car is going: " <<
    MyCar->MyWheels->GetSpeed() << endl;

  // Apply the brakes.
  MyCar->MyBrakes->Apply(20);
  cout << "Applying the brakes." << endl;
  cout << "The car is going: " <<
    MyCar->MyWheels->GetSpeed() << endl;

  // Stop the car.
  MyCar->MyBrakes->Apply(80);
  cout << "Applying the brakes." << endl;
  cout << "The car is going: " <<
    MyCar->MyWheels->GetSpeed() << endl;

  // Shut off the engine.
  MyCar->MyEngine->Stop();
  cout << "Engine Stopped" << endl;
  return 0;
}
```

The example code performs a few simple tasks using the various classes. You could always add more to your test code. The thing to notice is that everything goes through the Mediator class, MyCar. Here's the output from this example:

```
Engine Started!
The car is going: 20
Applying the brakes.
The car is going: 16
Applying the brakes.
The car is going: 0
Engine Stopped
```

3

Understanding Functional Programming

Contents at a Glance

Chapter **1**

Considering Functional Programming

This minibook describes a different sort of C++ programming in the form of the functional programming paradigm. A *paradigm* is a framework that expresses a particular set of assumptions, relies on particular ways of thinking through problems, and uses particular methodologies to solve those problems. You'll still use C++, but you use it in a manner that differs from the object-oriented programming (OOP) paradigms used in the previous minibook. Because many people are only now becoming aware of functional programming techniques, this chapter discusses how the functional and OOP paradigms differ.

The chapter also looks at some of the ways in which you change your programming style to use the functional programming paradigm. These style changes have some significant benefits when applied to certain kinds of development that rely heavily on math, perform various kinds of analysis, or work with technologies such as machine learning. You may not know it, but C++ is recommended as a language for both machine learning and deep learning in articles like the one at `https://towardsdatascience.com/top-10-in-demand-programming-languages-to-learn-in-2020-4462eb7d8d3e`. However, making it work in these environments requires use of functional programming techniques.

And finally in this chapter, you discover how to implement functional programming strategies using lambda expressions. This is one of the simplest ways to achieve what you want with a minimum of disruption to your standard programming practices if you're heavily involved in OOP. Later chapters delve more deeply into lambda expressions. This chapter just helps you get your feet wet.

REMEMBER

You don't have to type the source code for this chapter manually. In fact, using the downloadable source is a lot easier. You can find the source for this chapter in the \CPP_AIO4\BookIII\Chapter01 folder of the downloadable source. See the Introduction for details on how to find these source files.

Understanding How Functional Programming Differs

Functional programming has somewhat different goals and approaches than other paradigms use. Goals define what the functional programming paradigm is trying to do in forging the approaches used by languages that support it. However, the goals don't specify a particular implementation; doing that is within the purview of the individual languages.

REMEMBER

The main difference between the functional programming paradigm and other paradigms is that functional programs use math functions rather than statements to express ideas. This difference means that rather than write a precise set of steps to solve a problem, you use math functions, and you don't worry about how the language performs the task. In some respects, this makes languages that support the functional programming paradigm similar to applications such as MATLAB. Of course, with MATLAB, you get a user interface, which reduces the learning curve. However, you pay for the convenience of the user interface with a loss of power and flexibility, which functional languages do offer. Using this approach to defining a problem relies on the *declarative programming* style, which you see used with other paradigms and languages, such as Structured Query Language (SQL) for database management.

In contrast to other paradigms, the functional programming paradigm doesn't maintain state. The use of *state* enables you to track values between function calls. Other paradigms use state to produce variant results based on environment, such as determining the number of existing objects and doing something different when the number of objects is zero. As a result, calling a functional program function always produces the same result given a particular set of inputs, thereby making functional programs more predictable than those that support state.

Because functional programs don't maintain state, the data they work with is also *immutable,* which means that you can't change it. To change a variable's value, you must create a new variable. Again, this makes functional programs more predictable than other approaches and makes functional programs easier to run on multiple processors.

TECHNICAL STUFF

The capability to work on multiple processors is one area in which C++ excels. Most, possibly all, machines today have more than one core in their CPU, which allows for multiprocessing. Each *core* is essentially a single processor. Unlike many languages, C++ is uniquely positioned to make full use of the hardware, whether that hardware exists as a Graphics Processing Unit (GPU), Tensor Processing Unit (TPU), container, cloud, mobile device, or microcontroller. It's this low-level affinity for the hardware and significant speed advantage that makes C++ the top choice for the Java Virtual Machine (JVM) and the Chrome V8 Engine.

Imperative programming, the kind of programming that most developers have done until now, is akin to an assembly line, where data moves through a series of steps in a specific order to produce a particular result. The process is fixed and rigid, and the person implementing the process must build a new assembly line every time an application requires a new result. Object-oriented programming (OOP) simply modularizes and hides the steps, but the underlying paradigm is the same. Even with modularization, OOP often doesn't allow rearrangement of the object code in unanticipated ways because of the underlying interdependencies of the code.

REMEMBER

Functional programming gets rid of the interdependencies by replacing procedures with pure functions, which requires the use of immutable state. Consequently, the assembly line no longer exists; an application can manipulate data using the same methodologies used in pure math. The seeming restriction of immutable state provides the means to allow anyone who understands the math of a situation to also create an application to perform the math.

Using pure functions creates a flexible environment in which code order depends on the underlying math. That math models a real-world environment, and as our understanding of that environment changes and evolves, the math model and functional code can change with it — without the usual problems of brittleness that cause imperative code to fail. Modifying functional code is faster and less error prone than other programming paradigms because the person implementing the change must understand only the math and doesn't need to know how the underlying code works. In addition, learning how to create functional code can be faster as long as the person understands the math model and its relationship to the real world.

Functional programming also embraces a number of unique coding approaches, such as the capability to pass a function to another function as input. This capability enables you to change application behavior in a predictable manner that isn't possible using other programming paradigms.

CONSIDERING OTHER PROGRAMMING PARADIGMS

You might think that only a few programming paradigms exist besides the functional programming paradigm explored in this minibook, but the world of development is literally packed with them. That's because no two people truly think completely alike.

The reason for so many paradigms is that each one represents a different approach to the puzzle of conveying a solution to problems by using a particular methodology, all while making assumptions about things like developer expertise and execution environment. In fact, you can find entire sites that discuss the issue, such as the one at `https://cs.lmu.edu/~ray/notes/paradigms/`. Oddly enough, some languages (such as C++) mix and match compatible paradigms to create an entirely new way to perform tasks based on what has happened in the past. Here are just four of these other paradigms. Many languages in the world today use just these four paradigms, so your chances of encountering them are quite high.

- **Imperative:** Imperative programming takes a step-by-step approach to performing a task. The developer provides commands that describe precisely how to perform the task from beginning to end. During the process of executing the commands, the code also modifies application state, which includes the application data. The code runs from beginning to end. An imperative application closely mimics the computer hardware, which executes machine code. Machine code is the lowest set of instructions that you can create and is mimicked in early languages, such as assembler.

- **Procedural:** Procedural programming implements imperative programming, but adds functionality such as code blocks and procedures for breaking up the code. The compiler or interpreter still ends up producing machine code that runs step by step, but the use of procedures makes it easier for a developer to follow the code and understand how it works. Many procedural languages provide a disassembly mode in which you can see the correspondence between the higher-level language and the underlying assembler. Examples of languages that implement the procedural paradigm are C and Pascal.

- **Object-oriented:** The procedural paradigm does make reading code easier. However, the relationship between the code and the underlying hardware still makes it hard to relate what the code is doing to the real world. The object-oriented paradigm uses the concept of objects to hide the code, but more important, to make modeling the real world easier. A developer creates code objects that mimic the real-world objects they emulate. These objects include properties, methods, and events to allow the object to behave in a particular manner. Examples of languages that implement the object-oriented paradigm are C++ and Java. (The OOP paradigm is discussed in Book 2.)

- **Declarative:** Functional programming actually implements the declarative programming paradigm, but the two paradigms are separate. Other paradigms, such as logic programming, implemented by the Prolog language, also support the declarative programming paradigm. The short view of declarative programming is that it does the following: describes what the code should do, rather than how to do it; defines functions that are referentially transparent (without side effects); and provides a clear correspondence to mathematical logic.

Defining an Impure Language

Many developers have come to see the benefits of functional programming. However, they also don't want to give up the benefits of their existing language, so they use a language that mixes functional features with one of the other programming paradigms (as described in the "Considering Other Programming Paradigms" sidebar). For example, you can find functional programming features in languages such as C++, C#, and Java. When working with an impure language, you need to exercise care because your code won't work in a purely functional manner, and the features that you might think will work in one way actually work in another. For example, you can't pass a function to another function in some languages. The following sections help you understand why C++ is an impure functional language.

Considering the requirements

The basis of functional programming is lambda calculus (`https://brilliant.org/wiki/lambda-calculus/`), which is actually a math abstraction. Every time you create and use a lambda function, you're likely using functional programming techniques (in an impure way, at least). C++ supports lambda functions through the lambda expressions that later sections of this chapter explore.

In addition to using lambda functions, languages that implement the functional programming paradigm have some other features in common. Here is a quick overview of these features:

>> **First-class and higher-order functions:** First-class and higher-order functions both allow you to provide a function as an input, as you would when using a higher-order function in calculus.

>> **Pure functions:** A pure function has no side effects. When working with a pure function, you can

- Remove the function if no other functions rely on its output

- Obtain the same results every time you call the function with a given set of inputs

- Reverse the order of calls to different functions without any change to application functionality

- Process the function calls in parallel without any consequence

- Evaluate the function calls in any order, assuming that the entire language doesn't allow side effects

>> **Recursion:** Functional language implementations rely on recursion to implement looping. In general, recursion works differently in functional languages because no change in application state occurs.

>> **Referential transparency:** The value of a variable (a bit of a misnomer because you can't change the value) never changes in a functional language implementation because functional languages lack an assignment operator.

Understanding the C++ functional limitations

C++ is actually an extension of C. The original name of C++ was C with classes. So, theoretically, pure C++ is an OOP language. However, with the introduction of the Standard Library (see Book 5, Chapter 6 as well as Book 7 for more on the Standard Library), it becomes possible to add functionality to the language and make it more generic. The use of Standard Library enables you to use the functional programming paradigm in C++. However, even with Standard Library, you can't turn what started out as a procedural language and became an OOP language into a functional programming language. The best you can hope to achieve is a language that supports a number of paradigms — some of them in a general way.

What occurs in C++ for the most part is that you rely on the Standard Library to hide the nonfunctional programming components. For example, you can use constants in your C++ code to create an immutable environment. You use templates to create functions that don't rely on variables and therefore have no state. Using constants with methods can also help eliminate the problems with side effects. You see all these principles demonstrated as the chapter progresses. However, unlike a pure language, such as Haskell, these conventions aren't enforced in C++, and humans will routinely find ways around them when programming needs dictate.

Passing a function to a C++ function can also prove difficult unless you rely on the Standard Library. For example, you can use a transform to interact with a range of values by passing the transform a function. As part of the strategy of passing functions to other functions, you can rely on lambda expressions for simple needs. However, passing complex functions is possible as well. When working with complex functions, however, many developers encase them in a typedef to make the code easier to read.

To create a pure function in C++, you must eliminate both state and side effects, which can be quite difficult. The process becomes especially difficult when working with external data, such as a file or a data stream. Obviously, a function that works with external data won't produce the same output every time you call it, but you can still reduce the problems of both state and side effects.

Even the use of recursion in place of the usual for or other looping mechanism can prove difficult in C++. In many cases, recursion relies on the use of mutable variables to track when the recursion should end. Careful use of various recursion strategies can make the use of mutable variables unnecessary, but doing so can be error prone and difficult (sometimes making the code hard to read).

REMEMBER

The takeaway from this section is that you can use C++ in a functional manner, but it requires additional work to do so. The benefits of this approach are that multiprocessing applications are easier to create, the code is more concise, and the code is often easier to understand as well. In some cases, you can't use a functional programming style, especially when interacting with third-party libraries. However, if you work through coding issues using the Standard Library and some built-in C++ features, you can find yourself creating mostly functional code and obtaining the desired benefits from doing so.

Seeing Data as Immutable

Being able to change the content of a variable is problematic in C++. The memory location used by the variable is important. If the data in a particular memory location changes, the value of the variable pointing to that memory location changes as well. The concept of immutable data requires that specific memory locations remain untainted. To create immutable data in C++, you must use constant variables, as in

```
const double pi = 3.1415926;
```

The reason you need an immutable variable is that in a multiprocessing scenario, the value of the variable must be the same no matter which processor works with it. If x = 5 for one processor, it must equal 5 for all processors, and that value can never change. More important, the ability to change the value of a variable infers order, and functional programming techniques can't rely on a specific order to accomplish their goals. Finally, immutable variables are reliable. You don't have to worry about some bit of code, especially that from a hacker, modifying the values in your code because it seems like it might be a good idea. The following sections describe various forms of immutability in C++.

Working with immutable variables

The Immutable example, shown in Listing 1-1, demonstrates three techniques for creating immutable variables. In all three cases, you can rely on the variable's value to remain consistent and also rely on the compiler to complain about any changes.

LISTING 1-1: **Working with Constant Data**

```
#include <iostream>

using namespace std;

struct Immutable{
  int val{7};
};

int main() {
  const int *test1 = new int(5);
  *test1 = 10;

  const int test2{6};
  test2 = 11;

  const Immutable test3;
  test3.val = 12;

  cout << *test1 << test2 << test3.val << endl;
  return 0;
}
```

When you run this example, you see the following output in the Build Messages tab of the Code::Blocks compiler:

```
error: assignment of read-only location '* test1'
error: assignment of read-only variable 'test2'
error: assignment of member 'Immutable::val' in read-only
  object
```

You can extend what you see here in other ways to make variables and their associated data immutable. Of course, now you have another problem — that of performing basic tasks, such as adding two numbers. To perform these tasks, you must begin using additional variables as containers like this:

```
const int sum = *test1 + test2;
```

Working with immutability in classes and structures

It's essential to understand that immutability comes in several levels when working with C++ classes and structures. The Immutable2 example, shown in Listing 1-2, shows two levels of immutability. The first occurs in the Immutable structure, while the second occurs in main() when attempting to make a change.

LISTING 1-2: **Creating Immutable Structure Members**

```cpp
#include <iostream>

using namespace std;

struct Immutable {
  int val{1};

  void SayHi(string Name) const {
    Name = "Smith";
    val = 2;
    cout << Name << val << endl;
  }

  void ChangeVal() {
    val = 3;
    cout << val << endl;
  }
};
```

(continued)

LISTING 1-2:   *(continued)*

```
int main() {
  const Immutable Test;
  Test.ChangeVal();
  Test.SayHi("Sam");
  return 0;
}
```

Figure 1-1 shows the error messages you receive when you attempt to compile this application. The first error occurs because the SayHi() method attempts to change val internally. Notice that ChangeVal() makes a similar change without error because it's not a const method (as created by adding const after the method name and arguments to SayHi()). The second error occurs because the ChangeVal() call in main() attempts to change val through an external call.

FIGURE 1-1:
Seeing errors generated as the result of immutability in a structure.

However, say that you want to allow internal changes to val, yet continue to deny external changes to enforce functional programming. Adding mutable to the val declaration: mutable int val{1}; allows internal changes. Consequently, a new build will generate only the ChangeVal() call error in main(). If you comment out this call, you can see that the example will build and generate the following output: Smith2. (The downloadable source provides these commented changes.)

Now the question is why it's possible to change the Name value in SayHi(), if there aren't supposed to be any changes. To make Name unchangeable, you must declare it as const like this: void SayHi(const string Name) const. So, now you know how to add immutability at various levels within structures and classes (which work the same as structures, in this case).

Creating constant expressions

A constant expression, or constexpr, is a special kind of function that you can compute at compile time rather than runtime. You create the code, just as you would any code, but the compiler converts the code into an output before the application even runs, which means that this is one form of immutability that also lacks state. Listing 1-3 shows the ConstantExpression example that demonstrates how to create this kind of code. (This example won't run with any version of C++ less than 11; the "Configuring Code::Blocks for smart pointers" sidebar in Book 1, Chapter 8 tells you how to perform this setup.)

LISTING 1-3: **Creating Constant Expression Functions**

```cpp
#include <iostream>

using namespace std;

constexpr int factorial(int n) {
  return n <= 1 ? 1 : (n * factorial(n - 1));
}

template<int n>
struct FactOut {
  FactOut() {
    cout << n << endl;
  }
};

int main() {
  // You can use a number if desired.
  FactOut<15> Nothing1;

  // Computed at compile time.
  FactOut<factorial(4)> Nothing2;

  // Computed at runtime.
  cout << factorial(5) << endl;
  return 0;
}
```

TIP

This example adds some new features to the functional programming toolbox. For example, the factorial() function relies on recursion (where a function calls itself to perform a task) to perform its task. When n is something greater than 1, the function calls itself with a value of n - 1. Otherwise, it returns a value of 1 and the recursion unrolls itself by popping previous iterations from the stack.

REMEMBER

The FactOut structure uses a template parameter of template<int n> (the first place you see a template used in the book is the "Observers and the Standard C++ Library" section of Book 2 Chapter 4, but they're explained in more detail in Book 5 Chapter 5). So, whatever you provide for n, it must evaluate to an int. Fortunately, the factorial() function does evaluate to an int, so you can use it as input to the template. Of course, the compiler wouldn't know whether factorial() did provide an int output unless it computed it at compile time. This is one of the secrets of creating functional programs in C++: You need to think about templates. The FactOut structure contains nothing more than a constructor, and the constructor outputs the value provided as input to the template.

Here's how all this works; main() begins by providing an int value of 15 to FactOut. The next line supplies factorial(4) as input to FactOut, but FactOut needs an int value, so the compiler computes the value during compile time. At runtime, FactOut still sees an int value, but this time it's a computed int value. You can also use factorial() as a standard function, but in this case, the application computes the value at runtime.

WARNING

The variables Nothing1 and Nothing2 really do contain nothing. They satisfy the requirements of the compiler and nothing more. The compiler will raise an exception if you try to use them in your code. This isn't to say that you can't create other coded template forms that do offer some other level of functionality, but this form doesn't allow that functionality. Here is another form of FactOut in which you can use the resulting variables:

```
template<int n>
struct FactOut {
  int val;
  FactOut() {
    cout << n << endl;
    val = n;
  }
};
```

In this case, val contains the computed value of n. Consequently, you could use the variables you create like this: cout << Nothing1.val << endl;. However, now you're introducing a mutable variable again. To avoid problems, you'd need to declare Nothing1 as const FactOut<15> Nothing1;.

Considering the Effects of State

Application *state* is a condition that occurs when the application performs tasks that modify global data. An application doesn't have state when using functional programming. The lack of state has the positive effect of ensuring that any call to a function will produce the same results for a given input every time, regardless of when the application calls the function. However, the lack of state has a negative effect as well: The application now has no memory. When you think about state, think about the capability to remember what occurred in the past, which, in the case of an application, is stored as global data.

Avoiding state in any C++ application is nearly impossible. A problem area is any sort of file or stream data, which by nature changes. The FileLineCount example, shown in Listing 1-4, demonstrates two techniques for determining the number of lines in a file named Temp.txt. The first method, LineCount1(), relies on state to track the current number of lines and the current character. The second method, LineCount2(), doesn't directly contain any sort of tracking; theoretically, it has no state.

LISTING 1-4: **Avoiding the Use of State Directly**

```
#include <iostream>
#include <fstream>
#include <algorithm>

using namespace std;

int LineCount1(string filename) {
  int lineCount = 0;
  char c = ' ';

  ifstream thisFile(filename);

  while (thisFile.get(c)) {
    if (c == '\n')
      lineCount++;
  }

  thisFile.close();

  return lineCount;
}
```

(continued)

LISTING 1-4: *(continued)*

```
int LineCount2(string filename) {
  ifstream thisFile(filename);

  return count(
    istreambuf_iterator<char>(thisFile),
    istreambuf_iterator<char>(), '\n');
}

int main() {
  const string filename = "Temp.txt";

  cout << LineCount1(filename) << endl;
  cout << LineCount2(filename) << endl;
}
```

REMEMBER

When you call the two functions in main(), you get the same output. Line-Count2() actually does appear to have no state. However, unlike the constant expression example in Listing 1-3, count() doesn't perform the calculation during compile time. Doing so would be impossible because the number of times a newline in Temp.txt could change before the application runs. Consequently, the method shown in LineCount2() hides the use of state, but state information still resides at lower levels in the application. Unfortunately, this is about the best you're going to get from C++ in the way of state elimination.

TECHNICAL STUFF

Note that istreambuf_iterator<char>() is an *iterator*, a kind of function that moves through a series of entries in some sort of data structure. In this case, you ask istreambuf_iterator<char>() to look through the characters in thisFile one character at a time. Every time count() sees a newline character, '\n', it adds one to the count. Normally, you must supply a beginning point and an ending point to count(). The second call to istreambuf_iterator<char>() says to continue checking characters until count() reaches the end of the file.

Eliminating Side Effects

The term *declaration* has a number of meanings in computer science, and different people use the term in different ways at different times. For example, in the context of a language such as C++, a declaration is a language construct that defines the properties associated with an identifier. You see declarations used for defining all sorts of language constructs, such as types and enumerations. However, that's not how you use the term *declaration* in a functional programming sense. The following sections describe side effects in terms of declarations and functions in the functional programming sense of the term *declaration*.

Contrasting declarations and functions

When making a declaration in functional programming, you're telling the underlying language to do something. For example, consider the following statement:

1. Make me a cup of tea!

The statement tells simply what to do, not how to do it. The declaration leaves the execution of the task to the party receiving it and infers that the party knows how to complete the task without additional aid. Most important, a declaration enables someone to perform the required task in multiple ways without ever changing the declaration. However, when using a function (or method) named MakeMeTea (the identifier associated with the function), you might use the following sequence instead:

1. Go to the kitchen.
2. Get out the teapot.
3. Add water to the teapot.
4. Bring the pot to a boil.
5. Get out a teacup.
6. Place a teabag in the teacup.
7. Pour hot water over the teabag and let steep for five minutes.
8. Remove the teabag from the cup.
9. Bring me the tea.

REMEMBER

A *function* details what to do, when to do it, and how to do it. Nothing is left to chance and no knowledge is assumed on the part of the recipient. The steps appear in a specific order, and performing a step out of order will cause problems. For example, imagine pouring the hot water over the teabag before placing the teabag in the cup. Functions are often error prone and inflexible, but they do allow for precise control over the execution of a task, and you use them far more often in C++ than you use declarations.

Declarations do suffer from another sort of inflexibility, however, in that they don't allow for interpretation. When making a declarative statement ("Make me a cup of tea!"), you can be sure that the recipient will bring a cup of tea and not a cup of coffee instead. However, when creating a function, you can add conditions that rely on state to affect output. For example, you might add a step to the function that checks the time of day. If it's evening, the recipient might return coffee instead of tea, knowing that the requestor always drinks coffee in the evening based on the steps in the function. A function therefore offers flexibility in its capability to interpret conditions based on state and provide an alternative output.

Declarations are quite strict with regard to input. The example declaration says that a *cup* of tea is needed, not a pot or a mug of tea. The MakeMeTea function, however, can adapt to allow variable inputs, which further changes its behavior. You can allow two inputs, one called size and the other beverage. The size input can default to cup and the beverage input can default to tea, but you can still change the procedure's behavior by providing either or both inputs. The identifier, MakeMeTea, doesn't indicate anything other than the procedure's name. You can just as easily call it MyBeverageMaker.

TIP

One of the hardest issues in moving from imperative languages to functional languages is the concept of declaration. For a given input, a functional language will produce the same output and won't modify or use application state in any way. A declaration always serves a specific purpose and only that purpose.

The second hardest issue is the loss of control. The language, not the developer, decides how to perform tasks. Yet, you sometimes see functional code where the developer tries to write it as a function, usually producing a less-than-desirable result (when the code runs at all).

Associating functions with side effects

An essential difference between functions and declarations is that functions don't return a value in the same manner as declarations do. The previous paragraphs present a function that seems to provide the same result as the associated declaration, but the two aren't the same. The declaration "Make me a cup of tea!" has only one output: the cup of tea. The function has a *side effect* instead of a value. After making a cup of tea, the function indicates that the recipient of the request should take the cup of tea to the requestor. However, the function must successfully conclude for this event to occur. The function isn't returning the tea; the recipient of the request is performing that task. Consequently, the function isn't returning a value.

Side effects also occur in data. When you pass a variable to a function, the expectation in functional programming is that the variable's data will remain untouched — immutable. A side effect occurs when the function modifies the variable data so that upon return from the function call, the variable changes in some manner.

Removing side effects

Because of the nature of the language, you have no magic bullet to use to kill side effects in C++. However, through disciplined coding, you can remove the side effects by observing some basic rules:

>> Never modify the incoming data.

>> Never rely on external data or modify any data outside the function.

>> Ensure that the function produces precisely the same result every time you provide a specific input.

>> Target the function so that it does one thing well, rather than multiple things adequately.

>> Make the function small.

>> Never repeat code or use boilerplate code.

>> Use the switch statement rather than if...then statements.

>> Use only immutable data.

The NoSideEffects example, shown in Listing 1-5, demonstrates these principles. No matter what you do outside the function, nothing changes the result given a particular input.

LISTING 1-5: **Producing Code without Side Effects**

```
#include <iostream>
#include <vector>
#include <algorithm>

using namespace std;

int AddIt(const vector<int> Input,
          const int Start, const int End) {

  int Accumulate = 0;

  // Copy the full vector to a vector of the
  // correct size.
  vector<int> Process(End - Start);
  copy(&Input[Start], &Input[End], Process.begin());
```

(continued)

LISTING 1-5: **(continued)**

```
// Create a sum using a foreach loop.
for (int Element : Process)
  Accumulate += Element;
return Accumulate;
}

int main() {
  const vector<int> ThisVector = {12, 2, 4, 18, 7, 2};

  cout << "Sum of All Elements: " <<
    AddIt(ThisVector, 0, ThisVector.size()) << endl;
  cout << "Sum of Elements 1 through 4: " <<
    AddIt(ThisVector, 1, 5) << endl;
  return 0;
}
```

Everything in this example is handled as a constant except the `Accumulate` and `Process` variables inside the `AddIt()` function. Consequently, there are no side effects. Any changes occur only within `AddIt()`, and `AddIt()` will always produce the same output for a given input.

To process just the `ThisVector` elements that are needed for the summation, `AddIt()` creates a copy of the `Input` vector using the `copy()` function. (Don't worry about the use of a `vector` right now; you see them explained in detail in Book 5, Chapter 6.) Notice that by using Standard Library functionality, you can avoid the appearance of state for the most part in this function. Even the foreach loop (implemented as a special case of the `for` loop):

```
for (int Element : Process)
  Accumulate += Element;
```

avoids the usual state information needed to power the loop. Theoretically, you could create a recursive solution to this problem that wouldn't use state at all. Here's the output from the example:

```
Sum of All Elements: 45
Sum of Elements 1 through 4: 31
```

TECHNICAL STUFF

You might wonder why this example doesn't use an array instead of a vector. The problem with `std::array` is that you must provide an array size, such as `array<int, 6> ThisVector = {12, 2, 4, 18, 7, 2};` so that the array size is known at compile time. However, you don't know the size of the `Process` array at compile time because the call to `AddIt()` provides for a variable starting and ending point. One way around this issue would be to use a `constexpr` setup, as shown earlier in Listing 1-3.

Creating a declarative C++ example

Even though Listing 1-5 goes a long way toward making the C++ code easy to understand and considerably more bulletproof than you might otherwise expect, you can go one step further in that effort without resorting to anything odd in the way of coding. The `Declarative` example shown in Listing 1-6 relies on the Standard Library even further to eliminate the need for a separate function.

LISTING 1-6: **Using Declarative Programming Techniques**

```cpp
#include <iostream>
#include <array>
#include <numeric>

using namespace std;

int main() {
  array<int, 6> ThisArray = {12, 2, 4, 18, 7, 2};
  cout << "Sum of All Elements: " <<
    accumulate(ThisArray.begin(), ThisArray.end(), 0)
    << endl;
  cout << "Sum of Elements 1 through 4: " <<
    accumulate(&ThisArray[1], &ThisArray[5], 0) << endl;
  return 0;
}
```

This example uses the `std::accumulate()` function to perform the required work. There are a number of interesting functions of this sort in the `numeric` header, which you can see at `https://en.cppreference.com/w/cpp/header/numeric`. Notice that the majority of these functions require C++ 11, C++ 17, or even C++ 20 to use, so they're more appropriate for new development. The output from this example is precisely the same as the output from Listing 1-5; only the technique changes.

REMEMBER

One of the more interesting aspects of this example is that you work with an array and allow the underlying code to handle the how of creating the sum. This code doesn't worry about any sort of procedure at all; it simply tells the Standard Library to accumulate (sum) the values together.

Notice also the two methods used to provide the starting and ending points for the calculation. What you need is an address. The first call uses the begin() and end() functions to supply the address, and the second call relies on the address provided by the [] operator.

Understanding the Role of auto

Starting with C++ 11, you can use the auto keyword in place of a specific type declaration. The use of the auto keyword comes in handy when you don't know what data type to expect in advance. When you run the application, the runtime deduces the type of the variable so that you can work with it correctly. Using this technique helps you create flexible code, even if it does reduce the clarity of your code a little. The Auto example, shown in Listing 1-7, shows how to use this keyword to perform various tasks.

LISTING 1-7: **Using the auto Keyword**

```cpp
#include <iostream>
#include <typeinfo>

using namespace std;


void DisplayIt(auto Value) {
  cout << Value << " is of the " <<
    typeid(Value).name() << " type." << endl;
}

int main() {
  auto Hello1 = "Hello There!";
  string Hello2 = "Hello Again!";
  auto Number1 = 1234;
  int Number2 = 5678;
  auto Float1 = 12.34;
  float Float2 = 56.78;
  auto Boolean1 = true;
  bool Boolean2 = false;

  DisplayIt(Hello1);
  DisplayIt(Hello2);
  DisplayIt(Number1);
  DisplayIt(Number2);
```

```
DisplayIt(Float1);
DisplayIt(Float2);
DisplayIt(Boolean1);
DisplayIt(Boolean2);

return 0;
}
```

The code begins by creating a number of variables — with half using standard declarations and half using the auto keyword. It then calls DisplayIt() to display the variable value and type. By using the auto keyword, DisplayIt() can accept all these inputs and interact with them appropriately.

TIP

Even though this code works, it has a problem. The typeid() function often returns a mangled result depending on the compiler you use. Here's an example:

```
Hello There! is of the PKc type.
Hello Again! is of the NSt7__cxx1112basic_stringIcSt11char
  _traitsIcESaIcEEE type.
1234 is of the i type.
5678 is of the i type.
12.34 is of the d type.
56.78 is of the f type.
1 is of the b type.
0 is of the b type.
```

Although you can probably figure the i, d, f, and b entries out, the PKc entry is a mystery, and forget trying to determine the type of the next line that begins with NSt7. You'll likely want the output in human-readable form, which requires a few additional steps, starting with the addition of two new #include entries.

```
#include <memory>
#include <cxxabi.h>
```

The DemangleIt() function takes the mangled input from DisplayIt() and forms it into a human-readable string, as shown here:

```
string DemangleIt(const char* Mangled) {
  int Status;
  unique_ptr<char[], void(*)(void*)> Result(
    abi::__cxa_demangle(Mangled, 0, 0, &Status), free);
  return Result.get() ? string(Result.get()) : "Error";
}
```

The call to `abi::__cxa_demangle()` performs the actual result. What you receive is a `unique_ptr`, `Result`, that contains a pointer to the human-readable form of the type. If the `abi::__cxa_demangle()` call isn't successful, `Result` will contain a null pointer, and you can return a result of `"Error"` in place of the actual type string. To make this code functional, you need to modify `DisplayIt()`, as shown here:

```
void DisplayIt(auto Value) {
  cout << Value << " is of the " <<
    DemangleIt(typeid(Value).name()) << " type." << endl;
}
```

Now when you run the example, you see the output in human-readable form, which makes working with it a lot easier.

```
Hello There! is of the char const* type.
Hello Again! is of the std::__cxx11::basic_string<char,
  std::char_traits<char>, std::allocator<char> > type.
1234 is of the int type.
5678 is of the int type.
12.34 is of the double type.
56.78 is of the float type.
1 is of the bool type.
0 is of the bool type.
```

WARNING

At this point, you should notice something about using `auto`: You may not always get the expected type. In this case, the string declared using `auto` is of a different type than the string declared using `string`. The deduction process often relies on default types as well. For example, if you mean to use a `float`, but declare the variable as `auto`, the result will be a `double` instead because that's the default type.

Passing Functions to Functions

Sometimes you need to apply a process to a group of numbers, or you need to apply more than one process to a single number. In fact, sometimes you need to do both. When you encounter situations like this, the easiest method of dealing with them is to pass a function, the process you want to perform, to another function that handles the situation. In the sections that follow, you begin by seeing a simple example of performing this task on a single number using multiple processes. You also see how to apply a single process to a group of numbers in a technique called a *transform*, because you're transforming one series of numbers into another series of numbers.

Seeing a simple example of function input

At times, a single number represents a base value, but you must manipulate it in various ways to achieve a result. For example, you might need to find the correct process to use to optimize a particular set of values using a base value as a starting point. The FunctionFunction example, shown in Listing 1-8, demonstrates how to use this technique.

LISTING 1-8: **Passing a Function to a Function**

```cpp
#include <iostream>
#include <vector>

using namespace std;

int AddSome(int Value) {
  return Value + 10;
}

int DelSome(int Value) {
  return Value - 10;
}

int MulSome(int Value) {
  return Value * 10;
}

int DivSome(int Value) {
  return Value / 10;
}

typedef int(*FuncPtr)(int);

void ModIt(int Value, vector<FuncPtr> FuncArray) {
  int NumFunc = FuncArray.size();
  cout << "Processing " << NumFunc << " functions."
    << endl;

  for(int i = 0; i < NumFunc; i++)
    cout << FuncArray[i](Value) << endl;
}
```

(continued)

LISTING 1-8: *(continued)*

```
int main() {
  vector<FuncPtr> FuncArray =
    {*AddSome, *DelSome, *MulSome, *DivSome};
  ModIt(10, FuncArray);
  return 0;
}
```

In most cases when you use this technique, you create an array or vector of function pointers. Using a vector is more flexible because you don't have to predetermine the number of functions to pass — it can be any number up to the maximum size of the vector. To make this technique work, however, you must begin by creating a typedef that defines the form of each function pointer entry consisting of the

>> Return value, which is int

>> Pointer to the function in parentheses, which is (*FuncPtr)

>> Input parameters in parentheses, which is (int)

TIP

The *typedef*, the creation of a new name for a type of object, appears in quite a few places in the book. For example, in Book 4, Chapter 1 you see it used to work with a vector to process strings. Book 5, Chapter 1 demonstrates how to use a typedef with a multidimensional array. In fact, Book 5 is the place to go if you want to gain a full appreciation of all the uses for a typedef.

You define the vector as vector<FuncPtr> with a vector name, such as FuncArray. Creating the vector then becomes a matter of providing pointers to the four functions used for testing in this case: AddSome(), DelSome(), MulSome(), and DivSome(). These four functions don't do much, but they do help in testing.

The code calls ModIt() with the value you want to work with, which is 10, and the vector of function pointers, FuncArray. Inside ModIt(), the code calls each of the functions in turn with the supplied value and outputs the result onscreen. Here is the output from this example:

```
Processing 4 functions.
20
0
100
1
```

Using transforms

A transform allows you to process a series of values using a single function. Combining a series of transforms enables you to process a series of values using a series of functions in a particular order. You see transforms used in all sorts of ways, including to condition data and process video. The Transform example, shown in Listing 1-9, gives you an overview of how this technique works using the C++ range functionality.

LISTING 1-9: **Using a Transform on a Series of Data Points**

```cpp
#include <iostream>
#include <vector>
#include <algorithm>

using namespace std;

struct EvenPair {
  int Value;
  bool Even;
};

EvenPair IsEven(int Value){
  if (Value % 2 == 0)
    return EvenPair{Value, true};

  return EvenPair{Value, false};
}

int main(){
  vector<int> Values{1, 2, 3, 4};
  vector<EvenPair> Evens(Values.size());

  transform(Values.begin(), Values.end(),
            Evens.begin(), IsEven);

  for(auto isEven : Evens)
    if (isEven.Even)
      cout << isEven.Value << " is even." << endl;
    else
      cout << isEven.Value << " is odd." << endl;

  return 0;
}
```

This example uses the EvenPair structure to hold two variables that contain the original value you want to check and show whether that value is even. In main(), you begin by creating two vectors: one input, Values, and one output, Evens. The Evens vector will contain a list of the original values and a Boolean showing whether each value is even.

REMEMBER

The call to Transform() takes pointers to the beginning and ending of Values, the beginning of Evens, and the name of a function to use for the transformation. In this case, IsEven() receives an individual Value, determines whether it's even using the mod operator Value % 2, and then outputs a Value and Even pair.

After the transformation completes, a foreach loop checks each value in Evens and outputs an appropriate string. Here are the results:

```
1 is odd.
2 is even.
3 is odd.
4 is even.
```

Using Lambda Expressions for Implementation

A lambda expression is an unnamed function that you can use in place of a regular function reference. Using a lambda expression can make your code more readable by placing the function inline. Chapters 2 and 3 of this minibook cover lambda expressions in detail, but the Lambda example, shown in Listing 1-10, shows an alternative way to create the code displayed in Listing 1-9 in a shorter way.

LISTING 1-10: **Performing a Transform Using a Lambda Expression**

```
#include <iostream>
#include <vector>
#include <algorithm>

using namespace std;

struct EvenPair {
  int Value;
  bool Even;
};
```

```
int main(){
  vector<int> Values{1, 2, 3, 4};
  vector<EvenPair> Evens(Values.size());

  transform(Values.begin(), Values.end(),
            Evens.begin(), [](int Value) {
                return (Value % 2 == 0)
                  ? EvenPair{Value, true}
                  : EvenPair{Value, false};});

  for(auto isEven : Evens)
    if (isEven.Even)
      cout << isEven.Value << " is even." << endl;
    else
      cout << isEven.Value << " is odd." << endl;

  return 0;
}
```

The basic idea of this example is the same as the example in the "Using trans-forms" section, earlier in this chapter, except that it uses a lambda expression in place of the call to IsEven(). The lambda expression begins with a capture clause, [], which defines how to capture any required external variables. An empty capture clause says that the lambda expression can work only with variables that are local to it, which is Value in this case.

As with IsEven(), the lambda expression requires an int input, Value. The compiler deduces the output type based on the lambda expression code. However, you can specify the output type directly when needed using -> output_type. In this case, you'd use [](int Value) -> EvenPair in place of the code shown.

The output is one of two values, as determined by a ternary operator. When (Value % 2 == 0) is true, the output is EvenPair{Value, true}; otherwise, the output is EvenPair{Value, false}. The point is that this version is shorter than the version in Listing 1-9, so lambda expressions can make your code shorter and easier to understand when the function you want to use is small.

Chapter **2**

Working with Lambda Expressions

The "Using Lambda Expressions for Implementation" section of Chapter 1 of this minibook offers a brief overview of lambda expressions as they apply to transforms. However, lambda expressions can do considerably more than you discover in that section's example. Using lambda expressions isn't required to write good C++ code, but they can make your C++ code better and allow for certain optimizations in some cases. This chapter discusses in more detail how and when you use lambda expressions.

This chapter also describes the parts of a lambda expression. You may not ever use everything that a lambda expression has to offer, but it's good to know what's available. You might find that you can make your code even shorter and easier to understand by creating just the right type of lambda expression.

Finally, the chapter shows some examples of how to use lambda expressions for practical purposes such as sorting data. It also helps you understand some development nuances, such as throwing an exception when necessary. Even though this section isn't comprehensive, it provides enough basics for you to know how to use lambda expressions effectively. Chapter 3 of this minibook addresses some additional advanced examples.

You don't have to type the source code for this chapter manually. In fact, using the downloadable source is a lot easier. You can find the source for this chapter in the `\CPP_AIO4\BookIII\Chapter02` folder of the downloadable source. See the Introduction for details on how to find this book's source files.

Creating More Readable and Concise C++ Code

The lambda expression begins with the anonymous function, which actually existed before electronic computers. Alonzo Church (`https://history-computer.com/ModernComputer/thinkers/Church.html`) created the idea of an anonymous function in 1936, which is part of lambda calculus. One of the first computer languages to use anonymous functions was LISP, in 1958. Here are the kinds of anonymous functions you commonly run across in computer science:

>> Function literal

>> Lambda abstraction

>> Lambda expression

Of course, the target of this chapter is the lambda expression, but it pays to know about the other forms of anonymous function as well. All forms of anonymous function share one trait: They aren't associated with any sort of identifier. In other words, you typically use them for short, concise calculations that an application may need to perform only once. From a human perspective, using a lambda expression makes code simpler to understand by placing the function inline rather than in a separate block of code. This technique could lead to spaghetti code of the worst sort when used inappropriately, so some restraint is required on the part of the developer.

REMEMBER

From a computer language perspective, anonymous functions often enable you to clear the code of a plethora of one- or two-line function declarations. Some languages even require the use of anonymous functions for tasks such as binding events to callbacks or instantiating a function for particular values. However, this isn't the case in C++; everything you can do with a lambda expression, you can also do with a named function. When considering lambda expressions in C++, you gain these advantages:

>> **Greater efficiency:** The compiler doesn't have to create a stack frame for lambda expressions, so less underlying machine code is generated.

>> **Better readability:** Locating a one- or two-line named function consumes developer time and makes the code less readable because you don't see it in context.

>> **Fewer errors:** By making a function concise and targeted, it's possible to reduce coding errors because the function is also more understandable.

>> **Reducing frankenfunctions:** Using lambda expressions can help rid your code of those named functions that try to do too much using too many different styles and not accomplishing a great deal except confusing the developers who look at it. When thinking about frankenfunctions, think about those named functions that are put together from bits and pieces of one- or two-line functions and whose actions are differentiated using if...then or switch statements.

TIP

The most important concept to take away from this section is that lambda expressions don't replace named functions; they simply provide an alternative style that you can use to make your code better. Given that they represent a style and not a coding mandate, you need to work with them for a while to define a comfort level that makes sense in the applications you write.

Defining the Essential Lambda Expression

Because lambda expressions rely on math, rather than on coding technique, they have a form that is common across computer languages. You can't make a direct replacement of a lambda expression written in one language into another, but understanding the lambda expressions in both languages is easier because they have a similar form. The following sections discuss the C++ specific form of a lambda expression.

Defining the parts of a lambda expression

A lambda expression can take a number of forms. You saw one of those forms in the "Using Lambda Expressions for Implementation" section of Chapter 1 of this minibook. However, it's time to look at the full definition of the lambda expression:

```
[ captures ] <tparams> ( params ) specifiers exception
attr -> ret requires { body }
```

Not all of these elements are needed in every case, and some are available only in some versions of C++. With these limitations in mind, Table 2-1 provides a description of each of the elements (with a blank version column indicating that the element is available in all current versions).

TABLE 2-1   **Elements of a Lambda Expression**

Element	Minimum C++ Version	Description
captures	Various	Specifies how external variables are captured for use by the lambda expression. The default is to capture variables by reference. However, you can also create a copy of the variable. You can define a single policy for all variables or provide policies for individual variables. Starting with C++ 14, you can also provide a variable initializer in case the variable hasn't been initialized. The reference at https://en.cppreference.com/w/cpp/language/lambda#Lambda_capture offers additional details.
tparams	20	Provides a templated method of defining variable types. You use it to provide type names to the parameters of a generic lambda. This entry works much like the templates described at https://en.cppreference.com/w/cpp/language/templates. You may supply an optional requires clause to place constraints on the templated functionality.
params	Various	Defines the parameters passed into the lambda expression for processing. Starting with C++ 14, you can use default arguments and the auto keyword.
specifiers	Various	Modifies the manner in which the code interacts with captured external variables. The following keywords are available: mutable: Allows modification of the variables and objects, and the calling of object non-const members. constexpr (C++ 17 and above): Specifies that the function call operator is a constexpr (see the "Creating constant expressions" section of Chapter 1 of this minibook for details). consteval (C++20 and above): Specifies that the function call operator is an immediate function (see the "Defining an immediate function" section of Chapter 3 of this minibook for details).
exception	Various	Creates a dynamic exception specification (see the "Specifying that the lambda expression throws exceptions" section, later in this chapter) or defines a noexcept specifier (C++ 11 and above).
attr	11	Adds attributes to the function for implementation specifics, such as working on the GNU or IBM platforms. The discussion at https://en.cppreference.com/w/cpp/language/attributes provides additional details on using attributes.
ret		Indicates the return type of the lambda expression. If you don't include this element, the compiler will deduce the return type based on the code you provide.

Element	Minimum C++ Version	Description
requires	20	Defines requirements for template arguments that make it easier to choose the correct function overloads and template arguments. You use this element as an optional addition to tparams. The discussion at https://en.cppreference.com/w/cpp/language/constraints provides additional details.
body		Contains the function body — that is, the code that will actually execute.

Some common patterns are used to create lambda expressions so that you don't have to rely on the full version shown earlier in this section. Here are the most common forms:

» [captures] (params) -> ret { body }: Defines a const lambda, which is the most common form. All the captured variables are const in this case, and you can't modify them.

» [captures] (params) { body }: Specifies a const lambda in which the return type is deduced by the compiler. The compiler uses the function's return statement as a basis for making the deduction.

» [captures] { body }: Creates a lambda expression that requires no inputs. You can't use this form if the lambda expression makes use of the constexpr, mutable, exception specification, attributes, or trailing return type features.

Relying on computer detection of return type

The automatic detection feature of lambda expressions works much like the auto keyword for other types of declarations. In most cases, the automatic detection feature works fine because it relies on the most common or default type for the output.

WARNING

Unfortunately, as described in the "Understanding the Role of auto" section of Chapter 1 of this minibook, the automatic detection (deduction) on the part of the compiler doesn't always work precisely as planned. In addition, depending on how you define the function input to a function, you can get some strange results. Consequently, you always need to exercise care in the use of this feature. The ReturnDeduction example, shown in Listing 2-1, demonstrates how you can obtain different results based on whether you specify a return type or allow the computer to deduce it for you. (This example uses the same `DemangleIt()` function described in the "Understanding the Role of auto" section of Chapter 1 of this minibook.)

LISTING 2-1: **Deciding Between a Deduced or Specific Return Type**

```cpp
#include <iostream>
#include <typeinfo>
#include <memory>
#include <cxxabi.h>

using namespace std;

string DemangleIt(const char* Mangled) {
  int Status;
  unique_ptr<char[], void(*)(void*)> Result(
    abi::__cxa_demangle(Mangled, 0, 0, &Status), free);
  return Result.get() ? string(Result.get()) : "Error";
}

void ShowType(function<float(double)> lambda) {
  cout << "Input has a value of: " << lambda(2.6) << endl;
  cout << "Input has type of: " <<
    DemangleIt(typeid(lambda(2.6)).name()) << endl;
}

void ShowChar(function<char(int)> lambda){
  cout << "Input has a value of: " << lambda(7) << endl;
}

int main() {
  ShowType([](int x) -> int {return int(x * x);});
  ShowType([](double x) -> int {return int(x * x);});
  ShowType([](double x) -> double {return x * x;});
  ShowType([](double x) {return float(x * x);});
  ShowType([](double x) {return x > 2 ? true : false;});
  ShowType([](int x) -> char {return char(x * 10);});
  ShowChar([](int x) -> char {return char(x * 10);});
  return 0;
}
```

The input argument for the functions in this example is function<>. When using function<>, you specify a return type, even if the return type is void, and any input types, or empty parentheses, (), when the function doesn't need one. Part of the problem with both ShowType() and ShowChar() is that the function<> declaration doesn't allow use of auto, so you get whatever type you define, as you see later in the example.

The ShowType() and ShowChar() functions both show the value of lambda() when you provide a specific input value to the lambda expression. The ShowType() function also outputs the type of the value output by the function, and you'll see the importance of this output in a moment.

The lambda functions are of the two const types described in the "Defining the parts of a lambda expression" section, earlier in this chapter. Some specify a return type; others don't. Note that the first two lambda expressions both provide an int output, but one takes an int as input and the other takes a double. Playing with input and output types like this can help you understand the effects of decisions that you make when using lambda expressions. Note that the last three lambda expressions don't actually return a numeric type. The first of these returns a bool and the last two return char.

You probably think that one or more of these lambda expressions will fail, especially given the input values used in ShowType() and ShowChar(). However, they all do work, as shown in the somewhat surprising output here:

```
Input has a value of: 4
Input has type of: float
Input has a value of: 6
Input has type of: float
Input has a value of: 6.76
Input has type of: float
Input has a value of: 6.76
Input has type of: float
Input has a value of: 1
Input has type of: float
Input has a value of: 20
Input has type of: float
Input has a value of: F
```

The compiler seems adept at making the lambda expressions work even when they really shouldn't. For example, the first lambda expression accepts an int as input and produces an int as output, so the input is truncated, which results in an output of 4. The second lambda expression truncates the output as an int, so now you see 6 from what should be the same calculation, which should actually produce a value of 6.76, as shown in the next two outputs. The bool output is a value of 1 and the char output is a value 20, neither of which reflects their true types. However, the really odd thing is that the type of all these outputs is float (the default as explained in the next section); it doesn't matter what the lambda expression actually provided as output. The point is that you need to exercise care in the construction of both the lambda expression and the function that receives it to obtain the desired result.

Using the auto keyword with lambda expressions

The auto keyword can save you a great deal of pain when working with lambda expressions, plus it can help you avoid some common problems with getting the result you want. The UseAuto example, shown in Listing 2-2, is a reworking of the example in Listing 2-1, shown earlier. However, even though the example works in a similar manner, the output is different because of the use of auto.

| LISTING 2-2: | **Performing Tasks Using auto** |

```
#include <iostream>
#include <typeinfo>
#include <memory>
#include <cxxabi.h>

using namespace std;

string DemangleIt(const char* Mangled) {
  int Status;
  unique_ptr<char[], void(*)(void*)> Result(
    abi::__cxa_demangle(Mangled, 0, 0, &Status), free);
  return Result.get() ? string(Result.get()) : "Error";
}

void ShowData(auto lambda){
  cout << "Input has a value of: " << lambda(3.6) << endl;
  cout << "Input has type of: " <<
    DemangleIt(typeid(lambda(3.6)).name()) << endl;
}

int main() {
  ShowData([](int x) -> int {return int(x * x);});
  ShowData([](double x) -> int {return int(x * x);});
  ShowData([](double x) -> double {return x * x;});
```

```
ShowData([](double x) {return float(x * x);});
ShowData([](double x) {return x > 2 ? true : false;});
ShowData([](double x) -> char {return char(x * 10);});

return 0;
}
```

When you run this example, you see that the auto keyword enables you to obtain results specific to the input. Here is what you see in this case (which you can compare to the output in the previous section):

```
Input has a value of: 9
Input has type of: int
Input has a value of: 12
Input has type of: int
Input has a value of: 12.96
Input has type of: double
Input has a value of: 12.96
Input has type of: float
Input has a value of: 1
Input has type of: bool
Input has a value of: $
Input has type of: char
```

TIP

By giving up control over the form of the input to ShowData(), you also preserve the types of the various inputs. Each of the outputs is now of the correct type, and the char output (last) actually appears as a character rather than a number. However, there isn't a best solution — only the solution that works to meet your specific requirements. You therefore need to keep the function<> method described in the previous section in mind.

Lest you think that someone could pass anything to ShowData(), you can try, but you won't be successful. If you were to pass something like ShowData(14), the compiler would output an error message of 'lambda' cannot be used as a function. Even though you're using auto, the auto is still expecting a function as input.

Using lambda expressions as macros

You can assign a lambda expression to a variable and then use the variable as a kind of macro. This technique can make it a lot easier to perform some repetitive tasks that seem to appear everywhere, but take little code. The CreateMacro example, shown in Listing 2-3, demonstrates this approach.

LISTING 2-3: **Creating a Macro**

```
#include <iostream>

using namespace std;

int main(){
  auto f = [](auto Input) {cout << Input << endl;};

  f("Hello");
  f(221);
  f(true);
  f(99 / 3);
  f(char(65));
  f(int(15/4));
  return 0;
}
```

The code in this example creates a simple lambda expression that outputs the input expression, whatever it might be, to the screen. To make the macro work, you use auto in two contexts, both as the type of the variable holding the macro and as the input. Here's the output you see:

```
Hello
221
1
33
A
3
```

Developing with Lambda Expressions

The previous sections of the chapter give you an idea of how lambda expressions work. In the following sections of the chapter, you see how to implement certain lambda expression techniques in a more advanced manner that you might use within application code.

Using lambda expressions with classes and structures

You can use lambda expressions for a wide variety of tasks with both classes and structures. In most cases, the tasks have something to do with data manipulation, such as finding data elements or sorting items, but lambda expressions can also see use for various kinds of analysis. The LambdaForClass example, shown in Listing 2-4, stores a list of AnimalEntry entries in the Animals list found in the StoreAnimals class. The lambda expression that defines FindAnimals() helps locate a particular animal type and display the exhibits holding those animals in the zoo.

LISTING 2-4: **Interacting with Classes and Structures**

```
#include <iostream>
#include <list>
#include <algorithm>

using namespace std;

struct AnimalEntry {
  string Name;
  int CageLocation;
};

class StoreAnimals {
public:
  void FindAnimals(string Name);
  list<AnimalEntry> Animals;
};

void StoreAnimals::FindAnimals(string FindName) {
  for_each(Animals.begin(), Animals.end(),
    [FindName](AnimalEntry ThisEntry) {
      if (FindName == ThisEntry.Name)
        cout << ThisEntry.CageLocation << endl;
    }
  );
}

int main() {
  StoreAnimals Zoo;
```

(continued)

LISTING 2-4: *(continued)*

```
Zoo.Animals.push_back (AnimalEntry{"Hippo", 300});
Zoo.Animals.push_back (AnimalEntry{"Tiger", 301});
Zoo.Animals.push_back (AnimalEntry{"Tiger", 302});
Zoo.Animals.push_back (AnimalEntry{"Zebra", 303});

cout << "Finding hippo cages." << endl;
Zoo.FindAnimals("Hippo");

cout << "Finding tiger cages." << endl;
Zoo.FindAnimals("Tiger");
return 0;
}
```

An interesting part of this example is the use of a for_each() to iterate the entries in the Animals list. Even though this example iterates the entire list, you can also limit the search scope to specific records by providing a different beginning and ending point within the list.

This example also uses a simple capture, FindName, to obtain the name of the animal to locate. The next section of the chapter provides additional details on how captures work, but it uses a different approach than this example does. The lambda expression must also accept an individual entry, ThisEntry, of type AnimalEntry, from the for_each().

The main() code consists of creating a StoreAnimals object, Zoo, and populating the Animals list it contains with AnimalEntry objects. The code can then call Zoo. FindAnimals() to locate specific animals in the list. Here's the output from this example:

```
Finding hippo cages.
300
Finding tiger cages.
301
302
```

Working with the capture clause

You have many ways to use the capture clause, but one of the more interesting is to make your lambda expression a little more flexible. You can use the capture clause to help implement multiple behaviors by using a single lambda expression, as shown in the MultiTask example in Listing 2-5.

LISTING 2-5:
Performing Multiple Tasks by Using a Capture Clause

```cpp
#include <iostream>
#include <typeinfo>

using namespace std;

struct AddVal_t {};
typedef AddVal_t AddVal;

struct SubVal_t {};
typedef SubVal_t SubVal;

int main() {
  int Total = 0;

  auto ChangeNum = [Total](auto Type, int Value) mutable {
    if (is_same<decltype(Type), AddVal>::value) {
      Total += Value;
      return Total;
    } else if (is_same<decltype(Type), SubVal>::value) {
      Total -= Value;
      return Total;
    } else {
      throw -1;
    }
  };

  AddVal DoAdd;
  SubVal DoSub;

  cout << ChangeNum(DoAdd, 5) << endl;
  cout << ChangeNum(DoAdd, 6) << endl;
  cout << ChangeNum(DoSub, 4) << endl;
  try {
    cout << ChangeNum(5, 5) << endl;
  } catch (int e) {
    cout << "Error in Input!" << endl;
  }
  cout << Total << endl;
  return 0;
}
```

This example is actually capable of doing a number of things, and you should experiment with it. For one thing, you begin with two structures, AddVal_t and SubVal_t, that are now empty but could be expanded to provide additional functionality. The code defines two types: AddVal and SubVal, based on these structures.

The lambda expression depends on an external variable, Total, which is initialized to 0. The ChangeNum() declaration uses Total as a capture, and you'll see later in this section why that's important. The two input arguments, Type (defines what operation to perform) and Value (defines the amount of change), work just like any other set of arguments. The mutable element specifies that the code can change Total.

You could use phrases, numbers, or other methods of determining an action for this example, but the example uses types instead. If ChangeNum() receives an input of the appropriate type, it will perform the appropriate action. Because of the way that this code is structured, the action can be type specific. The call to is_same() determines whether the input type, Type, is the same as a base type, such as AddVal or SubVal. After the types are verified, the code performs type-specific tasks. If the type isn't present, ChangeNum() throws an exception.

To use the lambda expression, the code must create variables of the correct type. Normally, you'd initialize the variables, DoAdd and DoSub, but because the example uses an empty structure, you don't need to in this case. The code then calls ChangeNum() using various operations and values, including one incorrect call. Note that the code also checks the value of Total at the end. Here's the output you should see:

```
5
11
7
Error in Input!
0
```

Even though the lambda expression has tracked Total internally, it hasn't changed the external value at all. So, you see the expected outputs for each call, but the actual value of Total doesn't change. Of course, you also see the error output for incorrect inputs.

The method of capture is important. For example, you can initialize the capture should you want to do so. Change [Total] to read [Total = 5] and then rerun the code. The outputs now look like this:

```
10
16
12
Error in Input!
0
```

REMEMBER

The internal values of Total have changed, but the external value of Total remains 0. You can also change this behavior by changing [Total = 5] to read [&Total]. Note that you can't initialize Total if you also plan to access it by reference, so [&Total = 5] won't work. Here's the new output:

```
5
11
7
Error in Input!
7
```

Now the external value of Total reflects the manipulations of the lambda expression. Although writing even more complex lambda expressions than the one shown here is possible, you need to consider when you've reached the point where you should be using a standard function, rather than a lambda expression. Ideally, this example demonstrates the upper end of lambda expression complexity.

Sorting data using a lambda expression

Although a computer can deal with data in any order, humans require order to make sense of the data. The standard sorting functions provided with C++ work well with data in standard format, such as a single-column list. However, after you start adding structures or classes, the data is much harder to sort without help. The SortList example, shown in Listing 2-6, shows how to perform a single-column and a two-column sort on data formatted with a structure, Collect, into a Collectables list (a vector, in this case).

LISTING 2-6: **Performing Sorting Tasks**

```cpp
#include <iostream>
#include <vector>
#include <algorithm>

using namespace std;

struct Collect {
  string Name;
```

(continued)

LISTING 2-6: *(continued)*

```
    int Height;
    string Location;
};

int main() {
    vector<Collect> Collectables;
    Collectables.push_back ({"Statue", 40, "Basement"});
    Collectables.push_back ({"Statue", 30, "Basement"});
    Collectables.push_back ({"Mirror", 54, "1st Floor"});
    Collectables.push_back ({"Statue", 33, "1st Floor"});
    Collectables.push_back ({"Mirror", 33, "2nd Floor"});
    Collectables.push_back ({"Chair", 44, "1st Floor"});
    Collectables.push_back ({"Chair", 36, "2nd Floor"});

    auto SortRule1 = [](Collect S1, Collect S2) {
        return S1.Location < S2.Location;
    };

    auto SortRule2 = [](Collect S1, Collect S2) {
        if (S1.Location != S2.Location)
            return S1.Location < S2.Location;
        return S1.Name < S2.Name;
    };

    sort(Collectables.begin(), Collectables.end(),
        SortRule1);

    cout << "One Column Sort" << endl;
    for (auto s: Collectables)
        cout << s.Name << "\t" << s.Height << "\t"
            << s.Location << endl;

    sort(Collectables.begin(), Collectables.end(),
        SortRule2);

    cout << endl << "Two Column Sort" << endl;
    for (auto s: Collectables)
        cout << s.Name << "\t" << s.Height << "\t"
            << s.Location << endl;

    return 0;
}
```

The example begins by creating a vector of items to sort. It then creates two sort rules. Both SortRule1 and SortRule2 perform comparisons and return a bool value as to whether the comparison (the first item is less than the second item) is true. The difference is that SortRule2 performs the task on two columns of the list, so two levels of comparison are required. The code then calls sort() to perform the list sorting and relies on a foreach loop to display the result, which appears here:

```
One Column Sort
Mirror   54       1st Floor
Statue   33       1st Floor
Chair    44       1st Floor
Mirror   33       2nd Floor
Chair    36       2nd Floor
Statue   40       Basement
Statue   30       Basement

Two Column Sort
Chair    44       1st Floor
Mirror   54       1st Floor
Statue   33       1st Floor
Chair    36       2nd Floor
Mirror   33       2nd Floor
Statue   40       Basement
Statue   30       Basement
```

Specifying that the lambda expression throws exceptions

Exceptions can be a difficult part of your code to implement properly because an exception indicates that something unexpected has happened and the caller needs to take action. Early versions of lambda expressions include a throw() specification as part of the declaration, but the specification proved difficult to implement, and many programmers saw it as an awkward way to program. So, even though throw() is still an optional part of the specification, you don't generally see it used. In fact, you can't use it in C++ 20 because it has been deprecated and removed.

REMEMBER

The MultiTask example (refer to Listing 2-5) throws an exception when the caller doesn't provide an acceptable input of the correct type. Throwing an exception is still perfectly acceptable, and when you call outside functions from your lambda expression, these functions can throw exceptions, too. However, sometimes you really don't want the exception to occur because the unexpected situation is expected. To get past this problem, you can use noexcept() to disregard the exception, like this:

```
cout << noexcept(ChangeNum(5,5)) << endl;
```

Instead of an exception, the code outputs the captured value of Total, which is 0. This is the operator form of noexcept(). You also have access to a specifier version of noexcept() that isn't guaranteed to work with older versions of C++. It looks like this:

```
auto ChangeNum = [Total](auto Type, int Value) mutable
    noexcept {...}
```

In this case, the inability to throw an exception affects the lambda expression as a whole, along with any functions that it calls. Of course, now you don't know when exceptional conditions really do happen — the code simply outputs whatever answer it can, which is likely incorrect, when an unforeseen condition occurs.

Chapter **3**

Advanced Lambda Expressions

The previous chapter demonstrated tasks that you can perform using lambda expressions with most versions of C++ 11 and above. This chapter takes the next step by considering advanced tasks that you can perform using newer versions of C++. In fact, the first section is C++ 20 specific. Some of the remaining sections also work with C++ 17. The point is that if you're working with an older version of C++, most of what you see in this chapter won't work. Remember that you can test the examples in this chapter using Wandbox (https://wandbox.org/) if your C++ compiler doesn't provide the required C++ 20 functionality.

Also in this chapter, you look at new ways in which to use lambda expressions in C++ 20. Before C++ 20, you couldn't use a lambda expression in a context requiring an unevaluated expression, including the decltype() operator, which is the specific topic of this chapter. However, the techniques you learn can apply to other unevaluated contexts. Don't worry if you don't understand these terms just now; they're covered later in the chapter.

Older versions of C++ won't allow you to assign a lambda expression or make it constructible. Consequently, you can't do something like make two map objects (see the "Mapping your data" section of Book 5, Chapter 6 for details about maps) equal when the source map object contains a lambda expression. In addition, it's difficult to make the lambda expression a constructible part of the map declaration, so you end up re-creating it every time. This chapter looks at how C++ 20 fixes both of these issues.

The previous chapter explores captures of various types. However, you can summarize them as being by copy, reference, or `std::tuple`. The ability to send an arbitrary, packed list of data with a variable number of arguments requires the use of a *variadic template.* The final section of this chapter discusses the use of packs and demonstrates how C++ expands them to allow access. You use this sort of feature in places where the number of arguments is unknown until runtime. For example, you may have to deal with data that has a variable number of constraints placed on it.

REMEMBER

You don't have to type the source code for this chapter manually. In fact, using the downloadable source is a lot easier. You can find the source for this chapter in the \CPP_AIO4\BookIII\Chapter03 folder of the downloadable source. See the Introduction for details on how to find these source files.

Considering the C++ 20 Lambda Extensions

C++ 20 adds a number of lambda extensions. Some of these extensions appear as the chapter progresses. The remaining extensions appear in the following sections.

Defining an immediate function

An immediate function is associated with `consteval`, which often appears like this:

```
#include <iostream>

using namespace std;

consteval double sqr(float x) {
  return x * x;
}

int main()
{
```

```
  constexpr double MySquare = sqr(4.2);
  cout << MySquare << endl;
  return 0;
}
```

The value of `MySquare` is computed at compile time rather than runtime. `MySquare` occupies static memory space from the time the application begins to when it ends, and its value never changes.

The `consteval` specifier for a lambda expression has the same effect, but is often more flexible and concise. Here's the lambda expression version of the same code:

```
#include <iostream>

using namespace std;

int main()
{
  auto sqr = [](auto x) consteval {return x*x;};
  constexpr double MySquare = sqr(4.2);
  constexpr auto MySquare2 = sqr(20);

  cout << MySquare << endl;
  cout << MySquare2 << endl;
  return 0;
}
```

WARNING

As with the function version, the value of `MySquare` and `MySquare2` are both computed at compile time. Consequently, if you try to use a value that isn't known at compile time, the compiler generates an error message.

Using = and this in captures

The examples shown in the "Using lambda expressions with classes and structures" and "Working with the capture clause" section of Chapter 2 of this minibook demonstrate how to work with captures. Some captures aren't currently very readable. For example, both of these two captures imply `this`, which is a pointer to the current object, but `this` is explicitly stated only in one:

```
[=]
[=, *this]
```

The = operator says to capture all variables by copy. The this operator also captures the current object by copy. You use *this to capture the current object by reference, which means you can make changes to it. In C++ 20, you can now use [=, this] to make it clear that you are capturing both variables and the current object by copy, rather than by reference. You can also use [&, this], which indicates that you are capturing all variables by reference but capturing the object by copy.

Finding other changes

Sometimes, despite having the best understanding possible of lambda expressions, things just don't work when you code them and it appears that they should. Often, you find subtle changes to the specification that tell you why something is no longer working. For example, you can see some of these changes in the paper "P1091R2 Extending structured bindings to be more like variable declarations" at http://www.open-std.org/jtc1/sc22/wg21/docs/papers/2018/p1091r2.html.

Working in Unevaluated Contexts

An *unevaluated expression* is a full expression; it doesn't require evaluation at runtime. For example, the typeid, sizeof, noexcept, and decltype operators aren't evaluated. In addition, the C++ 20 requires-expressions (see https://en.cppreference.com/w/cpp/language/constraints) aren't evaluated. An *unevaluated context* is one in which C++ is looking for an unevaluated expression of some type. C++ 20 allows the use of lambda expressions in unevaluated expressions, template arguments, alias declarations, and typedef declarations.

To see how an unevaluated context works, the PriorityQueue example, shown in Listing 3-1, demonstrates how to add a lambda expression comparator within a decltype() to automatically sort the priority queue.

LISTING 3-1: **Defining a Priority Queue Comparator**

```
#include <iostream>
#include <queue>

using namespace std;

int main() {
```

```
priority_queue<
  int,
  vector<int>,
  decltype( [](int a, int b)->bool{return a>b;})> PQ;

PQ.push(10);
PQ.push(5);
PQ.push(8);
PQ.push(1);
PQ.push(11);

while (!PQ.empty()) {
  cout << PQ.top() << endl;
  PQ.pop();
}
}
```

A `priority_queue` is a *container adapter* (something that modified the behavior of a standard container, such as a `vector`) that makes performing lookups in a consistent manner possible. It does so at the expense of insertion and extraction times. However, if you perform mostly lookups, using a `priority_queue` can substantially improve application execution times.

This example creates a `priority_queue` that accepts `int` values as input, modifies the behavior of a `vector`, and uses a lambda expression within a `decltype()` as a comparator. The lambda expression is simple in this case — it just compares two values and returns `true` when the first value is greater than the second. The purpose of this `priority_queue` is to create a vector where the entries remain in sorted order at all times, making lookups faster.

After creating the `priority_queue`, the example pushes values in a random order. However, the `priority_queue` automatically sorts them for you. The code then uses a `while` loop to show the order in which the values are stored, as shown here:

```
1
5
8
10
11
```

Using Assignable Stateless Lambda Expressions

Until C++ 20, lambda expressions aren't constructible or assignable. A lambda expression is *constructible* if you use it to replace a structure similar to this one:

```
struct {
  template <typename X, typename Y>
  auto operator()(X x, Y y) const { return x > y; }
} greater;
```

A structure like this one would be used for performing tasks such as acting as a comparator for a map. A lambda expression is *assignable* if you can assign a source lambda to a target lambda, like this:

```
MyMap2 = MyMap1;
```

The idea is to make lambda expressions interchangeable with function objects. Using a lambda expression would be more concise and potentially easier to understand. The AssignLambda example, shown in Listing 3-2, demonstrates how to perform this task using a map.

LISTING 3-2: **Creating a Constructible Lambda and Then Assigning It**

```
#include <iostream>
#include <map>

using namespace std;

int main()
{
  auto greater = [](auto x, auto y) { return x > y; };
  map<string, int, decltype(greater)> MyMap1;

  MyMap1.insert(pair<string, int>("D", 12));
  MyMap1.insert(pair<string, int>("B", 4));
  MyMap1.insert(pair<string, int>("C", 8));
  MyMap1.insert(pair<string, int>("A", 1));
```

```
cout << "MyMap1 Content" << endl;
for (auto element : MyMap1)
  cout << element.first << "\t" << element.second
    << endl;

map<string, int, decltype(greater)> MyMap2;
MyMap2 = MyMap1;
MyMap1.insert(pair<string, int>("E", 23));
MyMap2.insert(pair<string, int>("F", 35));

cout << endl << "MyMap2 Content" << endl;
for (auto element : MyMap2)
  cout << element.first << "\t" << element.second
    << endl;
}
```

Compare this example with the one in Listing 3-1 and you'll note that the comparator, greater, appears as a separate element, enabling you to use the same comparator in multiple map instances without repeating the lambda expression code. As with the priority queue example, the use of a comparator will automatically sort the key/value pairs in the map as they're inserted.

What's especially interesting is that you can assign MyMap1 to MyMap2. However, MyMap2 is now copied from MyMap1. However, the content of MyMap1 and MyMap2 become separate after the copy process so that changes made to MyMap1 and MyMap2 are different beyond that point. Here's the output from this example:

```
MyMap1 Content
D    12
C    8
B    4
A    1

MyMap2 Content
F    35
D    12
C    8
B    4
A    1
```

Dealing with Pack Expansions

A *data pack* is a group of variables sent to a templated function in which the number of variables is unknown until runtime. Pack expansion is an essential part of dealing with a variable number of arguments. The following sections describe pack expansion using a number of examples so that you can see how the basic concept works.

Considering the template

Starting with C++ 11, you can send a variable number of arguments using a variadic template. To provide you with a basic idea of how this works, consider the code found in the VariadicTemplate example, as shown in Listing 3-3.

LISTING 3-3: **Using a Variadic Template**

```
#include <iostream>

using namespace std;

template<typename... Types>
size_t nargs(Types... args) {
  return sizeof... (args);
}

int main()
{
  cout << nargs(1, "3.5", true) << endl;
  cout << nargs(2, 4, "Hello", 1.1) << endl;
  cout << nargs() << endl;
  return 0;
}
```

The ... operator says that this code is variadic — meaning that the number of arguments and their types are unknown. The nargs() function receives a variable number of arguments in a single packed variable, args. All this function does is tell you the number of arguments passed, so you see the following output:

```
3
4
0
```

If you were to look at the first call, nargs(1, "3.5", true), the expansion of the function header would look like this:

```
template<int, const char*, bool>
size_t nargs(int param1, const char* param2, bool param3)
```

Using a variadic template doesn't preclude the use of known variables. For example, if you have a function with one known variable and a pack of unknown variables, the declaration might look like this:

```
template<typename T, typename... Types>
size_t nargs(T Parm, Types... args) {
```

Processing the variables using recursion

Variadic templates require a special kind of recursion to process. Unlike standard recursion, the function header for variadic recursion changes with each call because the number of variables is one less each time. Consequently, you create a base case as a separate function call. The VariadicTemplate2 example, shown in Listing 3-4, demonstrates this approach.

| LISTING 3-4: | **Processing the Variables in Variadic Templates** |

```
#include <iostream>

using namespace std;

template<typename T>
void ProcessArgs(T arg) {
  cout << arg << endl;
}

template<typename T, typename... Args>
void ProcessArgs(T ThisArg, Args... args) {
  cout << ThisArg << endl;
  ProcessArgs(args...);
}

int main()
{
  ProcessArgs(1, "Hello", true, 3.5);
  return 0;
}
```

In this case, each call to ProcessArgs() expands args, separating out one variable for display as ThisArg until only one variable is left (the base case), with the final variable, arg, displayed onscreen. The example will take any number of arguments of virtually any type that cout can display. Here's the output from this example:

```
1
Hello
1
3.5
```

Processing the variables using a lambda expression

Using a lambda expression with variadic templates can make certain tasks significantly easier. For example, you might want to know whether a particular group of numbers is all greater than 7. So, you construct a lambda expression, like this:

```
auto constraint = [](int x) {return x > 7;};
```

TIP

The lambda expression could perform any level of constraint checking, but in this case, it simply looks for an int input greater than 7. Note that this lambda expression looks specifically for an int value, which means that providing lists of values that don't include int values will produce an error message from the compiler.

As with the example in the previous section, the VariadicTemplate3 example, shown in Listing 3-5, relies on recursion. However, the recursion is a little more complex this time.

LISTING 3-5: **Checking on Constraints**

```
#include <iostream>
#include <typeinfo>

using namespace std;

auto constraint = [](int x) {return x > 7;};

template<typename T>
bool ProcessArgs(T arg) {
```

```cpp
    cout << "Value is: " << arg << endl;
    return constraint(arg);
}

template<typename T, typename... Args>
bool ProcessArgs(T arg, Args... args) {
    cout << "Value is: " << arg << endl;
    return constraint(arg) && ProcessArgs(args...);
}

int main()
{
    cout << "List contains only numbers above 7: "
        << (ProcessArgs(10, 11, 14, 8) ? "True" : "False")
        << endl << endl;

    cout << "List contains only numbers above 7: "
        << (ProcessArgs(10, 3, 6) ? "True" : "False")
        << endl;;
    return 0;
}
```

The example still outputs each of the values it processes. However, it also checks the constraint and returns true when the number is greater than 7. This extra level of processing is common in certain sciences, especially in statistical analysis, machine learning, or deep learning tasks. An advantage of this approach is that the code doesn't check every value if one value is out of range. The moment the code detects an incorrect value, it ends the recursion. Here's the output from this example:

```
Value is: 10
Value is: 11
Value is: 14
Value is: 8
List contains only numbers above 7: True

Value is: 10
Value is: 3
List contains only numbers above 7: False
```

4

Fixing Problems

Contents at a Glance

Chapter **1**

Dealing with Bugs

Who knows whether it's true, but as the story goes, back when the first computer was built over a half-century ago, it filled an entire room with circuitry (yet was about as powerful as one of those inexpensive calculators — the kind that perform only basic math). One day, the thing was misbehaving, and some brave engineers climbed deep into the thing. (The version we're thinking of has them wearing white radiation suits, of course.) Deep in The Bowels of the Machine (sounds like a movie title), they found none other than . . . an insect! A bug! It was a great big bug that had gotten messed up in the circuitry, causing the computer to malfunction. So the story goes, anyway. Today, we use the term *bug* to mean something that is wrong with an application. In this minibook, you discover how to track down bugs and fix them in your software. In this chapter, you see exactly what a bug is (and is not!), how bugs occur, and how you can try to avoid them.

REMEMBER

You don't have to type the source code for this chapter manually. In fact, using the downloadable source is a lot easier. You can find the source for this chapter in the \CPP_AIO4\BookIV\Chapter01 folder of the downloadable source. See the Introduction for details on how to find these source files.

It's Not a Bug. It's a Feature!

So you're using a word processor and suddenly the application freaks out and saves your file automatically. You didn't tell it to do that. Then you use the same copy of the word processor and try to do a copy-and-paste procedure (that's called a *use case*, by the way). Suddenly the Font dialog box pops up. And then later, you're sitting with your laptop at Starbucks, and it automatically begins the shutdown procedure. You didn't tell it to do that.

Bugs! Bugs! They're all bugs! Or are they? Seems that these pesky little incidents might be considered *features* by some programmers.

Some word processors have an optional *autosave* feature that causes the application to automatically save recovery information in case the computer goes dead. And that Font dialog box that popped up was a user mistake: You meant to press Ctrl+V, but your fingers slipped and caught the *D* key instead. As it happens, by default Ctrl+D opens the Font dialog box in some word processors. And newer versions of most operating systems understand laptop computers: When the battery is just about to be completely drained, the operating system saves the entire state of the machine to a giant file on the hard drive and shuts down. This is called *hibernation*. So these aren't bugs, after all. Now you can close that bug report you just sent to the vendor.

Now consider this: Suppose that you're using an application and in the middle of it, you get a message box that says something like `ExceptionError`. Then the application simply closes. All your work is lost. So you call tech support, and the helpful friend on the other end says, "You must have typed something it didn't like. This application has a built-in protection scheme whereby if you type something you're not supposed to, it shuts down." That's when the guy says, "It's a *feature*, not a bug!" Unfortunately, sometimes situations walk the fine line between bug and feature. No one would think that an application crashing could be considered a feature, but consider this instead: When your browser messes up, a message asks whether you want it to send the vendor a trouble report. *That's* a feature that handles bugs.

But the unnamed application that shut down definitely has a bug. And other applications have bugs. For example, you may have been quickly switching between browser windows, typing, resizing, doing things quickly as you go back and forth between the windows, when suddenly the browser crashes and you see the trouble-report message. That really is a bug: The application choked when you, the user, did something that the programmers did not anticipate.

Of course, you wonder why the application choked. In addition to not having planned for some particular input, the programmers might have simply messed up. They didn't include code to handle a rough situation (rapidly switching, resizing — that sort of thing), or perhaps they wrote code that did something wrong, such as free a pointer but then continue to use the memory address.

Here's an example of programmers not expecting something. Suppose that you write an application that reads a number from the console. The user types a single character for the first choice and another character for the second choice. The code might look like this:

```
char x, y;
cout << "Enter your first choice" << endl;
cin >> x;
cout << "Enter your second choice" << endl;
cout << x << endl;
cin >> y;
cout << y << endl;
```

It's a simple little code, but suppose that the user responds to the first request by typing an entire word, such as **Read,** rather than a single letter, such as **R.** The application would then take the letters e, a, and d and use them for the subsequent cin calls — something you might not have anticipated. The e would go into the cin >> y; line and get put in y. That's the bug of not anticipating something: You, the programmer, must make sure that your application can handle all situations. All of them. Every single one. But fortunately, there are ways around such problems, and you discover them in this chapter.

You can group these situations into the following categories:

>> Real features, not bugs at all

>> A situation that the programmers didn't anticipate

>> A mistake, plain and simple

Make Your Application Features Look Like Features

The last thing you want is to get calls from users complaining about a bug in your application that was, in fact, a feature. This can happen, and it does. But the technical-support people are embarrassed when they have to explain, "No, sir/ma'am. That really is the way it's supposed to work." It's also not fun for the technical-support people to be subjected to name-calling after this, especially when they didn't write the software — you did.

But programmers want to make everybody's lives easier (starting with our own, of course!), so building software so that it's easy to use and makes sense is best. The key, then, in creating software where the features actually look like features is to make it all sensible. Don't have your software start the Zapper automatically unless the user explicitly asks for the Zapper to come on:

> Smiling technical-support representative: "It's a feature! The Zapper comes on after the computer has been sitting idle for ten minutes."

> Angry customer: "Yes, but I would kind of like to be at least ten feet away from the thing when the Zapper starts up!"

> Smiling technical-support representative: "But why would you be sitting there for ten minutes and not using the computer if you're not away from it?"

> Angry customer: "I was reading the manual on how to configure the Zapper!"

You know the rest: Lawsuits follow and people get fired. Not a pretty sight, and that says nothing for the poor customer who was in the vicinity of the computer when the Zapper kicked in at full force.

REMEMBER

With features, the rules are simple: Let users choose which features they want to happen and when. If they don't want autosave, for example, let them turn it off. Let them configure the software, and don't let it do anything surprising.

Anticipating (Almost) Everything

When you write an application, try to anticipate the different things that users can do to your application — much of which may not exactly be associated with the proper use of your application. Most of this kind of protection — that is, ensuring that your application doesn't choke when the users do something you don't anticipate — that you build into your software centers around the *user interface*, the area where the users interact with your application. The following sections offer some details about user interface issues you might face.

Considering menus

If your application is a console-based application or if users can enter characters into text boxes in a windowing application, you must guard against invalid input. Take a look at this output from a hypothetical application:

```
What would you like to do?
    A. Add random information to the system.
    B. Boil information.
```

```
      C. Compress information.
      D. Delete the information.
      Your choice:
```

Now suppose that the user chooses *D* for Delete, and the following menu appears:

```
What would you like to delete?
      A. None of the data; forget it!
      B. Some of the data.
      C. Most of the data.
      D. All the data! Get rid of it all!
```

Now imagine that a user starts this application and sees the first menu. The user doesn't know whether to type **A** for the first choice or **Add** for the first choice. The user types **Add** and presses Enter. Oops. The A went to the first choice, and the system added the random information and printed the same first menu again. The d (the second character the user typed) then went to the choice Delete the information. That caused the second menu, the Delete menu, to appear. The third character that the user typed, d, caused the second menu's D selection to take place — All the data! Get rid of it all! — all in one shot, without the user's realizing what happened.

Oops! What was supposed to be Add turned into Add, Delete, Delete all the data. Not good! How can you avoid this kind of thing?

>> Restrict the user's choices.

>> Clearly state what the user should do.

>> Support multiple options.

>> Anticipate what could go wrong.

For example, you might tell the user to type only a single character, with a message such as this:

```
Please enter a single character for your choice:
```

But now, does the user have to press Enter afterward? This message suggests so. But maybe not. So you must be more specific. Maybe one of these examples would work better:

```
Type a single character and do not press Enter:
```

or

```
Type a single character and then press Enter:
```

But even these aren't good enough. First, you should generally allow the user to press Enter. Doing something automatically with a single keystroke may surprise the user. Further, you may want to support multiple options. If the user wants to choose option A in the menu, you might support any of the following for input:

» A

» a

» Add

» ADD

» add

This can all be wrapped up into some short code that looks like this:

```
string choice;
cin >> choice;
char ch = choice[0];
ch = toupper(ch);
switch (ch)
{
    case 'A':
        cout << "Adding random data..." << endl;
        break;
    case 'B':
        cout << "Boiling it down!" << endl;
        break;
    case 'C':
        cout << "Compressing!" << endl;
        break;
    case 'D':
        cout << "Deleting..." << endl;
        break;
}
```

Now the user can type any word, and the only thing that the application checks is the first letter. But if you don't like the idea that aompress can be taken as add and not compress, you can do something like this:

```
string choice;
cin >> choice;
choice = MyUppercase(choice);
if (choice == "A" || choice == "ADD")
{
```

```
        cout << "Adding random data..." << endl;
}
else if (choice == "B" || choice == "BOIL")
{
    cout << "Boiling it down!" << endl;
}
else if (choice == "C" || choice == "COMPRESS")
{
    cout << "Compressing!" << endl;
}
else if (choice == "D" || choice == "DELETE")
{
    cout << "Deleting..." << endl;
}
else
{
    cout << "I don't know that word" << endl;
}
```

This code looks for only the first letter or the exact word, and the letter can be in either uppercase or lowercase, while words can be in uppercase, lowercase, or mixed case. This choice is probably the best one. However, you may notice that the example uses a function called MyUppercase( ), which relies on a lambda expression (see Book 3, Chapter 1 for details about using lambda expressions) to perform the processing (you need C++ 20 or above to use this version, but you can also use a simple for loop to perform the task as well).

```
string MyUppercase(string str) {
  for_each(str.begin(), str.end(), [](char & c) {
    c = ::toupper(c);
  });
  return str;
}
```

Dealing with textual input

Be careful if you're dealing with a sophisticated application. Suppose that you are writing an application that looks up information in a database for a particular customer name. You could run into the following situations:

>> The names in the database are in all uppercase letters (for example, GEORGE WASHINGTON), and the user can enter names in mixed case (for example, George Washington).

>> The first and last names are stored separately, so your application must look in the database for the situation where the last name is Washington and the first name is George. The user, who doesn't know to enter just the last name, may enter both names into a single text box. Or you might allow the user to enter both names at one time, but the user doesn't realize that the last name was supposed to come first, or perhaps it was last name, and then a comma, and then the first name.

>> The user can type some spaces at the beginning or end of the name. The application then looks for an entry like " George Washington " and does not find it, because it's stored as "George Washington" (with no spaces before or after).

>> The user might include middle initials when the name is not stored in the database with middle initials.

All these problems are easy to avoid. Here are some tips:

>> You must know how the names are stored in the database before you look for them. If they are stored in all caps, you shouldn't require the user to enter them in all caps. Instead, accept words in any case and convert them to uppercase.

>> You must know whether the names are stored with the first name separated from the last. Then allow any format. If the user types **George Washington** (no comma), you can split the string at the space and pull out the first name and last name. But if the user types the name with a comma between the first and last names, you can split it at the comma and extract the last name and then the first name.

>> Spaces should not be a problem. You can strip the spaces off a string after a user types it in.

>> Your application should clearly tell the user whether to enter a middle name, a middle initial, or neither. If you are using text controls, don't even include a middle name field if you don't want a middle name. Or if you do, specify right on the window whether the user should type a middle initial or an entire middle name. If the entry is just an initial, you can remove a trailing period, or add it, depending on what's stored in the database.

All these steps will help make your application bulletproof. The idea is to encourage users to do things the way they prefer, but to prevent them from doing things in ways that your application doesn't like. If your application doesn't want middle initials, don't give users the opportunity to enter them.

Performing string processing

The StringProcess example in Listing 1-1 shows you how you can strip spaces, strip a possible period off the end of a middle initial, and split a string based on either spaces or commas. This example uses a special class called vector. The vector class is much like an array, except that the vector class is a bit more powerful: Because vector is a class, you can add things to it and remove things from it easily by using methods. vector is also a *template*, however, so when you declare it, you must state what type of variables you want it to hold. You put the variable types in angle brackets. The example declares it using strings, like this: vector<string>. To make your life simpler, the code uses a typedef to make an easier name for this type: StringList.

LISTING 1-1: **Processing Strings to Reduce Bugs**

```cpp
#include <iostream>
#include <vector>
#include <string.h>
#include <algorithm>

using namespace std;

typedef vector<string> StringList;
StringList Split(string orig, string delims) {
  StringList list;
  int pos;
  while((pos = orig.find_first_of(delims)) != -1) {
    list.push_back(orig.substr(0, pos));
    orig = orig.substr(pos + 1);
  }
  list.push_back(orig);
  return list;
}

string MyUppercase(string str) {
  for_each(str.begin(), str.end(), [](char & c) {
    c = ::toupper(c);
  });
  return str;
}

string stripspaces(string orig) {
  int left;
  int right;
```

(continued)

LISTING 1-1: *(continued)*

```
      // If string is empty, just return it.
      if (orig.length() == 0)
        return orig;

      // Strip right
      right = orig.find_last_not_of(" \t");
      if (right > -1)
        orig.resize(right + 1);

      // Strip left
      left = orig.find_first_not_of(" \t");
      if (left > -1)
        orig.erase(0, left);

      // If left still has a space, it
      // means the whole string is whitespace.
      // So just remove it all.
      if (orig[0] == ' ' || orig[0] == '\t')
        orig = "";

      return orig;
    }

    void ProcessName(string name) {
      StringList list;
      string first, middle, last;
      int size, commapos;

      name = stripspaces(name);
      commapos = name.find(",");
      if (commapos > 0) {
        // Name has a comma, so start with last name.
        name.erase(commapos, 1);
        list = Split(name, " ");
        size = list.size();
        if (size > 0)
          last = list[0];
        if (size > 1)
          first = list[1];
        if (size > 2)
          middle = list[2];
      } else {
```

```
      // Name has no comma, so start with first name.
      list = Split(name, " ");
      size = list.size();
      if (size > 0)
        first = list[0];
      if (size > 2) {
        middle = list[1];
        last = list[2];
      }
      if (size == 2)
        last = list[1];
    }
    // If middle name is just initial and period,
    // then remove the initial.
    if (middle.length() == 2)
      if (middle[1] == '.')
        middle.erase(1,1);

    // Convert all to uppercase
    first = MyUppercase(first);
    middle = MyUppercase(middle);
    last = MyUppercase(last);

    cout << "first: " << first << endl;
    cout << "middle: " << middle << endl;
    cout << "last: " << last << endl;
    cout << endl;
}

int main() {
  string name;
  name = "   Washington, George Zeus   ";
  ProcessName(name);
  name = "Washington, George Z.";
  ProcessName(name);
  name = "George Z. Washington";
  ProcessName(name);
  name = "George Zeus Washington";
  ProcessName(name);
  name = "George Washington";
  ProcessName(name);
  return 0;
}
```

Listing 1-1 is almost bug-proof, but it still doesn't handle some situations properly. For example, if somebody tries to process a string with a middle name, such as Zeus. (notice the period after the name), the application doesn't remove the period. Here are some other improvements you might make to this application:

>> **Eliminate improper characters:** You might make sure that no improper characters appear in the names. Do this processing after you find the first, middle, and last names; that way, you won't kill the attempt to find the data based on the presence of a single comma that might be needed to specify the name order. You can use various if statements to do this kind of thing.

>> **Handle more names than three:** Add a special precaution for the case of more than three names. Some people have lots of names (like 10 or 11, especially if they're members of British royalty). But if this application is to be used, for example, in an oil change operation, you probably won't see Charles Philip Arthur George, Prince of Wales coming through. How you handle the names depends on your particular situation.

>> **Perform initial processing:** Do some initial processing. Right after the user enters the names, make sure that the names are not empty strings — that is, "" (one pair of quotation marks with no space between them).

THE MYTH OF THE BULLETPROOF APPLICATION

Anyone who has spent time reviewing the trade press knows that many applications have recurring problems with bugs. Just as soon as the vendor fixes one bug, another bug turns up. Some developers may think that the developers at these companies are morons and are giving us all a black eye. However, these developers, more often than not, are just like us. Because they're human, and humans make mistakes — at both the developer and user ends of the application — applications will never become bug-free. Sure, you may be able to create a simple, nearly bulletproof application, but as application complexity increases, so do the number of interactions and the number of potential bugs. At some point, the number of interactions between application parts increases to the point that a bug-free application becomes impossible.

The bulletproof application is a myth. If you buy into this myth, you may be tempted to stop looking for bugs the moment the development staff can't find any more of them. Unfortunately, this attitude leads to headlines proclaiming your application as the next significant security hole. Don't buy into the myth of the bulletproof application — always be alert for potential errors.

Avoiding Mistakes, Plain and Simple

Even though many programmers take measures to prevent bugs, they still sometimes let problems slip through. However, if you're careful, you can avoid a lot of these problems. When you create software, you should be in the right frame of mind to watch for potential problems as you write the code. (Getting into the right frame of mind includes ensuring that you have enough sleep, avoiding distractions, and doing other things that help you concentrate on your work.)

The list of potential problems could probably go on and on for thousands of pages. However, the point is not to have a big checklist, but rather for you to review this list and start to recognize the things you need to do to write good code. Writing code is conscious and deliberate. It's similar to walking down a sidewalk and being vaguely aware of such things as whether cars are coming or whether you need to step over any holes. These hazards are always in the back of your mind as you carefully walk along. Writing code is the same way: Certain gotchas should stay in the back of your mind:

>> **Indexes:** Strings and arrays run from index 0 to 1 less than the length. Using a loop, such as for (i=0; i<=size; i++), is a common mistake. The less-than-or-equal-to symbol is incorrect, yet people make this mistake a lot. The scary thing is that sometimes the code will still function, and you end up overwriting something else. Worse, you might not catch this coding error, so it manifests itself as a bug in the application later.

>> **For every new, there's a delete:** Whenever you allocate an object using new, remember to free it. But forgetting the delete doesn't usually create noticeable bugs in your application (at least, not at the time they occur). Read the next item to see what's more likely to cause a noticeable bug.

>> **Remember what you deleted:** Worse than forgetting to delete an object is forgetting that you deleted it and continuing to use it. When you delete a pointer, make sure that you don't pass it to some other object that stores it away and plans to use it again.

>> **Don't forget to create an object:** You may have seen this one. An error message pops up that says:

```
The instruction at 0x00402119 referenced memory at
0x00000000. The memory could not be written.
```

This means that someone had a pointer variable and forgot to call new. You can generate this message with the following code:

```
int *x = 0;
*x = 10;
```

The code creates a pointer variable and initializes it to 0, meaning that it's not being used. But before calling new or setting the variable equal to an object's address, the code tries to stuff something into the memory it points to (which is address 0, something that the operating system doesn't like). The operating system responds with the error message. This bug appears far more than expected in commercial software.

These are just a few items to think about, but you can see that they deal mostly with memory issues, such as allocating memory and using it incorrectly. Most important, you can avoid them if you're conscientious about your programming. As you code, bear in mind the repercussions of what you're doing. And as crazy as this sounds, remember what you might be forgetting! Ask yourself whether you're forgetting to delete some pointers or whether someone else has a copy of the pointer you're about to delete. If you keep these things in mind, you should avoid some of the most common bugs.

Chapter **2**

Debugging an Application

I n this chapter, you discover how you can use a debugger to track down problems and bugs in your application. Sooner or later, things don't work the way you planned them. In this case, you have several plans of attack. One is to use a debugger to try to fix the application, which is the approach taken in this chapter. You could also use cause-and-effect analysis, probabilistic analysis, or logging application output. You can find articles online that describe all sorts of techniques, such as this one: https://dev.to/nikpoltoratsky/debugging-you-re-doing-it-wrong-10-techniques-to-find-a-bug-in-your-code-4f41. However, this chapter relies on the old standby of debugging and focuses on the Code::Blocks debugger.

REMEMBER

You don't have to type the source code for this chapter manually. In fact, using the downloadable source is a lot easier. You can find the source for this chapter in the \CPP_AIO4\BookIV\Chapter02 folder of the downloadable source. See the Introduction for details on how to find these source files.

Programming with Debuggers

A *debugger* is a special tool that you use for analyzing your code in various ways, including tracing the code line by line. (*Tracing* is the act of viewing the code execution flow in an application.) Take a look at the BuggyProgram example, shown in Listing 2-1. This is just a basic application with a main() and a couple of functions used to demonstrate the debugger.

LISTING 2-1: Tracing a Simple Application

```cpp
#include <iostream>
#include <cstdlib>

using namespace std;

int CountRabbits(int original) {
  int result = original * 2;
  result = result + 10;
  result = result * 4;
  cout << "Calculating " << result << endl;
  return result * 10;
}

int CountAntelopes(int original) {
  int result = original + 10;
  result = result - 2;
  cout << "Calculating " << result << endl;
  return result;
}

int main() {
  int rabbits = 5;
  int antelopes = 5;
  rabbits = CountRabbits(rabbits);
  cout << "Rabbits now at " << rabbits << endl;
  antelopes = CountAntelopes(antelopes);
  cout << "Antelopes now at " << antelopes << endl;
  //system("PAUSE"); // add this for Windows
  return 0;
}
```

When you run this application, you see the following output:

```
Calculating 80
Rabbits now at 800
Calculating 13
Antelopes now at 13
```

Now look closely at `main()` and follow it through, line by line. The first thing `main()` does is declare a couple of integers. Then `main()` calls the `CountRabbits()` function. The `CountRabbits()` function declares an integer and completes a few lines of calculations. Then the `CountRabbits()` function prints a message. Finally, it returns. When it's back in `main()`, the application prints another message and then calls the `CountAntelopes()` function. This function also declares an integer, completes some calculations, prints a message, and then returns. Back in `main()`, the application prints another message, and, finally, the application finishes.

This is a linear description of the entire process of this application. You can see these same steps by using a debugger. With a debugger, you see the computer moving line by line through your code. A debugger performs the first line of your application and then waits for you to tell it to perform the next line — and then the next, and the next, and so on, until the end of the application.

ADDING DEBUG AND SYMBOL INFORMATION

When you compile with debug information, the compiler adds debug and symbol information to the final executable file. This information includes data about the source code files, including the line numbers and the variable names. This is the primary difference between a *debug* version and a *release* version of your product: People typically don't include debug and symbol information in a version of the product that they release to the general public. One reason is that including it makes it too easy for competitors and hackers to reverse-engineer the product. (Another reason is that including the debug and symbol information makes the application run slower and consume more system resources.) However, the actual source code is not in the debug and symbol information; that stays in the source code file. The debug information, instead, just contains line numbers, which serve as references into the source code file. So hackers and competitors won't have the complete source to your application, but they will have variable names and other information that could make their job easier (and yours harder).

TIP

This example uses the debugger that comes with the Code::Blocks application. Even if you prefer to use another debugger, at least try the Code::Blocks debugger. It is a nice tool, and it's helpful to know how to use more than one debugger because they all have different feature sets. In addition, using the Code::Blocks debugger allows you to follow through the chapter's examples. Then you can return to whatever other tool you're using.

REMEMBER

You must know one important aspect before using a debugger: For the debugger to understand your code, you must compile it with debugging information. The compiler adds extra information into the final executable so that the debugger can locate your source code and variable information. Here's how you turn on debug information:

>> **Code::Blocks:** Choose Build➪Select Target➪Debug.

>> **Dev-C++:** Open the project and choose Tools➪Compiler Options. In the Settings tab, choose Linker in the left panel. Make sure that Generate Debugging Information entry is set to Yes.

>> **gcc under MinGW and Cygwin:** Add the –g option to the compiler. You will probably do this inside a `Makefile`.

TIP

After you change the compiler options to generate debug information, you must rebuild your project because the compiler and linker must regenerate object files and executable files with the debug information.

Running the debugger

After you have rebuilt your project, you can run the debugger. However, before you can do anything, you need to tell the debugger where to stop. Click immediately to the right of 22 in the source code editor, the line that reads int rabbits = 5;. You see a red octagon appear; it looks similar to a stop sign, but without the word *stop*. After you have the required configuration done, see the following sections to find out about the initial debugging process in more detail.

Performing an initial run

To start the debugger, click Debug/Continue on the Debugger toolbar (the right-pointing red arrow), choose Debug➪Start / Continue, or press F8. (If you click Run, the application runs as normal without entering debug mode.) When you start the debugger, you should see a screen like the one shown in Figure 2-1. (You also get a console window behind that screen. This console window contains the output for the application you are debugging.)

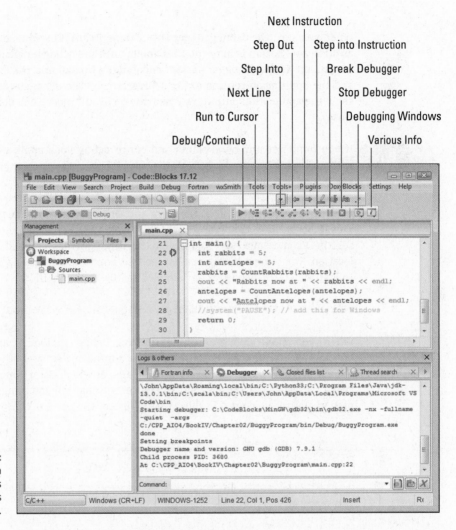

FIGURE 2-1:
The main
Code::Blocks
window shows
your source code.

Figure 2-1 shows two special features you need to successfully debug applications. The first is the red octagon, and the second is the yellow triangle. The red octagon is a *breakpoint* — a place where you want the debugger to stop. You add breakpoints to the Editing window by clicking the left side next to the instruction where you want to stop. When you click that spot again, the red octagon goes away, showing that you have cleared the breakpoint. You can place as many breakpoints as you want in the application, but you can place breakpoints only on instructions.

The yellow triangle is the *instruction pointer*, which shows the instruction that the debugger will execute next. As you tell the debugger to execute instructions, the yellow triangle moves. Whenever you start the application in debug mode, the yellow pointer automatically stops at each breakpoint. Figure 2-1 shows how the debugger looks when the yellow triangle stops at a breakpoint.

When you start the debugger again by clicking Debug/Continue, execution begins as if the application is in normal run mode until the debugger encounters another breakpoint. If the debugger doesn't encounter a breakpoint, the dialog box closes and the application returns to the source screen. The debugger doesn't pause to show the application output, as when you're in run mode. The dialog box simply closes.

REMEMBER

If you don't set any breakpoints and try to debug your application, it will run without letting you trace through the code. That is, the application will run as if you're not running it in the debugger.

Look at the Debugger tab of the Logs and Others window, shown in Figure 2-1. This tab contains debugging messages from your application. Whenever you see the At message, you know that the debugger has stopped at a particular location. The remainder of the message tells you where the debugger has stopped. In Figure 2-1, the debugger has stopped at line 22 of this file:

```
At C:\CPP_AIO4\BookIV\Chapter02\BuggyProgram\main.cpp:22
```

When you click Debug/Continue on the Debug toolbar again, you see a Continuing. . . message. Because this first run hasn't set any other breakpoints, the application continues to run until it ends, at which point you see some additional messages like those shown in Figure 2-2, that tell you things like the completion status, which is 0 in this case because of the return 0; line in the code.

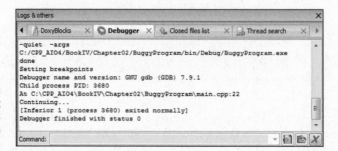

FIGURE 2-2:
Completing the run shows the application results.

TIP

Notice that the Debugger window provides you with all sorts of additional information. If you scroll up, you can see the build process and how it differs from a release build. When the build process completes, you see the done message, a Setting breakpoints message, a debugger information message, and the Process Identifier (PID) of the application process.

Reviewing the code line by line

Click Debug/Continue again to restart the application and debugger. The breakpoint you set earlier stops the application at line 22 again. Click Next Line, which is the third button on the Debugger toolbar. The button you want is the one with an icon with two squares and an arrow pointing from the first square to the second square. (You can also press F7.) The yellow triangle (instruction pointer) moves past the first assignment statement on line 22, which is int rabbits = 5;, to the second assignment statement on line 23. Notice that the Debugger window now contains a second At entry of At C:\CPP_AIO4\BookIV\Chapter02\BuggyProgram\main.cpp:23.

TIP

You can use options on the Debug menu in place of the buttons on the Debug toolbar. The Debug menu also shows shortcut keys for each of the debugging commands that support them.

Click Next Line. When you click the button, the instruction pointer advances to the next line. The computer will perform the second line in main(), which is this:

```
int antelopes = 5;
```

Click Next Line again. Now the instruction pointer is on the third line of main(), which looks like this:

```
rabbits = CountRabbits(rabbits);
```

This third line of main() is a function call, and now you have a choice. (*Don't* click Next Line!) You can either tell the computer to perform only what's inside this function without stopping on each line for you to see, or you can "step into it" and see the individual lines.

Click the fourth button from the left, the one called Step Into, which shows two squares and an arrow pointing between them. (Or press Shift+F7.) When you do, the instruction pointer moves into the CountRabbits() function. The highlight will be on the first line in that function:

```
int result = original * 2;
```

When the highlight moved into the function, the computer *stepped into* the function. Now think about the symbol for the icon that caused this to happen: The icon has squares and an arrow pointing between them. The two squares represent lines of code in the current function, and you go between them, or step into the called function. That's the idea behind the odd symbols. Notice also that the Debugger shows an appropriate At message of At C:\CPP_AIO4\BookIV\Chapter02\BuggyProgram\main.cpp:7.

Now, before stepping into this function — because you were clicking lines that were not functions but just individual lines — you used the Next Line button. But you could have used either the Next Line button or the Step Into button, because stepping into a function doesn't have much meaning on statements that are not functions.

TIP

Normally, you use the Next Line button by default and choose the Step Into button only when you specifically want to go into a function. The reason is that some lines of code that may not appear to be functions really are. For example, cout << "a"; is, in fact, a function, and you might not want to step into that code, because the source code for it might not be present or you simply might not be interested in the details of the function.

TIP

If you ever step into a function that you really don't want to trace, you can click the fifth Debugger toolbar button, Step Out, to get back to the previous function. The result is the same as if you had clicked Next Line when you were in the code that called the function. Keep the debugger running for the next section of the chapter.

Using the basic debugger functionality

The previous section tells you how to move from line to line within a code file. Here, you can see how the debugging features work. The following procedure takes you through the debugging process so that you can see the Code::Blocks debugger in action:

1. **Click Next Line three times until the instruction pointer appears on the cout line:**

```
cout << "Calculating " << result << endl;
```

This line writes output to the console, as shown in Figure 2-3. Remember, in addition to the main Code::Blocks window, you have a console window. That's where the output from this line goes.

2. **Click Next Line.**

The instruction pointer lands on the return statement.

3. **Click Next Line again.**

The instruction pointer is on the closing brace of the function. Note that Code::Blocks highlights both the opening brace and the closing brace in blue, as shown in Figure 2-4. This feature helps you see where a function begins and ends in the Integrated Development Environment (IDE).

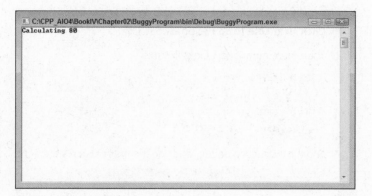

FIGURE 2-3:
Be sure to check
the output to
ensure that
it's what you
expected.

FIGURE 2-4:
The debugger
shows the
beginning
and end of
code blocks.

```cpp
main.cpp ×
 5
 6    int CountRabbits(int original) {
 7        int result = original * 2;
 8        result = result + 10;
 9        result = result * 4;
10        cout << "Calculating " << result << endl;
11        return result * 10;
12    }
13
```

4. **Click Next Line yet again.**

The instruction pointer returns to main( ), on the line following the call to the CountRabbits( ) function:

```cpp
cout << "Rabbits now at " << rabbits << endl;
```

5. **Click Next Line again.**

The instruction pointer is on the second function call:

```cpp
antelopes = CountAntelopes(antelopes);
```

6. **But this time, instead of stepping into the function, just press Next Line to step over it.**

The instruction pointer advances to the next line, which is this:

```cpp
cout << "Antelopes now at " << antelopes << endl;
```

Look at the console. The CountAntelopes( ) function contains a call to cout. You can see on the console that this cout line did its stuff:

```cpp
Calculating 13
```

You saw the output from the CountAntelopes( ) function because, although you stepped over the function, you didn't actually skip it. The debugger just didn't go through the function line by line.

7. **Click Next Line to do the final** cout **line.**

Your entire output now looks like this:

```
Calculating 80
Rabbits now at 800
Calculating 13
Antelopes now at 13
```

and the instruction pointer ends on the final return statement:

```
return 0;
```

8. **Click Next Line one more time, and the highlight is on the closing brace of** main().

Now things get just a little strange. There's really more code than you can see. When you compile and link your application, the linker includes some special start-up code that calls your main() function.

9. **Click Next Line one more time.**

The debugger moves out of your source file and into some assembly language code. The Debugger window shows the following message:

```
In __mingw_CRTStartup () ()
```

10. **Click a new button, Next Instruction (six buttons from the left on the Debugger toolbar), to advance to the next instruction.**

The Debugger window shows the following message again:

```
In __mingw_CRTStartup () ()
```

11. **To see what all this means, click Debugging Windows (ten buttons from the left on the Debugger toolbar) and choose Disassembly from the drop-down list box.**

Code::Blocks displays a new window called Disassembly, as shown in Figure 2-5. The numbers in your figure may differ from the screenshot, but the code is the same.

This is assembly, a human-readable form of the language that the computer understands. You don't have to know what all this means, but you can probably figure out that the line

```
0x4010ff call    0x430c40 <_cexit>
```

is where this code exits the application.

12. **To end the application, click the first button (Debug/Continue).**

Clicking Debug/Continue causes the application to run to the real end of your application (or to the next breakpoint) and then finish.

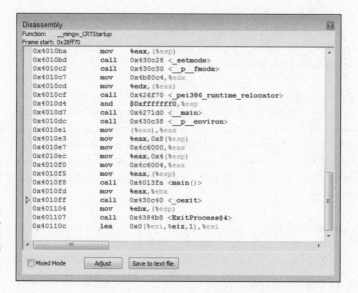

FIGURE 2-5:
The Disassembly
window displays
the assembly
language version
of your code.

That's how you step through your application line by line. But you can do a lot more with the application than you do in this section when you're stepping through it. You can look at the values in your variables, you can change the values of the variables, and you can get a list of all the function calls that led up to the current position in your application. You can do plenty, as explained in the remainder of this minibook.

Recognizing the parts of the Code::Blocks debugger

The Code::Blocks debugger displays the Debugger toolbar whenever you debug an application. The previous sections of this chapter discuss many of the buttons on the Debugger toolbar: Debug/Continue, Next Line, Next Instruction, Step Into, and Step Out. However, the toolbar contains a number of other interesting buttons you should know about.

Sometimes you examine a piece of code in the editor and want to see what the variables look like when you get to that point. To see what happens, place the text cursor at the place you want to stop (hovering the mouse cursor over the place you want to stop isn't enough) and click Run to Cursor (the second button on the Debugger toolbar). The debugger stops at the line where the cursor is resting. In this case, the text cursor acts as a kind of breakpoint for the debugger.

After you debug your application for a while and locate problems you want to fix, you may not want to run the rest of the application. When this situation occurs, simply click Stop Debugger (the button that looks like a box with an *X* in the middle). The debugger stops immediately. You can make any required changes and restart the debugger as normal.

Code::Blocks provides access to a number of debugging windows. In fact, you can see one of these windows previously in this chapter — the Disassembly window (refer to Figure 2-5). You access these windows by clicking the Debugging Windows button (the one that looks like a window, to the right of the Stop Debugger button) or by choosing Debug➪Debugging Windows. Later chapters in this minibook describe these windows in detail. Here is a quick summary of the windows for now:

>> **Breakpoints:** Presents all the breakpoints you've set in your application. Double-clicking a breakpoint entry takes you to that breakpoint in the editor. You can use this window also to remove one or more breakpoints.

>> **CPU Registers:** Shows the contents of the hardware registers in the processor. You won't normally need to view these registers unless you're performing low-level programming tasks (such as writing a device driver).

>> **Call Stack:** Displays the function calls used to get to the current point in the code.

>> **Disassembly:** Lets you see the underlying assembly language code. You won't normally need to view this information unless you're performing low-level programming tasks.

>> **Memory Dump:** Displays the precise way that the application stores data in memory, which may not look very much like the C++ view. This window is useful because it helps you understand how memory works and how your application uses memory. In some cases, knowing how a variable stores memory can help you locate problems with your code.

>> **Running Threads:** Shows a list of threads, other than the main thread, associated with the current application. You use this window for debugging multithreaded applications.

>> **Watches:** Displays a list of local variables and function parameters. You can also add other variables to monitor as a watch. In addition, you can create new statements, such as `rabbits + antelopes`, so you can see the total of the two variables. The Watches window is probably the most useful debugger window because it illustrates the C++ view of your data and shows how the application code manipulates that data.

The debugger also provides access to a number of information windows. You access these windows by clicking the Various Info button (the one with an *i* in italics far down on the left) or by choosing Debug➪Information. Here is a summary of the information windows:

>> **Current Stack Frame:** Shows the current stack frame information. C++ creates something called a *stack frame* when certain events occur, such as calling a function. This stack frame contains the data and data references for the current function. You won't normally need to view this information unless you're performing low-level programming tasks.

>> **Loaded Libraries:** Lists all the libraries loaded to run your application. It's important to know which libraries your application uses when you deploy it on other machines. In many cases, you may not even know that C++ requires certain libraries to run your application, so this window is exceptionally useful.

>> **Targets and Files:** Provides a detailed view of how the loaded libraries are used in your application. You won't normally need to view this information unless you're performing low-level programming tasks.

>> **FPU Status:** Displays the register information for the Floating-Point Unit (FPU) in your processor. At one time, the FPU was a separate chip, but now it appears as part of your main processor. The FPU is exceptionally adept at performing real number (versus integer) math. You won't normally need to view this information unless you're performing low-level programming tasks.

>> **Signal Handling:** Shows how Code::Blocks handles signals between the hardware and your application, such as an arithmetic exception or a segmentation fault. You won't normally need to view this information unless you're performing low-level programming tasks.

Debugging with Different Tools

You can use several tools for debugging your code. However, which compiler you usually use dictates which debugging tools you can use. For example, Microsoft Visual C++ has a really good debugger. But getting it to debug an application compiled with Dev-C++, for example, is difficult because different compilers use different forms of debugging and symbol information. The type used by the various breeds of gcc compilers is different from the type used by Microsoft Visual C++. Here are some of the debuggers that are available:

>> **Visual C++:** This debugger works similarly to the Code::Blocks debugger. It's primarily for debugging applications that were built by using Visual C++. However, if you are brave and need to debug something for which you have no code or symbol information, its support for assembly-code debugging is good.

» **gdb:** This is the standard debugger that ships with MinGW and Cygwin. It's a command-line tool, but you can use the Insight debugger with it so that you can use a graphical front end. This makes life a lot easier. But if you insist on using the command-line version, you can learn about it by typing **gdb** at the command prompt and then typing **help**.

» **Dev-C++:** Starting with Version 5, Dev-C++ has an integrated debugger that works similarly to the Insight debugger. You may want to give this a try. (If you're using a version of Dev-C++ prior to 5.0, you have to use the Insight debugger.)

Debugging a Code::Blocks Application with Command-Line Arguments

A *command-line argument* is something you type along with the command for an application at the command prompt. For example, when you type the **Dir** (directory listing command) at the command prompt, you can include additional information such as *.DOC, which will list all files with a .DOC extension. (If you use Dir *.DOC? instead, you also see any files with a .DOCX extension.) The full command Dir *.DOC consists of a command (Dir) and a command-line argument (*.DOC). The addition of command-line arguments allows you to extend the functionality of an application and make it do more. To test such an application, you need to be able to specify command-line arguments as part of the debugger environment.

Code::Blocks, like most other capable IDEs, provides the means for specifying command-line arguments. The "Setting the command-line parameters in Code::Blocks" sidebar in Book 1, Chapter 6 provides you with the basics of setting command-line arguments. However, a number of readers of previous editions of this book wanted more information. With this in mind, I wrote a more detailed description of how command-line arguments work as part of the post "Debugging a CodeBlocks Application with Command Line Arguments" for a previous edition of this book on my blog at http://blog.johnmuellerbooks.com/2011/11/01/debugging-a-codeblocks-application-with-command-line-arguments/. Please be sure to check out this blog post if you want additional information about precisely what is going on.

Chapter **3**

Stopping and Inspecting Your Code

Sometimes, code breaks. The word *break* has different meanings among the people using it in the coding world. When programmers talk about *breaking the code*, it may mean that the programmer made a mistake and the code no longer works. It could also mean that a change in a library causes the code to malfunction despite a lack of errors caused by the programmer. But this chapter uses a different definition for *break*. When you're debugging an application, you can have the application run until it gets to a certain line in the code. The debugger then stops at that line, and you can look at the values of variables, inspect the code, or even change the variables. When the application stops, that's called *breaking*. It stops on that particular line because you put a *breakpoint* on that line.

This chapter discusses setting and manipulating breakpoints in your code (if nothing else in your code is broken). You also inspect and modify various aspects of your code, such as variables, after your code stops at a breakpoint. You also see how to use *watches* to keep track of certain variables or expressions.

TIP

The examples in this chapter rely on the debugger supplied with the Code::Blocks IDE. If you use a different product, the debugger will probably work about the same but not precisely the same. For example, you can do everything shown here using Microsoft Visual C++. The keystrokes and mouse clicks may be different, but the features are present. Make sure to check the vendor documentation for precise details on using your debugger.

REMEMBER

To work through the examples in this chapter, you must compile with debug information turned on. (In Code::Blocks, you can compile with debug information by choosing Debug in the Build Target field of the Compiler toolbar. If you can't see the Compiler toolbar, choose View ⇨ Toolbars ⇨ Compiler to place a check mark next to the Compiler entry.) When you develop software, you should always have debug information on. That way, you're always ready to debug your code and fix things. Only when you're ready to release the product formally should you recompile it without debug information. (You should still perform a full test of the software again without debug information, just to make sure that it functions correctly.)

REMEMBER

You don't have to type the source code for this chapter manually. In fact, using the downloadable source is a lot easier. You can find the source for this chapter in the \CPP_AIO4\BookIV\Chapter03 folder of the downloadable source. See the Introduction for details on how to find these source files.

Setting and Disabling Breakpoints

A *breakpoint* is a place in your code where you tell the debugger to stop. The sections that follow discuss breakpoints. You use the Breakpoints sample code, shown in Listing 3-1, for these sections. Make sure that you compile it with debug information on.

LISTING 3-1: **Using an Application for Breakpoints and Inspections**

```cpp
#include <iostream>

using namespace std;

class BrokenMirror {
private:
  int NumberOfPieces;
public:
  int GetNumberOfPieces();
  void SetNumberOfPieces(int newamount);
  BrokenMirror() : NumberOfPieces(100) {}
};
```

```
int BrokenMirror::GetNumberOfPieces() {
  return NumberOfPieces;
}

void BrokenMirror::SetNumberOfPieces(int newamount) {
  newamount = newamount * 20;
  NumberOfPieces = newamount;
}

int main() {
  BrokenMirror mirror;
  mirror.SetNumberOfPieces(10);
  cout << mirror.GetNumberOfPieces() << endl;
  return 0;
}
```

Setting a breakpoint in Code::Blocks

Compile the application in Listing 3-1 (with debug information turned on). Look at the left margin of the window, to the right of the line numbers. Figure 3-1 shows a small octagon on line 14. When you view the IDE, this octagon is red. The red octagon is a breakpoint. To set this breakpoint in your own code, click in the area between the left margin and the code (or right-click the line of code and choose Toggle Breakpoint from the context menu), as shown in the figure on line 14. If you haven't done so, click the mouse in the left margin of the int Bro kenMirror::GetNumberOfPieces() line. You see a red octagon appear in the left margin. You just placed a breakpoint on that line.

Click again in the left margin of the same line. The red octagon disappears. When the octagon disappears, the breakpoint is gone.

Finally, click a third time, because for now you do want a breakpoint there.

Run the application by clicking the Debug/Continue button (the icon with the red, right-pointing arrow on it) on the Debugger toolbar. If you don't see the Debugger toolbar, choose View ⇨ Toolbars ⇨ Debugger to place a check mark next to the Debugger entry. (Don't click the Run button, which is the green right-pointing triangle on the Compiler toolbar, because choosing this option simply runs the application without debugging it.) When you click Debug/Continue, the console window may pop in front, so just click the Code::Blocks window to bring it back to the front.

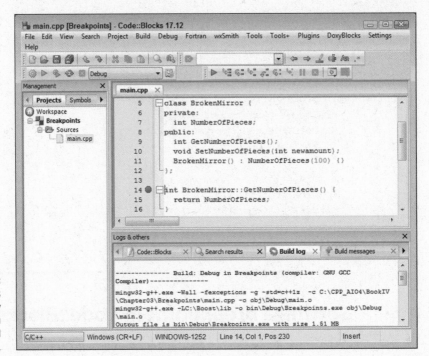

FIGURE 3-1:
Code::Blocks
displays any
breakpoints you
set using a red
octagon.

The application runs until it gets to the breakpoint you chose for the `int Broken Mirror::GetNumberOfPieces()` line, as shown in Figure 3-2. Note that execution actually ends with the opening curly brace because this is the beginning of execution for this function. The yellow, right-pointing triangle tells you the current instruction that the Code::Blocks debugger will execute. You can now click the Next Line button (the button with two squares and an arrow pointing from the upper square to the lower square) to move to the next line, or you can click Debug/ Continue to run the rest of the application.

Enabling and disabling breakpoints

You may have times when you have several breakpoints set and you want to turn them off momentarily but don't want to lose them because you may want to turn them back on later. You can do this by *disabling* the breakpoints. Disabling the breakpoint is faster than removing the breakpoints and then going back and finding them again to turn them back on. Use the following steps to disable a breakpoint:

1. **Right-click the red octagon on the left side of the editor and choose Edit Breakpoint from the context menu.**

You see the Edit Breakpoint dialog box, as shown in Figure 3-3.

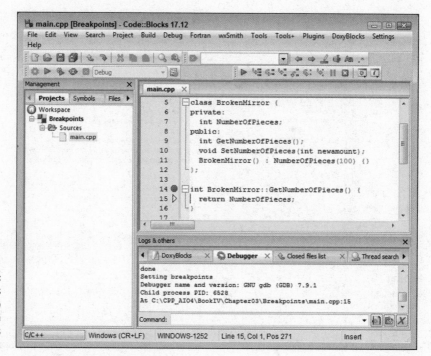

FIGURE 3-2:
Debug mode tells
Code::Blocks to
stop execution
when it reaches
the breakpoint.

FIGURE 3-3:
Use the Edit
Breakpoint dialog
box to enable
and disable
breakpoints.

2. **Clear the Enabled option and click OK.**

Code::Blocks disables the breakpoint so that it no longer stops application
execution.

Many debuggers show a disabled breakpoint using a hollow red circle (or sometimes an octagon). Code::Blocks turns the red octagon gray instead. However,
you'll still want to see that disabling the breakpoint actually does work. Set a new
breakpoint after the line that reads `return NumberOfPieces;` (on the curly brace).
Click Debug/Continue and you'll see that the debugger bypasses the first breakpoint and stops at the second, as shown in Figure 3-4.

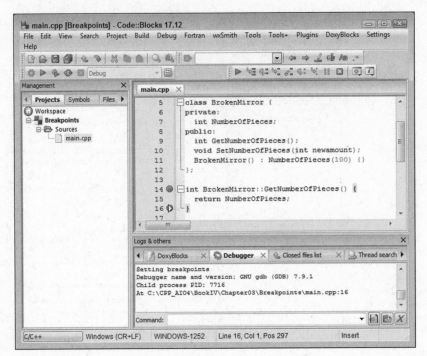

FIGURE 3-4:
Disabled
breakpoints
don't stop
application
execution.

In some cases, you want to enable or disable a number of breakpoints. Use the following steps to perform this task:

1. Choose Debug ➪ Debugging Windows ➪ Breakpoints.

You see the Breakpoints window, shown in Figure 3-5. The window shows the kind of breakpoint (with a red or gray octagon to tell you whether it's enabled or disabled), the breakpoint location, the line in the code file where the breakpoint appears, and the name of the debugger being used.

Breakpoints					
Type	Filename/Address	L...	Info	Debugger	
● Code	C:\CPP_AIO4\BookIV\Chapter03\Breakpoints\main.cpp	14	(index: -1)	GDB/CDB debugger	
● Code	C:\CPP_AIO4\BookIV\Chapter03\Breakpoints\main.cpp	16	(index: 2)	GDB/CDB debugger	

FIGURE 3-5:
Use the
Breakpoints
window to access
a number of
breakpoints
at one time.

2. **Right-click the breakpoint entry and choose one of the management options from the context menu.**

   The management options help you control one or more breakpoints. You can perform the following tasks using the management options:

   - Open the breakpoint in the editor so that you can see where it's located.

   - Edit the breakpoint, which displays the Edit Breakpoint dialog box, shown in Figure 3-3.

   - Remove the selected breakpoint.

   - Disable the selected breakpoint.

   - Add a bookmark so that you can find this location in the code with greater ease. When you choose this option, you see a right-pointing blue arrow between the line number and the code. Use the Edit⇨Bookmarks menu options to work with bookmarks.

   - Remove all the breakpoints you have set in the application.

Watching, Inspecting, and Changing Variables

When you stop at a breakpoint in an application, you can do more than just look at the code. You can have fun with it! You can look at the current values of the variables, and you can change them.

The `Breakpoints2` example, shown in Listing 3-2, is a sample application that you can use to try these examples of inspecting, changing, and watching variables. Please note that this application is similar to Listing 3-1, earlier in this chapter, but you should see some differences. Specifically, it adds a line to the `SetNumberOfPieces()` method:

```
newamount = newamount * 20;
```

The example adds a new function called `SpecialMath()` and an `i` variable to `main()` that is initialized to 10. The code then manipulates `i` and passes it into the `SetNumberOfPieces()` function.

LISTING 3-2: **Using an Application for Breakpoints and Inspections**

```cpp
#include <iostream>

using namespace std;

class BrokenMirror {
private:
  int NumberOfPieces;
public:
  int GetNumberOfPieces();
  void SetNumberOfPieces(int newamount);
  BrokenMirror() : NumberOfPieces(100) {}
};

int BrokenMirror::GetNumberOfPieces() {
  return NumberOfPieces;
}

void BrokenMirror::SetNumberOfPieces(int newamount) {
  newamount = newamount * 20;
  NumberOfPieces = newamount;
}

int SpecialMath(int x)
{
    return x * 10 - 5;
}

int main() {
  int i = 10;
  BrokenMirror mirror;

  i = i + SpecialMath(i);
  mirror.SetNumberOfPieces(i);
  cout << mirror.GetNumberOfPieces() << endl;

  // Clear this comment if you want the application to
  // stop to display the results.
  // system("PAUSE");
  return 0;
}
```

When you run this application by clicking Run, you should see an output value of 2100.

Watching the variables

To watch the variables in your application, follow these steps:

1. **Compile this application using a debug build (Build ⇨ Select Target ⇨ Debug) rather than a release build.**

2. **Set a breakpoint at the** int i = 10; **line in** main().

3. **Click Debug/Continue.**

4. **When the debugger stops at the breakpoint, choose Debug ⇨ Debugging Windows ⇨ Watches.**

   You see the Watches window, as shown in Figure 3-6. Notice that the Watches window automatically includes i and mirror. If you click the + next to mirror, you can drill down to see NumberOfPieces.

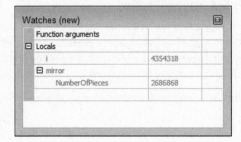

FIGURE 3-6:
The Watches window shows the value of variables and objects.

Notice that the values in i and NumberOfPieces are random because the code hasn't assigned values to them yet. The values you see will differ from those shown in Figure 3-6. This is the reason you never want to use a variable until after you assign a value to it. In this case, the variables are shown in red because C++ has just created them.

REMEMBER

Objects such as mirror contain not only variables but also other objects. When an object contains a child object, the child object will also have a plus sign next to it. To see the contents of this child object, simply click the plus sign next to it. You can keep drilling down until you reach the end of the object list.

5. **Click the Next Line button on the Debugger toolbar so that you are one line beyond the following line:**

```
int i = 10;
```

The application changes the value of i to 10, as shown in Figure 3-7. The variable is still shown in red because its value has just changed. However, notice that NumberOfPieces is now shown in black because its value hasn't changed since the last instruction.

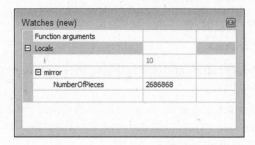

FIGURE 3-7: Assigning a value to i changes its value in the Watches window.

6. **Click Next Line on the Debugger toolbar.**

The entry for i turns black to show that it has remained stable during the execution of this command. However, NumberOfPieces is now shown in red and has a value of 100. The use of red for changed variables and black for unchanged variables makes it easy to determine which variables have changed.

7. **Click Debug/Continue.**

The application ends.

8. **Remove any breakpoints you've set in the example application.**

Changing values

Sometimes you need to verify that the application works as intended by simulating changes that might occur in the code. In many cases, this means changing a value from its default to the value you want to test. Fortunately, the Watches window provides the means to perform this task. Follow these steps to see how you can change variable values:

1. **Set a breakpoint at the** i = i + SpecialMath(i); **line in** main().

2. **Click Debug/Continue.**

3. **When the debugger stops at the breakpoint, choose Debug⇨Debugging Windows⇨Watches.**

   You see the Watches window (refer to Figures 3-6 and 3-7). The values of i and NumberOfPieces appear as before. However, you can't change these values; you can only view them.

4. **Type i in the first column of the last row of the Watches window and press Enter.**

   You see the current value of i, which is 10. Notice also that you see a variable type, int, in the third column, as shown in Figure 3-8. This entry is also in red because you've just added it to the Watches window.

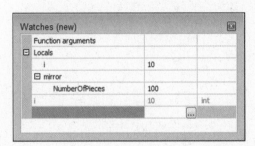

FIGURE 3-8:
Adding a watch to the window presents additional information.

5. **Select the value, 10, in the second column of the Watches window for the i you added, type 100, and click the next line of the Watches window.**

   Code::Blocks changes the value of i to 100. The i variable entry, which used to be black, has turned red because you changed the value. Notice that the copy of i in the Locals area has also changed in both value and color.

6. **Click Next Line three times so that the instruction pointer is on the line that reads**

   ```
   return 0;
   ```

   Notice that the output of the application (as well as the value of NumberOfPieces in the Watches window) has changed to 21900. Normally the output is 2100. The difference occurs because the value of i was changed.

7. **Click Debug/Continue.**

   The application ends.

Chapter **4**

Traveling About the Stack

D ebuggers can be powerful things. They can leap tall computer applications in a single bound and see through them to find all their flaws. The more you know about debuggers, the more you can put them to use. In this chapter, you see how to move about the stack, which provides you with a record of calls within your application, among other useful information.

This chapter also helps you view data in various ways. For example, in the previous chapter you got a quick view of local variables in the "Watching the variables" section. This chapter enhances your understanding of local variables. In addition, you see how threads and memory work, which offers another perspective of data and how code interacts with it. Finally, you get down to the nuts and bolts with assembly language, which is sort of the way that the computer sees your application, except with a human-readable twist.

REMEMBER

You don't have to type the source code for this chapter manually. In fact, using the downloadable source is a lot easier. You can find the source for this chapter in the \CPP_AIO4\BookIV\Chapter04 folder of the downloadable source. See the Introduction for details on how to find these source files.

Stacking Your Data

A stack is a common data structure in the computer world. When the operating system runs an application, it gives that application a *stack*, which is simply a big chunk of memory used to store data. But the data is stored just like a stack of cards (or a stack of pancakes if you prefer): With a stack of real cards, you can put a card on the top, and then another, and do that six times over; then you can take a card off and take another card off. You can put cards on the top and take them off the top. And if you follow these rules, you can't insert them into the middle or bottom of the stack. You can only look at what's on the top. A stack *data structure* works the same way: You can store data in it by *pushing* the data *onto* the stack, and you can take data off by *popping* it *off* the stack. And yes, because the stack is just a bunch of computer memory, sneaking around and accessing memory in the middle of the stack is possible. But under normal circumstances, you don't do that: You put data on and take data off.

TECHNICAL STUFF

What's interesting about the stack is that it works closely with the main CPU in your system. The CPU has its own little storage bin right on the chip itself. (It isn't in the system memory, or RAM; it's inside the CPU itself.) This storage bin holds what are called *registers.* One such register is the *stack pointer,* called the SP when working with 16-bits, ESP when working with 32-bits, or RSP when working with 64-bits. The names of the registers vary by register size. When the folks at Intel replaced the earlier chips with newer, more powerful chips, they made the registers bigger. You can see a listing of register names at https://docs.microsoft.com/en-us/windows-hardware/drivers/debugger/x64-architecture. The tutorial at https://www.tutorialspoint.com/assembly_programming/assembly_registers.htm provides additional information as well.@@@

The stack is useful in many situations and is used extensively behind the scenes in the applications you write. The compiler generates code that uses the stack to store:

>> Local variables

>> Function parameters

>> Function calling order

It's all stacked onto the stack and stuck in place, ready to be unstacked.

Moving about the stack

The Code::Blocks debugger, like most debuggers, lets you look at the stack. But really, you're not looking directly at the hardware stack. When a debugger shows you the *application stack*, it's showing you the list of function calls that led up to the application's current position in the application code. However, the application stack is a human-readable form of the hardware stack, and the debugger uses the hardware stack to get that information. So that's why programmers always call the list of function calls the *stack*, even though you're not actually looking at the hardware stack.

Figure 4-1 shows an example of the Call Stack window in Code::Blocks. To see the Call Stack window, simply choose Debug➪Debugging Windows➪Call Stack. You can see the Call Stack window in front of the main Code::Blocks window. No information appears in the Call Stack window until you start running an application.

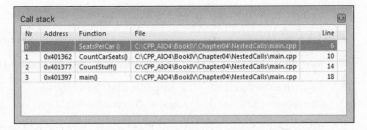

FIGURE 4-1:
The Call Stack window shows the function calls that led up to the current position.

You can try viewing the stack yourself. Look at the `NestedCalls` example, shown in Listing 4-1. This listing shows a simple application that makes several nested function calls.

LISTING 4-1: **Making Nested Function Calls**

```cpp
#include <iostream>

using namespace std;

int SeatsPerCar() {
    return 4;
}

int CountCarSeats() {
    return 10 * SeatsPerCar();
}
```

(continued)

| LISTING 4-1: | *(continued)* |

```
int CountStuff() {
    return CountCarSeats() + 25;
}

int main() {
    cout << CountStuff() << endl;
    // Remove the following comment to see the code
    // execute in the debugger.
    //system("PAUSE");
    return 0;
}
```

To try the Call Stack window, follow these steps:

1. **Compile this application (set the Build Target field to Debug).**

2. **Set a breakpoint at the** cout << CountStuff() << endl; **line.**

3. **Run the application in the Code::Blocks debugger by pressing F8.**

4. **Step into the** CountStuff() **function, and then into the** CountCarSeatsfunction(), **and then into the** SeatsPerCar() **function.**

   (Or, just put a breakpoint in the SeatsPerCar() function and run the application until it stops at the breakpoint.)

5. **Choose Debug⇨Debugging Windows⇨Call Stack.**

   A window like the one in Figure 4-1 appears. Note the order of function calls in the Call Stack window:

   ```
   SeatsPerCall()
   CountCarSeats()
   CountStuff()
   main()
   ```

   This information in the Call Stack window means that your application started with main(), which called CountStuff(). That function then called CountCarSeats(), which in turn called SeatsPerCall(). And that's where you are now. Code::Blocks places a red highlight on the current stack location — the block of code that the application is currently executing.

TIP

This window is handy if you want to know what path the application took to get to a particular routine. For example, you might see a routine that is called from many places in your application and you're not sure which part is calling the routine when you perform a certain task. To find out which part calls the routine, set a breakpoint in the function. When you run the application and the debugger stops at that line, the Call Stack window shows you the path the computer took to get there, including the name of the function that called the function in question.

In the Call Stack window, you can double-click any function name, and the Debugger moves the cursor to the function's body in the source code. This feature makes it easy for you to locate any function within the call stack and see why the code followed the path it did. Double-clicking only moves your view to the line on the call stack; the program is still stopped on the line at the top of the stack. When you switch to a new location in the call stack, the red bar moves to that location in the Call Stack window so that you can always keep track of where you are in the call stack.

REMEMBER

Stack features are common to almost all debuggers. It's not possible to say *all*, because some truly bad debuggers that don't have stack features are out there. But the good debuggers, including those built into Code::Blocks and Microsoft Visual C++, include features for moving about the stack.

Storing local variables

As you get heavily into debugging, it always helps to fully understand what goes on under the hood of your application. At this point, the text speaks on two levels:

>> Your C++ code

>> The resulting assembly code that the compiler generates based on your C++ code. (*Assembly* is the human-readable form of machine code that the processor on your machine understands.)

This chapter clearly states which level you're reading about. Suppose that you write a function in C++ and you call the function in another part of your application. When the compiler generates the assembly code for the function, it inserts some special code at the beginning and end of the function. At the start of the function, this special code allocates space for the local variables. At the end of the function, the special code de-allocates the space. This space for the variables is called the *stack frame* for the function.

This space for the local variables lives on the stack. The storage process works as follows: When you call your function, the computer pushes the return address of the caller onto the stack. After the computer is running inside the function, the special code that the compiler inserted saves some more of the stack space — just enough for the variables. This extra space becomes the local storage for the variables, and just before the function returns, the special code removes this local space. Thus, the top of the stack is now the return address. The return then functions correctly.

TECHNICAL
STUFF

This process with the stack frame takes place with the help of the internal registers in the CPU. Before a function call, the assembly code pushes the arguments to the function onto the stack. Then it calls the function by using the CPU's built-in `call` statement. (That's an assembly-code statement.) This `call` statement pushes the return address onto the stack and then moves the instruction pointer to the function address. After the execution is inside the function, the stack contains the function arguments and then the return address. The special function start-up code (called a *prolog*) saves the beginning of the stack frame address in one of the CPU registers, called the Base Pointer (BP) register. (As with SP, the name of BP can be EBP or RBP based on the register size.)

The prolog saves the value on the stack. The prolog code first pushes the BP value onto the stack. Then the prolog code takes the current stack pointer (which points to the top of the stack in memory) and saves it back in the BP register for later use. Then the prolog code adjusts the stack pointer to make room for the local variable storage. The code inside the function then accesses the local variables as offsets above the position of BP on the stack and the arguments as offsets below the position of BP on the stack.

Finally, at the end of the function, the special code (now called an *epilog*) undoes the work: The epilog copies the value in BP back into SP; this de-allocates the local variable storage. Then it *pops* the top of the stack off and restores this value back into BP. Now the top of the stack contains the function return address, which is back to the way it was when the function began. The next assembly statement is a `return`, which pops the top of the stack off and goes back to the address that the epilog code popped off the stack. Just think: Every single time a function call takes place in your computer, this process takes place.

TECHNICAL
STUFF

Inside the computer, the stack actually runs upside down. When you push something onto the stack, the stack pointer goes *down* in memory — it gets *decremented.* When you pop something off the stack, the stack pointer gets *incremented.* Therefore, in the stack frame, the local variables are actually *below* BP in memory, and you access their addresses by subtracting from the value stored in the BP register. The function arguments, in turn, are *above* the BP in memory, and you get their addresses by adding to the value stored in BP.

TECHNICAL
STUFF

The one topic not discussed in the preceding paragraph is the return value of a function. In C++, the standard way to return a value from a function is for the function's assembly code to move the value into the Accumulator, or AX, register (whose name also varies by register size). The calling code can inspect the AX register after the function is finished. However, if you are returning something complex, such as a class instance, things get a bit more complex. Suppose that you have a function that returns an object, but not as a pointer, as in the function header `MyClass MyFunction();`. Different compilers handle this differently, but when the gcc compiler that's a part of Code::Blocks, Dev-C++, MinGW, or Cygwin encounters something such as `MyClass inst = MyFunction();`, it takes the address of `inst` and puts it in AX. Then, in the function, it allocates space for a local variable, and in the `return` line it copies the object in the local variable into the object whose address is in AX. So when you return a non-pointer object, you are, in a sense, passing your object into the function as a pointer.

Debugging with Advanced Features

Most debuggers, including Code::Blocks, have some advanced features that are handy when you're tracing through your application. These features include the capability to look at *threads* (individual sequences of programmed instructions) and assembly code.

Viewing threads

If you are writing an application that uses multiple threads and you stop at a breakpoint, you can get a list of all current threads by using the Running Threads window. To open the Running Threads window, in the main Code::Blocks window choose Debug⇨Debugging Windows⇨Running Threads. A window showing the currently running threads opens. Each line looks something like this:

```
2 thread 2340.0x6cc  test() at main.cpp:7
```

The first number indicates which thread this is in the application; for example, this is the second thread. The two numbers after the word `thread` are the process ID and the thread ID in hexadecimal, separated by a dot. Then you see the name of the function where the thread is stopped, along with the line number where the thread is stopped.

Tracing through assembly code

If you feel the urge, you can view the actual assembly code. In some cases, you use the assembly code view to find particularly difficult bugs, or you might want to determine which of two programming techniques produces less code. In fact, you may just be curious as to how the compiler converts your code. To see the assembly code, choose Debug⇨Debugging Windows⇨Disassembly and you see the

Disassembly window. Check the Mixed Mode option when you want see a mix of C++ and assembly code, as shown in Figure 4-2. This approach makes it a lot easier to understand how Code::Blocks turns your C++ code into assembly language. Notice that the top of the window tells you the name of the function you're viewing and which file contains the function, and the C++ code includes line numbers so that you know precisely where you are in the source code.

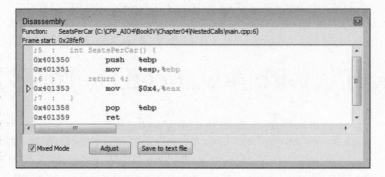

TIP

Some readers have noted that Code::Blocks will sometimes freeze when displaying the Disassembly window. The IDE will report that the disassembly is being loaded, but the process never completes. In this case, close the sample code and restart the IDE. In most cases, the disassembly will load on the second try.

The window shown in Figure 4-2 is the disassembly of the SeatsPerCar() function shown previously in Listing 4-1. Here's the function again so that you can compare it to Figure 4-2:

```
int SeatsPerCar() {
    return 4;
}
```

The following lines create the stack frame:

```
0x401350    push    %ebp
0x401351    mov     %esp,%ebp
```

TIP

You know that this is a 32-bit application because the disassembly uses the 32-bit register names throughout. If this were a 64-bit application, the register names would reflect the proper size, such as %rbp and %rsp.

After the code creates a stack frame, it moves a value of 4 (the return 4; part of the code) into EAX, as shown here:

```
0x401353    mov     $0x4,%eax
```

The code then pops EBP and returns to the caller (the CountCarSeats() function) using this code:

```
0x401358    pop     %ebp
0x401359    ret
```

Now, if you move into the CountCarSeats() function, you see assembly like that shown in Figure 4-3.

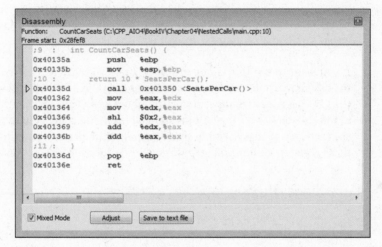

FIGURE 4-3: This Disassembly window shows the Count CarSeats() function code.

As before, the assembly code begins by creating a stack frame. It then issues a call to the SeatsPerCar() function. When the function returns, the assembly performs the multiplication part of the task. Finally, the code performs the usual task of placing the return value in EAX, popping EBP, and returning to the caller. Notice that what appears to be simple multiplication to you may not be as simple in assembly language. Say that you change the code to read

```
int CountCarSeats() {
    return 4 * SeatsPerCar();
}
```

The math is simpler now because you're using 4, which is easily converted into a binary value. Figure 4-4 shows the assembly that results from this simple change.

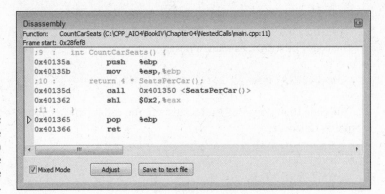

FIGURE 4-4:
Small C++ code changes can result in large assembly-code changes.

Now all the code does is perform a shift-left (SHL) instruction. Shifting the value in EAX left by 2 is the same as multiplying it by 4. The assembler uses the SHL instruction because shifting takes far fewer clock cycles than multiplication, which makes the code run faster. The result is the same, even if the assembly code doesn't quite match your C++ code.

If you want to see the values in the registers so that you can more easily follow the assembly code, choose Debug⇨Debugging Windows⇨CPU Registers. You see the CPU Registers window, shown in Figure 4-5. This window reflects the state of the registers at the current stopping point in the code. Consequently, you can't see each step of the assembly code shown in the Disassembly window reflected in these registers unless you step through the code, one instruction at a time.

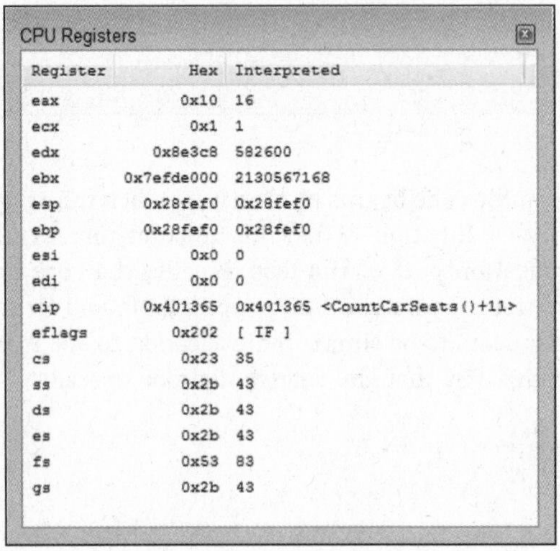

FIGURE 4-5:
Viewing the CPU registers can give you insight into how code interacts with the processor.

5
Advanced Programming

Contents at a Glance

Chapter **1**

Working with Arrays, Pointers, and References

When the C programming language, predecessor to C++, came out in the early 1970s, it was a breakthrough because it was *small*. C had only a few keywords. Tasks like printing to the console were handled not by built-in keywords but by functions. Technically, C++ still has few keywords, so it's still small. So what makes C++ big?

» Its libraries are huge.

» It's extremely sophisticated, resulting in millions of things you can do with the language.

In this chapter, you encounter the full rundown of topics that lay the foundation for C++: arrays, pointers, and references. In C++, these items come up again and again.

This chapter assumes that you have a basic understanding of C++ — that you understand the material in Books 1 and 2. You know the basics of pointers and arrays (and maybe just a teeny bit about references) and you're ready to grasp them thoroughly. When you finish this chapter, you'll have expanded on your knowledge enough to perform some intermediate and advanced tasks with relative ease.

You don't have to type the source code for this chapter manually. In fact, using the downloadable source is a lot easier. You can find the source for this chapter in the \CPP_AIO4\BookV\Chapter01 folder of the downloadable source. See the Introduction for details on how to find these source files.

Building Up Arrays

As you work with C++ arrays, it seems like you can do a million things with them. This section provides the complete details on arrays. The more you know about arrays, the less likely you are to use them incorrectly, which would result in a bug. (The following sections don't tell you about the std::array class described at https://en.cppreference.com/w/cpp/container/array. Instead, they discuss basic C++ arrays. Book 3, Chapter 1 provides a simple std::array example in the "Creating a declarative C++ example" section, and you get a more detailed look in the "Working with std::array" section in Chapter 6 of this minibook.)

Know how to get the most out of arrays when necessary — not just because they're there. Avoid using arrays in the most complex way imaginable.

Declaring arrays

The usual way of declaring an array is to line up the type name, followed by a variable name, followed by a size in brackets, as in this line of code:

```
int Numbers[10];
```

This code declares an array of 10 integers. The first element gets index 0, and the final element gets index 9. Always remember that in C++, arrays start at 0, and the highest index is one less than the size. (Remember, *index* refers to the position within the array, and *size* refers to the number of elements in the array.) To declare an array of indeterminate size, leave out the size value, like this:

```
int Numbers[];
```

In certain situations, you can declare an array without putting a number in the brackets. For example, you can initialize an array without specifying the number of elements:

```
int MyNumbers[] = {1,2,3,4,5,6,7,8,9,10};
```

The compiler is smart enough to count how many elements you put inside the braces, and then the compiler makes that count the array size.

Specifying the array size helps decrease your chances of having bugs. Plus, it has the added benefit that, in the actual declaration, if the number in brackets does not match the number of elements inside braces, the compiler issues an error. The following

```
int MyNumbers[5] = {1,2,3,4,5,6,7,8,9,10};
```

yields this compiler error:

```
error: too many initializers for 'int [5]'
```

But if the number in brackets is greater than the number of elements, as in the following code, you won't get an error. Instead, the remaining array elements aren't defined, so you can't access them. So be careful!

```
int MyNumbers[15] = {1,2,3,4,5,6,7,8,9,10};
```

You also can skip specifying the array size when you pass an array into a function, like this:

```
int AddUp(int Numbers[], int Count) {
    int loop;
    int sum = 0;
    for (loop = 0; loop < Count; loop++) {
        sum += Numbers[loop];
    }
    return sum;
}
```

This technique is particularly powerful because the AddUp() function can work for any size array. You can call the function like this:

```
cout << AddUp(MyNumbers, 10) << endl;
```

But this way to do it is kind of annoying because you have to specify the size each time you call in to the function. However, you can get around this problem. Look at this line of code:

```
cout << AddUp(MyNumbers, sizeof(MyNumbers) / 4) << endl;
```

With the array, the `sizeof` operator tells you how many bytes it uses. But the size of the array is usually the number of elements, not the number of bytes. So you divide the result of `sizeof` by 4 (the size of each `int` element).

But now you have that magic number, 4, sitting there. (By *magic number*, we mean a seemingly arbitrary number that's stuffed somewhere into your code.) So a slightly better approach would be to enter this line:

```
cout << AddUp(MyNumbers, sizeof(MyNumbers) / sizeof(int))
  << endl;
```

Now this line of code works, and here's why: The `sizeof` the array divided by the `sizeof` each element in the array gives the number of elements in the array. (You also see this technique demonstrated in the "Declaring and accessing an array" section of Book 2, Chapter 2.)

Arrays and pointers

The name of the array is a pointer to the array itself. The *array* is a sequence of variables stored in memory. The *array name* points to the first item. The following sections discuss arrays and pointers.

Seeing arrays as arrays and pointers

An interesting question about arrays and pointers is whether it's possible to use a function header, such as the following line, and rely on `sizeof` to determine how many elements are in the array. If so, this function wouldn't need to have the caller specify the size of the array.

```
int AddUp(int Numbers[]) {
```

Consider this function found in the `Array01` example and a `main()` that calls it:

```
#include <iostream>

using namespace std;

void ProcessArray(int Numbers[]) {
  cout << "Inside function: Size in bytes is "
    << sizeof(Numbers) << endl;
}

int main(int argc, char *argv[]) {
```

```
int MyNumbers[] = {1,2,3,4,5,6,7,8,9,10};
cout << "Outside function: Size in bytes is ";
cout << sizeof(MyNumbers) << endl;
ProcessArray(MyNumbers);
return 0;
}
```

When you run this application, here's what you see:

```
Outside function: Size in bytes is 40
Inside function: Size in bytes is 4
```

Outside the function, the code knows that the size of the array is 40 bytes. However, inside the function the size reported is 4 bytes. The reason is that even though it appears that you're passing an array, you're really passing a *pointer* to an array. The size of the pointer is just 4, and so that's what the final cout line prints.

Understanding external declarations

Declaring arrays has a slight idiosyncrasy. When you declare an array by giving a definite number of elements, such as

```
int MyNumbers[5];
```

the compiler knows that you have an array, and the sizeof operator gives you the size of the entire array. The array name, then, is *both* a pointer and an array! But if you declare a function header without an array size, such as

```
void ProcessArray(int Numbers[]) {
```

the compiler treats this as simply a *pointer* and nothing more. This last line is, in fact, equivalent to the following line:

```
void ProcessArray(int *Numbers) {
```

Thus, inside the functions that either line declares, the following two lines of code are *equivalent*:

```
Numbers[3] = 10;
*(Numbers + 3) = 10;
```

This equivalence means that if you use an extern declaration on an array, such as

```
extern int MyNumbers[];
```

and then take the size of this array, the compiler will get confused. Here's an example: If you have two files, numbers.cpp and main.cpp, where numbers.cpp declares an array and main.cpp externally declares it (as shown in the Array02 example), you will get a compiler error if you call sizeof:

```
#include <iostream>

using namespace std;

extern int MyNumbers[];

int main(int argc, char *argv[]) {
  cout << sizeof(MyNumbers) << endl;
  return 0;
}
```

In Code::Blocks, the gcc compiler gives this error:

```
error: invalid application of 'sizeof' to incomplete type
  'int []'
```

The solution is to put the size of the array inside brackets, such as extern int MyNumbers[10];. Just make sure that the size is the same as in the other source code file! You can fake out the compiler by changing the number, and you won't get an error. But that's bad programming style and just asking for errors.

REMEMBER

Although an array is simply a sequence of variables all adjacent to each other in memory, the name of an array is really just a pointer to the first element in the array. You can use the name as a pointer. However, do that only when you really need to work with a pointer. After all, you really have no reason to write code that is cryptic, such as *(Numbers + 3) = 10;.

The converse is also true. Look at this function:

```
void ProcessArray(int *Numbers) {
    cout << Numbers[1] << endl;
}
```

This function takes a pointer as a parameter, yet you access it as an array. Again, don't write code like this; instead, you should try to understand why code like this works. That way, you gain a deeper knowledge of arrays and how they live inside the computer, and this knowledge, in turn, can help you write code that works properly.

Differentiating between pointer types

Even though this chapter tells you that the array name is just a pointer, the name of an array of integers isn't the exact same thing as a pointer to an integer. Check out these lines of code (found in the `Array03` example):

```
#include <iostream>

using namespace std;

int main() {
  int LotsONumbers[50];
  int x;
  LotsONumbers = &x;
}
```

The code tries to point the `LotsONumbers` pointer to something different: something declared as an integer. The compiler doesn't let you do this; you get an error. That wouldn't be the case if `LotsONumbers` were declared as `int *LotsONumbers`; then this code would work. But as written, this code gives you a compiler error like this one:

```
error: incompatible types in assignment of 'int*' to 'int [50]'
```

This error implies the compiler does see a definite distinction between the two types, `int*` and `int[50]`. Nevertheless, the array name is indeed a pointer, and you can use it as one; you just can't do everything with it that you can with a normal pointer, such as reassign it. These tips will help you keep your arrays bug-free:

>> Keep your code consistent. If you declare, for example, a pointer to an integer, do not treat it as an array.

>> Keep your code clear and understandable. If you pass pointers, it's okay to take the address of the first element, as in `&(MyNumbers[0])` if this makes the code clearer — though it's equivalent to just `MyNumbers`.

>> When you declare an array, always try to put a number inside the brackets, unless you are writing a function that takes an array.

>> When you use the `extern` keyword to declare an array, also put the array size inside brackets. But be consistent! Don't use one number one time and a different number another time. The easiest way to be consistent is to use a constant, such as `const int ArraySize = 10;` in a common header file and then use that in your array declaration: `int MyArray[ArraySize];`.

Using multidimensional arrays

Arrays do not have to be just one-dimensional. Dimensions make it possible to model data more realistically. For example, a three-dimensional array would allow you to better model a specific place in 3-D space. The following sections discuss using multidimensional arrays.

Declaring a multidimensional array

You can declare a multidimensional array using a technique similar to a single-dimensional array, as shown in the Array04 example in Listing 1-1. The difference is that you must declare each dimension separately.

LISTING 1-1: **Using a Multidimensional Array**

```
#include <iostream>

using namespace std;

int MemorizeThis[10][20];

int main() {
  for (int x = 0; x < 10; x++) {
    for (int y = 0; y < 20; y++ ) {
        MemorizeThis[x][y] = x * y;
    }
  }

  cout << MemorizeThis[9][13] << endl;
  cout << sizeof(MemorizeThis) / sizeof(int) << endl;
  return 0;
}
```

When you run this, MemorizeThis gets filled with the multiplication tables. Here's the output for the application, which is the contents of MemorizeThis[9][13], and then the size of the entire two-dimensional array:

```
117
200
```

And indeed, 9 times 13 is 117. The size of the array is 200 elements. Because each element, being an integer, is 4 bytes, the size of the array in bytes is 800.

You can have many, many dimensions, but be *careful*. Every time you add a dimension, the size multiplies by the size of that dimension. Thus an array declared like the following line has 48,600 elements, for a total of 194,400 bytes:

```
int BigStuff[4][3][5][3][5][6][9];
```

And the following array has 4,838,400 elements, for a total of 19,353,600 bytes. That's about 19 megabytes!

```
int ReallyBigStuff[8][6][10][6][5][7][12][4];
```

If you really have this kind of a data structure, consider redesigning it. Any data stored like this would be downright confusing. And fortunately, the compiler will stop you from going totally overboard. Just for fun, try this giant monster:

```
int GiantMonster[18][16][10][16][15][17][12][14];
```

You'll get an error of:

```
error: size of array 'GiantMonster' is too large
```

Considering data type

The data type of your array also makes a difference. Here are some byte values for arrays of the same size, but using different types:

```
char CharArray[20][20];      // 400 bytes
short ShortArray[20][20];    // 800 bytes
long LongArray[20][20];      // 1,600 bytes
float FloatArray[20][20];    // 1,600 bytes
double DoubleArray[20][20];  // 3,200 bytes
```

Initializing multidimensional arrays

Just as you can initialize a single-dimensional array by using braces and separating the elements by commas, you can initialize a multidimensional array with braces and commas and all that jazz, too. But to do this, you combine arrays inside arrays, as in this code:

```
int Numbers[5][6] = {
    {1,2,3,4,5,6},
    {7,8,9,10,12},
    {13,14,15,16,17,18},
    {19,20,21,22,23,24},
    {25,26,27,28,29,30}
};
```

The hard part is remembering whether you put in five arrays containing six subarrays or six arrays containing five subarrays. Think of it like this: Each time you add another dimension, it goes *inside* the previous dimension. That is, you can write a single-dimensional array like this:

```
int MoreNumbers[5] = {
    100,
    200,
    300,
    400,
    500,
};
```

Then, if you add a dimension to this array, each number in the initialization is replaced by an array initializer of the form {1,2,3,4,5,6}. Then you end up with a properly formatted multidimensional array.

Passing multidimensional arrays

If you have to pass a multidimensional array to a function, things can get just a bit hairy. That's because you don't have as much freedom in leaving off the array sizes as you do with single-dimensional arrays. Suppose you have this function:

```
int AddAll(int MyGrid[5][6]) {
    int x,y;
    int sum = 0;
    for (x = 0; x < 5; x++) {
        for (y = 0; y < 6; y++) {
```

```
        sum += MyGrid[x][y];
      }
    }
  return sum;
}
```

So far, the function header is fine because it explicitly states the size of each dimension. But you may want to do this:

```
int AddAll(int MyGrid[][]) {
```

or maybe pass the sizes as well:

```
int AddAll(int MyGrid[][], int rows, int columns) {
```

But unfortunately, the compiler displays this error for both lines:

```
declaration of 'MyGrid' as multidimensional array
must have bounds for all dimensions except the first
```

The compiler is telling you that you must explicitly list all the dimensions, but it's okay if you leave the first one blank, as with one-dimensional arrays.

So this crazy code will compile:

```
int AddAll(int MyGrid[][6]) {
```

The reason is that the compiler treats multidimensional arrays in a special way. A multidimensional array is not really a two-dimensional array, for example; rather, it's an array of an array. Thus, deep down inside C++, the compiler treats the statement MyGrid[5][6] as if it were MyGrid[5] where each item in the array is itself an array of size 6. And you're free not to specify the size of a one-dimensional array. Well, the first brackets represent the one-dimensional portion of the array. So you can leave that space blank, as you can with other one-dimensional arrays. But then, after that, you have to give the subarrays *bounds*, a specific number of entries.

TIP

When using multidimensional arrays, it's often easier to think of them as an array of arrays. Either of the following function headers, for example, is confusing:

```
int AddAll(int MyGrid[][6]) {
int AddAll(int MyGrid[][6], int count) {
```

Working with Arrays, Pointers, and References

Here's a way around this problem: Use a `typedef`, which is cleaner:

```
typedef int GridRow[6];
int AddAll(GridRow MyGrid[], int Size) {
  int x,y;
  int sum = 0;
  for (x = 0; x < Size; x++) {
    for (y = 0; y < 6; y++) {
      sum += MyGrid[x][y];
    }
  }
  return sum;
}
```

The `typedef` line defines a new type called `GridRow`. This type is an array of six integers. Then, in the function, you're passing an array of `GridRow`s.

Using this `typedef` is the same as simply using two brackets, except it emphasizes that you're passing an array of an array — that is, an array in which each member is itself an array of type `GridRow`.

Arrays and command-line parameters

In a typical C++ application, the `main()` function receives an array and a count as *command-line parameters* — parameters provided as part of the command to execute that application at the command line. However, to beginning programmers, the parameters can look intimidating. But they're not: Think of the two parameters as an array of strings and a size of the array. However, each string in this array of strings is actually a character array. In the old days of C, and earlier breeds of C++, no `string` class was available. Thus strings were always character arrays, usually denoted as `char *MyString`. (Remember, an array and a pointer can be used interchangeably for the most part). Thus you could take this thing and turn it into an array — either by throwing brackets at the end, as in `char *MyString[]`, or by making use of the fact that an array is a pointer and adding a second pointer symbol, as in `char **MyString`. The following code from the CommandLineParams example shows how you can get the command-line parameters:

```
#include <iostream>

using namespace std;

int main(int argc, char *argv[]) {
  int loop;
```

```
  for (loop = 0; loop < argc; loop++) {
    cout << argv[loop] << endl;
  }
  return 0;
}
```

Before you build your application, add some command-line arguments to it by choosing Project➪Set Program's Arguments to display the Select Target dialog box, shown in Figure 1-1. Type these arguments (one on each line) in the Program Arguments field and then click OK.

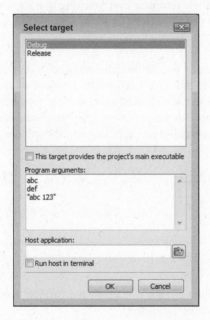

FIGURE 1-1:
Use the Select Target dialog box to add program arguments.

You see the following output when you run the application. (Note that the application name comes in as the first parameter and the quoted items come in as a single parameter.)

```
C:\CPP_AIO4\BookV\Chapter01\CommandLineParams\bin\Debug\
    CommandLineParams.exe
abc
def
abc 123
```

The first argument is always the name of the executable. The executable name can be accompanied by the `.exe` extension, the executable path, and the drive on which the executable resides. What you see depends on your IDE and compiler.

Allocating an array on the heap

Arrays are useful, but it would be a bummer if the only way you could use them were as stack variables. This section shows an exception to not treating arrays as pointers by telling how you can allocate an array on the heap by using the `new` keyword. (If you can't quite remember the difference between the stack and the heap, check out the "Heaping and Stacking the Variables" section in Book 1, Chapter 8.) But first you need to know about a couple of little tricks to make it work.

You can easily declare an array on the heap by using `new int[50]`, for example. But think about what this is doing: It declares 50 integers on the heap, and the `new` word returns a pointer to the allocated array. But, unfortunately, the makers of C++ didn't see it that way. For some reason, they based the array pointer type on the first element of the array (which is, of course, the same as all the elements in the array). Thus the call:

```
new int[50]
```

returns a pointer of type `int *`, not something that explicitly points to an array, just as this call does:

```
new int;
```

If you want to save the results of new `int [50]` in a variable, you have to have a variable of type `int *`, as in the following:

```
int *MyArray = new int[50];
```

In this case, an array name is a pointer and vice versa. So now that you have a pointer to an integer, you can treat it like an array:

```
MyArray[0] = 25;
```

Deleting an array from the heap

When you finish using the array, you can call `delete`. But you can't just call `delete MyArray;`. The reason is that the compiler knows only that `MyArray` is a pointer to an integer; it doesn't know that it's an array! Thus `delete MyArray` will only delete the first item in the array, leaving the rest of the elements sitting around on the heap, wondering when their time will come. So the makers of C++ gave us a special form of delete to handle this situation. It looks like this:

```
delete[] MyArray;
```

If you're really curious about the need for delete[] and delete, consider that there's a distinction between allocating an array and allocating a single element on the stack. Look closely at these two lines:

```
int *MyArray = new int[50];
int *somenumber = new int;
```

The first allocates an array of 50 integers, while the second allocates a single array. But look at the types of the pointer variables: They're both the same! They're both pointers; each one points to an integer. And so the statement

```
delete something;
```

is ambiguous if something is a pointer to an integer: Is it an array, or is it a single number? The designers of C++ knew this was a problem, so they *unambiguated* it. They declared and proclaimed that delete shall delete only a single member. Then they invented a little extra that must have given the compiler writers a headache: They said that if you want to delete an array instead, just throw on an opening and closing bracket after the word delete. And all will be good.

Storing arrays of pointers and arrays of arrays

Because of the similarities between arrays and pointers, you are likely to encounter some strange notation. For example, in main() itself, you have seen both of these at different times:

```
char **argc
char *argc[]
```

If you work with arrays of arrays and arrays of pointers, the best bet is to make sure that you completely understand what these kinds of statements mean. Remember that although you can treat an array name as a pointer, you're in for some technical differences. The following lines of code show these differences.

First, think about what happens if you initialize a two-dimensional array of characters like this:

```
char NameArray[][6] = {
  {'T', 'o', 'm', '\0', '\0', '\0'},
  {'S', 'u', 'z', 'y' , '\0', '\0'},
  {'H', 'a', 'r', 'r' , 'y', '\0'}
};
```

This is an array of an array. Each *inner* array is an array of six characters. The *outer* array stores the three inner arrays. (The individual content of an array is sometimes called a *member* — the inner array has six members and the outer array has three members.) Inside memory, the 18 characters are stored in one consecutive row, starting with T, then o, and ending with m and finally three copies of \0, which is the null character. But now take a look at this:

```
char* NamePointers[] = {
  "Tom",
  "Suzy",
  "Harry"
};
```

This is an array of character arrays as well, except that it's not the same as the code that came just before it. This is actually an array holding three pointers: The first points to a character string in memory containing Tom (which is followed by a null-terminator, \0); the second points to a string in memory containing Suzy ending with a null-terminator; and so on. Thus, if you look at the memory in the array, you won't see a bunch of characters; instead, you see three numbers, each being a pointer.

TIP

It's often helpful to see the content of memory as you work with arrays. To see memory in Code::Blocks, choose Debug⇨Debugging Windows⇨Memory Dump. You see the Memory window. Type & (ampersand) plus the name of the variable you want to view in the Address field and click Go. (You can also see the content of a specific memory address by typing its address, such as **0x28ff08**, or the memory pointed to by a register by typing $ plus the register name, such as **$sp**.)

TECHNICAL
STUFF

So where on earth (or in the memory, anyway) are the three strings, Tom, Suzy, and Harry when you have an array of three pointers to these strings? When the compiler sees string constants such as these, it puts them in a special area where it stores all the constants. These constants then get added to the executable file at link time, along with the compiled code for the source module. And that's where they reside in memory. The array, therefore, contains pointers to these three constant strings in memory. Now, if you try to do the following (notice the type of PointerToPointer)

```
char **PointerToPointer = {
  "Tom",
  "Suzy",
  "Harry"
};
```

you will get an error:

```
error: initializer for scalar variable requires one element
```

A *scalar* is just another name for a regular variable that is not an array. In other words, the `PointerToPointer` variable is a regular variable (that is, a scalar), not an array.

Yet, inside the function header for `main()`, you can use `char **`, and you can access this as an array. As usual, there's a slight but definite difference between an array and a pointer. You can't always treat a pointer as an array; for example, you can't initialize a pointer as an array. But you can go the other way: You can take an array and treat it as a pointer most of the time. Thus you can do this:

```
char* NamePointers[] = {
  "Tom",
  "Harry",
  "Suzy"
};
char **AnotherArray = NamePointers;
```

This code compiles, and you can access the strings through `AnotherArray[0]`, for example. Yet you're not allowed to skip a step and just start out initializing the `AnotherArray` variable like so:

```
char** AnotherArray = {
  "Tom",
  "Harry",
  "Suzy"
};
```

If you write the code that way, it's the same as the code shown just before this example — and it yields a compiler error! This is one (perhaps obscure) example in which the slight differences between arrays and pointers become obvious, but it does help explain why you can see something like this:

```
int main(int argc, char **argv)
```

CHAPTER 1 **Working with Arrays, Pointers, and References** 497 and you are free to use the `argv` variable to access an array of pointers — specifically, in this case, an array of character pointers, also called *strings.*

Building constant arrays

If you have an array and you don't want its contents to change, you can make it a constant array. The following lines of code, found in the `Array05` example, demonstrate this approach:

```
const int Permanent[5] = { 1, 2, 3, 4, 5 };
cout << Permanent[1] << endl;
```

This array works like any other array, except you cannot change the numbers inside it. If you add a line like the following line, you get a compiler error, because the compiler is aware of constants:

```
Permanent[2] = 5;
```

Here's the error you get when working in Code::Blocks:

```
error: assignment of read-only location 'Permanent[2]'
```

Arrays have a certain constancy built in. For example, you can't assign one array to another. If you make the attempt (as shown in the `Array06` example), the Code::Blocks compiler presents you with an `error: invalid array assignment` error message.)

```
int NonConstant[5] = { 1, 2, 3, 4, 5 };
int OtherList[5] = { 10, 11, 12, 13, 14 };
OtherList = NonConstant;
```

In other words, that third line is saying, "Forget what `OtherList` points to; instead, make it point to the `NonConstant` array, {1,2,3,4,5}!" The point is that arrays are always constant. If you want to make the array elements constant, you can precede its type with the word `const`. When you do so, the array name is constant, and the elements inside the array are also constant.

Pointing with Pointers

To fully understand C++ and all its strangeness and wonders, you need to become an expert in pointers. (Fortunately, many modern innovations in C++ are making the need to know pointers less of an issue — you have other means at your disposal, as discussed in Book 1, Chapter 8.) One of the biggest sources of bugs is when programmers who have a so-so understanding of C++ work with pointers and mess them up. But what's bad in such cases is that the application may run properly for a while and then suddenly not work. Those bugs are the hardest bugs to catch, because the user may see the problem occur and then report it, but programmers can't reproduce the problem. In this section, you see how you can get the most out of pointers and use them correctly in your applications so that you won't have these strange problems.

Becoming horribly complex

You could see a function header like this:

```
void MyFunction(char ***a) {
```

Yikes! What are all those asterisks for? Looks like a pointer to a pointer to a pointer to . . . something! How confusing. Some humans have brains that are more like computers, and they can look at that code and understand it just fine, but most people can't. The following sections help you understand how passing pointers to functions works.

Using a typedef

To understand the code, think about this: Suppose you have a pointer variable, and you want a function to change what the pointer variable points to. What this is saying is that the function wants to make the pointer point to something else, rather than change the contents of the thing that it points to. There's a big difference between the two. Any time you want a function to change a variable, you have to either pass it by reference or pass its address. This process can get confusing with a pointer. One way to reduce the confusion is to define a new type — using the typedef word. It goes like this (as shown in the Pointer01 example):

```
typedef char *PChar;
```

This is a new type called PChar that is equivalent to char *. That is, PChar is a pointer to a character.

Now look at this function:

```
void MyFunction(PChar &x) {
  x = new char('B');
}
```

This function takes a pointer variable and points it to the result of new char('B'). That is, it points it to a newly allocated character variable containing the letter B. Now, think this through carefully: A PChar simply contains a memory address — really. You pass it by reference into the function, and the function modifies the PChar so that the PChar contains a different address. That is, the PChar now points to something different from what it previously did.

To try this function, here's some code you can put in main() that tests MyFunction():

```
PChar ptr = new char('A');
PChar copy = ptr;
MyFunction(ptr);
cout << "ptr points to " << *ptr << endl;
cout << "copy points to " << *copy << endl;
```

The code creates two variables of type PChar: ptr and copy. It assigns a new char, 'A', to ptr and then copies the address of ptr to copy so that they both point to the same location in memory. At this point, then, ptr and copy both have the same memory address in them.

Next, the code calls MyFunction(), which changes where ptr points in memory. On return from the function, the code prints two characters: the character that ptr points to and the character that copy points to. Here's what you see when you run it:

```
ptr points to B
copy points to A
```

This means that MyFunction() worked! The ptr variable now points to the character allocated in MyFunction (a B), while the copy variable still points to the original A. In other words, they no longer point to the same thing: MyFunction() managed to change what the variable points to.

Using pointers to pointers

Now consider the same function, but instead of using references, try it with pointers. Here's a modified form (as found in the Pointer02 example):

```
typedef char *PChar;
void AnotherFunction(PChar *x) {
  *x = new char('C');
}
```

The parameter is really a `char **` in this case. You could create another `typedef` to handle it, as in `typedef char **PPChar;`. Because the parameter is a pointer, you have to dereference it to modify its value. Thus you see an asterisk, `*`, at the beginning of the middle line. Here's a modified `main()` that calls this function:

```
PChar ptr = new char('A');
PChar copy = ptr;
AnotherFunction(&ptr);
cout << "ptr points to " << *ptr << endl;
cout << "copy points to " << *copy << endl;
```

Because the function uses a pointer rather than a reference, you have to pass the address of the `ptr` variable, not the `ptr` variable directly. So notice that the call to `AnotherFunction()` has an ampersand, `&`, in front of the `ptr`. This code works as expected. When you run it, you see this output:

```
ptr points to C
copy points to A
```

This version of the function, called `AnotherFunction()`, made a new character called C. Indeed, it's working correctly: `ptr` now points to a C character, and `copy` hasn't changed. Again, the function pointed `ptr` to something else.

Avoiding typedefs

The previous examples created a `typedef` to make it much easier to understand what the functions are doing. However, not everybody does it that way; therefore you have to understand what other people are doing when you attempt to fix their code. So here are the same two functions found in the previous sections, `MyFunction()` and `AnotherFunction()`, but without `typedef`. Instead of using the new `PChar` type, they directly use the equivalent `char *` type:

```
void MyFunction(char *&x) {
  x = new char('B');
}

void AnotherFunction(char **x) {
  *x = new char('C');
}
```

To remove the use of the `typedef`s, all you do is replace the `PChar` in the two function headers and the variable declarations with its equivalent `char *`. You can see that the headers now look goofier. But they mean exactly the same as before: The first is a reference to a pointer, and the second is a pointer to a pointer.

Working with Arrays, Pointers, and References

But think about char **x for a moment. Because char * is also the same as a character array in many regards, char **x is a pointer to a character array. In fact, sometimes you may see the header for main() written like this

```
int main(int argc, char **argv)
```

instead of

```
int main(int argc, char *argv[])
```

Notice the argv parameter in the first of these two is the same type as we've been talking about: a pointer to a pointer (or, in a more easily understood manner, the address of a PChar). But you know that the argument for main() is an array of strings.

Using multiple typedefs

Now it's time to consider what happens when you have a pointer that points to an array of strings and a function that is going to make it point to a different array of strings. The Pointer03 example begins by creating the required typedefs:

```
typedef char **StringArray;
typedef char *PChar;
```

StringArray is a type equivalent to an array of strings. In fact, if you put these two lines of code before your main(), you can actually change your main() header into the following and it will compile:

```
int main(int argc, StringArray argv)
```

Now here's a function that will take as a parameter an array of strings, create a new array of strings, and set the original array of strings to point to this new array of strings:

```
void ChangeAsReference(StringArray &array) {
  StringArray NameArray = new PChar[3];
  NameArray[0] = "Tom";
  NameArray[1] = "Suzy";
  NameArray[2] = "Harry";
  array = NameArray;
}
```

Just to make sure that it works, here's something you can put in `main()`:

```
StringArray OrigList = new PChar[3];
OrigList[0] = "John";
OrigList[1] = "Paul";
OrigList[2] = "George";

StringArray CopyList = OrigList;
ChangeAsReference(OrigList);

cout << OrigList[0] << endl;
cout << OrigList[1] << endl;
cout << OrigList[2] << endl << endl;
cout << CopyList[0] << endl;
cout << CopyList[1] << endl;
cout << CopyList[2] << endl;
```

The code creates a pointer to an array of three strings. It then stores three strings in the array. Next, the code saves a copy of the pointer in the variable called `CopyList`, changes the `OrigList` pointer by calling `ChangeAsReference()`, and prints all the values. Here's the output:

```
Tom
Suzy
Harry

John
Paul
George
```

The first three outputs are the elements in `OrigList`, which were passed into `ChangeAsReference()`. They no longer have the values `John`, `Paul`, and `George`. The three original Beatles names have been replaced by three new names: `Tom`, `Harry`, and `Suzy`. However, the `Copy` variable still points to the original string list. Thus, once again, changing the pointer reference worked.

Working with string arrays using pointers

The previous section uses `typedefs` to work with string arrays, but you can also do it with pointers. Here's the modified version of the function, this time using said pointers (as shown in the `Pointer04` example):

```
void ChangeAsPointer(StringArray *array) {
  StringArray NameArray = new PChar[3];
```

```
    NameArray[0] = "Tom";
    NameArray[1] = "Harry";
    NameArray[2] = "Suzy";
    *array = NameArray;
}
```

As before, here's the slightly modified sample code that tests the function:

```
StringArray OrigList = new PChar[3];
OrigList[0] = "John";
OrigList[1] = "Paul";
OrigList[2] = "George";

StringArray CopyList = OrigList;
ChangeAsPointer(&OrigList);

cout << OrigList[0] << endl;
cout << OrigList[1] << endl;
cout << OrigList[2] << endl << endl;
cout << CopyList[0] << endl;
cout << CopyList[1] << endl;
cout << CopyList[2] << endl;
```

You can see that when the code calls ChangeAsPointer(), it passes the address of OrigList. The output of this version is the same as that of the previous version.

Here are the two function headers without using the typedefs:

```
int ChangeAsReference(char **&array) {
```

and

```
int ChangeAsPointer(char ***array) {
```

You may see code like these two lines from time to time. Such code isn't the easiest to understand, but after you know what these lines mean, you can interpret them.

TIP

Most developers use a typedef, even if it's just before the function in question. That way, it's clearer to other people what the function does. You are welcome to follow suit. But if you do, make sure that you're familiar with the non-typedef version so that you understand that version when somebody else writes it without using typedef.

Pointers to functions

When an application is running, the functions in the application exist in the memory; so just like anything else in memory, they have an address.

You can access the address of a function by taking the name of it and putting the address-of operator (&) in front of the function name, like this:

```
address = &MyFunction;
```

But to make this work, you need to know what type to declare `address`. The `address` variable is a pointer to a function, and the cleanest way to assign a type is to use `auto`, like this:

```
auto address = &MyFunction;
```

The traditional method is to use a `typedef` (as shown in the `FunctionPointer01` example). Here's the `typedef` you need:

```
typedef int(*FunctionPtr)(int);
```

It's hard to follow, which is why using `auto` is better, but the name of the new type is `FunctionPtr`. This defines a type called `FunctionPtr` that returns an integer (the leftmost `int`) and takes an integer as a parameter (the rightmost `int`, which must be in parentheses). The middle part of this statement is the name of the new type, and you must precede it by an asterisk, which means that it's a pointer to all the rest of the expression. Also, you must put the type name and its preceding asterisk inside parentheses. Now you're ready to declare some variables! Here goes:

```
FunctionPtr address = &MyFunction;
```

This line declares `address` as a pointer to a function and initializes it to `MyFunction()`. For this to work, the code for `MyFunction()` must have the same prototype declared in the `typedef`: In this case, it must take an integer as a parameter and return an integer. So, for example, you may have a function like this:

```
int TheSecretNumber(int x) {
  return x + 1;
}
```

Then you could have a main() that stores the address of this function in a variable — and then calls the function by using the variable:

```
int main() {
  typedef int (*FunctionPtr)(int);
  int MyPasscode = 20;
  FunctionPtr address = &TheSecretNumber;
  cout << address(MyPasscode) << endl;
}
```

Using the typedef approach has the advantage of specifying precisely what you want in the way of inputs, but the auto form is shorter and easier to understand. Here's main() using the auto form (you must be using C++ 11 or above to use this form):

```
int main() {
  int MyPasscode = 20;
  auto address = &TheSecretNumber;
  cout << address(MyPasscode) << endl;
}
```

Just so you can say that you've seen it, here's what the address declaration would look like without using a typedef:

```
int (*address)(int) = &TheSecretNumber;
```

The giveaway should be that you have two things in parentheses side by side, and the set on the right has only types inside it. The one on the left has a variable name. So this line is not declaring a type; rather, it's declaring a variable.

Pointing a variable to a method

When working with object-oriented programming (OOP), you need a way to access the methods within the object. Within an object's code, you use the this pointer to obtain the address of an object's method so that you can access the method instance data directly.

Remember that each instance of a class gets its own copy of the properties unless the properties are static. But methods are shared throughout the class. Yes, you can distinguish static methods from nonstatic methods. But doing so just refers to the types of variables they access: Static methods can access only static properties, and you don't need to refer to them with an instance. Nonstatic (that is, normal, regular) methods work with a particular instance. However, inside the memory, really only one copy of the method exists.

So how does the method know which instance to work with? The this parameter gets passed into the method to differentiate between instances. Suppose you have a class called Gobstopper that has a method called Chew(). Next, you have an instance called MyGum, and you call the Chew() method, like so:

```
MyGum.Chew();
```

When the compiler generates assembly code for this, it actually passes a parameter into the function — the address of the MyGum instance, also known as the this pointer. Therefore only one Chew() function is in the code, but to call it, you must use a particular instance of the class.

Because only one copy of the Chew() method is in memory, you can take its address. But to do so requires some sort of cryptic-looking code. Here it is, quick and to the point. Suppose your class looks like this:

```
class Gobstopper {
public:
  int WhichGobstopper;
  int Chew(string name) {
    cout << WhichGobstopper << endl;
    cout << name << endl;
    return WhichGobstopper;
  }
};
```

The Chew() method takes a string and returns an integer. Here's a typedef for a pointer to the Chew() function:

```
typedef int (Gobstopper::*GobMember)(string);
```

And here's a variable of the type GobMember:

```
GobMember func = &Gobstopper::Chew;
```

REMEMBER

As with other functions, you can use auto to make things simple when you work with C++ 11 or above. Here's the auto form of a variable that points to the Chew() method:

```
auto func = &Gobstopper::Chew;
```

If you look closely at the typedef, it looks similar to a regular function pointer. The only difference is that the class name and two colons precede the asterisk. Other than that, it's a regular old function pointer.

But whereas a regular function pointer is limited to pointing to functions of a particular set of parameter types and a return type, this function pointer shares those restrictions but has a further limitation: It can point only to methods within the class Gobstopper.

To call the function stored in the pointer, you need to have a particular instance. Notice that in the assignment of func in the earlier code, there was no instance, just the class name and function, &Gobstopper::Chew. So to call the function, grab an instance, add func, and go! The FunctionPointer02 example, shown in Listing 1-2, contains a complete example with the class, the method address, and two separate instances.

LISTING 1-2: **Taking the Address of a Method**

```
#include <iostream>

using namespace std;

class Gobstopper {
public:
  int WhichGobstopper;
  int Chew(string name) {
    cout << WhichGobstopper << endl;
    cout << name << endl;
    return WhichGobstopper;
  }
};

int main() {
  typedef int (Gobstopper::*GobMember)(string);
  GobMember func = &Gobstopper::Chew;

  Gobstopper inst;
  inst.WhichGobstopper = 10;

  Gobstopper another;
  another.WhichGobstopper = 20;

  (inst.*func)("Greg W.");
  (another.*func)("Jennifer W.");
  return 0;
}
```

The code begins by creating a typedef called GobMember, as discussed earlier in this section. It then creates a method pointer, func, to access the method. When using C++ 11 or above, you can replace these two lines with the much easier-to-understand single line:

```
auto func = &Gobstopper::Chew;
```

Of course, when you use this alternative, the compiler must deduce the correct types, which it may not always do correctly. Using the typedef gives you additional control at the cost of complexity.

The code then creates two instances of Gobstopper, inst and another. In both cases, it directly assigns a value to WhichGobstopper, which will vary depending on instance and accessed through this. The final section calls the Chew() method indirectly using func in each instance and assigns a name as the input string.

When you run the code, you can see from the output that it is indeed calling the correct method for each instance:

```
10
Greg W.
20
Jennifer W.
```

Now, when you hear "the correct method for each instance," what the statement really means is that the code is calling the same method each time but using a different instance. If you're thinking in object-oriented terms, consider each instance as having its own copy of the method. Therefore it's okay to say "the correct method for each instance."

Pointing to static methods

A *static method* is, in many senses, just a plain old function. The difference is that you have to use a class name to call a static function. But remember that a static method does not go with any particular instance of a class; therefore you don't need to specify an instance when you call the static function.

Here's an example class (as shown in the FunctionPointer03 example) with a static function:

```
class Gobstopper {
public:
  static string MyClassName() {
```

```
    return "Gobstopper!";
  }
  int WhichGobstopper;
  int Chew(string name) {
    cout << WhichGobstopper << endl;
    cout << name << endl;
    return WhichGobstopper;
  }
};
```

And here's some code that takes the address of the static function and calls it by using the address:

```
int main() {
  typedef string (*StaticMember)();
  StaticMember staticfunc = &Gobstopper::MyClassName;
  cout << staticfunc() << endl;
  return 0;
}
```

Note that the call `staticfunc()` doesn't refer to a specific instance and it doesn't refer to the class, either. The application just called it. Because the truth is that deep down inside, the static function is just a plain old function.

Referring to References

This section discusses how to use references and assumes that you already know how to pass a parameter by reference when you're writing a function. (For more information about passing parameters by reference, see Book 1, Chapter 8.) But you can use references for more than just parameter lists. You can declare a variable as a reference type. And just like job references, this use of references can be both good and devastating. So be careful when you use them.

Reference variables

Declaring a variable that is a reference is easy. Whereas the pointer uses an asterisk, *, the reference uses an ampersand, &. But it has a twist. You can't just declare it, like this:

```
int &BestReference; // Nope! This won't work!
```

If you try this, you see an error that says `BestReference declared as reference but not initialized`. That sounds like a hint: Looks like you need to initialize it.

Yes, references need to be initialized. As the name implies, *reference* refers to another variable. Therefore, you need to initialize the reference so that it refers to some other variable, like so (as shown in the `Reference01` example):

```
int ImSomebody;
int &BestReference = ImSomebody;
```

From this point on, the variable `BestReference` refers to — that is, is an *alias* for — `ImSomebody`. So, if you change the value of `BestReference`, as shown here:

```
BestReference = 10;
```

you'll really be setting `ImSomebody` to 10. Look at this code that could go inside `main()`:

```
int ImSomebody;
int &BestReference = ImSomebody;
BestReference = 10;
cout << ImSomebody << endl;
```

When you run this code, you see the output

```
10
```

That is, setting `BestReference` to 10 caused `ImSomebody` to change to 10, which you can see when you print the value of `ImSomebody`. That's what a reference does: It refers to another variable.

REMEMBER

Because a reference refers to another variable, that implies that you can't have a reference to just a number, as in `int &x=10`. In fact, the offending line has been implicated: You are not allowed to do that. You can have only a reference that refers to another variable.

Returning a reference from a function

It's possible to return a reference from a function. But be careful if you try to do this: You don't want to return a reference to a local variable within a function, because when the function ends, the storage space for the local variables goes away.

But you can return a reference to a global variable. Or, if the function is a method, you can return a reference to a property.

For example, here's a class found in the Reference02 example that has a function that returns a reference to one of its variables:

```
class DigInto {
private:
  int secret;
public:
  DigInto() { secret = 150; }
  int &GetSecretVariable() { return secret; }
  void Write() { cout << secret << endl; }
};
```

Notice that the constructor stores 150 in the secret variable, which is private. The GetSecretVariable() function returns a reference to the private variable called secret. The Write() function writes out the value of the secret variable. Lots of secrets here! And some surprises, too, which you discover shortly. You can use this class like so:

```
int main()
{
  DigInto inst;
  inst.Write();

  int &pry = inst.GetSecretVariable();
  pry = 30;
  inst.Write();

  auto &pry2 = inst.GetSecretVariable();
  pry2 = 40;
  inst.Write();
  return 0;
}
```

The example uses two kinds of references, one int and one auto (you must have C++ 11 or above installed to use the second type). Notice that using auto doesn't eliminate the need for the & to create a reference. If you were to write auto pry2 = inst.GetSecretVariable(); instead, you'd receive a warning message stating warning: variable 'pry2' set but not used. However, the code would still compile, and if you use the Build ➪ Build and Run option, you might not even notice the warning.

When you run this example, you see the following output:

```
150
30
40
```

Here's a look at the code in a little more detail. The first output line is the value in the secret variable right after the application creates the instance. But look at the code carefully: The variable called pry is a reference to an integer, and it gets the results of GetSecretVariable(). What is that result? It's a reference to the private variable called secret — which means that pry itself is now a reference to that variable. Yes, a variable outside the class now refers directly to a private member in the instance! After that, the code sets pry to 30. When the code calls Write() again, the private variable will indeed change. (The same sequence occurs when you use the auto variable pry2.)

Creating code like this is a bad idea because it provides access to a private variable. The GetSecretVariable() function pretty much wipes out any sense of the variable's actually remaining private. The main() function is able to grab a reference to it and poke around and change it however it wanted, as if it were not private!

That's a problem with references: They can potentially leave your code wide open. Therefore, think twice before returning a reference to a variable. Here's one of the biggest risks: Somebody else may be using this code, may not understand references, and may not realize that the variables called pry and pry2 have a direct link to the private secret variable. Such an inexperienced programmer might then write code that uses and changes pry or pry2 — without realizing that the property is changing along with it. Later on, then, a *bug* results — a pretty nasty one at that!

TIP

Because functions returning references can leave unsuspecting and less-experienced C++ programmers with just a wee bit too much power on their hands, it's a best practice to use caution with references. No, you don't have to avoid them altogether; it's simply a good idea to be careful. Use them only if you really feel you must. But remember also that a better approach in classes is to have member access functions that can guard the private variables.

However, now that you've received the usual warnings, know that references can be very powerful, provided that you understand what they do. When you use a reference, you can easily modify another variable without having to go through pointers — which can make life much easier sometimes. So, please: Use your newfound powers carefully.

Chapter **2**

Creating Data Structures

C++, being a computer language and all, provides you with a lot of ways to manipulate *data* — numbers, letters, strings, arrays — anything you can store inside the computer memory. To get the most out of C++, you should know as much as you can about the fundamental data types. This chapter covers them and how to use them.

This chapter refers to the ANSI standard of C++. ANSI is the American National Standards Institute. The information provided in this chapter deals with the ANSI standard (singular) of C++. Fortunately, the GNU gcc compiler that comes with Code::Blocks is ANSI-standard-compliant.

REMEMBER

You don't have to type the source code for this chapter manually. In fact, using the downloadable source is a lot easier. You can find the source for this chapter in the \CPP_AIO4\BookV\Chapter02 folder of the downloadable source. See the Introduction for details on how to find these source files.

Working with Data

In the sections that follow, you see how to manipulate data, consider the data types available to you, and discover how you can change one data type to another.

The great variable roundup

The ANSI C++ standard dictates the fundamental C++ types shown in Table 2-1.

REMEMBER

C++ includes a signed keyword, but you have little reason to use it because signed is assumed if you don't specifically use unsigned. Note that when you use unsigned, the size of the variable doesn't change: It takes the same number of bytes. Instead, the range *shifts*. For example, a short ranges from −32,768 to 32,767, so there are 65,536 possibilities. An unsigned short ranges from 0 to 65,535; again, there are 65,536 possibilities.

The precise values of some of these types, such as long double, can vary by compiler. The best way to ensure that you understand the limits of your compiler is to run a simple test. The VarTypes example, shown in Listing 2-1, demonstrates the maximum values for each data type found in Table 2-1.

TABLE 2-1:

ANSI C++ Character Types

Name	Size in Bytes	Range
char	1	−128 to 127
unsigned char	1	0 to 255
short	2	−32,768 to 32,767
unsigned short	2	0 to 65,535
int and long	4	−2,147,483,648 to 2,147,483,647
unsigned int and unsigned long	4	0 to 4,294,967,295
long long	8	−9,223,372,036,854,775,808 to 9,223,372,036,854,775,807
unsigned long long	8	0 to 18,446,744,073,709,551,615
bool	1	true/false
float	4	1.17549e-038 to 3.40282e+038
double	8	2.22507e-308 to 1.79769e+308
long double	12	3.3621e-4932 to 1.18973e+4932

LISTING 2-1: **Testing Maximum Type Values**

```cpp
#include <iostream>
#include <climits>
#include <cfloat>

using namespace std;

int main() {
  char Char = CHAR_MAX;
  unsigned char UChar = UCHAR_MAX;
  short Short = SHRT_MAX;
  unsigned short UShort = USHRT_MAX;
  int Int = INT_MAX;
  unsigned int UInt = UINT_MAX;
  long Long = LONG_MAX;
  unsigned ULong = ULONG_MAX;
  long long LongLong = LLONG_MAX;
  unsigned long long ULongLong = ULLONG_MAX;
  bool Bool = true;
  float Float = FLT_MIN;
  double Double = DBL_MIN;
  long double LDouble = LDBL_MIN;

  cout << "Char\t\t\t" << Char << "\t\t\t" <<
    sizeof(Char) << endl;
  cout << "Unsigned Char\t\t" << UChar << "\t\t\t" <<
    sizeof(UChar) << endl;
  cout << "Short\t\t\t" << Short << "\t\t\t" <<
    sizeof(Short) << endl;
  cout << "Unsigned Short\t\t" << UShort << "\t\t\t" <<
    sizeof(UShort) << endl;
  cout << "Int\t\t\t" << Int << "\t\t" <<
    sizeof(Int) << endl;
  cout << "Unsigned Int\t\t" << UInt << "\t\t" <<
    sizeof(UInt) << endl;
  cout << "Long\t\t\t" << Long << "\t\t" <<
    sizeof(Long) << endl;
  cout << "Unsigned Long\t\t" << ULong << "\t\t" <<
    sizeof(ULong) << endl;
  cout << "Long Long\t\t" << LongLong << "\t" <<
    sizeof(LongLong) << endl;
  cout << "Unsigned Long Long\t" << ULongLong << "\t" <<
    sizeof(ULongLong) << endl;
```

(continued)

LISTING 2-1: *(continued)*

```
cout << "Bool\t\t\t" << (Bool ? "True" : "False") <<
  "\t\t\t" << sizeof(Bool) << endl;
cout << "Float\t\t\t" << Float << "\t\t" <<
  sizeof(Float) << endl;
cout << "Double\t\t\t" << Double << "\t\t" <<
  sizeof(Double) << endl;
cout << "Long Double\t\t" << LDouble << "\t\t" <<
  sizeof(LDouble) << endl;
return 0;
}
```

REMEMBER

Notice the use of constants, such as CHAR_MAX, to set maximum values. When working with integers, you use the statement #include <climits>, which reads as include the file climits. You may see other headers used, but they may not include the ULLONG_MAX constant. When working with floating-point numbers, you #include <cfloat>. This example provides the following output:

Char	127	1
Unsigned Char	255	1
Short	32767	2
Unsigned Short	65535	2
Int	2147483647	4
Unsigned Int	4294967295	4
Long	2147483647	4
Unsigned Long	4294967295	4
Long Long	9223372036854775807	8
Unsigned Long Long	18446744073709551615	8
Bool	True	1
Float	1.17549e-038	4
Double	2.22507e-308	8

TIP

The char output will reflect a character, rather than a number, in all cases. Consequently, you may see a different character output on your display. Notice also the use of (Bool ? "True" : "False") to display a textual value, rather than a numeric value, for Bool.

Expressing variables from either side

Occasionally, when you look at error messages (or if you read the ANSI standard), you see the terms lvalue and rvalue. The *l* and *r* refer to left and right, respectively. In an assignment statement, an lvalue is any expression that can be on the left side of the equals sign, and an rvalue is an expression that can be on the right side of an equals sign.

REMEMBER

The terms lvalue and rvalue don't refer to what happens to be on the left side and right side of an assignment statement. They refer to what is allowed or not allowed on the left or right side of an assignment statement. You can have only lvalues on the left side of an assignment statement and rvalues on the right side of an assignment statement. Here are some examples, in which ploggle is an int type. This is allowed because ploggle is an lvalue:

```
ploggle = 3;
```

On the left side, you cannot have items that are strictly an rvalue. The following is not allowed because 2 is strictly an rvalue:

```
2 = ploggle;
```

The number 2 can't appear on the left (setting it equal to something else makes no sense), therefore it isn't an lvalue. In fact, anything you can set equal to something else is an lvalue.

The main reason you need to know these terms is their tendency to show up in error messages. If you try to compile the line 2 = ploggle, you see an error message similar to this one:

```
non-lvalue in assignment
```

If you don't know what the term lvalue means, these messages can be confusing. Although seeing the problem with 2 = ploggle is pretty easy, sometimes the problem is not that obvious. Look at this:

```
ChangeMe() = 10;
```

In most cases, putting a function call on the left doesn't make sense, so you don't do it. In other words, you must consider whether the expression ChangeMe() is considered an lvalue. Look at this code from the LValueAndRValue example:

```
#include <iostream>

using namespace std;

int uggle;
```

```
int &ChangeMe() {
  return uggle;
}

int main() {
  ChangeMe() = 10;
  cout << ChangeMe() << endl;
  return 0;
}
```

The function ChangeMe() returns a reference to an integer; this line is valid:

```
ChangeMe() = 10;
```

The expression ChangeMe() refers to the variable uggle, and thus this line of code stores 10 in uggle. You can still use ChangeMe() as a function, as shown in the next line with the cout, so it can still stand alone.

REMEMBER

The words lvalue and rvalue aren't C++ keywords. You don't type these into an application.

Casting a spell on your data

Although C++ has all these great data types, such as int and char, the fact is that the CPU just stores them as numbers. And sometimes you may have a character and need to use its underlying number. To do this, you can *cast* the data into a different type.

The way you cast is to take a variable of one type and type the variable's name, preceded by the other type you would like it to be. You put that other type in parentheses, as shown in the SimpleCast example that follows.

```
#include <iostream>

using namespace std;

int main() {
  char buddy = 'A';
  int underneath = (int)buddy;
  cout << underneath << endl;
  return 0;
}
```

When you run this code, you obtain an output value of 65. If you substituted a lowercase a, the output would be 97 because uppercase and lowercase letters have different numeric values.

Comparing casting and converting

The idea behind casting is to take some data and, without changing it, use it in another way. For example, you could have an array containing the characters Apple. But inside the memory, each letter is stored as a number. For example, the A is stored as 65, p is stored as 112, l as 108, and e as 101. Therefore, you use code like that found in the CastOrConvert example that follows when you want to cast each character to an integer:

```
char str[] = {'A','p','p','l','e','\0'};
cout << str << endl;

for (int x: str)
  cout << x << endl;
```

where str is the string Apple (notice the null value required to end the string). The for each loop casts each character in str, one at a time, to an int, and then prints it out onscreen. This act would print out the numerical equivalents of each letter, as shown here:

```
Apple
65
112
112
108
101
0
```

In other words, the code casts the characters to integers — but doesn't actually change any data.

Converting, however, is different. If you want to take the number 123, casting it to a string will not create a string 123. The string 123 is made up of three underlying characters. The numbers for the string 123 are 49, 50, and 51, respectively. Casting the number 123 into a char won't produce the string, "123". Instead, you would need to convert the number to a string using code like this, as shown in CastOrConvert.

```
int value = 123;
char strValue[4];
```

```
strValue[3] = '\0';
for (int counter = 2; counter >= 0; counter--) {
  strValue[counter] = (char)(value % 10 + 48);
  value = value / 10;
}
cout << strValue << endl;
```

In this case, the code works backward to create the string from the number by using a combination of integer division and modulus. The content in value is destroyed in the process, but strValue contains the correct string in the end. To get an idea of how this works, 123 % 10 = 3, while 123 / 10 = 12. The value 3 + 48 = 51 comes out to the char value '3' when cast. Of course, there is a much easier way to perform this task (you must #include <string>):

```
string EasyValue = to_string(123);
cout << EasyValue << endl;
```

As is true of most techniques, there are times when casting won't work as expected. One of those times come into play when converting between floats and integers. Instead of using a conversion function, the C++ compiler automatically converts from float to integer and vice versa if you try to cast one to the other. Ugh. That goes against the rest of the rules, so be careful. Here's an example of converting a float to an integer:

```
float f = 6.3;
int i = (int)f;
```

But the crazy part is that you can also do the same thing without even using the cast:

```
float f = 6.3;
int i = f;
```

WARNING

Casting and converting can both cause problems. For example, when casting between a float and an int, you have the potential for data loss. A float value of 0.123 will appear as an int value of 0. Whenever possible, use *built-in conversions* (those where you can simply make one data type equal to another data type, such as making an int variable equal to a char variable) to ensure that the output you receive truly represents the correct transition between one type and another. Later in this chapter, you also see how to use safe casting techniques with both dynamic_cast and static_cast. Unlike most languages, C++ won't protect you from yourself. For example, you can cast a pointer to some other type, even though such a cast doesn't make sense. You could even convert the address into a string if you want. C++ assumes that you want the low-level access that it can provide, so it also gives you the extra flexibility to perform tasks incorrectly.

UNDERSTANDING AND AVOIDING NARROWING CASTS

A *narrowing cast* is one in which you could lose data, such as casting a float into an int (you can lose the decimal part of the data) or a double into a float (double holds larger numbers). Unfortunately, standard implementations of most compilers don't necessarily warn you about narrowing casts, as is the case for the CastOrConvert example. However, you can overcome this issue by using the Guideline Support Library (GSL) described at https://www.modernescpp.com/index.php/c-core-guideline-the-guidelines-support-library. It includes the narrow cast, which throws an exception when some code you've written will result in a narrowing cast, such as that shown here:

```
double d = 9.9;
int i = narrow<int>(d);
```

This code will throw an exception because the cast will result in a narrowing of the data. The narrow_cast is an alternative that allows a narrowing cast because you've indicated that you're aware that narrowing will occur, as shown here:

```
double d = 9.9;
int i = narrow_cast<int>(d);
```

This time, you don't see an exception because you've indicated that you know the cast will result in a narrowing of the data. The Microsoft documentation at https://docs.microsoft.com/en-us/cpp/code-quality/c26472?view=vs-2019 provides some additional insights about GSL.

Casting safely with C++

The ANSI standard of C++ comes with all kinds of goodies that make life easier than it used to be. Casting is one example. Originally, you could just cast all you wanted and change from one data type to another, possibly causing a mess, especially if you take existing code and compile it under a different operating system or perhaps even under a different compiler on the same operating system. One type may have a different underlying representation, and then, when you convert it on one system, you get one thing; take it to a different system and you get something else. That's bad. It creates bugs!

So the ANSI standard for C++ gives some newer and better ways of casting between items of data. These include dynamic_cast, static_cast, and const_cast. (There is also a reinterpret_cast, but it's incredibly unsafe to use and therefore not demonstrated.)

Dynamically casting with dynamic_cast

When the makers of C++ came up with these new ways of casting, their motivation was this: Think in terms of conversions. A cast simply takes one data type and tells the compiler to treat it as another data type. So first ask yourself whether one of the conversions will work for you. If not, you can consider one of the new ways of casting.

But remember, a cast tells the compiler to treat some data as another type of data. But the new ways of casting prevent you from doing a cast that doesn't make sense. For example, you may have a class hierarchy, and you have a pointer to a base class. But because an instance of a derived class can be treated as an instance of a base class, this instance that you're looking at could actually be an instance of a derived class.

In the old style of C and C++ programming, you could just cast the instance and have at it:

```
DoSomethingCool( (derivedclass *) someptr );
```

This code assumes that someptr is of type pointer-to-base-class that, in fact, points to a derivedclass instance. It may point to derivedclass, but that depends on how you wrote the application. But, relying on assumptions rather than actual knowledge is a great way to create a buggy application.

However, with the new ANSI ways of casting, you can be sure that someptr points to a derivedclass instance. The DynamicCast example, shown in Listing 2-2, is a complete application that demonstrates a proper *down-cast* that uses a pointer to a base class and casts it down to a pointer of a derived class.

LISTING 2-2: **Casting Instances Dynamically for Safety**

```cpp
#include <iostream>

using namespace std;

class King {
protected:
  string CrownName;
public:
  virtual string &MyName() { return CrownName; }
  virtual ~King(){}
};
```

```
class Prince : public King {
public:
  string School;
};

void KingInfo(King *inst) {
  cout << "=========" << endl;
  cout << inst->MyName() << endl;
  Prince *asPrince = dynamic_cast<Prince *>(inst);
  if (asPrince != 0)
  {
    cout << asPrince->School << endl;
  }
}

int main() {
  Prince George;
  George.MyName() = "George I";
  George.School = "School of the Kings";
  KingInfo(&George);
  King Henry;
  Henry.MyName() = "Henry II";
  KingInfo(&Henry);
  return 0;
}
```

When you run this code, you see output that looks like this:

```
=========
George I
School of the Kings
=========
Henry II
```

Some strange things are going on in this code. Starting with main(), the code calls KingInfo(), first passing it the address of George (a Prince instance, derived from King) and then the address of Henry (a King instance).

The KingInfo() function first prints the information that is common to both due to inheritance using the MyName() function and prints the resulting name. Then comes the important part: the dynamic cast. To do the dynamic cast, the code calls dynamic_cast and saves inst (which can be of type King or Prince) in a pointer variable called asPrince. Notice the syntax of dynamic_cast. It looks like a template in that you include a type in angle brackets. Then you put the variable you want to cast in parentheses (in this case inst).

If the dynamic cast works, it returns a pointer that you can save as the type inside angle brackets. Otherwise, the dynamic cast returns 0. After calling dynamic_cast, the code tests the result against 0. If the result is not 0, the dynamic cast worked, which means that inst is of type Prince. Then, in the if block, the code retrieves and prints the School member, which is part of Prince, not King.

Notice the unique design of the King class in Listing 2-2. For dynamic_cast to work, the base class involved must have at least one virtual function. Thus the base class — and each of its derived classes — has a virtual table (also needed for dynamic_cast to work). In addition, the Code::Blocks compiler raises a warning message when you don't provide a virtual destructor:

```
warning: 'class King' has virtual functions but non-virtual
    destructor
```

Consequently, the example includes a virtual destructor as well. Notice also that this class uses good design by keeping CrownName private and providing an accessor function, MyName(), to it.

You don't need to use references in a class as shown here to make dynamic_cast work. But you do need at least one virtual function.

The fundamental difference between an old-style direct cast and a dynamic_cast is that the compiler generates code that automatically does an old-style cast, regardless of whether the cast is valid, during compile time. That is, the cast is hardcoded. But dynamic_cast tests the types at runtime. The dynamic cast may or may not work depending on the type of the object.

When you use a dynamic cast, you can cast either a pointer or a reference. The KingInfo() function shown previously in Listing 2-2 uses a pointer. Here's a modified form that uses a reference:

```
void KingInfoAsReference(King &inst) {
  cout << "=========" << endl;
  cout << inst.MyName() << endl;
  try {
    Prince &asPrince = dynamic_cast<Prince &>(inst);
    cout << asPrince.School << endl;
  } catch (...) { }
}
```

To make this version work, you have to use an *exception handler* (which is a way to deal with unusual situations; see Chapter 3 in this minibook for more information on exception handlers). The reason for using an exception handler is that with a pointer, you can simply test the result against 0. But with references, you have no such thing as a null reference or 0 reference. The reference must work or you get a runtime error. In C++, the way you can catch a situation that didn't work is by typing the word try, followed by your code that attempts to do the job, in braces. Follow that with the word catch and a set of parentheses containing three periods. Following that, you put braces — and possibly any code you want to run — just in case the earlier code didn't work.

This code doesn't do anything inside the catch block because the application will continue to work even if the call fails — the output simply lacks the school name. C++ requires that all try blocks are matched with a catch block, so you must include the catch block even when it doesn't do anything.

Statically casting with static_cast

The ANSI C++ standard includes a special type of cast that does no type checking. If you have to cast directly without the help of dynamic_cast, you should opt for static_cast instead of the old C-style cast.

When you want to do a static cast, call static_cast and follow it with angle brackets containing the type you want to cast to. Then put the item being cast inside parentheses, as in the following:

```
FinalType *f = static_cast<FinalType *>(orig);
```

The advantage of using static_cast is that it does some type checking at compile time, whereas old C-style casts do not. The compiler allows you to do static_cast only between related objects. You can do a static_cast from an instance of one class to an instance of a derived or base class. But if two classes are not related, you will get a compiler error. For example, suppose that you have these two lines of code:

```
class FinalType {};
class AnotherType {};
```

They're unrelated classes. Then, if you have these lines of code

```
AnotherType *orig = new AnotherType;
FinalType *f = static_cast<FinalType *>(orig);
```

and you try to compile the code, you get an error:

```
static_cast from 'AnotherType *' to 'FinalType *'
```

The following code, found in the StaticCast example, shows how to make the casting work:

```cpp
#include <iostream>

using namespace std;

class FinalType {};
class AnotherType : public FinalType {};

int main() {
    AnotherType *orig = new AnotherType;
    FinalType *f = static_cast<FinalType *>(orig);
}
```

The difference between static_cast and dynamic_cast is that static_cast does all its type checking at compile time; the compiler makes sure that the cast is okay. A dynamic_cast performs both runtime and compile time checks, so it's more comprehensive. Old C-style casts do none of this type checking.

If you're just doing a conversion between floating-point numbers and integers, you can do an old-style cast. (That's because an old-style cast is really a conversion, not a cast.) Alternatively, of course, you're welcome to use static_cast to get the same job done:

```cpp
float f = static_cast<float>(x);
```

Changing the constness of variables with const_cast

Sometimes you need to add or remove const from a variable in order to perform a cast. The variable itself doesn't change, but the cast output does. For example, if you want to send a const value to a function that doesn't accept a const value, you need to perform a const_cast. Likewise, you may have a volatile variable, one that is changed by code outside the current application. (This is a common process in embedded applications; see the article at https://www.tutorialspoint.com/What-does-the-volatile-keyword-mean-in-Cplusplus for more information.) You may need to cast the volatile variable as a common variable. The ConstCast example that follows shows both techniques:

```
#include <iostream>

using namespace std;

void PrintIt(int *out) {
  cout << "The value is: " << *out << endl;
}

int main() {
    volatile int X = 20;
    const int Y = 30;

    PrintIt(const_cast<int*>(&X));
    PrintIt(const_cast<int*>(&Y));
    return 0;
}
```

In the first case, if you were to try PrintIt(&X), you'd see error: invalid conversion from 'volatile int*' to 'int*' during compilation. Likewise, in the second case, PrintIt(&Y) would produce an error: invalid conversion from 'const int*' to 'int*' error message. Of course, neither X nor Y has its attributes removed; you simply strip the volatile or const attribute off for the purpose of sending the value to PrintIt().

Structuring Your Data

Before C++ came to life, C had something that was similar to classes, called *structures.* The difference was that structures had only properties — no methods. Here's an example of a structure:

```
struct Dimensions {
  int height;
  int width;
  int depth;
  int weight;
  int price;
};
```

This block of code is similar to a class; as you can see, it has some properties but no methods. Nor does it have any access control (such as public, private, or protected).

But not only did the designers of C++ add classes to C++, they also enhanced the structures in C++. So now you can use structures more powerfully in C++ than you could in C. The main change to structures in C++ is that they can have methods and access control. Thus, you can add to the Dimensions structure like so (making struct and class equivalent):

```
struct Dimensions {
private:
  int price;
public:
  int height;
  int width;
  int depth;
  int weight;
  int GetPrice() { return price; }
};
```

Then create an instance of Dimensions in your code like this:

```
Dimensions FirstIem;
Dimensions *SecondItem = new Dimensions;
```

REMEMBER

When the great founder of the C++ language (Bjarne Stroustrup) created C++, he enhanced structures to the point that classes and structures are *identical*, with one exception. Members of a structure are public by default. Members of a class, however, are private by default. Because the differences are so small, most C++ programmers today never even touch a structure, except to create an object that has only public properties.

In other words, programmers use struct for simple data types that are a collection of smaller data types. (That is, they use structs the same way C originally used them.) The sections that follow tell you about some of these data-structure issues.

TECHNICAL STUFF

If you're familiar with C and just learning C++, you may be interested to know that when you declare a variable that is a structure type, in C++ you need to give only the name of the structure. You no longer need the word struct in the declaration. Thus the following line will still compile in C++:

```
struct Dimensions another;
```

but all you really need is

```
Dimensions another;
```

Structures as component data types

A common use of structures is as an advanced data type made up of underlying data types. For example, a lot of operating systems that deal with graphics include libraries that require a `Point` structure. Typically, a `Point` structure is simply a grouping of an X-coordinate and a Y-coordinate, all in one package like this:

```
struct Point {
  int x;
  int y;
};
```

Then, when you need to call a function that requires such a structure — such as the function created for this example called `DrawDot()` — you would simply declare a `Point` and call the function, as in the following:

```
Point onedot;
onedot.x = 10;
onedot.y = 15;
DrawDot(onedot);
```

The `DrawDot` function would have a prototype that looks like this:

```
void DrawDot(Point pt);
```

Note that the function doesn't take a pointer to a `Point`, nor does it take a reference to a `Point`. It just gets right to the `Point` directly.

TIP

If you want, you can initialize the members of a structure the same way you would an array:

```
Point seconddot = { 30, 50 };
DrawDot(seconddot);
```

Equating structures

Setting simple structures that are equal to another structure is easy. The C++ compiler automatically handles this by copying the members one by one. The `EquateStruct` example, shown in Listing 2-3, is an example of this process in action.

LISTING 2-3: **Copying Structures Easily**

```cpp
#include <iostream>

using namespace std;

struct Point3D {
  double x;
  double y;
  double z;
};

int main() {
  Point3D FirstPoint = { 10.5, 22.25, 30.8 };
  Point3D SecondPoint = FirstPoint;

  cout << SecondPoint.x << endl;
  cout << SecondPoint.y << endl;
  cout << SecondPoint.z << endl;
  return 0;
}
```

TIP

Because structures are almost identical to classes, you can take Listing 2-2 and change the structure definition to the following class definition, and the application will continue to function the same:

```cpp
class Point3D {
public:
  double x;
  double y;
  double z;
};
```

No matter which form of the application you use, the output is simple. When you run this application, you see output similar to this:

```
10.5
22.25
30.8
```

Returning compound data types

Because simple structures are just a grouping of smaller data items, you can treat them as one chunk of data. For that reason, you can easily return them from functions without having to use pointers. The following function (found in the CompoundData example) shows how to return a structure:

```
Point3D StartingPoint(float x) {
  Point3D start;
  start.x = x;
  start.y = x * 2;
  start.z = x * 3;
  return start;
}
```

This function relies on the Point3D struct defined in the preceding section, "Equating structures." The following code shows how to use this function:

```
int main() {
  Point3D MyPoint = StartingPoint(5.2);
  Point3D OtherPoint = StartingPoint(6.5);

  cout << MyPoint.x << endl;
  cout << MyPoint.y << endl;
  cout << MyPoint.z << endl;
  cout << endl;
  cout << OtherPoint.x << endl;
  cout << OtherPoint.y << endl;
  cout << OtherPoint.z << endl;
}
```

These cout statements produce the following output:

```
5.2
10.4
15.6

6.5
13
19.5
```

Note that StartingPoint() creates a local variable, start, of type Point3D. This variable isn't a pointer or reference. The return is an unmodified start. Calling StartingPoint() copies the value of the returned structure into variables in main(), first MyPoint and then OtherPoint.

TECHNICAL STUFF

You may start to see some trouble in paradise when returning structures (or class instances, because they're the same thing). Returning a structure works, but what happens is sophisticated. When you create an instance of the structure in the function, you're just creating a local variable. That's definitely not something you want to return; it would sit on the stack as a local variable. But consider this call:

```
Point3D MyPoint = StartingPoint(5.2);
```

At the assembly level, `StartingPoint()` receives the address of `MyPoint`. Then at the end of the function, again at the assembly level, the compiled code copies the contents of `start` into the `MyPoint` structure by using the pointer to `MyPoint`. So `StartingPoint()` doesn't actually return anything; instead, the data is copied. Thus, if your structure includes a pointer variable (for example), you get a copy of the pointer variable as well — that is, your pointer variable will point to the same thing as the pointer in the function. That may or may not be what you want, depending on your situation. So be careful and make sure you fully understand what you're doing when you return a structure from a function!

Naming Your Space

It's often nice to be able to use a common name for a variable or other item without fear that the name will clash with a preexisting identifier. For example, somewhere in a header file, you may have a global variable called `Count`, and somebody else may want to make a variable called `Count` in an application that uses your header file. Or you may want to name a function `GetData()` — but you need to ensure that it doesn't conflict with another header that already has a `Get-Data()` function. These are examples of potential naming clashes (or sometimes called a name collision). The following sections describe how to create and use namespaces to your benefit.

Creating a namespace

You can use *namespaces* to group identifiers, such as all your classes, under a single name. If you called this group `Menagerie`, for example, `Menagerie` is your namespace. You would then put your classes inside it, as shown in the `Simple-Namespace` example:

```
namespace Menagerie {
  class Oxen {
  public:
```

```
      int Weight;
      int NumberOfTeeth;
   };

   class Cattle {
   public:
      int Weight;
      int NumberOfChildren;
   };
}
```

The names Oxen and Cattle are unique within the Menagerie namespace. You are free to reuse these names in other namespaces without worrying about a clash. Then, if you want to use either of the two classes outside the Menagerie namespace, you *fully qualify* the names of the classes, like so (notice the use of the double colons between Menagerie and Cattle):

```
Menagerie::Cattle bessie;
bessie.Weight = 643;
```

Unlike class and structure declarations, a namespace declaration doesn't have to end with a semicolon.

REMEMBER

Employing using namespace

If you plan to use the names in the Menagerie namespace without having to retype the namespace name each time, just put a line after the namespace declaration in the other namespace (but somewhere preceding the use of the names Cattle and Oxen in your code), like this:

```
using namespace Menagerie;
```

Then you can access the names as if they're not in a namespace:

```
Cattle bessie;
bessie.Weight = 643;
```

When you include a line that has using namespace, the compiler knows that the namespace is only for lines that follow the using namespace declaration. Consider the following code:

REMEMBER

```
void cattleranch() {
   Cattle x;
}
```

```
using namespace Menagerie;
void dairy() {
  Cattle x;
}
```

Here the first function won't compile because the compiler won't know the name Cattle. To get it to work, you have to replace Cattle with Menagerie::Cattle. But the second function will compile because you included using namespace Menagerie;.

The using namespace line is good only for lines that follow it. If you put using namespace inside a code block — inside curly braces { and }, as you would inside a function — the line applies only to lines that follow it within the same code block. Thus, in this case:

```
void cattleranch() {
    using namespace Menagerie;
    Cattle x;
}

void dairy() {
    Cattle x;
}
```

the compiler will be happy with the first function, cattleranch() but not with the second function, dairy(). The using namespace line is good only for the length of the cattleranch() function; it's inside that function's code block.

TIP

When you have a using namespace line, any variables or identifiers you create after that line don't become part of the namespace you're using. The using namespace line simply tells the compiler that if it finds an identifier it doesn't recognize, it should check next inside the namespaces you're using.

REMEMBER

When you have a using namespace line, you can follow it with more using namespace lines for other namespaces — and doing so won't cause the compiler to forget the previous using namespace line. Thus, if you have

```
using namespace Menagerie;
using namespace Ocean;
```

you can successfully refer to identifiers in both the Menagerie and the Ocean namespaces.

CREATING ONE NAMESPACE IN MANY PLACES

After you create a namespace, you can add to it later in your code if necessary. All you have to do is start the first block of code with (for example) namespace Menagerie { and then finish it with a closing brace. Then, later in your code, do the same line again — starting the block again with namespace Menagerie { and ending it with a closing brace. The identifiers in both blocks become part of the namespace Menagerie.

WARNING

However, now if there are multiple occurrences of the same name, you receive an error message saying that the reference to the name is ambiguous. The compiler then presents a list of namespaces that contain the name so that you can decide which one to use. You resolve the name clash by fully qualifying the name.

Using variables

You can put variables in a namespace and then later refer to them through the namespace, as in the following:

```
namespace Menagerie {
    int CattleCount;
}
```

And do it again later — for example, in your main() — like this:

```
Menagerie::CattleCount = 10;
```

But remember: A namespace is not a class! Only one instance of the CattleCount variable exists; it just happens to have a full name of Menagerie::CattleCount. You can't get away with creating multiple instances of Menagerie because it's a namespace. (Think of it like a surname: There could be multiple people named John, and to distinguish between them in a meeting at work, you might tack on their last names: John Squibbledash and John Poltzerbuckin.) Although the namespace name comes first in Menagerie::CattleCount, it's analogous to the last name. Two variables can be called CattleCount: one in the Menagerie namespace and one in the Farm namespace. Their full names are Menagerie::CattleCount and Farm::CattleCount.

Using part of a namespace

You can use only a portion of a namespace if desired. Using the `Menagerie` namespace declared earlier in this section, you could do something like this outside the namespace:

```
using Menagerie::Oxen;
Oxen ollie;
```

(Notice that no `namespace` word appears after `using`.) The first line tells the compiler about the name `Oxen`, and the second line creates an instance of `Oxen`. Of course, if you have `using namespace Menagerie`, the `using Menagerie::Oxen` isn't very useful because the `Oxen` name is already available from the `using namespace Menagerie` line.

REMEMBER

Think of a `using` declaration as pulling a name into the current namespace. Therefore, a declaration such as `using Menagerie::Oxen` pulls the name `Oxen` into the current namespace. The single name then lives in both namespaces.

To understand how one name becomes a part of two namespaces, consider the `Namespace` example, shown in Listing 2-4.

LISTING 2-4: **Pulling Names into Other Namespaces with the using Declaration**

```
#include <iostream>

using namespace std;

namespace A {
  int X;
}

namespace B {
  using A::X;
}

int main() {
  A::X = 2;
  cout << B::X << endl;
  return 0;
}
```

THE STANDARD NAMESPACE

Sooner or later, you're going to encounter something like this:

```
std::cout << "Hi" << std::endl;
```

You see this because normally `cout`, `cin`, `endl`, and everything else that comes from `#include<iostream>` is in a namespace called `std` (which is short for *standard*). Most developers don't want to write a namespace name and two colons every time for each occurrence of `cout` or `endl`. To avoid this problem you simply put

```
using namespace std;
```

at the beginning of your application, after the `include` lines. So if you look at the downloadable code, you see that line at the beginning of every application.

This code has two namespaces, A and B. The first namespace, A, has a variable called X. The second namespace, B, has a `using` statement that pulls the name X into that namespace. The single variable that lives inside A is now part of both namespaces, A and B. `main()` verifies this: It saves a value in the X variable of A and prints the value in the X variable of B with an output of:

```
2
```

A::X and B::X refer to the same variable, thanks to the `using` declaration!

Chapter **3**

Constructors, Destructors, and Exceptions

I n this chapter, you encounter three vital topics: constructors, destructors, and exceptions. Fully understanding what goes on with *constructors* (creating an object) and *destructors* (destroying an object) is very important. The better you understand how constructors and destructors work, the less likely you are to write class and structure code that doesn't function the way you expected and the more likely you are to avoid bugs.

Exceptions are important also in that they let you handle unexpected situations — that is, you can handle problems when they do come up. An exception can signal a program error, a missing resource, use input issues, or any number of other situations that the application code didn't expect. That's why it's called an exception — an exception to what was expected.

Many developers feel that constructors, destructors, and exceptions are extremely simple. In fact, many developers would doubt that these three topics could fill an entire chapter, but they can. After you read this chapter, you should have a good mastery of constructors, destructors, and exceptions.

REMEMBER

You don't have to type the source code for this chapter manually. In fact, using the downloadable source is a lot easier. You can find the source for this chapter in the \CPP_AIO4\BookV\Chapter03 folder of the downloadable source. See the Introduction for details on how to find these source files.

Constructing and Destructing Objects

As described in Book 2, Chapter 3, classes describe how to build objects. *Constructors* are methods that the application calls when it creates an instance. This topic appeared as early as the "Using an initializer" section of Book 1, Chapter 8, so you've already heard about them a few times. *Destructors,* on the other hand, are methods that the application calls when it deletes an instance. The "Starting and Ending with Constructors and Destructors" section of Book 2, Chapter 1 provides you with an overview of them. Both are essential to making classes complete by telling how to create and delete objects described by the class.

A single class can have multiple constructors. In fact, several kinds of constructors are available. There aren't as many kinds of destructors. (In fact, there's really only one.) In the sections that follow, you obtain all the necessary information to create both constructors and destructors.

Overloading constructors

You're allowed to put multiple constructors in your class. The way the user of your class chooses a constructor is by setting up the parameters in the variable declaration. Suppose you have a class called Clutter, and suppose you see the following two lines of code:

```
Clutter inst1("Jim");
Clutter inst2(123, "Sally");
```

These two lines have different types of parameters in the list. Each one is making use of a different constructor for the single class.

You can put multiple constructors in your class. The process of putting multiple constructors is called *overloading* the constructors. The Constructor01 example demonstrates how to create a Clutter class that has two constructors, as shown here:

```
class Clutter {
protected:
```

```
    string ChildName;
    int Toys;

public:
    Clutter(int count, string name) {
        ChildName = name;
        Toys = count;
    }

    Clutter(string name) {
        ChildName = name;
        Toys = 0;
    }
};
```

The compiler determines which overloaded constructor to use based on the parameters. Therefore, the overloaded constructors must differ by parameter lists, which means the number or type of parameters (or both); just changing the names doesn't count! If the parameter lists don't differ, the compiler can't distinguish them, and you'll get an error when it tries to compile the class definition.

REMEMBER

If your constructor doesn't have a parameter provided by other constructors, you should initialize the associated variable within the constructor code. For example, the second constructor doesn't include a parameter for Toys, so the constructor code initializes this variable to 0. As an alternative, you can use an initializer, as described in the "Initializing members" section of the chapter.

TIP

Having multiple constructors makes your class more flexible and easier to use. Multiple constructors give the users of your class more ways to use the class, allowing them to configure the instances differently, depending on the situation. Further, the constructors force the user to configure the instances only in the ways your constructors allow.

Initializing members

When C++ originally came out, any time you wanted to initialize a property, you had to put it inside a constructor. This created some interesting problems. The main problem had to do with references: You can put reference variables in a class, but normally reference variables must be initialized. You can't just have a reference variable floating around that doesn't refer to anything. But if you put a reference variable inside a class and create an instance of the class, the application will first create the instance and then call the constructor. Even if you initialize the reference in the first line of the constructor, there's still a moment when you have an uninitialized reference. The following sections help you build a class with an initializer, and you see the result of these efforts as the Constructor2 example.

Starting the ANSI approach simply

The ANSI standard uses a single approach for setting up properies: initializers. An *initializer* goes on the same line as the constructor in the class definition; or, if the constructor isn't *inline* — defined within the class code block — the initializer goes with the constructor in the code outside the class definition. Here's an example of how to add an initializer to a class (this section continues to build on this class):

```
class MySharona {
protected:
  int OneHitWonders;
  int NumberRecordings;
public:
  MySharona() : OneHitWonders(1), NumberRecordings(10) {}
};
```

When you create an instance of this class, the OneHitWonders member gets the value 1 and the NumberRecordings member gets the value 10. Note the syntax: The constructor name and parameter list (which is empty in this case) are followed by a single colon. The properties appear after that, each followed by an initial value in parentheses. Commas separate the properties. After the properties is the open brace for any code you want in the constructor.

REMEMBER

You can put any of the class properties in the initializer list, but you don't have to include them all. If you don't care to initialize some, you don't have to. Note also that you cannot put inherited members in the initializer list; you can include only members that are in the class itself.

Passing a variable

Initializers don't have to rely on static values. You can also pass these initial values in through the constructor. Here's a slightly modified version of the MySharona class. This time, the constructor has a parameter saved in the NumberRecordings member:

```
class MySharona {
protected:
  int OneHitWonders;
  int NumberRecordings;
public:
  MySharona(int Records) : OneHitWonders(1),
    NumberRecordings(Records) {}
};
```

By associating an initializer list with a constructor, you can have different initializers with different constructors. You're not limited to initializing the data the same way for all your constructors.

Accessing base constructors

You may have noticed that the member initialization follows a format similar to the way you initialize an inherited constructor. Look at how the following code calls the base class constructor:

```cpp
class MusicInfo {
public:
  int PhoneNumber;
  MusicInfo(int Phone) : PhoneNumber(Phone) {}
};

class MySharona : public MusicInfo {
protected:
  int OneHitWonders;
  int NumberRecordings;
public:
  MySharona(int Records) : OneHitWonders(1),
    NumberRecordings(Records),
    MusicInfo(8675309) {}
};
```

In the MySharona class, the properties get initialized, and the base class constructor gets called, all in the initialization. The call to the base class constructor is this portion:

```cpp
MusicInfo(8675309)
```

But note that the code passes a number into the constructor. The MusicInfo constructor takes a single number for a parameter, and it uses the number it receives to initialize the Phone member:

```cpp
MusicInfo(int Phone) : PhoneNumber(Phone) {}
```

Therefore, every time someone creates an instance of the class MySharona, the inherited PhoneNumber member is automatically initialized to 8675309. Thus you can create an instance of MySharona like this:

```cpp
MySharona CD(20);
```

This instance starts out having the member values OneHitWonders = 1, Number-Recordings = 20, and Phone = 8675309. The only thing the user can specify is the NumberRecordings member. The other two members are set automatically by the class.

However, you don't have to do it this way. Perhaps you want the users of this class to be able to specify the PhoneNumber when they create an instance. Here's a modified form that does it for you:

```
class MusicInfo {
public:
  int PhoneNumber;
  MusicInfo(int Phone) : PhoneNumber(Phone) {}
};

class MySharona : public MusicInfo {
protected:
  int OneHitWonders;
  int NumberRecordings;
public:
  MySharona(int Records, int Phone) : OneHitWonders(1),
    NumberRecordings(Records), MusicInfo(Phone) {}
};
```

Look carefully at the difference: The MySharona class now has two parameters. The second is an integer that's passed into the base class through the portion:

```
MusicInfo(Phone)
```

So to use this class, you might do something like this:

```
MySharona CD(20, 5551212);
```

This code snippet creates an instance of MySharona, with the members initialized to OneHitWonders = 1, NumberRecordings = 20, and PhoneNumber = 5551212.

Overloading the constructor

If you have overloaded constructors, you can have different sets of initializations. Look at one more modification to this final version of the Constructor02 example:

```
class MySharona : public MusicInfo {
protected:
  int OneHitWonders;
  int NumberRecordings;
```

```
public:
  MySharona(int Records, int Phone) : MusicInfo(Phone),
    OneHitWonders(1), NumberRecordings(Records) {}

  MySharona(int Records) : MusicInfo(8675309),
    OneHitWonders(1), NumberRecordings(Records)  {}
};
```

This class has two constructors from the combination of the previous two versions, so now you can use either constructor. You can create two variables, for example, each using a different constructor:

```
MySharona CD(20, 5551212);
MySharona OldCD(30);
cout << CD.PhoneNumber << endl;
cout << OldCD.PhoneNumber << endl;
```

When you run the `cout` lines, they have different values for the `PhoneNumber` member. The first passes a specific value; the second accepts a default value:

```
5551212
8675309
```

REMEMBER

You should initialize the base class values first. Otherwise the compiler is likely to display warning messages when you compile the application.

Using default values

If the only real difference in the different constructors is whether the user supplies a value (as was the case in the previous example), you can use a slightly better approach. Constructors (and any function in C++, really) can have default values. The `Constructor03` example shortens the previous examples by using default values. The result is the same:

```
class MySharona : public MusicInfo {
protected:
  int OneHitWonders;
  int NumberRecordings;
public:
  MySharona(int Records, int Phone=8675309) :
    MusicInfo(Phone), OneHitWonders(1),
    NumberRecordings(Records) {}
};
```

In the preceding code, the second parameter to the constructor has an equals sign and a number after it, which means that the user of the class doesn't have to specify this parameter. If the parameter is not present, it automatically gets the value 8675309.

You can have as many default parameters as you want in a constructor or any other function, but the rule is that the default parameters must come at the end. After you have a default parameter, all the parameters that follow must have a default value. Therefore, the following type of code is not allowed:

```
MySharona(int Records = 6, int Phone) :
    MusicInfo(Phone), OneHitWonders(1),
    NumberRecordings(Records) {}
```

There's a practical reason for this prohibition: When the user calls the constructor (by creating a variable of type MySharona, there is no way to leave out just a first parameter and have only a second one. It's not possible, unless C++ were to allow an empty parameter followed by a comma, as in MySharona(,8675309). Overloaded constructors (and other functions) must also differ by non-optional parameters. Otherwise, the compiler can't tell whether you're trying to use one function or another with some parameters omitted.

Adding a default constructor

A *default constructor* is a constructor that takes no parameters — the compiler generally creates it when you don't create any constructors. You can have a default constructor in a class in either of two ways: by coding it or by letting the compiler implicitly build one for you. Every class that lacks a constructor has a default constructor created by the compiler.

You've probably seen a default constructor before. This class has no constructor, so the compiler generates an implicit one for you. It works like this:

```
class Simple {
public:
  int x,y;
  void Write() {
    cout << x << " " << y << endl;
  }
};
```

Of course, the preceding class doesn't do much. It's the same as this:

```
class Simple {
public:
  int x,y;
  void Write() {
      cout << x << " " << y << endl;
  }

  Simple() {}
};
```

Recognizing that the default constructor is there, however, is important. And you need to realize when the compiler doesn't create a constructor automatically because you may run into some problems. Look at this modified version of the class (found in the Constructor04 example):

```
class Simple {
public:
  int x,y;
  void Write() {
    cout << x << " " << y << endl;
  }

  Simple(int startx) { x = startx; }
};
```

This class includes a constructor that takes a parameter. After adding this constructor, the class no longer gets an implicit default constructor from the compiler. Adding a line like this to main():

```
Simple inst;
```

causes the compiler to generate an error message like this:

```
In function 'int main()'
error: no matching function for call to 'Simple::Simple()'
note: candidate: Simple::Simple(int)
note:    candidate expects 1 argument, 0 provided
note: candidate: constexpr Simple::Simple(const Simple&)
note:    candidate expects 1 argument, 0 provided
note: candidate: constexpr Simple::Simple(Simple&&)
note:    candidate expects 1 argument, 0 provided|
```

If you remove the added constructor, this error goes away! Therefore, when you provide no constructors, the compiler gives you an implicit default constructor.

Now here's where you could run into trouble: Suppose you build a class and provide no constructors for it. You give the class to other people to use. They're using it in their code, all happy, making use of the default constructor. Then one day somebody else decides to enhance the class by adding a special constructor with several parameters. The rogue programmer adds the constructor and then makes use of it. Unfortunately, this also means that all the other people who were using the implicit default constructor suddenly start getting compiler errors! You can avoid this problem by explicitly including a default constructor, even if it does nothing:

```
class Simple {
public:
  int x,y;
  void Write() {
    cout << x << " " << y << endl;
  }

  Simple() {}
};
```

Then when someone adds a constructor with parameters, the default constructor will still be there. The added constructor will overload the default constructor:

```
class Simple {
public:
  int x,y;
  void Write() {
      cout << x << " " << y << endl;
  }

  Simple() {}
  Simple(int startx) { x = startx; }
};
```

Note that now this class has two constructors! And all will be happy, because everybody's code will still compile.

Functional constructors

Every once in a while, you may come across code that looks like this:

```
Simple inst = Simple(5);
```

It looks like a function call or like the way you would declare a pointer variable, except there's no asterisk and no new word. It's actually a functional syntax for calling a constructor. The right side creates a new instance of Simple, passing 5 into the constructor. This new instance gets copied into the inst variable.

TIP

This approach can be handy when you create an array of objects, where the array contains actual objects, not pointers to objects:

```
Simple MyList[] = { Simple(1), Simple(50), Simple(80),
    Simple(100), Simple(150) };
```

The approach seems a little strange because the variable MyList is not a pointer, yet you're setting it equal to something on the right. But this approach is handy because you may need a temporary variable. The Constructor05 example, shown in Listing 3-1, demonstrates how you can use the functional syntax to create a temporary instance of the class string.

| LISTING 3-1: | **Creating Temporary Instances with Functional Constructors** |

```
#include <iostream>

using namespace std;

void WriteMe(string str) {
  cout << "Here I am: " << str << endl;
}

int main() {
  WriteMe(string("Sam"));
  return 0;
}
```

When you compile and run this, you see this output:

```
Here I am: Sam
```

The code creates a temporary instance of the string class in main(). But as it turns out, an even shorter version of this code is available by calling WriteMe() like this:

```
WriteMe("Sam");
```

This code works out well because you don't even feel like you're working with a class called string. The parameter just seems like a basic type, and you're passing a character array, Sam. However, the parameter is an instance of a class. Here's how the code works. Suppose you have a class like the one found in the Constructor06 example and a function to go with it:

```
class MyNumber {
public:
  int First;
  MyNumber(int TheFirst) : First(TheFirst) {}
};

void WriteNumber(MyNumber num) {
  cout << num.First << endl;
}
```

WriteNumber() isn't a member of MyNumber. You can make any of the following calls to WriteNumber().

» Use a previously declared variable of type MyNumber:

```
MyNumber prime = 17;
WriteNumber(prime);
```

» Create a temporary instance, passing the value 23 into the constructor:

```
WriteNumber(MyNumber(23));
```

» Create a temporary instance, but do so implicitly:

```
WriteNumber(29);
```

The output from this example is

```
17
23
29
```

REMEMBER

You may wonder when your temporary variables get destroyed. For instance, if you call WriteNumber(MyNumber(23));, how long does the temporary MyNumber instance live on? The ANSI standard states that the instance is deleted at the end of the full expression.

WARNING

Be careful when using implicit temporary objects. Consider the following class and function found in the Constructor07 example:

```
class MyName {
public:
  string First;
  MyName(string TheFirst) : First(TheFirst) {}
};

void WriteName(MyName name) {
  cout << "Hi I am " << name.First << endl;
}
```

Seems straightforward. The `MyName` constructor takes a string, so it seems as though the following code should work:

```
WriteName("George");
```

Unfortunately, the compiler gives the following error message:

```
In function 'int main()':
error: could not convert '(const char*)"George"' from
    'const char*' to 'MyName'
```

Here's the problem: The compiler got shortsighted. The compiler considers the type of the string constant to be a `const char *` (that is, a pointer to a `const` character, or really a constant character array). There aren't any constructors that take a `const char *` parameter, but one does take a `string`, and the `string` class has a constructor that takes a `const char *` parameter. Unfortunately, the compiler doesn't fall for that, and it complains. To make the call work, you must adjust the

```
WriteName(string("George"));
```

This time it works. Now the compiler explicitly creates a temporary `string` instance. Using a temporary `string` implicitly creates a temporary instance of `MyName` class.

Calling one constructor from another

If you have some initialization code and you want several constructors to call it, you might try putting the code in one constructor and then having the other constructors call the constructor that has the initialization code. Unfortunately, this scenario won't work. When you have a constructor and write code to call another constructor from within it, such as this:

```
CallOne::CallOne(int ax)
{
   y = 20;
   CallOne();
}
```

where CallOne is your class, the code will compile but won't behave the way you may expect. The line CallOne(); isn't calling a constructor for the same instance! The compiler treats this line as a functional constructor, which creates a separate, temporary instance. When CallOne() ends, the application deletes the instance. You can see this behavior with the following class:

```
class CallOne {
public:
   int x,y;
   CallOne();
   CallOne(int ax);
};

CallOne::CallOne() {
   x = 10;
   y = 10;
}

CallOne::CallOne(int ax) {
   y = 20;
   CallOne();
}
```

When you create an instance by using the second constructor like this, the value of the y member of the instance will be 20, not 10:

```
CallOne Mine(10);
```

To people who don't know any different, it may look as though the y would first get set to 20 in the second constructor, and then the call to the default constructor would cause it to get changed to 10. But that's not the case: The second constructor is not calling the default constructor for the same object; it's creating a separate, temporary instance.

REMEMBER

If you have common initialization code that you want in multiple constructors, put the code in its own private or protected function (called, for example, `Init()`), and have each constructor call the `Init()` function. If you have one constructor call another constructor, it won't work. The second constructor will be operating on a separate instance.

Copying instances with copy constructors

One nice thing about C++ is that it lets you copy instances of classes. For example, if you have a class called `Copyable`, you can write code like this:

```
Copyable first;
Copyable second = first;
```

This code creates two instances, and `second` is a duplicate of `first`. The application accomplishes this by simply copying all the properties from `first` to `second`, which works well except that you may want to customize the behavior. For example, you may have a property that contains a unique ID for each instance. In your constructor, you may have code that generates a unique ID. The problem is that the previous sample doesn't call your constructor: It makes a duplicate of the object. Thus, your two objects have the same number for their supposedly unique IDs.

If you want control over the copying, you can create a copy constructor. A *copy constructor* is just a constructor that takes as a parameter a reference to another instance of the same class, as in this example:

```
Copyable(const Copyable& source);
```

When you copy an instance, your application calls this constructor. The parameter to this constructor is the instance you're copying. Thus, in the case of `Copyable second = first;`, the source parameter is `first`. And because it's a reference (which is required for copy constructors), you can access its members by using the dot notation (`.`) rather than the pointer notation (`->`).

The `Constructor08` example shown in Listing 3-2 is a complete application that demonstrates copy constructors.

LISTING 3-2:   **Customizing the Copying of Instances**

```cpp
#include <iostream>

using namespace std;

class Copyable {
protected:
  static int NextAvailableID;
  int UniqueID;
public:
  int SomeNumber;
  int GetID() { return UniqueID; }
  Copyable();
  Copyable(int x);
  Copyable(const Copyable& source);
};

Copyable::Copyable() {
  UniqueID = NextAvailableID;
  NextAvailableID++;
}

Copyable::Copyable(int x) {
  UniqueID = NextAvailableID;
  NextAvailableID++;
  SomeNumber = x;
}

Copyable::Copyable(const Copyable& source) {
  UniqueID = NextAvailableID;
  NextAvailableID++;
  SomeNumber = source.SomeNumber;
}

int Copyable::NextAvailableID;

int main() {
  Copyable take1 = 100;
  Copyable take2;
  take2.SomeNumber = 200;
  Copyable take3 = take1;
  cout << take1.GetID() << " "
       << take1.SomeNumber << endl;
  cout << take2.GetID() << " "
       << take2.SomeNumber << endl;
```

```
    cout << take3.GetID() << " "
         << take3.SomeNumber << endl;
    return 0;
}
```

You see the following output when you run this application:

```
0 100
1 200
2 100
```

You need to know two things about this code:

>> **Copy constructor with** const **instance.** C++ has a rule where you must have a constant instance to create a copy. If you leave off const, this line would not compile properly.

>> **Copying the propeterties manually from one instance to the other.** Now that the class has its own copy constructor, the computer will not copy the members as it would when the code lacks a copy constructor.

Listing 3-2 uses a *static* member to keep track of what the next available UniqueID is. Remember that a class shares a single static member among all instances of the class. Therefore, you have only one instance of NextAvailableID, and it's shared by all the instances of class Copyable.

When constructors go bad

Suppose that you're writing a class that will connect to the Internet and automatically download the latest weather report for the country of Upper Zamboni. The question is this: Do you put the code to connect to the Internet in the constructor or not?

People are often faced with this common design issue. Putting the initialization code in the constructor provides many advantages. For one, you can produce a usable instance without having to first create it and then call a separate method that does the initialization. In general, this approach works fine.

However, sometimes the initialization process can produce an error. For example, suppose that the constructor is unable to connect to the Internet. Remember: A constructor doesn't return a value. So you can't have it return, for example, a bool that would state whether it successfully did its work.

You have many choices for dealing with issues like Internet connections, and different people seem to have rather strong opinions about which choice is best. Here are the common options:

» **Just don't do it:** Write your constructors so that they create the object but don't do any work. Instead, put the work code in a separate method, which can return a `bool` representing whether it was successful.

» **Let the constructor do the work:** If the work fails (for example, it can't connect to the Internet), have the constructor save an error code in a property. When you create an instance, you can check the property to see whether it works.

» **Let the constructor do some more of the work:** If the work fails, throw an exception. In your code, then, you would wrap the creation of the instance with a `try...catch` block and include an exception handler. (See "Programming the Exceptions to the Rule," later in this chapter, for more information on `try...catch` blocks and exception handlers.)

WARNING

Each of these options comes with potential problems. For example, having a two-part creation and initialization process means that you depend on the developer to perform both steps. Using an error code means that you depend on the developer to check it. Raising exceptions during the creation process means that you're depending on the developer to wrap the code in a `try...catch` block. None of these options comes without risk.

Destroying your instances

Although constructors are versatile and people could seemingly write entire books on them, destructors are simple, and there's not a whole lot to say about them. But you do need to know some information to make them work properly. For example, destructors don't get parameters, and (like constructors) they do not provide return values.

Suppose you have a class that contains, as members, instances of other classes. When you delete an instance of the main class, you need to know that the contained instances will be deleted automatically. If your class contains actual instances (as opposed to pointers), they will get deleted. Look at this code from the `Destructor01` example:

```
class LittleInst {
public:
  int MyNumber;
  ~LittleInst() { cout << MyNumber << endl; }
};
```

```
class Container {
public:
  LittleInst first;
  LittleInst *second;
  Container();
};

Container::Container() {
  first.MyNumber = 1;
  second = new LittleInst;
  second->MyNumber = 2;
}
```

You see two classes, LittleInst and Container. The Container class holds an instance of LittleInst (the property called first) and a pointer to Little-Inst. The constructor sets up the two LittleInst instances. For first, it already exists, and all you have to do is configure first's MyNumber member. But second is just a pointer, so the code creates the instance before it can configure the second MyNumber member. Thus we have two instances, one a pointer and one a regular instance.

Now suppose you use these classes like so:

```
Container *inst = new Container;
delete inst;
```

Container has no destructor, so the concern is whether first and second get destroyed. Here's the output you see:

```
1
```

That's the output from the LittleInst destructor. The number 1 goes with the first member. So you can see that first was destroyed, but second wasn't.

REMEMBER

Here's the rule: When you delete an instance of a class, the members that are direct (that is, not pointers) are deleted as well. If you have any pointers, however, you must manually delete them in your destructor (or elsewhere).

Sometimes you may want an object to hold an instance of another class but want to keep the instance around after you delete the containing object. In that case, you wouldn't delete the other instance in the destructor.

Here's a modification to the `Container` class (found in the `Destructor02` example) that deletes the `second` instance:

```
class Container {
public:
  LittleInst first;
  LittleInst *second;
  Container();
  ~Container() { delete second; }
};
```

Then, when you run these two lines again:

```
Container *inst = new Container;
delete inst;
```

you see this output, which deletes both instances:

```
2
1
```

In the preceding output, you can see that it deleted the second instance first. The reason is that the application calls the destructor before it destroys the direct members. In this case, when the code deleted the `Container` instance, the application first called the destructor before deleting the `first` member. That's actually a good idea, because in the code for the destructor, you may want to do some work on the properties before they get wiped out.

Virtually inheriting destructors

You can (and should) make destructors virtual — unlike constructors (the constructor can't be virtual because when a constructor of a class is executed, there is no virtual table in the memory, which means no virtual pointer has been defined yet). The reason is that you can pass an instance of a derived class into a function that takes a base class, like this:

```
void ProcessAndDelete(DeleteMe *inst) {
  cout << inst->Number << endl;
  delete inst;
}
```

This function takes an instance of class `DeleteMe`, does some work on it, and deletes it. Now, suppose you have a class derived from `DeleteMe` — say, class `Derived`. Because of the rules of inheritance, you're allowed to pass the instance of `Derived` into this function. But by the rules of polymorphism (as described in the "Specializing with polymorphism" section of Book 2, Chapter 3), if you want the `ProcessAndDelete()` function to call an overloaded method of `Derived`, you need to make the method virtual. That's the case with all destructors as well. The `Destructor03` example, shown in Listing 3-3, demonstrates making destructors virtual.

LISTING 3-3: **Making the Destructors Virtual**

```
#include <iostream>

using namespace std;

class DeleteMe {
public:
  int Number;
  virtual ~DeleteMe();
};

class Derived : public DeleteMe {
public:
  virtual ~Derived();
};

DeleteMe::~DeleteMe() {
  cout << "DeleteMe::~DeleteMe()" << endl;
}

Derived::~Derived() {
  cout << "Derived::~Derived()" << endl;
}

void ProcessAndDelete(DeleteMe *inst) {
  cout << inst->Number << endl;
  delete inst;
}

int main() {
  DeleteMe *MyObject = new(Derived);
  MyObject->Number = 10;
  ProcessAndDelete(MyObject);
  return 0;
}
```

When you run this application, delete calls the destructor for Derived , which in turn calls the base class destructor. You can see how all this works thanks to the cout calls in the destructors. Here's the output:

```
10
Derived::~Derived()
DeleteMe::~DeleteMe()
```

The first line is the output from ProcessAndDelete(). The middle line is the output from the Derived() destructor, and the third line is the output from the DeleteMe() destructor. The code passes in a Derived instance, and the application calls the Derived destructor.

Now try this: Remove virtual from the DeleteMe destructor:

```
class DeleteMe {
public:
  int Number;
  ~DeleteMe();
};
```

When you compile and run the application, the application calls the base class destructor. Because ProcessAndDelete() takes a DeleteMe instance, you see this output:

```
10
DeleteMe::~DeleteMe()
```

ORDERING YOUR CONSTRUCTORS AND DESTRUCTORS

When you have constructors and destructors in a base and derived class and you create an instance of the derived class, remember the ordering: The computer first creates the members for the base class, and then the computer calls the constructor for the base class. Next, the computer creates the members of the derived class, and then the computer calls the constructor for the derived class.

The order for destruction is opposite. When you destroy an instance of a base class, first the computer calls the destructor for the derived class and then deletes the members of the derived class. Next, the computer calls the destructor for the base class and then deletes the members of the base class.

In the preceding example, the destructor isn't `virtual`; it's not able to find the proper destructor when you pass a `Derived` instance. So it calls the destructor for whatever type is listed in the parameter.

TIP

Getting into the habit of always making your destructors `virtual` is a good idea. That way, if somebody else writes a function, such as `ProcessAndDelete()`, you can be assured the function automatically calls the correct destructor.

Programming the Exceptions to the Rule

Constructors, Destructors, and Exceptions

An *exception* is an unexpected situation that occurs in your software. For example, if you try to write to a file, but somehow that file is corrupted and you can't, the operating system might *throw* an exception. Or you might have a function that processes some data, and if the function encounters corrupted data, it might throw an exception. The following sections get you started using exceptions.

Creating a basic try. . .catch block

The `Exception01` example, shown in Listing 3-4, is a sample of a function that throws an exception.

LISTING 3-4: **Throwing and Catching Exceptions**

```
#include <iostream>

using namespace std;

void ProcessData() {
  throw new string("Oops, I found some bad data!");
}

int main() {
  try {
    ProcessData();
    cout << "No problems!" << endl;
  } catch (string *excep) {
    cout << "Found an error. Here's the message.";
    cout << endl;
```

(continued)

LISTING 3-4: *(continued)*

```
    cout << *excep;
    cout << endl;
  }
  cout << "All finished." << endl;
  return 0;
}
```

You see the following text as output when you run this application:

```
Found an error. Here's the message.
Oops, I found some bad data!
All finished.
```

Look closely at what this application does. In main(), there's a call to ProcessData() inside a try...catch block. Because the call is inside a try... catch block, the computer calls the function; and if the function throws an exception, the application automatically comes back out of the function and goes into the catch block. The catch block receives the object that was thrown as a parameter, much like a parameter to a function.

But if ProcessData() doesn't encounter any problems and therefore doesn't throw an exception, the function will complete its work and the application will continue with the code after the function call. If there is no exception, then upon completion of ProcessData(), the computer executes the cout line after the ProcessData() call.

REMEMBER

Think of an exception handler as a way to detect unexpected events. When something unexpected happens, even if there is no fault in the code or the assumptions you make, the catch block can handle the situation or at least alert you to it. After the try...catch block completes, the application runs any lines that follow, regardless of whether an exception occurred. Thus, in all cases, Listing 3-4 executes the line

```
cout << "All finished." << endl;
```

In the listing, note that ProcessData() calls throw, meaning that it generates an exception. Normally, you probably wouldn't just have a function throw an exception for no reason, as this function does — it's included like this for the example. This particular throw looks like this:

```
throw new string("Oops, I found some bad data!");
```

The exception is thrown using a new `string` instance. You can create an instance of any class you want, and it can be either a pointer or a direct instance, depending on whether you prefer to work with pointers or references (it's your choice).

Now look at the `catch` block in Listing 3-4. Notice that it starts with this:

```
catch (string *excep)
```

REMEMBER

Because the function throws a pointer to a `string` instance, the `catch` block must accept a pointer to a `string` instance. Everything must match.

Normally you don't throw an exception of type `string`. Instead, you use one of the exception categories described at `https://en.cppreference.com/w/cpp/error`, such as `invalid_argument`, to standardize the exception. You can also create a custom exception category using a `struct` or a `class` that extends `std::exception`, as described at `http://peterforgacs.github.io/2017/06/25/Custom-C-Exceptions-For-Beginners/`. Note that some exception categories are available only to users of C++ 11, C++ 17, or above. Both C++ 17 and C++ 20 remove some exception categories, so it's important to verify the categories you use in your application.

When working with C++ 11 or above, the `catch` block parameter may also have attributes that control how you interact with it, such as making the parameter `const`. Catching exceptions by reference avoids some significant problems that can occur when catching exceptions by value, as described in the article at `https://riptutorial.com/cplusplus/example/9212/best-practice--throw-by-value--catch-by-const-reference`.

WARNING

Never throw an exception in a destructor. If an object's method throws an exception, the application calls the object's destructor before moving out of the `try...catch` block. When the destructor experiences an unexpected event and also throws an exception, the application sees that two exceptions are active at the same time and calls the `terminate()` function, which causes the application to stop running.

Using multiple catch blocks

You can have more than one `catch` block. Suppose that different types of exceptions could get thrown. For example, you might have a function like this to use with `ProcessData()` from the previous section:

```
void ProcessMore() {
    throw new int(10);
}
```

ProcessData() threw a pointer to a string, but this one throws a pointer to an integer. When you call the two functions, your try...catch block can look like this:

```
try {
  ProcessData();
  ProcessMore();
  cout << "No problems!" << endl;
} catch (string *excep) {
  cout << "Found an error. Here's the message.";
  cout << endl;
  cout << *excep;
  cout << endl;
} catch (int *num) {
  cout << "Found a numerical error. Here it is.";
  cout << endl;
  cout << *num;
  cout << endl;
}
cout << "All finished." << endl;
```

If you add this code and the ProcessMore() function to Listing 3-4, you want to comment out the throw line from ProcessData() if you want to see this application handle the integer exception. That's because the execution of the lines in the try block cease as soon as a throw statement occurs, and control transfers to the appropriate catch block. Which catch block gets the honor depends on the type of the object thrown.

Throwing direct instances

You can throw a direct instance that is not a pointer. This is called throwing an exception by value. However, you should avoid this practice for two reasons (which is why the technique isn't demonstrated here):

>> **Resource usage and time:** Throwing an exception by value means that the application must create a second copy of the object because the original object goes out of scope. You now have two copies of the exception object on the stack.

>> **The slicing problem:** If the catch clause is created to catch a super class object (the parent) and the exception thrower uses a derived class instead, the catch block receives only a copy of the super class object without any of the attributes intact. The super class object in the catch block doesn't have the values defined by the derived class, so if the thrown object includes any of those values they are lost.

The preferred method of throwing exceptions in newer versions of C++ is to use references in the catch block. (The throw line does not change.) It looks like this:

```
try {
  ProcessData();
  ProcessMore();
} catch (string &excep) {
  cout << excep;
} catch (int &num) {
  cout << num;
}
```

You may notice something just a little strange. For the integer version, the throw statement looks like this:

```
throw 10;
```

That is, the line of code is throwing a value, not an object. But the catch line looks like this:

```
catch (int &num) {
```

The catch statement is catching a reference. Normally you can have references only to variables, not to values! But it works here because inside the computer, the application makes a temporary variable, and that's what you're referring to in the catch block.

Catching any exception

If you want to write a general catch handler that will catch any exception and you don't care to actually catch the object that was thrown, you can write your handler like this:

```
try {
  ProcessData();
  ProcessMore();
  cout << "No problems!" << endl;
} catch (...) {
  cout << "An unknown exception occurred." << endl;
}
```

That is, instead of putting what is effectively a parameter in the catch header, you just put three dots, called an ellipsis. You can also use the ellipsis as a general exception catcher in addition to your other handlers. However, because the general exception handler is generic, you must place it last in the list. When creating a list of catch blocks, always move from most specific to least specific. Here's an example:

```
try {
  ProcessData();
  ProcessMore();
  cout << "No problems!" << endl;
} catch (string excep) {
  cout << "Found an error. Here's the message.";
  cout << endl;
  cout << excep;
  cout << endl;
} catch (int num) {
  cout << "Found a numerical error. Here it is.";
  cout << endl;
  cout << num;
  cout << endl;
} catch (...) {
  cout << "An unknown exception occurred." << endl;
}
```

WARNING

If your function calls throw an exception and you don't have any exception handler for it (because your catch blocks don't handle the type of exception being thrown or you don't have any try...catch blocks), your application will *stop*. The application prints the following message on the console and then immediately terminates the application:

```
abnormal program termination
```

TIP

These programming rules keep your users happily ignorant of exceptions:

>> Know when you're calling a function that could throw an exception.

>> When you're calling a function that could throw an exception, include an exception handler.

>> It doesn't matter how *deep* the exception is when it's thrown; somewhere, *somebody* needs to catch it. A function could call a function that calls a function that calls a function that calls a function that throws an exception. If no intermediate function has an exception handler, put one in your outer function.

Rethrowing an exception

When inside a catch block, a throw statement without anything after it simply rethrows the same exception. Although this reaction may seem a bit convoluted (and indeed it can be), you may have a function that contains a try...catch block that works with the object at a low level. However, the function may not have the resources or information to handle the exception, so it rethrows the exception to a function higher up that may have the required access. The calling function might have a try...catch block that can actually handle the exception. In other words, you might have something like the code found in the Exception02 example:

```cpp
#include <iostream>

using namespace std;

void Inner() {
  throw string("Error!");
}

void Outer() {
  try {
    Inner();
  } catch (string excep) {
    cout << "Outer caught an exception: ";
    cout << excep << endl;
    throw;
  }
}

int main()
{
  try {
    Outer();
  } catch (string excep) {
    cout << "main caught an exception: ";
    cout << excep << endl;
  }
  return 0;
}
```

In the preceding code, main() calls Outer(). Outer(), in turn, calls Inner(). Inner() throws an exception, and Outer() catches it. But main() also wants to catch the exception. So Outer() rethrows the exception. You do that by calling throw without anything after it, like this:

```cpp
throw;
```

When you run this application, you see the following output.

```
Outer caught an exception: Error!
main caught an exception: Error!
```

Using a standard category

Normally you use a standard category of exception whenever possible. Previous examples show one method of working with exceptions, but using a standard category means that you gain access to additional functionality and know how the recipient will interpret the exception. Also, using categories helps you create hierarchies of exceptions so that you handle the most detailed exception first. With these ideas in mind, the Exception03 example shows how to use an exception category of invalid_argument. You must have C++ 11 or above to use this example.

```cpp
#include <iostream>

using namespace std;

bool CheckInt(int value) {
  if (value > 5) {
    return true;
  } else {
    throw invalid_argument("Input too small!");
  }
  return false;
}

int main() {
  try {
    cout << (CheckInt(6) ? "OK" : "Not Right") << endl;
    cout << (CheckInt(5) ? "OK" : "Not Right") << endl;
  } catch (const invalid_argument& ex) {
    cerr << "Invalid Argument: " << ex.what() << endl;
  }
  return 0;
}
```

Notice that you use the same techniques as usual, such as calling throw to throw the exception. In this case, though, you're creating an exception object of type invalid_argument, which requires an input string detailing the error.

The catch block relies on a const invalid_argument reference, which is the most efficient and least error-prone method of passing exception information. Notice that you can call the what() method to obtain access to the error information. This example also shows how to use cerr to output the exception information to the standard error stream.

Chapter **4**

Advanced Class Usage

Classes are amazingly powerful. You can do so much with them. In this chapter, you discover many of the extra features you can use in your classes. But these aren't just little extras that you may want to use on occasion. If you follow the instructions in this chapter, you should find that your understanding of classes in C++ greatly improves, and you'll want to use many of these topics throughout your programming.

This chapter also discusses many of the issues that come up when you're deriving new classes and inheriting members. This discussion includes virtual inheritance and multiple inheritance, topics that people mess up a lot. As part of this discussion, you see the ways you can put classes and types inside other classes.

REMEMBER

You don't have to type the source code for this chapter manually. In fact, using the downloadable source is a lot easier. You can find the source for this chapter in the \CPP_AIO4\BookV\Chapter04 folder of the downloadable source. See the Introduction for details on how to find these source files.

Inherently Inheriting Correctly

Without inheritance, doing object-oriented programming (OOP) would be nearly impossible. Yes, you could divide your work into objects, but the real power comes from inheritance. However, you have to be careful when using inheritance or you can really cause yourself problems. In the sections that follow, you see different ways to use inheritance — and how to keep it all straight.

Morphing your inheritance

Polymorphism refers to using an object as an instance of a base class. For example, if you have the class `Creature` and from that you derive the class `Platypus`, you can treat the instances of class `Platypus` as if they're instances of class `Creature`. This concept is useful if you have a function that takes as a parameter a pointer to `Creature`. You can pass a pointer to `Platypus`.

However, you can't go further than that. You can't take a pointer to a pointer to `Creature`. (Remember that when creating a pointer to a pointer, the first pointer is the address of the second pointer variable.) So if you have a function such as this:

```
void Feed1(Creature *c) {
  cout << "Feed me!" << endl;
}
```

you're free to pass the address of a `Platypus` object, as in the following:

```
Platypus *plato = new Platypus;
Feed1(plato);
```

However, with a function that takes the address of a pointer variable (note the two asterisks in the parameter), like this:

```
void Feed2(Creature **c) {
  cout << "Feed me!" << endl;
}
```

you can't pass the address of a pointer to a `Platypus` instance, as in this example:

```
Platypus *plato = new Platypus;
Feed2(&plato);
```

If you try to compile this code, you get a compiler error.

Avoiding polymorphism

You don't always use polymorphism when you declare a variable, as shown in the previous section. If you do, you're declaring variables like this:

```
Creature *plato = new Platypus;
```

The type of `plato` is a pointer to `Creature`. But the object is a `Platypus`. You can create a `Platypus` from a `Creature` because a pointer to a base class can point to an object of a derived class. But now the compiler thinks that `plato` is a pointer to a `Creature` instance, so you can't use `plato` to call a `Platypus` method — you can use `plato` only to call `Creature` methods. For example, if your two classes look like this:

```
class Creature {
public:
  void EatFood() {
    cout << "I'm eating!" << endl;
  }
};

class Platypus : public Creature {
public:
  void SingLikeABird() {
    cout << "I'm siiiiiiinging in the rain!" << endl;
  }
};
```

the following code doesn't work:

```
Creature *plato = new Platypus;
plato->SingLikeABird();
```

Although the first line compiles, the second doesn't. When the compiler gets to the second line, it thinks that `plato` is an object of class type `Creature`, and `Creature` doesn't have a method called `SingLikeABird()`, so the compiler gets upset. You can fix the situation by casting, like this:

```
Creature *plato = new Platypus;
static_cast <Platypus *>(plato)->SingLikeABird();
```

If you want to save some work, start by declaring `plato` as type `Platypus`, as shown here:

```
Platypus *plato = new Platypus;
plato->SingLikeABird();
```

You may need to perform a cast at times. For example, you may have a variable that can hold an instance of an object or its derived object. Then you have to use polymorphism, as in the following code:

```
Creature *plato;
if (HasABeak == true) {
  plato = new Platypus;
} else {
  plato = new Creature;
}
```

This code defines a pointer to Creature. That pointer stores the address of either a Platypus instance or a Creature instance, depending on what's in the HasABeak variable.

But if you use an if statement like that, you shouldn't follow it with a call to SingLikeABird(), even if you cast it:

```
static_cast <Platypus *>(plato)->SingLikeABird();
```

The reason is that if the else clause took place and plato holds an instance of Creature, not Platypus, the plato object won't have a SingLikeABird() method. Either you get some type of error message when you run the application or you don't, but the application will mess up later. And those messing-up-later errors are the worst kind to try to fix.

Adjusting access

You may have a class that has protected members; and in a derived class, you may want to make these members public. You transition the members to public by adjusting the access. You have two ways to do this: One is the older way, and the other is the newer American National Standards Institute (ANSI) way, which is the method supported by the current version of the GNU Compiler Collection (GCC). If your compiler supports the newer way, the creators of the ANSI standard ask that you use the ANSI way.

In the following classes, Secret has a member, X, that is protected. The derived class, Revealed, makes the member X public. Here's the older way:

```
class Secret {
protected:
  int X;
};
```

```
class Revealed : public Secret {
public:
  Secret::X;
};
```

The code declares the member X public by providing the base class name, two colons, and then the member name. It didn't include any type information; that was implied. So in the class Secret, the member X is protected. But in Revealed, it's public.

Here's the ANSI way, which requires the word using. Otherwise, it's the same:

```
class Secret {
protected:
  int X;
};

class Revealed : public Secret {
public:
  using Secret::X;
};
```

Now, when you use the Revealed class, the inherited member X is public, but X is still protected in the base class, Secret.

Avoiding variable naming conflicts

If you want to make a protected member public in a derived class, don't just rede-clare the member. If you do, you end up with two properties of the same name within the class; and needless to say, that can be confusing! Look at the following two classes:

```
class Secret {
protected:
  int X;
public:
  void SetX() {
    X = 10;
  }
  void GetX() {
    cout << "Secret X is " << X << endl;
  }
};
```

```
class Revealed : public Secret {
public:
  int X;
};
```

The Revealed class has two int X members! Suppose you try this code with it:

```
Revealed me;
me.SetX();
me.X = 30;
me.GetX();
```

The first line declares the variable. The second line calls SetX( ), which stores 10 in the inherited X, because SetX( ) is part of the base class. The third line stores 30 in the new X declared in the derived class. GetX( ) is part of the base class, so it prints 10.

Having two properties of the same name is confusing. It would be best if the compiler didn't allow you to have two variables of the same name. But just because the compiler allows it doesn't mean you should do it. Having two variables of the same name is a perfect way to increase the chances of bugs creeping into your application.

Using class-based access adjustment

Suppose you have a class that has several public members, and when you derive a new class, you want all the public members to become protected, except for one. You can do this task in a couple of ways. You can adjust the access of all the members except for the one you want left public. Or, if you have lots of members, you can take the opposite approach. Look at this code:

```
class Secret {
public:
  int Code, Number, SkeletonKey, System, Magic;
};

class AddedSecurity : protected Secret {
public:
  using Secret::Magic;
};
```

The derived class inherits the base class as protected, as you can see in the header line for AddedSecurity. That means that all the inherited public members of `Secret` are protected in the derived class. But then the code promotes `Magic` back to `public` by adjusting its member access. Thus, `Magic` is the only public member of `AddedSecurity`. All the rest are protected.

REMEMBER

If you have a member that is private and you try to adjust its access to `protected` or `public` in a derived class, you quickly discover that the compiler won't let you do it. The reason is that the derived class doesn't even know about the member because the member is private. And because the derived class doesn't know about the member, you can't adjust its access.

Returning something different, virtually speaking

Two words that sound similar and have similar meanings in computer programming are overload and override. To *overload* means to take a function and write another function of the same name that takes a different set of parameters. To *override* means to take an existing function in a base class and give the function new code in a derived class. The function in the derived class has the same prototype as the base class: It takes the same parameters and returns the same type.

An overloaded function can optionally return a different type, but the parameters must be different from the original function, whether in number or type or both. The overloaded function can live in the same class or in a derived class. The idea here is to create what appears to be a single function that can take several types of parameters. For example, you may have a function called `Append()` that works on strings. By using `Append()`, you'd be able to append a string to the end of the string represented by the instance, or you could append a single character to the end of the string represented by the instance. Now, although it feels like one function called `Append()`, really you would implement it as two separate functions: one that takes a string parameter and one that takes a character parameter.

This section discusses one particular issue dealing with *overriding* functions (that is, replacing a function in a derived class). Generally, the overriding function must have the same parameter types and must return the same type as the original function. A situation exists under which you can violate this rule, although only slightly. You can violate the rule of an overriding function returning the same type as the original function if *all three* of the following are true:

>> The overriding function returns an instance of a class derived from the type returned by the original function.

>> You return either a pointer or a reference, not an object.

>> If you return a pointer, the pointer doesn't refer to yet another pointer.

TIP

Typically, you want to use this approach when you have a container class that holds multiple instances of another class. For example, you may have a class called Peripheral. You may also have a container class called PeripheralList, which holds instances of Peripheral. You may later derive a new class from Peripheral, called Printer, and a new class from PeripheralList, called PrinterList. If PeripheralList has a function that returns an instance of Peripheral, you would override that function in PrinterList. But instead of having it return an instance of Peripheral, you would have it return an instance of Printer. The Overriding-Derived example, shown in Listing 4-1, shows how to perform this task.

LISTING 4-1: **Overriding and Returning a Derived Class**

```cpp
#include <iostream>
#include <map>

using namespace std;

class Peripheral {
public:
  string Name;
  int Price;
  int SerialNumber;
  Peripheral(string aname, int aprice, int aserial) :
    Name(aname), Price(aprice),
    SerialNumber(aserial) {}
};

class Printer : public Peripheral {
public:
  enum PrinterType {laser, inkjet};
  PrinterType Type;
  Printer(string aname, PrinterType atype, int aprice,
    int aserial) :
    Peripheral(aname, aprice, aserial), Type(atype) {}
};

typedef map<string, Peripheral *> PeripheralMap;

class PeripheralList {
public:
  PeripheralMap list;
  virtual Peripheral *GetPeripheralByName(string name);
  void AddPeripheral(string name, Peripheral *per);
};
```

```cpp
class PrinterList : public PeripheralList {
public:
  Printer *GetPeripheralByName(string name);
};

Peripheral *PeripheralList::GetPeripheralByName
 (string name){
  return list[name];
}

void PeripheralList::AddPeripheral(
string name, Peripheral *per) {
  list[name] = per;
}

Printer *PrinterList::GetPeripheralByName(string name) {
  return static_cast<Printer *>(
    PeripheralList::GetPeripheralByName(name));
}

int main(int argc, char *argv[]) {
  PrinterList list;
  list.AddPeripheral(string("Koala"),
    new Printer("Koala", Printer::laser,
    150, 105483932)
  );
  list.AddPeripheral(string("Bear"),
    new Printer("Bear", Printer::inkjet,
    80, 5427892)
  );

  Printer *myprinter = list.GetPeripheralByName("Bear");
  if (myprinter != 0) {
    cout << myprinter->Price << endl;
  }
  return 0;
}
```

This example uses a special type called map, which is simply a container or list that holds items in pairs. The first item in the pair is called a *key,* and the second item is called a *value.* You can retrieve values from the map based on the key. This example stores a Peripheral (the value) based on a name, which is a string (the key).

The example uses a `typedef` to create the `map` by specifying the two types involved: first the key and then the value. The `typedef`, then, looks like this:

```
typedef map<string, Peripheral *> PeripheralMap;
```

This line creates a type of a `map` that stores a set of `Peripheral` instances and you can look them up based on a name. The code uses a notation similar to that of an array to put an item in the `map`, where `list` is the `map`, `name` is a `string`, and `per` is a pointer to `Peripheral`. The key goes inside square brackets, like this:

```
list[name] = per;
```

To retrieve the item, you refer to the `map` entry using brackets again, as in this line from the listing:

```
return list[name];
```

Listing 4-1 shows a `Printer` class derived from a `Peripheral` class. It also has a `container` class called `PrinterList` derived from `PeripheralList`. The idea is that the `PrinterList` holds only instances of the class called `Printer`. So the code overrides the `GetPeripheralByName()` function. The version inside `PrinterList` casts the item to a `Printer` because the items in the list are instances of `Peripheral`. If you were to leave this function as is, every time you want to retrieve a `Printer`, you'd get back a pointer to a `Peripheral` instead, and you'd have to cast it to a `(Printer *)` type. Overriding the `GetPeripheralByName()` function and performing the cast there is easier and more efficient.

TECHNICAL STUFF

The code in Listing 4-1 has a small bug: Nothing is stopping you from putting an instance of `Peripheral` in the `PrinterList` container. Or, for that matter, you could add an instance of any other class derived from `Peripheral` if there were more. But when you retrieve the instance in the `GetPeripheralByName()`, it's automatically cast to a `Printer`. That would be a problem if somebody had stuffed something else in there other than a `Printer` instance. To prevent a wrongful addition, create a special `AddPeripheral()` function for the `PrinterList` class that takes, specifically, a `Printer`. To do that, you would make the `AddPeripheral()` function in `PeripheralList` virtual and then override it, modifying the parameter to take a `Printer` rather than a `Peripheral`. When you do so, you hide the function in the base class. But that's okay: You don't want people calling the base class version because it can accept any `Peripheral`, not just a `Printer` instance. When you run this application, you should get an output value of 80 (the price of the printer named `Bear`).

Multiple inheritance

In C++, having a single base class from which your class inherits is generally best. However, it is possible to inherit from multiple base classes, a process called *multiple inheritance*.

Employing multiple inheritance

One class may have some features that you want in a derived class, and another class may have other features that you want in the same derived class. If that's the case, you can inherit from both through multiple inheritance.

REMEMBER

Multiple inheritance is messy and difficult to pull off properly. But when you use it with care, you can make it work. The DerivingTwoDiff example, shown in Listing 4-2, shows how to perform this task.

LISTING 4-2: **Deriving from Two Different Classes**

```cpp
#include <iostream>

using namespace std;

class Mom {
public:
  void Brains() {
    cout << "I'm smart!" << endl;
  }
};

class Dad {
public:
  void Beauty() {
    cout << "I'm beautiful!" << endl;
  }
};

class Derived : public Mom, public Dad {
};

int main(int argc, char *argv[]) {
  Derived child;
  child.Brains();
  child.Beauty();
  return 0;
}
```

When you run this code, you see the following output:

```
I'm smart!
I'm beautiful!
```

In the preceding code, the class Derived inherited the functions of both classes Mom and Dad. Because it did, the compiler allows a Derived instance, child, to call both functions. You use this approach to derive from multiple classes:

```
class Derived : public Mom, public Dad
```

You start with the base classes to the right of the single colon, as with a single inheritance, and separate the classes with a comma. You also precede each class with the type of inheritance, public.

Setting access in multiple inheritance

As with single inheritance, you can use inheritance other than public. But you don't have to use the same access for all the classes. For example, the following, although a bit confusing, is acceptable:

```
class Derived : public Mom, protected Dad
```

This means that public members derived from Dad are now protected in the Derived class, which also means that users can't call the methods inherited from Dad, nor can they access any properties inherited from Dad. If you used this type of inheritance in Listing 4-2, this line would no longer work:

```
child.Beauty();
```

If you try to compile it, you see the following error, because the Beauty() member is protected now:

```
'void Dad::Beauty()' is inaccessible
```

REMEMBER

When you work with multiple inheritance, be careful that you understand what your code is doing. Although it may compile correctly, it still may not function correctly, leading to the famous creepy-crawly thing called a bug.

Seeing multiple inheritance go wrong

Strange, bizarre, freaky things can happen with multiple inheritance. If both base classes have a property called Bagel, the compiler gets confused. Suppose you enhance the two base classes with a `Bagel` effect (as seen in the `DerivingTwo-Diff2` example):

```
class Mom {
public:
  int Bagel;
  void Brains() {
    cout << "I'm smart!" << endl;
  }
};

class Dad {
public:
  int Bagel;
  void Beauty() {
    cout << "I'm beautiful!" << endl;
  }
};

class Derived : public Mom, public Dad {
};
```

In the preceding code, each of the two base classes, `Mom` and `Dad`, has a `Bagel` member. The compiler will let you do this. But if you try to access the member, as in the following code, you get an error:

```
Derived child;
child.Bagel = 42;
```

Here's the error message we see in Code::Blocks:

```
error: request for member 'Bagel' is ambiguous
```

The message means that the compiler isn't sure which `Bagel` the code refers to: The one inherited from `Mom` or the one inherited from `Dad`. If you write code like this, make sure you know which inherited member you're referring to so you can fix the problem.

REMEMBER

Now this is going to look bizarre, but it's correct. Suppose you're referring to the `Bagel` inherited from `Mom`. You can put the name `Mom` before the word `Bagel`, separated by two colons:

```
child.Mom::Bagel = 42;
```

Yes, that really is correct, even though it seems a little strange. And if you want to refer to the one by Dad, you do this:

```
child.Dad::Bagel = 17;
```

Both lines compile properly because you removed any ambiguities. In addition, you can access them individually by using the same technique:

```
cout << child.Mom::Bagel << endl;
cout << child.Dad::Bagel << endl;
```

Virtual inheritance

At times, you may see the word virtual thrown in when deriving a new class, as in the following:

```
class Diamond : virtual public Rock
```

This inclusion of virtual is to fix a strange problem that can arise. When you use multiple inheritance, you can run into a crazy situation in which you have a diamond-shaped inheritance, as in Figure 4-1.

In Figure 4-1, you can see that the base class is Rock. The Diamond and Jade classes derive from Rock. At this point, the code uses multiple inheritance to derive the class MeltedMess from Diamond and Jade. Yes, you can do this. But you have to be careful.

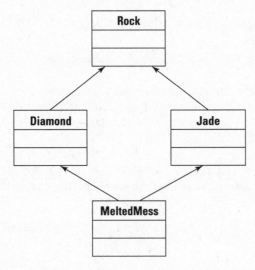

FIGURE 4-1:
Using diamond inheritance can be hard.

Understanding the diamond-shaped inheritance problem

Think about this: Suppose Rock has a public member called Weight. Then both Diamond and Jade inherit that member. Now when you derive MeltedMess and try to access its Weight member, the compiler claims that it doesn't know which Weight you're referring to — the one inherited from Diamond or the one inherited from Jade. You know that there should only be one instance of Weight, because it came from a single base class, Rock. But the compiler sees only one level up, not two.

To understand how to fix the problem, recognize what happens when you create an instance of a class derived from another class: Deep down inside the computer, the instance has a portion that is itself an instance of the base class. When you derive a class from multiple base classes, instances of the derived class have one portion for each base class. Thus an instance of MeltedMess has a portion that is a Diamond and a portion that is a Jade, as well as a portion that wasn't directly inherited from Rock.

Digging deeper, MeltedMess has both a Diamond in it and a Jade in it, and each of those in turn has a Rock in them, which means that the compiler sees two Rocks in MeltedMess. With each Rock comes a separate Weight instance. The Cracking-Diamonds example, shown in Listing 4-3, demonstrates the problem. This listing declares the classes Rock, Diamond, Jade, and MeltedMess.

LISTING 4-3: **Cracking Diamonds**

```
#include <iostream>

using namespace std;

class Rock {
public:
  int Weight;
};

class Diamond : public Rock {
public:
  void SetDiamondWeight(int newweight) {
    Weight = newweight;
  }
```

(continued)

LISTING 4-3:   *(continued)*

```
    int GetDiamondWeight() {
      return Weight;
    }
};

class Jade : public Rock {
public:
  void SetJadeWeight(int newweight) {
    Weight = newweight;
  }

  int GetJadeWeight() {
    return Weight;
  }
};

class MeltedMess : public Diamond, public Jade {
};

int main(int argc, char *argv[])
{
  MeltedMess mymess;
  mymess.SetDiamondWeight(10);
  mymess.SetJadeWeight(20);

  cout << mymess.GetDiamondWeight() << endl;
  cout << mymess.GetJadeWeight() << endl;
  return 0;
}
```

One member is called Weight, and it's part of Rock. The Jade and Diamond classes include two accessor methods, one to set the value of Weight and one to get it.

The MeltedMess class derives from both Diamond and Jade. The code creates an instance of MeltedMess and calls the four methods that access the supposedly single Weight member in Rock. The code calls the accessor for Diamond, setting Weight to 10. Then it calls the one for Jade, setting Weight to 20.

In a perfect world, in which each object only has one Weight, this would have first set the Weight to 10 and then to 20. When you print it, you should see 20 both times. But you don't:

```
10
20
```

Repairing the diamond-shaped inheritance problem

When you print the `Diamond` portion of the `MeltedMess` instance `Weight` in Listing 4-3, shown previously, you see 10. The `Jade` portion displays 20 instead. Therefore, `mymess` has two different `Weight` members. That's not a good thing.

To fix it, add the word `virtual` when you inherit from `Rock`. According to the ANSI standard, you put `virtual` in the two middle classes (as shown in the `CrackingDiamonds2` example provided with the downloadable source and explained in this section). This means `Diamond` and `Jade` in this case. Thus, you need to modify the class headers in Listing 4-3 to look like this:

```
class Diamond : virtual public Rock {
```

and this:

```
class Jade : virtual public Rock {
```

When you make these modifications and then run the application, you find that you have only one instance of `Weight` in the final `MeltedMess` class instance, `mymess`. It's not such a mess after all! Here's the output after making the change:

```
20
20
```

Now this makes sense: Only one instance of `Weight` is in the `mymess` object, so the following line changes the `Weight` to 10:

```
mymess.SetDiamondWeight(10);
```

Then the following line changes the same `Weight` to 20:

```
mymess.SetJadeWeight(20);
```

You can also access `Weight` directly now without error, so the accessor methods aren't strictly needed:

```
mymess.Weight = 30;
```

POLYMORPHISM WITH MULTIPLE INHERITANCES

If you have multiple inheritance, you can safely treat your object as any of the base classes. In the case of the diamond example, you can treat an instance of MeltedMess as a Diamond instance or as a Jade instance. For example, if you have a function that takes a pointer to a Diamond instance as a parameter, you can safely pass a pointer to a MeltedMess instance. Casting also works: You can cast a MeltedMess instance to a Diamond, Jade, or Rock instance. However, if you do, use the static_cast method like this to ensure the best outcome:

```
Rock casted = static_cast<Rock>(mymess);
cout << casted.Weight << endl;
```

Then the following lines print the value of the one Weight instance, 30:

```
cout << mymess.GetDiamondWeight() << endl;
cout << mymess.GetJadeWeight() << endl;
cout << mymess.Weight << endl;
```

REMEMBER

With a diamond inheritance, use virtual inheritance in the middle classes to ensure that they point to the correct type. Although you can also add the word virtual to the final class (in the example's case, that's MeltedClass), you don't need to.

Friend classes and functions

You may encounter a situation in which you want one class to access the private and protected members of another class. Normally, doing so isn't allowed. But it is if you make the two classes friends. C++ provides the friend keyword to override the normal class protections.

Use friend only when you really need to. If you have a class, say Square, that needs access to the private and protected members of a class called DrawingBoard, you can add a line inside the class DrawingBoard that looks like this:

```
friend class Square;
```

This code allows the code in Square to access the private and protected members of any instance of type DrawingBoard.

REMEMBER

In many cases, allowing complete access of one class by another class opens too many possibilities for bugs and security issues (among other things). Friend functions are a more limited form of the `friend` keyword because they limit access to a global function or a single method within a class. If you need to provide friend access for some reason, using a friend function is better. Listing 4-4 shows the `BestFriends` example that demonstrates both friend classes and friend functions.

LISTING 4-4: **Working with Friends**

```cpp
#include <iostream>

using namespace std;

class PAndP;

class Limited {
public:
  void ShowProtected(PAndP &);
};

class PAndP {
public:
  friend class Peeks;
  friend void Limited::ShowProtected(PAndP &X);
  friend void FriendFunction(PAndP &X);
protected:
  void IsProtected() {cout << "Protected" << endl;}
private:
  string var = "Var";
  void IsPrivate() {cout << "Private " << var << endl;}
};

class Peeks {
public:
  void ShowProtected(PAndP &X) {X.IsProtected();}
  void ShowPrivate(PAndP &X) {
    X.var = "From Peeks";
    X.IsPrivate();
  }
};

void Limited::ShowProtected(PAndP &X){
  X.IsProtected();
}
```

(continued)

LISTING 4-4: **(continued)**

```
void FriendFunction(PAndP &X) {
  X.IsProtected();
  X.var = "From FriendFunction";
  X.IsPrivate();
}

int main() {
  PAndP Hidden;
  Peeks ShowMe;
  Limited ShowMeAgain;

  ShowMe.ShowProtected(Hidden);
  ShowMe.ShowPrivate(Hidden);

  ShowMeAgain.ShowProtected(Hidden);

  FriendFunction(Hidden);
  return 0;
}
```

The private and protected (PAndP) class contains protected and private members that Peeks, Limited::ShowProtected(), and FriendFunction() access. Each of these entities takes a different route, and that route isn't always as obvious as it might be.

When working with the Limited class, coding order is important. You begin by creating a forward reference to class PAndP and then define the Limited class. However, you can't define Limited::ShowProtected() yet because the members of PAndP aren't known to the compiler and there isn't a way to create a forward declaration of them. Consequently, the actual code for Limited::ShowProtected() comes later, which is the only method in Limited that has access to PAndP. If you were to try accessing PAndP from any other member, the compiler would complain.

TIP

Creating the friend entries for Peeks and FriendFunction() is easier because you aren't dealing with just a part of the element. All you need are the friend entries in the PAndP class. Note that every method or function that interacts with PAndP receives a pointer to a PAndP instance to do so. The code in main() creates the required objects and accesses the PAndP protected and private members. You see the following output when you run this application:

FRIENDS OF A SAME CLASS

An instance of a class can access the private and protected members of other instances of the same class. The compiler allows you to do it. However, you normally want objects to remain isolated from each other for all sorts of reasons, including keeping bugs at bay and reducing security risks. It helps to think of the only situation in which this kind of activity is actually useful as a host and client, when one instance acts as a host to a client instance for something like creating a container for an object of the same type. To make this sort of access happen, you provide a pointer to another instance of the same class (the client) inside the host class, perhaps passed in as a parameter. The host class is free to modify any of the passed class members.

```
Protected
Private From Peeks
Protected
Protected
Private From FriendFunction
```

Using Classes and Types within Classes

Sometimes an application needs a fairly complex internal structure to get its work done. Three ways to accomplish this goal with relatively few headaches are nesting classes, embedding classes, and declaring types within classes. The following sections discuss the two most common goals: nesting classes and declaring types within classes. The "Nesting a class" section also discusses protection for embedded classes.

Nesting a class

You may have times when you create a set of classes with one class acting as the primary class while all the other classes function as supporting classes. For example, you may be a member of a team of programmers, and your job is to write a set of classes that log on to a competitor's computer at night and lower all the prices on the products. Other members of your team will use your classes in their applications. You're just writing a set of classes; the teammates are writing the rest of the application. The following sections consider the issues involved in performing this task, as well as a potential solution in the form of nested classes.

Considering the nesting scenario issues

In the classes you're creating, you want to make the task easy on your coworkers. In doing so, you may make a primary class, such as EthicalCompetition, that they will instantiate to use your set of classes. This primary class will include the methods for using the system. In other words, it serves as an *interface* to the set of classes.

In addition to the main EthicalCompetition class, you might create additional auxiliary classes that the EthicalCompetition class will use, but your coworkers won't interact with directly. One might be a class called Connection that handles the tasks of connecting to the competitor's computer. However, the Connection class may present these problems:

>> **Potential conflicts:** The class Connection may be something you write, but your organization may support another Connection class, and your coworkers might need to use that class.

>> **Privacy:** You may not want your coworkers using this special Connection class. Perhaps it has special functionality that would reveal too many organizational secrets, or you just want them using the main interface, the EthicalCompetition class.

To solve the unique name problem, you have several choices. For one, you can just rename the class something different, such as EthicalCompetitionConnection. But that's a bit long for a class used exclusively for internal needs. However, you could shorten the class name and call it something that's likely to be unique, such as ECConnection.

Yet at the same time, if the users of your classes look at the header file and see a whole set of classes, which classes they should be using may not be clear. (Of course, you would write some documentation to clear this up, but you do want the code to be at least somewhat self-explanatory.)

Understanding the nested class solution

One solution for dealing with both naming conflict and privacy issues for support classes is to use *nested* classes. With a nested class, you write the declaration for the main class, EthicalCompetition, and then, inside the class, you write the supporting classes, as in the following:

```
class EthicalCompetition {
private:
  class Connection {
  public:
```

```
      void Connect();
   };
public:
   void HardWork();
};
```

Note that this shows a class inside a class. Here's the code for the functions:

```
void EthicalCompetition::HardWork() {
   Connection c;
   c.Connect();
   cout << "Connected" << endl;
}

void EthicalCompetition::Connection::Connect() {
   cout << "Connecting..." << endl;
}
```

The header for the Connect function in the Connection class requires first the outer class name, then two colons, then the inner class name, then two colons again, and finally the function name. This follows the pattern you normally use where you put the class name first, then two colons, and then the function name. But in this case, you have two class names separated with two colons.

When you want to declare an instance of the Connection class, you do it differently, depending on where you are in the code when you declare it:

>> **Inside a method of the outer** EthicalCompetition **class:** You simply refer to the class by its name, Connection. Look at the method HardWork, with this line:

```
Connection c;
```

>> **Outside the methods:** You can declare an instance of the inner class, Connection, without an instance of the outer class, EthicalCompetition. To do this, you fully qualify the class name, like this:

```
EthicalCompetition::Connection myconnect;
```

This line would go, for instance, in the main() function of your application if you want to create an instance of the inner class, Connection.

However, you may recall that one of the reasons for putting the class inside the other was to shield it from the outside world, to keep your nosy coworkers from creating an instance of it. But so far, what you've done doesn't really stop them from using the class. They can just use it by referring to its fully qualified name, EthicalCompetition::Connection.

Creating an inner class definition

So far, you've created a handy grouping of the class, and you also set up your grouping so that you can use a simpler name that won't conflict with other classes. If you just want to group your classes, you can use a nested class. If you want to add higher security to a class so that others can't use your inner class, however, you have to create an *inner class definition.*

Here's a series of three tricks devoted to showing you how you create that inner class definition. For the first trick, you declare the class with a forward definition but put the class definition outside the outer class. Never put the inner class definition inside a private or protected section of the outer class definition; it doesn't work. The following code takes care of that declaration for you:

```
class EthicalCompetition {
private:
  class Connection;
public:
    void HardWork();
};

class EthicalCompetition::Connection {
public:
  void Connect();
};
```

Here, inside the outer class, is a header for the inner class and a semicolon that you use instead of writing the whole inner class; that's a forward declaration. The rest of the inner class appears after the outer class. To make this code work, you must fully qualify the class name, like this:

```
class EthicalCompetition::Connection
```

TIP

If you skip the word EthicalCompetition and two colons, the compiler compiles this class as though it's a different class. Later, the compiler will complain it can't find the rest of the Connection class declaration. The error is

```
error: aggregate 'EthicalCompetition::Connection c' has
    incomplete type and cannot be defined
```

Remember that message so that you know how to correct it when you forget the outer class name.

By declaring the inner class after the outer class, you can now employ the second trick. The idea is to write the inner class so that only the outer class can access the members. To accomplish this task, you make all the members of the inner class either private or protected and then make the outer class, EthicalCompetition, a friend of the inner class, Connection. Here's the modified version of the Connection class:

```
class EthicalCompetition::Connection {
protected:
  friend class EthicalCompetition;
  void Connect();
};
```

Only the outer class can access most of the Connection members now. However, even though the members are protected, nothing stops users outside EthicalConnection from creating an instance of the Connection class. To add this security, you employ the third trick, which is to create a constructor for the class that is either private or protected. When you change the constructor's access, following suit with a destructor is a good idea. Make the destructor private or protected, too. Even if the constructor and destructor don't do anything, making them private or protected prevents others from creating an instance of the class — others, that is, except any friends to the class. So here's yet one more version of the class:

```
class EthicalCompetition::Connection {
protected:
  friend class EthicalCompetition;
  void Connect();
  Connection() {}
  ~Connection() {}
};
```

This third trick completes the process. When someone tries to make an instance of the class outside EthicalCompetition (such as in main()), as in this:

```
EthicalCompetition::Connection myconnect;
```

you see the following message:

```
EthicalCompetition::Connection::~Connection()' is protected
```

You can still create an instance from within the methods of EthicalCompetition. The ProtectingEmbedded example, shown in Listing 4-5, contains the final application.

LISTING 4-5: **Protecting Embedded Classes**

```cpp
#include <iostream>

using namespace std;

class EthicalCompetition {
private:
  class Connection;
public:
  void HardWork();
};

class EthicalCompetition::Connection {
protected:
  friend class EthicalCompetition;
  void Connect();
  Connection() {}
  ~Connection() {}
};

void EthicalCompetition::HardWork() {
  Connection c;
  c.Connect();
  cout << "Connected" << endl;
}

void EthicalCompetition::Connection::Connect() {
  cout << "Connecting..." << endl;
}

int main(int argc, char *argv[]) {
  // Uncomment this line to see the access error.
  // EthicalCompetition::Connection myconnect;
  EthicalCompetition comp;
  comp.HardWork();
  return 0;
}
```

Here's the output from this example:

```
Connecting...
Connected
```

Types within classes

When you declare a type, such as an enum, associating it with a class can be convenient. For example, you may have a class called Cheesecake. In this class, you may have the SelectedFlavor property, which can be an enumerated type, such as Flavor:

```
enum Flavor {
  ChocolateSuicide,
  SquishyStrawberry,
  BrokenBanana,
  PrettyPlainVanilla,
  CoolLuah,
  BizarrePurple
};
```

Use this code to associate Flavor with a class:

```
class Cheesecake {
public:
  enum Flavor
  {
    ChocolateSuicide, SquishyStrawberry, BrokenBanana,
    PrettyPlainVanilla, CoolLuah, BizarrePurple
  };
  Flavor SelectedFlavor;

  int AmountLeft;
  void Eat() {
    AmountLeft = 0;
  }
};
```

You can use the Flavor type anywhere in your application, but to use it outside the Cheesecake class, you must fully qualify its name by lining up the class name, two colons, and then the type name, like this:

```
Cheesecake::Flavor myflavor = Cheesecake::CoolLuah;
```

An enum requires that you also fully qualify the enumeration. Using just Cool-Luah on the right side of the equals sign will cause the compiler to complain and say that CoolLuah is undeclared. The Cheesecake example, shown in Listing 4-6, demonstrates how we can use the Cheesecake class.

LISTING 4-6: **Using Types within a Class**

```cpp
#include <iostream>

using namespace std;

class Cheesecake {
public:
  enum Flavor {
    ChocolateSuicide, SquishyStrawberry, BrokenBanana,
    PrettyPlainVanilla, CoolLuah, BizarrePurple
  };
  Flavor SelectedFlavor;

  int AmountLeft;
  void Eat() {
    AmountLeft = 0;
  }
};

int main() {
  Cheesecake yum;
  yum.SelectedFlavor = Cheesecake::SquishyStrawberry;
  yum.AmountLeft = 100;
  yum.Eat();
  cout << yum.AmountLeft << endl;
  return 0;
}
```

REMEMBER

When you declare a type (using a typedef or an enum) inside a class, you don't need an instance of the class present to use the type. But you must fully qualify the name when you are using it from outside of the class. Thus, you can set up a variable of type Cheesecake::Flavor and use it in your application without creating an instance of Cheesecake.

In contrast to nested classes, you can make a type within a class private or protected. If you do so, you can use the type only within the class members. If you try to use the type outside the class (including setting a property, as in yum. SelectedFlavor = Cheesecake::SquishyStrawberry;), you get a compiler error.

TIP

You can also put a typedef inside your class in the same way you'd put an enum inside the class, as in the following example:

```
class Spongecake {
public:
  typedef int SpongeNumber;
  SpongeNumber weight;
  SpongeNumber diameter;
};

int main() {
  Spongecake::SpongeNumber myweight = 30;
  Spongecake fluff;
  fluff.weight = myweight;
  return 0;
}
```

Chapter **5**

Creating Classes with Templates

I f C++ programming has any big secret, it would have to be *templates*, which are entities that define either a family of functions or a family of classes. Templates seem to be the topic that beginning programmers strive to understand because they've heard about them and seem to think that templates are the big wall over which they must climb to ultimately become The C++ Guru. This chapter begins by showing you that creating and using basic templates need not be difficult.

The one thing you can be certain of is that knowing how to work with templates will open your abilities to a whole new world, primarily because the entire Standard C++ Library is built around templates. Further, understanding templates can help you understand all that cryptic code that you see other people posting on the Internet. This chapter also helps you understand how to access, use, and extend standard templates.

REMEMBER

You don't have to type the source code for this chapter manually. In fact, using the downloadable source is a lot easier. You can find the source for this chapter in the \CPP_AIO4\BookV\Chapter05 folder of the downloadable source. See the Introduction for details on how to find these source files.

Templatizing a Class

This section begins by showing you just how simple templates are to understand. It begins with a discussion of type, which you can skip if you already understand the concept fully. The next section deals with the need for creating templates based on a type.

Considering types

This section begins with the OldGasStation class. Remember, a class is a *type*. You can declare variables of the type. Thus you can declare a variable of type OldGasStation called, for example HanksGetGas. You can also create another variable of type OldGasStation; maybe this one would be called FillerUp. And, of course, you can create a third one; this one might be called GotGasWeCanFillIt. Each of these variables, HanksGetGas, FillerUp, and GotGasWeCanFillIt, are each instances of the type (or class) OldGasStation.

In the same way, you can make some instances of an existing type, say int. You can name one CheckingAccountBalance and another BuriedTreasuresFound. Each of these is an instance of the type int Although int isn't a class, it is a type.

Think about this so far: You have the two different types available to you. One is called OldGasStation and the other is called int. One of these is a type you make; the other is built into C++.

Focus on the one you create, OldGasStation. This is a type that you create by declaring it in your application when you write the code. The compiler takes your declaration and builds some data inside the resulting application that represents this type. After the application starts, the type is created, and it doesn't change throughout the course of the application.

REMEMBER

The variables in your application may change at runtime; you can create new instances of a type and delete them and change their contents. But the type itself is created at compile time and doesn't change at runtime. Remember this as one property of types in general. You need to keep this in mind when dealing with templates.

Defining the need for templates

Suppose that you have a class called MyHolder. This class will hold some integers. Nothing special, but it looks like this:

```
class MyHolder {
public:
  int first;
  int second;
  int third;
  int sum() {
    return first + second + third;
  }
};
```

This class is easy to use; you just create an instance of it and set the values of its members. But remember: After the application is running, the class is a done deal. But at runtime, you're free to create new instances of this class. For example, the following code creates ten instances of the class, calls sum( ), and prints the return value of sum( ):

```
MyHolder *hold;
int loop;
for (loop = 0; loop < 10; loop++) {
  hold = new MyHolder;
  hold->first = loop * 100;
  hold->second = loop * 110;
  hold->third = loop * 120;
  cout << hold->sum() << endl;
  delete hold;
}
```

This code creates an instance at runtime, does some work with it, and then deletes the instance. It then repeats this process for a total of ten times. Instances (or variables) are created, changed, and deleted — all at runtime. But the class is created at compile time.

Suppose you're coding away and you discover that this class MyHolder is handy, except it would be nice if you had a version of it that holds floats instead of ints. You could create a second class just like the first that uses the word float instead of int, like this:

```
class AnotherHolder {
public:
  float first;
  float second;
```

```
  float third;
  float sum() {
    return first + second + third;
  }
};
```

This class works the same way as the previous class, but it stores three `float` types instead of `int` types. But you can see, if you have a really big class, that this method would essentially require a lot of copying and pasting followed by some search-and-replacing — in other words, busywork. But you can minimize this busywork by using templates. Instead of typing two different versions of the class, type one version of the class that you can, effectively, modify when you need different versions of the class. Look at this code:

```
template <typename T>
class CoolHolder {
public:
  T first;
  T second;
  T third;
  T sum() {
    return first + second + third;
  }
};
```

Think of this templated class as a rule for a single class that does exactly what the previous two classes did. (Ignore the template declaration, `template <typename T>`, for now; it's explained in the "Understanding the template keyword" section of the chapter.) In this rule is a placeholder called `T` that is a placeholder for a type. Imagine this set of code; then remove the first line and replace all the remaining `T`'s with the word `int`. If you did that, you would end up with this:

```
class CoolHolder {
public:
  int first;
  int second;
  int third;
  int sum() {
    return first + second + third;
  }
};
```

This is, of course, the same as the earlier class called MyHolder, just with a different name. Now imagine doing the same thing but replacing each T with the word float. You can probably see where we're going with this. Here it is:

```
class CoolHolder {
public:
  float first;
  float second;
  float third;
  float sum() {
    return first + second + third;
  }
};
```

Again, this is the same as the earlier class called AnotherHolder, but with a different name. That's what a template does: It specifies a placeholder for a class. But it doesn't actually create a class . . . yet. You have to do one more thing to tell the compiler to use this template to create a class. You accomplish this task by writing code to create a variable or by using the class somehow. Look at this code:

```
CoolHolder<int> IntHolder;
IntHolder.first = 10;
IntHolder.second = 20;
IntHolder.third = 30;
```

This code tells the compiler to create a class by replacing every instance of T with int in the CoolHolder template. In other words, the compiler creates a class named CoolHolder<int>. These four lines of code create an instance of CoolHolder<int> called IntHolder and set its properties. The computer creates this class at compile time. Remember, types are created at compile time, and this example code is no exception to this rule.

TIP

Here's an easy way to look at a template. When you see a line like CoolHolder<int> IntHolder; you can think of it as being like CoolHolderint IntHolder. Although that's not really what the template is called, you are telling the compiler to create a new class. In your mind, you may think of the class as being called CoolHolderint, that is, a name without the angle brackets. (But remember that the name really isn't CoolHolderint. It's CoolHolder<int>.)

Creating and using a template

The previous section tells how to put a template together based on your requirements, so now it's time to put that template into action. The CoolHolder example, shown in Listing 5-1, contains a complete application that uses the CoolHolder template.

LISTING 5-1: **Using Templates to Create Several Versions of a Class**

```cpp
#include <iostream>

using namespace std;

template <typename T>
class CoolHolder {
public:
  T first;
  T second;
  T third;
  T sum() {
    return first + second + third;
  }
};

int main() {
  CoolHolder<int> IntHolder;
  IntHolder.first = 10;
  IntHolder.second = 20;
  IntHolder.third = 30;

  CoolHolder<int> AnotherIntHolder;
  AnotherIntHolder.first = 100;
  AnotherIntHolder.second = 200;
  AnotherIntHolder.third = 300;

  CoolHolder<float> FloatHolder;
  FloatHolder.first = 3.1415;
  FloatHolder.second = 4.1415;
  FloatHolder.third = 5.1415;

  cout << IntHolder.first << endl;
  cout << AnotherIntHolder.first << endl;
  cout << FloatHolder.first << endl;

  CoolHolder<int> *hold;
  for (int loop = 0; loop < 10; loop++) {
    hold = new CoolHolder<int>;
    hold->first = loop * 100;
    hold->second = loop * 110;
    hold->third = loop * 120;
```

```
    cout << hold->sum() << endl;
    delete hold;
  }
  return 0;
}
```

When you run this application, you see a bunch of results from calls to sum():

```
10
100
3.1415
0
330
660
990
1320
1650
1980
2310
2640
2970
```

Look closely at the code. Near the beginning is the same template shown previously. Remember that the compiler doesn't create a type for this template. Instead, the compiler uses it as a rule to follow to create additional types. That is, the code indeed serves as a template for other types, thus its name.

Understanding the template keyword

It's time to consider the template keyword in the template definition. Here's the first line of the template shown in Listing 5-1:

```
template <typename T>
```

All this means is that a template class follows and it has a type with a placeholder called T. Inside the class, anywhere a T appears, the compiler replaces it with the typename defined by T, such as int or float.

REMEMBER

The T is stand-alone; if you have it as part of a word, it won't be replaced. The standard practice is for people to use T for the placeholder, but you can use any identifier (starting with a letter or underscore, followed by any combination of letters, numbers, or underscores). In some cases, templates have more than one replaceable placeholder, each of which is unique.

To use the template, you declare several variables of types based on this template. Here's one such line:

```
CoolHolder<int> IntHolder;
```

This line declares a variable called IntHolder. For this variable, the compiler creates a type called CoolHolder<int>, which is a type based on the CoolHolder template, where T is replaced by int. Here's another line where the code declares a variable:

```
CoolHolder<int> AnotherIntHolder;
```

This time, the compiler doesn't have to create another type because it just created the CoolHolder<int> type earlier. But again, this line uses the same type based on the template, where T is replaced by int.

The example in Listing 5-1 creates another class based on the CoolHolder template. It's instantiated at FloatHolder:

```
CoolHolder<float> FloatHolder;
```

When the compiler sees this line, it creates another type by using the template, and it replaces T with the word float. So in this case, the first, second, and third properties of FloatHolder each hold a floating-point number. Also, the sum() method returns a floating-point number.

The following line uses the CoolHolder<int> type created earlier to declare a pointer to CoolHolder<int>, hold. Yes, you can do that; pointers are allowed:

```
CoolHolder<int> *hold;
```

Then the code that follows cycles through a loop to create new instances of type CoolHolder<int> by using the line

```
hold = new CoolHolder<int>;
```

The code accesses the members using the pointer notation, ->, like so:

```
hold->first = loop * 100;
```

REMEMBER

These are the basics of templates. They're really not as bad as people make them out to be. Just remember that when you see an identifier followed by angle brackets containing a type or class, it's a template.

Going Beyond the Basics

The previous section discusses template basics. However, templates are more flexible and powerful than you might imagine. The following sections discuss how you can move beyond the basics to add flexibility to your code.

Separating a template from the function code

In the earlier days of templates and C++, the rule was that you had to put the method code for a class template inside the template itself; you couldn't put a forward declaration in the template and then put the function code outside the template, as you could do with classes. However, the ANSI standard changed this situation and made putting the code outside the template legal. (It's important to know this fact because you may encounter convoluted-looking code that puts everything inside.) The ImFree example, shown in Listing 5-2, shows you how to separate the methods from the template.

LISTING 5-2: **Separating a Template from Function Code**

```cpp
#include <iostream>

using namespace std;

template <typename T>
class ImFree {
protected:
  T x;
public:
  T& getx();
  void setx(T);
};

template <typename T>
T &ImFree<T>::getx() {
  return x;
}

template <typename T>
void ImFree<T>::setx(T newx) {
  x = newx;
}
```

(continued)

LISTING 5-2: **(continued)**

```
int main() {
  ImFree<int> separate;
  separate.setx(10);
  cout << separate.getx() << endl;
  return 0;
}
```

Look closely at one of the methods:

```
template <typename T>
T &ImFree<T>::getx() {
    return x;
}
```

The first line is the same as the first line of the template definition. It's just the word template followed by the parameter in angle brackets.

The next line looks almost like you might expect it to. With classes, you put the function prototype, adding the class name and two colons before the function name itself, but after the return type. Here you do that, too; the sticky part is how you write the template name. You don't just give the name; instead, you follow the name with two angle brackets, with the parameter inside, like this: T &ImFree<T>::getx(). Note the <T> part.

TIP

Note that the getx() method returns a reference instead of a variable of type T. There's a good reason for doing it. In the main() function of Listing 5-2, you create the class based on the template with an integer parameter:

```
ImFree<int> separate;
```

However, you can create the class with some other class:

```
ImFree<SomeOtherClass> separate;
```

When you do that, you don't really want to return just an instance from the function, as in

```
T& getx() {
    return x;
}
```

Returning an instance copies the existing instance rather than return the existing instance. Using a reference means that the class user doesn't have to do any bizarre coding. For example, displaying the output using a cout is rather straightforward:

```
cout << separate.getx() << endl;
```

Including static members in a template

You can include static members in a template, but you need to be careful when you do so. Remember that all instances of a class share a single static member of the class. You can think of the static member as being a member of the class itself, whereas the nonstatic members are members of the instances.

Now, from a single template, you can potentially create multiple classes. This means that to maintain the notion of static members, you need to either get creative with your rules or make life easy by just assuming that each class based on the template gets its own static members. The easy way is exactly how this process works.

REMEMBER

When you include a static member in a template, each class that you create based on the template gets its own static member. Further, you need to tell the compiler how to store the static member just as you do with static members of classes that aren't created from templates. The StaticMembers example, shown in Listing 5-3, contains an example of static members in a template.

LISTING 5-3: **Using Static Members in a Template**

```
#include <iostream>

using namespace std;

template <typename T>
class Electricity {
public:
    static T charge;
};

template <typename T>
T Electricity<T>::charge;

int main() {
  Electricity<int>::charge = 10;
  Electricity<float>::charge = 98.6;
```

(continued)

LISTING 5-3: *(continued)*

```
Electricity<int> inst;
inst.charge = 22;

cout << Electricity<int>::charge << endl;
cout << Electricity<float>::charge << endl;
cout << inst.charge << endl;

return 0;
}
```

Note how you declare storage for the static member; it's the two lines in between the template and `main()`. You supply the same template header you would for the class and then specify the static member type (in this case, `T`, which is the template parameter). Next, you refer to the static member by using the usual `classname::member` name syntax. But remember that the class name gets the template parameter in angle brackets after it.

This code creates two classes based on the templates `Electricity <int>` and `Electricity <float>`. Each of these classes has its own instance of the static member; the `<int>` version contains `10` and the `<float>` version contains `98.6`. Then, just to show that there's only a single static member per class, the code creates an instance of `Electricity<int>` and sets its static member to `22`. Using a `cout` statement, you can see that the output for the two `Electricity<int>` lines are the same and the `Electricity<float>` output is different.

Parameterizing a Template

A template consists of a template name followed by one or more parameters inside angle brackets. Then comes the class definition. When you create a new class based on this template, the compiler obliges by making a substitution for whatever you supply as the parameter. Focus your eyes on this template:

```
template <typename T>
class SomethingForEveryone {
public:
    T member;
};
```

Not much to it: It's just a simple template with one member called, conveniently enough, member. However, notice in particular what's inside the angle brackets. This is the parameter: typename T. As with parameters in a function, the first is the type of the parameter (typename), and the second is the name of the parameter (T). Previous sections have illustrated how this all works. However, you don't always use typename; you can use other types, as described in the sections that follow.

Putting different types in the parameter

It turns out there's more to using parameters than meets the computer screen. You can put many more keywords inside the parameter beyond just the boring word typename. For example, suppose you have a class that does some comparisons to make sure that a product isn't too expensive for a person's budget. Each person would have several instances of this class, one for each product. This class would have a constant in it that represents the maximum price the person is willing to spend.

But there's a twist: Although you would have multiple instances of this class, one for each product the person wants to buy, the maximum price would be different for each person. You can create such a situation with or without templates. Here's a way you can do it with a template:

```
template <int MaxPrice>
class PriceController {
public:
  int Price;
  void TestPrice()
  {
    if (Price > MaxPrice)
    {
      cout << "Too expensive" << endl;
    }
  }
};
```

In this case, the template parameter isn't a type at all — it's an integer value, an actual number. Then, inside the class, you use that number as a constant. As you can see in the TestPrice function, the code compares Price to the MaxPrice constant. So this time, instead of using T for the name of the template parameter, the code views it as a value, not a type. The PriceController example, shown in Listing 5-4, contains a complete example that uses this template.

LISTING 5-4: **Using Different Types for a Template Parameter**

```cpp
#include <iostream>

using namespace std;

template <typename T>
class SomethingForEveryone {
public:
  T member;
};

template <int MaxPrice>
class PriceController {
public:
  int Price;
  void TestPrice(string Name)
  {
    if (Price > MaxPrice)
    {
      cout << Name << " too expensive!" << endl;
    }
  }
};

int main() {
  SomethingForEveryone<int> JustForMe;
  JustForMe.member = 2;
  cout << JustForMe.member << endl;

  const int FredMaxPrice = 30;
  PriceController<FredMaxPrice> FredsToaster;
  FredsToaster.Price = 15;
  FredsToaster.TestPrice("Toaster");
  PriceController<FredMaxPrice> FredsDrawingSet;
  FredsDrawingSet.Price = 45;
  FredsDrawingSet.TestPrice("Drawing set");

  const int JulieMaxPrice = 60;
  PriceController<JulieMaxPrice> JuliesCar;
  JuliesCar.Price = 80;
  JuliesCar.TestPrice("Car");
  return 0;
}
```

Each person gets a different class that reflects the maximum price they're willing to pay. You can see that Fred gets a class called `PriceController` `<FredMaxPrice>`. Julie, however, gets a class called `PriceController` `<JulieMax Price>`. And remember, these really are different classes. The compiler created two different classes, one for each item passed in as a template parameter. Also notice that the parameters are constant integer values. `FredMaxPrice` is a constant integer holding 30. `JulieMaxPrice` is a constant integer holding 60.

For the first one, `PriceController` `<FredMaxPrice>`, the code creates two instances. For the second one, `PriceController` `<JulieMaxPrice>`, the code creates one instance. In all instances, the code sets the price of the item and then calls `TestPrice()` with the item name. If the item is too expensive, the `PriceController` outputs a special message. Here's the output from this example:

```
2
Drawing set too expensive!
Car too expensive!
```

WARNING

When working with some older versions of C++, you can't use certain types, such as `float`, for your template. Doing so can cause the build process to fail with all sorts of odd messages. However, you also see the following message, which tells you precisely where the problem lies:

```
error: 'float' is not a valid type for a template non-type
    parameter
```

TIP

Starting with C++ 11, you can use `std::nullptr_t;` as a parameter type, as in `template <std::nullptr_t N>`. When working with C++ 20, you gain access to these types as well:

>> Floating-point type

>> Literal class type with the following properties:

- All base classes and nonstatic data members are public and non-mutable.

- The types of all base classes and non-static data members are structural types. Depending on the compiler, you might also be able to use a multidimensional array of the structural type.

TIP

A null pointer represents a special case that differentiates between 0 and an actual null (missing) value. Its actual representation is `(void *)0`, which makes it different from the C/C++ `NULL` value. You can see the null pointer discussed at `https://hackernoon.com/what-exactly-is-nullptr-in-c-94d63y6t` and `https://stackoverflow.com/questions/13665349/what-is-a-proper-use-case-of-stdnullptr-t-template-parameters`.

Creating Classes with Templates

PARAMETERIZING WITH A CLASS

When your template is expecting a class for its parameter (remember, a class, not an instance of a class), you can use the word `typename` in the template parameter. You then instruct the compiler to create a class based on the template by passing a class name into the template, as in `MyContainer<MyClass>inst;`. Typically, you use a container class as a template parameter if you have a template that you intend to hold instances of a class. However, instead of using `typename`, you use `class`, like so:

```
template <class T>
class MyContainer {
public:
    T member;
};
```

Including multiple parameters

You're not limited to only one parameter when you create a template. For example, the Standard C++ Library has a template called `map`. The `map` template works like an array, but instead of storing things based on an index as you would in an array, you store them based on a key and value pair. To retrieve an item from `map`, you specify the key, and you get back the value. When you create a class based on the `map` template, you specify the two types `map` will hold, one for the key and one for the value. These are types, rather than objects or instances. After you specify the types, the compiler creates a class, and inside that class you can put the instances.

To show how this works, instead of using the actual `map` template, the following example creates a template that works similarly to a `map`. Instances of classes based on this template will hold only as many items as you specify when you create the class, whereas a real `map` doesn't have any limitations beyond the size of the computer's memory. The `MultipleParameters` example, shown in Listing 5-5, demonstrates an alternative `map` template.

LISTING 5-5: **Using Multiple Parameters with Templates**

```
#include <iostream>

using namespace std;

template<typename K, typename V, int S>
class MyMap {
```

```
protected:
  K key[S];
  V value[S];
  bool used[S];
  int Count;

  int Find(K akey) {
    int i;
    for (i=0; i<S; i++) {
      if (used[i] == false)
        continue;
      if (key[i] == akey) {
        return i;
      }
    }
    return -1;
  }

  int FindNextAvailable() {
    int i;
    for (i=0; i<S; i++) {
      if (used[i] == false)
        return i;
    }
    return -1;
  }

public:
  MyMap() {
    int i;
    for (i=0; i<S; i++) {
      used[i] = false;
    }
  }

  void Set(K akey, V avalue) {
    int i = Find(akey);

    if (i > -1) {
      value[i] = avalue;
    }
    else {
      i = FindNextAvailable();
```

(continued)

LISTING 5-5: **(continued)**

```
        if (i > -1) {
          key[i] = akey;
          value[i] = avalue;
          used[i] = true;
        }
        else
            cout << "Sorry, full!" << endl;
      }
    }

  V Get(K akey) {
    int i = Find(akey);

    if (i == -1)
      return 0;
    else
      return value[i];
  }
};

int main() {
  MyMap<char,int,10> mymap;

  mymap.Set('X',5);
  mymap.Set('Q',6);
  mymap.Set('X',10);

  cout << mymap.Get('X') << endl;
  cout << mymap.Get('Q') << endl;
  return 0;
}
```

When you run this application, you see this output:

```
10
6
```

This listing is a good exercise — not just for your fingers as you type it in, but for understanding templates. Notice the first line of the template definition:

```
template<typename K, typename V, int S>
```

This template takes three parameters. The first is a type, K, used as the key for map. The second is a type, V, used as the value for map. The final is S, and it's not a type. Instead, S is an integer value; it represents the maximum number of pairs that map can hold.

The methods that follow allow the user of any class based on this map to add items to map and retrieve items from map. The example currently lacks functions for removing items; you might think about ways you could add such functions. You might even look at the header files for the map template in the Standard C++ Library to see how the designers of the library implemented a removal system.

Working with non-type parameters

Starting with C++ 11, you can use non-type parameters to define a template. The use of non-type parameters makes it possible to create templates that accept some interesting types of input, yet are more specific in some ways than general template types. Previous sections have shown how to use types for templates; here are some common non-types used for templates:

>> lvalue reference

>> nullptr

>> pointer

>> enumeration

>> integral

>> auto (some functionality provided starting with C++ 17 and enhanced with deduction of the class type in C++ 20)

One of the more interesting non-type parameters is an enumeration. You can use the enumeration to enforce things like kind selection or for verifying that a particular kind is in use. It also comes in handy for comparisons. The NonTypeParm example, shown in Listing 5-6, demonstrates techniques you can use when working with templates that rely on an enumeration.

LISTING 5-6: | **Using an Enumeration in a Template**

```
#include <iostream>

using namespace std;

enum StoreType {
```

(continued)

LISTING 5-6: **(continued)**

```
  Red,
  Blue,
  Green
};

template <typename V>
struct StoreOut {
  V Value;
  StoreType Kind;
};

template <StoreType K, typename V>
class StoreIt {
protected:
  V Value;
  StoreType Kind = K;
public:
  StoreIt() {
    Value = 0;
  }

  StoreIt(V value) {
    Value = value;
  }

  StoreOut<V>& getx();
  void setx(StoreType, V);
  string KindToString();
};

template <StoreType K, typename V>
StoreOut<V>& StoreIt<K, V>::getx() {
  StoreOut<V>* Out = new StoreOut<V>();
  Out->Value = Value;
  Out->Kind = Kind;
  return *Out;
}

template <StoreType K, typename V>
void StoreIt<K, V>::setx(StoreType newT, V newV) {
  Value = newV;
  Kind = newT;
}
```

```
template <StoreType K, typename V>
string StoreIt<K, V>::KindToString(){
  switch (Kind) {
    case Blue: return "Blue";
    case Green: return "Green";
    case Red: return "Red";
  }
  return "Not Found";
}

int main() {
  StoreIt<StoreType::Blue, int> Test;
  Test.setx(StoreType::Red, 5);

  StoreIt<StoreType::Red, int> Test2(6);

  cout << Test1.KindToString() << "\t" <<
    Test1.getx().Value << endl;
  if (Test1.KindToString() != "Blue")
    cout << "Test1 storage type changed." << endl;
  if (Test1.KindToString() == Test2.KindToString())
    cout << "Test1 and Test2 are of equal types." << endl;
  return 0;
}
```

This example stores two values: a storage type and a value. The StoreType enumeration contains the only values you can use as input: Red, Blue, and Green. You provide one of these values when creating the initial object and again when setting a value using setx(). Using this approach limits the number of object types that a caller can create to those that you expect.

TIP

The type could be anything. For example, if you create a car object and your company only supports certain paint colors, you could limit selection to those colors programmatically. This example simplifies the enumeration selection so that you can more easily see how it works.

Because the example stores two values, it needs a method for returning two values, which is the purpose of the StoreOut structure. The getx() method uses it to return data to the caller.

The actual StoreIt class declaration protects the two variables: Value, which can be of any type; and Kind, which must be a StoreType enumeration value. It also provides three methods: getx(), which returns a StoreOut structure;, setx(), which accepts the StoreType and value used to set the object values;

and `KindToString()`, which provides the utility service of changing a `StoreType` value to a string for output. The `setx()` and `getx()` methods work much the same as their counterparts in Listing 5-2. The `KindToString()` method uses a simple `switch` statement to perform the required translation.

The code in `main()` creates a `StoreIt` object, `Test1`, stores data in it, and then displays the values onscreen. The `main()` code also demonstrates some of the ways in which you might use this template class. For example, you could determine whether the `Kind` of `Test1` has changed. You could also determine whether `Test1` and `Test2` are the same `Kind` of object. Notice that `Test1` and `Test2` use different constructor types so that the `Kind` is created as part of the template, but `Value` is either a default value of 0 or a specific value of 6 in this case. Here's what you see as output:

```
Red     5
Test1 storage type changed.
Test1 and Test2 are of equal types.
```

Typedefing a Template

If there's a template that you use with particular parameters repeatedly, often just using `typedef` is the easiest way to go. For example, if you have a template like this

```
template <typename T>
class Cluck {
public:
  T Chicken;
};
```

and you use `Cluck <int>` repeatedly, employ the following:

```
typedef Cluck<int> CluckNum;
```

Then, anytime you need to use `Cluck<int>`, you can use `CluckNum` instead. Here's how:

```
int main() {
  CluckNum foghorn;
  foghorn.Chicken = 1;
  return 0;
}
```

TIP

Using `typedef` for templates makes the resulting class name look like a regular old class name, rather than a template name. In the preceding example, you use `CluckNum` instead of the somewhat cryptic `Cluck<int>`. And interestingly, if you're working as part of a team of programmers and the other programmers aren't as knowledgeable about templates as you are, they tend to be less intimidated if you `typedef` the template.

REMEMBER

When the compiler creates a class based on a template, people say that the compiler is *instantiating* the template. Even though most people use the word *instantiate* to mean creating an object based on a class, you can see how the template itself is a type from which you can create other types. Thus, a class based on a template is actually an instance of a template, and the process of creating a class based on a template is called *template instantiation*.

Deriving Templates

If you think about it, you can involve a class template in a derivation in at least three ways. You can:

>> Derive a class from a class template

>> Derive a class template from a class

>> Derive a class template from a class template

If you want to find out about these techniques, read the following sections.

Deriving classes from a class template

You can derive a class from a template, and in doing so, specify the parameters for the template. In other words, think of the process like this:

1. From a template, you create a class.

2. From that created class, you derive your final class.

Suppose you have a template called `MediaHolder`, and the first two lines of its declaration look like this:

```
template <typename T>
class MediaHolder
```

Then you could derive a class from a particular case of this template, as in this header for a class:

```
class BookHolder : public MediaHolder<Book>
```

Here you create a new class (based on MediaHolder) called MediaHolder<Book>. From that class, you derive a final class, BookHolder. The ClassFromTemplate example, shown in Listing 5-7, is an example of the class MediaHolder.

LISTING 5-7: **Deriving a Class from a Class Template**

```cpp
#include <iostream>

using namespace std;

class Book {
public:
  string Name;
  string Author;
  string Publisher;
  Book(string aname, string anauthor, string apublisher) :
    Name(aname), Author(anauthor), Publisher(apublisher){}
};

class Magazine {
public:
  string Name;
  string Issue;
  string Publisher;
  Magazine(string aname, string anissue,
    string apublisher) :
    Name(aname), Issue(anissue), Publisher(apublisher){}
};

template <typename T>
class MediaHolder {
public:
  T *array[100];
  int Count;
  void Add(T *item)
  {
    array[Count] = item;
    Count++;
  }
```

```cpp
  MediaHolder() : Count(0) {}
};

class BookHolder : public MediaHolder<Book> {
public:
  enum GenreEnum
    {childrens, scifi, romance,
     horror, mainstream, hownotto};
  GenreEnum GenreOfAllBooks;
};

class MagazineHolder : public MediaHolder<Magazine> {
public:
  bool CompleteSet;
};

int main() {
  MagazineHolder dl;
  dl.Add(new Magazine(
      "Dummies Life", "Vol 1 No 1", "Wile E."));
  dl.Add(new Magazine(
      "Dummies Life", "Vol 1 No 2", "Wile E."));
  dl.Add(new Magazine(
      "Dummies Life", "Vol 1 No 3", "Wile E."));
  dl.CompleteSet = false;
  cout << dl.Count << endl;

  BookHolder bh;
  bh.Add(new Book(
      "Yellow Rose", "Sandy Shore", "Wile E."));
  bh.Add(new Book(
      "Bluebells", "Sandy Shore", "Wile E."));
  bh.Add(new Book(
      "Red Tulip", "Sandy Shore", "Wile E."));
  bh.GenreOfAllBooks = BookHolder::childrens;
  cout << bh.Count << endl;
  return 0;
}
```

When you run this example, you see the magazine count of 3 first, and the book count of 3 second.

Deriving a class template from a class

A template doesn't have to be at the absolute top of your hierarchy; a template can be derived from another class that's not a template. When you have a template and the compiler creates a class based on this template, the resulting class will be derived from another class. For example, suppose you have a class called Super-Math that isn't a template. You could derive a class template from SuperMath. The TemplateFromClass example, shown in Listing 5-8, demonstrates how you can do this.

LISTING 5-8: **Deriving a Class Template from a Class**

```cpp
#include <iostream>

using namespace std;

class SuperMath {
public:
  int IQ;
};

template <typename T>
class SuperNumber : public SuperMath {
public:
  T value;

  T &AddTo(T another) {
    value += another;
    return value;
  }

  T &SubtractFrom(T another) {
    value -= another;
    return value;
  }
};

void IncreaseIQ(SuperMath &inst) {
  inst.IQ++;
}
```

```
int main() {
  SuperNumber<int> First;
  First.value = 10;
  First.IQ = 206;
  cout << First.AddTo(20) << endl;

  SuperNumber<float> Second;
  Second.value = 20.5;
  Second.IQ = 201;
  cout << Second.SubtractFrom(1.3) << endl;

  IncreaseIQ(First);
  IncreaseIQ(Second);
  cout << First.IQ << endl;
  cout << Second.IQ << endl;
  return 0;
}
```

The base class is called SuperMath, and it has a member called IQ. From Super-Math, the example derives a class template called SuperNumber that does some arithmetic. Later, the example adds an Incredible IQ-Inflating Polymorphism to use in this function:

```
void IncreaseIQ(SuperMath &inst) {
    inst.IQ++;
}
```

Note what this function takes as a parameter: A reference to SuperMath. Because the SuperNumber class template is derived from SuperMath, any class you create based on the template is, in turn, derived from SuperMath. That means that if you create an instance of a class based on the template, you can pass the instance into the IncreaseIQ() function. (Remember, when a function takes a pointer or reference to a class, you can instead pass an instance of a derived class.)

Deriving a class template from a class template

If you have a class template and you want to derive another class template from it, first you need to think about *exactly* what you're doing; the process takes place when you attempt to derive a class template from another class template. Remember that a class template isn't a class: A class template is a cookie-cutter that the compiler uses to build a class. If, in a derivation, the base class and the derived classes are both templates, what you really have is the following:

1. The first class is a template from which the compiler builds classes.

2. The second class is a template from which the compiler will build classes that are derived from classes built from the first template.

Now think about this: You create a class based on the base class template. Then you create a second class based on the second template. This process doesn't automatically mean that the second class derives from the first class. Here's why: From the first template, you can create many classes. When you create a class from the second template, which of those classes will it derive from?

To understand what's happening here, look at the TemplateFromTemplate example, shown in Listing 5-9. To keep the code simple, the example uses basic names for the identifiers. (Notice that we commented out one of the lines. If you're typing this, type that line in, too, with the comment slashes, because you'll try something in a moment.)

LISTING 5-9: **Deriving a Class Template from a Class Template**

```
#include <iostream>

using namespace std;

template <typename T>
class Base {
public:
  T a;
};

template <typename T>
class Derived : public Base<T> {
public:
  T b;
};

void TestInt(Base<int> *inst) {
  cout << inst->a << endl;
}

void TestDouble(Base<double> *inst) {
  cout << inst->a << endl;
}
```

```
int main() {
  Base<int> base_int;
  Base<double> base_double;

  Derived<int> derived_int;
  Derived<double> derived_double;

  TestInt(&base_int);
  TestInt(&derived_int);
  TestDouble(&base_double);
  TestDouble(&derived_double);

  //TestDouble(&derived_int);
  return 0;
}
```

The example has two functions, each taking a different class — and each class based on the first template, called Base. The first takes Base<int> * as a parameter, and the second takes Base<double> * as a parameter. When a function, such as TestInt() or TestDouble(), takes a pointer to a class, it can legally pass a pointer to an instance of a derived class, which means that you can create this variable:

```
Derived<int> derived_int;
```

You pass this variable to the function that takes a Base<int> and it compiles. That means that Derived<int> is derived from Base<int>. In the same way, Derived<double> is derived from Base<double>. When you run this code, it outputs four numbers: two int values and two double values.

To see how Derived<int> relies on Base<int>, uncomment the line TestDouble(&derived_int). When you do this, and you try to compile the listing, you see this message:

```
error: cannot convert 'Derived<int>*' to 'Base<double>*' for
    argument '1' to 'void TestDouble(Base<double>*)'
```

The error message says you can't pass a pointer to Derived<int> to a function that takes a pointer to Base<double>. That's because Derived<int> isn't derived from Base<double>.

REMEMBER

Templates aren't derived from other templates. You can't derive from templates because templates aren't classes. Rather, templates are cookie cutters for classes, and the class resulting from a template can be derived from a class resulting from another template. Look closely at the declaration of the second template class. Its header looks like this:

```
template <typename T>
class Derived : public Base<T>
```

The clue here is that the Derived template takes a template parameter called T. Then the class based on the template is derived from a class called Base<T>. But in this case, T is the parameter for the Derived template. See what happens if you create a class based on Derived, such as this one:

```
Derived<int> x;
```

This line creates a class called Derived<int>; then, in this case, the parameter is int. Thus the compiler replaces the Ts so that Base<T> in this case becomes Base<int>. So Derived<int> is derived from Base<int>.

Templatizing a Function

A *function template* is a function that allows the user to essentially modify the types used by a function as needed. For example, look at these two functions:

```
int AbsoluteValueInt(int x) {
    if (x >= 0)
        return x;
    else
        return -x;
}

float AbsoluteValueFloat(float x) {
    if (x >= 0)
        return x;
    else
        return -x;
}
```

To take the absolute value of an integer, you use the AbsoluteValueInt() function. But to take the absolute value of a float, you instead use the AbsoluteValueFloat() function. Of course, you need yet another function to support double or other types. Instead of having a separate function for double and a separate function for every other type, you can use a template like this:

```
template <typename T> T AbsoluteValue(T x) {
    if (x >= 0)
        return x;
    else
        return -x;
}
```

Now you need only one version of the function, which handles any numeric type, including double. The users of the function can, effectively, create their own versions of the function as needed. For example, to use an integer version of this function, you put the typename, int, inside angle brackets after the function name when calling the function:

```
int n = -3;
cout << AbsoluteValue<int>(n) << endl;
```

If you want to use the function for a float, you do this:

```
float x = -4.5;
cout << AbsoluteValue<float>(x) << endl;
```

Note the function template declaration. The real difference between the function template and a standard function is in the header:

```
template <typename T> T AbsoluteValue(T x)
```

Begin with the word template, a space, and an open angle bracket (that is, a less-than sign). These characters are followed by the word typename, a closing angle bracket (that is, a greater-than sign), and then an identifier name. Most people like to use the name T (because it's the first letter in *type*). At this point, you add the rest of the function header, which, taken by itself, looks like this:

```
T AbsoluteValue(T x)
```

REMEMBER

T represents a type. Therefore, this portion of the function header shows a function called AbsoluteValue that takes T as a parameter and returns T. Creating a function based on this template by using an integer, means that the function takes an integer parameter and returns an integer. When the compiler encounters a line like this:

```
cout << AbsoluteValue<float>(x) << endl;
```

it creates a function based on the template, substituting `float` anywhere it sees T. However, if you have two lines that use the same type, as in this:

```
cout << AbsoluteValue<float>(x) << endl;
cout << AbsoluteValue<float>(10.0) << endl;
```

the compiler creates only a single function for both lines.

Overloading and function templates

If you really want to go out on a limb and create flexibility in your application, you can use overloading with a function template. Remember, *overloading a function* means that you create two different versions of a single function. What you're doing is creating two separate functions that have different parameters (that is, either a different number of parameters or different types of parameters), but they share the same name. Look at these two functions found in the FunctionOverloadingAndTemplates example:

```
int AbsoluteValue(int x) {
  if (x >= 0)
    return x;
  else
    return -x;
}

float AbsoluteValue(float x) {
  if (x >= 0)
    return x;
  else
    return -x;
}
```

These functions are an example of overloading. They take different types as parameters. (One takes an `int`; the other takes a `float`.) Of course, you could combine these functions into a template:

```
template <typename T> T AbsoluteValue(T x) {
  if (x >= 0)
    return x;
  else
    return -x;
}
```

There really isn't any difference between the two examples. After all, you can use the following two lines of code either after the overloaded functions (without the type parameters) or after the function template:

```
cout << AbsoluteValue<int>(n) << endl;
cout << AbsoluteValue<float>(x) << endl;
```

In this case, n is an int and x is a float. However, the template is a better choice. If you use the overloaded form and try this code, you see an error:

```
cout << AbsoluteValue(10.5) << endl;
```

Even though 10.5 is a float you see an error message like this:

```
error: call of overloaded 'AbsoluteValue(double)' is ambiguous
```

The message contains AbsoluteValue(double), which means that the compiler thinks that 10.5 is a double, not a float. You can pass a double into either a function that takes an int or a function that takes a float. The compiler will just convert it to an int or a float, whichever it needs. Because the compiler thinks that 10.5 is a double, it can pass the value to either overloaded function version. So that leaves you with a choice: You can cast it to a float using (float)10.5; declare it a float using 10.5f; or create a third overloaded version of the function, one that takes a double.

Creating a template is easier than overcoming these sorts of errors. The second reason the template version is better: If you want a new type of the function, you don't need to write another version of the function.

However, you can also overload a function template. The OverloadedFunction-Template example, shown in Listing 5-10, contains an overloaded function template.

LISTING 5-10: **Overloading a Function Template**

```
#include <iostream>

using namespace std;

template <typename T> T AbsoluteValue(T x) {
  cout << "(using first)" << endl;
```

(continued)

LISTING 5-10:   *(continued)*

```
    if (x >= 0)
      return x;
    else
      return -x;
  }

  template <typename T> T AbsoluteValue(T *x) {
    cout << "(using second)" << endl;
    if (*x >= 0)
      return *x;
    else
      return -(*x);
  }

  int main() {
    int n = -3;
    cout << AbsoluteValue<int>(n) << endl;

    float *xptr = new float(-4.5);
    cout << AbsoluteValue<float>(xptr) << endl;
    cout << AbsoluteValue<float>(10.5) << endl;
    return 0;
  }
```

Passing a pointer (as in the second call to AbsoluteValue() in main()), uses the second version of the template. And just to be sure which version gets used and at what time during application execution, the example contains a cout line at the beginning of each function template. Here's what you see as output:

```
(using first)
3
(using second)
4.5
(using first)
10.5
```

From the middle two lines, you can see that the computer did indeed call the second version of the template.

You can make life a little easier by using a small trick. Most compilers let you leave out the type in angle brackets in the function template call itself. The compiler deduces what type of function to build from the template, based on the types that you pass into the function call. Here's an example main() that you can substitute for the main() in Listing 5-10:

```
int main() {
  int n = -3;
  cout << AbsoluteValue(n) << endl;
  float *xptr = new float(-4.5);
  cout << AbsoluteValue(xptr) << endl;
  cout << AbsoluteValue(10.5) << endl;
  return 0;
}
```

This code replaces AbsoluteValue<int>(n) with AbsoluteValue(n). When you run the modified code, you see the same output as when you run Listing 5-10.

Templatizing a method

When you write a template for a class, you can put function templates inside the class template. You simply declare a function template inside a class, as in the following found in the MemberFunctionTemplate example:

```
class MyMath {
public:
  string name;
  MyMath(string aname) : name(aname) {}

  template <typename T> void WriteAbsoluteValue(T x) {
    cout << "Hello " << name << endl;
    if (x >= 0)
      cout << x << endl;
    else
      cout << -x << endl;
  }
};
```

The WriteAbsoluteValue() method is a template. It's preceded by the word template and a template parameter in angle brackets. Then it has a return type, void, the function name, and the function parameter.

When you create an instance of the class, you can call the method, providing a type as need be, as in the following:

```
int main() {
  MyMath inst = string("George");
  inst.WriteAbsoluteValue(-50.5);
  inst.WriteAbsoluteValue(-35);
  return 0;
}
```

In the first call, the function takes a double (because, by default, the C++ compiler considers -50.5 a double). In the second call, the function takes an integer. The compiler then generates two different forms of the function, and they both become members of the class.

REMEMBER

Although you can use function templates as class members, you cannot make them virtual. The compiler won't allow it, and the ANSI standard forbids you from doing it. If you try to make the function template virtual, you get an error message that looks similar to this one:

```
'virtual' can only be specified for functions
```

Chapter **6**

Programming with the Standard Library

When you get around in the world of C++ programming, you encounter two different libraries that people use to make their lives easier. These two libraries are:

» Standard C++ Library

» Standard Template Library (STL)

In this case, *library* means a set of classes that you can use in your applications. These libraries include handy classes, such as `string` and `vector` (which is like an array — it's a list you use to store objects).

The difference between the Standard C++ Library and STL is that STL came first. STL was used by so many developers that the American National Standards Institute (ANSI) decided to standardize it. The result is the similar Standard C++ Library that is part of the official ANSI standard and now part of most modern C++ compilers. This chapter uses the Standard C++ Library, or simply the *Standard Library*. The concepts presented here also apply to STL, so if you're using STL, you can use this chapter.

You don't have to type the source code for this chapter manually. In fact, using the downloadable source is a lot easier. You can find the source for this chapter in the `\CPP_AIO4\BookV\Chapter06` folder of the downloadable source. See the Introduction for details on how to find these source files.

Architecting the Standard Library

When people start using the Standard Library, they often ask about the source code. They see the header files, but no `.cpp` files. There are no `.cpp` files. ANSI architected the Standard Library for ease of use and reliability.

The classes contain their functions inside the class definitions; there are no forward declarations. You don't add source files to your project or link in compiled libraries. Just add an include line for the libraries you want.

To see how this works for yourself, open any project file you're worked on to date that has `#include <iostream>` and relies on a `cout`/`endl` combination to output text. Right-click `endl` and choose Find Implementation of: 'endl' from the context menu. Code::Blocks will open the `ostream` file and take you to the implementation of `endl`, which basically outputs `'\n'` to the output stream, amid some other confusing code. When you scroll to the beginning of that file, you see:

```
/** @file include/ostream
 *  This is a Standard C++ Library header.
 */
```

There is no `.cpp` file involved. All of the code appears in the header.

Containing Your Classes

Computers need a place to store objects, so the Standard Library includes containers in which you can put objects. These special containers are called *container classes,* and the Standard Library implements them as templates. When you create an instance of a container class, you specify what class it holds.

When you specify the class in a container, you are saying that the container will contain instances of your specified class or of classes derived from your specified class. You must decide whether the container will hold instances of the class, pointers to the instances, or references to the instances.

Storing in a vector

The Vectors example, shown in Listing 6-1, demonstrates how to use a container class. This particular container is a data type called a vector, and it works much like an array.

LISTING 6-1: **Using Vectors as Examples of Container Classes**

```
#include <iostream>
#include <vector>

using namespace std;

int main() {
  vector<string> names;

  names.push_back("Tom");
  names.push_back("Dick");
  names.push_back("Harry");
  names.push_back("April");
  names.push_back("May");
  names.push_back("June");

  cout << names[0] << endl;
  cout << names[5] << endl;
  return 0;
}
```

You use vector as a template. That means that it's going to have a template parameter, which is string in this case. Note also the included header files. Among them are <vector> (with no .h after the filename). In general, you include the header file that matches the name of the container you are using. Thus, if there were such a thing as a container called rimbucklebock, you would type #include <rimbuck-lebock>. Or, if you use the container called set, you type #include <set>. When you run this example, you see two names as output:

```
Tom
June
```

There are a number of advantages to using a vector instead of a regular, plain old, no-frills array:

>> You don't need to know up front how many items will be going in it. With an array, you need to know the size when you declare it.

» You don't need to specifically deallocate a vector, as you do with a dynamically defined array.

» You can obtain the precise size of a vector, so you don't need to pass the size of the vector to a function.

» When a vector is filled, the underlying code allocates additional memory automatically.

» You can return a vector from a function. To return an array, you must dynamically define it first.

» You can add and remove items from the middle of a vector, something that you can't easily do with an array.

» You can copy or assign a vector directly.

Here are some things you can do with vector:

» Add items to the end of it.

» Access its members by using bracket notation.

» Iterate through it, either from beginning to end or from the end back to the beginning.

The Vectors2 example, shown in Listing 6-2, demonstrates how to use multiple vectors in a single application. You can see that each one holds a different type, specified in the template parameter. This example requires C++ 11 or above to use.

LISTING 6-2: **Creating More Advanced Vectors**

```
#include <iostream>
#include <vector>

using namespace std;

class Employee {
public:
  string Name;
  string FireDate;
  int GoofoffDays;
  Employee(string aname, string afiredate,
    int agoofdays) : Name(aname), FireDate(afiredate),
    GoofoffDays(agoofdays) {}
};
```

```
int main() {
  // A vector that holds strings
  vector<string> MyAliases;
  MyAliases.push_back(string("Bud The Sailor"));
  MyAliases.push_back(string("Rick Fixit"));
  MyAliases.push_back(string("Bobalou Billow"));
  for (auto entry : MyAliases)
    cout << entry << endl;

  // A vector that holds integers
  vector<int> LuckyNumbers;
  LuckyNumbers.push_back(13);
  LuckyNumbers.push_back(26);
  LuckyNumbers.push_back(52);
  for (auto entry : LuckyNumbers)
    cout << entry << endl;

  // A vector of default constructed ints.
  vector<int> Default(5);
  int i = 0;
  vector<int>::reverse_iterator rentry = Default.rbegin();
  for (; rentry != Default.rend(); rentry++)
    *rentry = ++i;
  for (auto entry : Default)
    cout << entry << endl;

  // A vector that holds Employee instances
  vector<Employee> GreatWorkers;
  GreatWorkers.push_back(Employee("George","123100", 50));
  GreatWorkers.push_back(Employee("Tom","052002", 40));
  for (auto entry : GreatWorkers)
    cout << entry.Name << endl;
  return 0;
}
```

After you compile and run this application, you see the following output from the cout statements:

```
Bud The Sailor
Rick Fixit
Bobalou Billow
13
26
```

```
52
5
4
3
2
1
George
Tom
```

TIP

Notice that this example relies on an iterated `for` loop for each of the vectors. Using an iterated `for` loop greatly reduces the amount of code you write. Plus, you don't have to worry about the size of the `vector` you're processing. All you concern yourself with are the individual entries.

The `Default` portion of the example is also interesting in that it declares a `vector` of a specific size and reverse-fills the vector from the end to the beginning. Consequently, `Default[0]` contains the value 5, rather than 1, as you might expect. To work backward, you must use a standard `for` loop.

Working with std::array

Sometimes you need a fixed-size array, but without the limitations of the built-in array. In this case, `std::array` may do the trick for you. It provides built-in functionality, such as knowing its own size, supporting assignment, and providing random access iterators. The `StdArray` example, shown in Listing 6-3, demonstrates two interesting ways that you can use `std::array`. You need C++ 17 or above to use this example.

LISTING 6-3: **Working with std::array to Overcome array Limitations**

```cpp
#include <iostream>
#include <array>
#include <algorithm>
#include <iterator>

using namespace std;

int main() {
  array<char, 5> Letters = {'a', 'b', 'c', 'd', 'e'};

  for (entry: Letters)
    cout << entry << endl;
```

```
reverse_copy(Letters.begin(), Letters.end(),
             ostream_iterator<char>(cout, " "));
return 0;
}
```

Notice that the declaration begins by providing the array type, char, and the number of array elements, 5, as template parameters. Letters contains five char values from 'a' through 'e'.

As shown in the example, you can use a standard iterated for loop to display the individual entries. However, you can also output the Letter content in other ways, such as by performing a reverse_copy() to the console with the ostream_iterator<char>(). The point is to avoid limiting yourself to one coding style when another will do the job better with fewer lines. Here's the output you see from the example:

```
a
b
c
d
e
e d c b a
```

Mapping your data

The Maps example, shown in Listing 6-4, demonstrates a type of container called a map. A map works much the same as a vector, except for one main difference: You look up items in vector by putting a number inside brackets, like this:

```
cout << names[0] << endl;
```

But with a map, you can use any class or type you want for the index (called a *key*), not just numbers. To create an entry, you use a *key* (the index) and a *value* (the data) as a pair.

LISTING 6-4: **Associating Objects with map**

```
#include <iostream>
#include <map>

using namespace std;
```

(continued)

LISTING 6-4: *(continued)*

```
int main() {
  map<string, string> marriages;
  marriages["Tom"] = "Suzy";
  marriages["Harry"] = "Harriet";

  cout << marriages["Tom"] << endl;
  cout << marriages["Harry"] << endl;
  return 0;
}
```

To use map, you declare a variable of class map, supplying two template parameters, the key class and the value class, which are both string in the example. To
store a map value, you place a key inside brackets and set it equal to a value:

```
marriages["Tom"] = "Suzy";
```

To retrieve that particular item, you supply the key in brackets:

```
cout << marriages["Tom"] << endl;
```

When you run this example, you see the following two strings as output:

```
Suzy
Harriet
```

REMEMBER

Even though the keys can be any type or class, you must specify the type or class
you're using when you set up map. After you do that, you can use only that type for
the particular map. Thus, if you say that the keys will be strings, you cannot then
use an integer for a key, as in marriages[3] = "Suzy";.

Containing instances, pointers, or references

One of the most common discussions you encounter when people start talking
about how to use the container templates is whether to put instances in the containers, pointers, or references. For example, which of the following should you
type?

```
vector<MyClass>
vector<MyClass *>
vector<MyClass &>
```

In other words, do you want your container to store the actual instance (whatever that might mean), a reference to the actual instance, or a pointer to the instance? To explore this idea, look at the Maps2 example in Listing 6-5. Here, you're trying out the different ways of storing things in map: instances, pointers, and references.

LISTING 6-5: **Making Decisions: Oh, What to Store?**

```
#include <iostream>
#include <map>

using namespace std;

class StoreMe {
public:
  int Item;
};

bool operator < (const StoreMe & first,
const StoreMe & second) {
  return first.Item < second.Item;
}

int main() {
  // First try storing the instances
  map<StoreMe, StoreMe> instances;
  StoreMe key1 = {10}; // braces notation!
  StoreMe value1 = {20};
  StoreMe key2 = {30};
  StoreMe value2 = {40};
  instances[key1] = value1;
  instances[key2] = value2;

  value1.Item = 12345;
  cout << instances[key1].Item << endl;
  instances[key1].Item = 34567;
  cout << instances[key1].Item << endl;

  // Next try storing pointers to the instances
  map<StoreMe*, StoreMe*> pointers;
  StoreMe key10 = {10};
  StoreMe value10 = {20};
  StoreMe key11 = {30};
  StoreMe value11 = {40};
```

(continued)

LISTING 6-5:   *(continued)*

```
  pointers[&key10] = &value10;
  pointers[&key11] = &value11;

  value10.Item = 12345;
  cout << (*pointers[&key10]).Item << endl;

  // Finally try storing references to the instances.
  // Commented out because it causes an error.)
//  map<StoreMe&, StoreMe&> pointers;
  return 0;
}
```

To create the instances of StoreMe, you use the braces notation. You can do that when you have no constructors. So the line

```
StoreMe key1 = {10};
```

creates an instance of StoreMe and puts 10 in the Item property. To create an individual instances entry, you need both a key and a value instance of StoreMe. You then use the key to provide a name for the value stored in the map. Consequently, instances contains two entries consisting of two StoreMe objects each. Here's what you see when you run the application:

```
20
34567
12345
```

This output doesn't precisely match expectations because the code changes the Item property in value1:

```
value1.Item = 12345;
```

When the code outputs the value of instances[key1].Item, you see an output of 20, not 12345. That means that the value stored in map is a copy, not the original. However, when the code changes the value in instances like this:

```
instances[key1].Item = 34567;
```

REMEMBER

the value portion of the instances entry does change. You see 34567 as output. Consequently, when working with map instances, you must modify the map entry directly.

Now that you've figured out that map is storing copies of what you put in it, the idea of storing a pointer should be clear: If you have a pointer variable and then you make a copy of it, although you have a separate pointer variable, the original and the copy both point to the same memory location. That's the idea behind the second part of Listing 6-5. You create pointers like this:

```
map<StoreMe*, StoreMe*> pointers;
```

Now this map stores pointer variables. Remember that a pointer variable just holds a number that represents an address. If two separate pointer variables hold the same number, it means that they point to the same object at the same address. Furthermore, because this map is holding pointers, it's holding numbers, not instances — something to think about. To store a value when using pointers, you need to use code like this:

```
pointers[&key10] = &value10;
```

Note the use of the ampersand (&) used as a reference operator to store addresses in map. It's now possible to change the Item member of one the value objects:

```
value10.Item = 12345;
```

that you print using this carefully parenthesized line:

```
cout << (*pointers[&key10]).Item << endl;
```

and you see this:

```
12345
```

REMEMBER

When working with map pointers, you modify the original variable to make a change because the map entries point to the original variable, rather than make a copy of it. However, as you can see, using map pointers also makes your code harder to read.

Don't worry just now about the bool operator < (const StoreMe & first, const StoreMe & second) function. This function is explained in the "Performing comparisons" section, later in this chapter.

Note that the following line is commented out:

```
// map<StoreMe&, StoreMe&> pointers;
```

It attempts to declare a map that holds references, but the code generates a compiler error instead. Try uncommenting the commented line and see the error message. Here's an example of what you might see (make sure to add the comment back in when you're done):

```
error: conflicting declaration 'std::map<StoreMe&,
    StoreMe&> pointers'
error: 'pointers' has a previous declaration as
    'std::map<StoreMe*, StoreMe*> pointers'
```

REMEMBER

References are out of the question because the map is making a copy of everything you put in it.

Working with copies

All C++ containers, not just maps, generally make copies of whatever you stick inside them as shown in the previous section. The Vectors3 example, shown in Listing 6-6, replicates the essential functionality of the Maps2 example shown in Listing 6-5.

LISTING 6-6: **The vector Version of the Maps2 Example**

```cpp
#include <iostream>
#include <vector>

using namespace std;

class StoreMe {
public:
  int Item;
};

int main() {
  vector<StoreMe> instances;
  StoreMe value1 = {20};
  StoreMe value2 = {40};
  instances.push_back(value1);
  instances.push_back(value2);

  value1.Item = 12345;
  cout << instances[0].Item << endl;
  instances[0].Item = 34567;
  cout << instances[0].Item << endl;
```

```
    vector<StoreMe*> pointers;
    StoreMe value10 = {20};
    StoreMe value11 = {40};
    pointers.push_back(& value10);
    pointers.push_back(& value11);

    value10.Item = 12345;
    cout << (*pointers[0]).Item << endl;
    return 0;
}
```

Oddly enough, the output from this example is precisely the same as the Maps2 example and for the same reason. Whether the container is a vector or a map doesn't matter; both of them hold copies of the objects or pointers you provide. Consequently, you can remember these two rules about deleting your original objects:

>> **When the container holds instances:** If you're putting instances in the container, you can delete the original instances after they're added. This is okay because the container has its own copies of the instances.

>> **When the container holds pointers:** If you're putting pointers in the container, you don't want to delete the original instances because the pointers in the container still point to these instances.

It's up to you to decide which method is better. But here are a couple of things to consider:

>> **Keeping instances around:** If you don't want to keep instances lying around, you can put the instances in the container, and it will make copies.

>> **Copyability:** Some classes, such as classes filled with pointers to other classes or classes that are enormous, don't copy well. In that case, you may want to put pointers in the container.

Comparing instances

When you work with classes that contain other classes (such as vector), you need to provide the class with a way to compare two things. The following sections describe how to provide comparison capability when working with containers.

Considering comparison issues

For humans comparing is easy, but it's not that easy for a computer. For example, suppose you have two pointers to string objects. The first points to a string containing abc. The second points to another string containing abc. When writing code, you must consider whether the two variables are equal:

» **Value:** When considering the value alone, the two string objects are equal.

» **Memory location:** When considering the pointer instead of the value, the two string objects aren't equal.

Now look at this code:

```
string *pointer3 = new string("abc");
string *pointer4 = pointer3;
```

These two pointers point to the same object, which means that the memory locations are equal. Because they point to the same object, they also contain the same string of characters. So, from a value perspective, they're also equal.

REMEMBER

You need to know this distinction because when you create a container class that holds instances of your object, often the class needs to know how to compare objects. This is particularly true in the case of map, which holds pairs of items, and you locate the items based on the first element of the pair — the key element. When you tell map to find an item based on a key, map must search through its list of pairs until it finds one such that the key in the pair is equal to the search term (key) you passed in to the search. However, you need to consider these essentials when working with the keys:

» When using the pointer approach, two keys could contain the same value but point to different memory locations. So, you must consider whether the key search is based on value or memory location.

» When sorting the keys to make them easier to access in order, you must consider whether value is the only criterion by which to make the sort order correct.

Here's an example. You create a class called Employee that contains these properties: FirstName, LastName, and SocialSecurityNumber. Next, you create a Salary class that contains payroll information for an employee. This class has properties MonthlySalary and Deductions.

With these two objects in place, you create a map instance, where each key/value pair contains an Employee instance for the key and a Salary instance for the value. To look up an employee, you would make an instance of Employee and fill in the FirstName, LastName, and SocialSecurityNumber properties. You then retrieve the value based on this key. There are two issues here:

>> You'd create an instance and allow map to find the key that matches the instance. It's essential to know whether map is looking for the exact same instance or one identical to it. When looking for the exact same instance, you need a pointer to the original object, not a new object that you fill in with values.

>> If map is looking for an instance identical to the object you create, the search will fail if the employee changed names (such as during a marriage). In this case, your code needs logic to tell map to make the match based on the SocialSecurityNumber, without worrying about the other properties.

REMEMBER

The bottom line is that you need code within your classes to determine how to make comparisons. The comparisons are made based on what you see as essential data traits. These traits vary by dataset because how you use the dataset varies. Consequently, you can't create a one-size-fits-all solution; you must consider each dataset individually.

Performing comparisons

The previous section provides details on two issues you must resolve when comparing objects. Here's how to resolve these two issues: If you're dealing with your own classes, in addition to setting up a container class, you also provide a function that compares two instances of your own class. Your comparison function can determine whether two classes are equal, the first is less than the second, or the first is greater than the second.

REMEMBER

At first, how less than and greater than can apply to things like an Employee class may not seem apparent. But the idea behind less than and greater than is to give the container class a way to determine a sort order. For example, you might choose to sort an Employee class in one of these ways:

>> Social Security number

>> Last name, first name

>> First name, last name

>> Employee ID

>> Address

>> Organizational department

The point is that the computer can't make this decision; you need to choose how you want the data to appear. After you decide how you want them sorted, you'd create a function that determines when one record is less than, equal to, or greater than the other. If you want the list to sort by name, you would make your function look strictly at the names. But if you want your list to sort by Social Security number, you would write your function to compare the Social Security numbers.

The Maps3 example, shown in Listing 6-7, contains a map class with a comparison function that determines whether two keys are equal.

LISTING 6-7: Containing Instances and Needing Functions That Compare Them

```
#include <iostream>
#include <map>

using namespace std;

class Emp {
public:
  string Nickname;
  string SSN;

  Emp(string anickname, string asocial) :
    Nickname(anickname),
    SSN(asocial) {}

  Emp() : Nickname(""), SSN("") {}
};

class Salary {
public:
  int YearlyInc;
  int Taxes;

  Salary(int aannual, int adeductions) :
      YearlyInc(aannual),
      Taxes(adeductions) {}

  Salary() : YearlyInc(0), Taxes(0) {}
};

bool operator < (const Emp& first, const Emp& second) {
  return first.Nickname < second.Nickname;
}
```

```
int main() {
  map<Emp, Salary> employees;

  Emp emp1("sparky", "123-22-8572");
  Salary sal1(135000, 18);
  employees[emp1] = sal1;

  Emp emp2("buzz", "234-33-5784");
  Salary sal2(150000, 23);
  employees[emp2] = sal2;

  // Now test it out!
  Emp emptest("sparky", "");
  cout << employees[emptest].YearlyInc << endl;
  return 0;
}
```

When you run this application, you see the YearlyInc member of the Salary value, where the key is an Employee with the name sparky:

```
135000
```

Now notice a couple things about this code. First, to locate the salary for Sparky, you don't need the Employee instance for Sparky. Instead, you create an instance of Employee and set up the Nickname member without worrying about the SSN member. Then you retrieve the value by using the bracket notation for map:

```
cout << employees[emptest].YearlyInc << endl;
```

The map code uses the less-than function to perform this task. The < function compares only the Nickname members, not the SSN member. Notice that this function must return a bool value and that you precede the < with the operator keyword, defining this as an *operator function* — one that defines an operation between operands. You could change things around a bit by comparing the SSN members like so:

```
bool operator < (const Emp& first, const Emp& second) {
  return first.SSN < second.SSN;
}
```

Then you can locate Sparky's salary based on the SSN:

```
Employee emptest("", "123-22-8572");
cout << employees[emptest].SSN << endl;
```

A single < function may not seem like enough to perform all the required comparisons, such as equality. However, the code calls the less-than function twice, the second time flip-flopping the order of the parameters; and if the function returns false both times, the computer determines that they are equal. Using this approach makes life easier because you need to provide only a single comparison function.

UNDERSTANDING THE DEFAULT < FUNCTION

Containers in the Standard Library have a default < function. If you don't supply a < function of your own, the container supplies this default < function for you. This default function relies on a template class called less. This template is simple: It includes a single method that returns the Boolean value:

```
x < y
```

For most basic types, the default works fine. For example, the compiler can easily use the default when you're working with integers. However, the compiler doesn't understand the < operator when working with custom classes unless you provide your own < operator function, as you see everywhere else in this chapter. However, because the container takes a class in its parameter that defaults to the class less, you can put together your own class and use that instead of writing your own < operator function. Here's a sample:

```
class MyLess {
public:
  bool operator()(const MyClass &x, const MyClass &y) const {
    return x.Name < y.Name;
  }
};
```

Then when you create, for example, a map, you pass this class as a third parameter, rather than relying on the default:

```
map<MyClass, MyClass, MyLess> mymap;
```

Then you don't need your own less-than function. The advantage of this approach is that you now have a standardized < function implementation to use everywhere, and it's especially helpful when working within a team environment.

Iterating through a container

Containers in the Standard Library provide an overview of the container's content. If you have a container filled with objects ,you normally get an overview of what's there, but being able to drill down into the details would be nice. You use an *iterator* to drill down into the container. An iterator works with a container to let you step object by object through the container. The following sections tell you about iterators and how to work with them.

Working with iterators

Each container class contains an embedded type called `iterator`. You use the fully qualified name to create an iterator instance. For example, if you have a `map` that holds integers and strings, as in `map<int, string>`, you create an `iterator` instance like this:

```
map<string, int>::iterator loopy
```

Although `loopy` is an instance of `iterator`, some serious `typedef`ing is going on, and, in fact, `loopy` is a pointer to an item stored inside the container. To initialize `loopy` to point to the first item in the container, you call the container's `begin()` method, storing the results in `loopy`. Then `loopy` will point to the first item in the container. You can access the item by dereferencing `loopy`; then, when you're finished, you can move to the next item by incrementing `loopy` like this:

```
loopy++;
```

You can use this technique in various ways, such as by using the call to `reverse_copy()` shown previously in Listing 6-3. You can tell whether you're finished by checking to see whether `loopy` points to the last item in the container. To do this, you call the container's `end()` method and compare `loopy` to the `end()` value. If it's equal, you're done. The following few lines of code perform these steps:

```
vector<string>::iterator vectorloop = Words.begin();
while (vectorloop != Words.end())
{
    cout << *vectorloop << endl;
    vectorloop++;
}
```

You can see the type used for the iterator, in this case called `vectorloop`, which is initialized by calling `begin()`. `vectorloop` is dereferenced to access\the data, and is then incremented to get to the next item. The `while` loop tests `vectorloop` against the results of end() to determine when the processing is complete. The Iterators example code, shown in Listing 6-8, shows a more complete example of how to use an iterator.

LISTING 6-8: **Iterating**

```cpp
#include <iostream>
#include <map>
#include <vector>

using namespace std;

int main() {
  // Iterating through a map
  map<string, int> NumberWords;
  NumberWords["ten"] = 10;
  NumberWords["twenty"] = 20;
  NumberWords["thirty"] = 30;

  map<string, int>::iterator loopy = NumberWords.begin();
  while (loopy != NumberWords.end()) {
    cout << loopy->first << " ";
    cout << loopy->second << endl;
    loopy++;
  }

  // Iterating through a vector
  vector<string> Words;
  Words.push_back("hello");
  Words.push_back("there");
  Words.push_back("ladies");
  Words.push_back("and");
  Words.push_back("aliens");

  vector<string>::iterator vectorloop = Words.begin();
  while (vectorloop != Words.end()) {
    cout << *vectorloop << endl;
    vectorloop++;
  }
  return 0;
}
```

When you compile and run this application, you see the following output:

```
ten 10
thirty 30
twenty 20
hello
there
ladies
and
aliens
```

Avoiding pointer problems

When you create a vector, it allocates some space for the data you put in it. When the memory fills with data, the vector resizes itself, adding more space. To perform this task, vector uses the old memory-shuffle trick where it first allocates a bigger chunk of memory; then it copies the existing data into the beginning of that bigger chunk of memory, and finally it frees the original chunk of memory.

WARNING

Saving the pointer you receive when you use the various iterator functions to access a certain vector item (giving you a pointer to the item) is a bad idea because, after vector allocates more memory, that pointer will no longer be valid. It will point to somewhere in the original memory block that's no longer being used. The IteratorPointer example, shown in Listing 6-9, helps you understand the ramifications of this problem.

LISTING 6-9: **Seeing the Pointer Problem in Action**

```cpp
#include <iostream>
#include <vector>

using namespace std;

int main() {
  vector<int> test{1, 2, 3};

  vector<int>::iterator i1 = test.begin();
  i1++;
  cout << &i1 << endl;

  test.push_back(4);

  vector<int>::iterator i2 = test.begin();
  i2++;
  cout << &i2 << endl;
}
```

When you run this example, the code creates test with space for three items. The code then prints the address of the second item. Adding just one item means that test has to resize. The code then prints the address for the second item. The outputs won't match because the pointer to the second item changed during the resizing process.

A map of pairs in your hand

When you iterate through map, you get back not just the value of each item nor do you get just the key of each item. Instead, you get back a pair of things — the key and the value together. These objects live inside an instance of a template class called Pair, which has two properties, first and second.

The first member refers to the key in the pair, and the second member refers to the value in the pair. When you iterate through map, the iterator points to an instance of Pair, so you can grab the key by looking at first and the value by looking at second. Be careful: Pair is the internal storage bin inside map. You're not looking at copies; you're looking at the actual data in map. If you change the data, as in this code

```
while (loopy != NumberWords.end())
{
    loopy->second = loopy->second * 2;
    loopy++;
}
```

you change the value stored in map — not a copy of it.

The Great Container Showdown

The sections that follow provide a rundown of containers available in the Standard Library. Each container has a different purpose. In the following sections, you see where you can use each of them.

Associating and storing with a set

First things first: set is not a mathematical set. If you have any background in mathematics, you've likely come across the notion of a set. In math, a set doesn't have an order to it. It's a group of well-defined distinct objects stored in a collection.

In the Standard Library, set has an order to it. However, like a math set, set doesn't allow duplicates. If you try to put an item in set that's already there, set will ignore your attempt to do so. The Sets example, shown in Listing 6-10, demonstrates how to use set.

LISTING 6-10: | **Using set to Look up Items**

```cpp
#include <iostream>
#include <set>

using namespace std;

class Emp {
public:
  string Nickname;
  string SSN;

  Emp(string anickname, string asocial) :
    Nickname(anickname),
    SSN(asocial) {}

  Emp() : Nickname(""), SSN("") {}
};

bool operator < (const Emp& first, const Emp& second) {
  return first.SSN < second.SSN;
}

ostream& operator << (ostream &out, const Emp &emp) {
  cout << "(" << emp.Nickname;
  cout << "," << emp.SSN;
  cout << ")";
  return out;
}

int main() {
  set<Emp> employees;

  Emp emp1("sparky", "123-22-8572");
  employees.insert(emp1);
  Emp emp2("buzz", "234-33-5784");
  employees.insert(emp2);
  Emp emp3("albert", "123-22-8572");
  employees.insert(emp3);
```

(continued)

LISTING 6-10: *(continued)*

```
Emp emp4("sputz", "199-19-0000");
employees.insert(emp4);

// List the items
set<Emp>::iterator iter = employees.begin();
while (iter != employees.end())
{
  cout << *iter << endl;
  iter++;
}

// Find an item
cout << "Finding..." << endl;
Emp findemp("", "123-22-8572");
iter = employees.find(findemp);
cout << *iter << endl;
return 0;
}
```

When you compile and run this example, you see the following output:

```
(sparky,123-22-8572)
(sputz,199-19-0000)
(buzz,234-33-5784)
Finding...
(sparky,123-22-8572)
```

Listing 6-10 includes an Employee class along with a < operator that compares the SSN member of two Employee instances. This comparison results in two things:

>> **Ordering:** The items in set are in Social Security number order. This isn't true with all containers, but it's the way a set works.

>> **Duplicates:** The set ignores any attempt to add two employees with matching SSN values (even if other properties differ).

You can see in this listing that the code tries to add two employees with the same SSN values:

```
Employee emp1("sparky", "123-22-8572");
employees.insert(emp1);
```

and

```
Employee emp3("albert", "123-22-8572");
employees.insert(emp3);
```

Later, when the code prints all the items in set, you see only the one for "sparky", not the one for "albert". set ignored the second employee.

Finding an item in set is interesting. You create an instance of Employee and fill in only the SSN value, because that's the only property that the < function looks at. Call find() to perform the search. The find() function returns an iterator because the iterator type is really a typedef for a pointer to an item inside set. To access the item, you dereference the pointer.

TIP

Listing 6-7 shows a handy function that lets you use the Employee instance with cout by overloading the insertion (<<) operator function. This function's header looks like this:

```
ostream& operator << (ostream &out, const Employee &emp) {
```

The first parameter represents cout, and the second is the output value. Inside this function, you write to cout the individual members of the Employee. It also helps to know that you can perform map comparisons as needed using the same technique found in the "Understanding the default < function" sidebar. This same technique works with a class, but it requires more coding to implement.

SHOWDOWN: MAPS VERSUS SETS

It's important to realize the difference between map and set. map lets you store information based on a key, through which you can retrieve a value. Listing 6-7, presented earlier in the "Performing comparisons" section, shows an example in which the key is an Emp instance and the value is a Salary instance. But with set, you can achieve something similar: Listing 6-10 could use a single class containing both Emp and Salary information. Also, you can see in Listing 6-10 that it's possible to look up the Emp instance based on nothing but a Social Security number. So in this sense, the Listing 6-10 example shows a map in which the key is a Social Security number and the value is the rest of the employee information. The fact is, you can often accomplish associations with set, as you can with map. The advantage to set is that you need to store only one instance for each item, whereas with map, you must have two instances, both a key and a value. The advantage to map is that you can use the nice bracket notation. The choice is yours.

Unionizing and intersecting sets

When you work with sets, you commonly do the following:

» Combine two sets to get the union (all the elements in both sets without any duplicates).

» Find the common elements to get the intersection (those unique elements that appear in both sets).

When you `#include` `<set>`, you automatically get a couple of handy functions for finding the union and intersection of some sets. The `Sets2` example, shown in Listing 6-11, demonstrates how you can find the intersection and union of two sets.

LISTING 6-11: **Finding an Intersection and a Union Is Easy!**

```
#include <iostream>
#include <set>
#include <algorithm>

using namespace std;

void DumpClass(set<string> *myset) {
  set<string>::iterator iter = myset->begin();
  while (iter != myset->end())
  {
    cout << *iter << endl;
    iter++;
  }
}

int main() {
  set<string> English;
  English.insert("Zeus");
  English.insert("Magellan");
  English.insert("Vulcan");
  English.insert("Ulysses");
  English.insert("Columbus");

  set<string> History;
  History.insert("Vulcan");
  History.insert("Ulysses");
  History.insert("Ra");
  History.insert("Odin");
```

```
set<string> Intersect;
insert_iterator<set<string> >
  IntersectIterate(Intersect, Intersect.begin());
set_intersection(English.begin(), English.end(),
  History.begin(), History.end(), IntersectIterate);
cout << "===Intersection===" << endl;
DumpClass(&Intersect);

set<string> Union;
insert_iterator<set<string> >
  UnionIterate(Union, Union.begin());
set_union(English.begin(), English.end(),
  History.begin(), History.end(), UnionIterate);
cout << endl << "===Union===" << endl;
DumpClass(&Union);
return 0;
}
```

When you run the code in Listing 6-11, you see this output:

```
===Intersection===
Ulysses
Vulcan

===Union===
Columbus
Magellan
Odin
Ra
Ulysses
Vulcan
Zeus
```

But as you can see, something a little bizarre is in the code. Specifically, this part isn't exactly simple:

```
insert_iterator<set<string> >
  IntersectIterate(Intersect, Intersect.begin());
```

This code is used in the call to set_intersection(). It's a variable declaration. The first line is the type of the variable, a template called insert_iterator. The template parameter is the type of set, in this case set<string>.

The next line is the instance name, IntersectIterate, and the constructor requires two things: the set that will hold the intersection (called Intersect) and an iterator pointing to the beginning of the set, which is Intersect.begin().

The variable that these two lines create is an iterator, which is a helper object that another function can use to insert multiple items into a list. In this case, the function is set_intersection(). The set_intersection() function doesn't take the sets as input; instead, it takes the beginning and ending iterators of the two sets, along with the IntersectIterate iterator declared earlier. You can see in Listing 6-11 that those are the five items passed to the set_intersection() function. After calling set_intersection(), the Intersect object contains the intersection of the two sets. set_union() works precisely the same way as set_intersection(), except it figures out the union of the two sets, not the intersection.

REMEMBER

To use set_intersection() and set_union(), you need to add #include <algorithm> to the top of your listing. This is one of the header files in the Standard Library.

TIP

If you find the code in Listing 6-11 particularly ugly, a slightly easier way to call set_intersection(), one that doesn't require you to directly create an instance of insert_iterator, is available. It turns out that a function exists that will do it for you. To use this function, you can remove the declarations for IntersectIterate and UnionIterate, and then instead call set_intersection(), like this:

```
set_intersection(English.begin(), English.end(),
    History.begin(), History.end(),
    inserter(Intersect, Intersect.begin()));
```

The third line simply calls inserter(), which creates an instance of insert_iterator for you. Then you can do the same for set_union():

```
set_union(English.begin(), English.end(),
    History.begin(), History.end(),
    inserter(Union, Union.begin()));
```

Listing with list

A list is a simple container similar to an array, except you can't access the members of list by using a bracket notation as you can in vector or with an array. You don't use list when you need to access only one item in the list; you use it when you plan to *traverse* through the list, item by item.

To add items to a list, use the list's push_front() method or its push_back() method. The push_front() function inserts the item in the beginning of the list, in front of all the others that are presently in the list. If you use push_front() several times in a row, the items will be in the reverse order from which you put them in. The push_back() function adds the item to the end of the list. So if you put items in a list by using push_back(), their order will be the same as the order in which you added them. Using insert() and splice() enables you to place items in other locations in the list. You use an iterator to find the location you want and then splice the new item at that location.

REMEMBER

For operations in which you need a pointer to an item in the list, you need to use an iterator. An *iterator* is simply a typedef for a pointer to an item in the list; however, it points to the item in the list, not the original item you added to the list. Remember, the containers hold copies. Thus, if you do an insert() into a list and point to an original item, that item won't be a member of the list, and the insert() won't work.

TIP

Although the list template includes an insert() function, this function has only very special uses. To use insert(), you must have a pointer to an item in the list — that is, you need to have an iterator that you obtain by traversing the list. It has no find() function, and so really the only time you would use the insert() function is if you're already working your way through the list. But if you do need to do an insert and you're willing to use iterators to move through the list to find the location where you want to put the new item, insert() will do the job.

The Lists example, shown in Listing 6-12, demonstrates lists by using a duck metaphor (as in, getting all your ducks in a row). This example creates a list, adds ducks, and then reverses it. Next, the code creates a second list and splices its members into the first list.

LISTING 6-12: **Handling Items in a List Template**

```
#include <iostream>
#include <list>

using namespace std;

class Duck {
public:
  string name;
  int weight;
  int length;
};
```

(continued)

LISTING 6-12: *(continued)*

```cpp
ostream& operator << (ostream &out, const Duck &duck) {
  cout << "(" << duck.name;
  cout << "," << duck.weight;
  cout << "," << duck.length;
  cout << ")";
  return out;
}

void Dump(list<Duck> *mylist) {
  list<Duck>::iterator iter = mylist->begin();
  while (iter != mylist->end())
  {
    cout << *iter << endl;
    iter++;
  }
}

list<Duck>::iterator Move(list<Duck> *mylist, int pos) {
  list<Duck>::iterator res = mylist->begin();
  for (int loop = 1; loop <= pos; loop++)
  {
    res++;
  }
  return res;
}

bool operator < (const Duck& first, const Duck& second) {
  return first.name < second.name;
}

int main() {
  list<Duck> Inarow;

  // Push some at the beginning
  Duck d1 = {"Jim", 20, 15}; // Braces notation!
  Inarow.push_front(d1);
  Duck d2 = {"Sally", 15, 12};
  Inarow.push_front(d2);

  // Push some at the end
  Duck d3 = {"Betty", 18, 25};
  Inarow.push_front(d3);
  Duck d4 = {"Arnold", 19, 26};
  Inarow.push_front(d4);
```

```cpp
        // Display the ducks
        cout << "===Ducks===" << endl;
        Dump(&Inarow);

        // Reverse
        Inarow.reverse();
        cout << "\n==Reversed==" << endl;
        Dump(&Inarow);

        // Create the second list.
        list<Duck> extras;
        Duck d5 = {"Grumpy", 8, 8};
        extras.push_back(d5);
        Duck d6 = {"Sleepy", 8, 8};
        extras.push_back(d6);

        // Display the extras list.
        cout << "\n===Extras===" << endl;
        Dump(&extras);

        // Determine the positions.
        list<Duck>::iterator first = Move(&extras, 0);
        list<Duck>::iterator last = Move(&extras, 2);
        list<Duck>::iterator into = Move(&Inarow, 2);

        // Perform the splicing.
        Inarow.splice(into, extras, first, last);
        cout << "\n==Extras After Splice==" << endl;
        Dump(&extras);
        cout << "\n==Inarow After Splice==" << endl;
        Dump(&Inarow);

        // Sort the list.
        Inarow.sort();
        cout << "\n===Sorted===" << endl;
        Dump(&Inarow);
        return 0;
}
```

Move() moves to a position in the list. This function may seem counterproductive because the list template doesn't allow random access. But you need three iterators to perform the splice: two to target the start and end position of the second list (the source list) and one to target the position in the first list used to hold the spliced members. Move( ) locates the target position.

Move( ) is a template function. However, when calling the function, you don't provide the type name in angle brackets; the compiler determines which class version to use based on the object type passed into the function as a parameter.

To use sort( ), you must provide a < operator function, as described in earlier examples. Here's the application output:

```
===Ducks===
(Arnold,19,26)
(Betty,18,25)
(Sally,15,12)
(Jim,20,15)

==Reversed==
(Jim,20,15)
(Sally,15,12)
(Betty,18,25)
(Arnold,19,26)

===Extras===
(Grumpy,8,8)
(Sleepy,8,8)

==Extras After Splice==

==Inarow After Splice==
(Jim,20,15)
(Sally,15,12)
(Grumpy,8,8)
(Sleepy,8,8)
(Betty,18,25)
(Arnold,19,26)

===Sorted===
(Arnold,19,26)
(Betty,18,25)
(Grumpy,8,8)
(Jim,20,15)
(Sally,15,12)
(Sleepy,8,8)
```

You can see the elements that were inside the two lists before and after the splice; the ducks moved from one list to another.

SHOWDOWN: LISTS VERSUS VECTORS

Lists provide sequential access, which means that you can't drop into the middle of the list and look at whatever item is stored there (as you can with a vector). If you want to look at the items in the list, you must start at the beginning or the end and work your way through it one item at a time. A vector allows random access using brackets, as in MyVector[3]. This requirement may seem like a disadvantage for the list, but the ANSI document says that "many algorithms only need sequential access anyway." Lists have definite advantages. The list template allows you to splice together multiple lists, and it has good support for sorting the list, for splicing members out of one list and into another, and for merging multiple lists.

Stacking the deque

A double-ended queue, deque (pronounced "deck"), container is a sequential list of items like vector and list. Like vectors and unlike lists, deques allow random access using bracket notation. Unlike vector, deque lets you *push* (insert) items at the beginning or end and *pop* (remove) items off the beginning or end. To create a deque that holds integers, do something like this:

```
deque<int> mydek;
mydek.push_front(10);
mydek.push_front(20);
mydek.push_back(30);
mydek.push_back(40);
```

Then you can loop through the deque, accessing its members with a bracket, as if it's an array:

```
int loop;
for (loop = 0; loop < mydek.size(); loop++) {
    cout << mydek[loop] << endl;
}
```

You can also grab items off the front or back of the deque. Here's an example from the front:

```
while (mydek.size() > 0) {
    cout << mydek.front() << endl;
    mydek.pop_front();
}
```

Two functions show up here, front() and pop_front(). The front() function returns a reference to the item at the front of the deque. The pop_front() function removes the item that's at the front of the deque.

Waiting in line with stacks and queues

Two common programming data structures are in the Standard Library:

>> **Stack:** You put items on top of a stack one by one — and you take items off the top of the stack one by one. You can add several items, one after the other, before taking an item off the top. This process is sometimes called a Last In, First Out (LIFO) algorithm.

>> **Queue:** A queue is like waiting in line at the post office — the line gets longer as people arrive. Each new person goes to the back of the line. People leave from the front of the line. Like the stack, the queue also has an alternate name: it's a First In, First Out (FIFO) algorithm.

To use the Standard Library to make a stack, you can use a deque, a list, or a vector as the underlying storage bin. Then you declare the stack, as in the following example:

```
stack<int, vector<int> > MyStack;
```

Or you can optionally use the default, which is deque:

```
stack<int> MyStack;
```

For a queue, you can't use vector because vectors don't include operations for dealing with the front of an item list. So, you can use either deque or list. Here's a line of code that uses list:

```
queue<int, list<int> > MyQueue;
```

Or here's a line of code that uses deque by default:

```
queue<int> MyQueue;
```

You normally perform three operations with a stack and a queue:

>> **push:** When you add an item to a stack or queue, you *push* the item. This action puts the item on top of the stack or at the back of the queue.

>> **peek:** When you look at the top of the stack or the front of the queue, you *peek*. The peek operation doesn't remove the item.

>> **pop:** When you remove an item from the top of a stack or from the front of the queue, you pop it off.

To peek at the front of a queue, you call the front() method. For a stack, you call the top() method. For pushing and popping, the queue and stack each include a push() function and a pop() function. The StackAndQueue example, shown in Listing 6-13, demonstrates both a stack and a queue.

LISTING 6-13: **Creating a Stack and a Queue**

```
#include <iostream>
#include <stack>
#include <queue>

using namespace std;

void StackDemo() {
  cout << "===Stack Demo===" << endl;
  stack<int, vector<int> > MyStack;
  MyStack.push(5);
  MyStack.push(10);
  MyStack.push(15);

  cout << MyStack.top() << endl;
  MyStack.pop();
```

(continued)

LISTING 6-13: *(continued)*

```
        cout << MyStack.top() << endl;
        MyStack.pop();

        MyStack.push(40);
        cout << MyStack.top() << endl;
        MyStack.pop();
}

void QueueDemo() {
        cout << "===Queue Demo===" << endl;
        queue<int> MyQueue;
        MyQueue.push(5);
        MyQueue.push(10);
        MyQueue.push(15);

        cout << MyQueue.front() << endl;
        MyQueue.pop();
        cout << MyQueue.front() << endl;
        MyQueue.pop();

        MyQueue.push(40);
        cout << MyQueue.front() << endl;
        MyQueue.pop();
}

int main() {
        StackDemo();
        QueueDemo();
        return 0;
}
```

REMEMBER

When you specify a container to use inside the stack or queue, remember to put a space between the closing angle brackets. Otherwise, the compiler reads it as a single insertion operator, >>, and gets confused. Here is the output from this example:

```
===Stack Demo===
15
10
40
===Queue Demo===
5
10
15
```

Copying Containers

Structures are easy to copy when using well-designed class libraries — meaning that each container class contains both a copy constructor and an equal operator. To copy a container, you either set one equal to the other or pass the first container into the constructor of the second. The CopyContainer example shown in Listing 6-14 demonstrates how to perform this task.

LISTING 6-14: **Copying Containers Couldn't Be Easier**

```cpp
#include <iostream>
#include <map>

using namespace std;

class Tasty {
public:
  string Dessert;
};

bool operator < (const Tasty & One, const Tasty & Two) {
  return One.Dessert < Two.Dessert;
}

class Nutrition {
public:
  int VitaminC;
  int Potassium;
};

int main() {
  map<Tasty, Nutrition> ItsGoodForMe;
  Tasty ap = {"Apple Pie"}; // Braces notation!
  Nutrition apn = {7249, 9722};
  Tasty ic = {"Ice Cream"};
  Nutrition icn = {2459, 19754};
  Tasty cc = {"Chocolate Cake"};
  Nutrition ccn = {9653, 24905};
  Tasty ms = {"Milk Shake"};
  Nutrition msn = {46022, 5425};

  ItsGoodForMe[ap] = apn;
  ItsGoodForMe[ic] = icn;
```

(continued)

LISTING 6-14: *(continued)*

```
ItsGoodForMe[cc] = ccn;
ItsGoodForMe[ms] = msn;

map<Tasty,Nutrition> Duplicate1 = ItsGoodForMe;
map<Tasty,Nutrition> Duplicate2(ItsGoodForMe);
ItsGoodForMe[ap].Potassium = 20;
Duplicate1[ap].Potassium =40;

cout << ItsGoodForMe[ap].Potassium << endl;
cout << Duplicate1[ap].Potassium << endl;
cout << Duplicate2[ap].Potassium << endl;
return 0;
}
```

You can see that Listing 11-14 contains two classes, Tasty and Nutrition. A map called ItsGoodForMe associates Tasty instances with Nutrition instances. The code copies map twice, using both an equals sign and a copy constructor:

```
map<Tasty,Nutrition> Duplicate1 = ItsGoodForMe;
map<Tasty,Nutrition> Duplicate2(ItsGoodForMe);
```

The code changes one of the elements in the original map to see what happens and prints that element, as well as the corresponding element in the two copies (one of which is also changed). Here's the output:

```
20
40
9722
```

The output implies that the maps each have their own copies of the instances — that there's no sharing of instances between the maps.

REMEMBER

Containers hold copies, not originals. That's true when you copy containers, too. If you put a structure in a container and copy the container, the latter container has its own copy of the structure. To change the structure, you must change all copies of it. The way around this is to put pointers inside the containers. Then each container has its own copy of the pointer, but all these pointers point to the same one-and-only object.

Creating and Using Dynamic Arrays

Sometimes you don't know the array size you need until runtime. The default arrays provided with C++ rely on static sizes. In other words, you need to know what size array you need at the time you write the code. Unfortunately, the real world is dynamic — it changes. The earlier sections of this chapter discuss a number of array alternatives, such as stacks, queues, and deques. However, these solutions all require that you use a library. They also tend to increase the memory requirements of your application and slow it down as well. You have another alternative in the form of dynamic arrays. The following sections describe dynamic arrays and show how to use them. You need a minimum of C++ 11 to use these examples.

A dynamic array relies on the *heap,* the common area of memory that your application allocates for use by your application's functions. (See the "Heaping and Stacking the Variables" section of Book 1 Chapter 8 for more details.) You create a pointer to a variable of the correct type and then allocate memory for the resulting array. The functionality for performing this task is found in the new header file, so you need to include it as part of your application. The DynamicArray example, shown in Listing 6-15, demonstrates the use of a dynamic array.

LISTING 6-15: **Creating and Using Dynamic Arrays**

```
#include <iostream>
#include <new>

using namespace std;

int main() {
  int HowMany;
  int* DynArray;
  cout << "How many numbers would you like?" << endl;
  cin >> HowMany;
  DynArray = new (nothrow) int[HowMany];

  if (DynArray == nullptr)
    cout << "Error: Could not allocate memory!";
  else {
    for(int i = 0; i < HowMany; i++)
      DynArray[i] = i;
```

(continued)

LISTING 6-15: *(continued)*

```
    cout << "Displaying entries:" << endl;
    for (int i = 0; i < HowMany; i++)
      cout << DynArray[i] << endl;

    delete[] DynArray;
  }
  return 0;
}
```

The example begins by creating variables to hold the number of array elements and the array itself, which is a pointer to an array of int elements. The application asks you how many array elements to create. It then uses the new operator to create the dynamic array, DynArray. Notice the technique used to do this. The new operator is followed by (nothrow). This tells the application that if there isn't enough memory to create the array, it should return a nullptr value, which is simply a pointer that doesn't point to anything.

WARNING

The (nothrow) method may not work with certain compiler versions, especially when using the GNU Compiler Collection (GCC). The (nothrow) still works for low memory conditions, but it doesn't work for conditions created explicitly as part of the application execution. In this case, you see a std::bad_array_new_length exception under these conditions:

>> The array length is negative

>> The total size of the new array would exceed implementation-defined maximum value

>> The number of initializer-clauses exceeds the number of elements to initialize

TIP

Normally, the application would display an incomprehensible error message that only geeks could love if there wasn't enough memory. Using the (nothrow) approach gives you the opportunity to handle the error differently. The application handles the error by displaying a human-readable error message if (DynArray == nullptr).

You work with a dynamic array just as you do any other array. The example shows how to fill the array with data and to display the data onscreen. The array has the same capabilities, advantages, and disadvantages of any other array. However, when you get done using the array, you need to use the delete[] operator to delete the dynamic array and free the memory it uses for some other purpose. The output from this example looks like this if you request four array elements:

```
How many numbers would you like?
4
Displaying entries:
0
1
2
3
```

Working with Unordered Data

Creating data that has a particular order is appealing because it's a) easier to search and b) it makes certain tasks, such as removing old elements, easier. However, creating an ordered set of information is also problematic because you need to spend time keeping it in order. Newer versions of C++ provide access to an unordered set that is both searchable and easy to maintain. It has the advantage of adding the data in any order in which it comes. Minimal overhead is associated with trying to keep the data in a particular order. The following sections provide an overview of using unordered data. You need a minimum of C++ 11 to use these examples.

Using std::unordered_set to create an unordered set

Like the other containers discussed in this chapter, an unordered_set provides a particular method for storing data in a manner that makes it easy to access later. In this case, you have access to functions that insert() and erase() elements from the container. A special function, emplace() enables you to add new elements only if the element doesn't exist. Otherwise, the unordered set will allow as many duplicates as you want (and you can easily count them using count()). You can also use the find() function to track down elements that you want. Special functions tell you when you're at the beginning or end of the set.

Manipulating unordered sets

The easiest way to see how an unordered set works is to create one. The UnorderedSet example, shown in Listing 6-16, demonstrates how to use the various unordered_set features to maintain a listing of colors.

LISTING 6-16: **Creating and Using Dynamic Arrays**

```cpp
#include <iostream>
#include <unordered_set>

using namespace std;

int main() {
  unordered_set<string> Colors;
  Colors.insert("Red");
  Colors.insert("Green");
  Colors.insert("Blue");

  if(Colors.find("Red")!= Colors.end())
    cout << "Found Red!" << endl;

  auto ReturnValue = Colors.emplace("Red");
  if(!ReturnValue.second)
    cout << "Red is Already in Set!" << endl;

  cout << "There are " << Colors.count("Red")
       << " Red entries." << endl;

  ReturnValue = Colors.emplace("Orange");
  if(!ReturnValue.second)
    cout << "Orange is Already in Set!" << endl;
  else
    cout << "Orange Added to Set!" << endl;

  Colors.erase("Red");
  if(Colors.find("Red")!= Colors.end())
    cout << "Found Red!" << endl;
  else
    cout << "Red Missing!" << endl;
  return 0;
}
```

The example begins by creating a new unordered_set, Colors. Notice that this is a template, so you need to provide a type for the information that the set will hold. The code uses the insert() function to add three colors to the set.

The find() function enables you to look for a particular value in the set. When the value is missing, the find() function returns end(), which means that the current position within the set is at the end.

This example uses the auto data type. ReturnValue is used to detect when a value that you want to add to the set using emplace() already exists. If the value already exists, unordered_set refuses to add it when you call emplace(). On the other hand, if you call insert(), unordered_set will add duplicate entries.

To remove entries from a set, you call erase() with the value you want to remove. In this case, the example removes the color Red. It then searches for Red using find(). As you might expect, Red isn't found this time. The output from this example is as follows:

```
Found Red!
Red is Already in Set!
There are 1 Red entries.
Orange Added to Set!
Red Missing!
```

Working with Ranges

C++ now offers support for ranges, which you can read about at https://en.cppreference.com/w/cpp/ranges. A *range* is the set of objects between a beginning point and an ending point. The concept of ranges depends on iterators. A *view* is an iteration that manages data in some manner, and a range acts on this iteration. The example in this section requires C++ 20. As mentioned elsewhere in the book, such as Book 1 Chapter 5, if your compiler doesn't offer C++ 20 support, you can use Wandbox (https://wandbox.org/).

The Ranges example, shown in Listing 6-17, gives you a starting point for working with both ranges and views in C++ 20. In this example, the code creates a vector, MyList, fills it with data, and then uses the ranges::size() method to determine the size MyList. The code then creates a view that filters MyList and places the result in Filtered. A for loop prints the result.

| LISTING 6-17: | **Working with Ranges and Views** |

```cpp
#include <iostream>
#include <vector>
#include <ranges>

using namespace std;
```

(continued)

LISTING 6-17: **(continued)**

```cpp
int main() {
  vector<int> MyList {9, 2, 1, 6, 3, 8, 4};
  cout << "There are " << ranges::size(MyList) <<
    " items in MyList" << endl;

  auto Filtered = MyList | views::filter([](int n){
    return n % 3 == 0; });
  cout << "Items divisible by 3: " << endl;
  for (int i : Filtered)
    cout << i << endl;
  return 0;
}
```

Filtered is a *range adapter*, which is an iterable range. To create this variable, you specify the list you want to use, such as MyList, a pipe symbol (|), and the view or views you want to create. This example uses views::filter(). When you want to create multiple views, you separate them with addition pipes. You can also find views that will transform your data, drop certain elements, split ranges, join ranges, and so on. Whatever the range adapter creates appears in Filtered. As the code shows, you iterate over the view using a standard for loop.

6
Reading and Writing Files

Contents at a Glance

Chapter **1**

Filing Information with the Streams Library

You've heard of rivers, lakes, and streams, and it's interesting just how many common words are used in computer programming. That's handy, because it lets programmers use words they already know with similar meaning. Using common terms makes it easier to visualize abstract concepts in a concrete way.

Most programmers think of a stream as a file — the type stored on a hard drive, Universal Serial Bus (USB) flash drive, or Secure Digital (SD) card. But streams go beyond just files. A *stream* is any type of data structure that you can access as a flow of data, essentially a sequence of bytes. Streams are used to access all sorts of devices, such as smart speakers. Rather than just fill a 500MB data structure and then drop it onto the hard drive, you write your data piece after piece; the information goes into the file.

Streams go further than a wide variety of devices, however. Opening an Internet connection and putting data on a remote computer usually requires a stream-based data structure. You write the data in sequence, one byte after another, as the data goes over the Internet like a stream of water, reaching the remote computer. The data you write first gets there first, followed by the next set of data you write, and so on.

This chapter discusses different kinds of streams available to you, the C++ programmer. In addition, you discover how to handle errors and use flags to modify how you open files.

REMEMBER

You don't have to type the source code for this chapter manually. In fact, using the downloadable source is a lot easier. You can find the source for this chapter in the \CPP_AIO4\BookVI\Chapter01 folder of the downloadable source. See the Introduction for details on how to find these source files.

Seeing a Need for Streams

When you write an application that deals with files, you must use a specific order:

1. Open the file.

Before you can use a file, you must open it. In doing so, you specify a filename.

2. Access the file.

After you open a file, you either store data into it (this is called *writing* data to the file) or get data out of it (this is called *reading* data from the file).

3. Close the file.

After you have finished reading from and writing to a file, you must close the file.

For example, an application that tracks your stocks and writes your portfolio to a file at the end of the day might do these steps:

1. Ask the user for a name of a file.

2. Open the file.

3. For each stock object, write the stock data to the file.

4. Close the file.

The next morning, when the application starts, it might want to read the information back in. Here's what it might do:

1. Ask the user for the name of the file.

2. Open the file.

3. While there's more data in the file, create a new Stock object.

4. Read an individual stock entry from the file.

5. Put the data into the Stock object.

6. Close the file.

REMEMBER

Here are a couple of reasons to close a file after you've finished using it:

>> **Other applications might be waiting to use the file.** Some operating systems allow an application to *lock* a file, meaning that no other applications can open the file while the application that locked the file is using it. In such situations, another application can use the file after you close it, but not until then.

>> **When you write to a file, the operating system decides whether to immediately write the information onto the hard drive or flash drive/SD card or to hold on to it and gather more information, finally writing it all as a single batch.** When you close a file, the operating system puts all your remaining data into the file. This is called *flushing* the file.

You have two ways to write to a file:

>> **Sequential access:** In sequential access, you write to a file or read from a file from beginning to end. With this approach, when you open the file, you normally specify whether you plan to read from or write to the file, but not both at the same time. After you open the file, if you're writing to the file, the data you write gets added continually to the end of the file. Or if you're reading from the file, you read the data at the beginning, and then you read the data that follows, and so on, up to the end.

>> **Random access:** With random access, you can read and write to any byte in a file, regardless of which byte you previously read or wrote. In other words, you can skip around. You can read some bytes and then move to another portion of the file and write some bytes, and then move elsewhere and write some more.

Back in the days of the C programming language, several library functions let you work with files. However, they stunk. They were cumbersome and made life difficult. So, when C++ came along, people quickly created a set of classes that made life with files much easier. These people used the stream metaphor we've been raving about. In the sections that follow, you discover how to open files, write to them, read from them, and close them.

Programming with the Streams Library

The libraries you use to work with streams are divided into various groups, each of which requires its own header. The libraries divide input and output into separate classes, as shown in Figure 1-1. In addition, the kind of input and output determines which header you use. The libraries also support specific commands that include `cin` and `cout` — the commands you have used for so many purposes so far.

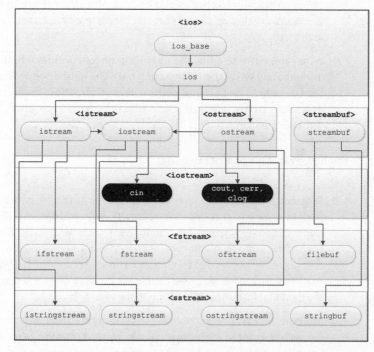

Now that you have a basic overview of how these various headers and commands work with the streams library to provide stream output, it's time to get the details. The following sections help you understand how to use code to create streams of data that could go to a file, Internet connection, or some other location, such as a smart speaker.

Getting the right header file

The streams library includes several classes that make your life much easier. It also has several classes that can make your life more complicated, mainly auxiliary classes that you rarely use. Here are three of the more common classes that you use:

>> ifstream: This is a stream you instantiate if you want to read from a file. The *if* part of the name stands for input file.

>> ofstream: This is a stream you instantiate if you want to write to a file. The *of* part of the name stands for output file.

>> fstream: This is a stream you instantiate if you want to both read and write to a file. The *f* part of the name stands for file (in a general sense, rather than specifically for input or output).

Before you can use the ifstream, ofstream, or fstream classes, you #include <fstream>. As with many C++ classes and objects, you find these classes inside the std namespace. Thus, when you want to use an item from the streams library, you must either

>> Prepend its name with std, as in this example:

```
std::ofstream outfile("MyFile.txt");
```

>> Include a using directive before the lines where you use the stream classes, as in this example:

```
using namespace std;
ofstream outfile("MyFile.txt");
```

Opening a file

Opening a file means to obtain access to a file on disk. The process of opening a file returns a variable that allows you to do things with that file, such as read or write it. You have two options for opening a file:

>> **Create a new file:** The file doesn't currently exist, so you must create a new one.

>> **Open an existing file:** The file does exist, so you open the existing one on disk.

Some operating systems treat these two methods as a single entity. The reason is that when you create a new file, normally you want to immediately start using it, which means that you want to create a new file and then open it. So the process of creating a file is often embedded right into the process of opening a file.

SEPARATING A PATHNAME

Everybody wants to be different and unique. The people who wrote Microsoft's MS-DOS operating system, instead of following in the tradition of using Unix's / for a pathname separator, decided to use \, thus adding the word *backslash* to the vocabularies of millions of people. So today, on Windows, you see such pathnames as `C:\MyDataFolder\MyMessyPath\DifficultToType\LetterToEditor.doc`. But on Unix, you see forward slashes, as in `/usr/something/LetterToEditor.doc`. In case you don't find this difference bad enough, think about what the backslash means in a string in C++. It means that another character follows, and the compiler interprets the two characters together as something else — a process called *escaping* the character. For example, \t means a tab, and \n means a newline character. To create a single backslash, you put two backslashes, which means that the earlier MS-DOS-style string must look like this if you use it in a C++ application:

```
"C:\\MyDataFolder\\MyMessyPath\\DifficultToType\\LetterToEditor.doc"
```

Yes, you must type every backslash twice if you want the compiler to get the correct string. But instead of doing this, you have a much better solution. Don't use backslashes at all, even if you're programming for Windows. When you write a C++ application on Windows, the libraries are smart enough to know that a forward slash works instead of a backslash. Therefore, you can use this string:

```
"C:/MyDataFolder/MyMessyPath/DifficultToType/LetterToEditor.doc"
```

In this book, you see the examples use the forward slash so that they work on both Unix and Windows.

When you open an existing file that you want to write to, you have several choices:

>> Erase the current contents; then write to the file.

>> Keep the existing contents:

- Write your information to the end of the file. This is called *appending* information to a file.

- Write your information to the beginning of the file. This is called *prepending* information to a file.

- Search for a particular location in the file and then add data at that point.

>> Overwrite all or part of the existing contents by replacing existing information with new information.

The `FileOutput01` example code, in Listing 1-1, shows you how to open a brand-new file, write some information to it, and then close it. (But wait, there's more: This version works whether you have the newer ANSI-compliant compilers or the older ones!)

Filing Information with the Streams Library

LISTING 1-1:   **Using Code That Opens a File and Writes to It**

```
#include <iostream>
#include <fstream>

using namespace std;

int main() {
  ofstream outfile("../MyFile.txt");
  outfile << "Hi" << endl;
  outfile.close();
  cout << "File Written!" << endl;
  return 0;
}
```

The short application in Listing 1-1 opens a file called `MyFile.txt`. (The `../` part of the file path places the file in the parent directory for the example, which is the `Chapter01` folder; see the "Finding your files" sidebar, in this chapter, for details.) The application opens the `MyFile.txt` file by creating a new instance of `ofstream`, which is a class for writing to a file. The next line of code writes the string `"Hi"` to the file. It uses the insertion operator, `<<`, just as `cout` does. In fact, `ofstream` is derived from the same class as `cout`, as shown in Figure 1-1, so anything you can do with `cout` you can also do with your file. When you finish writing to the file, you close it by calling the `close()` method.

If you want to open an existing file and append to it, you can modify Listing 1-1 slightly. All you do is change the arguments passed to the constructor, as follows:

```
ofstream outfile("MyFile.txt", ios_base::app);
```

The `ios::app` item is an enumeration inside a class called `ios`, and the `ios_base::app` item is an enumeration in the class called `ios_base`. The `ios` class is the base class from which the `ofstream` class is derived. The `ios` class also serves as a base class for `ifstream`, which is for reading files.

FINDING YOUR FILES

Whenever you open a new file, you must know where the file is, not just what the file is called. In other words, you need to supply both a *path* and a *filename,* not just a filename. You can obtain a path for your file in different ways, depending on your application. For example, you may be saving all your files in a particular directory; if so, you would then precede your filenames with that directory (that is, *path*) name. The string class makes this easy, as in this code:

```
const string MyPath = "c:\\GreatSoftwareInc";
string Filename = MyPath + "\\" + "MyFile.txt";
ofstream outfile(Filename);
```

Also, when you use a constant path, as shown in this example, you may, instead, store the pathname in an initialization file that lives on your user's computer, rather than *hardcode* it in your application as in this example. You may also include an Options window where your users can change the value of this path.

Paths can take on other forms. You don't need to create a *full path* to your file, which begins at the root directory of the hard drive and provides a complete description of every folder needed to access files. It's also possible to create a *relative path* to your file, which means using the current location as a starting point, using one or two periods as the starting point. Using one period (.) refers to the current directory and using two periods (..) refers to the parent directory. You can also combine periods.

- If you use .\MyData\MyFile.txt (with one period) as a path and the current directory is C:\GreatSoftwareInc\MyApp, the operating system looks for MyFile.txt in the C:\GreatSoftwareInc\MyApp\MyData folder.

- If you use ..\MyData\MyFile.txt (with two periods) as the path and the current directory is C:\GreatSoftwareInc\MyApp, the operating system looks for MyFile.txt in the C:\GreatSoftwareInc\MyData folder.

- If you use ..\..\MyData\MyFile.txt (with two sets of two periods) as the path and the current directory is C:\GreatSoftwareInc\MyApp, the operating system looks for MyFile.txt in the C:\MyData folder because now you're moving up two parent positions in the directory hierarchy.

Reading from a file

You can read from an existing file. You perform this task in a manner similar to using the cin object to read from the keyboard. The FileRead01 example, shown in Listing 1-2, opens the file created by Listing 1-1 and reads the string back in.

This example uses the parent directory again as a common place to create, update, and read files.

LISTING 1-2: **Using Code to Open a File and Read from It**

```
#include <iostream>
#include <fstream>

using namespace std;

int main() {
  string word;
  ifstream infile("../MyFile.txt");
  infile >> word;
  cout << word << endl;
  infile.close();
  return 0;
}
```

When you run this application, the string written earlier to the file in Listing 1-1 — Hi — appears onscreen.

Reading and writing a file

You may notice in Figure 1-1 that there is an fstream class that derives from iostream, which itself derives from both istream and ostream. Using the fstream class can save a lot of effort when you need to both read and write a file. The FileReadWrite01 example, shown in Listing 1-3, demonstrates how to both read and write the same file without closing the file handle first.

LISTING 1-3: **Reading and Writing a File Using a Single Handle**

```
#include <iostream>
#include <fstream>

using namespace std;

int main() {
  fstream outfile("../MyFile.txt",
                  ios::in | ios::out | ios::trunc);
  outfile << "Hi" << endl;
  outfile.flush();
```

(continued)

LISTING 1-3: **(continued)**

```
string Data;
outfile.seekg(0, ios::beg);
outfile >> Data;
outfile.close();

cout << "File Written!" << endl;
cout << Data << endl;
return 0;
}
```

The first part of this example works just like the example in Listing 1-1. You add opening modes to ensure that the handle works as anticipated: ios::in means that the file is open for input, ios::out means that the file is open for output, and ios::trunc means that the file is truncated (the old data is removed) before you add new data. Instead of closing the file, you call flush(), which ensures that the data actually appears on disk.

The example then creates an input string, Data, to receive information from the file. Before you can look at the file data, however, you must reposition the file pointer to point to the beginning of the file by using seekg(). A *file pointer* tells you the place where you will either read or write in a file. When you initially write to the file, the file pointer is at the end of the file, so to read the file you must reposition it to the beginning of the file. Notice that you now read the data just as you did in Listing 1-2.

Working with containers

You're not very likely to write single bits of data to a file in most cases. You usually want to work with something more complicated, like a container (Book 5, Chapter 6 tells you about various kinds of containers). The basic idea is to combine the file techniques in this chapter with the container techniques shown in Book 5, Chapter 6 to create an application that works with containers. Listing 1-4 shows the OutputVector example that demonstrates how to perform this task.

LISTING 1-4: **Saving a Vector to Disk**

```
#include <iostream>
#include <fstream>
#include <vector>

using namespace std;
```

```
int main() {
  vector<string> MyData;
  MyData.push_back("One");
  MyData.push_back("Two");

  ofstream outfile("../MyData.txt");
  for (Element : MyData)
    outfile << Element << endl;
  outfile.close();
  cout << "File Written!" << endl;
  return 0;
}
```

The example begins by creating a vector, MyData, that stores two strings. It then opens a file for output and uses a for loop to process the MyData elements one at a time. Each element appears on a separate line, which allows you to read the input file one line at a time to recreate the original vector from the disk file.

Handling Errors When Opening a File

When you open a file, all kinds of things can go wrong. A file lives on a physical device — a fixed disk, for example, or perhaps a flash drive or SD card — and you can run into problems when working with physical devices. For example:

>> Part of the disk might be damaged, causing an existing file to become corrupted.

>> You might run out of disk space.

>> The directory doesn't exist.

>> Your application doesn't have the right permissions to create a file.

>> Removable media is missing.

>> Network connection is down.

>> File is locked.

>> The filename was invalid — that is, it contained characters that the operating system doesn't allow in a filename, such as * or ?.

If you try to open a file for writing by specifying a full path and filename but the directory does not exist, the computer responds differently, depending on the operating system you're using. If you're unsure how your particular operating system will respond, try writing a simple test application that tries to create and open a nonexistent path like /abc/def/ghi/jkl/abc.txt. Then one of the following will happen:

>> The operating system will generate an error (the default for Windows).

>> The operating system will create the required path and file.

If you want to determine whether the ostream class was unable to create a file, you can call its fail() method. This method returns true if the object couldn't create the file. That's what happens when a directory doesn't exist. The DirectoryCheck01 example, shown in Listing 1-5, demonstrates an example of using the fail() method.

LISTING 1-5: **Returning True When ostream Cannot Create a File**

```cpp
#include <iostream>
#include <fstream>
using namespace std;
int main()
{
    ofstream outfile("/abc/def/ghi/MyFile.txt");
    if (outfile.fail()) {
        cout << "Couldn't open the file!" << endl;
        return 0;
    }
    outfile << "Hi" << endl;
    outfile.close();
    return 0;
}
```

When you run this code, you should see the message Couldn't open the file! when your particular operating system doesn't create a directory. If it does, your computer will open the file and write Hi to it.

As an alternative to calling the fail() method, you can use an operator available in various stream classes. This is !, fondly referred to as the *bang* operator, and you would use it in place of calling fail(), as in this code:

```cpp
if (!outfile)
{
```

```
cout << "Couldn't open the file!" << endl;
return 0;
}
```

REMEMBER

Like any good application, your application should do two things:

1. Check whether a file creation succeeded.

2. If the file creation failed, handle it appropriately. Don't just print a horrible message like Oops! Aborting!. Instead, do something friendlier — such as presenting a message telling users that there's a problem and suggesting that they might free more disk space. (There are other reasons not covered in this book, such as lack of rights to the area of disk where the file is written — you need to perform application testing to locate all the possible reasons a file creation might fail and then provide error handling for each potential issue.)

Flagging the ios Flags

When you open a file by constructing a stream instance, you can modify the way the file will open by supplying flags. In computer terms, a *flag* is simply an indicator whose presence or lack of presence tells a function how to do something. The flag appears in the constructor when working with a stream.

A flag looks like ios_base::app. This particular flag means that you want to write to a file, but you want to append to any existing data that may already be in a file. You supply this flag as an argument of the constructor for ofstream, as shown here:

```
ofstream outfile("AppendableFile.txt", ios_base::app);
```

You can see the flag as a second parameter to the constructor. Other flags exist besides app, and you can combine them by using the or operator, |. Following is a list of the available flags:

>> ios_base::ate: Use this flag to go to the end of the file after you open it. Normally, you use this flag when you want to append data to the end of the file.

>> ios_base::binary: Use this flag to specify that the file you're opening will hold binary data — that is, data that does not represent character strings.

>> ios_base::in: Specify this flag when you want to read from a file.

>> ios_base::out: Include this flag when you want to write to a file.

» `ios_base::trunc`: Include this flag if you want to wipe out the contents of a file before writing to it.

» `ios_base::app`: Include this flag if you want to append to the current file pointer position of the file (which is at the beginning when you first open the file). It's the opposite of `trunc` — that is, the information that's already in the file when you open it will stay there.

The `FileOutput02` example, shown in Listing 1-6, shows how to use a flag to append information to the output of Listing 1-1.

LISTING 1-6: **Appending to an Existing File**

```cpp
#include <iostream>
#include <fstream>

using namespace std;

int main() {
  string filename = "../MyFile.txt";
  ifstream check(filename);
  if (!check) {
    cout << "File doesn't exist.";
    return -1;
  } else {
    check.close();
  }

  fstream datafile(filename, ios_base::app);
  datafile << " There" << endl;
  datafile.close();
  cout << "File Written!" << endl;
  return 0;
}
```

TIP

This example begins by checking for the existence of the file. If the file doesn't exist (or you don't have permission to access it, making the file invisible to the application), the application won't create it to write to it. You can use this technique whenever you want to ensure that a file exists before you attempt to add data to it.

If the file exists, you want to close the file handle to it before you write to it by calling `check.close()`. You can then reopen the file for appending by adding the `ios_base::app` flag. The example outputs some additional text and closes the file.

Chapter **2**

Writing with Output Streams

Years ago, it was possible to have a personal computer with 3,000 bytes of memory. (Yes, that's three thousand bytes, not 3MB.) As an option, this computer came with a floppy disk drive that sat outside it. It didn't have a hard drive. Therefore, if you didn't have a hard drive but you wanted to use an application, you had to load the application from a floppy, type its name, and press Enter!

Nowadays, the notion of a computer without permanent storage is unthinkable. Not only do your applications appear in permanent storage in the form of files, but your applications also create files to store in permanent storage. In this chapter, you see the different ways you can write to a file in any permanent storage location: hard drive, removable device, network, online, or wherever else permanent storage is found.

REMEMBER

You don't have to type the source code for this chapter manually. In fact, using the downloadable source is a lot easier. You can find the source for this chapter in the `\CPP_AIO4\BookVI\Chapter02` folder of the downloadable source. See the Introduction for details on how to find these source files.

Inserting with the << Operator

Writing to a file is easy in C++. You're probably already familiar with how you can write to the console by using the cout object, like this:

```
cout << "Hey, I'm on TV!" << endl;
```

The cout object is a file stream. So, if you want to write to a file, you can do it the same way you would with cout: You just use the double-less-than symbol, called the *insertion operator*, like this: <<.

If you open a file for writing by using the ofstream class, you can write to it by using the insertion operator. The FileWrite01 example, shown in Listing 2-1, demonstrates how to perform this task.

LISTING 2-1: **Using Code to Open a File and Write to It**

```cpp
#include <iostream>
#include <fstream>

using namespace std;

int main() {
  ofstream outfile("../outfile.txt");
  outfile << "Look at me! I'm in a file!" << endl;

  int x = 200;
  outfile << x << endl;

  outfile.close();
  cout << "File Written" << endl;
  return 0;
}
```

OPERATING THE INSERTION OPERATOR

The insertion operator, <<, is an overloaded operator function. Inside the basic_ostream class, you can find several overloaded forms of the << operator function. Each one provides input for a basic type as well as for some of the standard C++ classes, such as string or one of its base classes. (Most libraries that ship with compilers are written by compiler vendors — who may implement their code slightly differently but get the same results.)

PLACING DATA IN SPECIFIC FOLDERS

Sometimes you want to place data in a specific common folder, such as the current working directory — the directory used by the application. C++ provides a method to obtain this information: getcwd(). This method appears in the <direct.h> header. Using the getcwd() method is relatively straightforward. You create a place to put the information, called a buffer, and then ask C++ to provide the information. The GetWorkingDirectory example demonstrates how to perform this task, as shown here:

```
#include <iostream>
#include <direct.h>

using namespace std;

int main() {
  char CurrentPath[PATH_MAX];
  getcwd(CurrentPath, PATH_MAX);
  cout << CurrentPath << endl;
  return 0;
}
```

As output, you should see the name of the directory that contains the application, such as C:\CPP_AIO4\BookVI\Chapter02\GetWorkingDirectory. The MAX_PATH constant is the maximum size that you can make a path. So, what this code is saying is to create a char array that is the size of MAX_PATH. Use the resulting buffer to hold the current working directory (which is where the name of the method getcwd() comes from). You can then display this directory onscreen or use it as part of the path for your output stream.

The first line inside main() creates an instance of ofstream, passing to it the name of a file called outfile.txt. The code then writes to the file, first giving it the string Lookit me! I'm in a file!, then a newline, then the integer 200, and finally another newline. After that, the code closes the file.

Formatting Your Output

If you're saving lists of numbers to a file, you may find that the process works better if the numbers are formatted in various ways. For example, you may want them all aligned on the right; or you might want your floating-point numbers to have a certain number of digits to the right of the decimal point. There are three elements to setting these formats:

>> **Format flags:** A *format flag* is a general style that you want your output to appear in. For example, you may want floating-point numbers to appear in scientific mode, or you may want to be able to print the words true and false for Boolean values rather than their underlying numbers. To do these tasks, you specify format flags.

>> **Precision:** This refers to how many digits are on the right of the decimal point when you print floating-point numbers.

>> **Field width:** This refers to how much space the numbers take (both floating point and integer). This feature allows you to align all your numbers.

TIP

The following sections discuss each of these elements. You can use format flags, along with precision and width specifiers, when writing to your files or outputting to the screen using cout. Because cout is a stream object in the iostream hierarchy, it accepts the same specifiers as output files.

Formatting with flags

Format flags enable you to tell the compiler how to output data you provide. To use the format flags, you call the setf() method for the stream object. (This can be either your own file object or the cout object.) For example, to turn on scientific notation, you would do this:

```
cout.setf(ios_base::scientific);
cout << 987654.321 << endl;
```

To turn off scientific mode, you call the unsetf() method:

```
cout.unsetf(ios_base::scientific);
cout << 987654.321 << endl;
```

If you're using your own file, you use code similar to that shown in Listing 2-2, as found in the FileWrite02 example.

LISTING 2-2: | **Writing Formatted Output**

```
#include <iostream>
#include <fstream>
```

```
using namespace std;

int main() {
  ofstream myfile("../numbers.txt");
  myfile.setf(ios_base::scientific);
  myfile << 154272.0 << endl;

  myfile << hex << showbase << 154272 << endl;

  myfile.unsetf(ios_base::hex);
  myfile << 154272 << endl;
  myfile.close();

  cout << "File Written" << endl;
  return 0;
}
```

When you run this code for writing to a file, the numbers.txt file contains the following output:

```
1.542720e+005
0x25aa0
154272
```

TIP

Each of the ios_base flags exists both as a format specifier and as a manipulator. (Don't worry about the precise differences for right now; Book 6, Chapter 5 explains manipulators in detail.)

The example begins by opening the file, setting the ios_base::scientific flag using setf(), and then outputting a floating-point value. Instead of using setf(), the next line uses the manipulator form of the hex flag to output an integer value. To see the hexadecimal value with the required base of 0x, you include the showbase flag. Finally, the example uses unsetf() to remove the ios_base::hex flag and outputs the same integer value as before. Whether you use the format specifier or the manipulator form of a flag, the flag remains set until you unset it.

REMEMBER

Table 2-1 tells about each of the flags you can use. Note that some flags affect only text, some affect only integers, and some affect only floating-point values. Setting a flag that doesn't affect a particular value type you want to output means that the value appears in its default form. However, you can or flags together using the | symbol to configure the output for multiple types.

TABLE 2-1   **ios_base Formatting Flags**

Flag	Type	Description
boolalpha	Independent	Setting this flag causes Boolean variables to write with the words true or false (or the equivalent words for your particular locale). Clearing this flag causes Boolean variables to write 0 for false or 1 for true. (The default is for this flag to be cleared.)
dec	Numerical Base	When you set this flag, your integers will appear as decimal numbers. To turn this off, you turn on a different *base*, either hex (for hexadecimal) or oct (for octal).
fixed	Float Format	This flag specifies that, when possible, the output of floating-point numbers will not appear in scientific notation. (Large numbers always appear as scientific notation, whether you specify scientific or fixed.)
hex	Numerical Base	With this flag, all your integers appear in hexadecimal format. To turn this off, choose a different base — dec or oct.
internal	Adjustment	The text is padded to fill an output field using a specific fill character.
left	Adjustment	When you turn on this flag, all numbers will be left-aligned with a width field. (See "Setting the width and creating fields," later in this chapter, for information on how to set the width.)
oct	Numerical Base	When you turn on this flag, your integers will appear in octal format.
right	Adjustment	With this flag, all your numbers will be right-aligned with a width field.
scientific	Float Format	When you specify this flag, your floating-point numbers always appear in scientific notation.
showbase	Independent	When you turn on this flag and print an integer, the integer will be preceded with a character that represents the base — decimal, hexadecimal, or octal. That can be good because the number 153 can represent 153 in decimal or 153 in hexadecimal (which is equivalent to 339 in decimal) or 153 in octal (which is equivalent to 107 in decimal).
showpoint	Independent	With this flag, your floating-point numbers have a decimal point, even if they happen to be whole numbers. (That is, a floating-point variable that contains 10.0 will print as 10. with a decimal point after it. Without this flag, it will just print as 10 with no decimal point.)
showpos	Independent	Normally, a negative number gets a minus sign before it, and a positive number gets no sign before it. But when you turn on this flag, each of your positive numbers will get a plus sign before it.
skipws	Independent	Skips the leading white space in some output operations so that left-aligned text is actually left aligned.
unitbuf	Independent	When you turn this on, your output will flush after each output operation. In other words, the library doesn't accumulate a certain amount of output before writing it in batches. Instead, the library writes all the output out each time you use the insertion operator, <<.

Flag	Type	Description
uppercase	Independent	When you write hexadecimal or scientific numbers, the various letters in the number appear as uppercase. Thus, the letters *A, B, C, D, E,* and *F* will appear in capitals in a hexadecimal number, and the *E* representing the exponent in scientific notation prints as a capital *E*. When this is not set, you get lowercase letters for hexadecimal numbers and *e* for the exponent in scientific notation.

Table 2-2 shows the manipulator forms of some flags. The table shows three columns: the flag, the manipulator to turn on the flag, and the manipulator to turn off the flag.

TABLE 2-2

Using ANSI-Standard Manipulators and Demanipulators

Flag	Manipulator	Demanipulator
boolalpha	boolalpha	noboolalpha
showbase	showbase	noshowbase
showpoint	showpoint	noshowpoint
showpos	showpos	noshowpos
skipws	skipws	noskipws
uppercase	uppercase	nouppercase
fixed	fixed	scientific
scientific	scientific	fixed

The scientific flag and fixed flag are opposites: fixed turns off scientific, and scientific turns off fixed. The default if you don't specify either is fixed. You don't use these flags together, such as, cout.setf(ios_base::scientific | ios_base::fixed);, because doing so can create some unusual and unusable results.

Six manipulators aren't in Table 2-2 because they don't have a demanipulator. Instead, they are three-way:

» **Bases:** dec, hex, and oct. Only one base can be active at a time. Activating a base automatically switches off the other bases.

» **Alignments:** internal, left, and right. Only one alignment can be active at a time. Activating an alignment automatically switches off the other alignments.

Specifying a precision

When you write floating-point numbers to a file or to `cout` (that is, numbers stored in `float` or `double` variables), having all the numbers print with the same number of digits to the right of the decimal point is often handy. This feature is called the *precision.*

Don't confuse this use of the word *precision* with the idea that `double` variables have a greater precision than `float` variables. This use of precision specifies the number of digits printed to either the file or `cout`. The value inside the variable doesn't change, nor does the precision of the variable's type.

To set or read the precision, call the stream's `precision()` function. If you call `precision()` with no parameters, you can find out the current precision. Or to set the precision, pass a number specifying how many digits you want to appear to the right of the decimal point. For example, the following line sets the precision of an output:

```
cout.precision(4);
```

The output of `cout << 0.33333333 << endl;` would take this rounded off form:

```
0.3333
```

If you don't set the precision, the stream will have a default precision, probably six, depending on your particular compiler. Precision has an interesting effect if you use it with the `showpoint` format flag. In the scientific community, these three numbers don't have the same precision, even though the first two have the same number of digits to the right of the decimal point:

```
3.5672
8432.2259
0.55292
```

Scientists consider precision to mean the same number of total digits, not counting leftmost 0's to the left of the decimal (as in the final of the three). Therefore, a scientist would consider the three following numbers to have the same precision because they all have four digits. (Again, for the final one, you don't count the 0 because it's to the left of the decimal point.)

```
3.567
8432.
0.1853
```

It also doesn't count rightmost zeros used as placeholders. For example 123,000 normally only has three significant digits: 1, 2, and 3. The three zeros are place-holders and don't provide any interesting information. However, 123,000.0 has seven significant digits because the .0 tells something about the precision of the number.

Scientific folks call these significant digits. You can accomplish significant digits with an output stream by combining precision with the showpoint flag. The PrecisionFunction example, shown in Listing 2-3, contains an example of showpoint and precision() working together in perfect harmony.

LISTING 2-3: **Using the Precision Function to Work with the showpoint Format Flag**

```
#include <iostream>

using namespace std;

int main() {
  cout.setf(ios_base::showpoint);
  cout.precision(4);

  for (int i=1; i<=10; i++) {
      cout << 1.0 / i << endl;
  }

  cout << "\n" << 2.0 << endl;
  cout << 12.0 << endl;
  cout << 12.5 << endl;
  cout << 123.5 << endl;
  cout << 1234.9 << endl;
  cout << 12348.8 << endl;
  cout << 123411.5 << endl;
  cout << 1234111.5 << endl;

  // Precision with zeros on the right.
  cout << "\n" << 123000 << endl;
  cout << 123000.0 << endl;
  cout << 123.0e3 << endl;

  // Only available C++ 17 and above
  // Use the -fext-numeric-literals switch.
  cout << 0x1E078p0 << endl;
  return 0;
}
```

When you run this application, here's the output you see:

```
1.000
0.5000
0.3333
0.2500
0.2000
0.1667
0.1429
0.1250
0.1111
0.1000

2.000
12.00
12.50
123.5
1235.
1.235e+004
1.234e+005
1.234e+006

123000
1.230e+005
1.230e+005
1.230e+005
```

The preceding output has a couple of interesting cases:

» The lines that read:

```
1.235e+004
1.234e+005
1.234e+006
```

of the preceding output are scientific notation to maintain four significant digits.

» The last four lines show how C++ handles int versus float values. The float values come in three forms: default, scientific notation, and hexadecimal notation with an exponent (p0). This last form is only available in C++ 17 and above, and you must include the -fext-numeric-literals switch on the Other Compiler Options tab of the Global Compiler Settings dialog to use it. If you wanted to make the int into a float, you'd need to replace 123000 with (float)123000.

>> The ninth line from the end, 1235., is rounded up from 1234.9 because of this line:

```
cout << 1234.9 << endl;
```

The precision() function has an associated manipulator. Instead of calling precision() as a function, you can use it as a manipulator. But the manipulator's name is slightly different: It's setprecision(). To use it, you include this header:

```
#include <iomanip>
```

These two lines cause the same thing to happen:

```
cout.precision(4);
cout << setprecision(4);
```

Setting the width and creating fields

This is where you can start making the numbers and data all nice and neat by aligning them in columns. To align your data, use the width() method for the stream or cout, passing the width of the field, like this:

```
cout.width(10);
```

Then, when you print a number, think of the number as sitting inside a field 10 spaces wide, with the number wedged against the right side of these 10 spaces. For example, look at this:

```
cout.width(10);
cout << 20 << endl;
```

This code produces this output:

```
        20
```

Although seeing this fact in the printed text is hard, this 20 is pushed to the right of a field of spaces 10 characters wide. That is, because the 20 takes two character spaces, there are eight spaces to the left of it.

TIP

If you prefer, you can have the numbers pushed to the left of the field. To do so, set the left format flag by using setf() or use the left manipulator.)

For the width manipulator, setw(), you can alternatively add #include <iomanip> and then use the manipulator:

```
cout << setw(10);
```

WARNING

Because of some oddities in the libraries, when you set the width, it stays that way only for the next output operation. Call it forgetful, if you will. Therefore, suppose you have code that looks like this:

```
cout.width(10);
cout << 20 << 30 << endl;
```

Only the first output, 20, has a field width of 10. The 30 just takes as much space as it needs. Therefore, these lines of code produce this output, which is probably not what most people would intend:

```
        2030
```

This is why it's preferable to use the manipulator form: You precede each output item with a width specification. Try this instead:

```
cout << setw(10) << 20 << setw(10) << 30 << endl;
```

which writes this to cout:

```
        20        30
```

The WidthFunction example in Listing 2-4 shows the great things you can do when you set the width.

LISTING 2-4: **Setting the Width of a Field Using the setw Manipulator or Width Function**

```
#include <iostream>
#include <iomanip>
#include <fstream>

using namespace std;

int main() {
  ofstream sals("../salaries.txt");
```

```
sals << setprecision(2) << fixed << left;
sals << setw(20) << "Name" << setw(10) << "Salary";
sals << endl;

// 19 hyphens, one space
sals << "------------------- ";

// 10 hyphens
sals << "----------" << endl;

sals << setw(20) << "Hank Williams";
sals << setw(10) << 28422.82 << endl;
sals << setw(20) << "Buddy Holly";
sals << setw(10) << 39292.22 << endl;
sals << setw(20) << "Otis Redding";
sals << setw(10) << 43838.55 << endl;
sals.close();

cout << "File Written" << endl;
return 0;
}
```

When you run Listing 2-3, you get a file called `salaries.txt`, like this:

```
Name                Salary
------------------- ----------
Hank Williams       28422.82
Buddy Holly         39292.22
Otis Redding        43838.55
```

The first field, Name is 20 characters wide. You use only 19 hyphens to give the appearance of a space between the two fields. In fact, the two fields are wedged against each other with no space between them.

TIP

If you wanted to run Listing 2-4 but display each salary in scientific format, as in 2.8e+04, you need to use `sals.setf(ios::scientific);` and `sals.setf(ios::left);` after removing the fixed modifier.

TIP

The example uses the `left` format flag so that the data in each field is aligned to the left end of the field. By default, each field is aligned to the right.

REMEMBER

Although you can specify the field width, you're actually specifying a minimum. If the characters in the output are less than the field width, the runtime library will pad them with spaces to make them that minimum size. If they are bigger than that width, the library doesn't chop them off to make them fit. If you add letters to the Hank Williams line in Listing 2-4 (like this: `sals << setw(20) << "Hank WilliamsABCDEFGHIJ";`), the output looks like the following example instead. The Hank Williams line runs beyond the 20 characters into the next field.

```
Name                 Salary
------------------- ----------
Hank WilliamsABCDEFGHIJ28422.82
Buddy Holly          39292.22
Otis Redding         43838.55
```

Chapter **3**

Reading with Input Streams

You have a file that you wrote to, but you need to read from it. After all, what good is a file if it's just sitting on your hard drive collecting dust?

In this chapter, you learn how you can read from a file. This task begins by extracting the data. You can perform this task using extraction operators, just as you use insertion operators in the previous chapter.

Reading a file is tricky because you can run into some formatting issues. For example, you may have a line of text in a file with a sequence of 50 digits. You may not know whether those 50 digits correspond to 50 one-digit numbers, 25 two-digit numbers, or some other combination. When you create the file, you probably know its format, but the fun part is getting your C++ application to properly read from files you didn't create. The file might contain 25 two-digit numbers, in which case you make sure that the C++ code doesn't just try to read one enormous 50-digit number.

REMEMBER

You don't have to type the source code for this chapter manually. In fact, using the downloadable source is a lot easier. You can find the source for this chapter in the \CPP_AIO4\BookVI\Chapter03 folder of the downloadable source. See the Introduction for details on how to find these source files.

Extracting with Operators

When you read from a file, you can use the *extraction* operator, >>. This operator is easy to use, as long as you understand that using the extraction operator does come with some caveats. For example, suppose you have a file called Numbers.txt with the following text on one line (you need the Numbers.txt file to work with this chapter's example code):

```
100 50 30 25
```

You can easily read these numbers into memory using the FileRead01 example code shown in Listing 3-1.

LISTING 3-1: **Reading a File Into Memory Using the Extraction Operator**

```cpp
#include <iostream>
#include <fstream>
#include <string.h>

using namespace std;

int main() {
  string weight;
  string height;
  string width;
  string depth;

  ifstream MyFile("../Numbers.txt");
  if (!MyFile) {
    cerr << "File couldn't be opened!" << endl;
    cerr << "Error Code: " << strerror(errno) << endl;
    return -1;
  }

  MyFile >> weight;
  MyFile >> height;
  MyFile >> width;
  MyFile >> depth;

  cout << "Weight = " << weight << "\r\n";
  cout << "Height = " << height << "\r\n";
  cout << "Width  = " << width << "\r\n";
  cout << "Depth  = " << depth;
```

```
    MyFile.close();
    return 0;
}
```

Each of the variables holds just one string element. To read all four numbers, you need to extract the data four times. The input file, Numbers.txt, has its numbers separated with spaces. You can also separate them with newline characters, like this:

```
100
50
30
25
```

The application doesn't care. It looks for *white space*, which is any number of spaces, tabs, and newlines. You could format the data so it looks like the following example, and the application will still read them in correctly.

```
100        50
                    30
    25
```

REMEMBER

When you are dealing with the standard input object, cin, the same rules about white space apply: If you read in four numbers, as in the following example, the cin object, like the ifstream object, will separate the numbers based on the white space.

WARNING

Users make common mistakes that can cause your application to fail or possibly display incorrect information:

>> If the user accidentally inserts a space into the input stream, whether from the console or a file, the computer sees the space as the beginning of a new string.

>> Sometimes users forget to add white space, which means that two values mash together and the computer sees them as a single entity.

>> A user might try to separate values using commas, semi-colons, or other non-white-space characters.

>> Missing values, where the user simply leaves the data out, is also a problem.

Consequently, when you encounter problems with the input data, looking for additional white space, missing white space, or missing values is a good place to begin.

REMEMBER

When you read information from a file, make sure that you clearly define the information order. In other words, make sure that you have agreed upon a protocol for the information. Otherwise, you'll likely end up with errors and mistakes.

This example includes error trapping for opening the file. This error trapping requires the addition of `#include <string.h>` (note the inclusion of the `.h`). After creating `MyFile` and opening the file with the constructor, the code checks for a file handle in `MyFile`. If `MyFile` is empty, the code outputs error information to `cerr`, the standard error output, and provides a human-readable output error, such as `No such file or directory`.

If the file opening process succeeds, the code reads in each of the data values using the extraction operator. It then outputs the values in a nicely formatted form and closes the file. When you run the application, you see the result of reading the file:

```
Weight = 100
Height = 50
Width  = 30
Depth  = 25
```

WHAT'S A PROTOCOL?

You have a list of numbers: 1600 20500 1849 20240. No matter how you look at these numbers, they don't mean anything. You need a protocol. As defined in this chapter, a *protocol* is simply a rule for how to format and order data. It describes the required content of a data stream. A protocol in general defines rules for exchanging information of any sort between computers (think of it as a diplomatic role). The two systems negotiate the exchange of data based on standardized rules.

As it happens, the first number in the set of numbers is the street address of the White House in Washington, DC, and the second number is the zip code for the White House. The third number is the street address of the main office for the National Park Service headquarters, and the fourth is the National Park Service zip code.

Further, a protocol dictates how you respond after receiving data. You may send back a single number 1, which means that you received the data properly, and the other party may send a single 0, which means that you won't receive further information. That's a protocol, and protocols are useful when reading data, whether it's from a file or over the Internet.

Encountering the End of File

Files end. The ending creates a condition called the *EOF*, which stands for End of File. When you read from a file, you need to know when you reach the end. If you know the file size, you can write your application so that it knows exactly when to stop. So here are the cases covered in this section:

>> Read to the end of the file by knowing the file size.

>> Read until the EOF marker without knowing the file size.

You, the programmer, know the format of the file you're reading. (Perhaps your application even wrote the file and now you're writing the part of the application that reads it.) Your format might start with a *size* entry. The application begins by reading this number and configuring itself to read the specified number of entries. This approach requires the file creator to start by writing the size before the rest of the data and to agree to this format.

Using the record count approach

The record count approach has the advantage of letting you know from the outset how many records to read. The `FileRead02` example consists of three source code files (Book 1, Chapter 7 tells you how to employ multiple files in a single project. You see `main.cpp` in Listing 3-2. It provides the coordination to write two files and then read them back into memory. Listing 3-3 shows the `writedata.cpp` code used to write data to disk. Listing 3-4 shows the `readdata.cpp` code used to read the data from disk.

LISTING 3-2: **Coordinating the Writing and Reading Process**

```
#include <iostream>

using namespace std;

int WriteFile(string filename, int count, int start);
int ReadFile(string filename);

int main() {
  cout << "Writing the files." << endl;
  if (WriteFile("../nums.txt", 5, 100) == -1)
    return -1;
  cout << "Files written successfully." << endl;
```

(continued)

LISTING 3-2: **(continued)**

```
cout << "\nReading the files.\n" << endl;
if (ReadFile("../nums.txt") == -1)
  return -1;
cout << "\nFiles read successfully." << endl;

return 0;
}
```

LISTING 3-3: ## Writing the Data to Disk with the Number of Records

```
#include <iostream>
#include <fstream>
#include <string.h>

using namespace std;

int WriteFile(string filename, int count, int start) {
  ofstream outfile(filename);
  if (!outfile) {
    cerr << "File couldn't be opened!" << endl;
    cerr << "Error Code: " << strerror(errno) << endl;
    return -1;
  }

  outfile << count << endl;

  for (int i=0; i<count; i++) {
    outfile << start + i  << endl;
  }

  outfile.close();
  return 0;
}
```

LISTING 3-4: ## Reading the Data from Disk Using the Number of Records

```
#include <iostream>
#include <fstream>
#include <string.h>
```

```
using namespace std;

int ReadFile(string filename) {
  ifstream infile(filename);
  if (!infile) {
    cerr << "File couldn't be opened!" << endl;
    cerr << "Error Code: " << strerror(errno) << endl;
    return -1;
  }

  int count = 0;
  infile >> count;
  cout << "File: " << filename << endl;
  cout << "This file has " << count << " items." << endl;

  int num = 0;
  for (int i=0; i<count; i++) {
    infile >> num;
    cout << num << endl;
  }

  infile.close();
  return 0;
}
```

All three of the code files include rudimentary error handling. It's important to consider what errors might happen (even those that seem impossible) and then add code to deal with them. The manner in which this application is written ensures that the data files are at least accessible, but not much else. A production application would also ensure that the data is in the correct format, order, and range (among other application-specific checks).

The data writing process begins by writing the number of records as the first entry in nums.txt. It then uses a for loop to write the specified number of values to disk. The values start at the point specified by start and end after reaching count.

The data reading process begins by opening the file and reading the first record, which should be the number of items in the file. The code outputs the filename and record count for you. This part of the example uses a for loop to read the individual values and display them on screen. When you run this application, you'll see the following output.

```
Writing the files.
Files written successfully.

Reading the files.

File: ../nums.txt
This file has 5 items.
100
101
102
103
104

Files read successfully.
```

Using the EOF check approach

Another possibility for reading and writing a file is that you continue reading data from the file until you reach the end of the file. You do this by testing
the istream or ifstream object for the EOF. The FileRead03 example uses the
same approach as the one in the previous section for breaking the code into
three parts. Listing 3-2 has main.cpp (yes, this example uses precisely the same
main() as before), Listing 3-5 contains writedata.cpp, and Listing 3-5 contains
readdata.cpp.

LISTING 3-5: **Writing the Data to Disk without the Number of Records**

```cpp
#include <iostream>
#include <fstream>
#include <string.h>

using namespace std;

int WriteFile(string filename, int count, int start) {
  ofstream outfile(filename);
  if (!outfile) {
    cerr << "File couldn't be opened!" << endl;
    cerr << "Error Code: " << strerror(errno) << endl;
    return -1;
  }

  for (int i=0; i<count; i++) {
    outfile << start + i  << endl;
```

```
  }

  outfile.close();
  return 0;
}
```

TIP

By comparing Listing 3-3 with Listing 3-5, and Listing 3-4 with Listing 3-6, you can see that this approach uses fewer lines of code and is somewhat simpler to read. Of course, you don't get the number of records as an immediate output either. Whether the extra coding needed to accommodate the number of records is worthwhile depends on how you use the data. For example, you might need the number of records to create an array to store the data.

LISTING 3-6: **Reading the Data from Disk Using EOF**

```
#include <iostream>
#include <fstream>
#include <string.h>

using namespace std;

int ReadFile(string filename) {
  ifstream infile(filename);
  if (!infile) {
    cerr << "File couldn't be opened!" << endl;
    cerr << "Error Code: " << strerror(errno) << endl;
    return -1;
  }

  int num;
  cout << "File: " << filename << endl;

  do {
      infile >> num;
      cout << num << endl;
  } while (!infile.eof());

  infile.close();
  return 0;
}
```

The data writing process is about the same in both cases. The only thing that Listing 3-5 is missing is the number of records output, which amounts to two lines of code.

However, the data reading process is different. When working with a file that contains the number of records, you can rely on a for loop and extract the data a precise number of times. Listing 3-6 shows that you use a do...while loop to accomplish the same thing when you don't know the number of records. The reason you use a do...while loop is to allow processing of a record, and then immediately check for the EOF marker using eof() before attempting to process the next record.

REMEMBER

You often see files processed using a while loop. The problem with this approach is that you now have to track a logical variable that specifies when the processing completes. Using a do...while loop is simpler and less error prone.

Reading Various Types

Reading files may not always be as straightforward for the computer as it is for humans. The computer needs specific rules for reading a file. The following sections discuss this issue and provide a demonstration for you to consider.

Understanding data reading issues

Reading a file can get complicated when you want to read spaces. Suppose you have two strings that you want to write to a file:

```
"I'll have a steak for dinner."
"I will have the Smiths for dinner, too."
```

Now suppose you wrote these to a file as one big, long, line to get "I'll have a steak for dinner. I will have the Smiths for dinner, too." Later, you want to read back in these two strings, but you can't follow this process:

```
string first, second;
infile >> first;
infile >> second;
```

If you do this, the variable first will hold I'll, and the variable second will hold have because, when you read in strings, the ifstream and istream classes use spaces to break (or *delimit*) the strings.

Even if you could somehow use the `ifstream` class to go past the spaces, it wouldn't know when it has reached the end of the first string because it doesn't view a period as anything special. You must write your application to follow this protocol: A string ends with a period. That protocol is fine, because ending with a period is the case with these two strings. However, you may need to process just sequences of words, like this:

```
"poodle steak eat puddle"
"dinner Smiths yummy"
```

And then, when you write these two strings to a file, you end up with this text inside the file:

```
poodle steak eat puddle dinner Smiths yummy
```

Or worse, you may get this text, which contains no space between the two strings:

```
poodle steak eat puddledinner Smiths yummy
```

TIP

When working with data that doesn't form sentences, you may not be limited to strings. You could be processing numbers, vectors, special classes, and so on. So, even though you see words strung together here, you need to think outside the box. Here's what you need to do to solve the problem of reading complex data in various forms:

1. Create a protocol. Here are some choices for your protocols:

   - You can write each string on a separate line, and when you read the file, you will know that each line is a separate string.

   - You can delimit each data element with a particular character. Then you would split your strings based on those delimiters.

2. Develop code to implement the same protocol for both reading and writing.

Writing and reading string-type data

When working with strings that form sentences or that you can separate into groups, your best bet is to work with them as strings separated by newline characters. The WriteReadString example, shown in Listings 3-7 (`main.cpp`), 3-8 (`WriteString.cpp`), and 3-9 (`ReadString.cpp`), writes and reads data (not just sentences) as elements separated by newline characters and read back in the same way. This represents the easiest method for writing complex data to disk.

LISTING 3-7: **Coordinating the Writing and Reading of Complex Data**

```cpp
#include <iostream>

using namespace std;

void ClearFile(string Filename);
int WriteData(string Filename, string Text);
int ReadData(string Filename);

int main() {
  string const file = "../strings.txt";

  ClearFile(file);
  cout << "Data file cleared." << endl;

  int Result = WriteData(file, "Some data to write.");
  Result = WriteData(file, "Some more data to write.");
  Result = WriteData(file, "Third time's a charm.");
  if (Result == 0)
    cout << "Data written successfully!\n" << endl;

  if (ReadData(file) == 0)
    cout << "\nData read successfully!" << endl;

  return 0;
}
```

LISTING 3-8: **Clearing the Data File and Writing Complex Data to It**

```cpp
#include <iostream>
#include <fstream>

using namespace std;

void ClearFile(string Filename) {
  ofstream DataFile;
  DataFile.open(Filename, ios_base::trunc);
  DataFile.close();
}

int WriteData(string Filename, string Text) {
  ofstream DataFile(Filename, ios_base::app);
```

```
        if (DataFile.is_open()) {
          DataFile << Text << endl;
        } else {
          cerr << "Unable to open file." << endl;
          return -1;
        }

        DataFile.close();
        return 0;
      }
```

Reading the Complex Data

```
#include <iostream>
#include <fstream>
#include <string.h>

using namespace std;

int ReadData(string Filename) {
  ifstream DataFile(Filename);
  if (!DataFile) {
    cerr << "File couldn't be opened!" << endl;
    cerr << "Error Code: " << strerror(errno) << endl;
    return -1;
  }

  string Data = "";
  while (getline(DataFile, Data)) {
    cout << Data << endl;
  }

  DataFile.close();
  return 0;
}
```

Many of the techniques you see in these code listings also appear in the previous examples of this chapter. However, instead of treating the data as separate elements, this example works with strings. This difference in data complexity requires a few changes.

Because the WriteData() function writes data and closes the file each time, appending the new data to the end of the file (using ios_base::app), you need a method of clearing the data file as needed. The ClearFile() function performs this task by opening the file, truncating it using ios_base::trunc, and closing it without writing anything to it.

The ReadData() function can't depend on an EOF check as was used in previous examples to determine the end of file. This example uses a while loop that checks the return value from the getline() function. When getline() reaches the EOF, the eof bit is set (meaning that getline() returns false) and the while loop ends. Compare this approach to the do...while loop used in Listing 3-6.

Writing and reading structured data

Structured data can appear in quite a few forms, but most of these structured forms require use of delimiters. A common type of delimited data file is the Comma Separated Value (CSV). It has a number of protocols to consider, but for the purpose of the example, the data file uses commas between fields and newline characters between rows. The WriteReadStucture example, shown in Listing 3-10, provides you with a simple view of how to work with this type of data.

LISTING 3-10: **Writing and Reading Structured Data**

```
#include <iostream>
#include <fstream>
#include <sstream>

using namespace std;

struct Box {
  string Name;
  int Height;
  int Width;
  int Depth;
  double Weight;

  friend ostream& operator << (ostream& Out, Box Data);
};

ostream& operator << (ostream& Out, Box Data) {
  Out << Data.Name << ",";
  Out << Data.Height << ",";
  Out << Data.Width << ",";
  Out << Data.Depth << ",";
  Out << Data.Weight << "\n";
```

```
      return Out;
    }

    int main() {
      string const file = "../boxes.txt";

      Box SamBox;
      SamBox.Name = "Sam's Box";
      SamBox.Height = 4;
      SamBox.Width = 5;
      SamBox.Depth = 6;
      SamBox.Weight = 7.8;

      ofstream OutFile(file, ios_base::app);
      OutFile << SamBox << endl;
      OutFile.close();

      Box InData;
      int Field = 0;
      string InString;
      stringstream ISS;
      ifstream InFile(file);

      while(getline(InFile, InString, ',')){
        switch (Field) {
        case 0:
          InData.Name = InString;
          break;
        case 1:
          ISS << InString;
          break;
        default:
          ISS << " " << InString;
          break;
        }

        Field++;
      }
      InFile.close();

      ISS >> InData.Height >> InData.Width >> InData.Depth
          >> InData.Weight;

      cout << "Name: " << InData.Name << endl;
```

(continued)

LISTING 3-10:　*(continued)*

```
cout << "Height: " << InData.Height << endl;
cout << "Width: " << InData.Width << endl;
cout << "Depth: " << InData.Depth << endl;
cout << "Weight: " << InData.Weight << endl;

return 0;
}
```

This example begins by creating a Box structure that contains a number of data types (making it harder to work with). It then defines an << operator function to allow easy output of the data to a file. You may see other methods of creating output for structured data, but this is the simplest approach in most cases. The main() code begins by opening the file and using the << operator to output the data to it.

Getting the data read back into a new Box structure, InData, is a little more difficult. This example makes use of a stringstream, ISS, to allow for easy conversion from string form to numeric form.

TIP

The magic in the approach used in this example is that it relies on getline() to use a delimited approach to reading the file. Each read stops at either a comma or a newline. Consequently, each read represents a single field within the data file, whether that field is part of a new row or not.

When the field is a Name, you can input the data directly into the InData structure. However, for other fields, the InString input data is actually placed within ISS. Spaces between entries make it possible for ISS to keep each of the data values separate. Field keeps track of the current field number so that the switch processes each field properly.

After the processing is complete (there is only one record, in this case), the code uses another form of streaming to send the numeric values from ISS to each of the InData numeric fields in the correct type. Now that InData contains the original information, the code produces this output:

```
Name: Sam's Box
Height: 4
Width: 5
Depth: 6
Weight: 7.8
```

» Creating and deleting directories

» Getting the contents of a directory

» Copying and moving, and why they are related

» Moving and renaming files and why they are similar

Chapter **4**

Building Directories and Contents

Native C++ versions before version 17 provide no functions for creating directories and getting the contents of a directory. (C++ 17 and above provides access to the `filesystem` library, but it isn't implemented in most compilers yet.)You need to know two points about this situation:

» There really is a good reason for this lack. C++ is a general-purpose language. Issues that deal with directories are specific to individual operating systems. Thus it doesn't make sense to include such features in C++.

» Some brave rebels have added some functions — and these functions exist in most C++ implementations. These additions are important; otherwise, you'd have to call in to the operating system to create or modify a directory.

C++ has a holdover from the C programming language in the header file `stdio.h` that includes functions for renaming and removing files and directories. In addition, it supports a function used to create a temporary file.

WARNING

This chapter presents you with ways to manipulate directories and files. (I tested these routines only for the GNU GCC compiler that comes with the Code::Blocks product for OS X, Linux, and Windows. If you're working with a different compiler or operating system, try the examples out. They probably will work.)

For the examples in this chapter, you need to add both `#include <stdio.h>` and `#include <io.h>` to the beginning of the source code file. (Please don't confuse this file with `ios.h`. That's not the right one to use just now.) If you're working with a compiler other than Code::Blocks, you're not guaranteed to find `io.h` in your `include` directory, but you should look for it.

You don't have to type the source code for this chapter manually. In fact, using the downloadable source is a lot easier. You can find the source for this chapter in the `\CPP_AIO4\BookVI\Chapter04` folder of the downloadable source. See the Introduction for details on how to find these source files.

Manipulating Directories

You have a couple functions to use for creating and deleting directories. These functions are in the `io.h` header file.

Creating a directory

If you want to create a directory, you can call the `mkdir()` function. If the function can create the directory for you, it returns a 0. Otherwise, it returns a nonzero value, such as 1. Here's some sample code (found in the `MakeDirectory` example) that uses this function:

```cpp
#include <iostream>
#include <stdio.h>
#include <io.h>

using namespace std;

int main() {
  if (mkdir("../abc") != 0)
    cout << "Directory not created." << endl;
  else
    cout << "Directory created." << endl;

  return 0;
}
```

USING THE FILESYSTEM LIBRARY

Most compilers today don't support the `filesystem` library, even if you have C++ 17 or above installed. However, Wandbox (https://wandbox.org/) does provide marginal support for the `filesystem` library, so you can begin experimenting with it using the documentation found at https://en.cppreference.com/w/cpp/filesystem. The `filesystem::path` (https://en.cppreference.com/w/cpp/filesystem/path) support is essential to making the library work. The problem with working on Wandbox is that you don't have access to an actual directory. Consequently, you end up experimenting with code like this (found in the `FileSystem` example):

```
#include <iostream>
#include <filesystem>

using namespace std;
namespace fs = std::filesystem;

int main() {
  fs::path APath(".");
  cout << "Exists: " << fs::exists(APath) << endl
       << "Root Name: " << APath.root_name() << endl
       << "Root Path: " << APath.root_path() << endl
       << "Relative Path: " << APath.relative_path() << endl;
  return 0;
}
```

Notice that this code simplifies typing the information by creating a namespace variable, `fs`, to access the `filesystem` library. The code begins by creating a path (the example uses the current path to avoid problems). It then starts querying the path for information, such as whether that path exists and the relative path. Unfortunately, the output is a little disappointing (but at least the current path exists):

```
Exists: 1
Root Name: ""
Root Path: ""
Relative Path: "."
```

TIP

This example uses a forward slash (/) in the call to `mkdir()` for compatibility reasons. In Windows, you can use either a forward slash or a backslash. After you run this example the first time, you should see a new directory named abc added to the /CPP_AIO4/BookVI/Chapter04 directory on your system. If you run the example a second time, you receive the "Directory not created." message because the directory already exists.

It would be nice to create an entire directory-tree structure in one fell swoop — doing a call such as mkdir("/abc/def/ghi/jkl") without having any of the abc, def, or ghi directories already existing — but each parent directory must exist before you attempt to create a child directory. The function won't create a jkl directory unless the /abc/def/ghi directory exists. That means you have to break this call into multiple calls: First create /abc. Then create /abc/def, and so on.

If you do want to make all the directories simultaneously, you can use the system() function, as described in "Using the quick-and-dirty method" section, later in this chapter. If you execute system("mkdir \\abc\\def\\ghi\\jkl");, you can make the directory in one fell swoop.

Deleting a directory

To delete a directory, you call the rmdir() function, passing the name of the directory. If you want to find out whether it worked, test its results against 0. Here's some sample code as found in the DeleteDirectory example:

```cpp
#include <iostream>
#include <stdio.h>
#include <io.h>

using namespace std;

int main() {
  if (rmdir("../abc") != 0)
    cout << "Directory not deleted." << endl;
  else
    cout << "Directory deleted." << endl;

  return 0;
}
```

After you run this example, the /CPP_AIO4/BookVI/Chapter04/abc directory that you created in the previous section goes away. Make sure you verify that the directory is added and removed as expected. If you run this example a second time, you see the "Directory not deleted." message because you can't delete a directory that doesn't exist.

This approach works only if the directory is empty. If the directory has at least one file or directory in it, the function can't remove the directory — and returns a nonzero result.

Getting the Contents of a Directory

A directory usually contains multiple files as well as other directories. Getting a list of contents can be complicated. You don't just call a single function and get something back. The following procedure tells how the process of getting directory content works:

1. Call `_findfirst()`, passing it a pathname and a pattern for the files whose names you want to find.

    For example, pass `*.*` to get all files in the directory, or `*.txt` to get all files ending in `.txt`. Also pass it a pointer to a `_finddata_t` structure.

2. Check the results of `_findfirst()`.

    If `_findfirst()` returned –1, it didn't find any files (which means you're finished). Otherwise it fills the `_finddata_t` structure with the first file it found, and it will return a number that you use in subsequent calls to the various find functions.

3. Look at the `_finddata_t` structure to determine the name of the file, and other information such as create date, last access date, and size.

4. Call `_findnext()` and pass it the following values: the number returned from `_findfirst()` and the address of a `_finddata_t` structure

    If `_findnext()` returns –1, it found no more files; you can go to Step 5. Otherwise look at the `_finddata_t` structure to get the information for the next file found. Then repeat Step 4.

5. Call `_findclose()` and pass it the number returned from `_findfirst()`.

    You're all finished.

This is the process used in the days of programming with older languages. Most languages today hide these details from view, but you still follow this process when using an older version of C++. The GetDirectoryContents example in Listing 4-1 shows how to implement a directory listing.

LISTING 4-1: **Using Code to Read the Contents of a Directory**

```
#include <iostream>
#include <io.h>
#include <time.h>

using namespace std;
```

(continued)

LISTING 4-1: *(continued)*

```cpp
string Chop(string &str) {
  string res = str;

  int len = str.length();
  if (str[len - 1] == '\r')
    res.replace(len - 1, 1, "");

  len = str.length();
  if (str[len - 1] == '\n')
    res.replace(len - 1, 1, "");

  return res;
}

void DumpEntry(_finddata_t &data) {
  string createtime(ctime(&data.time_create));
  cout << Chop(createtime) << "\t";
  cout << data.size << "\t";

  if ((data.attrib & _A_SUBDIR) == _A_SUBDIR)
    cout << "[" << data.name << "]" << endl;
  else
    cout << data.name << endl;
}

int main() {
  _finddata_t data;
  int ff = _findfirst ("../*.*", &data);

  if (ff != -1) {
    int res = 0;

    while (res != -1) {
      DumpEntry(data);
      res = _findnext(ff, &data);
    }

    _findclose(ff);
  }
  return 0;
}
```

You can see how main() follows the previously outlined steps. Each data structure uses its own function called DumpEntry(). The DumpEntry() function prints the file information. Here's what you should see when you run the application (the current directory entry, the parent directory entry, and directories containing the examples for this chapter; your list may vary slightly):

```
Sun Jul 26 15:04:51 2020    0           [.]
Sun Jul 26 15:04:51 2020    0           [..]
Sun Jul 26 16:12:09 2020    0           [DeleteDirectory]
Sun Jul 26 15:04:51 2020    0           [FileSystem]
Sun Jul 26 16:24:47 2020    0           [GetDirectoryContents]
Sun Jul 26 16:03:32 2020    0           [MakeDirectory]
```

The DumpEntry() function tests whether the item is a directory. This is another old (but reliable) way to program: You check for the presence of a particular bit in the middle of the attrib member of the structure, like this:

```
if ((data.attrib & _A_SUBDIR) == _A_SUBDIR)
  cout << "[" << data.name << "]" << endl;
else
  cout << data.name << endl;
```

The Chop() function removes an extraneous carriage return that the ctime() function adds to the end of the string it creates. Otherwise, the information after the date has to start on the next line of text, which isn't what the example needs.

Copying Files

When you copy a file from one location to another, you actually create a new file and fill it with the same contents as the original file. To perform this task, you have to read each byte from the first file and write it to the second. To make matters worse, copying a file means you have to make sure that you copy it exactly the same, that you don't accidentally tack an extra 0 or two at the end of the file, or an extra carriage return or linefeed at the end of the file (which could happen when you copy a text file). The two files should be identical — not only contain the same information, but also be the same size.

These are the basics, but most good copy routines do more. They give the new file a date that matches the date of the original file, and they set all the attributes, such as read-only, the same. There are a few ways to perform a copying task, but the following sections provide two of them.

Copying with windows

If you're programming in Windows, you can use an easy method to perform copying tasks: the CopyFile function. To use it, you include the line #include <windows.h> in your application. Then you just do the following:

```
CopyFile("c:/dog.txt", "c:/dog2.txt", TRUE);
```

This code copies from c:/dog.txt to c:/dog2.txt. The final parameter, TRUE in all capitals, is a preprocessor macro defined somewhere in the bowels of the Windows header files. You have to use either TRUE or FALSE when calling any of the Windows functions. When the early versions of Windows were around, no bool type existed, so resourceful developers defined their own TRUE and FALSE as integers. That final parameter in CopyFile() tells the function what to do if the file you're copying to already exists: TRUE means don't overwrite the existing file; just abort. FALSE means overwrite it.

Using the quick-and-dirty method

There's another way you can copy a file, and you can use this to also move, delete, and rename files. However, this method isn't portable: The code is operating-system specific, which means that a Windows application won't run on Linux and vice versa. You can execute any DOS or Unix-shell commands by using the system() function. For example, this code pauses the display:

```
system("PAUSE");
```

This code runs the pause command, which prints the message

```
Press any key to continue . . .
```

and waits for you to press a key. Because the system() function can run any shell command, you can use it to call the copy command, like this:

```
system("copy c:\\abc.txt c:\\def.txt");
```

Note that the command uses the backslash, not a forward slash due to limitations in the Windows command processor. If you're using some other platform, you need to consider the needs of the platform when formatting commands.

Moving and Renaming Files and Directories

You may have a file called

```
dog1.txt
```

and need to rename it to

```
temp\dog1.txt
```

This doesn't look like a valid way to rename a file. Notice that the file started out being called dog1.txt, and afterward it's still called dog1.txt. Rather than being renamed, the file appears to have moved to a new location — the temp subdirectory. The reason this is called a rename is that the file's real name is the entire pathname and filename together. For this reason, you can move and rename by files and directories using the same function. Of course, the path must exist. If you try to rename c:\dog1.txt to c:\temp\dog1.txt and there's no c:\temp directory, the rename fails and you get an error message.

The RenameFile example renames a file. Note that you must create a dog1.txt file and a temp directory in the \CPP_AIO4\BookVI\Chapter04\RenameFile folder for this example to work.

```cpp
#include <iostream>
#include <stdio.h>

using namespace std;

int main() {
  if (rename("dog1.txt", "dog2.txt") == 0)
    cout << "Renaming dog1.txt to dog2.txt." << endl;

  if (rename("dog2.txt","dog1.txt") == 0)
    cout << "Renaming dog2.txt to dog1.txt." << endl;

  if (rename("dog1.txt","temp/dog2.txt") == 0)
    cout << "Renaming dog1.txt to temp/dog2.txt." << endl;
```

```
    if (rename("temp/dog2.txt","dog1.txt") == 0)
      cout << "Getting back to start with dog1.txt."
        << endl;

  return 0;
}
```

The example uses the `rename()` function, passing first the old filename and then the new filename. The first call renames the file from `dog1.txt` to `dog2.txt`. The second call renames it from `dog2.txt` to `dog1.txt`. Finally, the code moves the file to the `temp` directory, but only if you created it. When you run this example, you see the following output:

```
Renaming dog1.txt to dog2.txt.
Renaming dog2.txt to dog1.txt.
Renaming dog1.txt to temp/dog2.txt.
Getting back to start with dog1.txt.
```

TIP

You can also give the file a new filename when you move it, as in this code:

```
rename("dog1.txt","temp/cat.txt")
```

REMEMBER

There are conditions under which the rename operation won't work:

» You're renaming the file to move it to a new directory, but that directory does not exist. In this case, create the directory before you move the file.

» You're renaming a file but some other file in the current directory already exists under that name. In this case, either delete the other file or (better yet) make your application ask its users what they want it to do: Delete the old file (that is, "overwrite it")? Abort the operation?

» You're renaming a file to move it to a new directory, but there's already a file by that name in that directory. In this case, as in the previous example, get your application to ask the users what to do — overwrite or abort?

» The file is locked by another application, such as when you open the file for editing.

TIP

Renaming also works with directories. You can move directory names around just as if they were files. But there's a catch: If any application has a file open within that directory, the `rename()` function won't work. The operating system lets you move or rename a directory only if you're not accessing any files inside the directory.

Chapter **5**

Streaming Your Own Classes

The C++ stream classes can read and write all sorts of goodies, such as integers, characters, strings, floating-point numbers, and Boolean variables. But sooner or later, being able to stream one of your own classes (like the following) would be nice:

```
MyClass x;
cout << x << endl;
```

C++ has a good reason not to have done this already: The compiler and library can't predict on their own how you want to stream your class using cout. (The example in the "Writing and reading structured data" section of Chapter 3 of this minibook shows one technique for accomplishing this task by overriding the << operator.) Here are some examples:

» The name of the class followed by the values of the public properties.

» The private properties.

» Derived values or some other information related to the class.

Therefore, you should make the class streamable. This chapter shows you how to do it. But keep in mind that you have (at least) two separate reasons why you may want to make a class streamable:

>> To provide a format for writing the object to a text stream.

>> To save the information in an object so that you can read it back in at a later date, thereby reconstructing the object. A class with this feature is called a *persistent* class.

This chapter covers both. You also discover how you can create your own manipulators. Remember, a *manipulator* is this kind of code:

```
cout << endl;
```

That is, the endl is the manipulator that adds a newline to the end of a stream. You can make your own manipulators that manipulate the stream in various ways, as you see later in this chapter.

REMEMBER

You don't have to type the source code for this chapter manually. In fact, using the downloadable source is a lot easier. You can find the source for this chapter in the \CPP_AI04\BookVI\Chapter05 folder of the downloadable source. See the Introduction for details on how to find these source files.

Streaming a Class for Text Formatting

When dealing with instances of one of your classes, the ability to use the insertion (<<) and extraction operators (>>) is nice. To use these operators, you overload them to work with your class properties. However, when people first find out about overloading the insertion and extraction operators, the process often seems so much harder than it really is.

When working with streams, you might hear that converting data or an object to a stream is called *serialization*, while converting a stream back to data or an object is called *deserialization*. (Note that the information from the following sections is combined with the CustomManipulator example in Listing 5-1 to provide a more complete example.)

Understanding the process

If you have a class, say, `Microwave`, and you have an instance of this class, say, `myoven`, all you do to accomplish the overloading of an operator is code a function that takes a stream parameter and an instance of your class, and writes the property values of the object to the stream. Then you can code one of the following lines:

```
cout << myoven;
outfile << myoven;
```

You can also code an operator that reads from a stream. All you do is write a function that reads the property values from a stream if you want to code one of the following lines:

```
cin >> myoven;
infile >> myoven;
```

Remember that `cout << myoven` actually calls a function called `<<`. Here's the function header:

```
ostream &operator <<(ostream &out, Microwave &oven)
```

Overriding the insertion and extraction operators isn't as hard to remember as you may think when you consider these issues:

» Every type you use for the operator override is a reference, which makes sense when you look at `cout << myoven`. The second parameter, `myoven`, isn't a pointer. In addition, you normally don't want to pass objects around directly, so that leaves only one possibility: passing it by reference.

» The function must return the stream that it's working with. Returning the stream allows you to chain operators together, like this:

```
cout << "hi" << myoven << 123 << endl;
```

» The operator function takes two parameters. You can see their order when you look at the order of `cout << myoven`. The first is the stream; the second is your class. Thus, when you put this all together, you get the function header described earlier.

Considering the insertion implementation

To create a new insertion function, you write to the stream passed into it. In general, you write class properties to the stream. However, you can add formatting or other values as needed. You decide how the output looks when you write the object to a stream. So if this is your `Microwave` class:

```
class Microwave {
public:
  int HighVoltageRadiation;
  int RadioactiveFoodCount;
  int LeakLevel;
  string OvenName;
};
```

Then your insertion function may look like this:

```
ostream &operator <<(ostream &out, Microwave &oven)
{
  out << "High Voltage Radiation: ";
  out << oven.HighVoltageRadiation << endl;
  out << "Radioactive Food Count: ";
  out << oven.RadioactiveFoodCount << endl;
  out << "Leak Level: ";
  out << oven.LeakLevel << endl;
  out << "Oven Name: ";
  out << oven.OvenName << endl;
  return out;
}
```

Here are some points to consider about the preceding code:

>> The example takes complete liberty with how the object looks on the stream. Each property provides a description, a colon, a space, and then a value. Then entries use endl so that each property appears on a separate line. The point is that the output can appear however you need it to appear.

TIP

>> The code returns the same output stream that came in as the first parameter (modified with the class data, of course).

>> When writing to the stream, the code writes to out, not to cout. Writing to cout would cause the function to fail when used with a file. When coding myfile << myoven, the information would go to cout, not into the file.

This function accesses only the public properties of the `myoven` instance. As it stands, the function can't access the private properties because it isn't a member of `Microwave`. To access the private properties, make this function a friend of `Microwave` by adding this code inside the `Microwave` class:

```
friend ostream &operator <<(ostream &out,Microwave &oven);
```

Considering the extraction implementation

The previous section tells you how to override the insertion operator. Here's a similar function for using the extraction operator to read from a stream (this function doesn't match the earlier insertion code, so it can't read text that was written by the earlier code):

```
istream &operator >>(istream &in, Microwave &oven)
{
    in >> oven.HighVoltageRadiation;
    in >> oven.RadioactiveFoodCount;
    in >> oven.LeakLevel;
    in >> oven.OvenName;
    return in;
}
```

You can see that the format of this function is like that of the insertion operator: The function returns a reference to the stream, and for parameters, the function takes a reference to a stream and a reference to a `Microwave` object.

As before, you have complete freedom on how you want to read the data in. The code reads in each member separately. So, if you call this function by using `cin`, like this

```
cin >> myoven;
```

then — when you run this line — you can type the member values on one line with spaces, or on separate lines, or any combination:

```
1234 5555
1054 "Buzz"
```

WARNING

There are always caveats when it comes to input, and overriding the extraction operator is no different. The `istream` you receive isn't guaranteed to provide all the data elements you need, in the correct order and in the right form. In some respects, you depend on the user or other data source to provide the information according to whatever protocol you've created. Consequently, unlike writing to a stream, reading from a stream involves some level of risk, so you need to provide robust error trapping.

Manipulating a Stream

A lot of people see this kind of thing:

```
cout << "Hello" << endl;
```

and wonder what on Earth endl is. After all, it's not a destination like cout — it's something else. The sections that follow discuss endl and other kinds of *manipulators*, which are special functions that interact with streams in specific ways using the insertion and extraction operators.

What's a manipulator?

A manipulator is actually the address of a function. To clarify exactly what endl is, think about this:

```
cout << endl;
```

The << operator function in this case is an overloaded insertion operator function that receives two parameters, cout and endl. The first parameter, cout, is an instance of ostream. The second parameter, endl, is the address of a function. When you type a function name, but don't include parentheses, you're giving the address of the function rather than calling the function.

So, in the standard header files is an overloaded insertion function that takes both an ostream and the address of a function. Now the thing about function addresses is that the type of a function pointer is based on the function's return type and parameter types. Thus, pointers to these two functions have the same type:

```
void WriteMe(int x, char c);
void AlwaysAndForever(int y, char x);
```

Even though the names of the parameters are different, the types of the parameters are the same. That's why pointers to the two functions have the same type. But pointers to the following two functions don't have the same type:

```
void SomethingForNothing(int x);
int LeaveMeAlone(int y, int z);
```

The functions don't have the same type because their prototypes are different. The first takes a single integer as a parameter and returns a void. The second takes two integers as parameters and returns an integer. Here's the prototype for the endl function:

```
ostream& endl(ostream& outs);
```

This function takes a reference to `ostream` and returns a reference to `ostream`. And here's a `typedef` for a pointer to this function:

```
typedef ostream& (*omanip)(ostream&);
```

This `typedef` defines a new type called `omanip`, which is a pointer to a function that takes as a parameter a reference to `ostream` and returns a reference to `ostream`. Therefore, if you have a variable of type `omanip`, you can set it to the address of the `endl` function.

For the `endl` manipulator to work, you need an overloaded insertion operator function that takes two parameters: first a reference to `ostream` (for `cout`) and then `omanip`. The second parameter must be a reference to `omanip` because the second item in `cout << endl` is of type `omanip`.

REMEMBER

If you're not clear on why `endl` is of type `omanip`, think about this: There's a function called `endl`, and to call that function, you would type its name, an opening parenthesis, some parameters, and then a closing parenthesis. But if you leave off the parentheses, you're just taking the address of the function. And the type `omanip`, defined earlier, is exactly that: an address to a function. But on top of being an address, the `endl` function's prototype matches that for the `omanip` type.

Here's a possibility for the header of the overloaded insertion operator:

```
ostream& operator<<(ostream& out, omanip func);
```

You can see the parameters that this function takes: First, it takes a reference to `ostream` and then `omanip`. Consequently, to implement `endl`, two functions are involved. Here are their headers:

```
ostream& endl(ostream& outs);
ostream& operator<<(ostream& out, omanip func);
```

When you type `cout << endl`, you're not calling the `endl` function. Instead, you're calling the `operator<<` function because `endl` by itself — without parentheses — is nothing more than the address of the `endl` function. And the address is of type `omanip`. Here's the `operator<<` function in its entirety:

```
ostream& operator<<(ostream &out, omanip func) {
    return (*func)(out);
}
```

The `func` parameter contains the address of `endl`. The code shown ends up calling `endl` and supplying it with `out`. You could use this approach for any function that matches the `omanip` type. Using this approach relies on function pointer syntax. As long as you know what is involved, you normally don't need to delve too far into the details. However, if you'd like more details, check out the article at `https://www.cprogramming.com/tutorial/function-pointers.html`.

This isn't the only way to accomplish coding a manipulator, as explained in the following section, "Writing your own manipulator." That section uses a slightly different approach that works equally well. But the technique described in this section is quite common, and you need to know how it works.

Writing your own manipulator

You can write your own manipulators in several ways. The goal is to allow for this type of code:

```
cout << mymanipulator;
```

and this line causes a function such as the following to get called:

```
ostream &operator << (ostream &out, somespecialtype a);
```

Several `operator<<` functions are natively available; ultimately, they differ in the second parameter type, `somespecialtype`. Whatever `mymanipulator` is, it must be the `somespecialtype` type as well. This type must be unique or the compiler will complain.

The "What's a manipulator?" section (earlier in this chapter) gives you the details on how the `endl` manipulator works, but that amount of detail is a bit too complicated. The example in this section creates a unique type, and the manipulator is an object of that type. As with other manipulators, function pointers work well. But for the function pointer to be unique, its parameter types must be unique. The example uses that as the parameter for the function, like this:

```
struct FullOvenManip {};
void FullOvenInfo(FullOvenManip x) {}
```

Check this sample carefully. The code uses a structure called FullOvenManip. This structure has nothing in it; its sole purpose in life is to provide for a unique set of parameters. The FullOvenInfo() function takes this structure as a parameter. The point is to create a unique prototype.

You can now provide an overloaded operator << function. That function takes a pointer to the FullOvenInfo() function. But to do that, you use typedef:

```
typedef void(*FullPtr)(FullOvenManip);
```

TIP

This line of code creates a type called FullPtr, which is a pointer to a function that takes a FullOvenManip parameter and returns a void. When writing your own manipulators, don't shy away from using typedef. The manipulator concept is confusing and can be a serious struggle for many developers to keep straight. By using a typedef, you can simplify your life a bit. Here's the overloaded operator << function header:

```
ostream &operator << (ostream &out, FullPtr);
```

You can see the second parameter: It's a FullPtr. And look at this code:

```
cout << FullOvenInfo;
```

The FullOvenInfo item is also a FullPtr because it's a pointer to a function that takes a FullOvenManip(). The CustomManipulator example, in Listing 5-1, shows how these elements work together.

LISTING 5-1: **Using Manipulators**

```
#include <iostream>
#include <fstream>
#include <map>

using namespace std;

class Microwave {
    friend ostream &operator <<(ostream &out,
                                Microwave &oven);
public:
    int HighVoltageRadiation;
    int RadioactiveFoodCount;
    int LeakLevel;
    string OvenName;
```

(continued)

LISTING 5-1: *(continued)*

```cpp
  typedef map<ostream *, bool> FlagMap;
  static FlagMap Flags;
};

Microwave::FlagMap Microwave::Flags;

ostream &operator <<(ostream &out, Microwave &oven) {
  bool full = true;
  Microwave::FlagMap::iterator iter =
    Microwave::Flags.find(&out);

  if (iter != Microwave::Flags.end()) {
    full = iter->second;
  }

  if (full) {
    out << "High Voltage Radiation: ";
    out << oven.HighVoltageRadiation << endl;
    out << "Radioactive Food Count: ";
    out << oven.RadioactiveFoodCount << endl;
    out << "Leak Level: ";
    out << oven.LeakLevel << endl;
    out << "Oven Name: ";
    out << oven.OvenName;
  } else {
    out << oven.HighVoltageRadiation << ",";
    out << oven.RadioactiveFoodCount << ",";
    out << oven.LeakLevel << ",";
    out << oven.OvenName;
  }
  return out;
}

istream &operator >>(istream &in, Microwave &oven) {
  in >> oven.HighVoltageRadiation;
  in >> oven.RadioactiveFoodCount;
  in >> oven.LeakLevel;
  in >> oven.OvenName;
  return in;
}

struct FullOvenManip {};
```

```
void FullOvenInfo(FullOvenManip x) {}

typedef void(*FullPtr)(FullOvenManip);

ostream &operator << (ostream &out, FullPtr) {
  Microwave::Flags[&out] = true;
  return out;
}

struct MinOvenManip {};

void MinOvenInfo(MinOvenManip x) {}

typedef void(*MinPtr)(MinOvenManip);

ostream &operator << (ostream &out, MinPtr) {
  Microwave::Flags[&out] = false;
  return out;
}

int main() {
  Microwave myoven;
  myoven.HighVoltageRadiation = 9832;
  myoven.RadioactiveFoodCount = 7624;
  myoven.LeakLevel = 3793;
  myoven.OvenName = "Burnmaster";

  cout << myoven << endl;
  cout << "============" << endl;
  cout << FullOvenInfo << myoven << endl;
  cout << "============" << endl;
  cout << MinOvenInfo << myoven << endl;

  return 0;
}
```

The code in Listing 5-1 creates two manipulators, one called FullOvenInfo() and one called MinOvenInfo(). When you use one of these manipulators, as in the following line, you call the overloaded operator << function:

```
cout << FullOvenInfo << myoven << endl;
```

The FullOvenInfo() function works with a map to keep track of which stream you're manipulating. The map lives as a static member in the Microwave class. So when you use the FullOvenInfo() manipulator on cout, the map's item for cout gets a value of true from operator<<() as Microwave::Flags[&out] = true;. And when you use the MinOvenInfo() manipulator on cout, the map's item for cout gets a value of false from that manipulator's operator<<() function.

Using the map may not make sense at first. The idea is that you may be working with multiple streams, such as one for an ofstream file and one for cout, and you may want some streams to show the full information via the FullOvenInfo() manipulator — and some other streams to show the minimal information via the MinOvenInfo(). The map is based on the stream. In the overloaded operator << function that prints a Microwave object, you see how the code checks the map for a true or false for the current stream.

TIP

Note that cout << FullOvenInfo does not actually send any output to cout; it just modifies cout so future output of a Microwave object will use the full format. Then the next part of the statement, << myoven, sends the Microwave object to cout. When you run this application, you see this output:

```
High Voltage Radiation: 9832
Radioactive Food Count: 7624
Leak Level: 3793
Oven Name: Burnmaster
============
High Voltage Radiation: 9832
Radioactive Food Count: 7624
Leak Level: 3793
Oven Name: Burnmaster
============
9832,7624,3793,Burnmaster
```

The output shows the same object three times. The first one demonstrates the default: If you provide no manipulators, you get a full listing. This need is handled in the overloaded operator <<() for printing a Microwave object:

```
bool full = true;
Microwave::FlagMap::iterator iter =
  Microwave::Flags.find(&out);

if (iter != Microwave::Flags.end()) {
  full = iter->second;
}
```

Remember that `iterator` is really a pointer to the `map` entry. The code calls `find()` to determine whether the item is inside the `map` entry. If it's not, `find` returns `Flags.end()`. And if the code doesn't return `Flags.end()`, that means it found the item in the `map`. So in that case, the code uses `iter->second` to obtain the value.

But notice what happens if the code doesn't return `Flags.end()`, meaning that the stream wasn't found in the `map`. Then the application sticks with the default value for `full`, which is `true`:

```
bool full = true;
```

So you can see that these output lines will function properly:

```
cout << myoven << endl;
cout << "============" << endl;
cout << FullOvenInfo << myoven << endl;
cout << "============" << endl;
cout << MinOvenInfo << myoven << endl;
```

The first line with `myoven` line uses the default, which is a full listing. The second line with `myoven` says to definitely output a full listing, using the `FullOvenInfo()` manipulator. The third line with `myoven` outputs a minimal listing using the `MinOvenInfo()` manipulator.

7
Advanced Standard Library Usage

Contents at a Glance

Chapter **1**

Exploring the Standard Library Further

The Standard Library is one of the most important parts of the C++ developer's toolkit because it contains a host of interesting functions that let you write great applications. The Standard Library originally started as the Standard Template Library (STL), and a number of companies, including Silicon Graphics, Inc. (SGI) and IBM, distributed it for everyone to use. The International Standards Organization (ISO) eventually took over STL, made a few minor changes to it, added some additional features, and renamed it the Standard Library.

REMEMBER

The STL and the Standard Library are two separate entities. As the Standard Library has grown, it has also become more different from the STL. Consequently, when you work with C++ today, you likely work with the Standard Library and, to avoid confusion, shouldn't refer to it as the STL. In fact, the Standard Library and the STL use different headers — again, to avoid confusion (you can see a heading listing at https://en.cppreference.com/w/cpp/header). The site at https://www.tutorialspoint.com/What-s-the-difference-between-STL-and-Cplusplus-Standard-Library provides a short discussion of the differences between the Standard Library and STL that includes additional details.

This chapter offers an overview of the Standard Library and shows you some examples of how to use it. However, if you don't see what you want here, don't worry; later chapters have additional examples, and you can always refer to the Standard Library documentation for even more examples. Before the chapter moves on to any examples, however, you need to know what the Standard Library contains, so the first section of this chapter gives you a list of Standard Library function categories.

REMEMBER

You don't have to type the source code for this chapter manually. In fact, using the downloadable source is a lot easier. You can find the source for this chapter in the \CPP_AIO4\BookVII\Chapter01 folder of the downloadable source. See the Introduction for details on how to find these source files.

Considering the Standard Library Categories

The Standard Library documentation uses a formal approach that you're going to find difficult to read and even harder to understand; it must have been put together by lawyers more interested in the precise meaning of words rather than the usability of the document. This immense tome (1,300+ pages) requires quite a bit of time to review. Fortunately, you don't have to wade through all that legal jargon mixed indiscriminately with computer jargon and the occasional bit of English. This chapter provides the overview you need to get going quickly.

The best way to begin is to break the Standard Library into smaller pieces. You can categorize the Standard Library functions in a number of ways. One of the most common approaches is to use the following categories:

Algorithms	Atomic Operations (C++ 11 and above)	C Compatibility
Concepts (C++ 20 and above)	Containers	Coroutines (C++ 20 and above)
Filesystem (C++ 17 and above)	Input/Output	Iterators
Localization	Numerics	Ranges (C++ 20 and above)
Regular Expressions (C++ 11 and above)	Strings	Thread Support (C++ 11 and above)
Utilities		

Note that this table doesn't include the *Standard Library Extensions*, additions that add specialized (non-general) functionality, which appear at https://en.cppreference.com/w/cpp/experimental/lib_extensions_2. The following sections provide a brief description of each of these categories and tell what you can expect to find in them. Knowing the category can help you locate the function you need quickly on websites that use these relatively standard category names.

Algorithms

Algorithms perform data manipulations such as replacing, locating, or sorting information. You've already seen some algorithms used in the book because it's hard to create a substantial application without using one. There aren't any types in the Algorithms category. The following is a list of common algorithm functions

(functions removed since C++ 11 and above don't appear in the list even if you can use them in an older version of C++):

adjacent_find	all_of (C++ 11 and above)	any_of (C++ 11 and above)
binary_search	clamp (C++ 17 and above)	copy
copy_backward	copy_if (C++ 11 and above)	copy_n (Updated C++ 11)
count	count_if	equal
equal_range	fill	fill_n
find	find_end	find_first_of
find_if	find_if_not (C++ 11 and above)	for_each
for_each_n (C++17 and above)	generate	generate_n
includes	inplace_merge	is_heap (Updated C++ 11)
is_heap_until (C++ 11 and above)	is_partitioned (C++ 11 and above)	is_permutation (C++ 11 and above)
is_sorted (Updated C++ 11)	is_sorted_until (C++ 11 and above)	iter_swap
lexicographical_compare	lexicographical_compare_three_way (C++ 20 and above)	lower_bound
make_heap	max	max_element
merge	min	min_element
minmax (C++ 11 and above)	minmax_element (C++ 11 and above)	mismatch
move (C++ 11 and above)	move_backward (C++ 11 and above)	next_permutation
none_of (C++ 11 and above)	nth_element	partial_sort
partial_sort_copy	partition	partition_copy (C++ 11 and above)
partition_point (C++ 11 and above)	pop_heap	prev_permutation

push_heap	remove	remove_copy
remove_copy_if	remove_if	replace
replace_copy	replace_copy_if	replace_if
reverse	reverse_copy	rotate
rotate_copy	sample (C++ 17 and above)	search
search_n	set_difference	set_intersection
set_symmetric_difference	set_union	shift_left (C++ 20 and above)
shift_right (C++ 20 and above)	shuffle (C++11 and above)	sort
sort_heap	stable_partition	stable_sort
swap	swap_ranges	transform
unique	unique_copy	upper_bound

In addition to the ‹algorithm› header entries found in the previous table, C++ 17 and above users have access to the ‹execution› header entries in the table that follows. This functionality is still part of the Algorithms category but appears in a different header. An *execution policy* determines whether your code executes in sequence (the normal approach) or in parallel. Executing code in parallel, whenever possible, makes your application run significantly faster.

is_execution_policy	parallel_policy	parallel_unsequenced_policy
sequenced_policy	unsequenced_policy (C++ 20 and above)	

Atomic operations

An *atomic operation* is a code block that executes as a single concurrent entity without the use of locking mechanisms. There are several benefits to using atomic operations:

>> Because the atomic operation is indivisible, it's free of *data races* where:

- Two or more threads in a single process access the same memory location concurrently

- At least one of the thread accesses is for writing

- The threads don't use any exclusive locks to control their accesses to that memory

» which results in nondeterministic behavior. The changes made by the threads vary run-by-run.

» Application development is significantly easier because you don't have to manage locks.

» There is a smaller risk of data-related errors.

You must have C++ 11 or above to use this feature. The following table contains the Atomic Operations category functions.

atomic_compare_ exchange_strong	atomic_compare_ exchange_strong_ explicit	atomic_compare_ exchange_weak
atomic_compare_ exchange_weak_ explicit	atomic_exchange	atomic_exchange_ explicit
atomic_fetch_add	atomic_fetch_add_ explicit	atomic_fetch_and
atomic_fetch_and_ explicit	atomic_fetch_or	atomic_fetch_or_ explicit
atomic_fetch_sub	atomic_fetch_sub_ explicit	atomic_fetch_xor
atomic_fetch_xor_ explicit	atomic_flag_clear	atomic_flag_clear_ explicit
atomic_flag_notify_ all (C++ 20 and above)	atomic_flag_notify_ one (C++ 20 and above)	atomic_flag_test (C++ 20 and above)
atomic_flag_test_ and_set	atomic_flag_test_ and_set_explicit	atomic_flag_test_ explicit (C++ 20 and above)
atomic_flag_wait (C++ 20 and above)	atomic_flag_wait_ explicit (C++ 20 and above)	atomic_init (Deprecated in C++ 20)
atomic_is_lock_free	atomic_load	atomic_load_explicit

atomic_notify_all (C++ 20 and above)	atomic_notify_one (C++ 20 and above)	atomic_signal_fence
atomic_store	atomic_store_explicit	atomic_thread_fence
atomic_wait (C++ 20 and above)	atomic_wait_explicit (C++ 20 and above)	kill_dependency

C Compatibility

A C compatibility header provides you with access to functionality that came with the original C language. For example, you find special math functions like pow( ) (raises a number to the given power) in the <math.h> header.

WARNING

All the C compatibility headers are deprecated at this point, which means you can still use them, but not for long. You should instead use the Utilities category equivalents. For example, the <ctime> header replaces the <time.h> header (note that the <ctime> header lacks the .h file extension).

Concepts

C++ 20 adds the capability to provide predicates that express a generic algorithm's expectations through *concepts*. You use a concept to formally document the constraints on a template to enforce certain behaviors. In addition, because the compiler knows the constraints at the outset, it can usually compile your application faster. The article at https://isocpp.org/blog/2016/02/a-bit-of-background-for-concepts-and-cpp17-bjarne-stroustrup provides more details about the potential for concepts. You could also read the fuller discussion at https://www.stroustrup.com/good_concepts.pdf. The following table provides a listing of Concepts category functions.

assignable_from	common_reference_with	common_with
constructible_from	convertible_to	copy_constructible
copyable	default_initializable	derived_from
destructible	equality_comparable	equality_comparable_with
equivalence_relation	floating_point	integral
invocable	movable	move_constructible

predicate	regular	regular_invocable
relation	same_as	semiregular
signed_integral	strict_weak_order	swappable
swappable_with	totally_ordered	totally_ordered_with
unsigned_integral		

Containers

Containers work just like the containers in your home — they hold something. You've already seen containers at work in other areas of this book. For example, both queues and deques are kinds of containers. The Containers category doesn't contain any functions, but it does contain a number of types including those in the following table (types are removed because C++ 11 and above don't appear in the list even if you can use them in an older version of C++).

array (C++ 11 and above)	deque	forward_list (C++ 11 and above)
list	map	queue
set	span (C++ 20 and above)	stack
unordered_map (C++ 11 and above)	unordered_set (C++ 11 and above)	vector

Coroutines

A *coroutine* is a new feature in C++ 20 that allows a function to suspend execution and resume its task later. The function stores the data needed to allow task resumption separately, rather than on the stack. This feature helps support sequential code that executes asynchronously, such as nonblocking I/O, without requiring use of callbacks. You can find an example of a coroutine at https://blog.panicsoftware.com/your-first-coroutine/. The following table contains the Coroutines category classes.

coroutine_handle	coroutine_traits	noop_coroutine_handle
noop_coroutine_promise	std::hash<std::coroutine_handle>	suspend_always
suspend_never		

Filesystem

Before C++ 17, C++ lacked the ability to perform some basic file system tasks, such as determining the existence of a path. The Filesystem category provides functionality needed to work with file systems on a local system. You can see an example of the <filesystem> header in use in the "Using the filesystem Library" sidebar in Book 6, Chapter 4. The article at https://www.codingame.com/playgrounds/5659/c17-filesystem provides additional examples. The following table lists the Filesystem category classes.

copy_options	directory_entry	directory_iterator
directory_options	file_status	file_time_type
file_type	filesystem_error	path
perm_options	perms	recursive_directory_ iterator
space_info		

Input/Output

The Input/Output category is an old friend in this book because you see it used in every example. Not every heading in this category appears in the book, but most do in some form. The following table provides a listing of the Input/Output category headers, which make it possible to access various forms of I/O.

cstdio	fstream	iomanip
ios	iosfwd	iostream
istream	ostream	sstream
streambuf	strstream (Deprecated in C++ 98)	syncstream (C++ 20 and above)

Iterators

Iterators enumerate something. When you create a list of items and then go through that list checking items off, you're enumerating the list. Using iterators helps you create lists of items and manipulate them in specific ways. The kind of iterator you create is important because some iterators let you go forward only, some can go in either direction, and some can choose items at random. Each kind of iterator has its specific purpose.

The Iterators category includes a number of classes. These classes determine the kind of iterator you create in your code and the capabilities of that iterator. The following is a list of the iterator classes (classes removed since C++ 11 and above don't appear in the list even if you can use them in an older version of C++):

`back_insert_iterator`	`bidirectional_iterator` (handled as concept in C++ 20 and above)	`bidirectional_iterator_tag`
`common_iterator` (C++ 20 and above)	`contiguous_iterator_tag` (C++ 20 and above)	`counted_iterator` (C++ 20 and above)
`default_sentinel` (C++ 20 and above)	`forward_iterator` (handled as concept in C++ 20 and above)	`forward_iterator_tag`
`front_insert_iterator`	`incremental_traits` (C++ 20 and above)	`indirect_result_t` (C++ 20 and above)
`indirectly_readable_traits` (C++ 20 and above)	`input_iterator` (handled as concept in C++ 20 and above)	`input_iterator_tag`
`insert_iterator`	`istream_iterator`	`istreambuf_iterator`
`iter_common_reference_t` (C++ 20 and above)	`iter_difference_t` (C++ 20 and above)	`iter_move` (C++ 20 and above)
`iter_reference_t` (C++ 20 and above)	`iter_rvalue_reference_t` (C++ 20 and above)	`iter_swap` (C++ 20 and above)
`iter_value_t` (C++ 20 and above)	`iterator` (Deprecated C++ 17)	`iterator_traits`
`move_iterator` (C++ 11 and above)	`move_sentinel` (C++ 20 and above)	`ostream_iterator`
`ostreambuf_iterator`	`output_iterator` (handled as concept in C++ 20 and above)	`output_iterator_tag`
`projected` (C++ 20 and above)	`random_access_iterator` (handled as concept in C++ 20 and above)	`random_access_iterator_tag`
`reverse_iterator`	`unreachable_sentinel_t` (C++ 20 and above)	

Localization

When you write applications for multiple languages, the application needs to know how to handle these languages correctly. The Localization category classes won't automatically convert your text to the other language. You need to perform any needed translation yourself. However, it does help you perform these tasks:

» Character classification

» String collation

» Numeric, monetary, and date/time formatting and parsing

» Message retrieval

REMEMBER

For most applications today, you use the ⟨locale⟩ header. If you have older applications that rely on the C language localization functionality that used to appear in local.h, you use ⟨clocale⟩ instead. C++ 11 introduced the ⟨codecvt⟩ header for converting Unicode character sets. This functionality is deprecated in C++ 17 — use the codecvt class in the ⟨locale⟩ header instead. The following table shows the ⟨local⟩ header classes.

codecvt	codecvt_base	codecvt_byname
collate	collate_byname	ctype
ctype_base	ctype_byname	ctype⟨char⟩
locale	messages	messages_base
messages_byname	money_base	money_get
money_put	moneypunct	moneypunct_byname
num_get	num_put	numpunct
numpunct_byname	time_base	time_get
time_get_byname	time_put	time_put_byname
wbuffer_convert (Added C++ 11, deprecated C++ 17)	wstring_convert (Added C++ 11, deprecated C++ 17)	

Numerics

The Numerics category is immense, as you might imagine. It provides access to all sorts of functions to perform math-related tasks. The most basic of the associated headers is ⟨cmath⟩, which contains basic math functionality, such as obtaining the absolute value of a number using the abs function. The following table lists the Numerics category headers.

Header	C++ version	Short description
`<bit>`	C++ 20 and above	Bit manipulation
`<cfenv>`	C++ 11 and above	Floating point environment access
`<cmath>`		Common math functions
`<complex>`		Complex number operations
`<numbers>`	C++ 20 and above	Math constants
`<numeric>`		Operations on values in ranges
`<random>`	C++ 11 and above	Random number generation
`<ratio>`	C++ 11 and above	Compile-time rational math
`<valarray>`		Interacts with arrays of values

Ranges

Being able to work efficiently with ranges of values is important in reducing the amount of code you write and ensuring that the code you do write is easy to understand. Most modern languages provide shortcuts for working with ranges of values, and the C++ 20 standard adds this functionality to C++.

TIP

Unfortunately, as of this writing, no major compilers or libraries actually implement this functionality, so you need to download and install the range-v3 library (`https://github.com/ericniebler/range-v3/`) to actually use it. This library is the basis for ranges support in C++ 20. (Using this library is outside the scope of this book; however, you can find documentation for it at `https://ericniebler.github.io/range-v3/`.)

This particular category is designed to work with *views*, which describe what you want to see as output. For example, if you want to sort a range in reverse order, you provide a view that describes this need, such as `views::reverse(v)`, where v is a vector containing the range you want to interact with. A sort might then look like `ranges::sort(views::reverse(v));`.

Ranges also work with concepts, described in the "Concepts" section of this chapter. A concept defines the sort of range you work with. The following table lists range concepts.

bidirectional_range	common_range	contiguous_range
forward_range	input_range	output_range
random_access_range	range	sized_range
view	viewable_range	

After you have a range, an idea of how you want to see it, and a task in mind, you can use the various ‹ranges› header classes to perform work. The following table shows the classes associated with the standard for this header.

borrowed_iterator_t	borrowed_subrange_t	dangling
iterator_t	range_difference_t	range_reference_t
range_rvalue_reference_t	range_size_t	range_value_t
ref_view	sentinel_t	subrange
view_interface	views::all	views::all_t
views::common (common_view)	views::counted	views::empty (empty_view)
views::filter (filter_view)	views::iota (iota_view)	views::join (join_view)
views::reverse (reverse_view)	views::single (single_view)	views::split (split_view)
views::take (take_view)	views::transform (transform_view)	

You can also customize the manner in which ranges work using customization point objects. The following table lists these objects found in the std::ranges namespace.

ranges::begin	ranges::data	ranges::empty
ranges::end	ranges::rbegin	ranges::rend
ranges::size		

Regular Expressions

Regular expression support appears in C++ 11 and above. It helps you look for patterns in strings. For example, you can ensure that email addresses and telephone numbers are in the right format before someone enters them into a database, reducing a few data errors in the process. You can also use regular expressions to perform search-and-replace operations. The following table contains the Regular Expression category classes.

basic_regex	match_results	regex_error
regex_iterator	regex_token_iterator	regex_traits
sub_match		

Strings

The Strings category provides a wide range of support for strings in C++. You have seen many examples of the ‹string› header, the most commonly used header, in use in this book. Humans understand strings quite well, but computers handle characters and, therefore, strings as numbers. To make strings easier to use, you need library support. The following table lists the String category headers and their purpose.

Header	C++ Version	Short Description
‹cctype›		Determines the category of narrow (char) characters.
‹charconv›	C++ 17 and above	Conversion to and from characters.
‹cstring›		Narrow character string handling functions.
‹cuchar›	C++ 11 and above	C-style Unicode character conversion functions.
‹cwchar›		Wide and multibyte character string-handling functions.
‹cwctype›		Determines the category of wide (wchar_t) characters.
‹format›	C++ 20 and above	String formatting functionality.
‹string_view›	C++ 17 and above	Basic string view handling class.
‹string›		Basic string handling class.

Thread Support

Multithreaded applications allow an application to apparently perform more than one task at a time. Obviously, the actual simultaneous execution of tasks on a system relies on the number of processors or cores it contains, but multithreading enables you to share processors in a manner that lets you perform tasks efficiently. Parallel and threaded execution of tasks falls into a category of development called *concurrency*, which isn't covered in this book, but you can find a basic article on it at `https://isocpp.org/wiki/faq/cpp11-library-concurrency`.

Utilities

Utilities are functions and types that perform small service tasks within the Standard Library. The functions include `min()`, `max()`, and the relational operators. The types include `chart_traits` (the traits of characters used in other Standard Library features, such as `basic_string`) and `pair` (a pairing of two heterogeneous values). The following table lists the various essential headers provided as part of the Utilities category, their associated C++ version, and a short description. If no C++ version is supplied, you can use the header in all current versions of C++.

Header	C++ version	Short description
`<any>`	C++ 17 and above	Provides support for the any class for objects that hold instances of any `CopyConstructible` type.
`<bitset>`		Implements constant-length bit arrays.
`<chrono>`	C++ 11 and above	C++ time utilities.
`<compare>`	C++ 20 and above	Supports the three-way (spaceship) operator.
`<csetjmp>`		Passes control to a particular execution context.
`<csignal>`		Passes signals (messages) between various application elements.
`<cstdarg>`		Handles variable-length argument lists.
`<cstddef>`		Standard macros and typedefs.
`<cstdlib>`		General-purpose utilities for program control, dynamic memory allocation, random numbers, sort, and search.
`<ctime>`		C-style time and date utilities.

Header	C++ version	Short description
<functional>		Provides function objects, function invocations, bind operations, and reference wrappers.
<initializer_list>	C++ 11 and above	Provides the means to initialize containers other than array, such as vector, list, and map.
<optional>	C++ 17 and above	A wrapper for a variable that may or may not contain an object.
<source_location>	C++ 20 and above	Identifies the location of source code.
<tuple>	C++ 11 and above	Allows creation of tuples.
<type_traits>	C++ 11 and above	Obtains compile-time type information.
<typeindex>	C++ 11 and above	Provides a wrapper around a type_info object for use as an index in associative and unordered associative containers.
<typeinfo>		Obtains runtime information.
<utility>		Basic utility functions.
<variant>	C++ 17 and above	Provides support for variant type variables.
<version>	C++ 20 and above	Supplies implementation-dependent library information.

Parsing Strings Using a Hash

Hashes are an important security requirement for applications today. A *hash* creates a unique numeric equivalent of any string you feed it. Theoretically, you can't duplicate the number that the hash creates by using another string. A hash isn't reversible — it isn't the same as encryption and decryption.

A common use for hashes is to send passwords from a client to a server. The client converts the user's password into a numeric hash and sends that number to the server. The number varies daily depending on some formula that both client and server know. The server verifies the number, not the password. Even if people are listening in, they have no way to ascertain the password from the number;

therefore, they can't steal the password for use with the target application. Other examples of hash use are to:

» Verify a file's hash to a previously saved hash value to ensure no one has modified the file.

» Compare two files to ensure they're most likely the same.

» Make dictionary searches fast.

Code::Blocks provides excellent support for hashes. However, in order to use it, you must enable support for C++ 11 extensions using the technique found in the "Working with ranges" section of Book 1, Chapter 5. After you enable the required support, you can create the HashingStrings example shown here to demonstrate the use of hashes.

```cpp
#include <iostream>
#include <unordered_map>

using namespace std;

int main() {
  hash<const char*> MyHash;
  cout << "The hash of \"Hello World\" is:" << endl;
  cout << MyHash("Hello World") << endl;
  cout << "while the hash of \"Goodbye Cruel World\" is:"
    << endl;
  cout << MyHash("Goodbye Cruel World") << endl;
  return 0;
}
```

The example begins by creating a hash function object, MyHash. You use this function object to convert input text to a hash value. The function object works just like any other function, so you might provide the input text as MyHash("Hello World"). Hashes always output precisely the same value given a particular input. Consequently, you should see the following output from this example.

```
The hash of "Hello World" is:
4952133
while the hash of "Goodbye Cruel World" is:
4952192
```

REMEMBER

Hashes have uses other than security requirements. For example, you can create a container that relies on a hash to make locating a particular value easier. In this case, you use a key/value pair in a *hash map* using `unordered_map<>`. The `HashMap` example, shown next, illustrates how to create a hash map:

```cpp
#include <iostream>
#include <unordered_map>
#include <string.h>

using namespace std;

struct eqstr {
  bool operator()(const char* s1, const char* s2) const
  {
    return strcmp(s1, s2) == 0;
  }
};

int main() {
  unordered_map<const char*, int,
    hash<const char*>, eqstr> Colors;
  Colors["Blue"] = 1;
  Colors["Green"] = 2;
  Colors["Teal"] = 3;
  Colors["Brick"] = 4;
  Colors["Purple"] = 5;
  Colors["Brown"] = 6;
  Colors["LightGray"] = 7;
  cout << "Brown = " << Colors["Brown"] << endl;
  cout << "Brick = " << Colors["Brick"] << endl;
  // This key isn't in the hash map, so it returns a
  // value of 0.
  cout << "Red = " << Colors["Red"] << endl;
}
```

An unordered (hash) map requires four inputs:

>> Key type

>> Data type

>> Hashing function

>> Equality key

The first three inputs are straightforward. In this case, the code uses a string as a key type, an integer value as a data type, and hash<const char*> as the hashing function. You already know how the hashing function works from the previous example in this section.

The equality key class is a little more complex. You must provide the hash map with a means of determining equality. In this case, the code compares the input string with the string stored as the key. The eqstr structure performs the task of comparing the input string to the key. The structure must return a Boolean value, so the code compares the strcmp function to 0. When the two are equal, meaning that the strings are equal, eqstr returns true.

REMEMBER

The example goes on to check for three colors, only two of which appear in the hash map Colors. In the first two cases, you see the expected value. In the third case, you see 0, which indicates that Colors doesn't contain the desired key. Always reserve 0 as an error indicator when using a hash map, because the hash map will always return a value, even if it doesn't contain the desired key. The output from this example is

```
Brown = 6
Brick = 4
Red = 0
```

Obtaining Information Using a Random Access Iterator

Most containers let you perform random access of data they contain. For example, the RandomAccess example shows that you can create an iterator and then add to or subtract from the current offset to obtain values within the container that iterator supports:

```
#include <iostream>
#include <vector>

using namespace std;

int main() {
  vector<string> Words;
  Words.push_back("Blue");
  Words.push_back("Green");
```

```
    Words.push_back("Teal");
    Words.push_back("Brick");
    Words.push_back("Purple");
    Words.push_back("Brown");
    Words.push_back("LightGray");
    // Define a random iterator.
    vector<string>::iterator Iter = Words.begin();
    // Access random points.
    Iter += 5;
    cout << *Iter << endl;
    Iter -= 2;
    cout << *Iter << endl;
    return 0;
}
```

In this case, the vector, Words, contains a list of seven items. The code creates an iterator for Words named Iter. It then adds to or subtracts from the iterator offset and displays the output onscreen. Here is what you see when you run this example:

```
Brown
Brick
```

Sometimes you need to perform a special task using a random-access iterator. For example, you might want to create a special function to summate the members of vector or just a range of members within vector. In this case, you must create a specialized function to perform the task as follows because the Standard Library doesn't include any functions to do it for you, as shown in the RandomAccess2 example:

```
#include <iostream>
#include <vector>

using namespace std;

template <class RandomAccessIterator>
float AddIt(RandomAccessIterator begin,
            RandomAccessIterator end) {
  float Sum = 0;
  RandomAccessIterator Index;
  // Make sure that the values are in the correct order.
  if (begin > end)
  {
    RandomAccessIterator temp;
```

```
      temp = begin;
      begin = end;
      end = temp;
   }
   for (Index = begin; Index != end; Index++)
      Sum += *Index;
   return Sum;
}

int main() {
   vector<float> Numbers;
   Numbers.push_back(1.0);
   Numbers.push_back(2.5);
   Numbers.push_back(3.75);
   Numbers.push_back(1.26);
   Numbers.push_back(9.101);
   Numbers.push_back(11.3);
   Numbers.push_back(1.52);

   // Sum the individual members.
   float Sum;
   Sum = AddIt(Numbers.begin(), Numbers.end());
   cout << Sum << endl;
   Sum = AddIt(Numbers.end(), Numbers.begin());
   cout << Sum << endl;

   // Sum a range.
   vector<float>::iterator Iter = Numbers.begin();
   Iter += 5;
   Sum = AddIt(Iter, Numbers.end());
   cout << Sum << endl;
   return 0;
}
```

This example builds on the previous example. You still create a vector, Numbers, and fill it with data. However, in this case, you create an output variable, Sum, that contains the summation of the elements contained in Numbers.

AddIt() is a special function that accepts two RandomAccessIterator values as input. These two inputs represent a range within the vector that you want to manipulate in some way. The example simply adds them, but you can perform any task you want. The output is a float that contains the summation.

AddIt() works as you expect. You call it as you would any other function and provide a beginning point and an end point within vector. The first two calls to AddIt sum the entire vector, and the third creates an iterator, changes its offset, and then sums a range within vector. Here is the output from this example:

```
30.431
30.431
12.82
```

REMEMBER

A random-access iterator can go in either direction. In addition, you can work with individual members within the container supplied to iterator. As a result, the functions you create for iterator must be able to work with the inputs in any order. How you handle this requirement depends on the kind of function you create.

Locating Values Using the Find Algorithm

The Standard Library contains a number of functions to find something you need within a container. Locating what you need as efficiently as possible is always a good idea. The four common find() algorithms are

» find()

» find_end()

» find_first_of()

» find_if()

The algorithm you use depends on what you want to find and where you expect to find it. You'll likely use the plain find() algorithm most often. The FindString example shows how to locate a particular string within vector. You can use the same approach to locate something in any container type:

```cpp
#include <iostream>
#include <vector>
#include <algorithm>

using namespace std;

int main() {
  vector<string> Words;
  Words.push_back("Blue");
```

```
Words.push_back("Green");
Words.push_back("Teal");
Words.push_back("Brick");
Words.push_back("Purple");
Words.push_back("Brown");
Words.push_back("LightGray");

vector<string>::iterator Result =
  find(Words.begin(), Words.end(), "LightGray");
if (Result != Words.end())
  cout << *Result << endl;
else
  cout << "Value not found!" << endl;

Result = find(Words.begin(), Words.end(), "Black");
if (Result != Words.end())
  cout << *Result << endl;
else
  cout << "Value not found!" << endl;
}
```

The example starts with a vector containing color strings. In both cases, the code attempts to locate a particular color within vector. The first time the code is successful because LightGray is one of the colors listed in Words. However, the second attempt is thwarted because Black isn't one of the colors in Words. Here's the output from this example:

```
LightGray
Value not found!
```

WARNING

Never assume that the code will find a particular value. Always assume that someone is going to provide a value that doesn't exist and then make sure you provide a means of handling the nonexistent value. In this example, you simply see a message stating that the value wasn't found. However, in real-world code, you often must react to situations in which the value isn't found by

>> Indicating an error condition

>> Adding the value to the container

>> Substituting a standard value

>> Defining an alternative action based on invalid input

TIP

You can use the find() algorithm for external and internal requirements. Even though the example shows how you can locate information in an internal vector, you can also use find() for external containers, such as disk drives.

Using the Random Number Generator

Random number generators fulfill a number of purposes. Everything from games to simulations require a random number generator to work properly. Randomness finds its way into business what-if scenarios as well. In short, you need to add random output to your application in many situations. Creating a random number isn't hard. All you need to do is call a random number function, as shown in the RandomNumberGenerator example:

```
#include <iostream>
#include <time.h>
#include <stdlib.h>

using namespace std;

int main() {
  // Always set a seed value.
  srand((unsigned int)time(NULL));
  int RandomValue = rand() % 12;
  cout << "The random month number is: "
    << RandomValue + 1 << endl;
  return 0;
}
```

REMEMBER

The Standard Library uses *pseudorandom* number generators: The numbers are distributed such that you appear to see a random sequence, but given enough time and patience, eventually the sequence repeats. In fact, if you don't set a seed value for your random number generator (or set it to a specific number), you can obtain predictable sequences of numbers every time. Most people use the time or some other automatically changing numeric source to set the seed value to make it more unpredictable. Here is typical output from this example:

```
The random month number is: 7
```

TIP

The first line of code in main() sets the seed by using the system time. Using the system time ensures a certain level of randomness in the starting value — and therefore a level of randomness for your application as a whole. If you comment out this line of code, you see the same output every time you run the application.

The example application uses rand() to create the random value. When you take the modulus of the random number, you obtain an output that is within a specific range — 12 in this case. The example ends by adding 1 to the random number because there isn't any month 0 in the calendar, and then outputs the month number for you.

Working with Temporary Buffers

Temporary buffers are useful for all kinds of tasks. Normally, you use them when you want to preserve the original data, yet you need to manipulate the data in some way. For example, creating a sorted version of your data is a perfect use of a temporary buffer. The TemporaryBuffer example shows how to use a temporary buffer to sort some strings:

```cpp
#include <iostream>
#include <vector>
#include <memory>
#include <algorithm>

using namespace std;

int main() {
  vector<string> Words;
  Words.push_back("Blue");
  Words.push_back("Green");
  Words.push_back("Teal");
  Words.push_back("Brick");

  int Count = Words.size();
  cout << "Words contains: " << Count << " elements."
    << endl;

  // Create the buffer and copy the data to it.
  pair<string*, ptrdiff_t> Mem =
    get_temporary_buffer<string>(Count);
  uninitialized_copy(Words.begin(), Words.end(),
                     Mem.first);

  // Perform a sort and display the results.
  sort(Mem.first, Mem.first+Mem.second);
  for (int i = 0; i < Mem.second; i++)
     cout << Mem.first[i] << endl;
```

```
// Show that the original list is unchanged.
cout << "\nShowing Words Hasn't Changed" << endl;
for (int i = 0; i < Count; i++)
  cout << Words[i] << endl;
return 0;
}
```

The example starts with the now familiar list of color names. It then counts the number of entries in Words and displays the count onscreen.

At this point, the code creates the temporary buffer using get_temporary_ buffer(). The output is Mem of type pair, with the first value containing a pointer to the string values and the second value containing the count of data elements. Mem doesn't contain anything — you have simply allocated memory for it.

The next task is to copy the data from Words to Mem using uninitialized_copy(). Now that Mem contains a copy of your data, you can organize it using the sort() function. The final step is to display the Mem content onscreen. Here is what you'll see:

```
Words contains: 4 elements.
Blue
Brick
Green
Teal

Showing Words Hasn't Changed
Blue
Green
Teal
Brick
```

Chapter **2**

Working with User-Defined Literals (UDLs)

P revious chapters have discussed literals as a kind of constant. For example, in the expression X = 5, the number 5 is a literal constant. The constant X stands in for the value 5 in application code. Using a literal enables you to create code that states the use of a value clearly, rather than having code that is filled with mystery values that no one can figure out. In addition, using literals lets you change constant values in one place, rather than in each place they're needed in an application.

Up to this point, you have used every other kind of literal constant in the various examples except for User-Defined Literals (UDLs). Unlike other kinds of literal constants, a UDL isn't defined as part of the C++ compiler — you create UDLs as needed to make your code more readable and easier to manage. In some cases, UDLs come with the libraries you use in C++, such as the Standard Library. This chapter does discuss UDLs that come as part of the Standard Library, but it also looks at how you'd create your own UDLs as needed.

REMEMBER

UDLs aren't part of older C++ specifications. In fact, they first made an appearance in C++ 11. This means that you must configure Code::Blocks to use the features provided by C++ 11 by using the technique found in the "Working with ranges" section of Book 1, Chapter 5. If you don't perform the configuration for each example in this chapter, you see error messages telling you that the default setup doesn't provide the desired support.

There are also some small, but important, changes for UDLs in C++ 20 that aren't covered in this chapter because they're used at a more detailed level. You can read about these tweaks to UDLs at `https://en.cppreference.com/w/cpp/language/user_literal`.

REMEMBER

You don't have to type the source code for this chapter manually. In fact, using the downloadable source is a lot easier. You can find the source for this chapter in the `\CPP_AIO4\BookVII\Chapter02` folder of the downloadable source. See the Introduction for details on how to find these source files.

Understanding the Need for UDLs

The whole point of literals is to make code more readable and easier to maintain. However, built-in literals are limited to a few data types, summarized as follows:

>> Integer

>> Floating-point

>> Character

>> String

>> Boolean

>> Pointer

>> UDL

Sometimes you need a literal of a type other than these built-in types, and that's where UDLs come into play. Unlike variables, the value of a UDL is always known at compile time. The compiler substitutes whatever value you define for the UDL with the actual value in the code. The purpose of the UDL is to make the code easier for the human developer to read and understand. After that task is completed, the compiler is free to use the actual value referenced by the UDL in the compiled code so that the application doesn't need to convert it during runtime. Your application therefore runs faster and uses fewer resources while remaining easy to read.

REMEMBER

Built-in literals are straightforward because they're based on core types. A UDL can be as complex as you need it to be to express a real-world data type. For example, if you're involved in a field that uses imaginary numbers, you can create a UDL to fulfill that need. You can also perform data conversions and other tasks that would be time consuming to perform in other ways. You can even create side effects, such as performing some sort of output, using a UDL.

Prefixes and suffixes

Saving time and effort is part of the reason you use literals. There is a shorthand way to create literals and ensure that you obtain the correct constant type. Many of the standard literals provide you with a prefix or suffix that you can use to tell the compiler how to interpret them. Precisely how the prefix or suffix is interpreted depends on how you use it. For example, a suffix of U could mean an unsigned int when used with an int value, while a prefix of U could mean a char32_t const pointer when used with a character string. Table 2-1 shows a listing of the prefixes and suffixes that most compilers support.

TABLE 2-1   **Standard Prefixes and Suffixes**

Data Type	Prefix	Suffix	Resultant Type
int		U or u	unsigned int
int		L or l	long
int		UL, Ul, uL, ul, LU, Lu, lU, or lu	unsigned long
int		LL or ll	long long
int		ULL, Ull, uLL, ull, LLU, LLu, llU, or llu	unsigned long long
double		F or f	float
double		L or l	long double
char	L		wchar_t
char	U		char32_t
char	U		char16_t
String	L		wchar_t const*
String	U		char32_t const*
String	U		char16_t const*

Using the prefixes and suffixes can save you considerable time. The PrefixesAnd-Suffixes example in Listing 2-1 demonstrates how you'd employ them to create variables of various sorts.

LISTING 2-1: **Creating Literals Using Prefixes and Suffixes**

```
#include <iostream>
#include <typeinfo>
#include <cxxabi.h>

using namespace std;
using namespace abi;

char* Demangle(const char* Object) {
  int Status;
  char* RealName;
  RealName = __cxa_demangle(Object, 0, 0, &Status);
  return RealName;
}

int main() {
  auto Int1 = 23;
  auto Int2 = 23L;
  auto Int3 = 23U;
  auto Int4 = 23u;

  auto String1 = "Hello";
  auto String2 = L"Hello";
  auto String3 = U"Hello";
  auto String4 = u"Hello";

  cout << Int1 << endl
    << Demangle(typeid(Int1).name()) << endl;
  cout << Int2 << endl
    << Demangle(typeid(Int2).name()) << endl;
  cout << Int3 << endl
    << Demangle(typeid(Int3).name()) << endl;
  cout << Int4 << endl
    << Demangle(typeid(Int4).name()) << endl;

  cout << String1 << endl
    << Demangle(typeid(String1).name()) << endl;
  cout << String2 << endl
    << Demangle(typeid(String2).name()) << endl;
```

```
cout << String3 << endl
    << Demangle(typeid(String3).name()) << endl;
cout << String4 << endl
    << Demangle(typeid(String4).name()) << endl;
return 0;
}
```

TIP

The Demangle() function is GCC specific. Most C++ compilers *mangle* (modify the spelling of) keywords and type information to make an application harder for someone to *reverse-assemble* (convert from machine language back into C++ source code). To determine type information, you use the typeid() function to create a typeinfo structure. The name() function returns the type name found in this structure to display it onscreen. However, this name is mangled, so you must use the Demangle() function to change it back to its original readable form.

Most of the examples in this chapter rely on the auto keyword to automatically detect the variable type created by a UDL. This keyword is an important feature for newer C++ applications that make use of the new extensions that the language provides. You can read about the auto keyword in the "Using the auto keyword with lambda expressions" section of Book 3, Chapter 2. In this case, the code uses the auto keyword to detect the output of the literal prefix or suffix so that the variable is automatically the correct type for a situation. When you run this application, you see the following output:

```
23
int
23
long
23
unsigned int
23
unsigned int
Hello
char const*
0x46e02c
wchar_t const*
0x46e038
char32_t const*
0x46e02c
char16_t const*
```

Even though the data is the same in every case, the variables used to hold the data differ because of the prefix or suffix used to create the variable. Notice that the same prefix or suffix has different effects depending on the type of the variable to which it's applied. In addition, sometimes the case of the prefix or suffix matters (as in working with a string).

Differentiating between raw and cooked

There are many ways to define literals. Of course, the kind of information that a literal affects is the most common method. However, literals can also be raw or cooked. A *raw* literal receives input from the application source and doesn't interpret it in any way. This means that the information is interpreted character by character, precisely as the sender has presented it. *Cooked* literals interpret the sender's input and automatically perform any required conversions to make the data usable to the recipient.

The easiest way to see this principle in action is through an example. The RawAndCooked example, shown in Listing 2-2, demonstrates the technique used to create either raw or cooked string processing.

LISTING 2-2: **Using Raw and Cooked String Processing**

```
#include <iostream>

using namespace std;

int main() {
  auto Cooked = "(Hello\r\nThere)";
  auto Raw = R"(Hello\r\nThere)";
  cout << Cooked << endl;
  cout << Raw << endl;
}
```

Most of the time when you see the \r\n combination, you know that the application will output a carriage return and linefeed combination. This is the cooked method of processing a string. The string is interpreted and any escape characters converted into *control characters* (characters that are normally regarded as commands, rather than data, such as the carriage return). However, notice how the Raw string is created. The R in front of the string tells the compiler to create the variable without interpreting the content. Here's the output you see from this example:

```
(Hello
There)
Hello\r\nThere
```

REMEMBER

Notice that the cooked form does output the parentheses, but the raw form doesn't. The parentheses are required as part of the raw form input. As you might imagine, the cooked form outputs the \r\n combination as control characters, while the raw form outputs the actual characters.

Working with the UDLs in the Standard Library

Even though you can currently create UDLs for the basic types described in the "Understanding the Need for UDLs" section, earlier in this chapter, there are many situations in which developers need UDLs for classes as well. In some cases, these classes are part of the Standard Library. Rather than have a number of non-standard implementations of these UDLs, the standards committee decided to add the UDLs directly to the Standard Library. You can read the details in the "User-defined Literals for Standard Library Types" at `http://www.open-std.org/jtc1/sc22/wg21/docs/papers/2013/n3531.pdf`. Consistent and standardized UDLs are now attached to some classes. The following sections describe the more important classes and show how to use them.

std::basic_string

The `std::basic_string` class enables you to work with sequences of `char`-like objects. The class currently has templates defined for

>> `char`

>> `wchar_t`

>> `char16_t`

>> `char32_t`

Working with User-Defined Literals (UDLs)

However, the class could easily be extended for other kinds of characters. In addition, the templates let you specify character traits and the method used to store the data in memory. The essential idea behind the basic_string is to enable you to accommodate a variety of character types within one character class to simplify coding.

In C++ 14, the Standard Library includes built-in literal support for basic_string. All you need to do is add the s suffix to a string to create one. However, it's important to get an idea of how all this works behind the scenes. The BasicString example, shown in Listing 2-3, demonstrates three techniques for creating a basic_string object.

LISTING 2-3: **Three Techniques for Creating a basic_string**

```
#include <iostream>
#include <typeinfo>
#include <cxxabi.h>

using namespace std;
using namespace abi;

string operator"" _s(const char * str, unsigned len) {
  return string{str, len};
}

char* Demangle(const char* Object) {
  int Status;
  char* RealName;
  RealName = __cxa_demangle(Object, 0, 0, &Status);
  return RealName;
}

int main() {
  basic_string<char> StdString = "A standard string.";
  auto AutoString = "This is an auto string."_s;
  auto UDLString = "This is a UDL string."s;

  cout << StdString << endl <<
    Demangle(typeid(StdString).name()) << endl;
  cout << AutoString << endl <<
    Demangle(typeid(AutoString).name()) << endl;
  cout << UDLString << endl <<
    Demangle(typeid(UDLString).name()) << endl;
  return 0;
}
```

This example performs three essential levels of conversion so that you can see the progression from one to another. In the first case, you see the straightforward method for creating a simple basic_string object, StdString. As you can see, it works just like any other template. The second case relies on a C++ 11 type operator definition to emulate the UDL that is included as part of C++ 14. The "Creating Your Own UDLs" section of this chapter tells you all the details about creating such an operator. All you really need to know for now is that the operator makes it possible to use a shortcut when creating basic_string objects. The third case shows the C++14 version of the same _s definition, but this one is built right into the Standard Library so you don't have to do anything special to use it. In all three cases, you create the same basic_string object type, but the technique differs each time. When you run this example, you see the following output:

```
A standard string.
std::__cxx11::basic_string<char, std::char_traits<char>,
   std::allocator<char> >
This is an auto string.
std::__cxx11::basic_string<char, std::char_traits<char>,
   std::allocator<char> >
This is a UDL string.
std::__cxx11::basic_string<char, std::char_traits<char>,
   std::allocator<char> >
```

TECHNICAL STUFF

There seems to be some confusion online as to how the raw and cooked versions of basic_string should work. In looking at the _s and s operators, the code already provides both raw and cooked implementations. For example, if you used this code with the _s operator:

```
auto RawString = R"(This is a\r\nraw string.)";
auto CookedString = "This is a\r\ncooked string.";
cout << RawString << endl;
cout << CookedString << endl;
```

you'd see the following output:

```
This is a\r\nraw string.
This is a
cooked string.
```

The s operator works in the same manner. So, you can use either raw or cooked strings with the same operator and receive the appropriate results.

std::complex

A *complex number* consists of a real number and an imaginary number that are paired together. (Just in case you've completely forgotten about complex numbers, you can read about them at http://www.mathsisfun.com/numbers/complex-numbers.html.) Real-world uses for complex numbers include:

>> Electrical engineering

>> Fluid dynamics

>> Quantum mechanics

>> Computer graphics

>> Dynamic systems

There are other uses for complex numbers, too, but this list should give you some ideas. In general, if you aren't involved in any of these disciplines, you probably won't ever encounter complex numbers. However, the Standard Library provides full support for complex numbers, just in case you do need them.

As with the BasicString example, this example shows the progression from a standard declaration to the C++ 14 suffix. The ComplexNumber example, shown in Listing 2-4, demonstrates all three stages so that you can see how both the C++ 14 suffix and the C++ 11 UDL forms work.

LISTING 2-4: **Three Techniques for Creating a complex Number**

```
#include <iostream>
#include <complex>

using namespace std;

complex<long double> operator"" _i(long double Value) {
  return complex<double>(0, Value);
}
int main() {
  complex<double> StdComplex(0, 3.14);
  auto AutoComplex = 3.14_i;
  auto UDLComplex = 3.14i;
  auto NonZeroRealPart = 2.01 + 3.14i;

  cout << StdComplex.real() << "\t"
    << StdComplex.imag() << endl;
  cout << AutoComplex.real() << "\t"
    << AutoComplex.imag() << endl;
```

```
cout << UDLComplex.real() << "\t"
  << UDLComplex.imag() << endl;
cout << NonZeroRealPart.real() << "\t"
  << NonZeroRealPart.imag() << endl;
return 0;
}
```

The example declares variables of all three types and assigns values to them. It also creates a version of a variable with a non-zero real part so you can see how to perform this task. You provide the real part plus the imaginary part as two values. It then displays both the real and imaginary parts of the number. When you run this example, you see the following output:

```
0       3.14
0       3.14
0       3.14
2.01    3.14
```

You can create three kinds of complex numbers. The following list shows the suffixes used for each type:

>> **i:** double

>> **if:** float

>> **il:** long double

The `auto UDLComplex = 3.14i;` form of declaration generates an error when you use the `-fext-numeric-literals` switch with the GNU GCC Compiler. You see this switch demonstrated in the "Specifying a precision" section of Book 6 Chapter 2. When performing tasks such as using hexadecimal notation with an exponent, you need to use one of the other complex number declaration types instead.

std::chrono::duration

The `chrono::duration` class serves to mark the passage of time. It answers the question of how much time has elapsed between two events. Developers use it for all sorts of time-related purposes.

REMEMBER

A `chrono::duration` object relies on a second as the standard duration between ticks. A *tick* is a single time duration interval. Using the standard setup, each tick equals one second. However, you can use the `ratio` object to define a new tick duration. For example, if you define `ratio<60>`, each tick lasts one minute. Likewise, defining `ratio<1, 5>` sets each tick to last one fifth of a second.

You can also change one interval to another using `duration_cast` with either a standard interval, such as `chrono::seconds`, or any interval `typedef` that you want to create. For example, `typedef chrono::duration<double, ratio<1, 5>> fifths;` defines an interval called fifths.

There is a lot more to talk about with the `chrono::duration` class, but you now have enough information to work with the Duration example, shown in Listing 2-5. As with previous examples, this one shows a progression from defining a variable directly, to using a custom UDL, and finally the built-in support that C++ 14 provides.

LISTING 2-5: **Three Techniques for Creating a chrono::duration**

```
#include <iostream>
#include <chrono>

using namespace std;

chrono::duration<unsigned long long> operator"" _m(
    unsigned long long Value) {
  return chrono::duration<int, ratio<60>>(Value);
}

int main() {
  chrono::duration<int, ratio<60>>StdTime(20);
  auto AutoTime(20_m);
  auto UDLTime(20min);

  cout << chrono::duration_cast<chrono::seconds>(StdTime)
    .count() << endl;
  cout << chrono::duration_cast<chrono::seconds>(AutoTime)
    .count() << endl;
  cout << chrono::duration_cast<chrono::seconds>(UDLTime)
    .count() << endl;
  return 0;
}
```

The example demonstrates a few features of the `chrono::duration` class. However, it focuses again on the progression from defining the variable by hand to using a shortcut to perform the task. Notice that the UDL relies on an integer value in this case, rather than a floating-point type. The value of 20 minutes is converted to seconds for output. As a result, you see these values when you run the application:

```
1200
1200
1200
```

The Standard Library supports a number of suffixes for `chrono::duration` when you use C++ 14. The following list shows the individual suffixes and tells you what they mean:

>> **h:** Hours

>> **min:** Minutes

>> **s:** Seconds

>> **ms:** Milliseconds

>> **us:** Microseconds

>> **ns:** Nanoseconds

Creating Your Own UDLs

The Standard Library, coupled with the built-in features of C++, provide you with an interesting array of literals. However, the true value of literals becomes more obvious when you create your own. There are many different needs you can address using UDLs, but three common needs are supporting data conversions, making custom types easier to work with, and obtaining desired side effects without the usual number of coding problems.

Although built-in or Standard Library literals come in both prefix and suffix form, you can create only the suffix form when defining your own literals. In addition, the suffix must begin with an underscore. The underscore serves to help prevent conflicts with existing suffixes and to ensure that other developers know that the literal is a custom (nonstandard) form.

Developing a conversion UDL

You can encapsulate conversions within a UDL. All you need to do after you create such a UDL is provide the appropriate suffix when defining the constant to obtain the result you want. The CustomUDL01 example, in Listing 2-6, demonstrates a technique for defining a conversion that changes the radius input to the area of a circle in the constant.

LISTING 2-6: **Defining a Data Conversion UDL**

```
#include <iostream>

using namespace std;

constexpr long double operator""
  _circ(long double radius) {
  return radius*radius*3.141592;
}

int main() {
  double x = 5.0_circ;
  cout << "The circle's area is: " << x << endl;
  return 0;
}
```

To create the UDL, the example relies on a constexpr with a return value of a long double and an input value, radius, of a long double. The equation for computing the area of a circle is πr^2. As you can see, the example performs the correct computation as part of the constexpr.

REMEMBER

Whenever you create a custom UDL, the compiler forces you to use the largest type for the conversion. What this means is that you must use a long double for floating-point literals and unsigned long long for integer literals. Even if you later choose to use a smaller type, as is done in this example by declaring x as a double, the literal itself must employ the largest possible type.

To declare a UDL of the new type, the example creates x, which uses the _circ suffix. It then outputs the result onscreen. When you run this example, you see that the correct value has been placed in x, as shown here:

```
The circle's area is: 78.5398
```

Developing a custom type UDL

A lot of the code you encounter relies on custom types that are hard to follow and understand. Creating a UDL to simplify the code makes things clearer and reduces the potential for error. The CustomUDL02 example, shown in Listing 2-7, shows a custom type, the operator used to create the UDL, and how the UDL is used to define a literal.

LISTING 2-7: **Creating a UDL for a Custom Type**

```
#include <iostream>

using namespace std;

struct MyType {
  MyType (double Input):Value(Input){}
  double Value;
};

MyType operator"" _mytype (long double Value) {
  return MyType(Value);
}

int main() {
  auto UDLType = 145.6_mytype;
  cout << UDLType.Value << endl;
  return 0;
}
```

For this technique to work, you must create a constructor for your type that accepts the number of inputs required to configure the type. At minimum, the constructor must accept one type or the input value the user provides is lost. The custom type need not support the same size data type as required by the operator, but they must be of the same sort. For example, you couldn't transition a long double to an int.

When you run this example, you see an output value of 145.6, which is the value you input to the custom type. You can handle fairly complex setups using this approach. The user of your custom type obtains the capability to create clear code that's easy to follow and interpret, even when the underlying types are complex.

Using a custom UDL for side effects

One of the most interesting uses for UDLs is to create *side effects* (an operation other than the usual or normal operation, either to make the application shorter and more efficient or to provide added flexibility). You want to define a certain kind of operation that takes place as a result of defining the literal. What you get is still a literal, but a literal that doesn't necessarily denote a value that you plan to use later. The CustomUDL03 example, shown in Listing 2-8, shows one such nontraditional use.

LISTING 2-8: **Using UDLs to Create an Interesting Side Effect**

```
#include <iostream>

using namespace std;

void operator"" _countdown (unsigned long long Value) {
  for (int i = Value; i >= 0; i--)
    cout << i << endl;
}

int main() {
  5_countdown;
  return 0;
}
```

Notice that the _countdown operator isn't attached to something that you'd normally associate with a value. In fact, it doesn't return a value at all. What you get instead is a side effect. When you run this example, you see this output.

```
5
4
3
2
1
0
```

What has happened is that the compiler has replaced 5_countdown with individual cout statements, one for each iteration of the loop. You end up with six cout statements that output the values between 5 and 0 (in reverse order). The side effect UDL opens all sorts of interesting possibilities for creating code that simplifies certain repetitive tasks in a manner that makes their use obvious.

Chapter **3**

Building Original Templates

C++ has been around for many years. Because of its longevity, C++ templates abound. In fact, it may seem that there is a template for every practical purpose. However, the templates that are available to the developer community through standardized and third-party resources usually reflect generalized needs. The individual company you work for (or you as a developer) may have specialized needs that a generalized template can't address.

REMEMBER

Every programming tool in existence offers a certain amount of flexibility. The reason you see so many generalized tools is that someone developed them and the community as a whole decided to adopt them. Never think that you can't create your own tools. After all, someone created the generalized tools you work with daily. Creating a custom tool requires nothing special, just time and thought on your part.

The trick to creating a customized tool is to think the process through, just as you would for any application you create. The fact that you'll use this customized tool to create multiple applications means that you must apply a higher standard to its design and the code it contains than you would for one-time applications. A mistake in a customized tool can spell errors in every application you create using it, so this code must work well.

This chapter addresses the thought process behind templates first and then shows some typical template examples. The examples help demonstrate ways in which you can use templates to create better applications that require less code because the templates you create meet your needs more completely than any generalized template can. After you see the template examples, you discover the techniques used to place a number of templates in a library. Finally, you discover how to use the template library to create applications.

The examples in this chapter discuss significant template creation and use details. However, they're designed to work with a broad range of C++ versions simply because templates are most useful when they support more than the latest version. However, C++ 17 and 20 do provide some interesting additional features, such as type deduction (see the "Understanding the Role of auto" section in Book 3, Chapter 1 for details) and you can read about them in the article at `https://dzone.com/articles/c-template-story-so-farc11-to-c20`.

REMEMBER

You don't have to type the source code for this chapter manually. In fact, using the downloadable source is a lot easier. You can find the source for this chapter in the `\CPP_AIO4\BookVII\Chapter03` folder of the downloadable source. See the Introduction for details on how to find these source files.

Deciding When to Create a Template

The first step in creating a template is deciding whether your idea will generate a useful template. Most developers have thousands of creative thoughts that translate into ideas during their careers; however, only a few of these ideas are exceptionally useful. By determining whether the template you want to create is a good idea at the outset, you waste less time on bad ideas and have more time to create that truly useful idea. Before you begin creating a new template, consider the following questions:

>> **Is there a generic template that is close enough to meet your needs?** A good template idea is unique — it does something more than perform a useful task; it performs a new kind of useful task. Template ideas that fail the uniqueness test usually consume many resources for a small payoff.

>> **Will you use the template more than once?** Some template ideas are so tuned to a particular project that the developer ends up using them precisely once, which means that the template never provides a payback on the investment to create it.

>> **Will the template save more time than you use to create it?** Templates can become complex. In fact, some templates are complex enough that you'd save time by not writing them at all. The reason to use templates is to save time and effort, so a complex template tends to require a larger payback period than a simple one.

>> **Is there a third-party template you can buy (or, better yet, obtain free) that nearly meets your need?** Someone else may have already had your good idea, or something very close to it. Before you invest time in creating a template, you should spend time researching online. Obtaining a third-party template that's close to what you want is always more time efficient than creating a custom template on your own.

>> **How generic is the template you want to create?** Many good template ideas are simply too specific, which limits their adaptability to other situations. You want to create a unique template, but one that can meet a range of organizational needs.

>> **Is your template concept complete?** Developers often envision only a piece of a template. For example, if you create a math template, you should actually create a library that contains all the equations you plan to use with your applications. Designing a template that contains a single equation is never worthwhile because other developers will have to finish the work you started.

>> **Do you have the skills to create the template?** Not everyone is a good template designer. A template designer must define a template that goes beyond the original expectations because someone will almost certainly use the template in unexpected ways. The best templates adapt to new situations that the originator never considered. Consequently, creating a template requires a different sort of mindset than creating an application.

REMEMBER

A little research at the outset can save significant time, effort, and replicated development. C++ has been around for a long time (at least in computer terms), so you can choose from a wealth of existing code. Always determine in advance whether the template you want to create is worth the effort and will make life easier for other developers.

Defining the Elements of a Good Template

Book 5, Chapter 5 offers some insights into basic template creation techniques. However, that introductory chapter doesn't address what makes for a good template. The template you create has to look professional and work as expected. The first decision you have to make is what kind of template to create. You can choose among these three types:

>> **Function:** A function represents the simplest way to create a template and eases debugging requirements. You can group functions in libraries to make them easier to access. However, functions often lack depth, and you can't coordinate activities between them as easily as you can between the elements of an object.

>> **Structure:** A structure provides the best speed in many cases and can reduce the amount of system resources required, depending on how you define the structure. Remember that C++ allocates memory for the entire structure, but structures also present opportunities for optimization that you don't get with a class.

>> **Class:** A class provides the greatest flexibility because you can express the template using all the elements that a class can provide — methods, properties, and events. You can inherit classes to create new classes. In short, if you have a complex idea to implement, classes are the way to do it.

The second decision you have to make is how to weight design factors when creating the template. C++ offers myriad ways to accomplish any given task. For example, you have multiple ways to create a function. However, one method is normally superior to the others simply because it offers some particular benefit. Consider these requirements when choosing the kind of template to create:

>> **Security:** "Simplicity" often translates into "easier to secure." In general, functions are easier to secure than structures, which are easier to secure than classes. However, you can easily write an insecure class if you use the wrong approach. Secure templates often require additional checks that can affect reliability (the template tends not to allow specific actions when these actions affect security) and speed (additional code always slows template execution).

>> **Reliability:** The options you choose will affect the reliability of the template you create. A reliable template produces consistent results for any data type supplied to it. In some cases, ensuring reliability means adding checks to the template, which increases complexity. The additional code affects both the security and the speed of the template.

>> **Speed:** Templates save the developer time. However, if the resulting template produces slow code, you can be sure that users will complain and the developer will end up rewriting some code to improve application speed. A fast template is usually small and performs the task precisely. The additional checks required to ensure secure and reliable operation always affect speed negatively, so you must work to achieve a balance.

>> **Usage:** Some templates are so difficult to use that it's hard to imagine that even the originator uses them. If a developer can't determine how to use your template, no one will ever use it, and your effort is wasted. Consequently, you must design the template such that it meets security, reliability, and speed goals without becoming overly difficult to use.

>> **Time:** Every time you design a new piece of software, a time element is involved. It's essential to decide whether the template will ultimately save enough development time to offset the development cost of creating and testing it. A template that you intend to use only a few times may not be worth the effort.

>> **Maintenance:** Someone will have to maintain the code used to create the template. A good template is one in which the code is relatively straightforward. Of course, you need to add comments to the code that explain how the code works — and fully document the template design. Most templates see some level of redesign during their lifecycles. They evolve as developers use the template and discover new ways to incorporate it into applications.

REMEMBER

The best template is the one that seems obvious. Consider the article about the invention of the safety pin at `https://lemelson.mit.edu/resources/walter-hunt`. The safety pin seems obvious, but someone still had to invent it because no one else had thought about it. When you create a template and someone tells you that it seems like an obvious idea, don't get mad. Be glad. You've joined the ranks of people who thought of something that fulfills an obvious need, but no one thought about your idea before you did.

The third decision you must make is how inclusive to make the template. In some cases, you want to create a template that can handle a range of situations. However, a template can quickly become unwieldy and difficult to manage. A good template is balanced; it includes the elements you need, but nothing beyond.

Creating a Basic Math Template

With a math template, you usually need access to a wealth of calculations but may use only one or two of those calculations at a time. For example, when calculating your mortgage, you don't need to know the amortization calculation. However, you might need the amortization calculation the next week when thinking about a retirement plan. In short, the calculations all have a purpose, and you need them all, but you don't need them all at the same time. Because of the way you use math templates, they work best as a series of function templates. The `MathTemplate` example, in Listing 3-1, shows how to create the series of functions.

LISTING 3-1: **Defining a Series of Function Templates**

```cpp
#include <iostream>
#include <cmath>

using namespace std;

template<typename T> T Area(T height, T length) {
  return height * length;
}

const double PI = 4.0*atan(1.0);

template<typename T> T CircleArea(T radius) {
  double result;
  result = PI * radius * radius;
  // This version truncates the value.
  return (T)result;
}

template<typename T> T TriangleArea(T base, T height) {
  double result;
  result = base * height * 0.5;
  return (T)result;
}

int main() {
  cout << "4 X 4 Areas:" << endl;
  cout << "Square: " << Area<int>(4, 4) << endl;
  cout << "Circle: " << CircleArea<int>(2) << endl;
  cout << "Triangle: " << TriangleArea<int>(4, 4) << endl;
  cout << "Using a value of pi of: " << PI << endl;
  return 0;
}
```

The calculations could consist of any math calculation. The point of the example is that using functions makes each of the calculations discrete, easy to use, and easy to manage. When you run this example, you see the following output:

```
4 X 4 Areas:
Square: 16
Circle: 12
Triangle: 8
Using a value of pi of: 3.14159
```

Note that `CircleArea<int>(2)` uses half the value of the other calculations as input. That's because you calculate the area of a circle using the equation $\pi \times r^2$. If you want to see other area and volume equations, check out the website at `http://www.aquatext.com/calcs/calculat.htm`.

TIP

For consistency, you could change the circle equation to read like this:

```
radius = radius / 2;
result = PI * radius * radius;
```

Dividing the input by 2, essentially changing the diameter to a radius, means that you could call the equation using the same number as all the other area calculations: `CircleArea<int>(4)`. Whichever approach you choose, you need to document how the template works so that other developers know how to use it.

You should also note that the circle and triangle calculations perform a bit of type coercion to ensure that the user gets the expected results back by modifying the `return` statement to read `return (T)result;`. The type conversions are needed to keep your templates from generating warning messages. It's important to note that the approach used in the example truncates the result when the template returns an `int`.

TECHNICAL STUFF

You may see examples online that don't calculate the value of π. Instead, these examples use `M_PI`, which supposedly appears in `<cmath>` or `<math.h>`. You can use either header. However, if you try to access `M_PI`, the compiler will complain that it can't find the value. This is because most compilers today use strict ANSI (American National Standards Institute) conventions, and `M_PI` isn't part of that convention. To access `M_PI`, you must add `#undef __STRICT_ANSI__` before `#include <cmath>` in your file. Of course, now you're also dragging in all the non-ANSI features, so in most cases, it's just better to calculate π to keep your code cleaner.

Building a Structure Template

Structure templates have many interesting uses, such as creating a data repository that doesn't depend on a particular type. The `StructureTemplate` example, shown in Listing 3-2, shows one such use.

LISTING 3-2: **Creating a Template from a Structure**

```cpp
#include <iostream>

using namespace std;

template<typename T> struct Volume {
  T height;
  T width;
  T length;

  Volume() {
    height = 0;
    width = 0;
    length = 0;
  }

  T getvolume() {
    return height * width * length;
  }

  T getvolume(T H, T W, T L) {
    height = H;
    width = W;
    length = L;
    return height * width * length;
  }
};

int main() {
  Volume<int> first;
  cout << "First volume: " << first.getvolume() << endl;
  first.height = 2;
  first.width = 3;
  first.length = 4;
  cout << "First volume: " << first.getvolume() << endl;

  Volume<double> second;
  cout << "Second volume: "
    << second.getvolume(2.1, 3.2, 4.3) << endl;
  cout << "Height: " << second.height << endl;
  cout << "Width: " << second.width << endl;
  cout << "Length: " << second.length << endl;
  return 0;
}
```

In this case, the structure contains height, width, and length data values that the code can use to determine volume. The structure includes a constructor to initialize the values, so even if someone calls getvolume() without initializing the structure, nothing bad will happen. The structure allows independent access of each of the data values. You can set or get them as needed.

The getvolume() function is overloaded. You can call it with or without input values. The code in main() tests the structure thoroughly. Here's what you see as output from this example:

```
First volume: 0
First volume: 24
Second volume: 28.896
Height: 2.1
Width: 3.2
Length: 4.3
```

You can use structures for another interesting purpose. The C++ standard says you can't create a typedef template. For example, the following code produces an error when you try to compile it:

```
template<typename T>
typedef map<string, T> MyDef;
```

When you try to compile this code in Code::Blocks, you see the following error:

```
error: template declaration of 'typedef'
```

However, you can define a typedef within a structure template. The Structure-Template2 example code, in Listing 3-3, shows a variation of the example found in Listing 6-4 of Book 5, Chapter 6.

LISTING 3-3: **Using a Structure to Define a typedef**

```
#include <iostream>
#include <map>

using namespace std;

template<typename T> struct MyDef {
  typedef map<string, T> Type;
};
```

(continued)

LISTING 3-3: *(continued)*

```
int main() {
  MyDef<string>::Type marriages;
  marriages["Tom"] = "Suzy";
  marriages["Harry"] = "Harriet";
  cout << marriages["Tom"] << endl;
  cout << marriages["Harry"] << endl;
  return 0;
}
```

This example overcomes the C++ limitations by placing the `typedef` within the struct, `MyDef`. The same structure can hold any number of `typedef` entries.

TIP

Using a `typedef` in this manner makes it easier to work with `map`. All you need to worry about is the value type; the key type is already defined as `string`. Except for the `marriages` declaration, this example works precisely the same as the example in Book 5, Chapter 6. It still outputs the following results:

```
Suzy
Harriet
```

Developing a Class Template

Class templates perform the heavy lifting of the template types. You use a class template to define objects of nearly any size. Classes are larger and more complex than the other techniques demonstrated in the chapter so far. In most cases, you use classes to represent complex objects or to perform tasks ill suited for function or structure templates.

REMEMBER

You normally code classes in a separate file using the name of the class as the filename. The class definition appears in a header file, while the code appears in a code file. To make things a bit easier to understand, this chapter eschews the normal setup and shows the entire example using a single file.

The example shows a specialized queue implementation. It includes many of the features of a standard queue and then adds a few features to meet special development needs. Queues and other containers tend to contain complex code, but you also need to use them with a variety of data types, making a class template the perfect implementation. The `ClassTemplate` example, shown in Listing 3-4, shows the code for this example.

LISTING 3-4: **Creating a Specialized Queue**

```cpp
#include <iostream>
#include <vector>

using namespace std;

template<typename T> class MyQueue {
protected:
  vector<T> data;
public:
  void Add(T const &input);
  void Remove();
  void PrintString();
  void PrintInt();
  bool IsEmpty();
};

template<typename T> void MyQueue<T>::Add(T const &input){
  data.push_back(input);
}

template<typename T> void MyQueue<T>::Remove() {
  data.erase(data.begin());
}

template<typename T> void MyQueue<T>::PrintString() {
  vector<string>::iterator PrintIt = data.begin();
  while (PrintIt != data.end()) {
    cout << *PrintIt << endl;
    PrintIt++;
  }
}

template<typename T> void MyQueue<T>::PrintInt() {
  vector<int>::iterator PrintIt = data.begin();
  while (PrintIt != data.end()) {
    cout << *PrintIt << endl;
    PrintIt++;
  }
}

template<typename T> bool MyQueue<T>::IsEmpty() {
  return data.begin() == data.end();
}
```

(continued)

LISTING 3-4: *(continued)*

```
int main() {
  MyQueue<string> StringQueue;
  cout << StringQueue.IsEmpty() << endl;
  StringQueue.Add("Hello");
  StringQueue.Add("Goodbye");
  cout << "Printing strings: " << endl;
  StringQueue.PrintString();
  cout << StringQueue.IsEmpty() << endl;
  StringQueue.Remove();
  cout << "Printing strings: " << endl;
  StringQueue.PrintString();
  StringQueue.Remove();
  cout << StringQueue.IsEmpty() << endl;

  MyQueue<int> IntQueue;
  IntQueue.Add(1);
  IntQueue.Add(2);
  cout << "Printing ints: " << endl;
  IntQueue.PrintInt();
  return 0;
}
```

The example starts with the class MyQueue. Note that data is a vector, not a queue as you might expect. A queue is an adapter — as such, it doesn't provide support for many of the features found in containers, such as vector. One of these features is the use of iterators.

REMEMBER

This example uses an iterator for printing, so it relies on a vector rather than a queue as a starting point. Whenever you create your own specialized version of a common construct, make sure you begin with the right object. Otherwise, you might find the experience of creating the new class frustrating at a minimum, and impossible in the worst case.

MyQueue includes the capability to add, remove, and print elements. In addition, you can check whether a queue is empty or full. You have already seen the code for these tasks in other parts of the book.

You might wonder about the code used for printing. The example includes separate methods for printing strings and integers, which might seem counterintuitive. After all, why not simply declare the iterator as follows so that it accepts any data type:

```
vector<T>::iterator PrintIt = data.begin();
```

The problem is that the iterator requires a specific data type. Consequently, you must declare it as shown previously in Listing 3-4. Otherwise you get this unhelpful error message:

```
error: expected ';' before 'PrintIt'
```

At some point, you want to test this new class using steps similar to those found in main(). The test checks whether the queue actually does detect the empty and filled states, determines how adding and removing elements works, and checks whether the print routines work. Here is the output from this example:

```
1
Printing strings:
Hello
Goodbye
0
Printing strings:
Goodbye
1
Printing ints:
1
2
```

Considering Template Specialization

Some templates don't go together quite as easily as you might expect because they express a concept that doesn't translate the same way for every data type. For example, when you use stringify to turn a data type into its string representation, the technique differs based on data type. When using stringify on an int, you might use the following template (as shown in the StringifyInt example):

```
#include <iostream>
#include <sstream>

using namespace std;

template<typename T>
inline string stringify(const T& input) {
  ostringstream output;
  output << input;
  return output.str();
}
```

```
int main() {
  // This call works as expected.
  cout << stringify<int>(42) << endl;
  // This call truncates.
  cout << stringify<double>(45.6789012345) << endl;
  return 0;
}
```

The stringify() function accepts any data type and simply uses an ostring-stream to convert input to a string. This approach works fine for the first call in main(), which is an int. However, when the code uses it for a double, the result is truncated, as shown here:

```
42
45.6789
```

TIP

You can fix this problem by adding special handling for a double. Here is the modified form of the example (as shown in StringifyDouble) that accommodates a double:

```
#include <iostream>
#include <sstream>
#include <iomanip>
#include <limits>

using namespace std;

template<typename T>
inline string stringify(const T& input) {
  ostringstream output;
  output << input;
  return output.str();
}

template <>
inline string stringify<double> (const double& input) {
  ostringstream output;
  const int sigdigits = numeric_limits<double>::digits10;
  output << setprecision(sigdigits) << input;
  return output.str();
}
```

```
int main() {
    cout << stringify<int>(42) << endl;
    cout << stringify<double>(45.6789012345) << endl;
    return 0;
}
```

When you run this example, you see the expected result because the double form of the template uses setprecision to modify the ostringstream value. As a result, you see the following output:

```
42
45.6789012345
```

WARNING

As things sit with C++ today, you must create a special template for each data type that requires it. Theoretically, if C++ ever gets a typeof() function, you could detect the data type and add a switch to perform specialized processing within a single template. The typeid() function demonstrated in the "Prefixes and suffixes" section in Chapter 2 of this minibook could work as a substitute for typeof(), but it's vendor-specific and not implemented in every version of C++. If you choose to use the typeid() function, make sure you know which compiler your organization will use to compile the application code.

TIP

You may have also noticed the inline keyword used for the template in this example. The inline keyword tells the compiler to place the code created by the template in line with the code in which it appears, rather than out of line as a separate function call. In some cases, such as this stringify() function, the result is code that executes faster. The compiler is under no obligation to comply with the inline keyword. In addition, you want template code placed out of line when it must perform some level of instantiation or it doesn't represent critical path code that the application can call often.

Creating a Template Library

You won't normally create a template and stick it in your application project file. The previous examples in this chapter put everything together for ease of explanation, but in the real world, templates usually reside in a library. Code::Blocks provides several kinds of library projects. This chapter looks at the *static library* — a library that is added into the application. Templates always reside in static libraries.

REMEMBER

Code::Blocks also supports dynamic link libraries (DLLs) and shared libraries that more than one application can use at a time. However, you can't place template code inside a DLL or shared library unless you create specific instances of the template because templates require the preprocessor to work and DLLs are pre-compiled code. Working with DLLs and shared libraries is more complex than working with static libraries, and you won't normally need the ability to share the library when creating a console application. See the "Defining your first project" section of Book 1, Chapter 3 for details about the various project types that Code::Blocks supports.

Defining the library project

Creating a library project is only a little different than creating a console application. The following steps describe how to create a library project:

1. Choose File ⇨ New ⇨ Project.

You see the New From Template dialog box, shown in Figure 3-1.

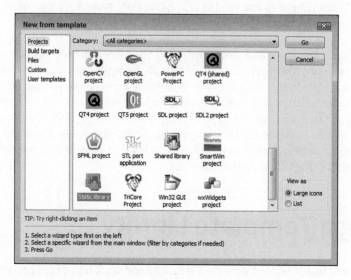

FIGURE 3-1:
Provide a
description of
your project for
Code::Blocks.

2. Highlight the Static Library icon on the Projects tab and then click Go.

You see the Welcome page of the Static Library wizard.

3. Click Next.

You see a list of project-related information fields, as shown in Figure 3-2. These questions define project basics, such as the project name.

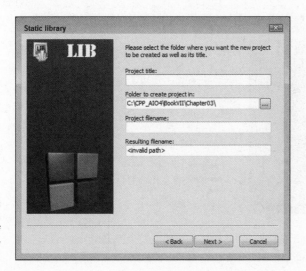

FIGURE 3-2:
Provide a
description of
your static library
for Code::Blocks.

4. **Type a name for your project in the Project Title field.**

   The example uses MathLibrary as the project title. Notice that the wizard automatically starts creating an entry for you in the Project Filename field.

5. **Type a location for your project in the Folder to Create Project In field.**

6. **(Optional) Type a project filename in the Project Filename field.**

7. **Click Next.**

REMEMBER

   You see the compiler settings, shown in Figure 3-3. This example uses the default compiler settings. However, it's important to remember that you can choose a different compiler, modify the locations of the debug and release versions of the project, and make other changes as needed. Code::Blocks provides the same level of customization for libraries as it does for applications.

8. **Change any required compiler settings and click Finish.**

   The wizard creates the application for you. It then displays the Code::Blocks IDE with the project loaded. This template creates a main.c file rather than a main.cpp file. Note that the Static Library project main.c file includes some sample code to get you started. You could compile this library and test it now.

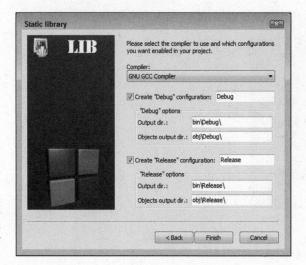

FIGURE 3-3:
Change the
compiler settings
to meet your
project needs.

Configuring the library project

The static library starts with a standard C file. To make this library work well with templates, you need to delete the C file, add a C++ file, and add a header file. The following steps describe how to perform this process:

1. **Right-click** main.c **in the Projects tab of the Management window and choose Remove File From Project from the context menu that appears.**

   Code::Blocks removes the file from the project tree.

2. **Choose File ➪ New ➪ File.**

   You see the New from Template dialog box, shown in Figure 3-4.

3. **Highlight the C/C++ Header icon and click Go.**

   You see the Welcome page of the C/C++ Header wizard.

4. **Click Next.**

   The wizard asks you to provide the header configuration information (see Figure 3-5).

5. **In the Filename with Full Path field, type** MathLibrary.h, **click the ellipsis (. . .) button, and then click Save.**

   Code::Blocks adds the complete project path to the filename you chose. Notice that Code::Blocks also supplies an entry for the Header Guard Word field. This word ensures that the header isn't added more than once to a project.

6. **Click All and then click Finish.**

   The C/C++ Source wizard adds the file to your project. You're ready to begin creating a template library.

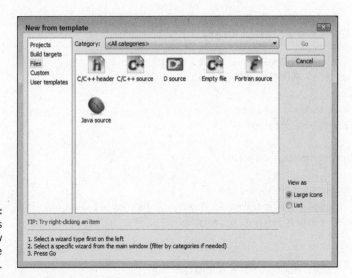

FIGURE 3-4:
Add new files
using the New
from Template
dialog box.

FIGURE 3-5:
Define the header
requirements.

Coding the library

At this point, you have what amounts to a blank header file in a static library project. Your static library could conflict with other libraries, so it's important to add a namespace to your code. The example uses MyNamespace, but normally you'd use something related to you as a person or your company, such as MyCompanyInc. The MathLibrary heading, in Listing 3-5, shows what you need to create the library used for this example.

LISTING 3-5: **Creating a Static Library**

```
#ifndef MATHLIBRARY_H_INCLUDED
#define MATHLIBRARY_H_INCLUDED

#include <iostream>
#include <cmath>

using namespace std;

namespace MyNamespace {
  template<typename T> T Area(T height, T length) {
    return height * length;
  }

  const double PI = 4.0*atan(1.0);
  template<typename T> T CircleArea(T radius) {
    double result;
    result = PI * radius * radius;
    // This version truncates the value.
    return (T)result;
  }

  template<typename T> T TriangleArea(T base, T height) {
    double result;
    result = base * height * 0.5;
    return (T)result;
  }
}

#endif // MATHLIBRARY_H_INCLUDED
```

As you can see, this is a portable form of the math library discussed in the "Creating a Basic Math Template" section, earlier in this chapter. Of course, the library form has changes. You have the usual #define statements and the use of a namespace to encapsulate all the code. Notice that the namespace comes after all the declarations.

Using Your Template Library

You have a shiny new template library. It's time to test it. The MathLibraryTest console application uses MathLibrary to display some area information. The output is the same as in the "Creating a Basic Math Template" section, earlier in this chapter. Listing 3-6 shows the test code used for this example.

LISTING 3-6:	**Testing the Static Library**

```
#include <iostream>
#include "..\MathLibrary\MathLibrary.h"

using namespace std;
using namespace MyNamespace;

int main() {
  cout << "4 X 4 Areas:" << endl;
  cout << "Square: " << Area<int>(4, 4) << endl;
  cout << "Circle: " << CircleArea<int>(2) << endl;
  cout << "Triangle: " << TriangleArea<int>(4, 4) << endl;
  cout << "Using a value of pi of: " << PI << endl;
  return 0;
}
```

When you use your own libraries, you need to tell the compiler where to find them. Because you likely created the example library in the same folder as the test application, you can use the simple path shown in Listing 3-6.

Because the library relies on a namespace, you must also include using namespace MyNamespace; in the example code. Otherwise, you'll spend hours trying to figure out why the compiler can't locate the templates in your library. You access and use the template library much as you did before.

Chapter **4**

Investigating Boost

As your skill with C++ improves, you find that you need additional functionality that doesn't come with the Standard Library. For example, the simple act of checking a string for specific character sequences (such as a telephone number pattern) can prove difficult. You can do it, but most developers will think that someone else has certainly crossed this bridge before. The answer to the question of where to find the additional code you need is third-party libraries. One of the most popular C++ libraries is Boost, which is the topic of this chapter and the next.

Two book chapters can't serve as a complete reference to an entire library — especially not a set of libraries the size of Boost. This particular chapter (Chapter 4) has a set of more limited goals. It introduces you to Boost and helps you understand why Boost may be helpful to your development efforts. It also shows you how to obtain and install Boost, demonstrates some Boost tools, and finally helps you create your first application using Boost. Chapter 5 picks up where this chapter leaves off and helps you use Boost to build some interesting applications. In short, these two chapters combined provide you with an overview of a library that you should consider spending more time discovering.

REMEMBER

Libraries are simply repositories of code. Consequently, any library can help you produce applications faster and with fewer errors. However, not all libraries are created with the same quality of code. Many developers use the Boost libraries because they provide high-quality code — so high quality that some of Boost is being standardized for inclusion in the Standard Library. The bottom line is that you must choose the libraries you want with care and look at both quality and price (when price is an issue).

REMEMBER

You don't have to type the source code for this chapter manually. In fact, using the downloadable source is a lot easier. You can find the source for this chapter in the \CPP_AIO4\BookVII\Chapter04 folder of the downloadable source. See the Introduction for details on how to find these source files.

Considering the Standard Library Alternative

As a developer, you encounter a vast number of libraries designed to overcome C++ deficiencies or limitations. Boost is one of the most popular libraries, but you can find many others. Looking at the list found at https://en.cppreference.com/w/cpp/links/libs, you soon discover that you could easily find yourself buried in libraries. Some of these libraries provide resources for exotic programming needs, and you should peruse them before creating your own custom library, as discussed in the previous chapter of this minibook. However, this section essentially comes down to the question of whether to use the Boost library or to stick exclusively with the Standard Library, both of which support general needs.

Understanding why the Standard Library contains Boost features

Boost has maintained a high standard for using the latest C++ features over the years. You can find more than a few articles and discussions online covering Boost classes that moved to the Standard Library after testing. Unfortunately, it's hard (or perhaps impossible) to find a complete listing. The discussion at https://stackoverflow.com/questions/8851670/which-boost-features-overlap-with-c11 is one of the most interesting because it shows that some Boost features are *backported* (an act of taking features from a newer version of a piece of software and adding them to an older version of the same software) from the

Standard Library (rather than the other way around). Check out the site at `https://caiorss.github.io/C-Cpp-Notes/boost-libraries.html` as well, because it's more complete than most sources. When thinking about these moves, C++ 11 uses these Boost features, among many others:

>> `std::regex`

>> `std::tuple`

>> `std::function`

>> Threading

>> Smart pointers

Each version of C++ with its associated Standard Library comes with new additions. When you move to C++ 17, you see these additions from Boost (along with many others):

>> Vocabulary types: `std::variant`, `std::any`, and `std::optional`

>> `string_view`

>> Searchers: Boyer Moore and Boyer Moore Horspool

>> `std::filesystem`

>> Special math functions

>> Template enhancements

The main point here is that Boost is a proving ground, while the Standard Library tends to act as a repository for tested functionality. If your goal is to build stable applications that use tested techniques, Boost may not be the solution you're looking for. However, when you need to implement the latest C++ features, you really need to use Boost.

Defining the trade-offs of using the Standard Library

As mentioned in the previous section, the Standard Library tends toward using stable techniques. You therefore don't necessarily find the best solution to a problem in the Standard Library if C++ is deficient in an area at the outset. However, you need to consider the transitional phase of an application, where it can move from using Boost to the Standard Library. Consider these sites that provide insights from people who moved from using Boost to the Standard Library when the Standard Library received updates from Boost that made it a good solution:

- » Bitcoin: `https://github.com/bitcoin/bitcoin/projects/3`
- » Tronic: `https://github.com/performous/performous/issues/39`
- » GoogleCodeExporter: `https://github.com/jbeder/yaml-cpp/issues/264`

REMEMBER

In reviewing these sites, you find that the transition wasn't necessarily seamless or error free, but it was doable. Fortunately, you can also find articles about making the move, such as this one on `std::filesystem` for C++ 17 developers: `https://www.bfilipek.com/2019/05/boost-to-stdfs.html`.

Many people also feel that Boost provides better productivity over the Standard Library. To a certain extent, this perception makes sense because Boost provides access to the latest C++ features in an easily used form. You don't have to write new functions to use the latest C++ features; Boost provides them for you. Articles like the one at `http://linuxcursor.com/open-source-gnu/01c-boost-libraries-can-increase-productivity` supply additional reasons for the productivity boost, which include the use of strict code-writing guidelines.

You should consider the trade-offs no matter which library you choose to use. Despite the problems of using older functionality, potentially introducing errors into your code by transitioning, and a drop in productivity, the essential reasons to use the Standard Library in place of Boost are the following:

- » The Standard Library is part of the compiler, so it's easy to access and is guaranteed to work.
- » The standards committee approves the Standard Library, so you can be sure that compatibility is stronger.
- » The concepts and techniques in the Standard Library are time tested, so you know that what you're using is less likely to break over time.
- » Boost developers are part of the Standard Library effort as well, so you can be sure that they've had time to work out kinks in Boost that won't appear in the Standard Library.

Understanding Boost

One of the best things about Boost is that the library itself is free. The Boost website, `https://www.boost.org/`, makes a point of letting developers know that they won't pay anything for using Boost, even in a commercial setting. In addition, Boost doesn't have any expenses, so you probably won't ever need to pay for it. You need to download Boost 1.73 (the version used for this book) from the `https://www.boost.org/users/history/version_1_73_0.html` site before proceeding with the rest of this chapter (you see installation instructions later in the chapter after the explanation of Boost features). You should probably read the associated Getting Started guide (the index page is at `https://www.boost.org/doc/libs/1_73_0/more/getting_started/index.html`) so that you know how to perform the installation for your platform. A number of people and organizations contribute to Boost. You can check out their pictures at `https://www.boost.org/users/people.html`.

REMEMBER

However, don't get the idea that Boost is completely free. If you want commercial-level support, you'll pay for it, just as you would with any other product. Only the library itself is free. The following sections describe some of the details of Boost.

Boost features

You might think that Boost couldn't really be all that complete if you can get it for free. Actually, Boost includes a significant number of features — far more features than the average developer will use in writing typical applications. It's interesting to note that you probably have an application on your system that relies on Boost: Adobe Acrobat. That's right; major applications do rely on Boost because it's a feature-rich application development library. In fact, you can see entire lists of applications you know and use at `https://www.boost.org/users/uses.html` (simply choose one of the categories, such as Shrink Wrapped Boost, to see the applications in that category).

The current version of Boost contains in excess of a hundred libraries in categories that meet an incredible number of needs (new libraries are added all the time). You can see a list of these libraries at `https://www.boost.org/doc/libs/1_73_0/`. In some cases, you'll need only Boost to meet all your development needs. Because these libraries meet specific conformity requirements, you never find yourself calling a function one way with one library and another way when using a different library.

TIP

In addition to libraries, Boost also provides a number of tools to make your development experience more enjoyable. Most of this chapter discusses these specialized tools. Because you get the source code for all the tools, you can build a version of the tool for every platform in your organization, which means that every developer can use the same toolset. Using a common toolset reduces training time and tends to improve the consistency of development output.

Licensing

The Boost license is friendly to individual users, consultants, and organizations. Even if you work in an enterprise environment, you can use Boost for free. The developers behind Boost are concerned enough about legal matters that they continue working on the license so that usage requirements are easy to understand. You can find a copy of the current license at `https://www.boost.org/users/license.html`.

REMEMBER

The Boost license and the GNU General Public License (GPL) differ in some important ways. The most important consideration for organizations is that the Boost license lets you make changes to the libraries without having to share these changes with anyone. You get to keep your source code secret, which is a big plus for organizations that create commercial applications.

Paid support

When working with Boost, you gain access to the source code and community support. For some organizations, the lack of a formal support mechanism is a problem. Fortunately, you can also get paid support from BoostPro Computing (https://github.com/boostpro). Most important, BoostPro Computing offers formal training in using Boost, which means that your organization can get up to speed quickly. You can find additional companies that provide Boost support at https://www.boost.org/community/.

Obtaining and Installing Boost for Code::Blocks

Before you can use Boost, you need to download it. The examples in this chapter rely on version 1.73.0 of the library, which you can obtain at https://www.boost.org/users/history/version_1_73_0.html. You get the entire Boost library in a single 173MB download (when obtained in .zip format). There are downloads for Windows and Unix (which you can use for both Mac and Linux development).

The Boost documentation appears at https://www.boost.org/doc/libs/1_73_0/. You can download the documentation as a .pdf from https://sourceforge.net/projects/boost/files/boost-docs/, but this source is outdated with 1.56.0 as the latest version.

You can download binaries for Windows systems if you want the library prebuilt from https://sourceforge.net/projects/boost/files/boost-binaries/. Unfortunately, the 1.73.0 binaries work only with Microsoft Visual C++. Code::Blocks developers will need to compile their own version of the product, which is actually the best way to go for everyone because you avoid compatibility issues that way.

Unpacking Boost

The first step in gaining access to Boost is to unpack the Boost 1.73.0 library file (boost_1_73_0.zip) that you downloaded earlier. The unzipped files add up to around 613MB, so it can take a while for the library to unpack. When working with Code::Blocks, you want to unpack this library into the \CodeBlocks\boost_1_73_0\ folder for ease of access. The documentation often refers to the boost_1_73_0\ folder as the Boost root directory, or $BOOST_ROOT. When you unpack the Zip file, you see the following folders (some of the folders, such as lib\, will be empty):

- » **boost\:** Contains all the Boost header files.

- » **doc\:** Provides a subset of the Boost documentation. If you want complete documentation, you must either download the separate Boost Docs file or use the website directly.

- » **lib\:** Contains all the Boost precompiled libraries after you build them. This folder won't contain any files (or may not even exist) when you unpack the Boost library.

- » **libs\:** Provides a root folder for all the Boost library headers. Here is a small sampling of a few of them:

  - **libs\accumulators\:** Contains a library of incremental statistical computation functions. In addition, you use this library for general incremental calculations.

  - **libs\algorithm\:** Contains algorithms that build on the string functionality found in the Standard Library. These algorithms provide functionality such as trimming, case conversion, predicates, and find/replace functions. You also find a min/max library that lets you determine the minimum and maximum of an expression in a single call (among other things).

  - **libs\any\:** Contains a library that helps you interact with variables in a manner reminiscent of scripting languages. You don't need this capability all the time, but it's handy when you want to do things such as convert between an int and string using a simple lexical_cast.

  - **libs\array\:** Provides an extension to basic array functionality so that you get some of the advantages of using a vector without the performance hit that using a vector can introduce.

  - **libs\more libraries:** Boost contains more than a hundred libraries. You'll want to check them all out.

- » **more\:** Holds policy and other important documents. The most important document at the outset is getting_started.html, which provides essential information for getting started using Boost. The index.htm file provides access to basic information about Boost, such as the licensing policy.

- » **status\:** Provides access to a Boost-wide test suite. Generally, you won't need the contents of this folder unless you plan to augment the Boost libraries in some way.

- » **tools\:** Contains a wealth of tools you use when working with Boost. Much of this chapter tells you about these tools. You must build the tools before you can use them. Each folder contains complete instructions, but you can also find an example of building the tools later in this section.

Using the header-only libraries

No matter which platform you work with, the header-only libraries are ready for use immediately after you unpack Boost. These libraries appear in the `boost_1_73_0\boost\` directory. Each library is contained in a separate subdirectory, and you access the library through its header file. Boost 1.73.0 supports 146 different header-only libraries that address all sorts of issues, such as incremental statistical computation. (That particular area is covered by the accumulators library, which is found in the `accumulators\` subdirectory.)

REMEMBER

Having access to the library doesn't mean that you'll know how to use it right out of the box, but the Boost folks do make an effort to supply you with good documentation so that you can discover how to use Boost. Look in the `boost_1_73_0\libs\` directory and you see another set of subdirectories containing the names of libraries, such as `accumulators\`. Each of these subdirectories contains a minimum of three subdirectories:

>> **doc:** The documentation for understanding and using the library. Access the documentation for an individual library by opening the `index.htm` file in its subdirectory. Access the documentation for Boost as a whole by opening the `libraries.htm` (or `index.html`) file found in the `boost_1_73_0\libs\` directory.

>> **example:** A somewhat simple application that demonstrates how to use the library. (The example is designed to show both usage and functionality, so some complex libraries have larger examples to demonstrate them.) Some libraries include multiple examples to fully demonstrate the library's functionality.

>> **test:** A test suite that you can use to ensure that any changes you make to Boost won't break the library or cause undesirable side effects.

Depending on the needs of the library, you may find additional subdirectories that contain other information or resources, such as tools. Some of the libraries require additional processing before you can use them. The next section of the chapter describes the building process so that you have a complete Boost installation. Make absolutely certain that you build the libraries before you proceed.

Building the libraries

The Boost library relies on code in headers. Using this approach means that if you include the header in your code, you already have everything you need to use the

Boost library. However, these few Boost libraries, including these common libraries, require separate compilation:

>> Boost.Chrono

>> Boost.Context

>> Boost.Filesystem

>> Boost.GraphParallel

>> Boost.IOStreams

>> Boost.Locale

>> Boost.MPI

>> Boost.ProgramOptions

>> Boost.Python (See the Boost.Python build documentation before building and installing it.)

>> Boost.Regex

>> Boost.Serialization

>> Boost.Signals

>> Boost.System

>> Boost.Thread

>> Boost.Timer

>> Boost.Wave

REMEMBER

If you have used previous versions of Boost, throw out everything you know because this latest version uses a completely different (and much easier) process to build the libraries — and it works the same on any platform. The process isn't any faster, unfortunately, but then again, Boost is a huge library.

The following steps help you build the libraries and create a centralized store of Boost information for your applications. These steps assume that you're using Code::Blocks as your IDE and that you've installed it using the instructions in Book 1, Chapter 1. You may need to modify the steps if you used some other installation process, rely on a different IDE, or work with certain 64-bit systems.

1. **Open a command prompt or terminal window using the technique appropriate for your platform.**

For example, when working with Windows, you choose Start ⇨ Programs ⇨ Accessories ⇨ Command Prompt. (Depending on your version of Windows, you may need to press the Windows key, type **cmd**, press Enter, and then select Command Prompt App from the list presented.) When working with a Mac, you navigate to the /Applications/Utilities window and double-lick Terminal. The method of opening a terminal window in Linux varies with the distribution you use.

2. **Type** CD /CodeBlocks/boost_1_73_0 **and press Enter.**

   The command processor takes you to the Boost directory.

3. **(Optional) If you haven't already created a path to the Code::Blocks compiler at the command line or terminal, create one.**

   For example, when working with Windows, type **path = C:\CodeBlocks\ MinGW\bin;%path%** and press Enter.

4. **Type** bootstrap gcc **and press Enter.**

   You see a message, Building Boost.Build engine, at the command prompt or terminal window for a few seconds. After the Boost.Build Engine is complete, you see additional text telling you how to use the resulting B2 command.

5. **Type** b2 **and press Enter.**

   Go get a cup of coffee. The installation process takes between 5 and 20 minutes depending on your system. This command prompt installs Boost using the default options and in the default directory. For example, you find Boost installed in the C:\Boost directory on a Windows system. It appears in the /usr/local/Boost directory on Mac and most Linux systems. When the process is complete, you find the new Boost folder complete with header and library files appropriate for your system.

WARNING

Older sites will tell you to build the Boost function using the --toolset=gcc command-line switch with b2 to perform various tasks. Using this command-line switch will result in an error with the newest versions of Boost. Make sure you leave this command line switch out unless you actually need it. In fact, it's usually better to use b2 alone and only add the --toolset command-line switch if an error occurs.

Testing the installation

At this point, you have the unpacked Boost files as a subdirectory under your Code::Blocks installation and a set of built libraries in the Boost directory (wherever it might appear on your system). You may initially think that you can get rid of one or the other set of files, but this isn't the case. The files you unpacked include documentation and example code that isn't part of the built libraries. The following steps help you test your installation by building the Boost.Timer library, which relies on both sets of files, so having both sets in place is important. (You can modify these instructions to build other libraries as well.)

BOOST INSTALLATION ON CERTAIN 64-BIT SYSTEMS

You may find that the build process in Step 4 of the procedure in the "Building the libraries" section fails. Generally, these steps work fine, but if you're working with certain 64-bit systems, you may find that they fail completely. The main problem could occur because you're using the wrong version of Code::Blocks for the book. Choose Help ⇨ About and verify that the version number you're using is 17.12 and that the Information tab shows Release 12.12 rev. 11256 in the Version field and 1.33.0 in the SDK Version field. If these values are wrong, you have the wrong version of Code::Blocks installed and may find that this chapter doesn't work at all.

If you have a 64-bit system (it says that you have a 64-bit install on the About dialog), you might still need to use an alternative installation procedure, as described at `https://gist.github.com/zrsmithson/0b72e0cb58d0cb946fc48b5c88511da8`. You shouldn't have to reinstall your copy of MinGW; simply move down to the Install Boost part of the page. The Boost settings accessed using Settings ⇨ Compiler (and described in the "Testing the installation" section of the chapter) will differ, as shown here:

- Search Directories: Compiler: `\boost\include\boost-1_68`

- Search Directories: Linker: `C:\boost\lib`

- Toolchain Executables: Compiler's installation directory: `C:\MinGW`

- Toolchain Executables: C Compiler: `g++.exe`

- Toolchain Executables: C++ Compiler: `g++.exe`

- Toolchain Executables: Linker for Dynamic Libs: `g++.exe`

- Linker Settings: Link Libraries: `C:\boost\lib\libboost_regex-mgw81-mt-sd-x64-1_68.a`

Note that this procedure uses Boost 1.68, not Boost 1.73, so you may still experience problems, but this process could provide an alternative for making the examples in this chapter work. It's also important to note that the locations of header files and other application development necessities will differ from those in this chapter for your installation.

1. **Locate the** `C:\CodeBlocks\boost_1_73_0\libs\regex\example\timer`
   folder on your system.

2. **Double-click the** `regex_timer.cpp` **file.**

   Code::Blocks automatically opens the file for you. If you attempt to compile the
   file at this point, Code::Blocks displays a considerable number of errors. The
   errors aren't due to problems with the code, but with issues in the configuration. You need to configure Code::Blocks to work with this example.

3. **Choose Settings ⇨ Compiler.**

   You see the Compiler Settings dialog box, shown in Figure 4-1. You need to
   perform three configuration tasks to make the example usable:

   ● Tell Code::Blocks where to find the Boost include (header) files.

   ● Tell Code::Blocks where to find the Boost library files.

   ● Configure Code::Blocks to add the required libraries to the application.

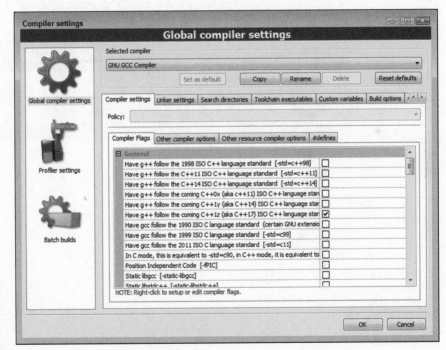

FIGURE 4-1:
Use the Compiler
Settings dialog
box to configure
Code::Blocks to
use Boost.

4. **Select the Search Directories tab.**

   You see three subtabs: Compiler, Linker, and Resource Compiler.

5. **Click Add in the Compiler subtab.**

   You see an Add Directory dialog box like the one shown in Figure 4-2.

FIGURE 4-2:
Add appropriate
search directories
for Boost header
and library files.

6. **Type the location of the Boost header files in the Directory field.**

   As an alternative, you can click the Browse button to use a Browse for Folder dialog box to find them. The files are normally located in the C:\CodeBlocks\ boost_1_73_0\boost folder.

7. **Click OK.**

   You see the search folder added to the Compiler tab, as shown in Figure 4-3.

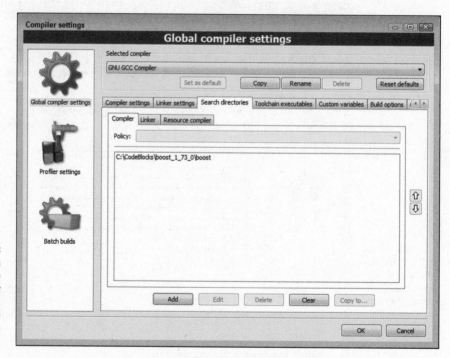

FIGURE 4-3:
The Search
Directories tab
will display any
compiler, linker,
or resource
compiler search
locations.

8. **Click Add in the Linker subtab.**

You see the Add Directory dialog box (refer to Figure 4-2).

9. **Type the location of the Boost library files in the Directory field and then click OK.**

The Boost library files are typically located in the `C:\CodeBlocks\boost_1_73_0\libs` directory. After you click OK, you see the directory added to the Linker tab.

10. **Select the Linker Settings tab.**

This tab contains two lists — one for link libraries and another for linker options.

11. **Click Add.**

Code::Blocks displays the Add Library dialog box, shown in Figure 4-4. This example requires use of the `libboost_regex-mgw6-mt-d-x32-1_73.a` library file.

Investigating Boost

FIGURE 4-4:
The example requires the use of a special library.

12. **Click the Browse button, locate the library you need to use, and click Open.**

The `libboost_regex-mgw6-mt-d-x32-1_73.a` library is normally found in the `C:\CodeBlocks\boost_1_73_0\bin.v2\libs\regex\build\gcc-6.2.0\debug\address-model-32\link-static\threading-multi\visibility-hidden\` directory.

13. **Click OK.**

You see the library file added to the Link Libraries list, as shown in Figure 4-5.

14. **Click OK.**

The Compiler Settings dialog box closes.

15. **Build the application by choosing Build ⇨ Build.**

The application should build without warnings or errors. If you see warnings or errors, ensure that you've added both header and library search paths, and the required library file.

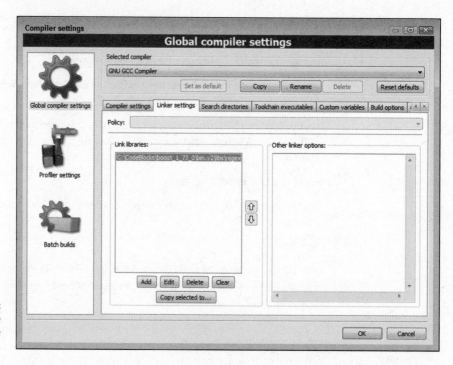

FIGURE 4-5:
The needed file appears in the Link Libraries list.

At this point, you have a shiny new application to try. This is an example application that is provided as part of Boost that shows how to work with regular expressions. (It serves to test the development environment to ensure that everything works.) Now it's time to see the application in action.

1. **Click Run.**

   You see the example start. The example asks you to type an expression. A simple string works fine.

2. **Type** Hi **when asked to enter an expression and press Enter.**

   The example asks you to provide a search string.

3. **Type** Hi there! **and press Enter.**

   You see the results shown in Figure 4-6. The times may be different because they depend on the processing speed of your system and a number of other factors.

4. **Type** quit **and press Enter.**

5. **Type** quit **(a second time) and press Enter twice.**

   The application ends. At this point, you know you can create, build, and use Boost applications on your system. You can close Code::Blocks without saving anything.

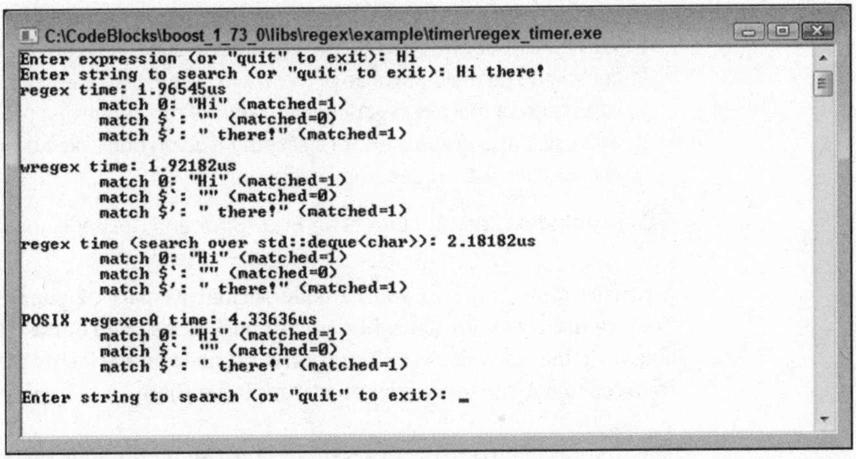

FIGURE 4-6:
The example
displays
the result
of the search.

Creating the Boost Tools

It's always nice when a vendor provides tools for making it easier to work with a product, and Boost is no exception. You find these tools in the \boost_1_73_0\ tools directory. The sections that follow this one describe a number of these tools in detail, but here is a quick list of the tools you get:

» **Boost.Build:** Helps you build applications that use Boost by automating some of the process from the command line. This product is actually an add-on for an updated version of Boost.Jam, which used to appear as a separate product.

» **Inspect:** Determines whether there are any errors in the Boost directory hierarchy. Errors in the directory hierarchy can cause the automatic Boost features to work incorrectly.

» **BoostBook:** Provides the developer with a fast and easy method for accessing the Boost documentation. It relies partially on DocBook (https://docbook. org/), the eXtensible Stylesheet Language (XSL), and some Boost functionality. This tool is used by some Boost libraries.

» **bcp:** Extracts subsets of Boost for use with your application. To perform this task, bcp also provides a method for determining which parts of Boost your code relies upon and it also makes it possible to print reports of Boost usage (including any required licensing information).

» **QuickBook:** Generates BoostBook XML files. This tool provides a WikiWiki (wiki) style documentation geared toward C++ documentation requirements. A *wiki* is a collection of hypertext documents. Wiki pages are collaborative and allow all users or registered users to change the content in these collections, which makes them different from a collection of static hypertext documents. It relies on simple rules and markup for providing output formatting.

>> **Wave:** Preprocesses your C/C++ application code. You can use it with any compiler. The main purpose of the Wave preprocessor is to check the expansion of macros in your code as part of the debugging process. You can also use it as a preprocessor replacement if you don't like how the preprocessor supplied with your compiler works.

>> **AutoIndex:** Creates indexes for BoostBook and DocBook documents.

All these tools come in source code format as part of your Boost installation. They're not ready for use when you unpack Boost. Of course, the lack of executable code makes sense considering the number of platforms that Boost supports. In order to use the tools, you must first build them.

The first task is to create a version of Boost.Build for your system. You use Boost.Build to build all the other tools. The following steps describe how to build Boost.Build:

1. **Open a command prompt or terminal window using the technique appropriate for your platform.**

   For example, when working with Windows, you choose Start⇨Programs⇨Accessories⇨Command Prompt. When working with a Mac, you navigate to the /Applications/Utilities window and double-click Terminal. The method of opening a terminal window in Linux varies with the distribution you use.

2. **Type** CD \CodeBlocks\boost_1_73_0\tools\build **and press Enter.**

   This is the Windows version of the command. For other platforms, you need to change directories to the directory that contains the Boost 1.73 tools. The command processor takes you to the Boost.Build directory.

3. **(Optional) If you haven't already created a path to the CodeBlocks compiler at the command line or terminal, create one.**

   For example, when working with Windows, type **path = C:\CodeBlocks\ MinGW\bin;%path%** and press Enter.

4. **Type** bootstrap gcc **and press Enter.**

   You see a message, Building the B2 engine (along with a lot of other text), at the command prompt or terminal window for a few seconds. When the Boost.Build compilation is complete, you see additional text telling you how to use the resulting B2 command.

5. **Type** b2 --prefix=*DIR* install **and press Enter.**

   You must replace the placeholder text *DIR* shown previously with the location you want to use to install Boost.Build. For example, if you have a Windows system and want to install Boost.Build in C:\Boost.Build, you type **b2 --prefix= C:\Boost.Build install** and press Enter.

REMEMBER

6. **Add Boost.Build to the path using the command for your particular platform.**

For example, when working with Windows, type **path=C:\Boost.Build\ bin;%path%** and press Enter.

Now that you have an application to build the Boost tools, you can build the tools themselves. A number of the tools come with build directories or build files in their main directory. In those directories are the instructions required to create the tools. For example, look in the \CodeBlocks\boost_1_73_0\tools\auto_ index\build directory and you see a Jamfile.v2 file. This is the file that contains the instructions for building the AutoIndex tool. Likewise, you find a Jamfile.v2 file in the \CodeBlocks\boost_1_73_0\tools\bcp folder. (The file is in the main directory, rather than a build directory in this case.). No matter where the Jam- file.v2 file is located, you use it to build the associated tool.

REMEMBER

However, the easiest method to build the tools is to build them all at one time. A special Jamfile.v2 file is located in the \CodeBlocks\boost_1_73_0\tools directory. You use it to create all the tools simultaneously, using the following steps.

1. **Open a command prompt or terminal window using the technique appropriate for your platform.**

2. **Type** CD \CodeBlocks\boost_1_73_0\tools **and press Enter.**

The command processor takes you to the main tools directory.

3. **(Optional) If you haven't already created a path to the CodeBlocks compiler at the command line or terminal, create one.**

For example, when working with Windows, type **path = C:\CodeBlocks\ MinGW\bin;%path%** and press Enter.

4. **(Optional) If you haven't already created a path to Boost.Build at the command line or terminal, create one.**

For example, when working with Windows, type **path=C:\Boost.Build\ bin;%path%** and press Enter.

5. **Type** b2 **and press Enter.**

Be patient; the build process will take several minutes. The executable files for Inspect (inspect.exe), bcp (bcp.exe), and QuickBook (quickbook.exe) will automatically appear in the \CodeBlocks\boost_1_73_0\dist\bin directory on your system after the build process is complete. BoostBook content appears in the \CodeBlocks\boost_1_73_0\dist\share\boostbook directory.

Using Boost.Build

Boost.Build is a complex tool that helps you create fully functional applications that rely on Boost using your compiler, such as GCC. Boost.Build provides an automated command-line approach to performing tasks that some developers prefer, especially when performing repetitive tasks where the IDE simply gets in the way. You have already used Boost.Build several times in this chapter to build the Boost libraries, a specific version of Boost.Build for your compiler, as well as the Boost tools. The following sections provide some helpful hints and tips for working with Boost.Build.

Getting a successful build

Every time you use the b2 command at the command prompt or terminal window, you use Boost.Build. A few rules to remember when using Boost.Build are

>> Ensure that you have a path set up to your compiler.

>> Ensure that you have a path set up to Boost.Build.

>> Use the --prefix option to place the output in a specific directory.

REMEMBER

If you know these rules, you'll avoid the problems that plague many developers who are new to Boost.Build. The bbv2.html file contained in the \CodeBlocks\ boost_1_73_0\doc\html directory contains complete documentation for Boost. Build. This is where you find a complete list of the Boost.Build properties and options. In addition, the documentation tells you how to perform various build types, such as applications and libraries. If you find that the bbv2.html file link is broken, it's a known issue that's documented at https://github.com/boostorg/website/issues/451. You can try the online alternative at https://boostorg.github.io/build/manual/master/index.html instead.

Creating your own example

It's time to see Boost.Build at work. To do this, you create a folder on your system where you can place a .cpp file. The example for this section appears in the Hello folder of the downloadable source as hello.cpp. The code for this example is really simple. It outputs a message to the computer screen, as shown here:

```cpp
#include <iostream>

using namespace std;

int main()
```

```
{
    cout << "Hello, I am your computer talking." << endl;
    return 0;
}
```

You don't even need to use Code::Blocks to perform this task. Any editor that produces plain-text output will work fine. For example, you could use Notepad to produce the code in Windows.

To use Boost.Build, you also need create a `jamfile.v2` file, which is just another plain-text file that you can create using Notepad or another text editor. The resource at `https://www.boost.org/doc/libs/1_33_1/doc/html/bbv2/advanced/jamfiles.html` makes things look a bit complex, but for this example, it comes down to a single line of text:

```
exe Hello : hello.cpp ;
```

Notice the space between `cpp` and `;`. You must include this space or the build process will fail. The error message isn't very helpful either. It tells you that you've encountered an odd escape character and then the end of file. All that this file says is to create an executable named `Hello` from `hello.cpp`.

To perform the build, you open a command prompt in the folder you chose, type **b2 --toolset=gcc**, and press Enter. The output tells you what Boost.Build does:

```
...found 8 targets...
...updating 5 targets...
gcc.compile.c++ bin\gcc-6.2.0\debug\hello.o
gcc.link bin\gcc-6.2.0\debug\Hello.exe
...updated 5 targets...
```

The fourth line tells you the location of the file: `bin\gcc-6.2.0\debug\`. When you go to this directory, you can type **Hello**, press Enter, and see the expected output. You can do a lot more than this section tells you, but it provides you with a very basic idea of how Boost.Build works.

Using Inspect

Many organizations want to make changes to the Boost library to ensure that the library meets their needs or to augment the Boost library to meet a new requirement. Whenever you change something, there is a chance that the change will cause compatibility issues because it doesn't meet the Boost library guidelines. In addition, a developer might introduce errors into the Boost library that others will find difficult to fix. The Inspect utility enables you to scan for potential Boost library errors after you make a change to it.

Start Inspect from the directory that you want to check. To make this process more efficient, make sure to set a path to the copy of Inspect that you built in the "Creating the Boost Tools" section of the chapter using the method appropriate for your platform. For example, when working with Windows, you type **path = C:\ CodeBlocks\boost_1_73_0\dist\bin;%path%** and press Enter.

Inspect looks for errors in the current directory and all subdirectories. You can try it by checking the library files you find out how to build in the "Building the libraries" section, earlier in this chapter. These files usually appear in the \Code-Blocks\boost_1_73_0\boost directory. Normally, Inspect performs a complete check of the libraries. However, you can modify Inspect behavior using the following command-line switches to perform specific tests:

>> -license

>> -copyright

>> -crlf

>> -end

>> -link

>> -path_name

>> -tab

>> -ascii

>> -apple_macro

>> -assert_macro

>> -deprecated_macro

>> -minmax

>> -unnamed

>> -version-string *version_message*

You can use any number of these command-line switches. If you forget the Inspect command-line switches, type **Inspect -help** and press Enter. Inspect shows you a list of the command-line switches that you can use for testing.

Inspect also provides a number of command-line switches that affect how it performs tests. The following list describes these command-line switches:

>> –cvs: Performs a check of only the cvs directory and ignores all other files.

>> –text: Outputs the results in pure text format. This option is especially useful when you want to save the results to a text file for later analysis. Otherwise, Inspect formats the output as HTML. Figure 4-7 shows a typical report. Click the links to see details about a particular test, such as the licensed status of each file within a particular directory.

FIGURE 4-7:
Inspect normally outputs its reports as HTML.

TIP

Inspect outputs information to the default output device, which is normally the console (your display). Seeing HTML in text form on a display isn't particularly helpful. Most platforms offer some type of redirection feature so that you can see the output to a file. For example, on a Windows system, you can type **Inspect > MyReport.html** and press Enter to output the results to a file named MyReport.html.

>> –brief: Reduces the amount of output text to the minimum required to indicate success or failure of the various tests.

>> –version–string *version_message*: Reduces the amount of output text by locating entries with a specific version string (as defined by *version_message*). What you're normally looking for is the version string provided with the library, such as 1_73_0 for the 1.73.0 version.

REMEMBER

Inspect is sensitive about the ordering of command-line switches. You must place the –cvs, –text, or –brief command-line switch first, followed by the test switches; otherwise, Inspect displays an error message. The website at https://www.boost.org/doc/libs/1_73_0/tools/inspect/index.html tells you more about working with Inspect.

Understanding BoostBook

The world abounds with documentation formats — everything from .docx files produced by Word to the seemingly ubiquitous .pdf file. Of all the documentation formats, the most universal and compatible is the lowly .txt file. However, .txt files lack formatting (except for control characters like tab, carriage return, and linefeed), which means that they limit you solely to words, which may not be enough to describe your documentation. Because you can choose from so many different file formats, and formatting code can prove especially difficult, the Boost library relies on a special document format called BoostBook.

REMEMBER

Documentation seems to be the bane of developers everywhere. No one seems to want to write the documentation, and the attempts at documentation often leave readers with more questions than answers. BoostBook won't make you a good writer. Although it does help you produce highly formatted documentation with a standardized format, it can't overcome deficiencies in writing skill. When creating documentation for your project, the best writer in your group is still the unsurpassed choice for documentation tasks.

If you have installed the Boost library using the instructions in the "Obtaining and Installing Boost for Code::Blocks" section of this chapter, you already have access to BoostBook. However, as with some other Boost utilities, you need to know a bit about Python to use this feature. In addition, you need an Apache server setup and must also download a number of other utilities. In short, even though BoostBook is accessible from a Boost library perspective, you still need to do some work to make this feature useful. The instructions at https://www.boost.org/doc/libs/1_73_0/doc/html/boostbook/getting/started.html describe the additional steps you need to perform.

BoostBook relies on XML to hold the content you want to place in the document. The use of XML is the reason you must install the DocBook eXtensible Stylesheet Language (XSL) (http://docbook.sourceforge.net/) and DocBook Document Type Definition (DTD) (http://www.oasis-open.org/docbook/xml/4.5/) support. You can see the XML used for BoostBook at https://www.boost.org/doc/libs/1_73_0/doc/html/boostbook/documenting.html. Check the main BoostBook page at https://www.boost.org/doc/libs/1_73_0/doc/html/boostbook.html for additional information.

If you performed the steps in the "Creating the Boost Tools" section of the chapter, you already have access to all the functionality needed to use BoostBook. The files you require appear in the CodeBlocks\boost_1_73_0\dist\share\boostbook directory of your system. These files help you perform the required formatting.

TIP

Even if you choose not to use BoostBook for your project, you do need to create a common documentation format. Using BoostBook may prove complicated for the Windows developer; the originators seem to have meant this documentation format more for Unix and Linux developers. However, it's still a useful documentation format, and you should consider it. If you find BoostBook lacking, you need to create a custom format or suffer the consequences of a poorly documented application.

Using QuickBook

QuickBook is an add-on for BoostBook. This utility started as someone's weekend project. Originally, QuickBook outputted simple HTML documents. However, now it outputs XML in BoostBook format so that you can quickly generate documentation that links with the rest of the documentation for your project. As described by the author at https://www.boost.org/doc/libs/1_73_0/doc/html/quickbook.html, QuickBook is a WikiWiki-style documentation tool. It's important to note that some people simply call it a Wiki (https://en.wikipedia.org/wiki/Wiki) or Wiki-Wiki or even Wiki Wiki. All the terms mean the same thing.

Before you use QuickBook, you generate a documentation file. You can see an example of such a file at https://www.boost.org/doc/libs/1_73_0/tools/quickbook/doc/quickbook.qbk. For a complete syntax summary for QuickBook, look at https://www.boost.org/doc/libs/1_73_0/doc/html/quickbook/syntax.html.

At this point, you're probably wondering why you should use QuickBook at all, because you have to generate a document file for it anyway. Here are the reasons why many developers use QuickBook instead of relying on BoostBook directly:

>> The QuickBook syntax is easier to read and use than writing XML.

>> You can use QuickBook to generate non-Boost documentation.

>> It's relatively easy to convert other documentation formats into QuickBook syntax.

QuickBook is a command-line utility. You find it in the `\CodeBlocks\ boost_1_73_0\dist\bin` directory after generating the Boost tools. (See the "Creating the Boost Tools" section, earlier in this chapter, for details.) Here are the command-line switches you can access when working with QuickBook:

>> **--help:** Displays a help message showing all the command-line switches, as well as the command-line syntax.

>> **--version:** Displays version information about QuickBook.

>> **--no-pretty-print:** Disables XML printing and uses plain text instead.

>> **--strict:** Performs additional checks for issues such as sections that aren't closed and square brackets that don't match any tags or templates.

>> **--no-self-linked-headers:** Generates plain headers, which makes creating the files easier but also prevents someone from right-clicking the header and copying a link to it.

>> **--indent** *arg*: Defines the number of spaces to use for indents (as specified by arg).

>> **--linewidth** *arg*: Defines the number of characters in a single line.

>> **--input-file** *arg*: Specifies the name of the input file.

>> **--output-format** *arg*: Allows the creation of boostbook, html, or onehtml output. The default is boostbook.

>> **--output-file** *arg*: Specifies the name of the output file.

>> **--output-dir** *arg*: Specifies the output directory path for html files.

>> **--no-output:** Allows checking of the documentation syntax without outputting the boostbook, which saves time during debugging.

>> **--output-deps** *arg*: Specifies the name of the output dependency file.

» **--ms-errors:** Specifies that QuickBook should use the Microsoft Visual Studio style of errors and warnings in the output message format. This option can make QuickBook easier for Microsoft Visual Studio developers to use and understand.

» **--include-path** *arg*: Adds the selected path to the include path. You may use this command-line switch multiple times to add multiple paths.

» **--define** *arg*: Defines a QuickBook macro. This feature is often used for conditional compilation.

» **--image-location** *arg*: Specifies the location of any image elements in order to read SVG details.

Using bcp

The bcp (Boost copy) utility helps you make Boost more manageable. You can use it to

» Copy one or more Boost modules to another location so that you can use a subset within an application.

» List all the elements within a module.

» Create an HTML report about module content that includes:

- License information

- Files without licensing information

- Files without copyright information

- Copyright information

- Dependency information for individual files

Theoretically, you can also use bcp to scan your application for a listing of elements needed to run the application. The output report includes all the information in a standard bcp report for a Boost module. You use one of four command-line syntaxes to work with bcp, as shown here:

```
bcp [options] module-list output-path
bcp --list [options] module-list
bcp --list-short [options] module-list
bcp --report [options] module-list html-file
```

Each of these command-line syntaxes performs a different task: copy, listing, short listing, and reporting. These command lines can accept a number of options, as described in the following list:

» **--boost=*path***: Defines the path to the Boost library.

» **--scan:** Treats the modules as a non-Boost file for the purpose of scanning file dependencies. You always use this option with your own applications.

» **--cvs:** Copies only files under Concurrent Versions System (CVS) version control.

» **--unix-lines:** Uses Unix-style line endings for the output. You won't ever use this command-line switch on a Windows system but may need it on Unix, Linux, and Macintosh systems.

» **--namespace=*name***: Rename the Boost namespace and associated library names to the value specified by *name*.

» **--namespace-alias:** Makes the namespace boost an alias of the namespace set with the --namespace command-line switch.

Using bcp is relatively straightforward. For example, if you want a listing of files for the regex library, change directories to \CodeBlocks\boost_1_73_0 and then use the following command line:

```
bcp --list regex > Out.txt
```

The bcp utility looks in the \CodeBlocks\boost_1_73_0 directory for Boost applications. In this case, the output appears in Out.txt. You should always use file redirection because the output is too large to read at the command prompt.

Say that you want a report about the regex module instead of a simple listing. In this case, you use the following command line:

```
bcp --report regex MyReport.html
```

Creating a report can take a while. Eventually, you see an HTML report like the one shown in Figure 4-8. You can discover more about bcp at https://www.boost.org/doc/libs/1_73_0/tools/bcp/doc/html/index.html.

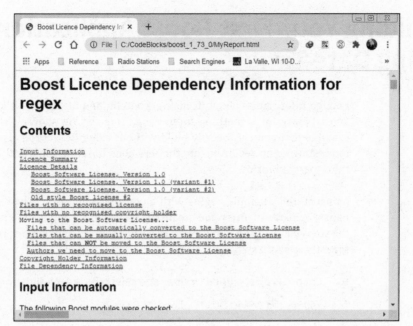

FIGURE 4-8:
The bcp utility
can output some
nice-looking
reports about
Boost modules.

Using Wave

The Wave utility is a preprocessor for the Boost library. Using a preprocessor can significantly speed the compilation process because a preprocessor compiles the library portion of the application. After you compile it the first time, you need not compile the library again. Theoretically, you can use Wave with any C++ compiler; however, you probably won't need it with compilers such as Code::Blocks and Microsoft Visual Studio because these products include their own preprocessor. You can find more information about the Wave utility at `https://www.boost.org/doc/libs/1_73_0/libs/wave/doc/wave_driver.html`.

There is more to the Wave utility than meets the eye, however. The Wave utility relies on the Wave library. This library ships as part of Boost, and you can use it in your applications as you do any other library. The website at `https://www.boost.org/doc/libs/1_73_0/libs/wave/index.html` tells you more about the Wave library.

Building Your First Boost Application Using Date Time

Enough information about licensing, content, and utilities — it's time to use the Boost library for something interesting. This section shows a simple date/time example that you can't easily build without using Boost. You also discover some interesting setup requirements that are good to know when you work with other third-party libraries.

As usual, this example begins with a console application. The example uses the name FirstBoost. After you create the new console application project following the steps you've used to create all the other console applications in the book, perform these setup steps:

1. **Choose Project ⇨ Build Options and select the Search Directories tab.**

You see the Project Build Options dialog box.

2. **Highlight FirstBoost in the left pane. Click Add.**

Code::Blocks displays the Add Directory dialog box, shown in Figure 4-9.

3. **Click the Browse button to display the Browse for Folder dialog box and highlight the \CodeBlocks\boost_1_73_0 folder on your hard drive. Click OK.**

A dialog box appears asking whether you want to maintain the entry as a relative path. *Relative paths* specify a location using the current location as a starting point. The alternative is an *absolute path,* which specifies a location based on the root directory of your hard drive. In most cases, absolute paths are less likely to get broken.

4. **Click No.**

Code::Blocks adds the folder you selected to the Add Directory dialog box.

5. Click OK.

You see the folder for the Boost library, as shown in Figure 4-10. (Your path could vary from the one shown in the screenshot, depending on the platform you use and how your copy of Boost was set up). Make sure you select the correct folder; otherwise, the compiler won't be able to find the Boost library or the headers won't compile correctly because they point to the wrong location on the hard drive.

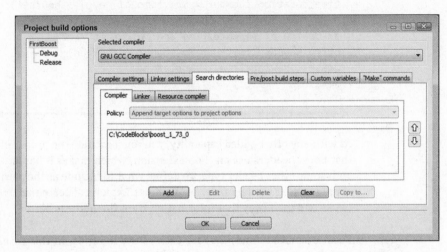

FIGURE 4-10:
Make sure you set the environment to use Boost.

6. Click OK.

The application environment is ready to use with the Boost library.

Now that you have the environment configured, you can begin working with Boost. Listing 4-1 shows a date/time example that displays the current time and then a modified date/time.

LISTING 4-1: Using Boost to Create a Simple Date/Time Example

```
#include <iostream>
#include "boost/date_time/posix_time/posix_time.hpp"

using namespace std;
using namespace boost::posix_time;
using namespace boost::gregorian;

int main() {
  // Obtain the current date and time.
```

(continued)

LISTING 4-1: **(continued)**

```
ptime Now = second_clock::local_time();
cout << Now << endl;

// Get the date and adjust it for tomorrow.
date TheDate = Now.date() + days(1);

// Get the time and adjust for an hour from now.
time_duration TheHour = Now.time_of_day() + hours(1);

// Create a new date/time and output it.
ptime NewDateTime = ptime(TheDate, TheHour);
cout << NewDateTime << endl;
return 0;
}
```

As with any other added capability, you must include the proper library files. Note that Boost headers use an .hpp extension, which makes it harder to confuse them with some other header type. To define what to include as the path to your library, simply look at the hierarchy in Windows Explorer. Locate the .hpp file you want to use and then copy that information from the Address bar.

REMEMBER

Boost provides namespaces for each of the libraries. In this case, the ptime and time_duration classes appear in the boost::posix_time namespace and the date class appears in the boost::gregorian namespace. If you find that your application won't compile, it usually means that you've missed a namespace and need to consider where each of the classes in your application comes from.

The application code begins by creating a variable, Now, that contains the current time, which you obtain using the second_clock::local_time() method. It then displays the current time. The ptime class includes methods for interacting with every time element: years, months, days, hours, minutes, seconds, and so on. The example shows a few of the interactions you can perform. When you run this application, the second time you see is one day and one hour ahead of the current time.

» **Using Tokenizer to break strings into tokens**

» **Converting numbers to other data types**

» **Using Foreach to create improved loops**

» **Using Filesystem to access the operating system**

Chapter **5**

Boosting up a Step

The Boost library is vast. It's doubtful that a typical developer will ever use everything that Boost has to offer. Of course, before you can pick and choose what you want to use, you need to know it exists. Browsing through the help file can reveal classes that you need to add to your toolkit to produce good applications. This chapter helps by taking you on a whirlwind tour of the major Boost categories. Don't expect this chapter to discuss everything — Boost is simply too large for that. If you want to see a list of what Boost has to offer, check out

» **All classes in alphabetical order:** https://www.boost.org/doc/libs/1_73_0

» **Categorized list:** https://www.boost.org/doc/libs/1_73_0?view=categorized

TIP

In addition to reviewing the examples in this chapter and looking through the Help file, it also pays to browse the Boost directory for examples. For example, if you look at the \CodeBlocks\boost_1_73_0\libs\regex\example directory, you find three examples of how to use RegEx, one of which is demonstrated in the "Testing the installation" section of Book 7, Chapter 4. Every example directory contains a Jamfile.v2 that you can use to build the examples using Boost.Build. If you still haven't found the example you need, check online for more examples — Boost is extremely popular. Even Microsoft has gotten into the act by providing examples at `https://devblogs.microsoft.com/cppblog/using-c-coroutines-with-boost-c-libraries/`, `https://marketplace.visualstudio.com/items?itemName=AdamWulkiewicz.GraphicalDebugging`, and `https://docs.microsoft.com/en-us/visualstudio/test/how-to-use-boost-test-for-cpp?view=vs-2019`.

Before you begin working through the examples in this chapter, make sure you know how to configure your development environment to use Boost. The "Testing the installation" and "Building Your First Boost Application Using Date Time" sections of Book 7, Chapter 4 tell how to configure Code::Blocks to use Boost. The "Building Your First Boost Application Using Date Time" section also provides you with a simple example that gets you started working with Boost.

REMEMBER

You don't have to type the source code for this chapter manually. In fact, using the downloadable source is a lot easier. You can find the source for this chapter in the `\CPP_AIO4\BookVII\Chapter05` folder of the downloadable source. See the Introduction for details on how to find these source files.

Parsing Strings Using RegEx

Regular expressions are an important part of today's computing environment. You use them to perform *pattern matching*, where the application finds a series of matching characters in a string. For example, if you want the user to enter values from 0 through 9 and nothing else, you can create a pattern that prevents the user from entering anything else. Using patterns in the form of regular expressions serves a number of important purposes:

>> Ensures that your application receives precisely the right kind of input

>> Enforces a particular data input format (such as the way you input a telephone number)

>> Reduces security risks (for example, a user can't input a script in place of the data you wanted)

WARNING

Some developers make the mistake of thinking that a regular expression can prevent every sort of data input error. However, regular expressions are only one tool in an arsenal you must build against errant input. For example, a regular expression can't perform range checking. If you want values between 101 and 250, a regular expression will ensure that the user enters three digits; however, you must use range checking to prevent the user from entering a value of 100.

DEFINING THE PATTERN

The RegEx library provides a number of methods for creating a pattern. For example, if you want the user to input only lowercase letters, you can create a range by using [a–z]. The example in this chapter shows how to create a simple three-digit numeric input. However, you can create a pattern for nearly any use. For example, a telephone number pattern might appear as ([0–9] [0–9] [0–9]) [0–9] [0–9] [0–9]–[0–9] [0–9] [0–9] [0–9], where a telephone number of (555) 555-5555 is acceptable, but a telephone number of 555-555-5555 isn't. The RegEx library reference appears at https://www.boost.org/doc/libs/1_73_0/libs/regex/doc/html/index.html.

This chapter doesn't provide you with a full explanation of all the patterns you can create. In fact, there are different flavors of regex patterns, so you want to be sure that a pattern you see online will actually work with the library that you're using for your application. The best place to start discovering the basics of Boost-compatible patterns is at https://www.boost.org/doc/libs/1_73_0/libs/regex/doc/html/boost_regex/syntax.html. It's important to note that older versions of Boost supported only the Perl syntax; newer versions support POSIX basic and POSIX extended syntax as well. Boost provides a wealth of pattern types.

How you use the pattern is just as important as how you create the pattern. For example, you can use RegEx_match to obtain a precise match. However, if you want to search only for a value, you use RegEx_search instead. The usage reference appears at https://www.boost.org/doc/libs/1_73_0/libs/regex/doc/html/boost_regex/ref.html.

Defining the pattern for a regular expression can prove time consuming. However, after you create the pattern, you can use it every time you must check for a particular input pattern. The following sections describe how to work with the RegEx (*regular expressions*) library.

Adding the RegEx library

Most of the Boost library works just fine by adding headers to your application code. However, a few components, such as RegEx, require a library. Before you can use a library, you must build it. The instructions for performing this task appear in the "Building the libraries" section of Book 7, Chapter 4. After you build the library, you must add it to your application.

USING BOOST LIBRARIES ON CERTAIN 64-BIT SYSTEMS

If you performed the Boost installation for your system using the techniques found in the "Boost Installation on Certain 64-bit Systems" sidebar in Book 7 Chapter 4, then you may not have any library files to use because they won't build. However, that means skipping the instructions in this section. In this case, you can try a header-only example using the code in the next section of the chapter to see if RegEx will work on your system. In at least some cases, it will work, but you may lose functionality provided by the library. When problems occur, you'll see an error message telling you there is a configuration (or sometimes other) error and that the Boost RegEx library is missing. The example in the "Accessing the Operating System Using Filesystem" section won't run on a 64-bit system using the alternative configuration.

Two techniques exist for adding the required headers and libraries to an application. The first technique is to add it to the compiler settings, as you do for the "Testing the installation" section of Book 7, Chapter 4. The second technique is to add the settings to a specific project. You use the first technique when you work with Boost for a large number of projects and require access to all libraries. The second technique is best when you use Boost only for specific projects and require access only to specific libraries. The following steps show you how to perform the project–specific setup for any library, not just the RegEx library:

1. **Use the Project wizard to create a new project.**

   Nothing has changed from the beginning of this book; every application begins with a new project. The next section discusses the RegEx example, and you can use that project name as a starting point here.

2. **Choose Project⇨Build Options.**

   Code::Blocks displays the Project Build Options dialog box.

3. **Select the project name, such as RegEx, in the left pane.**

4. **Select the Linker Settings tab.**

   You see a number of linker settings, including a Link Libraries list, which will be blank.

5. **Click Add.**

   Code::Blocks displays the Add Library dialog box, shown in Figure 5-1.

6. **Click the Browse button — the button sporting an opening file folder.**

   You see the Choose Library to Link dialog box.

FIGURE 5-1:
Select the library
you want to add.

7. **Using the dialog box, navigate to the library of your choice, such as** `libboost_regex-mgw6-mt-x64-1_73.a` **(the release version of the library), select the library, and then click OK.**

The Boost library files are typically located in the `\CodeBlocks\boost_1_73_0\bin.v2\libs\` directory. When you click OK, you see a dialog box that asks whether you want to keep this as a relative path.

REMEMBER

Relative paths specify a location using the current location as a starting point. The alternative is an *absolute path,* which specifies a location based on the root directory of your hard drive. In most cases, absolute paths are less likely to get broken.

8. **Click No.**

You see the absolute path for the selected library, such as `libboost_regex-mgw6-mt-x64-1_73.a,` added to the File field of the Add Library dialog box.

9. **Click OK.**

After you click OK, you see the absolute path for the library added to the Linker Settings, as shown in Figure 5-2.

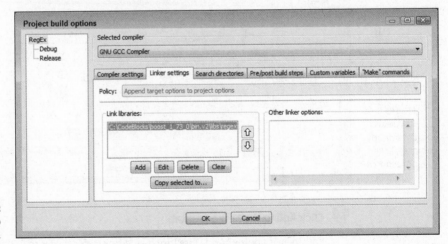

FIGURE 5-2:
Add the library to
the application.

10. **Click the Search Directories tab.**

    You see three subtabs: Compiler, Linker, and Resource Compiler.

11. **Click Add in the Compiler subtab.**

    You see an Add Directory dialog box like the one shown in Figure 5-3.

FIGURE 5-3:
Add appropriate
search directories
for Boost header
and library files.

12. **Type the location of the Boost header files in the Directory field.**

    As an alternative, you can click the Browse button to use a Browse for Folder dialog box to find them. The files are normally located in the \CodeBlocks\ boost_1_73_0\boost folder.

13. **Click OK.**

    You see the search folder added to the Compiler tab, as shown in Figure 5-4.

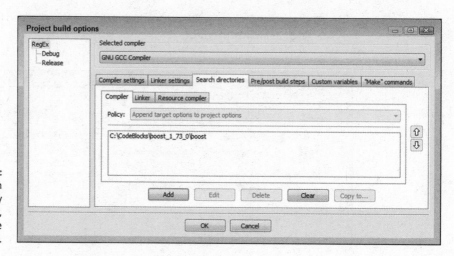

FIGURE 5-4:
The search
location for any
compiler, linker,
or resource
compiler.

14. **Click Add in the Linker subtab.**

    You see yet another Add Directory dialog box (refer to Figure 5-3).

15. Type the location of the Boost library files in the Directory field and then click OK.

The Boost library files are typically located in the \CodeBlocks\boost_1_73_0\ bin.v2\libs directory. After you click OK, you see the directory added to the Linker tab.

16. Click OK.

The selected library is ready for inclusion in your application.

Creating the RegEx code

Using a regular expression is relatively straightforward. All you do is create the expression and then use it with a function to perform specific kinds of pattern matches. The function you choose is important because each function performs the pattern matching differently. The RegEx example code, shown in Listing 5-1, demonstrates how to create a regular expression and then use it in two different ways to determine whether user input is correct.

LISTING 5-1: **Performing Matches and Searches Using RegEx**

```
#include <iostream>
#include "boost/regex.hpp"

using namespace std;
using namespace boost;

int main() {
  char MyNumber[80];
  cout << "Type a three-digit number: ";
  cin >> MyNumber;

  regex Expression("[0-9][0-9][0-9]");
  cmatch Matches;

  // Perform a matching check.
  if (regex_match(MyNumber, Matches, Expression)) {
    cout << "You typed: " << Matches << endl;
  } else {
    cout << "Not a three-digit number!" << endl;
  }
```

(continued)

LISTING 5-1: *(continued)*

```
// Perform a search check.
if (regex_search(MyNumber, Matches, Expression)) {
  cout << "Found: " << Matches << endl;
} else {
  cout << "No three-digit number found!" << endl;
}
return 0;
}
```

In this case, the code begins by adding the proper header, RegEx.hpp, and the proper namespace, boost. In many cases, you can get by without doing much more than performing these two steps in your code. It then performs three steps:

1. Get some user input. Even though the prompt tells the user to enter a three-digit number, C++ doesn't enforce this requirement.

2. Create the regular expression. This example needs a set of three ranges for numbers: [0–9] [0–9] [0–9]. Using ranges works well for a number of tasks, and you use them often when creating a regular expression.

3. Perform the pattern match. The example uses RegEx_match( ), which performs a precise match, and RegEx_search( ), which looks for the right characters anywhere in the input. Both functions require three input values: the value you want to check, an output variable of type cmatch that tells where the match is found, and the regular expression.

To see how this code works, you must perform a series of three tests. First, run the application and type **0** as the input. Naturally, typing 0 means that the code will fail and you see this output:

```
Not a three-digit number!
No three-digit number found!
```

Run the application again and type **123** as the input to see

```
You typed: 123
Found: 123
```

So far, there isn't much difference between the two functions, which is why you need the third test. Run the application and type **ABC123XYZ** as the input to see:

```
Not a three-digit number!
Found: 123
```

This final test shows that the RegEx_search( ) function finds the three-digit value in the string. Obviously, the RegEx_search( ) function is great when you need to locate information but not good when you need to secure it. When you need a precise pattern match, use RegEx_match( ) instead.

Breaking Strings into Tokens Using Tokenizer

Humans view strings as a sentence or at least a phrase. Mixtures of words create meaning that we can see in a moment.

REMEMBER

Computers, on the other hand, understand nothing. A computer can perform pattern matching and do math, but it can't understand Kipling (read more about this fascinating author at https://www.poetryfoundation.org/poets/rudyard-kipling). It's because of this lack of understanding that you must tokenize text for the computer. A computer can perform comparisons on individual *tokens*, usually single words or symbols, and create output based on those comparisons.

The compiler you use relies on a *tokenizer*, an application component that breaks text into tokens, to turn the text you type into machine code the computer can execute. However, the tokenizer appears in all sorts of applications. For example, when you perform a spelling check on a document, the word processing application breaks the text into individual words using a tokenizer, and then compares those words to words in its internal dictionary.

The Tokens example, shown in Listing 5-2, shows a method for creating tokens from strings. This basic technique works with any phrase, string, or series of strings. You'll normally process the tokens after you finish creating them.

LISTING 5-2: **Creating Tokens from Strings**

```
#include <iostream>
#include "boost/tokenizer.hpp"

using namespace std;
using namespace boost;

int main() {
  string MyString = "This is a test string!";
  tokenizer<> Tokens(MyString);
```

(continued)

LISTING 5-2:   *(continued)*

```
// Display each token on screen.
tokenizer<>::iterator Iterate;
for (Iterate = Tokens.begin(); Iterate != Tokens.end();
   Iterate++)
   cout << *Iterate << endl;
return 0;
}
```

The tokenizer template places the tokenized form of MyString in Tokens. The application now has a set of tokens with which to work. To see the tokens, you must iterate through them by creating a tokenizer<>::iterator, Iterate. The application uses iterator to output the individual tokens. When you run this application, you see the following output:

```
This
is
a
test
string
```

TIP

This example shows a basic routine that you can use for just about any need. However, you might need some of the extended capabilities of the tokenizer class. Check out the materials at https://www.boost.org/doc/libs/1_73_0/libs/tokenizer/doc/index.html for more information about both the tokenizer and the tokenizer<>::iterator.

Performing Numeric Conversion

Numeric conversion isn't hard to perform — it's *accurate* numeric conversion that's hard to perform. Getting the right result as you move from one type of number to another is essential. Sure, you probably won't notice too much if your game score is off by a point or two, but you'll definitely notice the missing dollars from your savings account. Worse yet, when taking a trip into space, a rounding error can definitely ruin your day as you head off toward the sun rather than Planet Earth.

The Boost library includes the converter template, which makes converting from one kind of number to another relatively easy. The converter template includes all kinds of flexibility. The Convert example, shown in Listing 5-3, presents two different levels of converter template usage.

WHY NUMERIC CONVERSION IS NECESSARY

Humans don't differentiate between one kind of number and another — seeing 1 is about the same as seeing 1.0. The computer, however, does make a differentiation between numbers at two levels:

- Integer versus floating-point
- Size

The integer part of the equation comes into play because of the early processors in PCs, which could perform only integer math. For floating-point math, you had to buy a separate math coprocessor. Today, the math coprocessor comes with the processor, but integer and floating-point math still occur in different areas of the processor. When the processor performs integer math, it uses different registers and capabilities than when it performs floating-point math. So the conversion between integer and floating-point data is more than philosophical; it involves using physically different areas of the processor.

The size issue determines how large the integer or floating-point value is. Again, the difference is physical. Early processors could handle only 8 bits of data at a time, then 16 bits, and on to 32 bits, and finally the 64 bits of today. (You can even read about an AMD 128 bit processor at https://www.tweaktown.com/news/68872/rick-morty-uses-128-bit-amd-cpu-3-584-825-480gb-ram/index.html.) Using larger numbers in older processors required a number of additional tasks in software, so using larger numbers incurred a significant performance penalty.

Today, with memory and processor register size no longer a concern, large numbers are also no longer a concern, except that you must observe the historical reasons for using numbers of a specific size. In addition, you sometimes gain benefits from a reliability, security, or speed perspective in using a smaller number. The important consideration in working with numbers is that you must observe the correct conversion techniques when you want to obtain the correct results.

LISTING 5-3: **Converting from double to int**

```
#include <iostream>
#include "boost/numeric/conversion/converter.hpp"

using namespace std;
using namespace boost;
using namespace boost::numeric;
```

(continued)

LISTING 5-3: **(continued)**

```
int main() {
  typedef converter<int, double> Double2Int;
  double MyDouble = 2.1;
  int MyInt = Double2Int::convert(MyDouble);

  cout << "The double value is: " << MyDouble << endl;
  cout << "The int value is: " << MyInt << endl;

  // See what happens with a larger value.
  MyDouble = 3.8;
  MyInt = Double2Int::convert(MyDouble);
  cout << "The double value is: " << MyDouble << endl;
  cout << "The int value is: " << MyInt << endl;

  // Round instead of truncate.
  typedef conversion_traits<int, double> Traits;
  typedef converter<int, double, Traits,
    def_overflow_handler, RoundEven<double> >
    Double2Rounded;
  MyInt = Double2Rounded::convert(MyDouble);
  cout << "The int value is: " << MyInt << endl;
  return 0;
}
```

The example begins by creating a converter object, Double2Int. This first object shows the minimum information that you can provide — the target (int) and source (double) values. The default setting truncates floating-point values (float and double among them) to obtain an int value. To perform a conversion, the code relies on the convert method, which requires a variable of the required source type as an argument.

REMEMBER

The converter template includes support for four kinds of rounding. You must use the correct kind of rounding to match your application requirements. Imagine what would happen to calculations if you used truncation when rounding is really the required operation. The following list describes all four kinds of rounding that converter supports:

>> Trunc: Removes the decimal portion of the value (rounds toward 0)

>> RoundEven: Rounds values up or down as needed such that the ending value is even (also called banker's rounding). Consequently, 1.5 rounds up to 2, while 2.5 rounds down to 2.

>> `Ceil`: Rounds the value up toward positive infinity when the decimal portion is greater than 0

>> `Floor`: Rounds the value down toward negative infinity when the decimal portion is greater than 0

The second `converter` object, `Double2Rounded`, shows the template requirements to choose the kind of rounding that the object performs. In this case, you supply five arguments to the template (the `converter` template accepts up to seven arguments; see `https://www.boost.org/doc/libs/1_73_0/libs/numeric/conversion/doc/html/boost_numericconversion/converter___function_object.html`):

>> Target

>> Source

>> `conversion_traits`, which include the target and source types as a minimum

>> Overflow handler, which determines how the object handles conversions that result in an overflow (the default is `def_overflow_handler`)

>> Rounding template object (which includes the rounding source type)

The process for using the extended form of the `converter` template is the same as the simple form shown earlier in the example. However, you must now create a `conversions_traits` object (`Traits` in this case) and provide the required input information. (See more examples of using `conversion_traits` at `https://www.boost.org/doc/libs/1_73_0/libs/numeric/conversion/doc/html/boost_numericconversion/conversion_traits___traits_class.html`.) As before, you rely on the `convert` method to perform the conversion process. Here's the application output:

```
The double value is: 2.1
The int value is: 2
The double value is: 3.8
The int value is: 3
The int value is: 4
```

The last two lines show the difference in rounding the value `3.8` using `Trunc` and `RoundEven`. See `https://www.boost.org/doc/libs/1_73_0/libs/numeric/conversion/doc/html/index.html` for more about numeric conversion.

Creating Improved Loops Using Foreach

Writing efficient loops is a requirement if you want your application to perform optimally. Interestingly enough, many loops use a certain amount of *boilerplate* code (code that is essentially the same every time you write it, but with small nuances).

REMEMBER

Templates and other methodologies described in this book provide a means to overcome the boredom of writing essentially the same code. However, none of the examples to date has shown a tried-and-true method: macros. A *macro* is essentially a substitution technique that replaces a keyword with the boilerplate code you'd normally write. Macros normally appear in uppercase, such as BOOST_ FOREACH, which is the macro used in this section of the chapter. Instead of typing all the code associated with a macro, you simply type the macro name and the compiler does the rest of the work for you.

TECHNICAL STUFF

The magic behind the BOOST_FOREACH macro is that it creates all the iteration code you normally create by hand. In other words, you aren't providing any less code to the compiler; you simply let the macro write it for you. The Boost library still relies on the Standard Library for_each algorithm; you avoid writing all the code you used to write when using the algorithm. See https://www.boost.org/doc/libs/1_73_0/doc/html/foreach.html for more about the BOOST_FOREACH macro. The ForEach example, in Listing 5-4, shows how to use a BOOST_FOREACH loop to iterate through a vector.

LISTING 5-4: **Creating a BOOST_FOREACH Loop**

```
#include <iostream>
#include <vector>
#include "boost/foreach.hpp"

using namespace std;
using namespace boost;

int main() {
  vector<string> names;
  names.push_back("Tom");
  names.push_back("Dick");
  names.push_back("Harry");
  names.push_back("April");
  names.push_back("May");
  names.push_back("June");
```

```
BOOST_FOREACH(string Name, names)
    cout << Name << endl;

cout << endl << "Backward:" << endl;
BOOST_REVERSE_FOREACH(string Name, names)
    cout << Name << endl;
return 0;
}
```

This example begins by creating a vector. In fact, it's the same vector as the one used for the Vectors example in Book 5, Chapter 6, Listing 6-1. In this case, the example then creates a BOOST_FOREACH loop that iterates through names. Each iteration places a single value from names into Name. The code then prints the single name.

An interesting feature of the Boost library is that you can reverse the order of iteration. In this case, the code uses a BOOST_REVERSE_FOREACH loop to go in the opposite direction — from end to beginning. The technique is precisely the same as going forward. Here's the application output:

```
Tom
Dick
Harry
April
May
June

Backward:
June
May
April
Harry
Dick
Tom
```

As you can see, iterating forward and backward works precisely as you expect. The BOOST_FOREACH and BOOST_REVERSE_FOREACH macros support a number of container types:

>> Any Standard Template Library (STL) container

>> Arrays

>> Null-terminated strings (char and wchar_t)

>> STL iterator pair (essentially a range)

>> boost::iterator_range<> and boost::sub_range<>

TIP

The macro STL container support is generalized. Any object type that supports these two requirements will work:

>> Nested iterator and const_iterator types

>> begin() and end() methods

Accessing the Operating System Using Filesystem

Working with files and directories is an important part of any application you create. Book 6 shows some standard techniques you use to work with both files and directories. However, these methods can become cumbersome and somewhat limited. Boost augments your ability to work with the file system using the Filesystem library. Creating and deleting both files and directories becomes a single call process. You can also perform tasks such as moving and renaming both files and directories.

The most important addition that Boost makes is defining a method to obtain error information from the operating system. This feature is found in the System library, which you must include as part of your application. Among other capabilities, the System library enables you to convert a numeric error that the operating system returns into a human-readable form. Unfortunately, the System library is still a work in progress, so this chapter can't demonstrate how to use it in any great detail.

You must add references to the libboost_filesystem-mgw6-mt-x32-1_73.a and libboost_system-mgw6-mt-x32-1_73.a files using the technique found in the "Adding the RegEx library" section, earlier in this chapter, for the example to work. The project file may require that you change the library setting to match your system. When you set up this application properly, you should see two libraries on the Linker Settings tab of the Project Build Options dialog box, as shown in Figure 5-5.

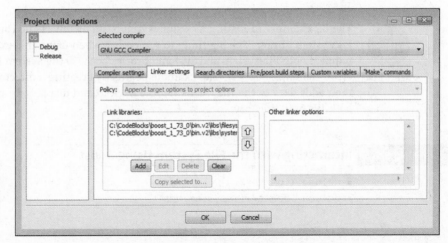

THE FILESYSTEM LIBRARY AND THE STANDARD LIBRARY

The developers of the Boost library continuously add to its capabilities. Some of the additions developers make are so useful that they end up in the Standard Library. The Filesystem library is one of these useful elements. In fact, it appears as part of C++ 17, as described in the article at https://www.fluentcpp.com/2019/11/22/how-c17-benefits-from-boost-libraries-part-two/.

Of course, standardized libraries require discussion from multiple groups, not just the Boost developers. Consequently, the Boost library you use today may not be precisely the same library you see added to the Standard Library. It's important to keep up with the proposed technical changes to the Boost library as they move to the Standard Library by reviewing the documentation online.

The movement of code from one setting to another tends to confuse developers because they suddenly find that a favorite library has seemingly disappeared. These developers also question whether they should continue using the old library or move to the new one. In all cases, you want to use the Standard Library when you can because the Standard Library is fully supported by a standards group, and is, well, standard. Consequently, when you begin creating new applications based on C++ 17 or above, you may want to consider moving from Boost to the Standard Library for the Filesystem library needs. (Ensure that your compiler also provides the required support.)

REMEMBER

The OS example in Listing 5-5 shows only a modicum of the capabilities of the Filesystem library. The big thing to remember when using this example is that it requires both Filesystem and System libraries because the System library provides error-handling support. The example begins by creating a directory and a file. It then adds data to the file, reads the file back in and displays it, and then deletes both file and directory.

LISTING 5-5: ## Interacting with the File System Using Boost

```
#include <iostream>
#include "boost/filesystem.hpp"

using namespace boost::filesystem;
using namespace std;

int main() {
  if (! exists("Test")) {
    create_directory(path("Test"));
    cout << "Created Directory Test" << endl;
  } else
    cout << "Directory Test Exists" << endl;

  if (! exists("Test/Data.txt")) {
    boost::filesystem::ofstream File("Test/Data.txt");
    File << "This is a test!";
    File.close();
    cout << "Created File Data.txt" << endl;
  } else
    cout << "File Data.txt Exists" << endl;

  if (exists("Test/Data.txt")) {
    cout << "Data.txt contains "
         << file_size("Test/Data.txt")
         << " bytes." << endl;
    boost::filesystem::ifstream File("Test/Data.txt");
    string Data;
    while (! File.eof()) {
      File >> Data;
      cout << Data << " ";
    }
    cout << endl;
```

```
    File.close();
  } else
    cout << "File Data.txt Doesn't Exist!" << endl;

  if (exists("Test/Data.txt")) {
    remove(path("Test/Data.txt"));
    cout << "Deleted Data.txt" << endl;
  }

  if (exists("Test")) {
    remove(path("Test"));
    cout << "Deleted Test" << endl;
  }

  return 0;
}
```

The first feature you should notice about this example is that it constantly checks to verify that the file or directory exists using the exists() function. Your applications should follow this pattern because you can't know that a file or directory will exist when you need to work with it, even if your application created it. A user or external application can easily delete the file or directory between the time you create it and when you need to work with it again.

To create a directory, you use create_directory(), which accepts a path as input. You create a path object using path(). Many of the other Filesystem library calls require a path object as well. For example, when you want to remove (delete) either a file or directory, you must supply a path object to remove(). Interestingly enough, remove() does remove a file without creating a path object, but it won't remove a directory. The inconsistent behavior can make an application that incorrectly uses remove() devilishly difficult to debug.

Notice that the example uses the boost::filesystem::ofstream and boost::filesystem::ifstream classes. If you try to compile the application without using the fully qualified name of the classes, you get an ambiguous reference error from Code::Blocks. Using the Boost version of the classes ensures maximum compatibility and fewer errors. Here is what you see when you run this application:

```
Created Directory Test
Created File Data.txt
```

```
Data.txt contains 15 bytes.
This is a test!
Deleted Data.txt
Deleted Test
```

One final element to look at in this example is `file_size()`, which reports the size of the file in bytes. The Filesystem library provides a number of helpful statistics that you can use to make your applications robust and reliable. As previously mentioned, you want to spend time working with this library because it contains so many helpful additions to the standard capabilities that C++ provides.

Index

Symbols

– (subtraction symbol), 60

–– (minus minus)
  decrement operator, 84, 92
  prefix/postfix operators, 85
  switch prefix, 166

! (bang), 92

!= (not equal to) operator, 107–108

(pound), 92, 96

% (percent sign) modulus operator, 86

& (ampersand), 92
  reference operator, 197, 220, 496, 501, 505, 510, 647

&& (and) operator, 110–111

( ) (parentheses), 65–66, 92, 202

* (star; asterisk), 92, 501
  dereference operator, 201
  multiplication symbol, 60, 84
  pointer variables, 205, 220

. (dot) operator, 92, 250, 555

. . . (ellipsis)
  general exception catcher, 567
  variadic operator, 422

/ (forward slash), 92
  division symbol, 60, 86
  in pathnames, 688, 729
  switch prefix, 166

/* */ (delimiters), 271

// (double slash), 270–271

: (colon)
  conditional operators and comparisons, 99
  range operator, 128

:: (two colons)
  classes and functions, 337, 575, 583, 593

scope resolution operator, 238

; (semicolon), 59, 153, 234

? (question mark), 99

@ (at sign), 92

[ ] (square brackets), 92, 388

\ (backslash), 66, 90–92, 688, 734

^ (caret), 93

{ } (curly braces), 53, 55, 92–93

|| (or) operator, 110–111

~ (tilde), 92

+ (addition symbol), 60, 78, 97

++ (plus plus)
  increment operator, 81, 92
  prefix/postfix operators, 85

++i (pre-increment) operator, 126

+= (plus equal) notation, 81, 96

< (less than)
  less than operator, 108–109
  operator function, 653–654, 668

< > (angle brackets), 93, 181–182

<< (insertion) operator, 59–60, 102, 223, 300, 661, 672, 698–699, 726, 738–741

<= (less than or equal to) operator, 108

= (equals sign), 75, 417–418

= 0 (pure specifier), 333–334

== (equal equal), 92
  equal to operator, 108–109

<=> (spaceship) operator, 109–110, 216

> (greater than) operator, 108–109

-> (arrow) operator, 245, 247, 250, 555, 608

>= (greater than or equal to) operator, 108

>> (extraction) operator, 102, 223, 277, 284, 712–714, 738, 741

" " (double quotes), 59, 67, 90, 93, 181–182

' ' (single quotes), 88, 90

\0 (null) character, 89

A

absolute paths, 846, 853

abstract classes, 333–334

abstract virtual methods, 334

Acronym Finder, 48

AddFiles example, 170

AddInteger example, 78–79

AddInteger2 example, 79–81

addition symbol (+), 60, 78, 97

AddOne example, 149

AddOne( ) function, 149–153

AIDE (Android IDE), 33–34

Alexander, Christopher, 336

algorithms, Standard Library, 755–757

allocating/deallocating memory
  defined, 205
  using new operator, 208

American National Standards Institute (ANSI), 515–516

ampersand (&), 92
  reference operator, 197, 220, 496, 501, 505, 510, 647

and (&&) operator, 110–111

Android IDE (AIDE), 33–34

AndroidForums, 42

angle brackets (< >), 93, 181–182

anonymous functions, 398

N

\n (newline) character, 89–91

Named Return Value Optimization (NRVO), 192

Namespace example, 538

namespaces, 534–539

  creating, 534–535

  creating in many places, 537

  defined, 179

  putting variables in, 537

  using namespace line, 535–537

  using part of, 538–539

nargs() function, 422

narrowing casts, 523

nested loops, 136–138

  break and continue statements inside, 137

  defined, 136

NestedCalls example, 471–472

nesting classes, 591–596

  inner class definitions, 594–596

  issues with, 592–594

Netbeans IDE, 26

new operator, 188, 206–211, 245, 441, 494, 676

newline (\n) character, 89–91

noexcept() function, 414

NonTypeParm example, 619–621

NoSideEffects example, 385–386

not equal to (!=) operator, 107–108

(nothrow), 676

NRVO (Named Return Value Optimization), 192

null (\0) character, 89

NULL, setting pointers to, 211

null pointers, 190, 615

nullable references

  optional pointers for, 191

  raw pointers for, 189

nullopt object, 216–217

numeric conversion, 858–861

O

object aliases, 267–268

  creating, 266–267

  defined, 266

ObjectAlias example, 266–267

object-oriented programming (OOP), 227–268, 312, 316

  arrays, 302–308

  cin object, 277–281

  classes, 227–268

    accessing members, 241–244

    class definitions, 230, 234, 238, 241

    const parameters, 251–252

    constructors, 259–264

    defined, 230, 240

    destructors, 260–262

    header files, 230, 232, 240–241

    hierarchies of, 264–268

    implementing, 232–237

    instances, 230, 234–237

    methods, 232, 235–241, 256–259

    modeling, 232

    names and filenames, 230

    object aliases, 267–268

    objects, 227–229, 240, 249–251

    parts of, 240–241

    properties, 231, 235, 241

    raw pointers and, 244–248

    singleton, 230

    smart pointers and, 248–249

    source files, 230, 240–241

    this pointer, 252–256

  comments, 270–272

  constants, 292–295

  defined, 372

design patterns, 335–366

  mediator pattern, 349–366

  observer pattern, 341–349

  origin of, 336

  singleton pattern, 337–340

functional programming vs., 371

objects, 309–334

  collection objects, 311–313

  defined, 309–310

  encapsulation, 316–322

  hierarchies of, 322–334

  mailbox system example, 310–315

  naming, 311

passing functions to functions, 371

preprocessor directives, 282–291

random numbers, 300–302

switch statements, 295–298

type conversion, 272–277

objects, 309–334

  collection objects, 311–313

  defined, 141, 240, 309–310

  encapsulation, 316–322

    APIs, 316

    defined, 316

    process for, 318–319

    properties, 316–322

  hierarchies of, 322–334

    abstract classes, 333–334

    establishing, 322–324

    overriding methods, 330–332

    polymorphism, 332–333

    protecting members when inheriting, 324–330

  mailbox system example, 310–315

    classes and instances, 314

    Mailbox objects, 314–315

    Mailboxes collection object, 311–313

Q

R

\r (carriage return) character, 90–91, 281

rand() function, 223, 301–302

random access iterator, 771–774

random number generators, 776–777

random numbers, 223, 300–302

RandomAccess example, 771–772

RandomNumber example, 301

RandomNumberGenerator example, 776

ranges, 679–680
  defined, 679
  range adapters, 680
  Standard Library, 764–765

Ranges example, 679–680

ranges::size() method, 679–680

raw literals, 784–785

raw pointers
  classes and, 244–248
  creating using initializers, 206–208
  creating using new keyword, 206–208
  defined, 188
  freeing (deleting), 209–211
  problems with, 189–191
  uses for, 188–189

RawAndCooked example, 784

reactive programming, 312

ReadConsoleData example, 278–280

ReadPointer example, 200

ReadString example, 102–103

recursion, 374–375, 379, 423–424

Reddit, 41

Reference01 example, 511

Reference02 example, 512

references, 510–513
  defined, 512
  forward references, 159–161, 237
  nullable references
    optional pointers for, 191
    raw pointers for, 189
  reference variables, 510–511
  relative references, 246
  returning from functions, 511–513

referential transparency, 374

RegEx example, 855–856

regular expressions
  parsing strings with, 850
    adding RegEx library, 851–855
    creating code, 855–857
    pattern matching, 850–851
  Standard Library, 766

reinterpret_cast, 523

relative paths, 846, 853

relative references, 246

remainder (modulus), 78, 86

rename() function, 736

RenameFile example, 735–736

replace() function, 164–165

RepLit IDE, 35

requires element, 401

reset() function, 215–216, 248–249

ret element, 400

Return Value Optimization (RVO), 192

return values
  defined, 150–151
  type of, 152

ReturnDeduction example, 401–402

ReturnPointer example, 221–222

reverse_copy() function, 642–643, 655

reverse-assembly, 783

Rextester.com IDE, 35

right flag, 702–703

rmdir() function, 730

ROOT, 30

runtime libraries, 208

runtime polymorphism, using raw pointers for, 189

rvalue term, 517–519

RVO (Return Value Optimization), 192

S

SayHello project, 55–60

scalars, 497

scientific flag, 702–703

SDL (Simple DirectMedia Layer), 29

seekg() function, 692

semicolon (;), 59, 153, 234

serialization, 738

set class, 658–661

set_intersection() function, 663–664

set_union() function, 664

setf() method, 700–701, 707, 709

sets, 658–661
  intersecting, 662–664
  looking up items, 659–661
  maps vs., 661
  unionizing, 662–664
  unordered, 677–679
    creating, 677
    manipulating, 677–679

Sets example, 658–661

Sets2 example, 662–663

setters, 316–317
  defined, 316
  property vs. method approach, 319
  reasons for using, 317

About the Authors

Luca Massaron is a data scientist and a marketing research director who specializes in multivariate statistical analysis, machine learning, and customer insight, with over a decade of experience in solving real-world problems and generating value for stakeholders by applying reasoning, statistics, data mining, and algorithms. From being a pioneer of web audience analysis in Italy to achieving the rank of top ten Kaggler on kaggle.com, he has always been passionate about everything regarding data and analysis and about demonstrating the potentiality of data-driven knowledge discovery to both experts and non experts. Favoring simplicity over unnecessary sophistication, he believes that a lot can be achieved in data science by understanding and practicing the essentials of it. Luca is also a Google Developer Expert (GDE) in machine learning.

John Mueller is a freelance author and technical editor. He has writing in his blood, having produced 114 books and more than 600 articles to date. The topics range from networking to artificial intelligence and from database management to heads-down programming. Some of his current books include discussions of data science, machine learning, and algorithms. His technical editing skills have helped more than 70 authors refine the content of their manuscripts. John has provided technical editing services to various magazines, performed various kinds of consulting, and writes certification exams. Be sure to read John's blog at http://blog.johnmuellerbooks.com/. You can reach John on the Internet at John@JohnMuellerBooks.com. John also has a website at http://www.johnmuellerbooks.com/. Be sure to follow John on Amazon at https://www.amazon.com/John-Mueller/.

Luca's Dedication

I would like to dedicate this book to my family, Yukiko and Amelia, to my parents, Renzo and Licia, and to Yukiko's family, Yoshiki, Takayo and Makiko.

John's Dedication

Over the years, a great many people have been kind to me and believed in my work. Otherwise, I wouldn't have made it to where I am now. This book is for them in thanks for all they have done.

Luca's Acknowledgments

My greatest thanks to my family, Yukiko and Amelia, for their support and loving patience. I also want to thank Simone Scardapane, an assistant professor at Sapienza University (Rome) and a fellow Google Developer Expert, who provided invaluable feedback during the writing of this book.

John's Acknowledgments

Thanks to my wife, Rebecca. Even though she is gone now, her spirit is in every book I write, in every word that appears on the page. She believed in me when no one else would.

Russ Mullen deserves thanks for his technical edit of this book. He greatly added to the accuracy and depth of the material you see here. Russ worked exceptionally hard helping with the research for this book by locating hard-to-find URLs and also offering a lot of suggestions. The code was also exceptionally difficult to check in this book and I feel he did an amazing job doing it.

Matt Wagner, my agent, deserves credit for helping me get the contract in the first place and taking care of all the details that most authors don't really consider. I always appreciate his assistance. It's good to know that someone wants to help.

A number of people read all or part of this book to help me refine the approach, test application code, verify the extensive text, and generally provide input that all readers wish they could have. These unpaid volunteers helped in ways too numerous to mention here. I especially appreciate the efforts of Eva Beattie who provided general input, read the entire book, and selflessly devoted herself to this project.

Finally, I would like to thank Katie Mohr, Susan Christophersen, and the rest of the editorial and production staff.

Publisher's Acknowledgments

Associate Publisher: Katie Mohr

Project and Copy Editor: Susan Christophersen

Technical Editor: Russ Mullen

Editorial Assistant: Matthew Lowe

Production Editor: Tamilmani Varadharaj

Cover Image: © Terminator3D / Getty Images